Selected Documents Relating to

LAW REFORM IN NORTH CAROLINA

during the Nineteenth Century

Selected Documents Relating to

LAW REFORM IN NORTH CAROLINA

during the Nineteenth Century

✦

*with Numerous Documents
from Surrounding Centuries
to Provide Historical Context*

compiled by

Thomas P. Davis
and
J. Barrett Fish

Raleigh, N.C.
2024

© 2024 North Carolina Office of Archives and History
All rights reserved.

ISBN: 978-0-8652-6507-3 (hardback)
ISBN: 978-0-8652-6508-0 (paperback)
ISBN: 978-0-8652-6509-7 (ebook)

NORTH CAROLINA DEPARTMENT OF NATURAL AND CULTURAL RESOURCES
D. Reid Wilson
Secretary

OFFICE OF ARCHIVES AND HISTORY
Dr. Darin J. Waters
Deputy Secretary

DIVISION OF HISTORICAL RESOURCES
Ramona Bartos
Director

HISTORICAL RESEARCH OFFICE
Ansley Herring Wegner
Research Supervisor

NORTH CAROLINA HISTORICAL COMMISSION
David Ruffin (2029)
Chair

The Honorable Newell Clark (2027)	Dr. Valerie A. Johnson (2027)
Shana Bushyhead Condill (2025)	Dr. Susanna M. Lee (2029)
Dr. David Dennard (2027)	Susan Phillips (2025)
Samuel B. Dixon (2025)	W. Noah Reynolds (2029)
Barbara Groome (2025)	Barbara B. Snowden (2029)

Emeriti: Mary Lynn Bryan, Kemp P. Burpeau, Alan D. Watson

Front Cover Photo: Photograph of code commissioners Victor C. Barringer, A. W. Tourgée, and William B. Rodman. Reproduced with permission of the Chautauqua County Historical Society, Westfield, N.Y.

In memory of

Raymond Mason Taylor (1933–2018)
Librarian of the North Carolina Supreme Court Library from 1964 to 1977, who wrote,

If government is to be "of laws and not of men," its laws must be recorded and preserved in an orderly manner that will make them accessible to all who are concerned with government.

Table of Contents

Dedication	v
Epigraphs	xii
Foreword	xiii
Acknowledgments	xv
Editorial Methodology	xvii
List of Images	xix
Epigraphs	xx
Preface	xxi
Epigraphs	xxiv
General Introduction	xxv

PART I: EARLY DOCUMENTS — 1

Epigraphs	2
Introduction to Early Documents	3
Document I–1: Charter, 1663	3
Document I–2: Charter, 1665	4
Document I–3: The Grand Model, 1669	6
Document I–4: Nine Confirmed Laws, 1669[–1670]	9
Document I–5: The Queen's Peace, 1711	9
Document I–6: Revisal, 1715	10
Document I–7: The Queen's Peace, 1715	13
Document I–8: Provincial Laws in Force, 1731	14
Document I–9: Revisal, 1746	14
Document I–10: English Law in Force, 1749	15
Document I–11: Court Act, 1760	17
Document I–12: Declaration and Resolves, 1774	18
Document I–13: Declaration of Rights, December 17, 1776	19
Document I–14: Constitution, December 18, 1776	22
Document I–15: Revisal Ordinance, December 21, 1776	26
Document I–16: Reception Ordinance, December 22, 1776	27
Document I–17: Reception Statute, May 9, 1777	27
Document I–18: Court Act, December 24, 1777	28
Document I–19: Reception Statute, December 24, 1777	29
Document I–20: Reception Statute, 1778	29
Document I–21: Equity Jurisdiction, 1782	30
Document I–22: Court Act, 1786	31
Document I–23: Trial by Jury, 1787	31
Document I–24: Revisal, 1787	32
Document I–25: Iredell's Preface, 1791	33
Document I–26: Martin's Preface, 1792	36
Document I–27: Iredell on Natural Justice, 1798	38

PART II: ANTEBELLUM PERIOD — 41

Epigraphs — 42
Introduction to Antebellum Period — 43
Document II–1: Meetings of the Judges, November 18, 1799 — 43
Document II–2: Court of Errors and Appeals, December 26, 1799 — 43
Document II–3: The Court of Conference, 1801 — 46
Document II–4: Haywood's Preface, 1808 — 47
Document II–5: State Military Laws, 1808 — 50
Document II–6: Rush on American Jurisprudence, 1815 — 51
Document II–7: Bentham's Letter, 1817 — 53
Document II–8: Revisal, 1817 — 55
Document II–9: Office of Reporter, 1818 — 56
Document II–10: H. Potter's Report, 1819 — 56
Document II–11: Gaston's Report, 1819 — 59
Document II–12: Taylor on the Common Law, 1820 — 63
Document II–13: British Statutes in Force, 1821 — 64
Document II–14: Taylor on the Common Law, 1823 — 69
Document II–15: Hawks's Preface, 1823 — 71
Document II–16: Taylor's Preface, 1824 — 72
Document II–17: Revisal on Administrators and Executors, 1825 — 74
Document II–18: Henderson on the Common Law, 1825 — 74
Document II–19: R. Potter on Social Contract, 1825 — 75
Document II–20: Hawks's Digested Index, 1826 — 76
Document II–21: Manly to Graham, 1827 — 77
Document II–22: Devereux on Humphreys, 1827 — 78
Document II–23: Resolution on Full Revisal, January 2, 1827 — 79
Document II–24: Resolution on Full Revisal, November 27, 1827 — 80
Document II–25: Resolution on Subject Revisal, December 7, 1827 — 80
Document II–26: Resolution on Subject Revisal, December 12, 1827 — 80
Document II–27: Bill on Subject Revisal, January 7, 1828 — 81
Document II–28: Resolution on Subject Revisal, November 26, 1828 — 81
Document II–29: Bill on Full Revisal, December 1828 — 81
Document II–30: Common and Statute Law on Subject Revisal, January 1829 — 82
Document II–31: Commissions for Common and Statute Law Subject Revisal, May 1829 — 83
Document II–32: Resolution on Subject Revisal, December 1829 — 84
Document II–33: Index, 1829–1830 — 84
Document II–34: Bill on Full Revisal, December 1830 — 84
Document II–35: Friends of Liberty Address, 1830 — 85
Document II–36: Unwritten Code of the People, 1832 — 88
Document II–37: Governor Swain's Message, 1833 — 89
Document II–38: Moore's Argument, 1834 — 90
Document II–39: Commission Report, 1834 — 95
Document II–40: Joint Select Committee Report, 1835 — 97

Document II-41: Commission Report, 1836	99
Document II-42: Revised Statutes, 1837	101
Document II-43: Revised Statutes' Preface, 1837	107
Document II-44: Swaim's Preface, 1841	110
Document II-45: Administration of Justice, 1845	111
Document II-46: Smith's Preface, 1846	114
Document II-47: Nash on the Common Law, 1849	115
Document II-48: Pearson on the Common Law, 1850	116
Document II-49: Pearson on the Common Law, 1851	116
Document II-50: Nash on Local Practice, 1853	118
Document II-51: Revised Code's Preface, 1854	118
Document II-52: Eaton's Preface, 1854	120
Document II-53: Battle on the Common Law, 1855	122
Document II-54: Pearson on the Common Law, 1856	122
Document II-55: Cantwell on Criminal Law, 1856	123
Document II-56: Battle on the Common Law, 1864	126
Document II-57: About the Judges of Our First Supreme Court (1819–1829)	126
Document II-58: About Judge John Hall (1767–1833)	127
Document II-59: About Mr. Archibald Henderson (1768–1822)	127
Document II-60: About Chief Justice Taylor (1769–1829)	128
Document II-61: About Mr. George Badger (1795–1866)	130

PART III: CODE COMMISSION ERA — 133

Epigraphs	134
Introduction to Code Commission Era	135
Document III-1: Laws in Force, October 18, 1865	135
Document III-2: Report on Freedmen's Code, January 22, 1866	136
Document III-3: Freedmen's Code, March 10, 1866	139
Document III-4: Merger of Law and Equity, February, 25, 1868	141
Document III-5: Code Commissioners, March 13, 1868	142
Document III-6: Constitution, April 21–23, 1868	143
Document III-7: Rodman to Holden, May 5, 1868	144
Document III-8: Tourgée to Rodman, June 8, 1868	145
Document III-9: Field to Tourgée, 1868	146
Document III-10: First Report of the Code Commissioners, July 15, 1868	146
Document III-11: The Judicial System, July 29, 1868	149
Document III-12: Pearson to Rodman, August 6, 1868	150
Document III-13: The Code Commission, August 8, 1868	150
Document III-14: Tourgée and the Code Commission, August 13, 1868	152
Document III-15: C.C.P. Preface, August 25, 1868	152
Document III-16: Second Report of the Code Commissioners, August 31, 1868	153
Document III-17: Pearson to Rodman, September 24, 1868	155
Document III-18: The Code Commission, November 6, 1868	156
Document III-19: The Code Commission, December 9, 1868	158

Document III–20: The Code Commission, December 18, 1868 — 158
Document III–21: The Code Commission, December 19, 1868 — 158
Document III–22: Schenck's Diary, December 23, 1868 — 159
Document III–23: Meeting of Bench and Bar, December 24, 1868 — 159
Document III–24: Suspension of Provisions on Contract, 1869 — 160
Document III–25: Meeting of Bench and Bar, January 8, 1869 — 161
Document III–26: Superior Courts and Clerks, January 25, 1869 — 161
Document III–27: Practice of Law, February 15, 1869 — 162
Document III–28: Schenck's Diary, March 8, 1869 — 163
Document III–29: Report of the Code Commissioners, March 20, 1869 — 163
Document III–30: Rodman to Tourgée, July 21, 1869 — 167
Document III–31: Barringer to Rodman, November 15, 1869 — 167
Document III–32: Bill for a Penal Code, 1869 — 168
Document III–33: Call for Convention, 1869–1870 — 171
Document III–34: Pearson on Judicial Legislation, 1870 — 178
Document III–35: Commissioners' Response, January 25, 1870 — 178
Document III–36: Report of the Code Commissioners, March 1870 — 181
Document III–37: New Code Commissioner, July 30, 1870 — 183
Document III–38: Bill Dissolving Code Commission, September 29, 1870 — 184
Document III–39: Report of the Code Commissioners, November 1870 — 184
Document III–40: Report of the Code Commissioners, December 18, 1870 — 188
Document III–41: Law Library of the Supreme Court Separated, 1871 — 193
Document III–42: Caldwell to Graham, March 7, 1871 — 193
Document III–43: Supreme Court Reporter Abolished, 1872 — 194
Document III–44: Battle's Report on Revisal, 1872 — 195
Document III–45: Constitutional Amendment Dissolving Code Commission, 1873 — 196
Document III–46: Constitutional Amendment on Procedure, 1875 — 197
Document III–47: Tourgée's Notes, 1878 — 198
Document III–48: Rodman to Tourgée, January 8, 1878 — 227
Document III–49: Phillips about Tourgée, July 18, 1878 — 228
Document III–50: About Mr. Lucien Holmes (1797–1871) — 228
Document III–51: About Judge Mitchell (1800–1876) — 230
Document III–52: About Chief Justice Pearson (1805–1878) — 230
Document III–53: About Mr. Joseph Wilson (1810–1884) — 232
Document III–54: About Judge Manning (1830–1899) — 233
Document III–55: About Judge Tourgée (1838–1905) — 235

PART IV: APPLIED DEMOCRACY — 237
Epigraphs — 238
Introduction to Applied Democracy — 239
Document IV–1: North Carolina Supreme Court Library, 1883 — 239
Document IV–2: Commission Report on *The Code*, 1883 — 240
Document IV–3: Clark's Preface, 1884 — 241
Document IV–4: Battle's History, 1889 — 241

Document IV–5: Field to Clark, 1892 — 244
Document IV–6: Clark's Preface, 1892 — 244
Document IV–7: Rodman to Clark, 1892 — 245
Document IV–8: Office of the Reporter, 1893 — 245
Document IV–9: Clark's Preface, 1895 — 246
Document IV–10: Manning's Commentaries, 1899 — 246
Document IV–11: Hinsdale on Codification, 1900 — 247
Document IV–12: Clark's Preface, 1900 — 249
Document IV–13: Shepherd's Speech, 1900 — 251
Document IV–14: Revisal's Preface, 1905 — 252
Document IV–15: Tourgée on the Common Law, 1908 — 254
Document IV–16: Winston's Speech, 1913 — 262
Document IV–17: Clark's Speech, 1914 — 266
Document IV–18: Prohibition on Local Acts, 1917 — 269
Document IV–19: Clark/Mordecai Exchange, 1917 — 270
Document IV–20: Winston's Speech, 1919 — 271
Document IV–21: Consolidated Statutes' Preface, 1920 — 274
Document IV–22: Pound on the Common Law, 1920 — 275
Document IV–23: Clark's History of Reprints, 1920 — 279
Document IV–24: Varser's Address, 1920 — 282
Document IV–25: Investigation of State Printing, 1923 — 282
Document IV–26: Adams's Evolution of Law, 1924 — 283
Document IV–27: About Chief Justice Clark (1846–1924) — 286
Document IV–28: About Chief Justice Shepherd (1847–1910) — 287
Document IV–29: About Dean Samuel Mordecai (1852–1927) — 290
Document IV–30: Winston's Autobiography, 1937 — 291
Document IV–31: Pound's Speech, 1958 — 291

EPIGRAPHS — 292
AFTERWORD — 293
BIBLIOGRAPHY — 295
FURTHER READING — 311
TABLE OF CASES AND ACTS CITED — 315
TABLE OF DOCUMENTS EXCERPTED — 319
DOCUMENT CREDITS — 327
ABOUT THE EPIGRAPHS — 329
ABOUT THE COMPILERS — 333
NOTES — 335
INDEX — 377

Our people have taken fast hold of the idea that some legal reform is necessary.

—Code Commissioners

We live in a period of uncommon excitement. The spirit of the age is restless, presumptuous, and revolutionary. The rapidly increasing appetite for wealth,—the inordinate taste for luxury, which it engenders,—the vehement spirit of speculation, and the selfish emulation which it creates,—the growing contempt for slow and moderate gains,—the ardent thirst for pleasure and amusement,—the diminishing reverence for the wisdom of the past,—the disregard of the lessons of experience, the authority of magistracy, and the venerable institutions of ancestral policy,—are so many bad symptoms of a diseased state of the public mind.

—Chancellor James Kent

*I labored under the comfortable illusion that, in order to secure wise and just government, all I had to do was to remove all restrictions on the free and full expression of the popular will. . . . There were still many restraints on their will, retained from old monarchical and aristocratic institutions; such as an independent judiciary, and the English common law with its subtilties [*sic*] and technicalities.*

—Mr. Orestes Brownson

[T]he liberal and socialistic revolutions of Europe during the last sixty or seventy years [i.e., since the French Revolution,] have to some extent had a philanthropic origin. . . . All these movements to popularize government, to mitigate penal codes, to redress political and social grievances, and to elevate the poorer and more numerous classes, although for the most part failing of their object, have originated in benevolent sentiment, though perverted to base, selfish purposes by their chief managers.

—Mr. Orestes Brownson

The imagination of the age was intent on history; its conscience was intent on reform.

—Professor George Santayana

Foreword

The life of the law has not been logic: it has been experience. The felt necessities of the time, the prevalent moral and political theories, intuitions of public policy, even the prejudices which judges share with their fellow-men have had a good deal more to do than the syllogism in determining the rules by which men should be governed. The law embodies the story of a nation's development through many centuries, and it cannot be dealt with as if it contained only the axioms and corollaries of a book of mathematics. In order to know what it is, we must know what it has been, and what it tends to become.

—Justice Oliver Wendell Holmes Jr.

In nineteenth-century North Carolina "the felt necessities of the time" evoked a penchant, a passion, at times an obsession, for the codification of laws. Much of the bench and bar of the time placed a high value on the "writtenness" of law.

Arguably the most ambitious of the nineteenth-century codifiers was Jeremy Bentham, an English philosopher. Bentham tendered his codification services at the national level to United States President James Madison. Undeterred by Madison's rebuff, he wrote the governors of the American states, offering "the outline of a complete body of law for the use of any political state." He apparently got no takers, but the idea had taken hold in at least one of the former British colonies, North Carolina.

Captioned as a nineteenth-century documentary history, this work actually commences with foundational documents from earlier times and ends with some from the early twentieth century. Its focus and major content, though, is indeed the nineteenth century, when the legal system of the newly minted state was feeling its way toward maturity and modernity.

Early times found the state wrestling with the question of incorporation of the law of the Mother Country. It adopted the law of England, if not inconsistent with its basic precepts, and that remains the law of North Carolina. Yet then, as now, issues could arise as to which laws of England applied and which did not. Before approving provisions on the structure of government, the new state adopted a Declaration of Rights as a preface, rooted in the notion that governmental power was vested in, and derived from, the people. There would be no hereditary aristocracy in this former English colony.

This volume details the several "revisals" of state law, from Justice James Iredell's early one (1787) to those of William Horn Battle (1837, 1872) and beyond. Tracing them here would serve no purpose. They await the interested reader in the pages that follow.

The passion for—obsession with—codification was not universal, however; in 1871 David Caldwell, Guilford County legislator and delegate to the 1868 state constitutional convention, informed former governor William A. Graham that he would not practice law while *The Code of Civil Procedure* was in effect. Caldwell accused the "Radical Judges," particularly the "carpetbagger" Judge Albion W. Tourgée, a staunch advocate of codification, of "partial rascality and fraud."

Judges, too, could be intransigent. Anderson Mitchell, a superior court judge from 1868 to 1875, did not like the code practice and refused to study it. Older lawyers in particular found it difficult to reconcile themselves to the new order.

Selected Documents Relating to Law Reform in North Carolina during the Nineteenth Century is a beneficial addition to the lore of North Carolina legal history and jurisprudence. Scholars and teachers should welcome it. Practicing attorneys may find utility in its pages. It is a work that should be of interest to all who care about history.

Tom Davis and Barrett Fish, the compilers, deserve commendation for their diligent collection efforts over a long period of time. Their commentary on the documents and their context is also insightful and enlightening.

WILLIS P. WHICHARD
Chapel Hill, N.C.
November 2023

Acknowledgments

This compilation was conceived and developed, and much of the research and transcription accomplished, while the Public Services Section of the North Carolina Supreme Court Library consisted of Mr. Thomas P. Davis, librarian; Mr. J. Barrett Fish, assistant librarian for public services; and Ms. Jennifer L. Bentley-Davis, library assistant. Many years later, Ms. Audrey Kellogg, library technical assistant, helped proof the transcriptions of the documents. During that time, the library had also been fortunate to employ interns and short-term or temporary employees who contributed to the production of this work. We acknowledge and appreciate the cheerful assistance received from Mr. Stephen Webb, Mr. Russell S. Michalak, Ms. Amanda Jo Gwaltney, Ms. Morgan Stoddard, and Ms. Marion Grabarak-Matthews.

Late in the life of this project, when the compilers began to consider whether to publish the work, former justice Willis P. Whichard, who is a longtime friend of the library, strongly encouraged us to offer the manuscript for publication. That encouragement grew into support, advice, and even assistance in procuring a copy editor, Ms. Donna Kelly, co-editor of the third volume of *The Papers of James Iredell* and editorial assistant with the John Dickinson Writings Project. Were it not for the gracious support of Justice Whichard, this compilation might have remained in manuscript form in a vertical file in the library. We also received the selfless support of Mr. Fred Wood of the appellate computing department of the Supreme Court of North Carolina. Mr. Wood volunteered his personal time and his vast expertise as a programmer and database administrator for an important aspect of this project: the organization and presentation of sources excerpted and cited so that the manuscript could be efficiently proofread. We thank him for his assistance.

Finally, we acknowledge and thank the following institutions whose collections have proven valuable to us:

- Chautauqua County Historical Society, Westfield, N.Y.
- Davis Library, University of North Carolina at Chapel Hill
- North Carolina Collection, Wilson Special Collections Library, University of North Carolina at Chapel Hill
- North Carolina Supreme Court Library
- Southern Historical Collection, Wilson Special Collections Library, University of North Carolina at Chapel Hill
- Special Collections, Joyner Library, East Carolina University
- State Archives of North Carolina
- State Library of North Carolina

Editorial Methodology

Excerpts of documents in this compilation range from a charter by a king witnessed in 1663 in Westminster, England, to a speech by a retired academic given in 1958 in Myrtle Beach, South Carolina. As one can easily imagine, documents originating at such disparate points of time and place, and occupying such different levels of dignity, will vary in acceptable spellings, abbreviations, and punctuation. Furthermore, some documents transcribed for this compilation had been published, while others had not. Of the published documents, some were produced locally before the province of North Carolina had a printing press (e.g., early eighteenth-century acts of assembly), others were printed both in draft and final forms (e.g., legislative edition and final edition of codifications), and still others were reprinted (e.g., newspaper reprints of reports of the code commissioners). The existence of various copies and printings of a published document may introduce variations in its content. Of the unpublished documents, handwriting and method of preservation affect the quality of transcription (e.g., microform of letters to and from Albion Tourgée). Given these complications, the compilers here list the most important points of decision in their editorial methodology:

- Final original sources are preferred to drafts and reprints
- Archaic letters, spellings, and abbreviations are preserved (e.g., "defence")
- British spellings are preserved
- Contractions, abbreviations, and capitalization are retained
- Spaces before colons and semi-colons are removed
- Errors in spelling are not corrected or marked with [*sic*] unless the compilers thought these errors might be mistaken for editorial errors (e.g., a repeated word)
- E-acute (É or é) is used in the spelling of "Tourgée," except when the name appears in a contemporary document without the é
- A cedilla is used under the "c" in "François," even where it is not used in the original document
- Editorial notes are in brackets and italics, for example: [*illegible*]
- Words added by the compilers are in brackets, for example: [Lords Proprietors]
- Words guessed at by compilers are in brackets with a question mark, for example: [and?]
- Note references contained in original documents are omitted in this compilation unless the content of the notes referenced is also provided in the compilation
- Margin notes are omitted
- The general physical appearance of the excerpted documents has not been fully reproduced, but every attempt has been made to retain font size, italics, bold, etc. when possible
- Because of typesetting constraints, some of the fonts, spacing, and alignment were standardized. As a result, some of the handwritten and published documents look different when compared to the originals.
- Transcriptions of handwritten documents retain crossed-out words and insertions, following the standard practice of documentary editing
- Headline style is used for titles (books, acts, etc.) even when lowercase words appear therein

Each of the documents in this compilation is prefaced by a document number, a document title (accompanied by year or date), and remarks by Mr. Davis, one of the compilers. The remarks, which are set off in brackets, provide historical context and point out important themes raised by that document. While the remarks and the document title should adequately orient the reader to the document, a technically correct and shortened bibliographic entry for each document is provided in the Table of Documents Excerpted.

The Bibliography includes all of the sources consulted in the compilation of this book. Some entries refer to chapters or parts of books as well as the books themselves. Newspapers are listed, but not all of the individual articles are included. Primary sources are listed by collection but not by individual item. This decision was made to save space and prevent duplication. Individual cases and acts are listed in the Table of Cases and Acts Cited and not repeated in the Bibliography. In Part I, individual acts come from either the *Colonial Records* or the *State Records*. Because they are the standardized shortened version of these important sources for use in historical works, only the volume and page number are provided for each reference, and the editors of each series are omitted. Some entries are listed by date instead of alphabetically, for example, meetings of the bar association or legislative sessions.

Notes are placed at the end of the compilation. They may provide substantive commentary, cross-references, and references to sources. As mentioned above, sources are cited in a shortened form in both the Tables and the Notes, while full citation information is provided in the Bibliography. Citations within notes are shortened to author and page number. Ellipses within brackets are used in shortening many of the citations to acts and laws that appear in both the Tables and the Notes. They are also used to shorten many of the lengthy titles of works for which a full citation appears in the Bibliography.

Because this publication is geared toward an audience familiar with legal writing, editing has deviated somewhat from *The Chicago Manual of Style* (17th edition). Several notes may occur within one sentence, clause, or paragraph rather than at the end of the sentence. Notes appear at the back of the book, instead of at the end of each Part, and they follow *The Bluebook* style for cross-referencing and parenthetical information. Each shortened citation is followed by the legal citation in brackets. There are occasions where a double ending parentheses is used instead of using brackets.

List of Images

Front cover: Code commissioners Victor C. Barringer, A. W. Tourgée, and William B. Rodman

IMAGE	PAGE	DOCUMENT
John Locke	7	I-3
Title page of *Swann's Revisal*	16	I-10
James Iredell Sr.	34	I-25
François-Xavier Martin	38	I-26
Dr. Calvin Jones	50	II-4
John Louis Taylor	72	II-15
Thomas P. Devereux	78	II-21
Page 1 of Index to acts, 1829–'30	85	II-33
James Iredell Jr.	106	II-42
Frederick Nash	117	II-49
William H. Battle	125	II-55
William B. Rodman	145	III-7
Richmond M. Pearson	157	III-18
First page of a handwritten report of code commissioners	192	III-40
Albion W. Tourgée	198	III-46
Page 75 from Albion W. Tourgée, *The Code of Civil Procedure of North Carolina*	209	III-47
Samuel Phillips	229	III-50
Walter Clark	243	IV-4
James E. Shepherd	250	IV-12
Robert W. Winston	272	IV-20
Samuel F. Mordecai	289	IV-28

The legal muckraker of today wields but a feeble pen in comparison with his predecessor of the first half of the last century.

—Dean Roscoe Pound

During the first fifty years of this Court [the Supreme Court of North Carolina] it lived under the practice and procedure formulated in feudal ages by the judges, who for the most part were not lawyers, but priests of the Catholic Church or laymen.

—Chief Justice Walter Clark

The enactment of that Code of Procedure at once threw the whole question of the law of procedure into the hands of the Legislature . . . and the consequence was that amendment after amendment, scores of them, were made by every succeeding Legislature. . . . It is not right to throw these questions of procedure into the hands of the Legislature. They should have been left under the control of the courts. It is the courts who apply the rules by which controversies are carried on before them, and, of course, those who are to apply the rules, are best able to understand them, best able to enunciate them, and best able to reshape them if they need it.

—James Coolidge Carter, Esq.

From time to time [the common law] may be altered and supplemented in many respects by judicious legislation, but let not this great heritage, the growth of centuries, and so rich in blessings to the people, be marred by the iconoclast, who generally comes in the guise of the reformer.

This I feel sure will not be done in North Carolina as long as we cherish the memories of Taylor, Henderson, Nash, Ruffin, Pearson and other eminent jurists, whose labors have added a new and brighter lustre to our unwritten or Common Law.

—Chief Justice James E. Shepherd

Preface

We have chosen a title for this compilation that is complicated and general: *Selected Documents Relating to Law Reform in North Carolina during the Nineteenth Century*. We are obliged, therefore, to explain it, describing with some precision the subject of this collection of documents and the principle of selection that sustains it.

The documents gathered here cover much less ground than some readers might hope, this false hope arising with the vaguely ambitious expression, "relating to law reform." To the innocent reader, law reform might conjure up any number of socially compelling initiatives, both in court administration[1] and in the enlightenment of substantive law.[2] While these initiatives were debated in North Carolina during the nineteenth century, as portions of documents in this compilation attest, these are not the aspects of reform with which we are here chiefly concerned. The point of this work, rather, is to elaborate the impact on North Carolina's legal history of the nineteenth-century obsession with *codification* as the necessary means of achieving these reforms.[3]

We refer nevertheless to law reform rather than to codification because a direct reference to codification may evoke too narrow a theme in the minds of prospective readers. In fact, documents relating to codification inevitably clarify not only what codification is, a systematic written arrangement of public-general acts of a sovereign authority in force in a jurisdiction, but also what it is not. The simplest explication of codification presumes by way of contrast such familiar jurisprudential norms as natural law in its classical,[4] scholastic,[5] and modern[6] incarnations, as well as classical common law as articulated in the seventeenth century by Sir Edward Coke and Sir Matthew Hale,[7] and in the next century by Thomas Wood and Sir William Blackstone.[8] These traditional norms lurk in the background of documents advocating reform by codification.

Now, this call for reform is rarely a dispassionate one: it is typically an impatient, mocking rejection of sacred custom and traditional moral science.[9] By what means, then, the great bemocked may wonder, is the burden of mankind's experience and the wisdom of its past to be displaced? The response is unequivocal: reform would proceed by extension of a newer sort of scientific method[10] from physics to the humanities,[11] undermining and dismissing as prejudice the natural hierarchical priorities and distinctions of local human judgments, and preferring, if not too quickly adopting,[12] a leveling equality of passion and political will.[13] Radical debaters, aiming to dissolve the moral realism[14] of Greek, Roman, Catholic, and early Protestant traditions, champion the rejection of practical reason[15] on the ground that its ideals are merely subjective, and champion the acceptance of raw passions on the ground that these allegedly quantifiable intensities—that is, objective entities—may serve as buildingblocks for a new moral science.[16]

From this perspective, codification in the nineteenth century is a phase of positivism that relates to the natural law and the classical common law traditions as a reformation, and documents relevant to codification therefore inevitably shed light on the traditional formations to which codification is a reaction.[17] In sum, then, our selections cover more ground than a reference to codification might have suggested to the uninitiated, even while covering less ground than the notion of law reform will certainly suggest to many contemporary readers.

Our use of temporal and geographical qualifications in our chosen title may mislead readers in other ways. Though our title would confine this work to law reform in the nineteenth century, we have seen fit to include quite a few documents from before that century. Our excuse for drawing the reader's attention to bits of documents from earlier centuries—some dating from before Tennessee country was ceded to the federal government and some even from before the province of Carolina split permanently into its northern and southern governments—is that these excerpts introduce themes which recur during the codification movement, even if these themes display different hues as they bloom in successive seasons. Among these perennial objects of concern are the distrust of attorneys *per se* and of judges in the exercise of their discretion; the commitment to writtenness, publication, and even public reading of laws and organic provisions by appropriate officers or bodies; the weariness over the reception conundrum and the concomitant issue of which received laws remained in force at any given time;[18] and the hesitation in allowing a role for the *philosophes* in developing a rational plan of government. In order to understand better the drive for codification, we think it is worth pausing to note that these themes, for one reason or another, have dominated law reform in North Carolina since its founding.

Our explanation for having reprinted so many documents from the early twentieth century, on the other hand, may strain credulity—at least until one looks with particularity at some of the items in question. For instance, even though it was published posthumously, the inclusion of Judge Tourgée's "The Unwritten Law and Why It Remains Unwritten" needs no apology, we think, as Judge Tourgée is among either the heroes or the villains of our story and a truly nineteenth-century figure who happened to live into the first decade of the twentieth century. Colonel Hinsdale's entry is from 1900, which is not too much of a stretch, especially since it reviews prior statutory codifications and because it concludes that North Carolina should stay the course and not attempt to codify the common law: in other words, it is the perfect epitaph for this compilation. Justice Adams's and Justice Varser's entries we admit seem quite late, but we have excerpted aggressively, retaining those portions of each document which deal mainly with a historical account of law reform during the prior century. We assert precisely the same point in defense of our inclusion of Dean Pound's speech in 1920 to the annual meeting of the North Carolina Bar Association.

Chief Justices Shepherd and Clark, like Judge Tourgée, lived across centuries. As each of these men had neared the pinnacle of his career in the nineteenth century, it seems not too gross a departure from the scope of our work to include late selections which reveal their opinions about codification. In fact, the decision by Chief Justice Clark to take up the mantle of codification near the very end of the nineteenth century, going so far as to correspond on the topic with the avid Benthamite reformer, David Dudley Field, Esq., of New York,[19] is an essential piece of the tale we tell, and we have included all we can find that might bear on the hardening of the chief justice's opinions about codification. The entries for Professor Mordecai and Judge Winston are largely of importance as attacks on Chief Justice Clark's position, but for that reason strongly relate to a key element in our story, even if appearing in print after that tale technically ends. For these reasons, we think that allowing entries in this compilation to extend beyond 1899 is not terribly misleading, that extending entries to the date of death of Chief Justice Clark in 1924 is not intolerable, and that allowing narrow exceptions even to this standard is justifiable.

While we may have strained the trust of our intended audience by our use of the expression "law reform" and possibly more so by our alleged limitation to documents from "North Carolina during the Nineteenth Century," neither of these abuses is as thoroughly misleading as the term "selected" in our title. A selection, if it is to be of use to the casual reader, implies knowledge approaching expertise and interest of unquestioned depth, such that the culling of materials testifies to the editors' unprejudiced and scholarly commitment to the subject matter. We are afraid, though, that this compilation reveals knowledge and commitment far less than it does an excess of local pride. One of the early motivations in pursuing this project was the insignificant number of references to North Carolina sources in Professor Perry Miller's masterpiece, *The Legal Mind in America*,[20] in Professor Charles Warren's opus, *A History of the American Bar*,[21] and in Mr. Charles Cook's contemporary study, *The American Codification Movement*.[22] One might say with only a little exaggeration that these curious snubs set us on the course of collecting pertinent documents.[23]

Pride alone, though, would not have kept us so vigilant. Our second great motivation was an abundance of questions from judges and lawyers of the appellate courts of North Carolina that required us to gain a better understanding of the state's 1868 Constitution and *The Code of Civil Procedure* of the same year. Passage of the Reconstruction Constitution and of this code were radical changes in North Carolina, merging law and equity and thus raising the question of the scope of trial by jury in civil actions,[24] lopping off the removal jurisdiction of the supreme court in equity cases,[25] empowering the clerk of the superior court to act as "the Court" in ordinary civil cases,[26] and abandoning the rotation of superior court judges. Many intractable issues arose, and arose quickly, and many decisions were made and opinions published which challenge understanding unless one remembers how very foreign code pleading was to jurists who in late 1868 found themselves elected to the bench by the people, and to practitioners[27] who had either trained in the old common law procedure or had just exchanged a double eagle for a new law license.[28] The opinions to which we refer appear in the *North Carolina Reports* and sometimes cause difficulty for contemporary judges and attorneys.[29]

Having explained our reservations about our chosen title, we observe now that in one respect this choice of title is fortuitous. By collecting documents concerned with law reform, and not merely with the codification of common law, we provide local material worthy of study from early in the nineteenth century, despite the fact that codification of the common law was not at first the flashpoint in North Carolina that it was in other jurisdictions. Law reform by codification was known here, both of statute law[30] and of common law,[31] but no local worthy seems to have advanced the latter idea with the force of a Thomas Grimké of South Carolina or a Robert Rantoul of Massachusetts.[32] Rather, North Carolina quietly followed New York in the 1820s and 1830s, codifying its acts of assembly and toying with the notion of codification of private substantive law but never declaring by general statute wide swaths of the common law; and, even more quietly, North Carolina overlooked the famously unsettling reform of civil procedure imposed in New York in the 1840s, perhaps because North Carolina's agricultural, practical, and political character[33] had always allowed for a more casual common law practice than had industrial, literary, and intellectual New York. This skipped phase of procedural law reform was quickly imposed on North Carolina during Reconstruction, and it did then become a flashpoint for bench and bar. The code commissioners who by constitutional mandate imposed this reform, though, were ousted by constitutional amendment before they could make much progress in the codification of private substantive law in this state. Much later in the century, during the period of Applied Democracy, Chief Justice Clark would revive the notion of codification, advocating the adoption in North Carolina of the substantive codes written and partially adopted in New York.[34] And in the early part of the twentieth century, while Chief Justice Clark continued to speak sharply of the necessity of codifying the common law,[35] progressive law reformers in North Carolina advanced the sort of action that democratic law reformers had shied away from in the early decades of the nineteenth century: the state constitution was amended to restrict further the power of the general assembly to pass private, special, and local acts, encouraging its members to pass general statutes in displacement of the common law and to rely upon legislatively established executive agencies to govern the state with particularity; the Committee on Law Reform of the newlyformed North Carolina Bar Association advocated for the adoption by the general assembly of sundry uniform laws (that is, "American" statute law) and for reliance by the supreme court upon restatements of the "American" common law; and an Institute of Government was established at the state university which took for its mission the teaching of the new law to government officials throughout the state.[36] Thus, in North Carolina, law reformers succeeded in codifying the state's acts of assembly and in abrogating common law procedure in the nineteenth century but did not firmly set the stage for the displacement of the precedents of the courts until early in the twentieth century.

Tom Davis
Raleigh, N.C.
June 2024

[N]either the common law, nor any other code yet devised by man, could foresee and specify every case that might arise, and thus supersede the use of reason in the ordinary affairs of life . . .

—Chief Justice John Louis Taylor

[C]odification is not simply morally impracticable, but philosophically impossible.

—James Coolidge Carter, Esq.

Enactment has taken the place of living social instinct, and the ideals which that instinct projects, which are the sole criteria of justice, may be thwarted rather than helped by that codification.

—Professor George Santayana

The law is . . . a complex science. It is a tax which we pay for freedom. . . . A brief and simple code of laws is adapted only to a simple state of society. . . . The law, as a science, is only a collection of general principles, founded on the moral law, and in the common sense of mankind, and applied to particular cases as they arise, by the diligence of the bar and the erudition of the courts. . . .

—Chancellor James Kent

[N]othing, except matters of mere form and arbitrary regulations, should ever become a written law, till it has already existed among the people as an unwritten rule of conduct.

—Editor of *American Jurist and Law Magazine*

A judge has a discoverable generic character and ruling motives; his past decisions, by force of personal vanity and inertia, will suggest his decisions in future; and when the public too has come to take his habits of judgment for granted, common law has been born.

—Professor George Santayana

I fear from the experience of the last twenty-five years that morals do not of necessity advance hand in hand with the sciences.

—President Thomas Jefferson

General Introduction

This compilation is divided into four parts—Early Documents, Antebellum Period, Code Commission Era, and Applied Democracy—the focus of which is law reform in North Carolina during the nineteenth century. The story told by the documents collected here is easily summarized.

During the Antebellum Period, the state's general assembly established an appellate court—its judges having no trial duties—to supervise the adaptation of the inherited colonial common law to current local conditions.[37] At about the same time, a call for codification of common law was heard internationally from law reformers.[38] By codification they meant a systematic written arrangement of public-general acts of a sovereign authority in force in a jurisdiction. In North Carolina, neither codification of common law procedure nor of common law substance attracted much attention during this period, but codification of the session laws of the general assembly and the statutes of Great Britain remaining in force locally did garner support.[39]

Soon after the Civil War, the era of the code commission kicked off in North Carolina with a new state constitution. This constitution provided for the popular election of supreme court justices and grounded the jurisdiction of the supreme court in fundamental law, thereby denying the general assembly its immediate control over the membership, power, and continued existence of this precedent-setting court.[40] The revamped fundamental law of the state, though, also established a commission apparently authorized to assist the general assembly in displacing common law precedents by codification.[41] The code commission successfully introduced codifications of civil and criminal procedure which were necessary to fill the void left by the new constitution's merger of law and equity and by its repeal of common law pleading and equity pleading.[42] But codification of the substance of the unwritten common law—what today we recognize as property, tort, contract, and criminal law—failed to materialize during the short lifespan of the commission. Nevertheless, by the end of the nineteenth century, during the period of Applied Democracy, the general assembly significantly increased its legislative output,[43] and newly-elected progressive members of the supreme court noticeably weakened the common law, both by overruling precedents[44] and by revamping the course of study required of applicants for a law license.[45]

The story told through the documents of this compilation, then, focuses on the relative importance of the general assembly and the supreme court in the development of the law of North Carolina in the nineteenth century. This story, though, must be placed in its broad historical context in order to show what was at stake in settling the relative importance of these institutions.

Codification had long and famously served legal systems on the European continent. For instance, the emperor Justinian ordered the codification of Roman law shortly after the fall of the western Roman territories.[46] A millennium later, early in the Reformation, Johann von Schwarzenberg provided a codification of German criminal law.[47] In 1804, Napoleon had French law codified.[48] And over the opening third of the nineteenth century, Jeremy Bentham—an English philosopher who during the French Revolution was declared an "honorary citizen" of France[49]—would offer his services as codifier to the world.[50]

The last two of these examples of codification, the one an accomplished codification and the other a sincere offer to codify, occurred in nineteenth-century Europe, its intellectuals continuing to be pulled by the Enlightenment thinking of the eighteenth century in their conceptions of society, government, and law. One intellectual ideal of this age of reason was the use of classification in scientific thinking.[51] Thus, the writers of common law treatises attempting to see through the dense forest of English municipal law, as well as the writers of codes attempting to codify it, thought to make law rational by classifying its authoritative judgments.[52]

Beyond displaying a penchant for systemization, though, intellectuals who applied Enlightenment reasoning to the "law declaring" of courts, and those who applied such reasoning to the "law making" of assemblies, parted ways. Writers who classified the rules of the English common law courts held tightly to the thread of tradition, respecting the reasonable customary practices from which the unwritten law of the realm had arisen, while writers who advocated for classified statutory bodies of law cleaved to a rationality more akin to mathematical science.[53] Enlightened codifiers thereby laid claim to another intellectual ideal of reason: universality or generality. They took law to be essentially statutory, that is, imposed from above and from outside the consciousness of any particular people or of any particular jurisdiction, no matter that for the time being particular sovereigns had to adopt codes for particular peoples.[54] The primacy of general statute, as opposed to the customary law of a people declared by courts in particular cases and comprising a legal tradition specified under natural and divine law, characterized three secular philosophies spawned during the Enlightenment and dominant in nineteenth-century intellectual circles: socialism, utilitarianism, and transcendentalism.[55]

In American jurisdictions in the nineteenth century, both the trio of secular philosophies that had found expression during the Enlightenment, with their commitment to general statute by general assemblies, and the common law tradition, with its commitment to declaration of custom by courts, influenced those who governed. The colonial common law had been inherited in American states in the eighteenth century insofar as consistent with state constitutions.[56] These constitutions established popular sovereignty and declared freedoms of the people,[57] but two understandings of the relation of the people to society, government, and law existed in the minds of American political theorists. On one understanding, colonial society, government, and law properly remained that of the state, though consciously modified in light of the revolt against an overreaching and abusive imperial authority, so that the sovereign that governed traditional society under state law was now the people. Governing by convention of the people or through their elected assembly was under and subject to a modified colonial common law of each jurisdiction,[58] just as governing by the English sovereign, according to revered precedents of its unwritten constitution, was under and subject to English common law[59]: the rule of law remained constitutionally fundamental. On another understanding,[60] sovereign individuals were a pre-societal reality, supreme in any society they voluntarily created and under any government they consciously established, their governing will not hampered by the inherited body of declared law.[61] The people, on the latter understanding, exercised this general governing will in public assembly, where together they embarked on true freedom, whatever in their progressively more enlightened public opinion that might happen to be.[62]

These competing conceptions of popular sovereignty and contrasting roles of the institutions of the people's government—courts committed to rationalizing and localizing the common law while keeping a keen eye on tradition, the lessons of history, and the fundamental importance of cabining governing authority by declared law; and assemblies committed to imposing a rational system of law from outside the known practice of the people while keeping a keen eye on the scientific vistas opened by the secular philosophies that had exploded onto the world from the cannon of the French Revolution[63]—might not sit well together. The courts might continue to treat legislation as merely in the service of the ancient common law tradition, that is, as protecting its morally reasonable principles by cautiously and occasionally responding to evasions of its rules by wicked men.[64] And assemblies might treat the common law—even the rationally categorized common law stabilized by a strong doctrine of precedent[65]—as an illegitimate invasion of the popular will as expressed in popular opinion, a usurpation properly addressed by attacks on the judiciary and on the common law it expounded. As one nineteenth-century radical American transcendentalist had written,

> I labored under the comfortable illusion that, in order to secure wise and just government, all I had to do was to remove all restrictions on the free and full expression of the popular will.... There were still many restraints on their will, retained from old monarchical and aristocratic institutions; such as an independent judiciary, and the English common law with its subtilties [sic] and technicalities.[66]

Law reforms instituted in the nineteenth century to disrupt the common law tradition and to hold the judiciary more accountable to the passing popular will included the popular election of judges,[67] the abandonment or revamping[68] of the educational requirements to practice law,[69] and, of course, the codification of the common law.[70]

And so, what took the form of a battle between assembly and court was in substance a battle between advocates of divergent political philosophies. In North Carolina in the nineteenth century, then, what was at stake in settling the relative importance of the general assembly and the supreme court was control over the foundation and concomitant character of the state's society, government, and law.

Tom Davis
Raleigh, N.C.
June 2024

Part I

Early Documents

[T]he Laws of England are the Laws of this Government . . . and it is hereby Enacted and declared that the common Law is and shall be in force in this Government . . .

—The Queen's Peace, 1711

Whereas in pursuance of an Act of Assembly made & ratified the 6th day of November last past the ancient standing laws of this Government have been carefuly [sic] revised.

—Revisal, 1715

An Act for appointing Commissioners to revise and print the Laws of this Province, and for granting to His Majesty, for defraying the Charge thereof, a Duty on Wine, Rum, and distilled Liquors . . .

—Revisal, 1746

Be it ordained by the representatives of the Freemen of North Carolina in Congress assembled . . ., That Thomas Jones, Samuel Johnston, Archibald Maclaine, James Iredell, Abner Nash, Christopher Neale, Samuel Ashe, Waightstill Avery, Samuel Spencer, Jasper Charlton, and John Penn, Esquires, . . . are hereby appointed to revive . . . all such statutes and acts of the Assembly as are or have been in force and use in North Carolina and . . . consistent with the Genius of a Free People . . .

—Revisal Ordinance, 1776

[T]he said commissioner is hereby authorised and directed in revising and collecting said Acts, to leave out all laws repealed or obsolete, all private Acts and all Acts on which no question of property can arise; and further the said commissioner is hereby required to see the said Acts printed in the same order and in the same words in which they now stand . . .

—Revisal, 1787

Introduction to Early Documents

In this first part of *Selected Documents Relating to Law Reform in North Carolina during the Nineteenth Century* are gathered early documents in the legal history of the province, colony, and state of North Carolina. This early period runs from the provincial founding through nearly the end of the eighteenth century.

While this selection of early documents hardly covers the field of law reform in the seventeenth and eighteenth centuries, its documents raise important themes encountered in law reform in the nineteenth century. The first three documents compiled here, all of which are from the seventeenth century, introduce the notion of written fundamental law, which perhaps foreshadows the constitution-making of 100 years hence. These and other documents here excerpted also show the influence of the English law on the province and the state. Rising democratic sentiment is evident in the commitment to compilation of laws in force in the eighteenth century, which by relatively wide distribution relieves the people from ignorance of their laws and from the discretion of magistrates. The extension of juries to equity proceedings shortly after American Independence also protects the people from excessive exercise of discretion by magistrates. A continuing theme in the early history of the state, exemplified in this collection by the court acts of 1760 and 1786, is a distrust of attorneys.

Document I–1 Charter, 1663

[By this charter of 1663, King Charles II purported to grant to named subjects—the Lords Proprietors[71]—the province of Carolina,[72] thereby enlarging the empire and spreading Christianity. The Lords Proprietors of this remote and dangerous land would relate legally to the King of England as did "any bishop of Durham."[73] Their relationship to the "barbarous" non-Christian peoples encountered in America—peoples who the King contended had not planted the lands across the ocean—might devolve, he warned, into one of war.[74]]

THE FIRST CHARTER GRANTED BY KING CHARLES THE SECOND, TO THE LORDS PROPRIETORS OF CAROLINA.

CHARLES the Second, by the grace of God, king of England, Scotland, France and Ireland, Defender of the Faith, &c., To all to whom these present shall come: Greeting:

1st. Whereas [the Lords Proprietors], being excited with a laudable and pious zeal for the propagation of the Christian faith, and the enlargement of our empire and dominions, have humbly besought leave of us, by their industry and charge, to transport and make an ample colony of our subjects, natives of our kingdom of England, and elsewhere within our dominions, unto a certain country hereafter described, in the parts of America not yet cultivated or planted, and only inhabited by some barbarous people who have no knowledge of Almighty God. . . .

4th. To have, use, exercise and enjoy, and in as ample manner as any bishop of Durham in our kingdom of England, ever heretofore have held, used or enjoyed . . . And them [the Lords Proprietors], we do by these presents . . . make, create and constitute the true and absolute Lords Proprietors of the country aforesaid . . . To have, hold, possess and enjoy the said country . . . to them [the Lords Proprietors], to be holden of us . . . as of our manner of East Greenwich in our county of Kent, in free and common soccage, and not in capite, or by knight service; yielding and paying yearly to us, our heirs and successors, for the same, the yearly rent of twenty marks of lawful money of England, at the feast of All Saints, yearly forever, . . . and also the fourth part of all gold or silver ore, which, within the limits aforesaid, shall from time to time happen to be found.

5th. And that the country . . . may be dignified by us with as large titles and priviledges as any other part of our dominions and territories in that region, Know ye, that we . . . incorporate and ordain the same into a province, and call it the Province of Carolina . . .

15th. And because that in so remote a country, and scituate among so many barbarous nations, and the invasions as well of salvages as of other enemies, pirates and robbers, may probably be feared; therefore we . . . do give power, [to the persons named], by themselves, or their captains, or other their officers, to levy, muster and train all sorts of men, of what condition or wheresoever born, in the said province for the time being, and to make war and pursue the enemies aforesaid, as well by sea as by land, yea, even without the limits of the said province, and by God's assistance to vanquish and take them, and being taken to put them to death by the law of war, or to save them at their pleasure; and to do all and every other thing, which unto the charge of a captain general of an army belongeth, or hath accustomed to belong, as fully and freely as any captain general of an army hath or ever had the same. . . .

IN WITNESS, &C.

WITNESS the King, at Westminster, the four and twentieth day of

March, in the fifteenth year of our reign, (1663.)

PER IPSUM REGEM.

Document I–2   Charter, 1665

[The charter of 1665,[75] granting from king to named subjects—the Lords Proprietors—the province of Carolina, relied upon such feudal notions as liege people[76] and the tenurial relationships of common socage, tenure *in capite*, and knight's service.[77] The Lords Proprietors held lands with the privileges and immunities of any bishop of Durham, which was reminiscent of the charter of Maryland,[78] where the proprietor was a "virtually independent feudal lord, with but very slight obligation to the crown."[79] The Carolina charter empowered the provincial government to enact laws, both public and particular, so long as these were consonant with reason and were as similar as would be convenient to the customs of England. This restriction by reason and custom strongly suggested the common law tradition which, along with the natural law tradition under which the common law had emerged, would suffer vociferous attack by nineteenth-century, positivistic reformers intent upon codification.[80] The charter also enabled the Lords Proprietors to enact constitutions with the assent of the local freemen.]

THE SECOND CHARTER GRANTED BY KING CHARLES THE SECOND,
TO THE PROPRIETORS OF CAROLINA, DATED THE THIRTIETH DAY OF JUNE,
IN THE SEVENTEENTH YEAR OF HIS REIGN, A. D., 1665.

CHARLES the second, by the grace of God, of Great Britain, France and Ireland, King, Defender of the Faith, &c. WHEREAS, by our letters patent, bearing date the twentyfourth [*sic*] day of March, in the fifteenth year of our reign, we were graciously pleased to grant unto [the Lords Proprietors] all that province, territory, or tract of ground, called Carolina . . .

Now know ye, That we, at the humble request of the said grantees . . . we are graciously pleased to enlarge our said grant unto them, according to the bounds and limits hereafter specified, and in favour to the pious and noble purpose of the said [the Lords Proprietors], all that province, territory or tract of land, situate, lying and being within our dominions of America aforesaid; . . . together with all and singular the ports, harbours, bays, rivers and inlets . . . ; and also, all the soils, lands, fields, woods, mountains, ferns, lakes, rivers, bays and islets . . . ; with the fishings of all sorts . . . ; and moreover all veins, mines and quarries . . . ; and furthermore, the patronage and advowsons of all the churches and chapels . . . ; together with license and power to build and found churches, chapels and oratories . . . ; and to cause them to be dedicated and consecrated, according to the ecclesiastical laws of our kingdom of England; together will all and singular the like and as ample rights, jurisdictions, privileges, prerogatives, royalties, liberties, immunities, and franchises of what kind soever . . . : to have, hold, use, exercise, and enjoy the same, as amply, fully and in as ample manner, as any Bishop of Durham, in our kingdom of England, ever heretofore had, held, used, or enjoyed, or of right ought or could have, use, or enjoy: and them the said [Lords Proprietors], their heirs and assigns, we do, by these presents, for us, our heirs and successors, make, create, and constitute, the true and absolute lords and proprietors of the said province or territory, and of all other the premises; . . . ; to hold, possess, and enjoy the said province, territory, islets, and all and singular other the premises, to them the said [Lords Proprietors]; to be holden of us, our heirs and successors, as of our manor of East Greenwich, in Kent, in free and common socage, and not in capite, or by knight's service . . .

. . . Know ye therefore moreover, That we . . . do grant full and absolute power, by virtue of these presents, . . . for the good and happy government of the said whole province or territory, full power and authority, to erect, constitute, and make several counties, baronies, and colonies, of and within the said provinces, territories, lands, and hereditaments, . . . with several and distinct jurisdictions, powers, liberties, and privileges: and also, to ordain, make, and enact, and under their seals, to publish any laws and constitutions whatsoever, either appertaining to the public state of the whole province or territory, or of any distinct or particular county, barony, or colony, or of or within the same, or to the private utility of particular persons, according to their best directions, by and with the advice, assent and approbation, of the freemen of the said province or territory, or of the freemen of the county, barony, or colony, for which such law or constitution shall be made, or the greater part of them, or of their delegates or deputies, whom, for enacting of the said laws, when, and as often as need shall require, we will, that the [Lords Proprietors] shall, from time to time, assemble in such manner and form as to them shall seem best; and the same laws duly to execute, upon all people within the said province or territory, county, barony, or colony . . . ; yea, if it shall be needful, and the quality of the offence require it, by taking away member and life, either by them the said [Lords Proprietors], or their deputies, lieutenants, judges, justices, magistrates, or officers, whatsoever . . . in such manner and form as unto the said [Lords Proprietors] shall seem most convenient: and also, to remit, release, pardon, and abolish, whether before judgment or after, all crimes and offences whatsoever against the said laws; and to do all and every thing and things, which, unto the complete establishment of justice, unto courts, sessions, and forms of judicature, and manners of proceeding therein, do belong, although in these presents express mention is not made thereof; and by judges to him or them delegated, to award process, hold pleas, and determine, in all the said courts and places of judicature, all actions, suits, and causes whatsoever, as well criminal as civil, real, mixt, personal, or of any other kind or nature whatsoever: which laws so as aforesaid to be published, our pleasure is, and we do enjoin, require, and command, shall be absolutely firm and available in law; and that all the liege people of us, our heirs and successors, within the said province or territory, do observe and keep the same inviolably in those parts, so far as they concern them, under the pains and penalties therein expressed, or to be expressed: *Provided nevertheless*, That the said laws be consonant to reason, and as near as may be conveniently, agreeable to the laws and customs of this our realm of England. . . .

And we will also, and of our especial grace, for us, our heirs and successors, do straitly enjoin, ordain, constitute, and command, that the said province and territory shall be of our allegiance; and that all and singular the subjects and liege people of us, our heirs and successors, transported or to be transported into the said province, and the children of them, and such as shall descend from them there born, or hereafter to be born, be, and shall be denizens and lieges of us, our heirs and successors, of this our kingdom of England, and be in all things, held, treated and reputed, as the liege, faithful people of us, our heirs and successors, born within this our said kingdom, or any other of our dominions; and may inherit or otherwise purchase and receive, take, hold, buy and possess, any lands, tenements, or hereditaments, within the said places, and them may occupy and enjoy, sell, alien, and bequeath; as likewise, all liberties, franchises, and privileges, of this our kingdom, and of other our dominions aforesaid, may freely and quietly have, possess, and enjoy, as our liege people, born within the same, without the molestation, vexation, trouble, or grievance, of us, our heirs and successors: any act, statute, ordinance, or provision, to the contrary notwithstanding. . . .

And because it may happen that some of the people and inhabitants of the said province cannot, in their private opinions, conform to the public exercise of religion, according to the liturgy, forms and ceremonies of the church of England, or take and subscribe the oaths and articles made and established in that behalf; . . . our will and pleasure therefore is, and we do, by these presents . . . give and grant unto the said [Lords Proprietors] full and free license, liberty and authority, by such ways and means as they shall think fit, to give and grant unto such person and persons, inhabiting and being within the said province or territory, hereby . . . such indulgences and dispensations, in that behalf, for and during such time and times, and with such limitations and restrictions, as they the said [Lords Proprietors] shall, in their discretion, think fit and reasonable: and that no person or persons unto whom such liberty shall be given, shall be any way molested, punished, disquieted, or called in question, for any differences in opinion, or practice in matters of religious concernments, who do not actually disturb the civil peace of the province, county or colony, that they shall make their abode in: but all and every such person and persons may, from time to time, and at all times, freely and quietly have and enjoy his and their judgments and consciences, in matters of religion, throughout all the said province or colony, they behaving themselves peaceably, and not using this liberty to licentiousness, nor to civil injury, or outward disturbance of others; any law, statute or clause, contained or to be contained, usage or custom of our realm of England, to the contrary hereof, in any wise notwithstanding.

And in case it shall happen, that any doubts or questions shall arise, concerning the true sense and understanding of any word, clause, or sentence contained in this our present charter; we will, ordain and command, that in all times, and in all things, such interpretations be made thereof, and allowed in all and every of our courts whatsoever, as lawfully may be adjudged most advantageous and favorable to the said [Lords Proprietors] . . .

WITNESS ourself, at Westminster, the thirtieth day of June, in the seventeenth year of our reign.

PER IPSUM REGEM.

DOCUMENT I–3   THE GRAND MODEL, 1669

[Like the charters of Carolina of 1663 and 1665, *The Fundamental Constitutions of Carolina*, often referred to as the *Grand Model*, had a distinctly feudal flavor. Its five instantiations[81] contained explicitly anti-democratic language[82] and have been called "an elaborate governmental plan drawn up . . . to regulate the aristocratic and democratic elements of society,"[83] thus emphasizing its foundation in the pre-modern English constitutional theory of mixed government.[84]

The *Grand Model*, like other modern constitutions, set out the public law of the polity in written form. Unfortunately, it constituted a polity that had no prior existence and thus no basis in the life of a people.[85] For this reason, it has been said, the plan of government ultimately failed and has justly earned the criticism of commentators in later generations. For example, in a letter from 1837 concerning codification of the common law, Charles Sumner criticized this "code" known to him as Locke's *Fundamental Constitutions*:

> The subject of codification is beginning to excite a strong interest in our country. . . . Among us, the *codification* proposed is simply *revision* and *redaction*,—the reduction of a portion of the vast mass of decided cases (*Jurisprudence des arrets*) to a written text,—thus establishing, as it were, a *stratum* of written law, which will give firmness and solidity to that portion which remains *unwritten*. By such a course, it seems to me that we, in a great degree, avoid the evils pointed out by Savigny and the Historical School. We still preserve the historical features of the law, not presuming to frame a *new* system from *new* materials without consulting the previous customs, habits, and history of the country. The error of Jeremy Bentham and of John Locke was in supposing that they, in their closets, could frame *de novo* a code for a people. Locke prepared a code, a century ago, for one of the North American colonies, which proved a signal failure. . . .[86]

The criticism that law, especially fundamental law, must be naturally concomitant with the society which it characterizes, and not a theoretical system drafted remotely by closet philosophers, has often been echoed by commentators.[87] Justice Story cemented this viewpoint for American posterity by including the notion in one of his more widely-read commentaries.[88] Later in the century, the Honorable Kemp Battle, president of the University of North Carolina in Chapel Hill, noticed the same theme.[89] Critics of the codification

The famed philosopher John Locke contributed to the drafting of *The Fundamental Constitutions of Carolina* while serving as secretary to Carolina Proprietor Anthony Ashley Cooper, First Earl of Shaftesbury. Photograph of engraving after portrait of John Locke by Godfrey Kneller in 1697. (*Credit*: State Archives of North Carolina, Raleigh)

of the private substantive law adopted this theme in debates in later decades of the nineteenth century, especially in New York.[90]

The Fundamental Constitutions of Carolina evidenced a distrust of lawyers, of the multiplicity of laws, and of commentary and exposition on the law. It placed value upon the writtenness of law, which allowed for accessibility, public reading, and authoritativeness of the documents that comprised the law.]

THE FUNDAMENTAL CONSTITUTIONS OF CAROLINA, DRAWN UP BY JOHN LOCKE, MARCH 1, 1669.
(see Locke's Works, 8th edition, volume 10, page 175.)

OUR sovereign Lord the King, having out of his royal grace and bounty, granted unto us the Province of Carolina, with all the royalties, properties, jurisdictions and priviledges of a County Palatine, as large and ample as the County Palatine of Durham, with other great Priviledges; for the better settlement of the government of the said place, and establishing the interest of the Lords Proprietors with equality, and without confusion; and that the government of this Province may be made most agreeable to the Monarchy under which we live, and of which this Province is a part; and that we may avoid erecting a numerous democracy: We, the Lords and proprietors of the Province aforesaid, have agreed to this following form of government, to be perpetually established amongst us, unto which we do oblige ourselves, our heirs and successors, in the most binding ways that can be devised. . . .

70th. It shall be a base and vile thing, to plead for money or reward; nor shall any one, (except he be a near kinsman, nor farther off than cousin german to the party concerned) be permitted to plead another man's cause, till before the judge, in open court, he hath taken an oath that he doth not plead for money or reward, nor hath, nor will receive, nor directly, nor indirectly, bargained with the party whose cause he is going to plead, for money, or any other reward for pleading his cause. . . .

74th. At the opening of every Parliament, the first thing that shall be done, shall be the reading of these Fundamental Constitutions, which the Palatine and Proprietors, and the rest of the members then present, shall subscribe. Nor shall any person whatsoever, sit or vote in the Parliament, till he hath that session subscribed these Fundamental Constitutions, in a book kept for that purpose, by the clerk of the parliament. . . .

76th. No act or order of Parliament shall be of any force, unless it be ratified in open parliament during the same session, by the Palatine or his deputy, and three more of the Lords Proprietors or their deputies; and then not to continue longer in force, but until the next biennial Parliament, unless in the meantime it be ratified under the hands and seals of the Palatine himself, and three more of the Lords Proprietors, themselves, and by their order published at the next biennial Parliament.

77th. Any Proprietor or his deputy may enter his protestation against any act of the Parliament, before the Palatine or his deputy's consent be given as aforesaid; if he shall conceive the said act to be contrary to this establishment, or any of these Fundamental Constitutions of the Government. And in such case, after full and free debate, the several estates shall retire into four several chambers, the Palatine and Proprietors into one; the Landgraves into another; the Casiques into another; and those chosen by the Precincts into a fourth; and if the major part of any of the four estates shall vote that the law is not agreeable to this establishment, and these Fundamental Constitutions of the Government, then it shall pass no farther, but be as if it had never been proposed. . . .

79th. To avoid multiplicity of laws, which by degrees always change the right foundations of the original government, all acts of Parliament whatsoever, in whatsoever form passed or enacted, shall at the end of a hundred years after their enacting, respectively cease, and determine of themselves, and without any repeal, become null and void, as if no such acts or laws had ever been made.

80th. Since multiplicity of comments, as well as of laws, have great inconveniences, and serve only to obscure and perplex; all manner of comments and expositions, on any part of these Fundamental Constitutions, or on any part of the common or statute laws of Carolina, are absolutely prohibited. . . .

117th. A true copy of these Fundamental constitutions shall be kept in a great book, by the register of every precinct, to be subscribed before the said register. Nor shall any person of what degree or condition soever, above seventeen years old, have any estate or possession in Carolina, or protection or benefit of the law there, who hath not, before a precinct register, subscribed these fundamental constitutions in this form:

"I, A. B., do promise to bear faith, and true allegiance, to our sovereign Lord King Charles the second, his heirs and successors, and will be true and faithful to the Palatine and Lords Proprietors of Carolina, their heirs and successors; and with my utmost power, will defend them and maintain the government, according to this establishment in these fundamental Constitutions." . . .

120th. These fundamental constitutions, in number a hundred and twenty, and every part thereof, shall be and remain, the sacred and unalterable form and rule of government of Carolina forever. Witness our hands and seals the first day of March, 1669.

Document I-4   Nine Confirmed Laws, 1669[-1670]

[During its early years, when Carolina could not fully put into practice its provincial constitution known as the *Grand Model* for want of a sufficient number of people in the province, the Lords Proprietors instructed the Governor and Council of Albemarle, with the consent of the Assembly, to make

such laws as you shall from time to time find necessary, which laws being ratified by you and any three of our five deputys shall be in force as is in that case provided in the Twelfth and other Articles of our fundamentall constitutions in forme of Government.[91]

Nine laws were ratified and confirmed by the Lords Proprietors on January 20, 1670, then passed again on October 15 of that year.[92] In 1715, the general assembly of the northeast part of the province would reconfirm six of these nine laws, the other three by then being obsolete.[93]]

ACTS OF THE ASSEMBLY OF ALBEMARLE RATIFIED
AND CONFIRMED BY THE PROPRIETORS,
20 JANUARY, 1669–1670.

(Colonial Entry Book No. 20, pp. 48–52.)

An Act Prohibiting Sueing of Any Person Within 5 Years. . . .
An Act Concerning Marriages. . . .
An Act Concerning Transferring of Rights. . . .
An Act Exempting New Comers from Paying Levys for One Yeare. . . .
An Act Against Ingrocers. . . .
An Act Concerning Defraying the Charges of the Governor and Councell. . . .
An Act What Land Men Shall Hould in One Devidend. . . .
An Act for the Speedier Seating of Land. . . .
An Act Prohibiting Strangers Tradeing With the Indians. . . .

The foregoing acts weare [*sic*] past again the 15th of October and sent per Mr. Nixon.

Document I-5   The Queen's Peace, 1711

[Although the status of English law in force in the province of North Carolina is often traced to an act of 1715,[94] the state records of North Carolina contain an act of 1711 on the same subject,[95] which appears in part below.

The 1711 act aimed to remedy disputes about the extent to which English laws were in force in North Carolina, a colony experiencing severe disturbances described in the act as "revolutions"—disturbances purportedly to Queen Anne's peace, the peace of the Lords Proprietors not being mentioned. The act asserted that the province was a member of the crown of England and that the province's charter limited the power of making local laws by two standards, consonance with reason and agreeableness to the "Laws and Customs" of England, which led the drafters of the act to conclude that the "Laws of England," insofar as compatible with provincial ways of living and trade, were the laws of North Carolina.[96] Given this conclusion, the general assembly declared that the "common Law" was and would continue to be in force in North Carolina.[97] Additionally, it declared that the "statute Laws of England"[98] pertaining to seven specified subjects were in force in North Carolina as well, even when the crown-in-Parliament had failed to name the colony with particularity in statutes on these subjects.[99]]

1711.

Chapter I.

An Act for the better and more effectual preserving the Queen's peace, and the establishing a good and lasting foundation of Government in North Carolina.

Whereas several revolutions have heretofore happened in this colony . . . ; And what has most nearly concerned us, are the late unhappy dissensions amongst ourselves in this Colony, whereby injustice and Oppression took place, and overspread our Colony. . . . We therefore the Commons assembled do pray that it may be Enacted. And be it Enacted by his Excellency the Palatin and Lords Proprietors, by and with the advice and consent of this present General Assembly and the authority thereof, and it is hereby Enacted, . . .

II. And be it Enacted by the authority aforesaid what person soever shall act in any place of profit or trust as aforesaid, without being so qualified shall forfeit the sum of one hundred pounds. . . . Provided . . . moreover what person or persons who hereafter shall equivocate, alter, add to, or diminish any word or clause, of the oaths appointed to be taken by Law shall be deemed and held guilty of forgery and high crimes, and shall be punished accordingly.

III. And whereas this Province is annexed to and declared to be a member of the Crown of England, yet notwithstanding disputes do often arise concerning the Laws of England, how far they are in force in this Government; and it appearing by the Charter that the power therein granted of making Laws are limited with the expression Viz. Provided such Laws be consonant to reason, and as near as may be agreeable to the Laws and Customs of Our Kingdom of England, from whence it is manifest that the Laws of England are the Laws of this Government, so far as they are compatible with our way of living and Trade, Be it therefore Enacted by the authority aforesaid, and it is hereby Enacted and declared that the common Law is and shall be in force in this Government except such part of the practice in the issueing out and return of Writts, and proceedings in the Court of Westminster which for want of several Officers, cannot be put in execution, which ought to be supplied by Rules of the General Court of this Government, being first approved of by the Governor in Council which shall be good in Law from time to time till it shall be altered by Act of Assembly.

IV. And be it further Enacted and Declared by the authority aforesaid that all statute Laws of England made for maintaining the Queen's Royal Prerogative and the security of her royal person and succession of the Crown, and all such Laws made for the establishment of, church and the Laws made for granting Indulgencies to protestant dissenters, and all Laws providing for the privilege of the people and security of trade as also statute Laws made for Limitation of Actions and for preventing vexatious Lawsuits, and for preventing immorality and frauds, and confirming Inheritances and Titles of Land are and shall be in force here, altho' this province or the plantations in general are not therein named. . . .

EDWARD HYDE
W. GLOVER
THO: POLLOCK
RICHD. SANDERSON
N. CHEVIN
THO. BOYD.

WM. SWAN Speaker.

Document I-6 Revisal, 1715

[In the general assembly, which convened November 17, 1715 and adjourned January 19, 1716,[100] "all the laws were revised and re-enacted . . . , and the common law of England was declared in full force in North Carolina."[101] This revisal would be referred to as the "book of Laws"[102] or the "Law Book."[103] Historian Francis L. Hawks described this revisal:

Thus, in the manuscript volume now before us, we find at a biennial assembly held in 1715, these *words placed in front* of all the enactments: "These following laws, being in number fifty-seven, were read three times and ratified in open assembly." This was a revisal of the whole body of statute law; and *at the close is a statement* that the revision had been made by authority: and a special enactment repeals all former laws not particularly excepted by their titles, and confirms the whole as "the body of the laws of the government." The volume contains also all the excepted laws, as well as those marked in the earliest printed revisal as then "obsolete."[104]

The statement Hawks noticed "at the close" of the manuscript volume was the last act in the revision, entitled An Act for the Confirmation of the Laws. It contained sixteen sections (reprinted below).

The 2nd section of this act of confirmation repealed all laws "heretofore made within this Province" except those continued and revised by their particular titles. The 6th section of this act of confirmation announced that "these following Laws . . . are hereby revived & continued." The 7th–12th sections then named six acts with particularity, and the 13th section listed the six confirmed laws, bringing the total number of laws continued to twelve. Additionally, the 14th section added an indefinite number of acts to this list when it continued any "Act relating to the Publick funds or bills of Credit, any Act of Naturalization, or any other private Acts." The final two sections of the act of confirmation demanded that the revision be accessible to the people and read by the clerks of court each year.

The list of laws which Hawks described as located "in front" of the manuscript volume appears in the state records as "North Carolina SS."[105] This document ratified the revisal of 1715 by listing the titles to fifty-seven of the sixty-six public acts comprising that revision. The nine public acts which were not listed in this ratifying document were:

- the six confirmed laws (chapters 1–6 of the revisal);[106]
- the act concerning escheats (chapter 30 of the revisal);[107]
- the act concerning the Queen's Peace (chapter 31 of the revisal);[108] and
- the act concerning surveying (chapter 33 of the revisal).[109]

Like the fifty-seven public acts listed by the ratifying document, the text of these nine acts appeared in full in separate chapters of the revisal, and, as noted above, were specifically continued and revised by sections 7, 8, 10, and 13 of the Act of Confirmation (chapter 66 of the revisal).[110]

Thus began in Carolina the periodic compilation of the statutes in force in North Carolina and thus continued (in chapter 31 of the revisal) the acknowledgment of the authority of the law of England as the foundation of Carolina law.]

CHAPTER LXVI.

An Act for the Confirmation of the Laws passed this Session of Assembly & for repealing all former Laws not herein particularly Excepted.

I. Whereas in pursuance of an Act of Assembly made & ratified the 6th day of November last past the ancient standing laws of this Government have been careful[l]y revised.

II. Be It Therefore Enacted by his Excellency the Pallatine & the rest of the true & absolute Lords, &c.

And it is hereby Enacted that all laws heretofore made within this Province such only Excepted as by their particular titles are hereby Expressly continued & revised are, and stand hereby repealed, annulled & void, & that all laws now made, passed and confirmed this present Session of Assembly together with such other as are hereafter mentioned to be continued shall be of full force & shall be hence forward deemed taken & adjudged as the body of the Laws of this Government & no other heretofore made.

III. And to prevent Disputes which may hereafter arise for or by reason of any Act or Acts, thing or things heretofore done or acted which might have been held & Claimed by Virtue of any Law hereby repealed, or Intended to be repealed.

IV. Be It Further Enacted, by the Authority aforesaid that all and every other act or acts, thing or things heretofore awarded, passed & done or which might have been held and claimed in pursuance to any law or act of Assembly hereby repealed & Intended to be repealed shall be good, valid & Effectual in the law to all intents & purposes whatsoever as if the said Laws and every of them were Continued & in force.

V. And saving Likewise to all persons the benefit and advantages of any suit or action already commenced, or Sued upon any Act or Acts hereby repealed, anything herein before to the Contrary notwithstanding.

VI. And Be It Further Enacted by the Authority aforesaid that these following Laws shall be, remain, and continue, and they are hereby revived & continued.

VII. An Act Concerning Escheat Lands & Escheators.

VIII. An Act for the better and more Effectual preserving the Queen's peace & establishing good and lasting foundation of Government, in North Carolina.

IX. An Act to promote the building a Court house to hold the Assembly in, at the fork of Queen Ann's Creek commonly called Matchacamak Creek in Chowan precinct.

X. An Act to regulate Divers abuses in the taking up land & to ascertain the method to be observed from henceforward in taking up and surveying of Land.

XI. An Act Impowering the Governor to appoint Commissioners to treat with all such Commissioners as shall be appointed by the Government of Virginia relating to the Indian affairs.

XII. An Act for the raising the sum of twenty four thousand pounds in publick bills of Credit for paying the remaining part of the Debts of the Government & for sinking the remaining part of the sum of twelve thousand pounds Publick bills of Credit with two years' Interest.

XIII. Provided always that this Act, nor anything therein Contained shall be construed, adjudged & taken or is & hereby meant or intended to annul, repeal or make void the six following Laws already confirmed by the Lords Proprietors the several titles whereof follows:

1st. An Act concerning Marriages.

2nd. An Act concerning transferring of rights.

3rd. An Act concerning the defraying the Charge of the Government & Council.

4th. An Act prohibiting strangers trading with the Indians.

5th. An Act for the speedy settlement of Land.

6th. An Act exempting new comers from paying Levys for one year.

XIV. And provided also, that this Act shall not Extend to make voyd, or annul, any Act or Clause of any Act relating to the Publick funds or bills of Credit, any Act of Naturalization, or any other private Acts, but that all and every such Act & acts are hereby Confirmed and ratified & that the Acts relating to the Publick funds or bills of Credit shall be and continue till they become absolute, or shall be afterwards declared voyd by act of the General Assembly any thing herein before to the contrary notwithstanding.

XV. And Be It Further Enacted by the Authority aforesaid that the Chief Justice and the Clerk of such & every precinct Court, shall take care, that the transcript, or book of Laws reposited in his or their Custody, shall be constantly laid open upon the Court table during the sitting of the Court for the perusal of such members of the Court or other persons Littigating Causes therein as shall have occasion so to do.

XVI. And Be It Further Enacted that the Clerk of each Court shall at the next Court after receipt thereof publickly & in open Court read over the same & so yearly at the first Court next following after the first day of May under the Penalty of five pounds for such neglect. And forasmuch as Mr.

CHARLES EDEN, Esq., Governor.

Signed by
N. CHEVIN,
W. REED,
CHR. GALE,
TOBIAS KNIGHT,
FRANCIS FOSTER,
    Lords Proprietors Deputies.

EDWARD MOSELEY, Speaker.

Document I–7 The Queen's Peace, 1715

[Chapter thirty-one of the *Revisal* of 1715 was nearly identical to the act concerning the Queen's peace of 1711, even mentioning the "Queen's Peace" and the "Queen's Royal Prerogative" after George I had succeeded Anne to the throne.[111] While changes in section numbering, punctuation, and capitalization occurred, the only significant variations in the 1715 act were that injustice and oppression were described as overtaking the *country*, rather than the *colony*, and that the jurisdiction of the act was limited by its text (i.e., not merely by the title of the act) to the northeast part of the province. A nearly contemporaneous act concerning the force of English law in Carolina passed in the "South-west part of this Province."[112] These acts varied significantly, though, the one for the southwest part of the province listing with particularity the English statutes in force there.[113]]

CHAPTER XXXI.

An Act for the more effectual observing of the Queen's Peace, and Establishing a good and lasting Foundation of Government in North Carolina.

I. Whereas several Revolutions have heretofore happened in this Colony . . . ; and what most nearly has concerned us, are the late unhappy Dissentions among ourselves in this Colony, whereby Injustice and Oppression took Place and Overspread our Country, our Trade decreased, and daily differences and Animosities increased, to the Ruin of Religion and our Liberties . . . :

II. We therefore, the Commons Assembled, do pray that it may be Enacted, And be it Enacted by his Excellency the Palatine, and the rest of the true and absolute Lords Proprietors of the Province of Carolina, by and with the Advice and Consent of the Members of the General Assembly, now met at Little River, for the North East part of the Province, and by the Authority of the same; And it is hereby Enacted, That any Person or Persons who shall, at any time after the Date hereof, speak any seditious Words or Speeches, or spread abroad false News, write or disperse scurrilous Libels against the present Government, . . . or that shall instigate others to Sedition . . . to contrive the Ruin and Disturbances of the Queen's Peace, and of the Safety and Tranquility of this Government; the said person or persons so offending, shall, and are to be reputed as utter Enemies to the Queen's peace, and the Welfare and Good of this Government; and shall be punished accordingly, . . . and be incapable of bearing any Office of Profit or Trust in this Government, for the space of Three Years . . .

V. And whereas, this Province is annexed to, and declared to be a Member of the Crown of England; yet, notwithstanding Disputes so often arise concerning the Laws of England how far they, are in Force in this Government; and it appearing by the Charter, that the Powers therein granted of making Laws, are limited with this Expression, viz.: "Provided, Such Laws be Consonant with Reason, and as near as may be, agreeable to the Laws and Customs of our Kingdom of England." From thence it is manifest, That the Laws of England are the Laws of this Government, so far as they are compatable with our Way of Living and Trade:

VI. Be it Therefore Enacted, by the Authority aforesaid, and it is hereby Enacted and Declared, That the common Law is, and shall be, in Force in this Government, except such part in the Practice, in the Issuing and Return of Writs, and Proceedings in the Court of Westminister [*sic*]; which for want of several Officers, cannot be put in Execution; which ought to be supplied by Rules of the General Court of this Government, being first approved of by the Governor and council, which shall be good in Law, from Time to Time, till it shall be altered by Act of Assembly.

VII. And be it further Enacted and Declared, by the Authority aforesaid. That all Statute Laws of England, made for maintaining the Queen's Royal Prerogative, and the Security of her Royal Person, and Succession of the Crown, and all such Laws made for the Establishment of the Church, and the Laws made for the Indulgence to Protestant Dissenters, and all Laws providing for the Priviledges of the People, and Security of Trade; as also, all Statute Laws made for Limitation of Actions, and Preventing of Vexatious Law Suits, and for preventing Immorality and Fraud, and confirming Inheritences and Titles of Land, are and shall be in Force here, altho' this Province, or the Plantations in general, are not therein named. . . .

Document I–8 Provincial Laws in Force, 1731

[After the surrender of the government of North Carolina by the Lords Proprietors to King George II, Sir Richard Everard held over as governor for a period of more than two years, and the local legislature met once, in November 1729, though the validity of the laws passed at that session were questioned and ultimately they were declared void.[114] The first royal governor in North Carolina, George Burrington, was commissioned in January 1730[115] and received his instructions in December 1730.[116] The twenty-fifth item of Burrington's instructions required that he and his council "take care that all Laws now in force [in North Carolina] be revived & considered and if there be anything either in the matter or style of them which may be fit to be retrenched or altered You are to represent the same to us with your opinion touching the said laws now in force. . . ." In his response to those instructions, reprinted below, Burrington reported on the laws passed by the hold-over government in November 1729, as well as on the laws in force in North Carolina, including five of the six confirmed laws,[117] an act concerning escheat lands, an act to regulate abuses in taking up and surveying lands, an act for raising money in public bills of credit, and the act for preserving the queen's peace from 1711.[118] Regarding the last of these acts, Burrington explained that some persons had held the 1711 act to be temporary, tied merely to the Cary Rebellion,[119] but that the better received opinion was that the 1711 act, which had been confirmed in the *Revisal* of 1715,[120] remained in force in North Carolina.]

These following are the Acts that were past in November 1729 after the King had purchased the Government of the Lords Proprietors, about the Validity of which Laws there has been such debates . . . but this hath been fully set forth in the Journalls & my Report.

[Here follows a list of the titles of eleven acts.]

THE SIX CONFIRMED LAWS.

These Laws following called the Confirmed Laws had been out of use and lost for above 20 years when upon a revival of the whole body of Laws in 1715 an old copy was produced and transcribed into the Law Book the original of them are entirely lost and they are become quite obsolete.

An Act concerning Marriages.
An Act transferring of Rights
An Act concerning the defraying the charge of the Governor & Councill
An Act prohibiting Strangers trading with the Indians
An Act for the speedy settlement of Lands

An Act concerning Escheat Lands and Escheators
This is a very old Law and not altered at the revisal in 1715. I am told that there are laws of this kind in most of His Maj[ty's] Colonies But whither two pence ⅌ [per] acre will be thought for the future a Comp[o]sition sufficient is submitted. The Law otherwise being very fittfor [sic] the Purpose.

An act for the more effectual preserving the Queen's Peace and establishing a good and lasting foundation of Government in North Carolina.

This was a Law after there had been Com[m]otions in the Country and People in Armes which was called Cary's Rebellion and after the Government was settled this Act was made for securing the same and by the manner of wording of it referring to the then present Government establish'd, hath been held by some to be a Law made for that time only but by being confirmed in 1715, And having been put in practice several times since It should seem to be the better received Opinion that it is sitll [sic] in force and in so turbulent a Place is a Law not ill suited for the purpose, and that part of it declaratory of the Laws of England being in force here seems well Provided. . . .

Document I–9 Revisal, 1746

[An act of 1746 requested that the provincial governor commission the persons specified to revise and compile the laws in force in the province and granted the commissioners a temporary monopoly in the sale of the compilation. When confirmed by the general assembly, the revisal would have the status of positive law and would supersede the laws on which it was based. The work of the commissioners under this act[121] became known as *Swann's Revisal* or the "Yellow Jacket,"[122] which was the first book printed in North Carolina. Beyond its status as an early compilation of statutes in force,[123] the Yellow Jacket is of interest because the purpose statement of the act commissioning it anticipated two themes that would be bandied about during the codification debates of the next century: relief of the ignorance of the people so that they might behave according to law and relief from the ignorance of the magistrates so that they would not tyrannize the people and would not rely too much upon their discretion.]

CHAPTER I.

An Act for appointing Commissioners to Revise and Print the Laws of this Province, and for granting to his Majesty, for defraying the Charge thereof, a Duty on Wine, Rum and distilled Liquors and Rice imported into this Province.

I. Whereas for want of the Laws of this Province being revised and printed, the Magistrates are often at a Loss how to discharge their Duty, and the People transgress many of them through want of knowing the same: Wherefore,

II. We pray it may be Enacted, And be it Enacted, by his Excellency Gabriel Johns[t]on, Esq., Governor, by and with the Advice and Consent of his Majesty's Council, and the General Assembly of this Province, and by the Authority of the same, That the Honourable Edward Moseley, Esq.; Samuel Swann, Esq.; the Honourable Enoch Hall, Esq.; and Mr. Thomas Barker, or the Majority of them, be, and they are hereby nominated and appointed Commissioners, to revise and print the several Acts of Assembly in Force in this Province.

III. And be it further Enacted, That the said Commissioners shall revise the said Acts of Assembly, and compile them in one Body, and make an Index, Marginal Notes, and References thereto, and shall lay the same before the next succeeding General Assembly after they shall have so revised and compiled them, to be ratified and confirmed . . .

IV. And be it further Enacted, That after the said Acts shall be revised and compiled by the said Commissioners, or the Majority of them, as aforesaid, and ratified and confirmed by the General Assembly, the same shall, with all convenient Speed, be printed, by the several Commissioners, or the Majority of them, who shall furnish and deliver several Books of the said Laws, well bound, and Lettered on the Back, to the several Officers, Offices, and Courts, hereinafter mentioned; that is to say, One to his Excellency the Governor, One for the use of his Majesty's Council, One for the use of the General Assembly, One for the use of the Secretary's Office, One for the use of the General Court, and One to each and every County Court respectively in this Province: And such only of the said Commissioners who shall revise the Laws as aforesaid, shall have and receive, for printing the said Acts, and furnishing and delivering the several Books aforesaid, the Sum of One Hundred Pounds, Proclamation Money; to be paid by the General Assembly, out of the Money arising by the Duty before mentioned; and also, the Benefit and Advantage of the sole Printing and Vending the Books of the said Laws, for and during the Space or Term of Five Years; and shall not take or receive above the sum of Fifteen Shillings, Proclamation Money, for each Book by them so printed. . . .

DOCUMENT I–10 ENGLISH LAW IN FORCE, 1749

[With this act of 1749, North Carolina attempted to list with particularity the English statutes in force in the colony—as South Carolina had done earlier in the century, well before the English king had purchased the province from the Lords Proprietors.[124] Unfortunately, North Carolina's foray into statute-listing was "either repealed or disapproved by the king" as too sweeping a repeal of British statutes.[125] So, while the act was printed in *Swann's Revisal*, it did not appear in later revisions of the laws.[126] The important and difficult issue of the scope of the reception of English statute law remained problematic in North Carolina until the mid-1830s.[127]

The act of 1749 also declared the common law of England to be in force in Carolina and thus is treated in *Swann's Revisal* as superseding the act concerning the Queen's peace from early in the century.[128] The act of 1749 presumed that English statutes in force in the colony had modified the common law of the colony, as had local constitutions, customs, and laws. Additionally, the act excepted ancient tenures from North Carolina's reception of the common law by enacting and declaring the English statute of 1660

A COLLECTION

OF

All the PUBLIC

ACTS OF ASSEMBLY,

OF

The PROVINCE of

NORTH-CAROLINA:

Now in FORCE and USE.

Together with the TITLES of all such LAWS as are Obsolete, Expir'd, or Repeal'd.

And also, an exact TABLE of the Titles of the ACTS in Force.

REVISED *by Commissioners appointed by an Act of the* GENERAL ASSEMBLY *of the said Province, for that Purpose; and Examined with the Records, and Confirmed in full Assembly.*

NEWBERN: Printed by JAMES DAVIS, M,DCC,LI.

In 1746, Samuel Swann was among the persons commissioned to revise the acts of assembly in force in the province. The revisal, published in 1751, was the first book printed in North Carolina. (*Credit*: Wilson Special Collections Library, University of North Carolina at Chapel Hill) concerning tenures "to be of as full Force in this Province, as if particularly enumerated by this Act [of 1749]."[129] The act of 1749 also excepted "that Part of the Common Law which relates to Matters Ecclesiastical which are inconsistent with, or repugnant to, the Settlement of the Church of *England* in this Province, by the Acts of Assembly thereof. . . ." Finally, in discussing who shall put in execution the common law of the province, the act recognized the court of chancery, which in Carolina consisted of the governor and his council.[130]]

CHAPTER I.

An Act to put in Force in this Province, the several Statutes of the Kingdom of England, or South-Britain, therein particularly mentioned. . . .

II. Be it therefore Enacted, by his Excellency Gabriel Johnston, Esq., Governor, by and With the Advice and Consent of his Majesty's Council, and General Assembly of this Province, and it is hereby Enacted, by the Authority of the same, That the several Statutes, and the several Paragraphs or Sections of the several Statutes of the Kingdom of England intituled [*sic*] as followeth, and made and Enacted in such Years of the Reigns of the Kings and Queens of England as before the Titles of the several Statutes, as in this Act set down, are, and are hereby to be in as full Force, Power, and Virtue, as if the same had been specially Enacted and made for this Province, or as if the same had been made and Enacted there in, by any General Assembly thereof: That is to say:

[Here follows a list of English laws declared to be in force in North Carolina, beginning with Magna Charta as issued in the 9th year of the reign of King Henry III, as well as sections III–V of this Act.] . . .

VI. And be it further Enacted, by the Authority aforesaid, That all and every Part of the Common Law of England, where the same is not altered by the above enumerated Acts, or inconsistent with the particular Constitutions, Customs, and Laws of this Province, excepting so much thereof as hath Relation to the ancient Tenures, which are taken away by the Act of Parliament [of 1660], . . . is hereby Enacted and declared to be of as full Force in this Province, as if particularly enumerated by this Act [of 1749]; and also excepting that Part of the Common Law which relates to Matters of Ecclesiastical, which are inconsistent with, or repugnant to, the Settlement of the Church, of England in this Province, by the Acts of Assembly thereof; be, and is hereby made and declared to be in as full Force and Virtue within this Province, as the same is, or ought to be, within the said Kingdom of England: And that the Governor for the Time being, with his Council, constituting a Court of Chancery in this Province, shall have Power to put in Execution, and cause to be put in Execution in this Province, so much of the said Common Law, (except as before excepted,) as the Lord Chancellor, or Lord Keeper of the Great Seal of Great Britain, may do in the Kingdom of England . . .

Document I-11 Court Act, 1760

[The distrust of attorneys and the need to control the activities of this privileged class of professionals was a continuing theme in the colonial history of North Carolina and in the codification debates of antebellum America. One scholar of colonial North Carolina asserted that the extant records reveal a chain of protests about lawyers:

> However the case may be and whether or not lawyers were regarded as of great importance by the early North Carolinians, it is a fact that we have few records to show how they were regarded as a class.
>
> Again, the few records which we do have are almost exclusively adverse to the lawyers. They form a chain of protests against the bar and of legislation passed with the intent to control and suppress its members.[131]

By 1760, "the people were determined that some action should be taken in regard to better control of lawyers. . . ."[132] A provision in the act excerpted below results from that determination. The Crown disapproved the act before 1762.[133]]

CHAPTER I.

An Act, for establishing Superior Courts of Pleas and Grand Sessions, and Regulating the Proceedings therein. . . .

LVII. And whereas, as well the Dignity of the Courts as the Security of the Suitors, depends greatly on the Capacity and Probity of Lawyers practicing in the same: Be it Enacted, by the Authority aforesaid, and it is hereby Enacted, That no Person who hath not already obtained a License, shall hereafter be admitted as an Attorney to practice the Law, or a Councellor to plead in the Superior or Inferior Courts in this Province, unless he shall first have been regularly examined as to his Knowledge in Matters of Law, and the Practice of Courts, by some one of the Judges of the Superior Courts; and shall have obtained a Certificate under the Hand of such Judge, recommending him to the Governor or Commander in Chief for the Time being, as properly qualified to practice the Law, or plead as aforesaid, and shall likewise have obtained a Certificate from the Justices of the Inferior Court of the County wherein he shall reside, certifying him to be a Person of good Character; and no License shall hereafter be granted to any Person to practice the Law, or plead in any of the Courts of Law or Equity, until such Certificates shall be by him obtained. . . .

Document I–12 Declaration and Resolves, 1774

[Delegates sitting in the First Continental Congress, including those representing the colony of North Carolina,[134] declared in this document their rights and liberties, while maintaining their loyalty to the mother country.[135] Grievances were stated, inconsistencies between past practices and the law were asserted, and redress was requested. In making this declaration, the deputies asserted that as Englishmen they do what "their ancestors in like cases have usually done, for asserting and vindicating their rights and liberties. . . ."[136] This particular example of the English practice of declaring rights is based on "the immutable laws of nature, the principles of the English constitution, and the several charters or compacts . . ."[137]

By natural law, English constitutional law, and positive foundational law of the colonies, the colonists claimed entitlement to the rights, liberties, and immunities of free and natural-born subjects within the realm of England. By this same authority, they asserted entitlement to: (1) the common law of England, including the privilege of being tried by their peers of the vicinage, (2) the English statutes as these existed at the time of colonization, and (3) the immunities and privileges granted and confirmed by royal charters or secured by the several codes of provincial laws. While this document did not receive the common law in any colony, it asserted that the common law was in force in each of the colonies, as were English statutes (broadly excepting eighteenth-century acts, many of which offended the colonial rights here asserted).

Beyond these general categories of legal right, the declaration and resolves also re-asserted specific rights which harken back to grievances recorded in the English Bill of Rights, including the rights to assemble, to petition the King, and to be free of standing armies.]

SELECT CHARTERS
AND OTHER DOCUMENTS
ILLUSTRATIVE OF
AMERICAN HISTORY
1606–1775 . . .

. . . No. 72. Declaration and Resolves of the
First Continental Congress
October 14, 1774

. . . The good people of the several colonies of New-Hampshire, Massachusetts-Bay, Rhode-Island and Providence Plantations, Connecticut, New-York, New-Jersey, Pennsylvania, Newcastle, Kent, and Sussex on Delaware, Maryland, Virginia, North-Carolina, and South-Carolina, justly alarmed at these arbitrary proceedings of parliament and administration, have severally elected, constituted, and appointed deputies to meet, and sit in general Congress, in the city of Philadelphia, in order to obtain such establishment, as that their religion, laws, and liberties, may not be subverted: Whereupon the deputies so appointed being now assembled, in a full and free representation of these colonies, taking into their most serious consideration, the best means of attaining the ends aforesaid, do, in the first place, as Englishmen, their ancestors in like cases have usually done, for asserting and vindicating their rights and liberties, DECLARE,

That the inhabitants of the English colonies in North-America, by the immutable laws of nature, the principles of the English constitution, and the several charters or compacts, have the following RIGHTS:

Resolved, N. C. D. 1. That they are entitled to life, liberty and property: and they have never ceded to any foreign power whatever, a right to dispose of either without their consent.

Resolved, N. C. D. 2. That our ancestors, who first settled these colonies, were at the time of their emigration from the mother country, entitled to all the rights, liberties, and immunities of free and natural-born subjects, within the realm of England.

Resolved, N. C. D. 3. That by such emigration they by no means forfeited, surrendered, or lost any of those rights, but that they were, and their descendants now are, entitled to the exercise and enjoyment of all such of them, as their local and other circumstances enable them to exercise and enjoy.

Resolved, 4. That the foundation of English liberty, and of all free government, is a right in the people to participate in their legislative council: and as the English colonists are not represented, and from their local and other circumstances, cannot properly be represented in the British parliament, they are entitled to a free and exclusive power of legislation in their several provincial legislatures, where their right of representation can alone be preserved, in all cases of taxation and internal polity, subject only to the negative of their sovereign, in such manner as has been heretofore used and accustomed: But, from the necessity of the case, and a regard to the mutual interest of both countries, we cheerfully consent to the operation of such acts of the British parliament, as are bona fide, restrained to the regulation of our external commerce, for the purpose of securing the commercial advantages of the whole empire to the mother country, and the commercial benefits of its respective members; excluding every idea of taxation internal or external, for raising a revenue on the subjects, in America, without their consent.

Resolved, N. C. D. 5. That the respective colonies are entitled to the common law of England, and more especially to the great and inestimable privilege of being tried by their peers of the vicinage, according to the course of that law.

Resolved, 6. That they are entitled to the benefit of such of the English statutes, as existed at the time of their colonization; and which they have, by experience, respectively found to be applicable to their several local and other circumstances.

Resolved, N. C. D. 7. That these, his majesty's colonies, are likewise entitled to all the immunities and privileges granted and confirmed to them by royal charters, or secured by their several codes of provincial laws.

Resolved, N. C. D. 8. That they have a right peaceably to assemble, consider of their grievances, and petition the king; and that all prosecutions, prohibitory proclamations, and commitments for the same, are illegal.

Resolved, N. C. D. 9. That the keeping a standing army in these colonies, in times of peace, without the consent of the legislature of that colony, in which such army is kept, is against law.

Resolved, N. C. D. 10. It is indispensably necessary to good government, and rendered essential by the English constitution, that the constituent branches of the legislature be independent of each other; that, therefore, the exercise of legislative power in several colonies, by a council appointed, during pleasure, by the crown, is unconstitutional, dangerous, and destructive to the freedom of American legislation.

All and each of which the aforesaid deputies, in behalf of themselves, and their constituents, do claim, demand, and insist on, as their indubitable rights and liberties; which cannot be legally taken from them, altered or abridged by any power whatever, without their own consent, by their representatives in their several provincial legislatures. . . .

Document I-13 Declaration of Rights, December 17, 1776

[Prepended to North Carolina's first constitution was its declaration of rights, which announced prominently that political power was vested in and derived from the people. While this provision made clear at least that political power was not vested in a monarch, it did not venture to elaborate on the fount of the people's political power. Did this distancing of political power from monarchy—*English* monarchy, in particular—disengage political power from divine law, natural law, and colonial common law entirely?[138] Or did this new vesting of political power rather substitute the people for the monarchs or aristocrats who had claimed or presumed divine right in recent centuries?[139] Or perhaps the representatives of the freemen in congress had in mind a more ancient view of English constitutional law: perhaps "the people" were under the inherited common law, even while they stood as the ultimate political power declared by the constitution of the fledgling republic. There followed in the state's declaration of rights another bold assertion: that no subset of the people was entitled to exclusive privileges. Presumably, this language barred legislation in favor of a hereditary aristocracy. Similarly, monopolies and perpetuities were declared contrary to the genius of this free state; and property of the soil was placed in the collective body of the people.

Having thus leveled the feudal estates which constituted traditional British mixed government, a separation of political power into abstract functional classes was announced in its stead.[140] Whether this theory derived directly and simply from Baron de Montesquieu or whether the freemen of North Carolina found inspiration elsewhere, perhaps from the English Revolution itself,[141] a government with separate powers would be expected to operate much differently than had colonial government in North Carolina. In fact, the contrast with past government was announced even more loudly by this document's declarations that the newly minted state of North Carolina was free, its government was free, its elections were free, and its press was free.

The declaration of rights not only distinguished North Carolina from its sometimes-abusive English heritage, but also embraced that heritage by harking back to rights declared at the English Revolution of late in the prior century, such as the right of the people's representatives to withhold consent to any proposed suspension of the laws by the government. Other rights preserved in North Carolina in the eighteenth century and declared by seventeenth-century English subjects had a much more ancient textual basis, such as the protection of freemen by the law of the land. Still other rights declared in North Carolina found their roots in Carolina's colonial experience, such as the right to worship God according to the dictates of one's conscience. In this way, bits and pieces of the English constitutional heritage found their way into a text that would soon be incorporated into North Carolina's new world, written constitution.]

1776.

THE DECLARATION OF RIGHTS....

A Declaration of Rights made by the Representatives of the Freemen of the State of North Carolina.

Section I. That all political Power is vested in and derived from the People only.

Section II. That the people of this State ought to have the sole and exclusive Right of regulating the internal Government and Police thereof.

Section III. That no Man or set of Men are entitled to exclusive or separate Emoluments or Privileges from the Community, but in Consideration of Public Services.

Section IV. That the Legislative, Executive and Supreme Judicial Powers of Government ought to be forever separate and distinct from each other.

Section V. That all Power of Suspending Laws, or the Execution of Laws, by any Authority without Consent of the Representatives of People, is injurious to their rights and ought not to be exercised.

Section VI. That Elections of Members to serve as Representatives in General Assembly, ought to be free.

Section VII. That in all criminal Prosecutions every Man has a Right to be informed of the Accusation against him, and to confront the Accusers and Witnesses with other Testimony, and shall not be compelled to give Evidence against himself.

Section VIII. That no Freeman shall be put to answer any criminal Charge, but by Indictment, Presentment, Impeachment.

Section IX. That no Freeman shall be convicted of any Crime, but by the unanimous verdict of a Jury of good and lawful Men, in open Court as heretofore used.

Section X. That excessive Bail should not be required, nor excessive Fines imposed, nor cruel or unusual punishment inflicted.

Section XI. That General Warrants whereby any Officer or Messenger may be commanded to search suspected Places, without Evidence of the Fact committed, or to seize any Person or Persons not named, whose offence is not particularly described and supported by Evidence, are dangerous to Liberty, and ought not to be granted.

Section XII. That no Freeman ought to be taken, imprisoned or disseissed of his Freehold, Liberties or Privileges, or outlawed or exiled, or in any Manner destroyed or deprived of his Life, Liberty or Property, but by the Law of the Land.

Section XIII. That every Freeman restrained of his Liberty is entitled to a Remedy to enquire into the Lawfulness thereof, and to remove the same if unlawful, and that such Remedy ought not to be denied or delayed.

Section XIV. That in all Controversies at Law respecting Property, the ancient Mode of Trial by Jury is one of the best Securities of the Rights of the People, and ought to remain sacred and inviolable.

Section XVI. [*sic*] That the Freedom of the Press is one of the great Bulwarks of Liberty, and therefore ought never to be restrained.

Section XVI. That the People of this State ought not to be taxed or made subject to the Payment of any Impost or Duty, without the Consent of themselves or their Representatives in General Assembly freely given.

Section XVII. That the People have a right to bear Arms for the Defence of the State; and as standing Armies in Time of Peace are dangerous to liberty, they ought not to be kept up; and that the military should be kept under strict subordination to, and governed by, the civil Power.

Section XVIII. That the People have a right to Assemble together to consult for their common good, to instruct their Representatives, and to apply to the Legislature for Redress of Grievances.

Section XIX. That all Men have a natural and unalienable Right to worship Almighty God according to the Dictates of their own Conscience.

Section XX. That for redress of Grievances and for amending and strengthening the Laws, Elections ought to be often held.

Section XXI. That a frequent Recurrence to fundamental Principles is absolutely necessary to preserve the Blessings of Liberty.

Section XXII. That no Hereditary Emoluments, Privileges or Honours ought to be granted or conferred in this State.

Section XXIII. That Perpetuities and Monopolies are contrary to the Genius of a free State, and ought not to be allowed.

Section XXIV. That retrospective Laws, punishing Facts committed before the Existence of such Laws, and by them only declared criminal, are oppressive, unjust, and incompatible with Liberty, wherefore no Ex post Facto Law ought to be made.

Section XXV. The Property of the Soil in a free Government, being one of the essential Rights of the collective Body of the People, it is necessary in order to avoid future Disputes, that the Limits of the State should be ascertained with Precision; and as the former temporary Line between North and South-Carolina was confirmed and extended by Commissioners appointed by the Legislatures of the two States, agreeable to the Order of the late King George the Second, in Council, that Line, and that only, should be esteemed the Southern Boundary of this State, as follows; that is to say, Beginning on the sea side, at a Cedar Stake at or near the Mouth of Little River, being the Southern extremity of Brunswick County, and runs from thence a North-West Course through the Boundary House, which stands in thirty-three Degrees fifty-six Minutes to thirty-five Degrees North Latitude; and from thence a West Course so far as is mentioned in the Charter of King Charles the Second, to the late Proprietors of Carolina: Therefore all the Territories, Seas, Waters, and Harbours, with their Appurtenances, lying between the Line above described and the Southern Line of the State of Virginia, which begins on the Sea Shore in thirty-six Degrees thirty Minutes North Latitude, and from thence runs West, agreeable to the said Charter of King Charles, are the Right and Property of the People of this State, to be held by them in Sovereignty, any partial Line without the Consent of the Legislature of this State, at any Time thereafter directed or laid out, in any wise notwithstanding. Provided always, That this Declaration of Right shall not prejudice any Nation or

Nations of Indians, from enjoying such Hunting Grounds as may have been, or hereafter shall be secured to them by any former or future Legislature of this State. And provided also, That it shall not be construed so as to prevent the establishment of one or more Governments Westward of this State, by consent of the Legislature. And provided further, That nothing herein contained, shall affect the Titles or Possessions of Individuals, holding or claiming under the Laws heretofore in Force, or Grants heretofore made by the late King George the Third, or his Predecessors, or the late Lords Proprietors, or any of them.

December the 17th Day, A. D. 1776, read the Third Time, and ratified in open Congress. Copy Test

R. CASWELL, President.
J. GLASGOW, Secretary.

Document I–14 Constitution, December 18, 1776

[Fearing anarchy and confusion after having shucked off their personal allegiance to King George III, the representatives of the freemen of North Carolina established a government in their newly independent state. They used writings to do it. They declared that all political power was derived from the people[142] and that the people had sole right to regulate government, among other shocking disavowals of European tradition. They established a legislative authority, elected by the people and called the general assembly, which would select public officers to perform some of the non-legislative functions of government.[143] The constitution required a general assembly of landed freemen but not of landed gentry, much less of nobility—that is, the general assembly would be classless and would regulate entails. Under this plan of government, the general assembly exercised fundamental control over public functionaries, from a governor and a few judges of little prestige, down to even humbler officers of the state, both military and civil. In choosing civil officers and placeholders to perform the duties of government, the representatives of the people selected from among the Protestant freemen of the state. Yet, no clergyman or preacher of the gospel could interfere in the business of the state by representing the people in the general assembly or by preaching treasonable or seditious discourses. And the general assembly could not establish in the state "any one Religious Church . . . in preference to any other."

While this form of government recognized colonial experience in its opening paragraphs, it failed to explain the constitution's relation to unwritten law, both private and public, under which Carolina had been established and grown. For instance, the writing did not acknowledge that the customary common law of England had been impliedly received in Carolina at the founding of the province during the reign of Charles II. The constitution maintained silence on this matter despite the fact that provincial assemblies during the reigns of Anne and of George I had declared the common law in force in North Carolina, basing their declarations on demonstrations from the language of the province's Restoration charters, and a colonial assembly during the reign of George II had made a similar declaration.[144] Nor did this written plan of government acknowledge that the king's subjects in North Carolina, through their representatives in the first continental congress, had relied upon the king's neglect of the common law in rallying for independence.[145] To what extent, then, did this revolutionary written plan of government displace the distinctly English unwritten law which the colonists had lived under and the neglect of which had served in part and at first as inspiration for their independence? If legitimacy in public law now demanded a written plan of government that differed markedly from charter arrangements, could private law be comprised of inherited colonial customs and acts developed under a government of proprietors feudally beholden to monarchs and their parliaments? In the body of the state constitution of 1776, the freemen did not address this question.

The question was addressed, though, by the representatives of the freemen as assembled in congress (that is, *not* by the senate or house of commons that would soon assemble in North Carolina and legislate as its general assembly) in declarations made both before and after passage of the constitution. Eleven days prior to passage of the state constitution, the representatives had declared various English constitutional precedents—fundamental rights, some formerly declared in writings and others not—to be rights in North Carolina.[146] And four days after passage of the state's constitution, the representatives declared that colonial law (in large part unwritten) remained the law of North Carolina until the "next session of General Assembly" insofar as this colonial law was consistent with the constitution's new form of government.[147]]

THE CONSTITUTION.
1776.

The Constitution or Form of Government agreed to and resolved upon by the Representatives of the Freemen of the State of North Carolina, elected and chosen for that particular Purpose, in Congress assembled, at Halifax, the Eighteenth Day of December, in the Year of our Lord One Thousand Seven Hundred and Seventy-six.

Whereas Allegiance and Protection are in their Nature reciprocal, and the one should of Right be refused when the other is withdrawn. And whereas George the Third, King of Great Britain, and late Sovereign of the British American Colonies, hath not only withdrawn from them his Protection, but by an Act of the British Legislature declared the Inhabitants of these States out of the Protection of the British Crown, and all their Property found upon the High Seas liable to be seized and confiscated to the Uses mentioned in the said Act. And the said George the Third has also sent Fleets and Armies to prosecute a cruel War against them, for the Purpose of reducing the Inhabitants of the said Colonies to a State of abject Slavery. In Consequence whereof, all Government under the said King within the said Colonies, hath ceased, and a Total Dissolution of Government in many of them hath taken Place. And whereas the Continental Congress having considered the Premises, and other previous Violations of the Rights of the good People of America, have therefore declared, that the Thirteen United Colonies are of Right, wholly absolved from all Allegiance to the British Crown or any other foreign Jurisdiction whatsoever, and that the said Colonies now are and forever shall be, Free and Independent States: Wherefore, in our present State, in order to prevent Anarchy and Confusion, it becomes necessary that a Government should be established in this state: Therefore, We, the Representatives of the Freemen of North Carolina, chosen and assembled in Congress for the express Purpose of framing a Constitution under Authority of the People, most conducive to their Happiness and Prosperity, do declare that a Government for this State, shall be established in Manner and Form following, to-wit,

Section I. That the Legislative Authority shall be vested in two distinct Branches, both dependant on the People, to-wit, a Senate and House of Commons.

Section II. That the Senate shall be composed of Representatives annually chosen by Ballot, one from each County in this State.

Section III. That the House of Commons shall be composed of Representatives annualy [sic] chosen by Ballot, two for each County, and one for each of the Towns of Edenton, New Bern, Wilmington, Salisbury, Hillsborough and Halifax.

Section IV. That the Senate and House of Commons, assembled for the Purpose of Legislation, shall be denominated the General Assembly.

Section V. That each Member of the Senate shall have usually resided in the County in which he is chosen, for one Year immediately preceding his Election; and for the same Time shall have possessed, and continue to possess, in the County which he represents, not less than three hundred Acres of Land in Fee.

Section VI. That each Member of the House of Commons shall have usually resided in the County in which he is chosen, for one Year immediately preceding his Election, and for Six Months shall have possessed, and continue to possess, in the county which he represents, not less than one hundred Acres of Land in Fee, or for the Term of his own Life.

Section VII. That all Freemen of the Age of twenty-one Years, who have been Inhabitants of any one County within the State twelve Months immediately preceding the Day of any Election, and possessed of a Freehold within the same County of fifty Acres of Land for six Months next before and at the Day of Election, shall be entitled to vote for a Member of the Senate.

Section VIII. That all Freemen of the Age of twenty-one Years, who have been Inhabitants of any County within this State twelve Months immediately preceding the day of any Election, and shall have paid public Taxes, shall be entitled to vote for Members of the House of Commons for the County in which he resides.

Section IX. That all Persons possessed of a Freehold in any Town in this State having a Right of Representation, and also all Freemen who have been Inhabitants of any such Town twelve Months next before and at the Day of Election, and shall have paid public Taxes, shall be entitled to vote for a Member to represent such Town in the House of Commons. Provided always, That this Section shall not entitle any

Inhabitant of such Town to vote for Members of the House of Commons for the County in which he may reside; nor any Freeholder in such County, who resides without or beyond the Limits of such Town, to vote for a Member for said Town.

Section X. That the Senate and House of Commons when met, shall each have power to choose a Speaker and other their Officers, be Judges of the Qualifications and elections of their Members, sit upon their own Adjournments from Day to Day, and prepare Bills to be passed into Laws: The two Houses shall direct Writs of Election for supplying intermediate Vacancies, and shall also jointly by Ballot adjourn themselves to any future Day and Place.

Section XI. That all Bills shall be read three times in each House before they pass into Laws, and be signed by the Speaker of both Houses.

Section XII. That every Person who shall be chosen a Member of the Senate or House of Commons, or appointed to any Office or Place of Trust, before taking his seat, or entering upon the Execution of his Office, shall take an Oath to the State; and all officers shall also take an Oath of Office.

Section XIII. That the General Assembly shall, by joint Ballot of both Houses, appoint Judges of the Supreme Courts of Law and Equity, Judges of Admirality [sic], and an Attorney-General, who shall be commissioned by the Governor, and hold their Offices during good Behaviour.

Section XIV. That the Senate and House of Commons shall have Power to appoint the Generals and Field-Officers of the Militia, and all Officers of the regular Army of this State.

Section XV. That the Senate and House of Commons, jointly at their first Meeting after each annual Election, shall by Ballot elect a Governor for one Year; who shall not be eligible to that Office longer than three Years in six successive Years: That no Person under thirty Years of Age, and who has not been a Resident in this State above five Years, and having in the State a Freehold in Lands and Tenements above the Value one Thousand Pounds, shall be eligible as Governor.

Section XVI. That the Senate and House of Commons, jointly at their first Meeting after each annual Election, shall by Ballot elect seven Persons to be a Council of State for one Year; who shall advise the Governor in the Execution of his Office; and that four Members shall be a Quorum: Their Advice and Proceedings shall be entered in a Journal to be kept for that Purpose only, and signed by the Members present; to any Part of which any Member present may enter his Dissent; and such Journal shall be laid before the General Assembly when called for by them.

Section XVII. That there shall be a Seal of this State, which shall be kept by the Governor, and used by him as occasion may require; and shall be called the Great Seal of the State of North Carolina, and be affixed to all Grants and Commissions.

Section XVIII. That Governor for the Time being, shall be Captain-General and Commander in Chief of the Militia; and in the Recess of the General Assembly, shall have Power, by and with the Advice of the Council of State, to embody the Militia for the public Safety.

Section XIX. That the Governor for the Time being, shall have Power to draw for and apply such Sums of Money as shall be voted by the General Assembly for the Contingencies of Government, and be accountable to them for the same; He also may, by and with the Advice of the Council of State, lay Embargoes, or prohibit the Exportation of any Commodity for any Term not exceeding thirty Days at any one Time, in the Recess of the General Assembly; and shall have the Power of granting Pardons and Reprieve., except where the Prosecution shall be carried on by the General Assembly, or the Law shall otherwise direct; in which Case he may, in the Recess, grant a Reprieve until the next Sitting of the General Assembly: And may exercise all other executive Powers of Government limited and restrained as by this Constitution is mentioned, and according to the Laws of the State: And on his Death, Inability, or Absence from the State, the Speaker of the Senate for the Time being, and in Case of his Death, Inability, or Absence from the State, the Speaker of the House of Commons shall exercise the Powers of the Governor, after such Death, or during such Absence or Inability of the Governor or Speaker of the Senate, or until a new Nomination is made by the General Assembly.

Section XX. That in every Case where any Officer, the Right of whose Appointment is by this Constitution vested in the General Assembly, shall during their Recess die, or his Office by other Means become vacant, the Governor shall have Power, with the Advice of the Council of State, to fill up such Vacancy by granting a temporary Commission, which shall expire at the End of the next Session of the General Assembly.

Section XXI. That the Governor, Judges of the Supreme Courts of Law and Equity, Judges of Admiralty, and Attorney-General, shall have adequate Salaries during their Continuance in Office.

Section XXII. That the General Assembly shall, by joint Ballot of both Houses, annually appoint a Treasurer or Treasurers for this State.

Section XXIII. That the Governor and other Officers offending against the State, by violating any Part of this Constitution, Mal-Administration or Corruption, may be prosecuted on the Impeachment of the General Assembly, or Presentment of the Grand-Jury of any Court of Supreme Jurisdiction in this State.

Section XXIV. That the General Assembly shall, by joint Ballot of both Houses, triennially appoint a Secretary.

Section XXV. That no Persons who heretofore have been, or hereafter may be, Receivers of Public Monies, shall have a Seat in either House of General Assembly, or be eligible to any office in this State, until such Person shall have fully accounted for and paid into the Treasury, all Sums for which they may be accountable and liable.

Section XXVI. That no Treasurer shall have a Seat in either the Senate, House of Commons or Council of State, during his Continuance in that Office, or before he shall have finally settled his Accounts with the Public, for all Monies which may be in his Hands at the Expiration of his Office belonging to the State, and hath paid the same into the Hands of the succeeding Treasurer.

Section XXVII. That no Officer in the regular Army or Navy, in the Service and Pay of the United States, of this or any other State, nor any Contractor or Agent for supplying such Army or Navy with Clothing or Provisions, shall have a Seat in either the Senate, House of Commons, or Council of State, or be eligible thereto; and any member of the Senate, House of Commons, or Council of State, being appointed to and accepting of such Office, shall thereby vacate his seat.

Section XXVIII. That no Member of the Council of State shall have a Seat either in the Senate or House of Commons.

Section XXIX. That no Judge of the Supreme Court of Law or Equity, or Judge of Admiralty, shall have a Seat in the Senate, House of Commons, or Council of State.

Section XXX. That no Secretary of this State, Attorney-General, or Clerk of any Court of Record, shall have a Seat in the Senate, House of Commons, or Council of State.

Section XXXI. That no Clergyman, or Preacher of the Gospel, of any Denomination, shall be capable of being a Member of either the Senate, House of Commons, or Council of State, while he continues in the exercise of the pastoral Function.

Section XXXII. That no Person who shall deny the being of God, or the Truth of the Protestant Religion, or the Divine Authority either of the Old or New Testament, or who shall hold Religious Principles incompatible with the Freedom and Safety of the State, shall be capable of holding any Office or Place of Trust or Profit in the Civil Department, within this State.

Section XXXIII. That the Justices of the Peace, within the respective Counties within this State, shall in Future be recommended to the Governor for the Time being, by the Representatives in General Assembly, and the Governor shall commission them accordingly: And the Justices, when so commissioned, shall hold their Offices during good Behaviour, and shall not be removed from Office by the General Assembly unless for Misbehaviour, Absence, or Inability.

Section XXXIV. That there shall be no Establishment of any one Religious Church in this State in Preference to any other; neither shall any Person, on any Pretence whatsoever, be compelled to attend any Place of Worship, contrary to his own Faith or Judgment; nor be obliged to pay for the Purchase of any Glebe, or the building of any House of Worship, or for the Maintenance of any Minister or Ministry, contrary to what he believes right, or has voluntarily and personally engaged to perform; but all Persons shall be at Liberty to exercise their own Mode of Worship. Provided, That nothing herein contained, shall be construed to exempt Preachers of treasonable or seditious Discourses from legal Trial and Punishment.

Section XXXV. That no Person in the State shall hold more than one lucrative Office at any one Time, Provided, That no Appointment in the Militia, or to the Office of a Justice of the Peace, shall be considered as a lucrative Office.

Section XXXVI. That all Commissions and Grants shall run in the Name of the State of North Carolina, and bear Test and be signed by the Governor; and all Writs run in the same Manner, and bear Test and be signed by the Clerks of the respective Courts; Indictments shall conclude, against the Peace and Dignity of the State.

Section XXXVII. That the Delegates for this State to the Continental Congress, while necessary, shall be chosen annually by the General Assembly, by Ballot, but may be superceded in the mean Time, in the same Manner; and no Person shall be elected to serve in that Capacity more than three Years successively.

Section XXXVIII. That there shall be a Sheriff, Coroner or Coroners, and Constables in each County within this State.

Section XXXIX. That the Person of a Debtor, where there is not a strong Presumption of Fraud, shall not be confined in Prison after delivering up, bona fide, all his Estate, real and personal, for the Use of his Creditors, in such Manner as shall be hereafter regulated by Law. All Prisoners shall be bailable by sufficient Sureties, unless for capital Offences, when the Proof is evident, or the Presumption great.

Section [X]L. That every Foreigner who comes to Settle in this State, having first taken an Oath of Allegiance to the same, may purchase, or by other just Means acquire, hold, and transfer Land or other real Estate; and after one Year's Residence, shall be deemed a Free Citizen.

Section XLI. That a School or Schools shall be established by the Legislature for the convenient Instruction of Youth, with such Salaries to the Masters paid by the Public, as many enable them to instruct at low Prices; and all useful Learning shall be duly encouraged and promoted in one or more Universities.

Section XLII. That no Purchase of Lands shall be made of the Indian Natives, but on Behalf of the Public, and by Authority of the General Assembly.

Section XLIII. That the future Legislature of this State shall regulate Entails in such a Manner as to prevent Perpetuities.

Section XLIV. That the Declaration of Rights is hereby declared to be Part of the Constitution of this State, and ought never to be violated on any Pretence whatever.

Section XLV. That any Member of either House of the General Assembly, shall have Liberty to dissent from, and protest against any Act or Resolve think injurious to the Public of any Individual, and have the Reasons of his Dissent entered on the Journals.

Section XLVI. That neither House of the General Assembly shall proceed upon public Business, unless a Majority of all the Members of such House are actually present; and that upon a Motion made and seconded, the Yeas and Nays upon any Question shall be taken and entered on the Journals; and that the Journals of the Proceedings of both Houses of the General Assembly, shall be printed and made public immediately after their Adjournment.

This Constitution is not intended to preclude the present Congress from making a temporary Provision for the well ordering of this State, until the General Assembly shall establish Government agreeable to the Mode herein before prescribed.

December the 18th Day, A. D. 1776, read the Third Time, and ratified in open Congress.

R. CASWELL, President.
J. GLASGOW, Secretary.

JAS. GREEN, JUN., Secretary.

Copy Test.

Document I-15 Revisal Ordinance, December 21, 1776

[In the ordinance appearing below, the representatives of the freemen of North Carolina assembled in congress assigned to eleven lawyers the duty: (1) to "revise and consider" the statutes and acts heretofore in force, and (2) to prepare bills consistent with the "Genius of a Free People" which the general assembly might consider at its next session. How did the representatives understand the scope of this commission? Did they hope the bills prepared by the commissioners would make a start at displacing the entire body of the colonial common law as well as revise the colonial statute laws and acts of assembly, all of which congress would soon receive as the law of North Carolina "until the next session of General Assembly"?[148] Or were the representatives' two commands to these eleven lawyers more tightly linked, such that bills offered by the revisors for consideration by the general assembly would aim only to Americanize colonial acts and British statutes in force in the colony? Many years later, Gov. David Swain reported that in accordance with this ordinance of 1776, the first two general assemblies which convened after American Independence "revised the whole body of the statute law."[149] And commissioners Iredell and Battle, in their preface to *The*

Revised Statutes of 1837, agreed that the statutes passed by these early legislatures were the fruit of the labor of at least some of the commissioners appointed by this ordinance.[150] The broadlyworded commission "to revise" the colonial statutes and acts, though, did not inspire the lawyers to offer to the general assembly a complete compilation of laws in force along the lines of *Swann's Revisal* of the preceding generation.

Under this ordinance of 1776, the representatives appointed only lawyers as commissioners. Given the commission's awesome responsibility—to judge which past usages were "consistent with the Genius of a Free People," this select group of attorneys must have commanded considerably more respect from their fellow freemen than did other members of the class of privileged professionals to which they belonged.[151]]

An Ordinance to appoint Certain Commissioners to revive the Statutes and Acts of Assembly heretofore in force and use in North Carolina and to prepare bills for the consideration of the next Assembly.

Be it ordained by the representatives of the Freemen of North Carolina in Congress assembled, and it is ordained by the authority of the same, That Thomas Jones, Samuel Johnston, Archibald Maclaine, James Iredell, Abner Nash, Christopher Neale, Samuel Ashe, Waightstill Avery, Samuel Spencer, Jasper Charlton, and John Penn, Esquires, be and they are hereby appointed to revive and consider all such statutes and acts of the Assembly as are or have been in force and use in North Carolina and to prepare such Bills to be passed into laws as may be consistent with the Genius of a Free People, that form of government which we have adopted, and our local situation and to lay the same before the next General Assembly for their approbation.

Read the third time and ratified in open Congress the twenty-first day of December, Anno Dom. 1776.

Document I-16 Reception Ordinance, December 22, 1776

[This ordinance receiving colonial law temporarily filled a perceived vacuum in law caused by the creation of the independent state of North Carolina. Beyond having a sunset provision, this ordinance was unusual in declaring goods to be achieved by its ordainment ("safety and good government") rather than evils to be remedied (doubts arising during revolutionary times[152]) by the reception of colonial law. The law received was restricted to what was "heretofore in use here" insofar as that law was not repugnant to independence.]

An Ordinance to inforce the Statute Laws and such part of the Common Law and Acts of Assembly heretofore in use here, also to enforce the Resolve of the Convention and Congresses of this State which have not had their effect.

Whereas it is absolutely necessary for the safety and good government of this State that Laws be immediately in force here; therefore,

Be it ordained by the Representatives of the freemen in Congress now assembled, and it is ordained by the authority of the same that all such Statutes and such parts of the Common Law and Acts of Assembly heretofore in use here and not destructive of, repugnant to or inconsistent with the freedom and Independence of this State, or the United States of America not abrogated, repealed, expired, or become obsolete, and all and every Resolve and Resolves of the several Congresses or Conventions of this State which have not had their effect or been repealed shall enure, continue and be in force until the next session of General Assembly and no longer.

And be it also ordained that all and every Resolve and Resolves heretofore Constituting Committees be and are hereby to all Intents and purposes repealed and abrogated.

Read three times and ratified in open Congress this 22d of December, 1776.

Document I-17 Reception Statute, May 9, 1777

[Being nearly identical to the reception ordinance of 1776,[153] this first reception statute after statehood allowed portions of the common and statute law, as well as acts of assembly heretofore in use, to endure, but only until the end of the next general assembly.]

CHAPTER XXV.

An Act for enforcing the Statute Laws and such parts of the Common Law and Acts of Assembly heretofore in use here, and also for enforcing the resolves of the Conventions and Congresses of this State, which have not had their effect, and for other purposes therein mentioned.

I. Whereas, it is absolutely necessary for the safety and good government of this State that Laws be immediately in force here, therefore,

II. Be it enacted by the General Assembly of the State of North Carolina, and by the authority of the same, that all such statutes and such parts of the Common Law and Acts of Assembly heretofore in use here and not destructive of, repugnant to or inconsistent with the freedom and independence of this State not abrogated, repealed, expired, become obsolete, or otherwise provided for, and all and every Resolve and Resolves of the several Congresses or Conventions of this State, which have not had their effect or been repealed shall enure, continue and be in force until the end of next session of General Assembly and no longer.

III. And be it further enacted by the authority aforesaid, that an act entitled an Act to prevent Card Playing, and other Deceitful Gaming, passed at New Bern in December, one thousand seven hundred and seventy, shall be and is hereby declared in be in full force until the end of the next session of the General Assembly.

Document I–18 Court Act, December 24, 1777

[By the court act of 1777, which mimicked the court act of a decade earlier,[154] the general assembly established a court consisting of three judges—presumably, judges appointed by joint ballot under section 13 of the state constitution of 1776,[155] and subject to the religious test of section 32[156]—to hear civil matters at law and criminal matters. The act defined the power and authority of the judges by reception of pertinent colonial law, except insofar as this colonial law might conflict with the new form of government or acts passed thereunder.]

CHAPTER II.

An Act for Establishing Courts of Law, and for Regulating the Proceedings therein.

Whereas it is necessary to a due and regular Administration of Justice that Courts be established in this State;

I. Be it Enacted by the General Assembly of the State of North Carolina, and it is hereby Enacted by the Authority of the same, That from and after the passing of this Act this State shall be, and it is hereby divided into Six several Districts, that is to say, the District of Wilmington, New Bern, Edenton, Halifax, Hillsborough, and Salisbury, in each of which a Court for the Trial of Causes, civil and criminal, shall be established, by the Name of the Superior Court of Law in the District where the same shall be held; and the said Courts shall consist of three Judges, being Men of Abilities, Integrity, and learned in the Law, who shall have Cognizance and legal Jurisdiction of all Pleas, real, personal, and Mixt; and also all Suits and Demands relative to Legacies, Filial Portions, and Estates of Intestates; all Pleas of the State, and criminal Matters, of what Nature, Degree, or Denomination soever, whether brought before them by original or Mesne Process, or by Certiorari, Writ of Error, Appeal from any Inferior Court, or by any other Ways or Means whatsoever: and they are hereby declared to have full Power and Authority to give Judgment, and to award Execution, and all other necessary Process thereupon; and shall have, use, exercise, and enjoy, the same Powers and Authorities, Rights, Privileges, and Preheminences, as were had, used, exercised, and enjoyed, by any former Judges in this Territory, except where it is, or may be otherwise directed by this, or any other Act, or where such Authorities, Rights, Privileges, or Preheminency, or any of them, may be inconsistent with, or repugnant to, the Form of Government and Constitution by Law established: And in Case of the Death or Absence of any of the said Judges, it shall and may be lawful for one or more of the same Judges, by himself or themselves, to hold any of the said Courts, and to take Cognizance, and give

Judgment, and award Execution, in the same Manner as all the said Judges might have done, had they been present. Provided always, That Demurrers, Cases agreed, special Verdicts, Bills of Exception to Evidence, and Motions in Arrest of Judgment, shall not be argued but before Two or more of the said Judges. . . .

Document I–19   Reception Statute, December 24, 1777

[This second reception statute had much in common with the first reception statute of 1777 and the reception ordinance of 1776,[157] continuing the law heretofore in force and use until the end of the next general assembly. Unlike the first reception statute and the reception ordinance, though, this statute framed the general assembly's action by doubts arising during revolutionary times as to what laws were in force, much as the 1711 and 1715 provincial reception acts had done, rather than by the necessity of "safety and good government."]

CHAPTER XIV.

An Act to enforce such Parts of the Statute and Common Laws as have been heretofore in Force and Use here, and the Acts of Assembly made and passed when this Territory was under the Government of the late Proprietors, and the Crown of Great Britain; and for reviving the several Acts therein mentioned.

I. Whereas Doubts may arise upon the Revolution in Government, whether any and what Laws continue in Force here: For Prevention of which,

II. Be it therefore Enacted by the General Assembly of the State of North Carolina, and it is hereby Enacted by the Authority of the same, That all such Statutes and Parts of Statutes, and such Parts of the Common Law, as were heretofore in Force and Use within this Territory, and all the Acts of the late General Assemblies thereof, or so much of the said Statutes, Common Law, and Acts of Assembly, as are not destructive of, or repugnant to; or inconsistent with, the Freedom and Independence of this State, and the Form of Government therein established, and which have not otherwise been provided for in Whole or in Part, not abrogated, repealed, expired, or become obsolete, are hereby declared to be in full Force within this State, and shall be observed accordingly.

III. And be it Enacted, by the Authority aforesaid, That one Act of the General Assembly made under the late Government, intituled, An Act for the more advantageous and easy Manner of obtaining Partitions of Lands in Coparcenary, Joint Tenancy, and Tenancy in Common; one other Act, intituled, An Act to prevent Card Playing, and other deceitful Gaming, passed at New Bern in the Month of December One Thousand Seven Hundred and Seventy, and since expired; and also one other Act, intituled, An Act for the Relief of Insolvent Debtors, with Respect to the Imprisonment of their Persons, made and passed at New Bern the Sixth Day of March, One Thousand Seven Hundred and Seventy Three, but since repealed by Proclamation; and the following Acts, passed last session of this present General Assembly, but which will expire with this Session, if not revived, to-wit, An Act to prevent hunting with a Gun by Fire Light in the Night; and An Act to prevent counterfeiting the Lottery Tickets of the United States, and other Purposes; and An Act to promote the recruiting Service, apprehending Deserters, and other Purposes therein mentioned; be, and are hereby revived, and declared to be in full Force, so far as the said Acts are not destructive of, repugnant to, or inconsistent with, the Freedom and Independence of this State, and the Form of Government therein established.

IV. And be it further Enacted, That this Act shall be, continue, and remain in full Force and Virtue, till the End of the next Session of Assembly, and no longer.

Document I–20   Reception Statute, 1778

[This third reception statute put to rest doubts as to what laws remained in force and use in the wake of the revolutionary change in government in the former colony of North Carolina. The scope of the reception included both English common law and statute law, as well as colonial acts of the assembly. Unlike the temporary reception statutes of 1777 and the reception ordinance of 1776, this 1778 statute contained no sunset provision.]

CHAPTER V.

An Act to enforce such Parts of the Statute and Common Laws as have been heretofore in Force and Use here; and the Acts of Assembly made and passed when this Territory was under the Government of the late Proprietors and the Crown of Great Britain, and for reviving the several Acts therein mentioned.

I. Whereas Doubts may arise, upon the Revolution in Government, whether any and what Laws continue in Force here: For Prevention of which,

II. Be it Enacted by the General Assembly of the State of North Carolina, and it is hereby Enacted by the Authority of the same, That all such Statutes, and such Parts of the Common Law, as were heretofore in Force and Use within this Territory, and all the Acts of the late General Assemblies thereof, or so much of the said Statutes, Common Law, and Acts of Assembly, as are not destructive of, repugnant to, or inconsistent with the Freedom and Independence of this State, and the Form of Government therein established, and which have not been otherwise provided for, in the Whole or in Part, not abrogated, repealed, expired, or become obsolete, are hereby declared to be in full Force within this State. . . .

Document I–21   Equity Jurisdiction, 1782

[This surprising statutory provision for trial by jury[158] on all issues of fact and the requirement of two judges to pass a final decree in equity proceedings[159] showed the people's deep distrust of judges and the felt need to cabin the exercise of judicial discretion. This act also demonstrated the great care taken by the general assembly with public monies: to keep costs down, the same judges in the same courts would wear two hats, law and equity.]

CHAPTER XI.

An Act for giving an Equity jurisdiction to the Superior Courts.

I. Whereas the courts of law, as at present established, are not equal to the redress of all kinds of injuries, but many innocent men are withheld of their just rights, and some deprived of them altogether, for want of a court or courts of equity;

II. Be it therefore enacted by the General Assembly of the State of North Carolina, and it is hereby enacted by the authority of the same, That from and after the expiration of the present session of the General Assembly, each Superior Court of law in this State shall also be and act as a court of equity for the same district, and possess all the powers and authorities within the same, that the court of chancery which was formerly held in this State under the late government used and exercised, and that are properly and rightfully incident to such a court, agreeable to the laws in force in this State, and not inconsistent with our present constitution. Provided, That no final decree shall be passed by any such court but where two of the judges at least are present.

III. And be it further enacted by the authority aforesaid, That the rules and methods of proceeding in the said courts shall be as follows . . . All matters of fact that shall come in issue between the parties shall be determined by a jury in the presence of the court, as in trials at law, and the trial shall be by the jury attending the superior court, or if they shall be discharged, it may be by a jury summoned instanter, (who are to be qualified as other jurymen) or a special jury may be summoned for that purpose with the consent of the parties, and approbation of the court, and the mode of proceding [sic] by such juries shall be the same in every respect as in trials at law; the same rules and methods to be observed in this case as have been practised upon questions of fact being submitted by a court of chancery to the decision of a common law jurisdiction. . . .

DOCUMENT I–22 COURT ACT, 1786

[Woe unto the "attorneys," again! The general assembly had lost patience with this privileged class of professionals because attorneys continued to abuse and distress the people. This act limited the presence in court of too many lawyers and protected *pro se* litigants from dismissal due to ignorance of arcane, scholastic forms of pleading.]

CHAPTER XIV.

An Act to Amend an Act Passed at New Bern, in December, One Thousand Seven Hundred and Eighty-Five, Entitled, "An Act for Encreasing the Jurisdiction of the County Courts of Pleas and Quarter Sessions, and of the Justices of the Peace Out of Court, and Directing the Time of Holding Courts in This State."

I. . . .
And whereas the frequent abuses of attornies have occasioned distress to many of the good people of this State:

II. Be it therefore Enacted, That it shall not be lawful for either plaintiff or defendant to employ in any matter or suit whatever more than one attorney to speak to any suit in court; and the courts in this State are hereby directed not to suffer more than one attorney as aforesaid in any matter whatever to plead for either plaintiff or defendant to any suit, under the penalty of a violation of this Act.

III. And be it Enacted, That in any matter or suit depending in court, it shall and may be lawful for either plaintiff or defendant to enter his own plea and defend his own cause, and that no instrument of writing which contains the substance, shall be lost or destroyed for want of form, any other law to the contrary notwithstanding. . . .

DOCUMENT I–23 TRIAL BY JURY, 1787

[The anonymous author of the pamphlet entitled "The independent, Citizen," excerpted below, objected to statutes that abridged the right to trial by jury in cases of confiscation and in certain small claims.[160] One of the offending confiscation statutes would soon be declared unconstitutional in *Bayard v. Singleton*.[161] Not only did the subject of the pamphlet relate to the litigation in *Bayard*, but also the author of the pamphlet addressed his argument to W. R. Davie, co-counsel for plaintiffs in *Bayard*. The argument of the pamphleteer placed the written law, both statutory and constitutional, in the bosom of the natural and common law, as well as within the English political history which defined fundamental rights. Evidently, in the view of the anonymous author, "there are unwritten principles of right and justice to which written constitutions and laws must conform."[162] This position, urged upon Davie and apparently made in support of loyalist plaintiffs in *Bayard*,[163] pointed out the error of premising legislative omnipotence in the government of North Carolina, but did not offer a remedy for legislative abuses of legislative power.[164]]

To the Honorable
W. R. Davie, Esq;
Counsellor at Law, one of the members
of the Federal Convention. . . .

July 30, 1787.

THE INDEPENDENT CITIZEN.　　　　　　　　　　　　　　　　　　　　　　　　　Number I.

. . . I HAVE ever understood it to be an acknowledged and granted principle, that on our ancestors landing in America, *British Laws and British Liberties* had emigrated with them, and that these laws and liberties were the *basis* upon which our Constitution was founded . . .

OUR ancestors ever considered the *trial by jury* as the *bulwark of liberty*, and the *fundamental right* of every freeman. . . . *[N]o other trial* can be esteemed *legal* or *impartial*.

... [It] is the unalienable right of freemen, according to the ancient law of the land. Nay, this particular *mode of trial* is so particularly attached to the *Laws of the Land*, that it is expressed and known by the general term, THE LAW OF THE LAND, LEX TERRÆ, as if there was no other law of the land but this one ...

NUMBER II. ...

NUMBER III. ...

... I am now asked with a sneer, *Cannot the Assembly do* ANY *thing?* ...

WITH this in our view, let us examine the supposed omnipotence of Assembly, it stands nearly upon the same footing with the parliament of England. ...

WE admit a *legal* dependence to this superior person or Assembly, but when dependence is defined as Judge Blackstone justly represents it to be an *obligation to conform to the will or law of the superior*, it ceases to be a legal dependence according to the common law and constitution of England, or according to our bill of rights.

To France and to the Frederician Code such definition of dependence is applicable, because in such despotic realms, the people acknowledge an inherent obligation to conform to the WILL or LAW of the superior. Under French, Prussian or Imperial government, WILL and LAW are synonymous. *Quod principi placuit legis habet vigorem* however wicked or iniquitous.

BUT this detestable Civilian maxim is not admitted by Freemen. Our laws acknowledge the Assembly for, the time being, to be the *superior* head of government. But the dependence which is thereby required from the *inferior* individual, or subject, is a *politic*, or *legal* dependence, and not *absolute* or *unlimited*. ...

THIS imaginary omnipotence of Assembly, that whatever is ordained must be law, without any exception of right or wrong, must be restrained within the bounds of *reason, justice,* and *natural equity*. ...

THE power and jurisdiction of the Assembly for making of laws &c. is not therefore so transcendent and absolute that it cannot be confined, *either for causes or persons within any bounds*, since the very bounds and limits of [the power and jurisdiction of the Assembly] are so very clearly defined ... that they fall within the judgment of every man who has common sense to distinguish good from evil, or right from wrong. ...

NUMBER IV. ...

SUPPOSE an act should be made to empower the Governor, without the advice of the Council, to appoint Judges, and other law officers, to hold their commissions, *during his pleasure*, instead of the appointed and legal condition *quamdiu bene se gesserint*, during good behaviour, thereby setting up will and pleasure, above law and justice which are the first and most essential rights of the people. Would not such an act attend to the utter subversion of the common law[?] ...

THE *law of reason*, is an universal law; any acts therefore which are contrary to nature, justice, morality, benevolence, are contrary to reason, that ray of divine nature and supreme law and consequently are null, and void, being mere corruptions, and not laws. ...

NUMBER V. ...

BUT, it was my intent to point out the error, and not to rectify the abuse ...

DOCUMENT I–24   REVISAL, 1787

[A 1776 ordinance on statutes in force[165] had not resulted in a formal revisal of the state's public laws, and an act of 1783, commissioning James Davis to produce a revisal, had never been executed.[166] The general assembly aimed again in 1787 to update *Swann's Revisal*.[167] It recited the necessity of a revisal of the laws in force in the state, commissioned James Iredell as the single revisor to accomplish the task,[168] specified inclusion of certain addenda materials in the work,[169] and confined the scope of the work to public laws.[170] The revisal was to be "printed in the same Order and in the same Words in which they now stand," such that the commissioner had neither power to introduce a subject-arrangement to the material nor to modernize arcane or obscure language. Finally, the printer was given a seven-year monopoly. Iredell undertook the commission and his revisal was confirmed during the first session of the general assembly in 1791.[171]]

CHAPTER IV.

An Act for Revising and Collecting the Acts of the General Assembly of the State of North Carolina.

Whereas it is necessary that the Acts of the General Assembly now in force in this State be revised and collected:

I. Be it Enacted by the General Assembly of the State of North Carolina, and it is hereby Enacted by the authority of the same, That James Iredell be, and he is hereby appointed a commissioner to revise and compile the Acts of the General Assemblies of the late province and present State of North Carolina, and to insert the charter from the crown of Great Britain, the Lords Proprietors great grant and the constitution of this State, together with the treaty of peace between Great Britain and the United States of America, and the confederation of the United States existing at the time such revisal shall be published; and further the said commissioner is hereby authorised and directed in revising and collecting said Acts, to leave out all laws repealed or obsolete, all private Acts and all Acts on which no question of property can arise; and further the said commissioner is hereby required to see the said Acts printed in the same order and in the same words in which they now stand, with marginal notes of the contents of each section, a marginal reference and a copious general index with reference to each Act and the contents of each section.

II. And be it further Enacted by the authority aforesaid, That the said commissioner be, and he is hereby authorised to agree and contract with a printer or printers to print and publish the said revisal, and furnish one copy to each county court within this State, two copies for the use of the General Assembly, and one to each superior court on account of the public; and such printer or printers shall be entitled to an exclusive right to print and sell the copies of such revisal for the space of seven years....

DOCUMENT I–25   IREDELL'S PREFACE, 1791

[In this preface, Commissioner James Iredell pointed out that his revisal of 1791 was the first "authentic general collection" of the statute law of North Carolina in almost forty years, and the first since independence. According to Iredell, *Swann's Revisal* served as a foundation to this collection of public statutes in force, though even that respected work had to be supplemented by certificates of repeal or disallowance by the king in council in a few cases. Additionally, some late provincial acts were difficult to find, forcing Iredell to resort to the files of the secretary of state. In a few cases the files of the secretary of state failed to contain the needed information, leaving Iredell to consult begrudgingly an unofficial collection of laws which had been printed just prior to the American Revolution.[172]]

PREFACE.

In consequence of the high trust with which I had the honour to be invested *(a)*, I have prepared in the best manner in my power the ensuing Collection. It would have been more answerable to my own wishes, and perhaps to the public expectation, had I possessed that degree of leisure which to make a work of such difficulty and importance perfectly correct, was absolutely indispensable. I flatter myself, however, that notwithstanding the frequent interruptions it has met with from my professional engagements and other causes, it will be found to contain every thing material towards a proper knowledge of those laws it was my duty to compile.

Immediately before accepting an appointment by President George Washington to serve on the United States Supreme Court, James Iredell Sr. completed the first revisal of public laws of the state of North Carolina in 1791. Photograph of 1889 engraving of James Iredell Sr. by Albert Rosenthal. (*Credit*: State Archives of North Carolina, Raleigh)

IN arranging this Collection, I have taken the liberty to deviate from the strict letter of the directions of the act which authorised it. My inducements, I hope, will be deemed a sufficient apology for my conduct in this respect. My error, if any, has consisted in publishing more than I was ordered to do, not less; and it appeared to me that if by that means I could render the Collection more useful, though it might occasion a temporary delay, it would be considered a pardonable one, and that I should be excused for preserving much useful matter which, by a literal compliance with my authority, I might have suppressed. Accordingly upon all subjects, where there seemed a probability that controversies might now subsist, I thought it proper to retain all the acts relating to those subjects, though some of them, or parts of some of them, were repealed. Such, for instance, are those interesting laws concerning *Entries* and *Confiscation*, upon which controversies may perhaps arise for some years to come. Many indeed of the existing laws on such subjects cannot be understood without a reference to the former. I was advised also by a very respectable and experienced friend of mine to retain all such parts at least of those acts concerning the division of counties as respected their boundaries, for though upon a strict construction they may be considered as private acts (a point, however, which under the peculiar circumstances of the law system, perhaps may well be deemed doubtful) yet it is of infinite importance to preserve an authentic testimonial of those boundaries, to guard against disputes that may arise concerning them hereafter.

THERE was one authority vested in me, which I confess I was afraid to exercise: I was directed "*to leave out all acts on which no question of property could arise.*" Though this expressed a confidence in me not a little flattering, I should have shewn myself very undeserving of it, if I had availed myself of so great a power without very clearly discerning that there was no hazard abusing it. I could not venture to repose so vain a confidence in my own judgment as to undertake to determine precisely what acts might give occasion to such questions, and what not. It would be a task perhaps difficult for any man, and if in the presumptuous exercise of so high an authority I had omitted any which it should have appeared afterwards it was material to have preserved, the error would have been fatal and irretrievable. On the other hand, by retaining all that was in force, leaving every part of it to be applied as circumstances might arise, this danger was avoided without any inconvenience attending it but that of a little longer delay in the publication, which I thought of inconsiderable moment compared to the danger of suffering so important a publication to be either erroneous or defective. *(b)*

I FEEL a concern for the necessity of apoligising for the imperfection of some of the marginal notes, and the incompleteness of the references in some instances, though these I believe are a very few. Having had to prepare this Collection in the midst of a great deal of professional business, I did not in all instances (as I have been since sensible) sufficiently attend to the examination of the marginal notes in former Collections of the laws from which part of this Collection was taken; and I made a few mistakes in references to other acts, which I discovered too late to correct in the body of the work. As the best atonement in my power to make for these inaccuracies, I have taken uncommon pains in the composition of the Index, which, I flatter myself, will be found both full and correct, and I must therefore make it a particular request that in any case of doubt, in referring to different acts, the Index may be consulted.

(a) See Page 609, ch. iv.—p. 634, ch. viii.

(b) After the publication had been begun, I stated this difficulty, together with the one above mentioned concerning the acts for dividing counties, and some other particulars, in a letter to the Speakers of the two Houses of the General Assembly, dated October 16th, 1789. In consequence of which the General Assembly, December 22, 1789, did me the honour to pass the follwinog [*sic*] vote:

"*Resolved*, That *James Iredell*, Esquire, be authorised to revise and publish the laws of this state, in such mode, form and manner, as his own knowledge and discretion may direct."

PART of this Collection having been prepared and printed before the session of 1789, and the references in that part accordingly being adapted to the laws as they stood at the close of the session of 1788, I thought it proper, in order to preserve an uniformity and prevent confusion, that the body of the laws should be prepared as they stood at that period. The public acts of the two additional sessions, of 1789 and 1790, are however contained in an Appendix, and where any of them interfere with former acts they are referred to in the Index. I had wished, and once intended, to have prepared a separate Index for them, but found I could not do so without occasioning a still further delay that I thought would be utterly unjustifiable.

CONSIDERING it my duty to derive my information from authentic materials only where they could be procured, I was very attentive in doing so. The edition of Mr. SWANN, published in 1752, having been confirmed by an act of Assembly *(a)*, was of course a sufficient voucher, and I followed it accordingly. But as between that period and the Revolution in 1776, no authentic general collection had been published, and I could not find all the individual printed copies, I applied to the Secretary of State, and obtained from him either the originals or copies of all the acts of Assembly between those two periods that were to be found in his office. I also obtained from him a certificate of all the instances of a repeal or disallowance by the King in Council of acts of Assembly under the royal government, so far as his office could afford such information (which was in a very few cases only) together with certified copies of the Declaration of Rights, and the Constitution of the state, and ordinances of 1776. Where any acts of Assembly previous to the Revolution were wanting, the deficiency was supplied from an edition of Mr. Davis, published in 1774. In every such instance a memorandum has been made of it. The acts of Assembly since the Revolution, and ordinances subsequent to the above, as also the Treaty of Peace with Great-Britain, and the ratification of the present Constitution of the United States, having been published by authority, I have deemed the printed copies so published a sufficient voucher for me.

During the publication of a great part of this work, and so long as it was practicable, I corrected every sheet of it myself. But the business of my profession requiring me to be frequently from home, I found I could not without a very inconvenient delay continue to do so, and therefore was under the necessity of relying on the care and accuracy of the Printers, of which I had reason to entertain a good opinion, and whose obliging disposition in the whole course of the publication I have experienced in a manner that deserves my most grateful acknowledgments. The duties of the high office to which I afterwards had the unexpected honour to be appointed, made it absolutely unavoidable for me to rely wholly on them for the correctness of the remaining part of the publication.

I have now only to add, that ever since I was honoured with the very important and flattering trust of the present publication, I have felt the most anxious desire to execute it with fidelity, and with all the accuracy it was in my power to command; that I submit the book, with diffidence, to the public judgment, fearful that its defects may not be considered sufficiently palliated by the causes for which I have endeavoured in some measure to account for them (so far as they are not ascribable to the humble capacity of the Editor), but at the same time with the hope that the state in general, and particularly those who know me best, will be persuaded that no man could engage in such a work with a heart more warmly attached to the people for whom it was principally intended, a people among whom I have long most happily lived, to whom I owe obligations that I shall ever acknowledge with gratitude and pride, and whose welfare and prosperity, wherever I am, and in whatever situation I may be placed, will be an unceasing object of my ardent wishes.

JA. IREDELL.

May 17, 1791.

(a) See Page 128. ch. vi.

Document I–26   Martin's Preface, 1792

[The list of accomplishments of Mr. François-Xavier Martin, even if limited to those projects undertaken on behalf of the people of North Carolina, is unquestionably impressive. In 1804, he produced an update to *Iredell's Revisal*;[173] he served as an unofficial reporter of decisions of North Carolina between 1795 and 1797;[174] prior to that service, he was commissioned by the general assembly to compile the state's private acts (which had been omitted from *Iredell's Revisal*) so that they would be "placed within the reach of every individual;"[175] and earlier still, he compiled under state authority the British statutes in force in North Carolina.[176]

The preface to this last-mentioned work, appearing below *en toto*, touched upon two themes characteristic of the phase of codification predominant between the wars with England. The first of these themes was resentment at having to continue to acknowledge the fact of one's heritage, traditions, and social history after victory in a civil war, reliance on British statutes being described by Martin as the "last seeming badge, and mortifying memento, of dependence" on Britain. The other prominent theme of the period mentioned here by Martin was the need for citizens to access and to know the letter of the written law. Martin hoped that this compilation of British statutes in force would "at least serve to disseminate the knowledge of a number of laws by which the people of this state are to be governed." Printing only the modern translation of the ancient texts served this end, especially when one treated many enactments of the late-medieval period as still in force, only pre-thirteenth-century statutes being too old to endorse authoritatively.]

PREFACE.

In obedience to a resolve of the Legislature, I have prepared this Collection: and now usher it into light, with all the diffidence that must naturally arise from a consciousness of insufficient abilities—a diffidence that is much heightened by the reflection that, notwithstanding it would have been my wish to have devoted my whole time to the undertaking from the moment I embarked in it, my attention has been frequently diverted by unavoidable occupations. However, I indulge the idea that whatever errors may be discovered will be found to be on the right side. Although I have, perhaps, suffered a few statutes to creep in, which might have been suppressed, I have omitted to insert none that were material.

To have been furnished with a clue to direct me through the vast dædalus of laws from which this collection is extracted, would have much eased my labour, and inspired me with some degree of confidence. Finding that no act of Assembly afforded it, and that many, even among the most respectable, professors of the law disagree in regard to the applicability of a number of British statutes, I have adopted and prosecuted the plan, that appeared to render the utility of the work least dependent on my own judgment, which, unmatured by age and unsupported by experience, could not be deemed a criterion.

I began at *Magna Charta*. The old statutes, before that period, are generally acknowledged to be rather a matter of mere curiosity, and scarcely an authentic record of any of them is extant. From thence to the seventeenth year of Charles the Second, the time at which the people of this country first legislated for themselves, I have inserted every statute unrepealed by subsequent acts, or which did not appear so glaringly repugnant to our system of government as to warrant its suppression. From the seventeenth of Charles, I have published such statutes as have been expressly enforced by act of Assembly, as those commonly called the statutes of jeofails, and the 5 Geo. 2, c. 7, which was intended by Parliament to operate in the British colonies of North-America, has ever been taken notice of by our courts of judicature, and was, I believe, for many years the only authority under which they issued writs of *fieri facias* against real estates.

All the statutes relating to the benefit of clergy have been preserved. They are a key that opens the way to the knowledge of a part of our criminal jurisprudence, which ought to be clearly known and understood.

Since the abolition of tenures fee-tail, the statutes respecting fines and recoveries may be said to have become obsolete. Those, nevertheless, with a few others, relative to that species of tenure, I have thought it improper to reject, as a great deal of property in this state is still secured under them: and in a few instances, an obsolete statute has been retained, having been deemed necessary for the illustration of others.

By such additions the collection has been swoln a little: but this inconvenience, I trust, will be fully compensated by the advantages that will result from it. The bar will have the opportunity of making their own application, and the bench will be able to judge with more safety.

I made use of *Hawkins'* and *Ruffhead*'s editions. The former being generally allowed to be the more respectable, I printed after it, except in very few instances indeed, when, not finding the translation in that, I resorted to the latter.

Many of the statutes were couched, at the time of their being enacted, in the latin or French language. I have been advised to print the translation only. I presume it will be deemed sufficient. Its long use seems to have given it a sort of prescriptive authority, and it is said to have been done, for the most part, with great learning and correctness.

I have prefixed to the work a table of chapters, containing, after the title of each, a reference to such statutes and acts of assembly on the same subject, as were proper to be considered. Should it fail in a few instances to give satisfaction, by recurring to the index, the reader will, no doubt, find what he vainly sought for in the table. I have endeavoured to make them both as copious and correct, as all the attention and accuracy it was in my power to command could render them.

Such is the plan which I thought would best answer the intentions of the legislature. I have prosecuted it in the best manner I was able. How far my endeavours have been attended with success remains to be decided. I cherish the hope that the necessity there was for such a publication will render it acceptable—

In the last decade of the eighteenth century, François-Xavier Martin compiled the private acts and the English statutes in force in North Carolina; in 1804, he updated *Iredell's Revisal* of 1791. Photograph of 1882 engraving of François-Xavier Martin. (*Credit:* State Archives of North Carolina, Raleigh)

even from the hands of one, who does not possess the talents which the importance of the subject required. It will at least serve to disseminate the knowledge of a number of laws by which the people of this state are to be governed, until, substituting acts of their own legislature to those their forefathers brought over from Great-Britain, they will shake off this last seeming badge, and mortifying memento, of dependence on her.

F. X. MARTIN.

Newbern, July 15, 1792.

DOCUMENT I–27   IREDELL ON NATURAL JUSTICE, 1798

[As he was executing his commission to revise the statute law of North Carolina, James Iredell was appointed to the Supreme Court of the United States by President George Washington. Iredell would serve for almost ten years on that court. In *Calder v. Bull*, a case from 1798 in which Justice Iredell contributed an opinion, he described natural justice as "abstract," "speculative," and "regulated by no fixed standard."[177] "The

Court cannot pronounce [an Act] to be void," he said, "merely because it is, in their judgment, contrary to the principles of natural justice."[178] In Iredell's view, the notorious fact that men may be biased in their own favor, for example, may not ground a judicial declaration that an act making a man a judge in his own cause is void, if that state's constitution had placed no limits on the legislative power.[179] Iredell did acknowledge that acts contrary to natural justice were an extraordinary evil. In fact, this was the reason, he argued, that the sovereign peoples of each state in convention wrote constitutions defining with precision the limitations on the legislative power. Judgments based on natural justice, though, were made by each branch of government in the exercise of its duties and could not be second-guessed by another branch of government. The judiciary could no more substitute its judgment about an act's conformance to natural justice than could the legislature substitute its judgment about a judicial decision's conformance to natural justice. A court could void an enactment, though, in a clear and urgent case of a general assembly acting *ultra vires*. That is to say, a court might compare what is written here with what is written there, and it may enforce the more fundamental positive law. Regarding speculations concerning unwritten precepts of natural justice, though, the general assembly was presumed to act justly; and whether it erred in its moral judgments would be determined by the people, who could redress such wrongs without the assistance of the courts.[180]]

August Term, 1798.

CALDER *et* WIFE, *versus* BULL *et* WIFE....

IREDELL, *Justice*. Though I concur in the general result of the opinions, which have been delivered, I cannot entirely adopt the reasons that are assigned upon the occasion....

But, let us, for a moment, suppose, that the resolution, granting a new trial, was a legislative act, it will by no means follow, that it is an act affected by the constitutional prohibition, that "no State shall pass any *ex post facto* law." I will endeavour to state the general principles, which influence me, on this point, succinctly and clearly, though I have not had an opportunity to reduce my opinion to writing.

If, then, a government, composed of Legislative, Executive and Judicial departments, were established, by a Constitution, which imposed no limits on the legislative power, the consequence would inevitably be, that whatever the legislative power chose to enact, would be lawfully enacted, and the judicial power could never interpose to pronounce it void. It is true, that some speculative jurists have held, that a legislative act against natural justice must, in itself, be void; but I cannot think that, under such a government, any Court of Justice would possess a power to declare it so. Sir *William Blackstone*, having put the strong case of an act of Parliament, which should authorise a man to try his own cause, explicitly adds, that even in that case, "there is no court that has power to defeat the intent of the Legislature, when couched in such evident and express words, as leave no doubt whether it was the intent of the Legislature, or no." 1 *Bl. Com.* 91.

In order, therefore, to guard against so great an evil, it has been the policy of all the *American* states, which have, individually, framed their state constitutions since the revolution, and of the people of the *United States*, when they framed the Federal Constitution, to define with precision the objects of the legislative power, and to restrain its exercise within marked and settled boundaries. If any act of Congress, or of the Legislature of a state, violates those constitutional provisions, it is unquestionably void; though, I admit, that as the authority to declare it void is of a delicate and awful nature, the Court will never resort to that authority, but in a clear and urgent case. If, on the other hand, the Legislature of the Union, or the Legislature of any member of the Union, shall pass a law, within the general scope of their constitutional power, the Court cannot pronounce it to be void, merely because it is, in their judgment, contrary to the principles of natural justice. The ideas of natural justice are regulated by no fixed standard: the ablest and the purest men have differed upon the subject; and all that the Court could properly say, in such an event, would be, that the Legislature (possessed of an equal right of opinion) had passed an act which, in the opinion of the judges, was inconsistent with the abstract principles of natural justice. There are then but two lights, in which the subject can be viewed: 1st. If the Legislature pursue the authority delegated to them, their acts are valid. 2d. If they transgress the boundaries of that authority, their acts are invalid. In the former case, they exercise the discretion vested in them by the people, to whom alone they are responsible for the faithful discharge of their trust: but in the latter case, they violate a fundamental law, which must be our guide, whenever we are called upon as judges to determine the validity of a legislative act....

Part II

Antebellum Period

He said, the rules of pedantry did not suit this country nor this age; that common sense had acquired a dominion in politics and religion, and was fast acquiring an absolute dominion in the law; that judges and lawyers should have the independence and magnanimity to strip off the veil of mystery from every branch of the law, and root out all the remains of a ridiculous pedantry; simplify the science, and make it intelligible, as far as possible, to the understanding of the common people.

—Judge Archibald D. Murphey

The [early] judges resolved to adhere to decided cases and settled principles. They had scant respect for the theory that because in the alien systems of continental Europe a judicial decision has no authoritative force in any other case, judicial precedents should be abolished and every question decided upon the basis of reason and common sense.

—Justice William J. Adams

Permit me to call your attention to an act . . . authorising the Governor to appoint two Commissioners to revise, digest, alter and amend all the statute and Common law in force in this State, relating to Executors and administrators . . . so far as to form a code or system . . . which shall be founded on principles of Justice, and suited to the true policy and present situation of the people of this State, etc.

—Gov. John Owen

The truth is, that not only the source but the very existence of our statute Law, is, as remarked by an elegant writer, with regard to the common Law, "as undiscoverable as the sources of the Nile." In such a state of things, the expounder of the Law alone is safe. . . . It is submitted to your wisdom to determine whether a legal system so perplexed, intricate and uncertain, is suited to the genius of our institutions, and the character of our citizens.

—Gov. David L. Swain

[T]he revisal now published . . . differs in its character from any heretofore executed.

—Commissioners to *The Revised Statutes*

Introduction to Antebellum Period

In this second part of *Selected Documents Relating to Law Reform in North Carolina during the Nineteenth Century* are gathered documents from the Antebellum Period. This period runs from about the beginning of the nineteenth century to the secession of North Carolina from the American Union.

At the period's beginning, legislators aim to reinvigorate precedent, which had been undermined by the court act of 1790. The state supreme court is established by the general assembly during this period and commitment to common law as adapted to local conditions is its mantra, despite attacks on the court and its members' salaries by democracy lovers and despite the drive for codification of the common law, which is evident throughout this period in other American jurisdictions. Chief Justice John Taylor leads the state supreme court from early in the nineteenth century to his death in 1829. He not only contributes to the development of the common law in North Carolina but is also an early innovator in the movement for codification of statute law, which is the other hallmark of this period in the state.

The themes raised by the documents excerpted in this second part of the compilation include distrust of judicial discretion, distrust of attorneys, preference for common-sense laws expressed in intelligible writings, interest in systematic arrangement of laws by subject matter, and insistence on widespread distribution of the laws. Democracy not only demands that the common citizen may know the law, but also presumes that the opinions and sentiments of the common citizen should inform government.

Document II–1   Meetings of the Judges, November 18, 1799

[The general assembly established biannual meetings of the judges of the superior courts in 1799, burdening the judges with the duty of arguing and determining open questions of law and equity from the circuits.[181] The meetings contemplated the attendance of neither parties nor attorneys, and required *seriatim* written opinions of the judges' determinations of these questions. At this time, the judges of the superior courts were John Louis Taylor, John Haywood, John Williams, and Spruce Macay. The meetings of the judges during the following two years had the additional purpose of trying notorious land fraud cases.[182]]

LAWS
OF
NORTH-CAROLINA. . . .

CHAPTER IV.

An Act *directing the Judges of the superior courts to meet together to settle questions of law or equity arising on the circuit, and to provide for the trial of all persons concerned in certain frauds.* . . .

IV. *And be it further enacted,* That the Judges at their said meeting, or any two of them, shall proceed to argue and determine all questions so as aforesaid brought before them, and shall set for ten days at each and every meeting unless the business shall be sooner finished; and each and every Judge at their said meeting shall give their final opinion in every case in writing, to be filed with the Clerk, and by him to be entered in a book kept for that purpose. . . .

Document II–2   Court of Errors and Appeals, December 26, 1799

[A debate took place in the general assembly in late 1799 over a bill to establish a court to review judgments and decrees of the trial courts.[183] The bill envisioned a permanent means for the common law to develop in the state, after the court act of 1790 had undermined the development of precedent by splitting the members of the court among eastern and western ridings, or circuits, and periodically rotating judges between the ridings.[184] This debate, as reported in the *Salisbury North-Carolina Mercury and Salisbury Advertiser*, aimed not only to develop the common law of North Carolina with circumspection, but also to put a check on the potential for tyranny and arbitrariness, not to mention indolence and neglect, of the four superior court judges. The bill failed.]

SALISBURY,

THURSDAY, DECEMBER 26, 1799.

Court of Error and appeals.

The Bill to establish a Court of Errors and Appeals, and to divide the Superior Courts of Law and Equity into four ridings, being on its second reading, in the Senate of this State, on Friday the 29th ult. the following Debate took place:

The bill having been read and put on its passage,

Mr. BLOUNT wished that the Gentleman who introduced this bill, or some other, would point out its utility. He saw the imperfections of our present Judicial System, and wished them remedied as much as any gentleman on that floor; but he distrusted his own judgment as to the proper remedy for them. He had his doubts whether this bill would furnish that remedy. He wished, however, for information, being friendly to the bill, if it could be shewn to be effectual.

Mr. JOHNSTON said, the want of some Court to which resort could be had in the last degree, must have been obvious to every man in this country, who had attended to the situation of our Judicial System, instead of suits being finally determined in the Courts in which they are commenced—some Court which should revise the proceedings of all other Courts; not only that our judges may become the more circumspect in the performance of their duty; but that there should be an opportunity afforded of revising and reconsidering cases which may have been wrongfully decided.

In cases where men are placed in independent situations, in which they are not responsible to any superior power, it some times happens that they become arbitrary and tyrannical in their proceedings. This bill, if passed into a law, will operate as a check upon Judges disposed to abuse their power; and even the best of men, when placed in a situation in which there is no check upon their conduct, often become indolent and neglectful of their duty; but, when they know there is a Court established to correct their errors or misconduct, they will be more guarded in their proceedings than they are at present.

The reason which had prevented him from attempting a remedy to this evil at an earlier period was this; when I practised at the bar, said Mr. J. we had only three Judges, who were obliged to attend every Court. To have formed them into a Court of Appeal, would, therefore, have obtained no remedy for the evil, since the Court would consist of the same men whose errors or faults were to be corrected; and when I considered the extreme reluctance—perhaps laudable reluctance—which some gentlemen have to every kind of expence, I was deterred from offer to form any separate establishment. The first time I found it in my power to bring forward a remedy for this grievance, was at the last session. We had then four Judges, and it appeared to me, that if the State were divided into four ridings, instead of two, the duty of the Judges would be so much lessened, that the Legislature might demand of them the additional duty of holding this new Court, without any increase of salary.

This expedient, Mr. J. said, might not be the best for curing the evil complained of; but it was the best and most practicable that has occured to me. He had, therefore submitted it to the consideration of the house; if they disapprove it, the bill would, of course, be rejected. He should be satisfied with having done his duty in bringing it forward. If any gentleman can furnish a better remedy, he would cheerfully give place to it, as he had no particular prejudice in favour of the system he had proposed. If any objections should be made to particular parts of the bill, he would endeavour to answer them; but as he found himself somewhat indisposed from a cold, he hoped other gentlemen, in favour of the bill, would speak to its general merits.

Mr. BLOUNT confessed he distrusted his own opinion with respect to the merits of this bill; and his asking for the information which had been given, was more for the satisfaction of other gentlemen than himself. Incapable as he acknowledged himself to be to remedy the evils of our present Judicial System, he thought he discovered a defect in the last clause of this bill, which he moved to amend by a proviso to this effect: "That the Judges respectively should ride in those districts where they last practised, and never afterwards ride in the same district."

The SPEAKER decided the motion out [of] order, the bill being upon its passage.

Mr. AVERY said, that whilst the bill [was] reading by paragraph, he forebore to [offer] any amendment to it, though if it were [to] pass, he thought it capable of amendment[,] as he felt, however, an inclination to [vote] against the bill altogether, had not attempted to amend it.

He rose with dissidence to speak to [the] merits of the bill. He was ready to acknowledge that there are great deficiencies in our present Judicial System, which [he] should be desirous of remedying, if it could [be] done in an objectionable manner; but [in] looking into this bill, he feared, if it passed, instead of its remedying the present defects, it would increase them.

It is well known, said Mr. A., that [a] great part of our Judicial business, is [done] in County Courts, and he found no [remedy] in this bill, for any errors which might be committed in judgments given in them[,] whereas, at present, appeals are made from those Courts to the Superior Courts. This bill contemplates that one Judge shall preside in this Court of Errors, and that no appeals shall be made from his decision. He did not think that there was complete safety in such a regulation.

With respect to the expence of holding these Courts. No compensation was mentioned for the Judges; but they could not be expected to [do] the business for nothing. Suppose the four Judges were to have 100l. each Court, that would be 800l. a year. This additional expence he should not object to, if the bill held out a complete remedy for the the evils complained of, but this does not appear to be the case. He knew many inconveniencies would result from carrying this act into effect particularly to citizens far removed from the seat of Government where the Courts are proposed to be held instead of being beneficial to such persons, would operate as their total ruin. Taking all these things into consideration, he should be inclined to vote against the bill, though as he had already promised, he had some suspicion of his own judgment with respect to it.

Mr. Johnston observed, that if the gentleman last up expected that this bill should have been perfect in all its parts, and had remedied every inconvenience experienced under our Judicial System, he expected more than he ought to have done. We ought not to look to mankind for perfection; the works of the Almighty are only completely so.

He wished the Gentleman from Burke, instead of objecting to the bill in toto, had proposed his amendments. The only general objection which had been stated, was that the courts would be held at a distance from some of our citizens. It would be impossible, Mr. J. said, to establish a Court of this kind in a situation where this objection might not be made. This is an inconvenience, said he, which the inhabitants of the country will be willing to submit to, in order to have secured to them, the due execution of the laws by which they hold their liberty and property. Under our present system said Mr. J. what is law at one place, is not at another. The opinions of Judges vary and the decision of one Judge is disregarded by another. But, when a Court, such as is now proposed, shall be established, which shall govern all the varying decisions which may be given in various parts of the State[,] some security will be had for the due administration of justice. Much, added Mr. [B.,] might be said on this subject, but from the difficulty I find in speaking, I shall leave to be said by others.

Mr. Irwin observed, it could not be [told] with any degree of certainty what would be the effect of this bill, as it was an entirely new measure. The great end of law is to obtain justice for individuals, and therefore the administration of justice ought to be made as convenient to the citizens at large as possible. But, instead of this, the present bill proposes to remove it as far from them as the State will admit of; and takes away the relief now afforded, without substituting a better; for he could not see that this Judge [on?] Appeal would be more likely to do justice than a Jury. When a trial has been had in a District or County Court, if the parties have not had a full and satisfactory trial, they can obtain a new hearing, which he thought a much easier way of coming at justice, than that proposed by this bill. Not one cause in ten tried in the District Courts, would ever be brought to this Court; it would afford relief, therefore, but in few instances. Besides, it could not be expected that this business should be done for nothing: it would doubtless be attended with considerable expence, and he thought for little purpose. It might, indeed, give advantages to the rich; but it would prove oppressive to the poor. When a man, full of money, had been unsuccessful in other Courts, he might carry his cause to a court such as is here proposed, where a poor man could not follow him. Believing as he did, therefore, that the bill, if passed, would not be productive of good, but the contrary, he should vote against it.

Mr. Avery made sum [sic] further objections to the bill, which were not distinctly heard.

Mr. Johnston replied to them, observing, that he was very unfortunate with respect to that gentleman; for though they agreed in opinion on questions of general politics, yet they generally differed on subjects of detail. In answer to the gentleman from Mecklenburg (Mr. Irwin) in relation to the expence of the proposed establishment, Mr. J. said no additional expence was contemplated; and as this establishment's proving an advantage to the rich, and the contrary to the boor man, the law, in general, he said was doubtless a great advantage to the poor man; it was made in order to protect the poor and weak against the oppressions of the opulent and strong—and this law, said he, is of the same kind.

Mr. Phifer said, it appeared to him, that his bill went to deny justice to the poorer class of the citizens; for how could a poor man travel 200 miles to attend a Court at this place? How is he to support the expence? Every gentleman in this house, said he, receives 25s. a day, for his services, and where is the poor man to get this sum to pay his lawyer, who, he supposed, would not be satisfied with less? If some revisions could be fixed in every District Court, citizens of every description would have some chance of justice being done to them.

Mr. Johnston wished to satisfy every gentleman, if he could. He allowed it would be inconvenient for some citizens to attend these Courts; but as to having the errors complained of corrected in the District Courts, it was out of the question; it would not have valuable effects proposed by this bill.

Mr. Irwin wished a case to be pointed out which would not be tried in a District Court, as well as in the Court of Errors and Appeals now proposed. If this were done, the usefulness of the bill would appear more evident.

The question being put on the second reading of the bill, there appeared a majority against it. Of course, it was rejected.

Document II-3   The Court of Conference, 1801

[In 1801, the general assembly extended the biannual meetings of the judges and named the meetings, "The Court of Conference." This act made explicit that no attorney shall speak or be admitted as counsel to the court. Both the original law[185] establishing the meetings of the judges and this extension to it anticipated that a judge in the case below would present the issues brought up for conference with his peers. This apparent concern with the cost of representation before a proposed court of errors had been expressed also in 1799 by members of the general assembly.[186] It is a sort of distrust of attorneys—it distrusts the need to use attorneys to achieve justice, even if it does not express a distrust of attorneys as a class of professionals.]

CHAP. XII.

An Act to continue longer in force, and to amend an act passed in the year one thousand seven hundred and ninety-nine, entitled "An act directing the Judges of the Superior Courts to meet together to settle questions of Law or Equity arising on the circuit, and to provide for the trial of all persons concerned in certain frauds."

WHEREAS the afore-recited act, in its provisions directing the Judges of the Superior Courts to meet together for the purpose of determining all questions of Law or Equity arising and remaining undetermined upon the circuit, has been found highly salutary and beneficial; and whereas the time of limitation of said act is soon to expire, and it appears to this General Assembly necessary that the same should be continued longer in force:

BE it therefore enacted by the General Assembly of the State of North-Carolina, and it is hereby enacted by the authority of the same, That the said act, so far as it regards the meeting together of the said Judges for the purposes aforesaid, be, and the same is hereby continued in force for three years longer; and the said meeting of the Judges shall be known by the name and stile of "The Court of Conference;" and the same shall be and continue for the time last aforesaid, under the same rules, regulations and restrictions, as are provided in and by the said recited act, except as is otherwise provided in this act.

II. *And be it further enacted by the authority aforesaid,* That the Judges of the said Court of Conference hereafter may and shall have power to sit at each and every term of the said Court, as long, not exceeding fifteen days (Sundays excepted) as the business of said Court shall require.

III. *And be it further enacted,* That no Attorney shall be allowed to speak, or admitted as Council in the aforesaid Court.

IV. *And be it further enacted,* That it shall be the duty of the Clerk of the said Court to permit any persons to search the records of his office, and give and make out copies of the same, to any person applying, for which he shall be entitled to the sames fees as the Clerks of the Superior Courts of this State; and on failure or refusal, the aforesaid Clerk shall be liable to the same penalties as are in such cases prescribed for the Clerks of the Superior Courts.

Document II-4 Haywood's Preface, 1808

[The first edition of *Haywood's Manual* was published in 1801. Extracted below is the preface to the second edition, which lists hundreds of subjects alphabetically arranged under which this unofficial manual distributed the sections of the public acts in force in the state. In contrast to this arrangement of materials, official revisals of the public laws in force in the state were organized chronologically, a practice that continued until *The Revised Statutes* of 1837 adopted an alphabetic arrangement.[187]

John Haywood, the author of this manual, was an unofficial reporter of opinions of the state's superior court and its court of conference,[188] as well as a judge of the superior court from 1793 to 1800. He later served in Tennessee as a judge and as a compiler of that state's statutes.]

PREFACE

All the public Acts and parts of public Acts, in force and use and in present operation, except a few relative to Boundaries, Divisions, &c. are contained in this volume, under the following heads:

Abatements,	Causeways,	Demurrer,	Foreigners,
Accessories,	Certificates,	Depositions,	Forfeitures,
Accidents,	Chairman,	Depreciation,	Forgery,
Account of Sales	Citizens,	Descents,	Fornication,
Acts of Assem.	Claims,	Devises,	Frauds & Fraudulent Conveyances,
Adm's. & Ex'rs.	Clerks of the Supreme, Superior & County Courts,	Disaffected,	Freehold,
Adjournment,	Clerk & Master in Equity,	Disclaimer,	Freemen,
Affidavits,	Clk. of the Court of Patents,	Discontinuance,	Free Negroes,
Allegiance,	Collectors of Arrears,	Door-keepers of the Assembly,	Funds,
Amendment,	Commissioner of Affidavits,	Door-keepers of the Council,	Gaming,
Appeals and Errors,	Commissions,	Dower,	Gaols.
Apprentices,	Commitment,	Draining of low Lands,	Garnishee,
Army Accounts,	Comptroller,	Drunkenness,	Gen. Assembly

Armies,	Conference,	Dueling,	Gifts;
Arrest,	Confiscation,	Elections,	Government,
Arrest of judgment,	Consul,	Embezzlement,	Governor,
Assembly.	Constables,	Emoluments,	Grants.
Assets,	Cont'g'. Fund,	Entails,	Guardian and Ward,
Assignment,	Continuance,	Entries,	Habeas Corpus
Attachment,	Conveyances,	Entry-takers & Surveyors,	Hides, Skins, and Furs.
Attorney,	Coopers,	Equity,	Hirings,
Attorney Genl.	Coroners,	Errors,	Hogs,
Auctioneers,	Corporations,	Errors in Grants, Deeds & Bills of Sale,	Honours,
Bail,	Costs,	Escape,	Horse-stealing
Banishment,	Council of State,	Escheats,	Horse-racing,
Bank,	Counterfeiting,	Estates-tail,	Hospit. money
Banks,	County Courts,	Evidence,	House-breaking,
Bastardy,	County Trustee,	Executions,	Hunting,
Bigamy,	County Wardens,	Executors,	Jailors,
Bill of Exception	Court-Houses,	Extinguishment	Ideots & Lunatics,
Bills of Exchange,	Court of Patents	Fairs,	Ieofails,
Bill of Rights,	Creditors,	Fayetteville,	Illegitimate Children,
Bills of Sale,	Criminals,	Fees,	Impeachment,
Births,	Cursing and Swearing,	Feme Covert,	Imprisonment,
Boats, &c.	Debtors,	Fences,	Indians,
Bonds,	Declaration,	Ferries,	Indictments,
Book Debts,	Deeds,	Fines,	Injunctions,
Boundaries,		Firewood,	Inquiry,
Bridges,		Firing Woods,	Insol. Debtors,
Burials,		Fish,	
Case agreed,			
Cattle, Horses, & Hogs,			

iv

Insol. Taxables,	Non pros.	Promiss. Notes,	Subpœna,
Inspections, and Inspectors,	Notaries,	Property,	Subpœna duces tecum,
Insurrections,	Notes, Bonds, and Orders,	Puis darrein continuance,	Suicide,
Interest,	Notice to public Debtors,	Punishment,	Sunday,
Intestates Estates,	Oaths,	Quakers,	Supreme Court,
Inventories,	Officers,	Quarantine,	Superior Courts,
Jointenancy,	Offices,	Ranger,	Sureties,

Joint & several Contracts,	Ordinaries,	Recognizances and Fines,	Surveyor,
Journals,	Orphans,	Record,	Swearing,
Iron Works,	Overseers,	Registers,	Taxes,
Issues in Equity	Overseers of Roads,	Registration,	Taxes for County Uses.
Judges,	Outlawry,	Religion,	Tender,
Judgmt. Bonds,	Oyer & Terminer,	Rentings,	Time,
Judgment by Default,	Papers destroyed,	Revenue,	Tobacco,
Jury,	Pardon & Oblivion.	Ridings,	Toll-Bridges,
Justices of the Peace,	Partition,	Rivers & Creeks	Tories,
Landings,	Patents,	Roads,	Towns,
Lands,	Patroles,	Runaways,	Treason,
Law of the Land	Penal Laws and Penalties,	Sailors,	Treasurer,
Laws,	People,	Salaries,	Treasurer of Public Buildings,
Law Books,	Perjury,	Sales & Auctions	Trespass,
Legacies,	Perpetuities,	Scire Facias,	Trustee,
Legislature,	Petitions,	Seals,	United States,
Libels,	Petitions to the Assembly,	Seamen,	University,
Liberties,	Physic,	Seat of Government,	Usury,
Limitations,	Pilots,	Secretary of State,	Vagrants,
Low Lands,	Pleas & Pleading	Servants,	Verdict,
Lunatics,	Pocoson,	Set-Off,	Vice and Immorality,
Maiming,	Polygamy,	Settlement,	View,
Majority,	Poor,	Sheriffs,	Wardens of the Poor,
Marriages,	Powers of Atty.	Sinking Fund,	Warrants.
Marriage Contracts,	Practice,	Slander,	Ways,
Members of Assembly,	Presentments,	Slaves,	Weights & Measures,
Military,	Press,	Soldiers,	Widows,
Militia,	Printer,	Solicitor-General,	Wids. of wounded Soldiers,
Mills,	Prisoners, Prisons & Stocks,	Speakers of the Assembly,	Wills,
Money,	Private Sec'ry.	Specific Articles,	Witnesses,
Monopolies,	Privileges,	Standard-Keeper,	Women,
Mortgages,	Prob. of Wills,	Stocks,	Woods,
Mulattoes,	Process,	Strays,	Wreck,
Names,	Processioners,	Subornation,	Writ of Error,
Ne exeat.			Writs.
Negroes,			

The second and third persons to hold the office of Adjutant-General of North Carolina, Edward Pasteur and Calvin Jones, advocated for the revision of the military laws of the state. Photograph of a portrait of Dr. Calvin Jones. (*Credit:* Marshall De Lancey Haywood)

Document II–5 State Military Laws, 1808

[A revisal of the state's military laws was the topic of a report from state Adjutant-General Calvin Jones[189] to the general assembly in late 1809, in which he enclosed a letter from state Adjutant-General Edward Pasteur to Gov. David Stone on the same topic from mid-1808. Pasteur recommended that the military laws not only be revised by the general assembly, but that they be "digested" and then formed into a "system," a guiding principle in the formation of such a "code" being "intelligible" language.[190] Thus, the vocabulary of the nineteenth-century codifiers was adopted by Pasteur many years before initiatives in statutory codification, partial or full,[191] foundered in the 1820s in North Carolina.]

... Received from the Adjutant-General, Calvin Jones, the following report:

To the Honorable the General Assembly of the State of North-Carolina.

GENTLEMEN,

I HAVE the honour, in conformity with the requisitions of law, to communicate herewith a general Return of the Militia of the State for the present year, with a Roster of the General and Field Officers....

It has been made my duty (and I chearfully [sic] perform it) to suggest to the Legislature whatever I shall deem calculated to improve the Militia. I hope I shall not be considered wanting in due respect to the labors of your honorable predecessors, when I say that I consider our Code of Militia Laws to be very defective, and that in my opinion they ought to undergo a thorough and entire revision....

As deservedly possessing higher authority than my own, I beg leave to refer to the sentiments expressed on this subject by my predecessor, General Pasteur, in his letter to his Excellency the Governor, of June 7th, 1808, as corresponding entirely with those which I entertain. An extract from that letter ... I hereto subjoin....

CALVIN JONES, Adjutant-General of
the North-Carolina Militia.

RALEIGH, Nov. 27, 1809.

Extract of a letter from General Pasteur to his Excellency the Governor, dated Newbern, June 7, 1808.

"IT is impossible to reflect upon the important rank which the wealth and population of this State entitles her to hold in the Union, without being struck with the inadequate means that have been employed to embody and give a useful direction to the immense natural resources she possesses. On every subject connected with the Militia particularly, a remissness seems to have prevailed, which, in the event of an actual invasion, would place the defences of the State on a most feeble and precarious footing, and expose all that is valuable in social life to a probable issue, which a patriotic mind cannot contemplate without a mingled emotion of astonishment and regret. Every thing possible to be achieved by Love of Country and undisciplined Valour might naturally be expected from the collective body of the People, contending for the Government of their choice, for the soil which contains the ashes of their Fathers, for their Wives and Children, for their "*altars and firesides*:" but history, experience and the passing occurrences of the day, forbid the expectation that Patriotism, however ardent, Valour however doubtless, can overturn veteran troops inured to the toils of war, accustomed to subordination, and supplying the deficiency of numbers, not less by unity of action than by celerity of movement. To place the Militia of this State in that respectable situation of discipline which can alone make an enemy feel their strength, it appears to me that the first essential step is to subject all the laws on that head to a complete revision, and by retaining the useful and expunging the inconvenient provisions, to form a system at once concise, intelligible, energetic. A measure so important ought to be conducted with great care and deliberation, and should previously be digested for the consideration of the Legislature. I would therefore most respectfully submit to the consideration of your Excellency, the propriety of recommending to the Legislature the plan of forming a Military Committee, to consist of such members of their body as are most experienced in such affairs, with instructions to project, during the recess, the outlines of such a code as the exigencies of the country demand, and its situation permits. Leisure would thus be afforded for obtaining information from all proper sources, the parts of the system could be adjusted with a view to their proper relation to each other, and to the whole. And what is of no slight importance, a mass of knowledge would be collected, highly useful in the ultimate decision of the Legislature."

DOCUMENT II-6 RUSH ON AMERICAN JURISPRUDENCE, 1815

[United States Attorney General Richard Rush's[192] speech in favor of codification of the common law was included in Chief Justice John Taylor's anonymously published *Carolina Law Repository*, so it was available for debate and discussion in North Carolina early in the nineteenth century.[193] In his speech, Rush may have used "code" to mean jurisprudence, or he may have meant statutory displacement of the common law.

The latter meaning seems likely, as he spoke with admiration of recent French codification, and he chided England for reforming medieval absurdities in a piecemeal manner, instead of by legislative inquest or by commission.]

AMERICAN JURISPRUDENCE.

Supposed to be written by Mr. Rush, Attorney-General of the United States.

. . . While the law with us is so copious, we are still willing to believe, that it has all the essential characteristics of a good code. That its comprehensiveness is the unavoidable result of our wants and the glorious evidence of our freedom. That its occasional darkness, supposed or real, is nothing more than belongs to all free codes in a greater or less degree, and is generally to be dispelled by the penetrating rays of a comprehensive knowledge. That above all, if in the unravelling and adjustment of complicated concerns, it may sometimes at first sight seem itself complicated, it never fails to throw a broad effulgence upon all the fundamental securities of the liberty and property of the citizen.

The English jurisprudence, with all it has to boast, was our first inheritance. But we hope it will not be thought we are presumptuous in supposing, that we have but secured to ourselves more signally its advantages, by shaking off, more freely than is done there, the shackles fixed upon it in early and rude periods. In making this remark, we think we shall largely carry with us the concurrence of informed and liberal readers, when it is applied to the whole criminal branch. When such sober minded and profound names as Hale, Blackstone, Romilly, and M'Intosh will agree, at epochs distant from each other, in condemning the deplorable severity of the English penal code, it may surely be permitted to others to join in the grateful opinion. Scarcely indeed does a year now pass over in which modern Parliaments are not paying homage to this opinion, by lopping off or mitigating some of the harsh and cruel features;—a work in which they have long ago been anticipated by the intelligent and humane wisdom of our own legislators. We still think, making all allowances for the exigencies of the two countries, that they have a great deal to do before they get to the point we have reached in this happy race of melioration. It cannot be said of us, as it is truly said of the English in reference to the numerous and small offences for which they punish capitally, that while, for centuries, every thing else had become dearer in its price among them, the life of man was continually allowed to grow cheaper.

The systems of law recently compiled for the French nation, if we will but abstract the political associations that go along with them, will challenge an almost universal judgment in their favor for the lights of ancient and modern wisdom so extensively intermingled in their formation. The imperialist bows to them from the auspices under which they were compiled; and Louis the Eighteenth, in his proclamation of January, 1814, speaks of them as containing, "under other modifications and names, the wisdom of all the ancient laws of France." If they do this they also do more. They embody much of the wisdom which the further experience of more recent times has evolved. It is gratifying to think, that the one which passes under the penal code of the French empire, is marked by many of the improvements familiar to the American states. To the Pennsylvanian it must be particularly so, when he finds that the law of homicide has been divided into the same degrees, and is couched in nearly the same terms, with the statute of that state upon this subject passed more than twenty years ago.*

Leaving the criminal branch, and bringing into view, the entire scope of jurisprudence in the two countries, we are disposed to place ours at the highest pitch in the comparison. If the advantage even be with us, we should say, in searching for the cause, that it is owing to our having gotten rid, in the greatest number of instances, of that feudal turn, and of those perplexed and cumbrous forms of the Norman day, which so long disfigured the admirable system upon which, by force or by artifice, they were incorporated. These, nothing but a prying eye, coupled with a resolution bold enough to lift up its hand against gray hairs, can ever effectually root out. "Time," says Lord Bacon, "is the greatest innovator; and if Time is always altering things for the worse, and Wisdom and Counsel do not sometimes alter them for the better, what will be the end thereof?" The English are rooting out these abuses; but perhaps, from a greater dread of touching the hoar that encircles the old trunk, seem more backward than we at tearing away the poisonous shoots which, at the subjugation of the true proprietors of the soil, were suffered to grow up rank around it. In the law of ejectment and entails; in the order of paying debts; in the law of descent, independent of the principle of primogeniture; in the liability of real estate to the demands of the creditor; in the law of executors and wills, with other points that might be enumerated, did not the nature of this discussion, which aims at nothing but drawing outlines, forbid, we think the liberal and less manacled judgment of the American states has outstripped the judicial wisdom of England in wholesome amendments. The luminous mind of Lord Mansfield did wonders towards many and obvious prunings. But much more remains to be accomplished; and perhaps his efforts, successful as they may have been, are in theory too bold for precedent even in his own meridian. Left to himself by the sluggishness of Parliament, he was forced to substitute a sort of judicial, for what would have been performed if not more efficaciously, more appropriately, by parliamentary legislation.

If the English would institute some legislative inquest, or set on foot some national commission, only once in a century, for the entire revisal of their admirable code, could it be, that in an enlightened age the father should never be able to succeed immediately as heir to the real estate of the son, or that, in the principal courts of the kingdom, land devised or descending to the heir, should not be liable to the simple contract debts of the ancestor or devisor, although the money was laid out in purchasing the very land? Surely common sense would too powerfully have pleaded for the abolition of the effect, after so long an extinction of the feudal cause. But these commissions of review, although sa[n]ctioned by the example of other great and enlightened nations both of ancient and modern times, an example which some of the American states have copied, have never been gone into by the English. While the rigors or absurdities of the Norman tyranny were yoked upon them in baneful heaps, during a single epoch, they seem, through an overstrained caution, little inclined to part with them, except one by one, in the tedious lapse of ages.

Not only has the nation been backward at any thing in the shape of a formal revisal of their code. It has been remarked also, as a fact somewhat curious, that, while the free states of Italy, in the 13th century, had their Consolato del Mare, of which they acknowledged their authority; Barcelona her Ordinances; Wisbuy and the Hanse-Towns, respectively, their Marine Codes; France, under Louis the Fourteenth, the same; and most other nations highly commercial, theirs,—Britain, the greatest naval power in the world, should never yet have any cemented naval or maritime collection compiled or published under the authority of the government. Different causes might be assigned, or different speculations hazarded, in accounting for this fact. Perhaps it has been the effect of accident; perhaps she has chosen to rely upon the compilations of other nations in connexion with her own statutory regulations and those of the crown. Or, possibly, the motive may have been generated by the vast and advantageous peculiarities of her political condition; and it may have been thought best not to confine within the restrictions or the certainties of a specific and stationary code, the rules of a commercial and warlike marine that has been so fast transcending, and that was so soon likely to draw entirely within the vortex of its own influence or control, that of every other country. Nothing is so apt as power, to flow over its bounds; and where its enterprizes are destined, in the plans or reveries of long-sighted and bold statesmen, to take a wide range it would be safest certainly, as with the press, to lay it under no previous restraints. These are but conjectures.

It is a subject of remark, scarcely less worthy to be alluded to, that this nation, so distinguished by great names in almost every branch of science, literature, and the arts, should yet be so barren in writers upon the public law. Few of her lawyers have soared beyond the fame of local learning. Of how little account, in the eyes of continental Europe, are her mere municipal jurists, may be gathered, in some slight degree—unless we look only at the humor of the idea—from Bynkershock's well known manner of speaking of the most valuable and profound of them all, my Lord Coke. He calls him, *Cocus quidam,—a certain Coke!*
(*To be continued.*)

* One of these codes, the commercial, has been translated into English by Mr. Du Ponceau of Philadelphia, who has added notes with his usual learning and ability. Mr. Rodman of New-York has translated the same code. We cannot help thinking that the latter gentleman would render an acceptable service to the public, by executing the plan he has intimated, of translating the whole of them, after the manner he has done the first. He has shown himself amply equal to the task; not as a translator merely, but as an ingenious anotator [*sic*] also.

Document II-7 Bentham's Letter, 1817

[The letter excerpted here from English philosopher Jeremy Bentham to the governor of each state in America raised many of the ideas prevalent in the codification debates in the states before the Civil War.

Its author, a student of the principles of legislation who is credited with having coined the word "codification," had failed in careers as a lawyer and politician, but was awarded French citizenship in 1792 due to his fame as a radical writer. Bentham was not a student of the American states, much less of North Carolina. He described America as a "Commonwealth" in the letter excerpted here and confessed therein to having first sent an offer to codify state laws to the President of the United States, rather than to the governors of the various states, because of his misapprehension of the Constitution of the United States. This misapprehension is ironic, as some writers, including Bentham himself, have understood constitutions to be "codifications" of organic or fundamental law. Apparently, this particular codification did more to obfuscate than to clarify the law for Mr. Bentham.

Compared to Chief Justice Lord Mansfield's broad, reforming, discretionary decisions, Bentham and Sir William Blackstone seem to represent diametrically opposed criticisms, the latter having restated in a scientifically-systematic treatise that portion of the unwritten law of England elaborated by past judicial and legal experts (i.e., to declare law in the context of England's legal traditions and a jurisprudence of natural law), and the former having boasted that someday he would certainly find a governmental authority to commission him to write a systematic series of statutes that would be applicable to any polity and all polities, and that would reach such a stage of completeness that it would cabin the discretion of judges like Mansfield, while allowing the necessary reforms that the common law—at least Blackstone's exposition of it—ignored on principle (i.e., to make law in reform of the legal tradition).[194] In seeking such a commission from North Carolina, Bentham's offer proceeded by an indirect route. The following letter and accompanying material were transmitted by Secretary of State John Quincy Adams to Gov. William Miller of North Carolina by a letter dated August 25, 1817:

> The books and pamphlets which accompany this letter, are transmitted to your Excellency at the request of their respective authors, Jeremy Bentham Esq[r]., of Queen Square Place, Westminster, & Robert Owen Esquire of Lanark. I shall have the honor of forwarding to your Excellency, some other of M. Bentham's publications from Washington.[195]

On November 10, 1817, the Secretary of State sent the governor the additional materials to which he had alluded in his letter of August:

> Before my late departure from England, I was requested by M. Jeremy Bentham to cause to be conveyed to you certain of his publications, upon subjects connected with various philanthropic and political institutions of society. In fulfil[l]ment of his wishes in this respect, I had some time ago, the honor of forwarding to you several publications of a similar nature, and I herewith transmit to you one small and one large Packet, which I hope may reach you safely, and the receipt whereof I will thank you to acknowledge to this Department.[196]

Weeks before the end of his term of office, on November 17, 1817, Governor Miller wrote to Secretary Adams:

> I have the honor to acknowledge the receipt of your letter of the 25th Ultimo, with the accompanying books and pamphlets, also your letter of the 10th Inst. with one large and one small package.[197]

The compilers have not located the materials sent by Adams; nor have they uncovered correspondence between Governor Miller and Mr. Bentham; nor have they found correspondence between Miller's successor, Gov. John Branch, and Mr. Bentham.]

No. VII.

CIRCULAR.—*To the Governor of the State of*

Queen-Square Place, Westminster,
London, June 1817.

Sir,—On the subject of Codification, an offer of mine, in the design of which, the State, over the councils of which your Excellency presides, was included, may be seen in a letter which I took the liberty to address to Mr. *Madison*, in his then character of President of your United States . . .

In the view taken of the subject by Mr. Madison, it happened not to be competent to the high situation at that time filled by him, to give to the offer in question the advantage of his sanction in any of the forms, which, for want of a sufficient acquaintance with the constitution of the United States, I had taken the liberty of submitting to his choice. Nevertheless, after so substantial an approbation as has been bestowed upon the offer in question, not only by those other distinguished citizens of your United Commonwealth, but by your late President himself, to wit, in and by the very letter in which he declined making, in a direct way, the proposed communication of it—I hereby take the liberty of submitting to your notice that same offer, as described in the accompanying letter to Mr. Madison, now printed for that purpose: and, forasmuch as of the twenty different States of which your Union is composed, if the offer in question has any claim to regard in any one, so has it in every other—hence the universality of the currency, which it has been my endeavour to give to it, and hence accordingly the word *circular*, by which an intimation of that endeavour is conveyed. . . .

On the occasion of the offer thus made, of the outline of a complete body of law for the use of any political state, as a work, which, though the foundations of it have so long ago been laid, remains yet to be completed,—it is matter of no small regret to me, that a correspondent number of copies, of a work containing a very considerable sample of the work now proposed to be executed, cannot accompany this address. . . . It is my ambition to approve myself, Sir, yours and your country's diligent and faithful servant,

JEREMY BENTHAM.

Document II-8 Revisal, 1817

[This act of 1817 commissioned a revisal and consolidation[198] of the positive law of North Carolina as a remedy for the difficulty laypersons encountered in determining which of the written laws were in force in North Carolina. Since the publication of François-Xavier Martin's 1804 update[199] to *Iredell's Revisal* of 1791,[200] the general assembly had passed many acts and had repealed or superseded many acts or sections of acts, some native and some British statutes in force in North Carolina. The commissioned revisal would simplify the task of determining the statutory law in force in North Carolina.]

CHAP. XVI.

An act for the revision of the Acts of the General Assembly.

WHEREAS, it is essentially necessary that the laws should exist in a form which will enable those who so wish to become acquainted with them, and from the multiplicity of the acts of the General Assembly of this state upon the same subjects, and from their being passed at different times and published as passed, it is very difficult for any but those who are professionally bred, to procure a knowledge of them: For remedy whereof,

BE *it enacted by the General Assembly of the State of North-Carolina, and it is hereby enacted by the authority of the same,*
That a committee of three persons be appointed by joint ballot of both houses, whose duty it shall be to revise and consolidate the public acts and parts of acts of the General Assembly of this state heretofore passed or which may be passed before the completion of their work: And whereas, from the phraseology of the act of one thousand seven hundred and seventy eight, chapter the fifth, doubts often arise what statutes of the parliament of Great Britain are in force in this state,

II. *Be it further enacted,* That it shall be the duty of said commissioners to enumerate and specify those statutes and parts of statutes of Great Britain which are in force within this state.

III. *And be it further enacted* That said commissioners shall be allowed such compensation as shall be judged adequate and proper, and that they report their proceedings to the succeeding General Assembly.

Document II–9 Office of Reporter, 1818

[The notion that all appellate opinions should be timely reported and distributed[201] sounded in favor of the common man's access to the law, which is the same bell rung by the more zealous codifiers in the early decades of the nineteenth century and by the symphony later performed by Jacksonian democracy. In other words, official reporting of opinions gave the impression of more writtenness of the unwritten law and assured that there was no collusion between monied parties and remote judges. Writtenness of opinions, though, may have tempted users of the law to treat these examples of moral and legal principle applied to facts (i.e., judgments made by practical reasoning) as akin to the conscious manipulations of statutory law,[202] rather than as declarations of law rooted in the reasonable customs of an upright people. Nonetheless, without explicitly touching upon the pros or cons of official reporting, the supplemental act of 1818 concerning the supreme court, excerpted below, created the judicial office of Reporter of the decisions of the supreme court.]

CHAPTER II.

An Act Supplemental to the Act Concerning the Supreme Court.

Be it enacted by the General Assembly of the State of North-Carolina, and it is hereby enacted by the authority of the same, . . .

XIII. *Be it further enacted*, That the Judges of the Supreme Court shall appoint some fit person as Reporter of the decisions of said Court, who shall be entitled to receive from the treasury of this State an annual compensation for his services, the sum of five hundred dollars: *Provided nevertheless*, The said compensation, shall not be paid unless said Reporter shall print and publish, or cause to be printed and published, in a neat type and on good paper the decisions of said Court, made during the time he shall act as such Reporter, within nine months after such decisions shall be made, and shall deliver eight copies of the decisions, so printed and published, to the Secretary of state without any expence to the state. Which copies shall be distributed as follows to wit: to the Secretary of the Governor, to the Clerk of the Supreme Court each one copy, to be retained in their office and handed over to their successors in office; and the residue of said copies shall be deposited in and become part of the Library of this state; and the said Reporter shall also deliver sixty two copies of said reports to be deposited one in the office of the Clerk of the Court of Pleas and Quarter Sessions of each county of the State.

Document II–10 H. Potter's Report, 1819

[*Potter's Revival*, called by its contemporaries the *New Revisal* or the *Revised Code*, was in the tradition of *Iredell's Revisal* of late in the prior century, and not an affirmative step in the direction of *The Revised Statutes* of the 1830s. While *Potter's Revisal* continued the tradition of state statutory revisals, it varied from its immediate predecessor on at least two points. While *Iredell's Revisal* had "collect[ed]," "compiled," and "revised" the whole body of the laws of the state,[203] *Potter's Revisal* "revise[d] and consolidate[d]" the "public acts and parts of acts" of the general assembly.[204] Furthermore, while the act to confirm *Iredell's Revisal* stated that that revisal could be "given in evidence, and received as such, in all the courts of law and equity within the state,"[205] the act to publish *Potter's Revisal* did not mention its status as evidence.[206]

In the report excerpted below, the Commissioners explained that they meant to present all portions of the acts that remained in force just as those portions were written. The fact that a single act may include many subjects did not dissuade them from their principle of presentation. Under no circumstances, then, would this work degenerate into a manual containing session laws broken into pieces according to subject.[207] Marginal references, though, would tie provisions on the same subject across acts.

The report also contained interesting attempts to clarify the question of statutory reception, the commissioners dividing the British statutes into two periods, 1225–1665 and 1666–1818, "1665" being the date of the second charter of Carolina, statutes at or before that date being received by the province on some theories of empire. The problem of reception loomed large in the early nineteenth century and served as one of the more persuasive arguments in the codification debates. The question of reception, of course, presented more than a hint of anti-English sentiment, but also raised very ordinary and important practical questions of access to information. Colonial statutes raised similar questions of access, this report explaining that the earliest extant act from colonial times bore the late date of 1715.

The commissioners signing this report were Henry Potter, John Louis Taylor, and Bartlett Yancey. Yancey had served as a state senator and congressman and is remembered for his role in the creation of the modern state supreme court[208] as well as for his support of the fair representation of the population of the western portion of the state. Potter, a federal district court judge for more than fifty years, is also remembered for his manual, *Office and Duty of the Justice of the Peace*.[209] Taylor's contribution to this revisal overlapped his duties as the first chief justice of the newly organized Supreme Court of North Carolina. He updated the revisal in a publication of 1827.[210] Taylor is also remembered for his nominal reports of decisions of the North Carolina courts (*Taylor's Reports*, 1799–1802; *Carolina Law Repository*, 1813–1816 (2 volumes); and *Term Reports*, 1816–1818) and for his codification of the laws of administrators and executors in 1824.[211]]

REPORT
Of the Commissioners appointed by an act of the Legislature of 1817,
to revise the laws of North-Carolina.

To the honorable the General Assembly of the State of North-Carolina.

The undersigned commissioners, appointed under the act of 1817, c. 16, to revise the public acts of the General Assembly, and to enumerate and specify the Statutes and parts of Statutes of Great-Britain, which are in force in the state, have the honor to Report, That they have finished the work committed to them, and hold it ready for inspection, and for such disposition of it as your honorable body may think proper to make.

The code, as revised, contains all the acts of Assembly from the year 1715, to 1818,* inclusive, which are now in force, together with some which have been repealed or superseded by subsequent acts, but which may be regarded as the foundation of some vested right, or as authorising some mode of proceeding, a reference to which may be necessary in the deduction and establishment of titles, or as the muniments, in some shape or other, of estates or interests; and these are carefully noted in the margin, as repealed, altered or obsolete, according to their true character. Wherever a repealed law did not appear necessary to be referred to, for these or other purposes of equal moment, it has been omitted, as an embarrassing incumbrance to the statute book; and should a resort to it ever be necessary, as indicating the progressive changes of the law, or as subsidiary to the investigations of the jurist or historian, it is still to be found in the compilation heretofore made.

The general course pursued by the commissioners has been, to take up each act singly, and to examine deliberately, in what respect it has been altered or modified by subsequent legislation, and to make distinct references to the date, chapter and section of any law, varying in any respect, the first enactment. The earliest law, therefore, on each subject, may be regarded as the foundation of a statutory system, of which the changes and ramifications are traceable by precise and discriminating marginal notices.

From the acts on the same subject afterwards passed, reference is made to those which are antecedent and subsequent; and every one to which the attention is directed, either contains within itself all the legislative provisions on the particular subject, or points, by an easy reference, to all other acts appertaining to the same system; and, to afford a greater facility to the enquirer, it is proposed to have but one series of chapters, and to insert them, with the dates of the acts, at the top of the pages in regular order. Thus the reader, instead of meeting a list of statutes described only by the year and chapter, is directed, at once, to the point he may be pursuing.

In adopting this plan, the commissioners considered that they were acting in furtherance of the views of the Legislature, as expressed in the act authorising the revision, and that the public interest and economy would be thereby promoted.

The arrangement of the acts under distinct heads, and in alphabetical order, has its advantages, and would be suitable for an abridgement or manual; but a revisal should contain every part of the act in force, without separating the different sections, and placing them under as many distinct heads as there are different subjects blended in the same act.

In giving construction to a statute, the intention of the Legislature is much better understood by an examination of the whole statute, than the particular clause which may more immediately relate to the question under consideration.

An alphabetical arrangement requires, necessarily, either that the sections be detached, or that the entire act be placed under several heads. In either event, it was considered, that the inconvenience would be greater than in the mode adopted. Another consideration was, that be due care and attention on the part of those who may hereafter superintend the printing of the public laws, the future acts of the General Assembly, by proper marginal references, may be made a continuation of the present revisal, and thereby supersede the expense of another.

Upon the other branch of the duty assigned to the commissioners, they have the honor further to Report: That they entered upon this task, under the direction of the general rule furnished by the act of 1778, c. 5, the substance of which is, that such British statutes as were in force before that period, and were not inconsistent with the freedom and independence of the State and the Constitution, and which have not been provided for in the whole or in part, nor abrogated, repealed, expired, or become obsolete, are thereby declared to be in full force.

In order to meet the enquiry, what statutes were in force before 1778, it became necessary to consider, in the first place, which of them began to operate with the first settlement of the country by emigrants from Great-Britain.

This event took place in 1665, the date of the charter of Charles the Second; and the colonists brought with them from the mother country, all such statutes then in force as were applicable to their situation, to the country, and their new way of life. Their infant settlements required a legislation of a character more simple, clear and determinate, than could be obtained by an indiscriminate adoption of the English statutes; a very large proportion of which were suitable to England alone, and could not without evident absurdity be extended to Carolina. Of this description, were the laws relative to the King's prerogative, the rights of the nobility and clergy, the trade and revenue of England, and even many of those sanguinary penal laws, whose policy, questionable even in a rich, commercial and populous country, must be ill adapted to the condition of a few agriculturalists, inhabiting a wilderness.

The next object of enquiry was, what statutes were extended to the colony after the date of the charter, either by the terms of the statutes themselves, and adopted here, or were enforced by legislative acts of the Proprietary, Regal or State Governments.

The charter to the lords proprietors invested them with the power of enacting laws with the assent of the freemen; but what was the course of proprietary legislation for the first fifty years after the settlement of the colony, there are no accessible means of ascertaining. In 1715, the date of the first acts which are extant, the legislature avow that it is often disputed how far the laws of England are in force in the colony; and to put an end to the doubts upon the subject, they deduce from the words of the charter, what perhaps would have more clearly resulted from the general principles of colonization, that the laws of England are the laws of the colony, so far as they are "compatible with our way of living and trade." But they go further, and adopt many statutes by general description, passed both before and after the settlement of the colony, which would not otherwise have been in force, either in consequence of any general principle, or as the necessary construction of the charter. Some of these were abrogated by the revolution, others became merged in the declaration of rights, which secured the privileges of the people in a more enlarged and effectual manner; and the residue have been superseded by laws, providing for the same subjects. There is one statute, however, passed after the date of the charter, which was adopted in 1715, under the designation of those which provided for the privileges of the people, which still retains its authority to a certain degree. The statute adverted to is the 31st Charles II, chapter 2nd, commonly called the *habeas corpus* act. Although the immunity of the subject from unjust imprisonment is proclaimed by magna charta and the petition of right, 3 Car. I. c. 1, and that of the citizen is still more strongly fortified by the declaration of rights, yet, with the exception of the habeas corpus act, there is neither statute nor act of Assembly which prescribes and enforces the method of obtaining the writ, and regulates the details of redress. There are many parts of this statute which are inapplicable to this state, but the substantial provisions of it are so important towards the effectual security of the liberty of the citizen, that it might be thought necessary by the legislature to modify and re-enact it.

Some other statutes passed posterior to the charter, are also now in force in this state, either because they were enforced in 1715, or at some later period, and are not incompatible with the constitution, and have not been repealed or otherwise provided for; or because they were originally made to extend to the state, and have been practically adopted. Of the former description, are the statutes for the amendment of the law; of the latter, are the 5th George II, c. 7, "An act for the more easy recovery of debts in his Majesty's plantations and colonies in America," of which the fourth section is in force; and the 12th George III, ch. 20, "An act for the more effectual proceeding against persons standing mute on their arraignment for felony or piracy."

The Commissioners are apprehensive that a detailed exposition of the reasons for inserting or omitting each particular statute, might be deemed tedious or unprofitable, but so far as the subject is susceptible of a general analysis, the result of the whole is, that when any British statute, passed between the years 1225, the earliest of the British statutes, and 1665, the date of the second charter of Charles II, to the proprietors of Carolina, in the seventeenth year of his reign, both inclusive, is not contained in the list, the reasons are, either,

1. Because it was unsuited to the condition of the colonies.
2. The same objects have been provided for, by the legislature of the Proprietary, Regal or State Government.
3. It has been annulled by the change from the Proprietary to the Regal Government, which took place in 1728, or by that from the Regal to the Independent Sovereignty established in 1776.

When any British statute, passed since 1665, is inserted in the list, the reasons are, either,

1. It has been enforced by some legislative act; or,
2. It has been extended by its terms to the colonies and adopted in practice.

The whole work is most respectfully submitted under the hope, that such imperfections as may be discovered in it, may meet with the candor and indulgence, which its intrinsic difficulty seems to bespeak.

H. POTTER,
J. L. TAYLOR,
B. YANCEY.

November 19, 1819.

---

* The acts of 1819 were afterwards included.

Document II–11 Gaston's Report, 1819

[The creation of the modern Supreme Court of North Carolina was a thorough break from prior state practice and with English practice.[212] A bill to create a purely appellate court, sponsored by Senators A. D. Murphey and Bartlett Yancey, and supported by Governor Miller, had failed in the prior year. A similar bill introduced by Senator William Gaston, the Federalist turned Whig, passed in 1818 with the strong support of Gov. John Branch.[213]

The more democratic forces in the state reviled the new court.[214] The presence of this aristocratic institution, divorced from the people by not riding circuit or trying cases, was made more palatable by giving it removal jurisdiction for equity cases. This removal jurisdiction would continue until adoption of the 1868 constitution.[215]]

JOURNAL OF THE SENATE.

Reports of Committees....

The select joint committee to whom was referred so much of the Governor's message as relates to the judiciary, have, in obedience to a resolution of the two Houses of the General Assembly, instructing them to enquire "whether any, and if any, what alterations are necessary to be made, respecting the Supreme Court and also whether the compensation allowed to the judges of the Supreme Court, be more than adequate for their services," made the enquiries directed by the resolution and respectfully report. As the resolution has not directed the attention of the committee to any specific alteration of the Supreme court, they have believed it proper to examine what are the objects to be promoted by such an establishment, and then to enquire whether these objects are attained by the court under it present organization.

The necessity of such a court results from the nature of the government under which we live. Ours is emphatically a government of laws, every individual, whatever his station in the community, is free to perform an act which the laws authorise, and no man is suffered to do what they prohibit. Since then, these are the universal and the only rules of action, it is indispensable that they be so expounded as that in their controul of civil conduct, they shall have a steady and uniform application. There is no mode by which the different tribunals of justice through the land, held by various persons with various degrees of intelligence can be made to concur in the same exposition of the public will, other than by establishing one Supreme court of judicature, which may conclusively pronounce in the last resort, on every difficulty arising in the interpretation of laws. Without an adequate establishment of this sort, liberty and property, the natural rights which men retain after society is formed, and the civil rights acquired by entering into society are unprotected and insecure.

The framers of our Constitution were aware that in some shape a Supreme court was indispensible. Without undertaking to prescribe its form, which might vary with the varying exigencies of the country, and might be safely confided to Legislative discretion, they seemed to have regarded its existence at all times, as a necessary adjunct of government. They have not said in so many terms that there shall be a Supreme court, but they have declared, "that the General Assembly shall, by joint ballot of both Houses, appoint Judges of the Supreme courts of law and equity, who shall be commissioned by the Governor, and hold their offices during their good behaviour," and they have further provided that "the Judges of the supreme courts of law and equity, shall have adequate salaries during their continuance in office."

For several years before the last session of the General Assembly, a supreme court existed in North Carolina, under a form which experience had shown to be defective. It was holden by the same Judges who presided in the superior courts, and took cognisance of appeals from their own decisions, or of questions they choose to transmit as doubtful and difficult. It would be a waste of time, to pronounce a condemnation of this system. Your committee believe that there is not an intelligent man among those whose attention has been directed to the subject, who does not know, nor a candid man who will not admit, that it was thoroughly inadequate for the purposes for which it was formed. Its duties were too varied, too vast, too momentous to be discharged by men whose time was principally occupied, and whose minds were worn out by other and sufficient employment. It wanted leisure, it wanted exemption from preconceived opinion, it wanted a thorough devotion of mind to its proper engagements, it wanted almost every requisite to make it what the people had a right to ask, an enlightened and consistent exposition of law, a faithful guardian of the rights of the citizen, and a correction of the errors of subordinate tribunals, its delays were ruinous, its haste was yet more pernicious, all classes of the community called for its amendment, and the only question was, in what mode could amendment best be made.

In strong and emphatic terms, the attention of the Legislature was called to the subject by the Governor. With an earnest and honest solicitude to do what was right, they bestowed on it their best consideration, and finally adopted the system which now obtains. The prominent and distinguished feature of this system, is the appointment of three Judges to hold the court, who are entirely distinct from those that preside on the circuits, to whom competent salaries are allowed, whose attention is confined to the business of the Supreme court, and whose duty it is to devote themselves wholly to it. Every decision on a question of law made in the State may be here reviewed on appeal, and upon every question thus brought before them, they are compelled to act finally and without delay. On the propriety of adopting this plan it was natural for the best men to differ, it was yet untried, its advantages could only be proved in theory, and prudent men with the most upright intentions, are often reluctant to trust to such demonstration. They are unwilling to change what exists, without an assurance that what is offered will be greatly better. They would rather endure the ills they have than fly to others which they know not of; but on the propriety of continuing it, a difference of opinion can scarcely be supposed; many, if not all of the reasons which then opposed its adoption, now operate for its continuance. It is the system by law established, and no law ought to be altered without an adequate cause. Every change produces its inconvenience; changes in the fundamental laws and great institutions of a State, are always followed by serious consequences, and he is unquestionably chargeable with rashness who adventures on them unnecessarily.

Your committee however are not deterred from recommending an alteration of the Supreme court establishment, by this negative reasoning merely. They believe that experience has tested its excellence, and shown that it is worthy to be cherished; they cordially join in the sentiment pronounced by the Governor, that "the salutary results anticipated from the system, have been realised, and that the extensive dispensation of justice flowing from it, while it reflects much credit on the members composing the court, reflects not less on the Legislature that had the courage and independence to establish it." Your committee find that the court under its improved form, has already settled many of the difficult and contested questions which has long agitated the community and embarrassed the rights of property; they have established important principles relative to the construction and execution of contracts in law and equity, they have given an authoritative interpretations to statutes and acts of Assembly, they have defined the jurisdiction of courts, and settled the rules which govern in the limitation of suits and revival of actions, they have ascertained the period when lands become subject to the lien of judgments, they have given certainty and consistency to the rules of evidence in cases of contested boundaries, and they have dispelled (it is confidently hoped forever,) the protentuous doubts and uncertainties which hung over the important subject of descent. One year has not passed since the court has been acting under its improved organization, and the committee believe it has already done more to render law what it ought to be, "a certain rule of civil conduct," than the judicial labours of the preceding twenty years have affected.

All the cases now receive a prompt attention, a patient hearing and a full deliberation. The docket is kept down, causes are disposed of at the first term, almost without an exemption, and the court is ready to receive those weighty and numerous equity suits, which have for so many years slept unheaded on the dockets of the courts in the west, and which the committee learn, are in preparation for their journey hither. Sufficiently long have the parties been mocked with a promise of hearing. In this court they will be heard, and it is this court only that they can obtain this boon.

In the main the committee have no doubt, but that the system has proved and will prove, eminently beneficial to the State; they are gratified also to perceive that a sister State, distinguished for her liberal and wise policy has discerned the advantages of such a system, and following our example, is disposed to realize them, in the language of her enlightened chief magistrate. South Carolina also finds, that the proper remedy for consistent and varying decisions, is the establishment of a court of errors and appeals, to be composed of Judges distinct from the Judges of the courts of law and equity, to have a superintending and controuling power over all the courts and to be the demier resort."

That the system will admit of amendment is readily conceded; like all human institutions, is stamped with that imperfection which characterise the works of man. Time will no doubt make manifest, defects as yet unnoticed, and suggest improvements not now foreseen. The committee however have not been sensible of defects, which render legislative interference at this session necessary, and without necessity, they deem it inexpedient to innovate on the plan. The system is now on its trial; it is in a course of fair, and it is believed, successful experiment; let the trial go on; let the experiment be conducted to a decisive issue. This its friends seem to have a right to ask, and this its candid opponents will not refuse to give. When it shall have acquired stability, it may be touched without danger; when we shall have seen its practical results, we can the better regulate its machinery; if any thing wrong be discovered, we can more certainly decide whether the fault be in the principle or in the details of the plan.

Directing their attention to the remaining branch of the resolution, the committee were at once arrested by considerations too obvious to be overlooked and too weighty to be disregarded. It is not now an enquiry what salaries shall be offered to induce men to engage in the public service. This was the enquiry at the last session, and it opened an unlimited range for every consideration of convenience, policy and economy. But this question was then settled. The constituted authorities fixed the compensation to be made to the judges of the supreme court before judges were appointed. The State proposed its terms, and these terms have been accepted. A contract was thus made between the State and the individuals appointed to this high office, which neither party can violate without guilt and reproach. The State is entitled to their best services, and if these be not rendered it may despoil them of their office; and on the other hand, they are entitled while they behave well, to the stipulated emolument, in consideration of which, they entered into the public employment. The question now is, will the State be faithless—will the State break its contract. The committee do not admit the supposition that this can be a question with the representatives of a moral and intelligent people.

It may be asked whether a case might not occur in which the General Assembly had so far betrayed the trust of their constituents, by making ruinous contracts on the part of the State, as to justify an infringement of such contracts by their successors? The committee will not say that in the nature of things, a case so monstrous cannot happen, but they owe it to their fellow-citizens, and to the character of the State, to declare that they regard it among moral impossibilities. If ever it should occur, the desperate nature of the case may indicate a remedy. There are occasions when contracts between individuals, however solemnly formed, are voidable on account of the force and fraud with which they were originally contaminated. But there is no casuistry more deceptive than that which draws from extreme and possible cases, rules for the government of ordinary conduct. The man is dishonest who violates his contracts, and the nature of the act will not be changed, tho' a State should descend to commit it. In the constitution of the United States, and in most of the State constitutions recently formed, the people have guarded against a perfidy of this sort to judic[i]al officers, by an express declaration that the salary of a judge shall not be diminished during his continuance in office. Though in the constitution of North-Carolina such a provision is not expressed in so many words, yet its spirit is unquestionably embodied there. "The judges shall hold their offices during good behaviour and they shall receive adequate salaries during their continuance in office." The obvious purport of these declarations, the moral sense of the community, and the universal usage under the constitution, are strong indications that a breach of faith by reduction of a stipulated salary is prohibited to us by the people. Whether the supposed excess in the compensation of the judges be an evil so enormous, so threat[e]ning to the existence or well being of the State, as to present a desperate case, justifying a departure from the established principles of morality, is a question which cannot be asked without a ludicrous effect. The utmost saving which the committee have heard of as contemplated to be clipped and pared from their salaries, is less than may be husbanded by shortening our session three days. It will not average twenty five dollars to a county. Is there a man in the community who values the character of his country, that will put this pittance, though he were to pay it all from his own pocket, in competition with the flighted faith of the State?

The committee do not, and cannot regard the question of salary as an open question; but if they did, they have no hesitation in s[a]ying that in their judgment the salary has not been fixed too high. To command confidence and respect, a seat on the bench of the supreme court, must be rendered worthy of the acceptance of the best talents in the country. The dearest interests of the citizens must not be trusted in the last resort, where there is no appeal, no revision to the adjudication of the second rate members of the bar. He who presides there, should have a purity above suspicion, and an intelligence not to be questioned. The State has a right to require, and it is her policy to demand from him, if necessary, an entire devotion of his time and his faculties to her service; she is bound therefore to pay him well, and to exempt him from the cares and embarrassments of private occupation. Seldom will any individual have a reputation sufficiently confirmed, to procure for him an elevation to this bench, who is not well advanced in years. What portion of intellectual exertion can be commanded for the public service from a judge, no longer young and active, perplexed by scanty means and numerous wants? He must either reside permanently at the seat of government, or spend here a considerable portion of his time. His station requires of him to live decently, and we know that the habits of society at this place will not permit that to be done without expense. Bound to explore thoroughly, and to search to the bottom, the various questions of difficulty arising in the administration of the law throughout the land, he is put to an annual charge in the purchase of books, which will surprise those who have not adverted to the circumstance, and makes no small deduction from his emoluments. If the judges of the supreme court perform their duties faithfully, their salaries are not more than adequate to their services; and if they should not perform their duties faithfully, their places ought to be filled with better men.

It comes not within the scope of the instructions to this committee to enquire into the salaries allowed to the judges of the superior courts. In every employment, public and private, civil and military, professional and mechanical, there is, and there must be, a difference of compensation between those in the highest and those in the subordinate stations. The former require talents of a higher grade than may suffice for discharging the functions of the latter, and it is an invariable rule that rare qualities command a comparatively high price. It is a rule eminently beneficial to society, by holding forth an adequate motive to industry, and the cultivation and improvement of the human powers. If however the difference between the salaries of the judges of the supreme and of the superior courts be thought disproportionate, the committee, satisfied that the former ought not be lessened, will not regret if an adequate addition be made to the latter.

The committee request to be discharged from the further consideration of the subject matter of the above mentioned resolution.

WM. GASTON, *Chairman.*

A true copy from the original in my office.

ROB'T. WILLIAMS, *C. S.*

Document II–12 Taylor on the Common Law, 1820

[Chief Justice John Taylor made a tremendous contribution to the development of the law of the state in the early nineteenth century.[216] To understand him is largely to understand the control of law reform in North Carolina during the Antebellum Period. While Taylor respected the principles and rules of the common law, surely to the delight of conservative political forces in North Carolina, he read harsh and inhumane statutory institutions which deviated from the common law (such as slavery) as narrowly as he thought possible, and he ushered in statutory codification for the state, surely to the delight of moderate political forces in North Carolina. Between 1798 and 1818, Taylor unofficially reported opinions of the state superior court, the court of conference, and the early supreme court. He was the first reporter in the state to employ headnotes.[217] By an act of 1817, he was appointed (along with Henry Potter and Bartlett Yancey) to revise the statute law of the state and list the statutes of England in force in the state.[218] This work was completed and published in 1821 and updated by Taylor in 1827.[219] At about the same time, he published a treatise on the duties of executors and administrators,[220] which was a statutory digest that foreshadowed the great change from chronologically arranged statutes in force to statutory codification, which was achieved in North Carolina about a decade later. Taylor had been elected by the general assembly to the superior court in 1798, served on the court of conference, and was chief justice of both the early and the modern Supreme Court of North Carolina, the position which he held at his death in 1829. His understanding of the common law is revealed in his appellate opinions, as in *State v. Tackett* from 1820, here excerpted.]

The State
v.
Tackett.
} From Wake....

Taylor, Chief-Justice, delivered the opinion of the Court: ...

The different degrees of homicide, they [the Legislature] left to be ascertained by the Common Law of the country—a system which adapts itself to the habits, institutions and actual condition of the citizens, and which is not the result of the wisdom of any one man, or society of men, in any one age, but of the wisdom and experience of many ages of wise and discreet men. ...

Document II–13 British Statutes in Force, 1821

[A table included in *Potter's Revisal* was the state's final attempt at listing the British statutes and parts of statutes in force in North Carolina. In 1837, *The Revised Statutes* would repeal "all the statutes of England or Great Britain heretofore in use in this State . . ."[221]]

STATUTES AND PARTS OF STATUTES
OF
GREAT BRITAIN,

REPORTED AS BEING IN FORCE IN THIS STATE, BY THE COMMISSIONERS APPOINTED UNDER THE ACT OF 1817, ENTITLED, "AN ACT FOR THE REVISION OF THE ACTS OF THE GENERAL ASSEMBLY."

Year and Reign.	Title of the Statutes, and Remarks.	Book & page of Ruffhead's edit.	
		VOL.	PAG.
20th Hen. 3, 1235, Chapter 7.	'Widows may bequeath the crop of their lands.'	1	16
Chap. 9.	'He is a bastard that is born before the marriage of his parents.'	1	19
21st Hen. 3, 1236.	'The day of the leap-year and the day before shall be holden for one day.'	1	20
3d Edw. 1, 1275. Chapter 9.	'All men shall be ready to pursue felons.' That part only of this statute is in force which corresponds with the title.	1	43
4th Edward 1, Statute 20, 1276.	'Of what things a coroner shall enquire.' This statute is in force except those parts which relate to the coroner's duty in the following points, viz: making enquiry as to the property of any person—treasure trove—appeals—deodands—wrecks—and except also that part which provides that lands shall remain in the king's hands, &c.	1	60
4th Edw. 1, 1276, Chap. 6	'By what words in a feoffment a feoffor shall be bound to warranty.'	1	63
6th Edw. 1, 1278, chap. 3.	'An alienation of land by tenant by the curtesy, with warranty, shall be void.'	1	65
6th Edw. 1, chapter 5.	'Several tenants against whom an action of waste is maintainable.'	1	66
Chap. 13.	'No waste shall be made hanging a suit for the land.'	1	69
13th Edw. 1, 1285, Chap. 1.	'In gifts in tail the donor's will shall be observed.' This statute is not in force, but a recurrence to it is often necessary in examining ancient titles.	1	78
Chap. 15.	'An infant cloined may sue by prochein amy.'	1	92
Chap. 14.	'The process in an action of waste. A writ to enquire of waste.'	1	92
13th Edw. 1, Chapter 18.	'He that recovereth debt may sue execution by fieri facias or eligit.'	1	93
Chap. 22.	'Waste maintainable by one tenant in common against another.'	1	94
Chap. 23.	'Executors may have a writ of accompt.'	1	95
Chap. 24.	'A writ of nuisance of a house, &c. levied and aliened to another. In like cases like writs grantable.' This statute is in force except those parts which relate to ecclesiastical persons.	1	95

Chap. 31.	'An exception to a plea shall be sealed by the justices.'	1	99
Chap. 34.	'It is felony to commit a rape. A married woman elopeth with an advouturer.' That part only of this statute is in force which enacts 'that if a wife willingly leave her husband, and go away and continue with the advouturer she shall be barred forever of action to demand her dower,' &c.	1	101
Chap. 39.	'The manner to deliver writs to the sheriffs to be executed. Returning of issues. Resistance of execution of process.' Those parts only of this statute are in force which give authority to the sheriffs to do certain things in case of resistance of the execution of process, and direct the punishment of those who resist the execution of process.	1	104
Chap. 45.	'The process of execution of things recorded within the year or after.'	1	109
Winchester, Chapter 1.	'Fresh suit shall be made after felons and robbers from town to town.'	1	112
18th Edw. 1, Statute 2.	'Statute of quo warranto.'	1	123
Statute 3.	'Another new statute of quo warranto.'	1	123
Chap. 3	'No feoffment shall be made to assure land in main.'	1	122
20th Edward 1, Statute 2.	'A statute of waste.'	1	126
33 Edw. 1, 1304.	'Who be conspirators and who champertors.' That part of this statute which relates to 'stewards and bailiffs of great lords' must be excepted.	1	149
1305. Statute 4.	'He that challengeth a jury or juror for the king must shew his cause.'	1	151
Statute 6.	'An ordinance for measuring of land.'	1	152
1st Edw. 2, 1307.	'In what cases it is felony to break prison, in what not.'	1	164
9th Edward 2nd, Chap. 16.	'The privilege of the church being demanded by the ordinary, shall not be denied to a clerk that hath confessed felony.'	1	171
2 Edward 3, 1328, Chap. 3.	'No man shall come before the justices, or go, or ride armed.'	1	197
4 Edward 3, 1330, Chap. 7.	'Executors shall have an action of trespass for a wrong done to their testator.'	1	203
Chap. 10.	'Sheriffs and goalers shall receive offenders without any thing taking.'	1	204
Chap. 11.	'Justices of assise shall enquire of maintainers, conspirators and champertors.'	1	204
5th Edw. 3, Chapter 10.	'The punishment of a juror, that is ambidexter and taketh money.'	1	210
Chap. 11.	'Process against those that be appealed, indicted or outlawed in one county, and remain in another.'	1	210

14th Edw. 3, Chapter 6.	'A record that is defective by misprision of a clerk shall be amended.'	1	224
Chap. 10.	'Sheriffs shall have the keeping of goals. A prisoner by duress becomes an approver.'	1	226
20th Edw. 3, 1346, Chap. 4.	'None shall maintain any quarrels but their own.'	1	247
25th Edw. 3, 1350, Chap. 3. Statute 5.	'No indictor shall be put upon the inquest of the party indicted.'	1	262
Chap. 5. Statute 5.	'Executors of executors shall have the benefit and charge of the first testator.'	1	263
Chap. 14.	'What process shall be awarded against him that is indicted of felony.' Only that part of this statute is in force which directs the issuing of a capias.	1	265
Chap. 16.	'The exception of non tenure of parcel shall not abate the whole writ.'	1	288
28th Edward 1354, Chap. 13.	'An inquest shall be de medietate linguæ where an alien is party.' That part of this statute only is in force which gives the inquest.	1	288
34th Edw. 3, 1360, Chap. 1.	'What sort of person shall be justices of the peace; and what authority they shall have.' That part only is in force which is distinguished by being between brackets.	1	299
Chap. 5.	'Auncel weight shall be put out. Buying and selling shall be by equal balance.'	1	300
Chap. 8.	'The penalty of a juror taking a reward to give his verdict.'	1	301
38th Edw. 3, 1363, Chap. 12	'The punishment of a juror taking reward to give his verdict; and of embraccors.'	1	320
50 Edw. 3, 1376, Chap. 6.	'Fraudulent assurances of lands or goods to deceive creditors shall be void.'	1	332
5th Rich. 2, 1381, Chap. 8.	'The penalty where any doth enter into lands where it is not lawful, or with force.'	1	352
9th Rich. 2, 1385, Chap. 3.	'A writ of error or attaint maintainable in the reversion.' This statute is in force so far only as it relates to a writ of error.	1	372
12th Rich. 2, 1388, Chap. 13	'The punishment of them which cause corruption near a city or great town to corrupt the air.'	1	382
15th Rich. 2, 1391, Chap. 2.	'The duty of justices of the peace where any forcible entry is made into lands.'	1	400
2 Henry 4, 1400, Chap. 7.	'In what case the plaintiff shall not be nonsuit if the verdict pass against him.'	1	437
Chap. 11.	'A remedy for him who is pursued wrongfully in the court of admiralty.'	1	438
4th Henry 4, 1402, Chap. 23.	'Judgments given shall continue until they be reversed by attaint or error.' In force, except by attaint.	1	453
5th Henry 4, 1403, Chap. 10.	'Justices of the peace shall imprison none but in the common gaol.'	1	459
11 Hen.4th, chapter 3.	'Records shall not be amended or repaired after judgment enrolled.' The second in force.	1	459

11 Henry 4, 1409, Chap. 9	'Jurors in indictments shall be returned by the sheriffs or bailiffs without the denomination of any.'	1	477
13th Hen. 4th 1411, Chap. 7	'The justices of the peace and the sheriffs shall arrest those which commit any riot, &c. and enquire of them and record their offences.'	1	480
2 Henry 5, 1414, Chap. 2.	'A *corpus cum causa*, or certiorari to remove him which is in execution at another man's suit.'	1	486
8th Henry 6, 1429, Chap. 9.	'The duty of justices of the peace where land is entered upon or detained with force.' Except the first section.	1	545
9th Henry 5, 1421, Chap. 4.	'The justices may amend defaults in records or process before judgment given.'	1	513
Chap. 12.	'No judgment or record shall be reversed for any writ, process, &c. rased. —What defects in records may be amended by the judges.'	1	550
Chap. 15.	'The justices may in certain cases amend defaults in records.'	1	553
10th Henry 6, 1432, Chap. 4.	'The penalty of him that maketh a false entry, that the plaintiff doth offer himself in person when he doth not.'	1	566
11th Hen. 6, 1433, Chap. 5.	'The remedy where a tenant granteth over his estate, taketh the profits and committeth waste.'	1	571
23 Henry 6, 1444, Chap. 9.	'No sheriff shall let to farm his county or any bailiwick. The sheriff's and bailiff's fees and duties in certain cases.' Only that part is in force which prohibits the letting to farm, &c.	1	608
31st Hen. 6, 1452, Chap. 9.	'A remedy for a woman inforced to be bound by statute or obligation.'	1	628
33 Henry 6, 1455, Chap. 1.	'A remedy for executors against servants that embezzle their master's goods after his death.'	1	629
3 Henry 7, 1486, Chap. 2.	'The penalty for carrying a woman away against her will that hath lands or goods.'	2	69
Chap. 10.	'All deeds of gift made to defraud creditors, shall be void.'	2	70
4th Henry 7, Chapter 13.	'Clergy shall be allowed but once, &c.' Part of this statute is in force, viz. that which disallows clergy a second time; and that which relates to the branding with a letter T.	2	77
Chap. 20.	'Actions popular prosecuted by collusion shall be no bar to those which be pursued with good faith.'	2	78
11th Hen. 7, 1494, Chap. 12.	'A mean to help and speed poor persons in their suits.'	2	85
Chap. 20.	'Certain alienations made by the wife, of the lands of her deceased husband, shall be void.'	2	96
19th Hen. 7, 1503, Chap. 13.	'Riot.' All that part of the statute is in force except what relates to summoning a jury and the issues.	2	102
6th Henry 8, 1514, Chap. 6.	'An act for the remitting prisoners with their indictments to the places where the crimes were committed.'	2	122
21st Hen. 8, 1529, Chap. 4.	'The sale of land by part of the executors lawful.'	2	137
Chap. 7.	'Servants embezelling their master's goods to the value of forty shillings or above, shall be punished as felons.'	2	141
Chap. 11.	'At what time restitution shall be made of goods stolen.'	2	142

Chap. 15.	'Fermors shall enjoy their leases against recoveries by feigned titles.'	2	147
23 Henry 8, 1531, Chap. 1.	'An act concerning convicts in petit treason, murder, &c.' That part of this statute which exempts the clergy from capital punishment is not in force, and except also petit treason.	2	158
25 Henry 8, 1533, Chap. 6.	'The punishment of the vice of buggery.' This act is made perpetual by 32, Hen. 8, C. 3.	2	181
27 Henry 8, 1535, Chap. 10.	'An act concerning uses and wills' except some local provisions.	2	226
32 Henry 8, 1540, Chap. 9.	'The bill of bracery and buying of titles,' except 1st and 5th sections.	2	280
Chap. 30.	'Mispleadings, Jeofails.' Made perpetual, 33 Hen. 8, C. 17.	2	293
Chap. 28.	'Lessees to enjoy the farm against the tenants in tail,' except. 4, 5 & 8 sections, and so much as applies to ecclesiastic rights.	2	291
Chap. 33.	'An act that wrongful disseisin is no descent in law.'	2	294
Chap. 34.	'Concerning grantees of reversions to take advantage of the conditions to be performed by the lessees.'	2	294
Chap. 37.	'For the recovery of arrearages of rent by executors of tenants in fee simple,' except the 2nd section and so much of the first as respects distraining for rent.	2	297
33 Henry 8, 1541, Chap. 1.	'A bill against them that counterfeit letters or privy tokens to receive money or goods in other men's names,' except 5th section.	2	303
37th Hen. 8, 1545, Chap. 8.	'The act that any indictment lacking these words, 'vi et armis,' shall be good.' This act is in force except the second section.	2	375
1 Edward 6, 1547, Chap. 12.	'An act for the repeal of certain statutes concerning treasons and felonies.' The 13th section is in force and part of the 10th.	2	392
2 & 3 Edw. 6, 1548, Chap. 24.	'An act for trial of murders and felonies, committed in several counties.'	2	422
5 & 6 Edw. 6, 1552, Chap. 9.	'An act for the taking away the benefit of clergy from certain offenders.'	2	446
Chap. 10.	'An act for the avoiding of clergy from divers persons.'	2	447
5th & 6th Edw. 6, 155, Chap. 16.	'Against buying and selling of offices.'	2	454
4th & 5th Ph. & Ma. 1557, Chap. 4.	'An act that accessaries in murder and divers felonies shall not have benefit of clergy,' except 2nd section.	2	503
8th Eliz. 1565, Chap. 4.	'An act to take away the benefit of clergy from certain offenders for felony.'	2	573
18th Eliz. 1576, Chap. 7.	'An act to take away clergy from the offenders in rape or burglary, and an order for the delivery of clerks convict without purgation.' The first section of this act is in force, except the part relative to forfeiture and outlawry.	2	615
Chap. 14.	'An act for reformation of jeofails.'	2	621
27th Eliz. 1585, Chap. 4.	'An act against covinous and fraudulent conveyances.' This act is in force except the 7, 8, 9, 10, 11 and 12 sections.	2	636

Chap. 5.	'An act for furtherance of justice, in cases of demurrer and pleadings.'	2	638
31st Eliz. 1589, Chap. 11.	'An act of explanation or declaration of the statute Octavo Regis' Hen. 6, concerning forcible entries, the indictments thereupon found.'	2	668
39th Eliz. 1597, Chap. 9.	'An act for taking away clergy from offenders against a certain statute made in the year of the reign of king Hen. 7th, concerning the taking away of women against their wills unlawfully.'	2	689
43d. Eliz. 1601, Chap. 4.	'An act to redress the misemployment of land, goods and stocks of money, heretofore given to certain charitable uses.'	2	708
21st Jacob. 1, 1623, Chap. 6.	'An act concerning women convicted of small felonies.' That part of the act is in force which allows benefit of clergy to women.	3	95
Chap. 13.	'An act for the further reformation of jeofails.'	3	99
Chap. 24.	'An act for the relief of creditors against such persons as die in execution.'	3	111
Chap. 15.	'An act to enable judges and justices of the peace to give restitution of possession in certain cases.'	3	100
16th & 17th Car. 2, Chap. 8.	'An act to prevent arrest of judgment and superceding executions.'	3	393
4th Anne, 1705, Chap. 16.	'An act for the amendment of the law and the better advancement of justice.'	4	205
31st Car. 2, Chap. 2.	'An act for the better security of the liberty of the subject, and for prevention of imprisonment beyond sea.'	3	397
17th Car. 2, 1665, Chap. 8.	'An act for avoiding unnecessary suits and delays.'	3	299
8th Anne, 1710, Chap. 20,	'An act for rendering the proceedings upon writs of mandamus, and informations in the nature of quo warranto, more speedy and effectual; and for the more easy trying or determining the rights of offices and franchises in corporations and bouroughs.' The 7th section of this act, extending the statutes of jeofails to mandamus and quo warrantos, is in force.	4	469
5th Geo. 1, 1718, Chap. 13.	'An act for the amendment of writs of error, and for the further preventing the arresting or reversing of judgments after verdicts.	5	201
5th Geo. 2, 1732, Chap. 7.	'An act for the more easy recovery of debts in his majesty's plantations and colonies in America.' The fourth section of this act is in force.	6	74
12th Geo. 3, 1772, Chap. 20.	'An act for the more effectual proceeding against persons standing mute on their arraignment for felony or piracy.'	11	379

Document II–14   Taylor on the Common Law, 1823

[In *State v. Hale*, Chief Justice John Louis Taylor struggled to do justice in a society based in significant part on gross injustice. When a people has inherited a colonial society that deviates entirely from the most fundamental principles of common law,[222] as where it inherits a slave society and proceeds to have its representatives pass acts in furtherance of that conscious deviation from basic justice, what power does a statutory appellate court have to do justice in cases involving slavery? Taylor did not seek a solution to this dilemma in the language used in the state constitution, with its declaration of rights made by its "freemen" and for its "freemen" and its "people." Rather, he turned to the common law from which the province, the colony, and the state had consciously deviated when instituting slavery. Taylor seems to have thought that where a question involving slavery had not been addressed by the general assembly, a gap existed in the deviant social plan. This gap in the extra-common law scheme, he suggested, could be filled by application of principles of the common law—i.e., by the use of legal reasoning from principles of justice and general rules of law.[223] And in employing this method of gap filling, Taylor would look both at past usage and at the recent trend in manners, public opinion, and social conscience[224] toward a more "benignant policy" that mitigates slavery, a trend fostered by the state's Christianity, of which the general assembly surely was apprised when it continued at statehood the unchristian institution of slavery. In *Hale*, then, the public peace had been broken by an attack by a stranger on an enslaved person, and this injustice the common law of crimes could reach, according to Taylor.[225] The common law justification of provocation might also reach a case of battery by a free man on an enslaved person, that common law doctrine suffering horrible distortion, though, due to the statutory existence of slavery in the state. In short, Taylor did not think his statutory appellate court had jurisdiction to contradict the general assembly, but where the court had room to operate, it could read the state's deviation from common law narrowly. And yet, contemporary lawyers may have wondered, when that conscious deviation by the general assembly was in utter contradiction to the humanity and human liberty which the common law protected, would the people's representatives object to even this narrow and halting reassertion of common law principle to fill gaps? Would this newborn statutory appellate court survive the more humane course which Taylor had mapped out for it? And when Taylor died six years later, did the general assembly seek a successor less likely to confront it so baldly? After Taylor's death, the general assembly elected Thomas Ruffin to fill the vacancy on its statutory supreme court.]

State *v.* Hale. } From Cumberland. . . .

TAYLOR, Chief-Justice. . . .

As there is no positive law, decisive of the question, a solution of it must be deduced from general principles, from reasonings founded on the common law, adapted to the existing condition and circumstances of our society, and indicating that result, which is best adapted to general expedience. Presumptive evidence of what this is, arises, in some degree, from usage, of which the Legislature must have been long since apprised, by the repeated conviction and punishment of persons charged with this offence.

It would be a subject of regret to every thinking person, if Courts of Justice were restrained, by any austere rule of judicature, from keeping pace with the march of benignant policy and provident humanity, which for many years, has characterised every Legislative act, relative to the protection of slaves, and which christianity, by the mild diffusion of its light and influence, has contributed to promote; and even domestic safety and interest equally enjoin. . . .

But though neither the common law, nor any other code yet devised by man, could foresee and specify every case that might arise, and thus supersede the use of reason in the ordinary affairs of life, yet it furnishes the principles of justice adapted to every state and condition of society. It contains general rules, fitted to meet the diversified relations, and various conditions of social man. Many of the most important of these rules, are not set down in any statute or ordinance, but depend upon common law for their support; of this description is the rule, that breaking the public peace is an offence, and punishable by fine and imprisonment. . . .

Mitigated as slavery is by the humanity of our laws, the refinement of manners, and by public opinion, which revolts at every instance of cruelty towards them, it would be an anomaly in the system of police which affects them, if the offence stated in the verdict were not indictable. . . .

Document II–15 Hawks's Preface, 1823

[North Carolina Supreme Court Reporter Francis L. Hawks was first a lawyer and afterwards a clergyman. Late in his life, long after he had moved from the state, he published a respected history of North Carolina's proprietary period.[226] Hawks served as the third official reporter of opinions of the Supreme Court of North Carolina, having succeeded A. D. Murphey and Thomas Ruffin. In the preface to his first volume of reports of cases, Hawks pointed out that a good reporter will personally listen to arguments of counsel and consult counsels' briefs, that he must report all opinions of the court (per statute), and he should report opinions timely. Hawks also stressed that his aim in reporting was "fidelity." Perhaps this ideal of fidelity contrasted with the content chosen by the early nominal reporters, who had included not only reports of cases but also extensive notes of the reporters,[227] as well as other documents meant to boost sales of their privately published books.[228]]

REPORTS OF CASES

ARGUED AND ADJUDGED

IN

THE SUPREME COURT

OF

North-Carolina,

DURING THE YEARS 1820 & 1821. . . .

PREFACE.

The Cases reported in this Volume were prepared in part by the former Reporter: the result of Mr. Ruffin's labours will be found in the first 248 pages of the book. The residue of the volume is by the present Reporter [Francis L. Hawks]; and, prepared as it was under many disadvantages, he is aware that it is not exempt from imperfections. Few of the arguments were heard by him, as they were made at a period when it was not his duty to report them; and with all the assistance which has been kindly afforded him by the Gentlemen of the Bar in furnishing their notes, he has yet to regret, that in many instances briefs were entirely lost, and it was not possible in others, to learn more of the argument than the name, perhaps, of some solitary case referred to. Anxious, since his appointment, to present as speedily as possible, the unreported decisions of the Court to the Profession, he had but little opportunity of revisal before publication. He aimed only at fidelity as a Reporter; and he cannot but believe there are defects, which, though now obvious to himself, yet were not so readily perceptible to a mind wearied with almost constant application to the business. With this statement, however, he submits the work to the candour of his brethren, and the object of his ambition will be attained, should it to them be useful. To some it may seem necessary to explain the insertion in the volume of Cases apparently unimportant, as involving principles the most common and of the most familiar application: the recollection of the members of the Bar will readily furnish an apology; the act under which the Reporter is appointed, leaves no discretion, but enjoins the publication of *all* the Cases.

NEWBERN, JULY, 1823.

John Louis Taylor helped to develop the state's common law while sitting as the first chief justice of the Supreme Court of North Carolina, clarified the state's statute law while serving as a commissioner on *Potter's Revisal* of public laws, and put to use his common law and statutory expertise in writing a statutory digest on executors and administrators. Photograph of portrait of John Louis Taylor. (*Credit:* State Archives of North Carolina, Raleigh)

Document II–16 Taylor's Preface, 1824

[Chief Justice John Louis Taylor published a statutory digest on the subject of wills, executors and administrators, provisions for widows, and distribution of intestates' estates in 1824, taking as his audience the "professional man," the "student," and "all descriptions of persons." This privately-produced work completely overlapped the subject matter of the legislative commission that would be given to his brother-in-law,

William Gaston, in the general assembly begun in the same year.[229] And being a digest—i.e., each chapter offering a three-fold package of black-letter rules, sections of pertinent acts in force, and notes of decisions on the subject of a chapter—this novel project contrasted markedly with the recently published *Potter's Revisal*,[230] in which Taylor and his fellow commissioners had transcribed all acts in force chronologically. Unlike a revisal, this statutory digest "attempt[ed] to systematize an interesting portion of the labours of the legislature . . . ,"[231] the term "systematize" being another way of saying "codify."[232] Prior reference works closest in kind to Taylor's treatise were *Haywood's Manual*,[233] which had organized the entire body of statutory law by subject, but had not provided annotations to opinions of the judiciary, and Martin's *Treatise on the Powers and Duties of Executors and Administrators*.[234]

Taylor's sort of reference tool served to deflect the reforming impulse of the early decades of the nineteenth century, which included a preference for acts of assembly over judicial decisions. His approach probably enjoyed success for two reasons. First, the members of the state's supreme court at the time viewed the common law as a system,[235] one presented in its English form by Sir William Blackstone's magnificently popular treatise, *Commentaries on the Laws of England*.[236] Second, various complaints lodged against the common law applied with equal vigor against acts of assembly. For example, like the judgments of the common law courts of England, some acts in force in North Carolina were British (and sounded British) and some were lost or difficult to locate;[237] furthermore, compilations of local acts of assembly were organized chronologically, and thus did not provide subject access to the acts and did not indicate repeal or obsolescence of provisions. While periodic revisals of statute law in North Carolina addressed the problem of repeal, only a true codification would also remedy the problem of chronological arrangement, only a good codification would settle the scope of the reception of British acts and modernize the language of ancient acts, and only a very useful codification would provide references to case law pertaining to each subject.

Taylor's statutory digest, limited in scope and unofficial though it was, took a step toward remedying these sorts of complaints concerning more than 100 years of legislative activity of the assembly in North Carolina. At the same time, by including precedents pertinent to each chapter of his statutory digest, his work advertised the contributions of the state's judiciary to an understanding of the law. In his preface to this work, the chief justice forewarned readers that not all of the precedents he cited were of equal weight, some of them having been established by the trial court judges on circuit, and promised researchers that weightier precedent would soon settle puzzles and cabin discretion as suits in equity and appeals in law and equity reached the newly established supreme court.

Taylor also mentioned in his preface that he was prepared to "digest other important titles in the statute book." In other words, well before the general assembly commissioned *The Revised Statutes*,[238] Chief Justice Taylor envisioned an annotated code of the state's statute law.]

PREFACE.

The following work is intended to combine, into one view, the numerous enactments which have been made on the subjects treated of, throughout a period of more than a century, and dispersed among more than forty statutes. They are subjects of great importance, and of frequent occurrence, in the affairs of men; but the difficulty of investigating many of them, is sometimes felt even by persons, to whom such pursuits are familiar; and by others who require information on the spur of the occasion, without the present means of obtaining legal advice, is often found absolutely insurmountable. If I shall have succeeded in facilitating the research of the professional man, and the student, and opening to all descriptions of persons, a ready access to the knowledge they seek, my object will be accomplished.

Some of the acts, relative to wills and revocations, are transcripts, or nearly so, from the statute of fraud and perjuries; and, therefore, some leading constructions on that statute have been cited, as explanatory of the meaning of our acts, and as serving to present a full view of the subject. But the mass of the regulations are of a local nature, on which no light could be thrown by foreign decisions, but pains have been taken to collect all the domestic ones, which are connected with the subject. At the same time, it must be remembered, that many of these have been pronounced on the circuit, under the multiplied disadvantages of a want of books and a pressure of business, and are not, therefore, of such decisive authority, as to preclude all future enquiry into their correctness. Some of them have even occurred in the course of the trial, without any previous notice to the counsel, and have demanded an immediate decision from the Court, without the necessary interval for reflection, or the search of authorities. These, as the best guides extant, must be received until better ones shall be furnished, by the points of law being agitated in the Superior Court, and carried thence, by appeal, to the Supreme Court, and finally determined there as the last resort, both in matters of law and equity. It is the intention of the Compiler, if this little work should be found useful and acceptable, to digest other important titles in the statute book, upon the same plan; and the collection of the whole, when completed, will give him an opportunity of improving the mode he has adopted, and of correcting any defective arrangement, which may not now be obvious to him.

The citations from the acts of Assembly, are to be understood as referring to the revisal, published by the Commissioners in 1821, up to the year 1820, inclusive. After that period the Pamphlet Laws are quoted by the letters P. L.

Document II–17 Revisal on Administrators and Executors, 1825

[With this 1825 act, the general assembly commissioned a revision and consolidation of the acts in force on administrators and executors,[239] naming William Gaston as commissioner.[240] Although Gaston was an expert on at least part of the laws to be revised,[241] he declined this commission.[242]]

CHAPTER XV.

An Act to provide for revising and consolidating the Acts of the General Assembly concerning Administrators and Executors

Be it enacted by the General Assembly of the State of North-Carolina, and it is hereby enacted by the authority of the same, That William Gaston, Esquire, be, and he is hereby appointed Commissioner to revise and consolidate all the public acts of the General Assembly of this State concerning the duties of Administrators and Executors, and report the same, with such alterations as may be necessary, in a clear and concise form, to the next General Assembly.

II. *And be if further enacted,* That the said William Gaston, Esquire, shall receive such compensation for his services as aforesaid, as may be judged adequate by the next General Assembly.

Document II–18 Henderson on the Common Law, 1825

[Judge Leonard Henderson viewed the English common law as the essence of the colonial common law inherited at statehood and developed thereafter by the decisions of the superior court, its conference of judges, and the statutory supreme court of North Carolina. Specifically, Henderson asserted that definitions at ancient common law were the state's legal definitions in their nature, all subsequent innovations being pragmatic deviations or unfortunate degradations of common law meaning.]

Smith
v.   } From Halifax. . . .
Campbell.

Henderson, Judge.— . . . I speak of these things at common law, that is in their nature . . .

DOCUMENT II–19   R. POTTER ON SOCIAL CONTRACT, 1825

[In his argument concerning the scope of jury trial in North Carolina civil cases under the state constitution, delivered in *Smith v. Campbell* and later elaborated for publication, firebrand attorney Robert Potter described the state constitution as evidence of a social compact that established a community of the people and the state government; and he identified the true method of its interpretation as one of founders' intent and not of expediency or practicality. While review of legislation by comparison to a written constitution paradigmatically exemplified modern jurisprudential trends and arguably grounded all law on a codification of sorts, the common law tradition—at least as it was re-envisioned in Enlightenment treatises—remained the context for understanding the founders' intent expressed in that document, and perhaps, contrary to Robert Potter's view, for the society allegedly compacted.]

ARGUMENT, &C.

The question to which I invite the attention of your honors, arises out of an action at law, which was brought before a single Justice of the Peace, upon a plain note of hand, for twenty-five dollars. . . .

I presume it is unnecessary to go into any arguments, to prove the paramount authority of the Constitution. I presume it is unnecessary to remind this Court, that forty-eight years ago, when our ancestors threw off the yoke of foreign domination, by dissolving the political bands which bound this country to Great-Britain, each individual here, possessed that portion of unbridled freedom, which exists in a state of nature, and must every where have existed, antecedent to the formation of Government, and that it was only by virtue of a solemn compact, at that time made and entered into between the people, the evidence of which is the Constitution, that that instrument acquired the power, of restraining or limiting in any degree, the free exercise and unconditional enjoyment of that liberty; in other words, that it is contains the *articles of agreement*, as to the *terms* on which the contracting parties, *the people*, consented to associate together as members of the same community, and that is only by virtue of certain of those articles, providing for the organization of the Legislature, and specifying the mode of its procedure, that its enactments carry with them the authority of law, how then can we place *particular* acts of the legislature, in competition with a fundamental principle of that Constitution, from which *all* its acts derive their validity; here the ingenuous mind, would at once pronou[n]ce the jurisdiction acts to be illegal; but to anticipate the fallacies of sophists, and to leave no loop, whereon to hang a doubt, let us return to that part of the Constitution especially violated, and illustrate with critical precision, the palpable conflict between every feature of it, and the jurisdiction acts. . . .

The Union generally, as well as this State in particular, is infested by a sect of politicians, not less powerful than plausible, who appear disposed, on all occasions, to make the Constitution speak any and every language, which *expediency* may seem to require. In settling a construction on any principle of the Constitution, they are influenced rather by a regard to the practical result that is to follow such construction, than by a pure and patriotic determination to carry into effect the true meaning and intention of the Constitution. The worshippers of power and pageantry may style the leaders of that sect *great* men; but *honest* men can only designate them as *distinguished villains*, who have found their way to office by *intrigue*, and sustain themselves there by *corruption*. Is it not shocking, is it not disgusting to every honest mind to hear the *expediency* of a measure *talked* of, when its *constitutionality* is under *consideration*? *Plain honest men*, can view in no other light than as *polished and brilliant knaves*, those advocates for national grandeur and magnificence, who *cant* about the *expediency* of their acts, as an apology for *deviating from the Constitution*, when too their very power thus to violate it, is derived from the Constitution itself, and is by the Constitution vested in them, upon the special trust and condition that they will defend it. I cannot derogate from the deep sense of reverential and filial regard, which I cherish towards the members of this Court, not only as public functionaries, but as men, by advancing an argument on the *expediency* of the decision, they are now called upon to make: satisfied that, on this occasion, as on all others, they will act under the impulse of the sublime sentiment *"justitia fiat, ruat cœlum."*

Document II–20 Hawks's Digested Index, 1826

[Supreme Court Reporter Francis L. Hawks published his digested index of North Carolina judicial decisions not long after the founding of the modern supreme court.[243] According to his preface, reprinted below, he acknowledged that the project was suggested to him by attorney Moses Mordecai.[244] Insofar as it is properly described as a modern digest, this finding aid for case law was contemporaneous with the first such tool produced in England,[245] and thus may represent a certain scientific way of thinking that pervaded the first quarter of the nineteenth century, somewhat analogously to codification of the positive law and presentation of the common law in comprehensive treatises. Arguably, the rise of the modern digest was a symptom of positivism in law: just as the nineteenth-century preference for the publication of a single "opinion of the court" suggested settled law where sundry justifications of judgments by seriatim opinions might not have suggested it, so a "digest of opinions of the court" suggested established categories of legal thought, settled language of the law, and trends of opinion. From these patterns, the bench and bar might induce legal rules, recognize exceptions based upon legally significant facts, and dismiss some opinions as outliers. And even if one were to think of the modern digest as a mere finding tool for persons who had not absorbed all the state's cases by reading law under an established attorney, such as laypersons and many students of the law during the early nineteenth century, Hawks's digest took some mystery out of the common law and provided useful entry points into cases published in hard-to-find nominal reports.

Relying in part upon the marginal notes of Judge John Louis Taylor's unofficial nominal reports,[246] Hawks's digested index grappled with points of law, important dicta, and notes of reporters from fourteen volumes of reports containing North Carolina judicial decisions.[247] The digest also indicated division on the bench, as well as denial or questioning of earlier cases, thus serving adequately as an early citator.]

PREFACE.

Having experienced the kindness of the profession on former occasions, the compiler of the following sheets hopes a favorable reception for this, the product of his leisure hours. The work was undertaken at the suggestion of one,* who was among the earliest professional friends of the author, of one who generously afforded him that advice and assistance, the want of which, at the commencement of professional life, is felt by all, and which none was more able than that friend to afford.

Of what has been attempted, it is proper some information should be given by the author; how far what has been attempted has been accomplished, it is for others to determine. The object was to present, in digested form, the points of law decided in North Carolina, and scattered through fourteen books of reports.† In the prosecution of this undertaking, the course pursued was, to read every case in the reports, and to make notes of the points decided, and of important *dicta*, in which brevity and perspicuity should be alike consulted. When the marginal note of the Reporter was, in the judgment of the Compiler, both brief and perspicuous he adopted it *verbatim*; where deficient in either quality, he abridged or altered it. In some of the reports, no marginal notes are given, and, consequently, the statement made of the points decided in them is by the compiler. After all, brevity was in some instances found not to be attainable but by the sacrifice of clearness, and in such cases, the statement will be found extended and particular, since it was thought better to be prolix than obscure.

The order of time in which the cases were decided has also been kept in view, and at the end of each paragraph will be found the year in which the decision was made. Thus may be traced the gradual changes of doctrine, and the fluctuations of judicial opinion. Where a doctrine to be found in some earlier case has been denied or questioned in a later decision, a note to that effect is added, and by following the paragraphs through the division, the law as now received will be found. And where, in the reports of Judge *Haywood*, he has appended a *quere* to the decision, it is noted. Where the Bench was divided, the names of the Judges deciding and dissenting are also given.

To the whole is added a complete list of the names of the cases reported, alphabetically arranged; by means of which, if the name of either party be remembered, the case may be found.

Lord Coke has remarked, that "for digesting of former laws into method and order, three things are requisite: judgment to know them, art to dispose them, and diligence to omit none of them;"[^] and the remark may with equal propriety be applied to digesting decisions.

That all these requisites will not be invariably found united in the present work, none can be more sensible than the author; and if that diligence which prevents omissions shall not be found wanting, the absence, even frequent, of judgment to know, and art to dispose, will not, by those who reflect on the difficulty of the undertaking, be thought an unpardonable defect.

It has not been in the power of the author, consistently with other and paramount engagements, to correct all the proof sheets; there are typographical errors, the most important of which are noticed in the list of *errata* at the end of the book.

My Lord Coke, in the preface before referred to, has "absolutely determined the advised and orderly reading over the books of reports at large, to be the right way to enduring and perfect knowledge; and to use abridgments as tables, and to trust only to the books at large; *neque enim prudentis arbitror sectari rivulos, ubi fontes ipsos petere liceat.*"

While this book can have no claim to be one of those, the reading of which is "the right way to perfect knowledge," it is believed to be not without merit, as a table by which the student and the practitioner may be guided to those "books at large," in which alone trust can be safely reposed.

In this humble character, and with this useful purpose, this Digest is submitted to the charitable judgment of a profession, distinguished not more for learning and acuteness, than for indulgent criticism.

Hillsborough, N. C. July, 1826.

---

* The late *Moses Mordecai, Esq.*
† Notes of a few decisions, &c. by F. X. Martin, 1 vol. Haywood's Reports, 2 vols. Taylor's Reports, 1 vol. Reports in the Court of Conference, 1 vol. Carolina Law Repository, 2 vols. North Carolina Term Reports, 1 vol. Murphey's Reports, 3 vols. and Hawks's Reports, 3 vols.
[^] Preface to 4th Reports.

Document II–21   Manly to Graham, 1827

[In the letter below, Mr. Matthias Evans Manly, who would one day serve as the last-elected antebellum member of the Supreme Court of North Carolina, reported to future governor William A. Graham a plan of attorney James West Bryan, Graham's former classmate at the University, for an unofficial, annotated manual of the entire state statute law, which would present each subject of legislation in an alphabetical arrangement.]

New Bern, Aug. 31st, 1827.

. . . John Stanly's health continues to improve. James Bryan has issued proposals to publish a new manual of the statute laws of the state. It is to be gotton [sic] up on Judge Haywood's plan precisely, with the addition of such decissions [sic] of the supreme court as affect the construction of acts. These are to be inserted in the body of the work, under the statutes to which they relate, in small print. The work will be printed and bound in Philadelphia; provided always a sufficient number of subscribers can be obtained to defray the expenses. Dr. Camey is still here, "cracking jokes." I am in good health—prospects *middling*.

Your Friend Forever.

Thomas P. Devereux served as reporter of opinions of the Supreme Court of North Carolina in the late 1820s and the 1830s. Thomas P. Devereux in his youth. (*Credit:* State Archives of North Carolina, Raleigh)

DOCUMENT II–22   DEVEREUX ON HUMPHREYS, 1827

[As officially reported in 1831 by Thomas P. Devereux, the *per curiam* decision in *Pike v. Armstead and Turner*, December Term 1827, included the note reprinted below.[248] This note contained an extract from a controversial book by the renowned English legal scholar, James Humphreys;[249] and this quotation from Humphreys' work is among the clearest acknowledgments of the more radical side of the codification movement in the early part of the nineteenth century by a member or officer of the state supreme court. That Devereux placed this note after opinions by Chief Justice Taylor and Judge Hall, in a case argued on one side by attorney George Badger and on the other by attorneys William Gaston and Gavin Hogg, is remarkable.

Humphreys' "work of high reputation," as Devereux described it, was published in Spring 1826. The title to the first edition contained the term "code," which was thought so offensive that it was abandoned in the edition of the following year in favor of the expression "systematic reform."[250] The book was not only cited by the official reporter of the Supreme Court of North Carolina, but also by the radical reformers responsible for the *Revised Statutes of New York*.[251] A worse blow to its reputation, the work was praised by philosopher Jeremy Bentham, and with good reason. Much to the shock of common law professionals, Humphreys suggested the abolition of tenures, uses, and passive trusts,[252] and advocated a civilian approach to the administration of law (i.e., codify the common law and do not allow precedents to be cited as authoritative).

Reporter Devereux had been educated at Litchfield in Connecticut, which may suggest connections to the northeastern states where Humphreys' work would have an immediate impact. Apparently, Devereux had attended Yale College, graduating in 1813.[253] It has been said that he was "a descendant of Jonathan Edwards, was a Trustee of the University of North Carolina, and Reporter of the Supreme Court."[254] It is unknown why he thought it would be "both useful and agreeable to the profession" to juxtapose Humphreys' ideas with the arguments and opinions of the leading lights of the North Carolina bench and bar.]

Robert Pike
v.
Starkey Armstead &
Thomas Turner.
} From Washington. . . .

☞ The Reporter, in making the following extract from a late Work of high reputation, does not wish to be understood as impeaching the decision of the Court in the above case; his sole object is to render the Work it is his duty to superintend, both useful and agreeable to the profession.

"Upon the enrol[l]ment act of *Hen. VII*, and the docketing and registering statutes, Equity has introduced, under the name of *notice*, a totally different construction, which has been nearly subversive of these descriptions of acts, and has raised a complicated system, much more grievous than any of the individual hardships meant to be redressed.

"They have determined, on the one hand, that a person buying an estate, *with notice*, of a prior incumbrance, *not registered*, shall, in equity, be bound by it, although he has duly registered his own conveyance. On the other hand, they have held, that a person having the legal estate as mortgagee, and advancing more money, *without notice*, of a second mortgage *duly registered*, shall hold, in respect of it, against the second mortgagee. In the former case, an unregistered deed is preferred to a registered one. In the latter, registration, even coupled with priority of time, is of no avail. It is indeed, urged, that the first mortgagee possesses that fiction termed the legal estate, and that both mortgagees are in *pari delicto*.—But, (passing the technical advantage,) if there be blame in the want of search, the second mortgagee affects only himself by it, whereas the first mortgagee affects also the second. In analogy to the foregoing resolutions, it is held in equity, that, although a judgment be not docketed, yet if a purchaser have notice of it before he completes, he shall be bound by it. He already possesses, it is said, that information which the statute [of William and Mary] intended to furnish him; but to this it might be replied, that he also knows an undocketed judgment is rendered void against himself; and that the judgment creditor might not have intended to rely upon the land contracted for. *Humphrey's on Real Property*, (1 *London Ed*. 154, 155.)

"I shall close with observing, that Courts of Equity have not thought fit to urge their doctrines upon notice, in opposition to decisions at law, that voluntary conveyances, are void under the statute of 27 *Eliz*. to prevent fraudulent conveyances, against subsequent purchasers *even with notice*, although the argument, that what the purchaser knew could never be a fraud upon him, is equally strong here as upon the registry and docketing acts. Neither have they interfered with the two successive acts for memorializing life annuities sold for money. Whatever may be the policy of these different acts, it does not appear that either the justice or the simplicity of the decisions upon them would have been improved by the introduction of the equitable doctrine of notice. *Ibid*. 160, 161."

༄ Document II–23 Resolution on Full Revisal, January 2, 1827 ༄

[With this resolution, Mr. David Swain, member of the house of commons, contemplated an official revisal of the entire body of statute laws in force, one where the laws would be arranged, revised, and digested by its commissioners.[255] Use of the terms "arranging" and "digesting" perhaps suggested a subject-arranged and annotated revisal, on the model of Chief Justice Taylor's statutory digest from 1824 in relation to wills, executors and administrators, provisions for widows, and the distribution of intestates' estates.[256]

The term "digest" had not been used to describe any of the state's prior revisals.[257] The resolution resulted in a bill, but the bill was postponed indefinitely.[258]]

JOURNAL OF THE HOUSE OF COMMONS....

Tuesday, January 2, 1827....

On motion of Mr. Swain,
Resolved, That the committee on the Judiciary be instructed to inquire into the expediency of providing by law for the arranging, revising and digesting the whole body of the public statute laws of North-Carolina, commencing with the latest English statutes in force in this State....

Document II–24   Resolution on Full Revisal, November 27, 1827

[With this resolution Mr. Enoch Foy, member of the house of commons, contemplated an official compilation of the entire body of statute laws in force arranged, revised, and digested by subject,[259] clarifying somewhat the resolution from late in the prior session by Mr. David Swain. The judiciary committee to which the resolution assigned this task for investigation rejected it.[260]]

JOURNAL OF THE HOUSE OF COMMONS....

Tuesday, November 27, 1827....

On motion of Mr. Foy,
Resolved, That the committee on the Judiciary be instructed to inquire into the expediency of providing by law for the arranging, revising and digesting the whole body of public and statute law of North-Carolina, commencing with the earliest English statute in force in this State, and for the compiling under one head all laws and clauses of laws in force on any one subject, with reference to the year when such laws were passed; and that they report by bill or otherwise....

Document II–25   Resolution on Subject Revisal, December 7, 1827

[In the resolution excerpted below, a senator sought a revisal and consolidation of acts of assembly on the narrow subject of the manner of sale of lands liable to taxes.[261] The resolution did not result in a bill on the subject.[262]]

JOURNAL OF THE SENATE....

Friday, December 7, 1827....

On motion of Mr. Shober,
Resolved, That the committee on the Judiciary be instructed to inquire into the expediency of revising and consolidating the different acts of Assembly, relative to the manner in which lands liable to taxes are to be sold, with such amendments as may be necessary to create more publicity of an intended sale, and a better notice to proprietors....

Document II–26   Resolution on Subject Revisal, December 12, 1827

[The resolution here provided inquired into "revising and consolidating" a narrow segment of the labors of the general assembly—the acts of assembly regarding public roads.[263] The house sent the resolution to the internal improvements committee, rather than through the normal route of the judiciary committee. The resolution did not result in a bill on the subject.[264]]

JOURNAL OF THE HOUSE OF COMMONS....

WEDNESDAY, DEC. 12, 1827....

On motion of *Mr.* Salmons,
Resolved, That the committee on Internal Improvements be instructed to inquire into the expediency of revising and consolidating the different acts of Assembly with regard to public roads, with such amendments as may be necessary to change the manner in which such roads are at present kept in repair; and that they report by bill or otherwise....

DOCUMENT II–27 BILL ON SUBJECT REVISAL, JANUARY 7, 1828

[Legislators offered sundry resolutions to amend the laws relating to executors and administrators during the 1827–'28 session of the general assembly, resulting in the house judiciary committee reporting a bill for "revising, digesting and amending" the laws on this subject matter.[265] The house approved the bill,[266] but the senate rejected it.[267]]

JOURNAL OF THE HOUSE OF COMMONS....

MONDAY, JANUARY 7, 1828.

A message from the Senate, informing that they had rejected the engrossed bill, entitled "A bill for revising, digesting and amending the law relative to executors and administrators; ..."

DOCUMENT II–28 RESOLUTION ON SUBJECT REVISAL, NOVEMBER 26, 1828

[The resolution below aimed to "amend, revise and consolidate" the acts of assembly concerning roads, bridges, and ferries.[268]]

JOURNAL OF THE HOUSE OF COMMONS....

WEDNESDAY, NOVEMBER 26, 1828....

On motion of Mr. Newland,
Resolved, That a select committee be raised, whose duty it shall be to amend, revise and consolidate the several acts of Assembly relating to roads, bridges and ferries and overseers and keepers thereof; and that they report by bill or otherwise....

DOCUMENT II–29 BILL ON FULL REVISAL, DECEMBER 1828

[Like the resolutions of 1827 to investigate the feasibility of revising the state laws (one of which had been introduced by Mr. David Swain, member of the house of commons from Buncombe County), a failed bill, tracked below in an excerpt of the legislative journals of 1828–'29, aimed to revise and digest the public statute laws of the state.[269] Swain showed interest in this 1828 bill. He would soon serve as governor and would lobby in a message to the general assembly for an act commissioning *The Revised Statutes*.[270]]

THE JOURNAL OF THE HOUSE OF COMMONS....

Tuesday, November 25, 1828...

On motion of Mr. T. Webb,
Resolved, That the committee on the Judiciary be instructed to inquire into the policy and expediency of providing by law for the revision of the Acts of Assembly of this State; and that they report by bill or otherwise....

Tuesday, December 2, 1828....

Mr. Nash, from the committee on the Judiciary, to whom was referred the resolution requiring them to inquire into the expediency of providing by law for the revision of the acts of Assembly of this State, reported, under the direction of the committee, a bill for revising and digesting the public statute laws of this State, and recommended its passage. The said bill was read the first time and passed, and, on motion, made the order of the day for Monday next, and be printed, one copy for each member of the Assembly....

Wednesday, December 10, 1828....

The bill for revising and digesting the public statute laws of this State, was read, and, on the motion of Mr. Swain, ordered to be laid on the table....

Saturday, December 13, 1828....

The bill for revising and digesting the public statute laws of this State, was read the second time and amended, and, on the motion of Mr. Potter, ordered to be laid on the table....

Monday, December 15, 1828....

The bill for revising and digesting the public statute laws of this State was read the second time and passed....

Tuesday, December 16, 1828....

The bill for revising and digesting the public statute laws of this State, was read the third time. Mr. Calloway moved to amend the bill. The question thereon was determined in the negative. Mr. Potter moved that the bill be indefinitely postponed. The question thereon was determined in the affirmative—yeas 70, nays 57. The yeas and nays demanded by *Mr.* Stedman....

Document II-30   Common and Statute Law on Subject Revisal, January 1829

[This act authorized the displacement of the statute law and common law of executors and administrators, as well as related law on heirs, devisees, and creditors of deceased persons' estates, with a digested "code" or "system."[271] No prior initiative of the general assembly has been located which aimed to codify officially any portion of the common law. Perhaps the publication of Chief Justice John Louis Taylor's statutory digest in 1824,[272] with its weaving together of state statutes and state precedents, made a codification of both common and statute law on this subject seem less radical to the general assembly. Still, this act of 1829, like earlier initiatives on this important subject matter,[273] bore no fruit, even though well-respected attorneys accepted the commission.[274]]

CHAPTER XXXVIII.

An act for revising, digesting and amending the laws relating to executors and administrators.

Be it enacted by the General Assembly of the State of North Carolina, and it is hereby enacted by the authority of the same, That the Governor of this State be, and he is hereby authorised and empowered to appoint two persons of competent skill and ability in the law, as commissioners, to revise, digest, alter and amend all the statute and common law in force in this State, relating to executors and administrators; and also to revise, digest, alter and amend so much of the statute and common law, concerning heirs, devisees, and creditors of deceased persons' estates, as shall be properly connected, in the opinion of said commissioners, with the law relating to executors and administrators, so as to form a code or system, on the title of executors and administrators, which shall be founded on principles of justice, and suited to the true policy and present situation of the people of this State.

II. *And be it further enacted,* That the said commissioners shall submit to the next General Assembly such code or system, so revised and digested, for its consideration; and after it shall have been approved by the Legislature, the said commissioners shall prepare the same for the press, and shall make an index of the matters contained therein.

III. *And be it further enacted,* That the said commissioners shall be allowed the time of one year to complete the duties assigned to them by this act, and that in the execution of those duties, they shall have free access to the State Library.

IV. *And be it further enacted,* That the said commissioners shall, for the services hereby required of them, be allowed such compensation as shall be deemed adequate and proper.

DOCUMENT II-31   COMMISSIONS FOR COMMON AND STATUTE LAW SUBJECT REVISAL, MAY 1829

[Gov. John Owen here offered commissions to attorneys Thomas Ruffin[275] and George Badger[276] to codify the statute and common law of executors and administrators, etc., contemplated by the act of January 1829. While Ruffin and Badger accepted the commissions, no report was filed by the commissioners in the time allowed by statute for its performance.[277]]

EXECUTIVE DEPARTMENT
No. CAROLINA May 22nd. 1829.

To Thomas Ruffin and Geo. E. Badger Esqrs.
Gentlemen,

Permit me to call your attention to an act passed at the last meeting of the General Assembly of this State, Chapter 38, authorising the Governor to appoint two Commissioners to revise, digest, alter and amend all the statute and Common law in force in this State, relating to Executors and administrators; and also to revise, digest, alter and amend so much of the statute and common law, concerning heirs, devisees, and creditors of deceased persons estates, as shall be properly connected in the opinion of said commissioners with the law relating to Executors and administrators, so far as to form a code or system on the title of Executors and administrators, which shall be founded on principles of Justice, and suited to the true policy and present situation of the people of this State, etc.

In the performance of that part of my duty growing out of this act, I desire to offer you the commission.

If it is important that this work be done at all, it is of the first importance that it be done well, and by those, in whose professional skill and attainments, the next Legislature will have confidence; and I certainly hazard nothing in saying, there are no gentlemen of the profession in the State, from whose hands such a work would be by them better received, and more freely and fully compensated.

I ask the favor of an answer as soon as convenient, and subscribe myself.

Most respectfully
Your obdt. servt.
Jno. Owen.

[Address: Raleigh.]

Document II-32   Resolution on Subject Revisal, December 1829

[Reprinted below is yet another resolution seeking a revisal and consolidation of a narrow subject of statute law—vacant lands.[278] The resolution failed in its aim.[279]]

JOURNAL OF THE HOUSE OF COMMONS....

Saturday, December 12, 1829....

On motion of Mr. Shipp,

Resolved, That the Judiciary committee be instructed to inquire into the expediency of revising, amending and consolidating all the laws now in force respecting surveyors, entry takers, and the entry of vacant and unappropriated lands; and that they report by bill or otherwise....

Document II-33   Index, 1829–30

[The index to the acts from the 1829–'30 legislative session provided access to statute law by subject, rather than merely by title.[280] It is true that a finding aid organized by subject may not signal the influence of minds contemplating the adoption and promotion of statutory codification. After all, various manuals, such as *Haywood's Manual*, presented the statute law by subject earlier in the nineteenth century.[281] But in light of the indexes to the public acts of the prior dozen volumes of session laws having provided access by title of act according to order of passage,[282] and in light of the intentionally chronological arrangement of *Potter's Revisal* in 1819,[283] the change in method of indexing may have had significance. This index provided subject access to both public acts and private acts in one finding aid for one session of the general assembly. The first page of the three-and-a-half-page index is reproduced on the facing page.]

Document II-34   Bill on Full Revisal, December 1830

[Late in 1830, a senator introduced yet another bill for revising the statute law of the state.[284] The bill was engrossed in the senate[285] but was postponed indefinitely by the house.[286]]

JOURNAL OF THE SENATE....

Thursday, December 9, 1830....

Mr. M'Kay also presented a bill for revising and digesting the public statute laws of this State; which was read the first time and passed....

First page of Index to acts, 1829–'30 scanned at the North Carolina Supreme Court Library (*Credit*: The compilers)

Document II-35 Friends of Liberty Address, 1830

[It was not uncommon for modern law reformers arguing from natural rights theories to take the elimination of slavery as one focus of law reform, blaming the metaphysic of modern natural law views and the common law worship of custom for toleration, if not espousal of slavery. The document excerpted here used both classical and humanitarian arguments in support of the abolition of slavery.[287] A strain of classical natural law sentiment slipped into the address when the Friends asserted that mankind had a subordinate nature, that politics must bow to morality, and that positive laws and common law must harmonize with and acquiesce in divine law and the law of nature. More modern sentiment was evident by the use of the expression "law of nature" and from the explicit references to "unalienable privileges" and the "natural rights of mankind." The Friends' appeal to reason and revelation, and to the notion that "a copy of [the law of nature] was furnished in the breast of every rational individual," recalled both traditions, as well as traditions even more ancient.

Mr. William Swaim, renowned publisher of the *Greensboro Patriot and Times*, was secretary to the board of managers of the Manumission Society in 1830. Apparently, he was not a Quaker, though he held a strong interest in the causes taken up by the Friends.[288] Professor Stephen Weeks of the University of North Carolina wrote of Mr. Swaim:

> Much anti-slavery matter was published by William Swaim, a young man of rare talent, in the Greensboro *Patriot*, a paper which he had just founded. Levi Coffin says: "He advocated the manumission of slaves, and though he met with a storm of opposition and was assailed by other papers, he continued his course boldly and independently. He received letters from various parts of the State full of threats and warnings. These he published in his paper, and replied to them in editorials. Many public speakers and writers engaged in discussion with him, but they could not cope with him, and generally retired from the combat much worsted."[289]

William Swaim's cousin, Benjamin Swaim,[290] was president of the Society after 1827 and publisher of *The Southern Citizen*.]

To the people of North-Carolina.

The Board of Managers of the Manumission Society of North-Carolina in General Association, feel in their indispensable duty, respectfully to address, not only their immediate constituents, but with them, the people of the State in general.

WILLIAM SWAIM, *Sec.*

Guilford, March 1830. . . .

ADDRESS, &c.

CAROLINIANS: . . .
Nor will doctrine of the injustice of absolute slavery lose any of its real weight by the consideration of its having the sanction of the Law, if we consider that all men are but subordinate beings, who are held bound to obey their Creator according to his own Laws, which he hath ordained, and by which he designs his creatures to be governed, among which that denominated the Law of nature (which is nevertheless a divine Law) may and ought to be regarded as having been instituted for the particular purpose to which we now apply it, and to which it has been applied by men of sound judgment and uncorrupted principles in every age; and to which it was particularly applied by the Fathers of our glorious liberty, as they have abundantly shown.* Nor dare any one doubt the validity of the Law of nature, any more than the right of its Almighty giver to a primary part in the government of mankind. It follows consequently that the principles set forth in the Law of nature for the government of mankind are *primary* or *constitutional* principles, and that the Laws enacted by men for their own government should harmonize with and acquiesce in them.

And as no authority can overreach that by which the law of nature is established, therefore no human Legislature, how lawfully soever it may be constituted, can deprive any individual, (he or she being one of God's creatures, and under his government) of any of those "*unalienable*" privileges guaranteed to him or her in the law of nature, otherwise than they are personally forfeited by the individual or individuals from whom they are taken, without offending the great Governor of the universe. Such laws are therefore founded in injustice, and ought to be repealed without delay, as they oppose *divine law*, and as such, must be offensive to the God of nature, whose wrath we necessarily incur by suffering them to exist.

Nor is this doctrine of the law of nature a mere chimera—it is a reality of which every rational man may have the most satisfactory evidence, even in his own breast: for it is there that this doctrine is fully authenticated and established. It was there that the writer's address discovered this principle. And there can be no doubt but, that the Patriots of 1776 discovered the same principle existing in their breasts in a similar manner. And in like manner, have good and Patriotic men in all ages discovered the same principle, in proportion as they received the aids of reason and revelation.* . . . Such being the dictates of human instinct—or to speak more correctly—such being the principles set forth in the law of nature, a copy of which is furnished in the breast of every rational individual, we are not surprized on finding them repeatedly set forth in the opinions and laws of men;—thus we know them, not only in the Declaration of American Independence, and in the Bill of Rights, but in some way or other set forth in some part of the Constitution or Laws of perhaps every State in the Union. . . . And our "*common law*," which is a primary ingredient in the "law of the land," mentioned in *Section 12*, of our declaration of rights, is said to be founded on "reason and the divine law," and is held to acquiesce in them in every instance, any former usage or decision to the contrary notwithstanding. The common law of this state, must therefore acquiesce in the provisions set forth in the law of nature, in all cases, when the "law of the land" is not rendered otherwise by some statute or special act passed either by the General Assembly of North Carolina, or by Congress; and that too, according to the Constitution of our State or of the United States, as the case may be, since the law of nature is evidently a *divine* law, and as such, must be supposed to harmonize with all other laws of *divine* origine [*sic*]; as it would be absurd to suppose two divine principles, opposed the one to the other. The law of nature, the law of reason, and consequently the *common* law of this State, (as we have shown,) all declare liberty to be the "birth right" of every human being. . . . On this subject we would say with *Plato*, that "No mortal can make laws to purpose" unless made in conformity with the divine *will*—that is, no human authority can give sanctity or justice to a law which violates the law of nature, or any other principle in the *will* of the Almighty ruler of the world. Such laws must therefore be a *curse* instead of a *blessing*, to those, by, and for whom they have been enacted. Neither are they sanctified by Judge Taylor's principle of necessity, since this great truth still remains, "*That* which is *morally wrong*, cannot be *politically right*." (C- J. Fox.)

But to return to the subject after this seeming digression:—If Judge Taylor has proved any thing in favor of the *presumption* of slavery, his arguments operate with as much *force* against those of the *mixed*, as against those of the *whole* blood; and the *presumption* of slavery is as unreasonable in relation to Africans of the "whole blood," as it is in relation to any colour that can possibly exist between "the two extremes of *black and white*." . . . It is therefore inconsistent with sound reason, with the divine Law, and consequently with the common law of this State, thus to trifle with the natural rights of mankind, and with God the great and sovereign donor of those rights, by making the mere colour of the skin, amount to a sufficient presumption against a fellow creature's liberty, and this "*mere presumption*" the means of depriving him of it. Is this just? Does conduct like this comport with the dignity and virtue of a "*free, christian*" and independent community?" . . .

---

* See Declaration of American INdependence and also Bill of Rights.

* In further confirmation of the above, we transcribe the following noble passage of Cicero cited by Lectantius out of his work DE REPUBLICA. . . ."From which it is clear" says Bishop Watson "that CICERO acknowledged a Law antecedent to all human civil institutions, and independent of them, binding upon all, constant and perpetual, the same in all times and places, not one thing at Rome and another at Athens; of an authority so high, that no HUMAN power had a RIGHT to alter or annul it; having God for its author, in his character of universal Master and Sovereign, taking hold of the very consciences of men, and following them with its animadversions, though they should escape the hand of man, and the penalties of human codes": here then is the LAW of nature fairly and fully apprehended. . . .

FINIS.

The committee appointed by the General Association of the Manumission Society of North-Carolina, to draw up an address to the people of the State, and to report the same to the Board of Managers of the said Society for publication, respectfully report the forgoing.

AMOS WEAVER, *Chairman.*

Document II–36   Unwritten Code of the People, 1832

[A commissioner for the statutory compilation reviewed in the document excerpted below is Judge John Haywood, author of *A Manual of the Laws of North-Carolina*,[291] who enjoyed a memorable legal career in North Carolina and in Tennessee.[292] According to the reviewer, the Tennessee legislature in 1825 had directed that commissioners "revise and digest all the statutes of Tennessee and North Carolina then in force, and of a public nature." So, while the work reviewed is *The Statute Law of Tennessee*, the reviewer freely embellished upon his themes with illustrations from the law of North Carolina, for example, when he discussed adverse possession and when he criticized *The Fundamental Constitutions of Carolina*.[293] The reviewer adopted a traditional—almost medieval—philosophy of law: law must move from the bottom up, from the usages of the people into the declarations of the courts and the assemblies.]

The Statute Laws of Tennessee, of a Public and General Nature, revised and digested by John Haywood *and* Robert L. Coobs, *by order of the General Assembly.* Knoxville. T. F. S. Heiskell. 1831. 2 vols. 8vo.

. . . Those who have no other pursuit before their eyes, but to show their wisdom in making laws, ought to consider that legislative enactments are rarely proper till the governed have already generally acted upon the rule which is about to be prescribed, or rather written. In other words, nothing, except matters of mere form and arbitrary regulations, should ever become a *written* law, till it has already existed among the people as an *unwritten* rule of conduct. Whatever is agreeable to the nature and condition of any people, will become a usage among them; and the statute book should be a record of those usages. It sometimes happens that if the legislature is tardy in transferring to the statute book the usages of the people, the courts themselves assume the function of that department. This has frequently occurred in England, where society is divided into two masses, one of which, though inferior in numbers, has been greatly superior in political influence. There the will of the uninfluential majority, suppressed in the halls of legislation, has acted itself out in the courts, long before it could find its way into the records of parliament. So powerful indeed has been this silent working of the causes of the advancement of society in that country, that the courts, as every lawyer knows, have virtually repealed acts of parliament, as the statute *de donis* and the statute of uses. This occurrence is not frequent with us, but examples are not wanting. For instance, our condition required a short term of limitation. This the legislature of North Carolina made seven years. But they drew the law upon an English model; and as the subject upon which the English statute operated was *actions* and not *rights*, so our statute was made in form to operate on actions not rights. But the situation of our people imperiously demanded that a *fair possession* should in a short period become a title. The legislature hesitated. The courts acted, and did not shun to declare that the legislature itself, which passed the act referred to, actually *intended* to act upon rights, not merely upon remedies. The act to which we allude is that of North Carolina of 1715. After a long struggle the courts at last declared that seven years' peaceable possession would give the possessor title to the extent of the boundaries mentioned in his deed, or color of title. This is against the words of the statute, and against the well settled English and American constructions of the words. But it has the saving virtue of being adapted to the condition of society. At last, but not till after the rule already existed, we may say, with strict propriety, in the unwritten code of the people, the legislature recognised and recorded it, in the Tennessee statute of 1819.

According to these principles, the acts of the legislature are to be regarded in the light of evidence, conclusive and uncontrollable, it is true, of the customs and usages which existed among the people at the period of their being embodied in the statute book.

Where a constitution designates a body of legislative magistracy, it simply appoints those, who, if they transcend not their duty, are to ascertain, and reduce into precise and definite rules, the customs of the people, and who are to write them out, and promulgate them authoritatively. In a country governed by usages or unwritten laws, the judicial magistrate declares what the custom is, or, more accurately, he decides the question which the litigants have made before him, according to his opinion of the usage, and his decision, if his tribunal be of the last resort, is conclusive evidence of the usage. Though a legislature were composed of the wisest men of the State in all human knowledge, yet their wisdom would be null if their laws should be made without reference to the nature and condition of the people for whom their labors were intended. Thus Locke's celebrated constitution of Carolina is only a monument of the utter futility of hypothetical (it does not deserve the name of theoretical,) legislation,—a lively memento of the singular preposterousness of attempting to form a people by laws.

Natural liberty is the power to do whatever is not prohibited by the laws of nature. Civil liberty is what remains of natural, after deducting the restraints of society. . . . To have the law-making power appointed by, and accountable to, the people, is a great security for liberty; but the manner in which the restraints of liberty are to be designated and published, is scarcely less important.

In the first place, those restraints should never be the cause of loss or inconvenience to the citizen. . . . The loss or inconvenience should be the effect of a transgression of a restraint . . . Hence the restraint should be prescribed; for there can be no transgression where there is no prohibition. . . .

In the second place, the law must not only be prescribed, that is, the restraint must not only be imposed, but it must be sufficiently done. To this end, it is not enough merely to write down the rule and promulgate it; for besides this, it should be so done as to be unequivocal. If the words of the legislature are dark, ambiguous, or doubtful, it opens the door to interpretation, and makes it necessary for the judiciary to enlighten the language, determine the meaning, ascertain the sense, of the legislature. In doing this, they truly exercise legislative functions. They are declaring that intention which the legislature ought to have sufficiently done. This is to exercise a broad discretion,—and it would be miraculous if some citizen should not, in the multifariousness of affairs, fall the victim to a rule, strictly *ex post facto*,—if the law, as declared by the court, should not be, to all intents and purposes, the cause of loss or inconvenience to him. . . .

Document II-37   Governor Swain's Message, 1833

[Gov. David Swain[294] justified his proposed reorganization of the state's revised laws[295] by the same arguments that democratic reformers had been using for years to advocate for the codification of the common law, perhaps deflecting radicalism down a slower and safer byway in the process, insofar as radical sentiment existed at all in the agricultural, anti-intellectual society of antebellum North Carolina.[296] It seems the conservative attorneys of North Carolina worried little about reforming the scholasticism of common law pleading or avoiding the inefficiencies of jury trials, perhaps because they did not follow the former with any rigor[297] and because they preferred to overindulge in the latter,[298] but the attorneys did worry about knowing and accessing the enacted law, both as inherited from England and as passed locally. As Swain complained regarding the conundrum of the reception of British acts in North Carolina, "not only the source but the very existence of our statute Law, is, as remarked by an elegant writer, with regard to the common Law, 'as undiscoverable as the sources of the Nile.' "]

MESGE.

To the General Assembly of the State of North Carolina:
GENTLEMEN: . . .

Among the various subjects which will come before you, the revision of the whole body of our public statute laws may be mentioned as deeply interesting to the community. The earliest statute in force in this State, was enacted in the year 1235, in the reign of Henry the third.—Our revised Code as it is termed, commences with the provincial laws passed by the General Assembly which sat at Little River in 1715, omitting the entire legislation of the mother country with regard to this State, during a period of four hundred and ninety years, and embracing more than a hundred entire statutes or parts of statutes. Of these many relate to the criminal law of the country, several create capital felonies or punish capitally, offences that were previously subject to a milder penalty; and yet, it is believed that complete copies of these enactments are not to be found in half a dozen libraries in the State. A part of those in force and many not in force, were published in Newbern, thirty years since, but the work did not equal public expectation and is now out of print. The lives, the liberty, and property of our citizens, are thus subject to the enactments of a government, widely dissimilar from ours, which few have read, or had it in their power to read. The legislation of nearly five centuries is a sealed book to the great body of the community, and in some degree even to the profession whose interest and duty render the study of the Law the business of life. It is but a short time since, the question whether a statute regulating the trial of an individual for a capital felony was in force in this State, became the subject of solemn argument before the Supreme Court, and called forth directly opposite opinions from the Judges. The truth is, that not only the source but the very existence of our statute Law, is, as remarked by an elegant writer, with regard to the common Law, "as undiscoverable as the sources of the Nile." In such a state of things, the expounder of the Law alone is safe. The Executive and Legislative Departments of the Government cease to be co-ordinate with the Judiciary, since the latter has not only the right to construe the whole body of legislation, but the privilege of declaring the existence within this State of any portion of the immense mass of British Statutes, enacted anterior to the period at which we began to legislate ourselves. I intend no disrespect to the Judiciary—the difficulty does not arise from a disposition on their part to encroach upon the other departments of the Government; but from an omission of the Legislature to perform its own functions. The task of revising and expense of publishing this Code, would be of little moment in comparison with its importance. The laws and journals of a single session are much more voluminous than such a work would be if properly executed.

A judicious legal reform should, however, extend to all the subsequent enactments, by which we are governed. Competent judges entertain the opinion that the bulk of our statute book might be lessened at least one third, by a repeal of statutes which are in effect obsolete, and others, the object of which has been attained by subsequent enactments. The whole of the legislation from 1715 to 1777, with the exception of the Statutes of Limitation, the Registry Acts, and a few others, might with propriety be expunged from our Code, as surplusage. Many subsequent Acts, and some of them connected with the criminal law, should share a similar fate. It is a capital felony, for instance, to counterfeit the notes of the Bank of North America, which have no circulation within this State—Various laws encumber the pages of the revisal, providing for the punishment of counterfeiting our revolutionary bills of credit, the necessity for which ceased years since with the existence of the bills themselves. An antiquary would at present be much more disposed to trace out their similitude than a counterfeiter.

Is it not strange, that our Revisal should exhibit to the citizen, various enactments to punish offences which cannot be committed, and conceal from his view innumerable penalties attached to actions, which he does not know to be wrong? It is submitted to your wisdom to determine whether a legal system so perplexed, intricate and uncertain, is suited to the genius of our institutions, and the character of our citizens. . . .

I have the honor to be, Gentlemen,
With high consideration,
Your obedient servant,

DAVID L. SWAIN.

Executive Department, North Carolina,
November 18th, 1833.

Document II–38 Moore's Argument, 1834

[Bartholomew Figures Moore, a counselor for the defendant, argued in the excerpt below that civil society must ultimately ground even the most unchristian and undemocratic aspect of its law upon human nature. Self-defense being as natural to the enslaved person as to the free, the killing of the master, Baxter, by the enslaved person, Will, should be manslaughter, not murder. And when Moore looked to the common law for the definition of "provoking cause," he again stressed that the principles of the common law were bottomed on human nature. When Moore invoked "the irresistible force of public sentiment" as "stronger than law," though, might he not have fallen into the ambiguities of democratic cant:[299] Was it enough that the strength of current sentiment was counter-acting the inertia of prior opinion? Would democratic society's changes in opinion inevitably progress morally? In relying on the progress of public opinion, had democratic society laid its treasure where neither moth nor rust destroys? Must not knowledge of practical good—perhaps bottomed ontologically on human nature[300]—condemn all unjust declarations of law as unreasonable, whenever and by whomever made?

Also arguing for the prisoner was attorney Samuel Mordecai. Arguing for the state was Attorney-General J. R. J. Daniel. Judge William Gaston wrote for the court.]

THE STATE v. NEGRO WILL, Slave of JAMES S. BATTLE....

DEC. 1834.

STATE
v.
WILL....

B. F. Moore, for the prisoner.— ...
The prisoner's counsel contends:—

First; That if Baxter's shot had killed the prisoner, Baxter would have been guilty of manslaughter at the least. And

Second; This position being established, the killing of Baxter under the circumstances stated is but manslaughter in the prisoner.

The first position would seem too plain to be argued; but as an opinion appears to be rapidly pervading the public mind, that *any* means may be resorted to, to coerce the perfect submission of the slave to his master's will; and that any resistance to that will, reasonable or unreasonable, lawfully places the life of the slave at his master's feet, it may be useful to attempt to draw the line, if there be any, between the lawful and unlawful exercise of the master's power....

It is not intended to combat the correctness of the decision in the *State* v. *Mann*, 2 Dev. 263, though that case leaves the slave, when his life is spared, in the slender guardianship of the "frowns and execrations" of a moral community against cruelty. That decision is not understood by me as some have expounded it. In declaring that a master cannot be indicted for a battery on his slave, the Court is not to be understood to affirm that he cannot be indicted for *any* offence which necessarily includes a battery. I apprehend the substance of their decision to be, that they will take no cognizance of any violence done to the slave by the master which does not produce death. It is true, there is a portion of the opinion of the Court which puts the slave entirely out of the pale of the law, and secures the master in a despotic immunity. In page 266, the Court say, "such obedience is the consequence of only uncontrolled authority over the body; there is nothing else which can operate to produce the effect; the power of the master must be absolute to render the submission of the slave perfect. In the actual condition of things it must be so, there is no remedy; this discipline belongs to the state of slavery; they cannot be disunited without abrogating at once, the right of the master and absolving the slave from his obligation." These expressions, it must be admitted, are clear beyond cavil in their meaning; and that they were selected to convey, with great accuracy, the opinions of the learned Judge who used them, may be well argued from the frank confession which he avows of their abhorrence. In truth, they do outlaw the slave, and legalise his destruction at the will of his master. It is believed, however, that they were never intended to cover the entire relation between master and slave. If they were, it is humbly submitted, that they are not only startling and abhorrent to humanity, but at variance with statute law and decided cases.... During its operations, it acknowledges no equal, who may check its will, and knows no superior afterwards, who may rightfully punish its deeds. The language of the Court does not strictly and precisely describe the relations of master and slave which subsisted in ancient Rome, and does now subsist in modern Turkey; a relation which this Court in the case of the *State* v. *Read*, did most emphatically denounce, as inhuman, unsuited to the genius of our laws, and unnecessary to protect the master in his legal rights. In that case, Judge HENDERSON fixes the true boundary of the master's power. It extends, says he, to securing the services and labours of the slave, and no farther. And he expressly declares that a power over the life of the slave is not surrendered by the law, because the possession of such a power is noways necessary to the purposes of slavery, and that his *life* is in the care of the law.

The idea of the *perfect* submission of the slave is in true accordance with the policy which should regulate that condition of life, wherever it may exist. But whether it will more certainly result from the *absolute* power of the owner, than from a *large* but *limited* authority, is questionable indeed. More especially, if it be true, as argued in the opinion already referred to, that the absolute power of the master, although left unrestrained by law, is checked and fettered by what is stronger than law, the irresistible force of public sentiment. If that force is now setting in a counter-current against the license of absolute power, either it is to be deprecated and stopped, or absolute power is most clearly proved to be unnecessary to the ends of slavery. The Courts of the country should foster the enlightened benevolence of the age, and interpret the powers which one class of the people claim over another, in conformity, not with the spirit which tolerates the barbarian who is guilty of savage cruelty, but with that which heaps upon him the frowns and deep execrations of the community. All domestic police must be regulated by the feelings and views of those who dispense it. If it be true then, that public sentiment will no longer tolerate excessive cruelties from the master, as is said by TAYLOR, Chief Justice, in *The State* v. *Hale*; by HENDERSON, Chief Justice, in *The State* v. *Read*; and by RUFFIN, Chief Justice, in *The State* v. *Mann*; and if it be true, likewise, that the relation between master and slave is to be discovered from the opinions and feelings of the masters, we cannot hear, without surprise, that it is necessary in the actual condition of things, to clothe the master with an uncontrolled and absolute authority over the body of the slave. . . .

It is further said in the *State* v. *Mann*, "that the slave, to remain a slave, must be made sensible, that there is no appeal from his master, that his power *in no one instance, is usurped*." The language here is equally explicit, and altogether as strong, as that before quoted. It denies to the slave the smallest attribute of a rational or feeling creature. It not only represses thought, and extinguishes all power to deliberate on any command of his master, however repugnant to natural justice it may be, and whether its execution is to affect himself or others; but it professes to control into perfect tameness the instinct of self-preservation. It would be difficult, and if it were easy, it would be lamentable, to accomplish the former; but it would be impossible to effect the latter. Such insensibility to life would defeat the very object of its inculcation, the value of the slave. For we can never hope to regulate this powerful instinct of nature, with an adjustment which will quietly yield all its love of life into the hands of a ferocious master, and yet preserve it against the world beside. But if it were desirable so far to annihilate it, the task is beyond the reach of human ingenuity, and not to be accomplished by the possession of absolute power, however fearfully enforced or terribly exercised. The relation of master and slave may repress all the noble energies and manly sentiments of the soul, and may degrade the moral being into a brute condition; and when this is done, we shall not be astonished to see the moral brute exhibiting the instinct natural to brute condition; . . .

I am arguing no question of abstract right, but am endeavouring to prove that the natural incidents of slavery must be borne with, because they are inherent to the condition itself; and that any attempt to restrain or punish a slave for the exercise of a right, which even absolute power cannot destroy, is inhuman, and without the slightest benefit to the security of the master, or to that of society at large. The doctrine may be advanced from the bench, enacted by the legislature, and enforced with all the varied agony of torture, and still the slave cannot believe, and will not believe, "that there is no one instance" in which the master's power is usurped. Nature, stronger than all, will discover *many* instances, and vindicate her rights at any and at every price. When such a stimulant as this urges the forbidden deed, punishment will be powerless to reclaim, or to warn by example. It can serve no purpose but to gratify the revengeful feelings of one class of people, and to inflame the hidden animosities of the other.

With great deference to the opinion already commented on, it would appear to me, that a conclusion directly the reverse, as to the necessity of absolute power in the master, should have been drawn from the premises. The slave can only expect to learn the law of the land, as respects the power of the owner over him, from the manner in which it is generally, and almost universally, administered by the owner. If their treatment is now so mild, or becoming so, as rarely to require the interposition of any tribunal for their protection, they will soon be taught by the conduct of their masters, if not already taught, that absolute power is not the master's right; and the consequence which may be expected will be, that the slave will be prepared to resist its exercise, when bad men attempt to commit the cruelties allowed by it. So important is it, that the Court should, as far as possible, conform their exposition of the rights of men with those sentiments of the public, which, by the Court, themselves, are admitted to be wholesome and just. And especially should they do so, when those rights are constituted by public opinion, and almost exclusively by that alone....

This brings us to the important question in this case. Was the prisoner *justly* so provoked by the shooting, *as under the influence of ordinary human frailty*, to cause his reason to be dethroned, and to be deprived of deliberation? Or, in the language of Judge HAYWOOD, in *Norris's case*, "was not the prisoner thereby deprived of the free and proper exercise of his rational faculties, owing to the fury of resentment, not unreasonably conceived?" If he was, that ends the question. Was it such a provocation, as, allowing for the disparity of the free and slave condition of men in this country, was well calculated, even in minds tolerably well regulated, to throw a man off his guard, and excite a furious anger? If so, the *State v. Merrill*, 2 Dev. 279 (RUFFIN's opinion) determines the fate of the prisoner. An appeal to human nature in its most degraded state, will answer, unhesitatingly, it was. No man can reason and respond otherwise. And it appears to me, that an appeal to the principles of law, as founded in the nature of man, and recognised for centuries, will leave not a particle of doubt. Can the prisoner be guilty of murder? Who can review the circumstances of the case, and in his candour pronounce that they carry in them, "the plain indication of a heart regardless of social duty, and fatally bent upon mischief?" If his case can be made to reach this standard definition of murder, what bosom is there which does not luxuriate in the poison of murderous thought? And in vain may nature plead her wrongs and the tempest of the passions, to excuse the indiscretion of her fitful moments. It may be murder; but if so, it must find its guilt, not in the human disposition, but in a policy that knows no frailty and shows no mercy. That policy is yet to be declared. I will not suppose its intended application to this case, and I shall, therefore, for the present, take the liberty of discussing the defence upon the received principles which define murder, and distinguish it from manslaughter....

Manslaughter wants one of the above intents which define murder. It implies an intent to kill or hurt, and that the intent is unjust, but supposes the absence of deliberation, or the presence of a *justly* provoking cause. (Cases illustrative of this definition, Bevil, 64, 65. 67 § 5, 68. 74 § 2, 76 § 3. *Stedman's case*, p. 80. *Carey's case*, p. 124.) But what is justly provoking cause? In our search for the meaning of the expression, we cannot consult the vague notions of men, as to insults. There would not only be no certainty in them as a guide, but they would strip men of all security for their lives. We must appeal to the common law as it has recognised excusable frailties. Its principles being bottomed on human nature civilised by legal restraints and legal privileges, adopt themselves with a happy facility, to all the changes and modifications of society, and to all the mutations in the relations of its parts. These principles having discarded the idea of legal provocation from words, have resolved the foundation of their existence into the protection of the person.

Self-preservation, being a prime law of nature, and indispensable to the first and permanent interests of society, the instinct is fostered instead of being checked. The policy of the law to cherish it, is what dispenses indulgence to an excess of force requisite to preserve it, and palliates an unnecessary homicide. If human institutions could so blunt this sense as to effectuate a law which should forbid blow for blow not threatening death, the introduction of slavery, to a great degree, would be already prepared. If, however, the degradation should stop at this point, still there would be a very ample scope for this powerful sense to act in, and a dangerous attack, or a blow menacing death, being out of the customary sufferance, would call up, in vigour, the unsubdued though mutilated sense, and surprise it into action. It is not the *object* of the law, in its regulation of the relation of master and slave, to destroy any portion of the instinct of self-preservation. On the contrary, it would be rejoiced to preserve it entire, but this is inconsistent with the subjection of the slave, without which he is valueless.... And hence it is too, that whenever the law, for the purpose of sustaining the relations of the several parts of society, deemed essential to the peace and safety of the whole, tolerates its partial suppression, it provides the best possible security against any abuse likely to occur because of its required extinction. Thus it gives to the wife, the protection of love and identity of welfare; to the child, the shield of affection; to the apprentice, the guaranty of a penal bond; and to the slave, the guard of interest. In the general, in proportion as these securities are weaker, that of the law itself ought to be stronger; and in proportion as the subjection in the one or the other of these relations, is required to be greater or less, so must the suppression of this instinct be greater or less. The subjection in the relation of slavery ought to be greater, and so ought the extinction of the instinct to be greater, than in any of the other relations. It is the legal duty of all who are subjects, in any one of them to adapt and conform this instinct to the extent necessary to maintain the relation; and if any one do not, he shall not plead its want of subjection in excuse of a deed occasioned by his neglect of duty. . . . In a word, in those bounds within which the law has enjoined it as a duty to curb the instinct of self-preservation, we are not allowed to display it, and if we do, the law cannot hear the defence of provocation; but all display of it out of those bounds, is admissible and is the effect of *legal* provocation. The law demands it as a duty that we should tame our passions to suit the condition which it has assigned us. It supposes that this duty will become habitual, and consequently of easy performance, that we will conform ourselves to its requirements. This, and this alone, is the true foundation of all the distinction between the master and the apprentice, between the freeman and the slave.

But having conformed ourselves to a given and required degradation, to an enjoined submission, we are ready by our very nature and habits, to resist any degradation or submission greatly beyond that which we have learned to acquiesce in as a *duty*. When a slave is required to bare his back to the rod, he does it, because it is usual; but when he is required to stand as a target for his master's gun, he is startled: no idea of duty sustains the requirement, and the unquelled portion of his instinct rouses his passions to resistance. . . .

When it is declared that a slave is a reasonable or human creature, as in *State* v. *Scott*, *State* v. *Hale*, and *State* v. *Read*, and that he is the subject of felony at common law; that murder and manslaughter both may be perpetrated on his person; that himself may commit both, it would seem to result that he was acknowledged to possess the human infirmities common to his species. That they must be palliated in some cases, even when the master is the victim, I hope I have satisfactorily shown. . . . But that not in a *single* relation in which the slave is placed by the law, is he debarred in *every* case of violence to his person, from feeling and pleading a legal provocation. . . .

Upon the whole, I cannot bring my mind to the conclusion, that this case is of higher grade than manslaughter, if of that; and whatever may be the prisoner's fate, I am free to declare, and with the most sincere candour, that I do not recognise in his conduct, the moral depravity of a murderer, nor any high degree of inaptitude to the condition of slavery. He was disobedient, it is true, and ran to avoid chastisement. Three-fourths of our slaves occasionally do this. He slew his overseer, it is true, after having been dangerously shot, pursued and overtaken. The tamest and most domestic brute will do likewise. And I feel, that if he must expiate the deed under the gallows, he will be a victim, not of his own abandoned depravity, but a sacrifice offered to the policy which regulates the relation of slavery among us. But before he is sacrificed, it may be useful to inquire into that policy. The interests of society demand that it should be fixed, and *permanently* fixed, that the master may know the extent of his authority, and the slave prepare himself to its accommodation.

No question can be more delicate, or attended with so many bad consequences if settled in error. It would be next to impossible for the judiciary to adjust this relation adversely to any strong and deliberate opinion entertained by the public mind. The momentum of this feeling acting through the juries of the country and the spirit of the legislature, would be too powerful, successfully to be encountered by the Courts. And in whatsoever decided current it might run, it would, finally, bear into its channel all interpretations of the law.

By a timely and judicious administration of the law, however, in relation to this subject, the Courts may effect much in the formation of public opinion, and at this time they may exert the opportunities afforded by their situation, in a most happy manner to impart fixedness and stability to those principles which form the true basis of the policy. They have of late frequently announced from the bench, the progression of humanity in the relation, and their clear conviction, that the condition of the slave was rapidly advancing in amelioration, under the benign influence of Christian precepts and the benevolent auspices of improving civilisation. It is believed, that these convictions were founded in truth, and the various laws on the statute book bring ample testimony to the fact. As far as slavery has been the subject of legislation for the last ninety years, it has been undergoing a gradual revolution in favour of the slave, and, it is confidently asserted, not adverse to the best interests of the master, or of the security of the public. In a popular government, we can nowhere look for more correct information of the state of the public mind, upon a subject deeply interesting to the people at large, than in their laws. The history of the legislation of the state for the last century on this subject, during which more than a dozen principal acts have been passed at intervals, is a history of a gradual progression in the improvement of the condition of the slave, in the protection of his person, his comforts, and those rights not necessary to be surrendered to his master. The length of time in which this evidence of a common sentiment has been continuing in one course, is irrefutable testimony of its being the true and deliberate sense of the community. . . .

It is not possible that there can be found, anywhere, a plainer manifestation of a decided intent to raise the consideration and standing of the slave, than is here exposed in the foregoing acts of the legislature. Will the Court disappoint this unequivocal intention? Will they rebuke the spirit of the age, and strike back this unfortunate race of men, advancing from the depths of misery and wretchedness, to a higher ground, under the shield of so much legislation enacted in their behalf?

Our laws furnish incontestable evidence of what *is* the enlightened sentiment of the state. The history of other nations affords a body of luminous information, to instruct us what that sentiment *should* be; and I feel no small pleasure in believing, that the legislative policy of our past and present day most fully accords with that course, which the long tried experience of bygone ages has distinctly marked out as the wiser and better one.

Upon this subject, the Baron Montesquieu has gathered the choicest materials of every age, clime, and nation. With a mind, formed in the mould of patience itself; strong by nature, and enriched with a philosophic cultivation, he hath executed the task of analysis with the most profound and discriminating sagacity. With no object in view, but the advancement of political knowledge, he hath unmasked all the forms of government, traced to the fountain the principles of their action, and exposed to the meanest capacity the deep and hidden reasons of all the diversified relations of man, and the true genius of the laws necessary to support them.

In his Spirit of Laws, vol. 1, p. 291, et seq. to 298, he treats of the subject of slavery, and informs us, as the result of his inquiries, that in governments whose policy is warlike, and the citizens ever ready with arms in their hands to quell attempts to regain liberty, slaves *may* be treated with great rigour and severity, without the hazard of servile wars; but that in republics, where the policy is essentially pacific, and the citizens devoted to the arts of peace and industry, the treatment of slaves *should* be mild and humane: that the power of the master should not be absolute, and that the slave should be put within the keeping of the law. If that candid and ingenious writer be not deceived in his conclusions, he has given us a hint for the regulation of our domestic servitude, the neglect of which may lead to the most fatal sequel. Our government is, perhaps, the most pacific on earth, and the citizens most addicted to the pursuits of civilised life. How inconsistent, then, will it be in us to adopt a policy in relation to our slaves, which must be either yielded up, or must change the habits and character of our people, and ultimately our form of government, with the blessings of liberty itself. . . .

In adjusting the balance of this delicate subject, let it not be believed that the great and imminent danger, is in overloading the scale of humanity. The Court must pass through Scylla and Charybdis; and they may be assured that the peril of shipwreck is not avoided, by shunning with distant steerage, the whirlpool of Northern fanaticism. That of the South is equally fatal. It may not be so visibly seen; but it is as deep, as wide, and as dangerous.

Mordecai, for the prisoner.—. . . .

DOCUMENT II-39   COMMISSION REPORT, 1834

[Excerpted below is a report of two of the commissioners of *The Revised Statutes*, James Iredell and William H. Battle, the third commissioner, Gavin Hogg, having been too ill to participate in its drafting. The commissioners awaited the appointment of Hogg's replacement by the general assembly and in the meantime laid plans for their revision. They aimed to revise the public statute laws of the state (that is, not to revise private acts or common laws), digesting and consolidating into one act the statute laws on a single subject and incorporating into the various subjects the British statutes still in force.[301] The commissioners planned to clean up phraseology and to bring all language into common modern English, so "the great mass of the people" would not find it unintelligible. They planned also to suggest to the general assembly any new provisions called for by "the altered state of our customs and manners" or due to the construction of statutes by the judiciary.]

Executive Department,
4th December, 1834.

To the General Assembly of the State of North Carolina.
Gentlemen:

I have the honor to transmit, herewith, a communication from James Iredell and William H. Battle, Esquires, two of the Commissioners appointed to revise the Public Statute Laws of this State.

I concur in all the opinions expressed by these gentlemen, and entertain sanguine hopes, that the duties confided to them will be discharged in a manner highly creditable to them, and eminently useful to the public. The appointment of a Clerk, as suggested, would, I am satisfied, not only facilitate and expedite the labors of the Commissioners, but greatly promote the convenience of the legislative body to which the work will be submitted for revision and confirmation. An appropriation of three hundred dollars, would afford adequate compensation for the labors of a competent clerk.

DAVID L. SWAIN.

REPORT.

To His Excellency, Governor Swain:

THE undersigned, appointed in conjunction with Gavin Hogg, Esq. by your commission, bearing date the fourteenth day of January, 1834, in pursuance of an Act of the General Assembly, passed at their last session, Commissioners to revise and digest the public statute law of this State,—

Respectfully Report:

That soon after their appointment, they convened in the city of Raleigh, made a cursory examination of the acts of Assembly and the British statutes in force in this State, and agreed upon the plan on which their revisal should be conducted. In these preliminary arrangements, they were assisted by Mr. Hogg; but they deeply lament what is already known to your Excellency, that the state of this gentleman's health, after long flattering him with the prospect that he would be able to discharge his portion of the duties of the commission, has at last entirely prevented him from any further prosecution thereof. Under these circumstances, the undersigned have proceeded alone, and have revised and digested many of the statutes in force in this State: But as the Legislature evidently intended to entrust this delicate task to *three persons*, they have not thought themselves warranted in submitting the result of the labours of *only two*. They, therefore, take the liberty of reporting what they have done—the plan on which they agreed; and a single revised statute as a specimen of that plan to your Excellency, that you may make such communication thereon you may deem right, to the General Assembly.

The undersigned have revised and consolidated the statutes upon many subjects—an enumeration of which, is not thought necessary; but their whole work, as far as it has gone, is subject to the examination of your Excellency, of the General Assembly, or of any Committee of that body; and verbal explanations, it wished for, will be cheerfully communicated.

Their plan has been simply to digest and consolidate into one Act, all the various statute laws relating to one subject, occasionally to alter vicious and inadvertent phraseology, and to insert in the body of the statute such new provisions as seemed to them to be manifestly proper. The whole of the statutes reported, must, of course, be again passed upon by the Legislature; and the undersigned have therefore felt the less reluctance, although seldom deviating from the will of the Legislature, heretofore expressed, to suggest, in the form of amendments, the new provisions which seemed to be called for, either by judicial decisions; by the evident haste in which the original act was drawn; or in case of old acts by the altered state of our customs and manners.

As regards the old British statutes, many of which are still in force here, we have, after mature deliberation, concluded to incorporate them in acts distributed according to the subjects to which they relate, clothing them in a modern garb. To report them in their original quaint and antiquated language, would be presenting to the Legislature a body of laws, unintelligible to the great mass of the people; and which few lawyers, however versed in black-letter learning, could understand without the aid of the commentaries which judicial construction has, from time to time, afforded. Many of them are in Norman French—a language originally corrupt, and now obsolete. For these reasons, we are led to believe, that these statutes should be translated into language more befitting the present time; and we are the more confirmed in this conclusion, by the fact, that in many States of the Union, the old British statutes, when believed important, have been re-modelled, and that, even in England, they are now undergoing a process, by which they can be suited to the present manners and customs, to the advanced state of knowledge and science, and to the understandings of the people, for whose use they are designed. In re-modelling these statutes, we shall pay careful attention to the judicial decisions, by which their meaning and construction have been established.

When this revision of the laws shall have been sanctioned by the Legislature, it is proposed, that, in its publication, there shall be an alphabetical arrangement of its contents, as the best means of facilitating the researches of those who may have occasion to examine it. A short Index of the Contents of all the sections of an act, will be placed at its head, and marginal notes also affixed to each separate section. References, where necessary, will be made from one subject to another, and also to judicial decisions. All the other requisitions of the act, under which this revision is made, shall likewise be complied with.

Without intending to cast the slightest censure upon those who prepared the revisal now in use, we must be permitted to remark, that many of the acts which it includes, are either repealed, or obsolete: And that we believe the Revisal we shall submit, containing only the acts to be in future operation, and comprising all the laws since the year 1820, will not occupy more than one volume, equal in size to one of the present Revised Code.

We, with deference, submit another remark to your better judgment: Our labors will be much accelerated, and we believe the convenience of the Legislature promoted, by authorizing the appointment of a clerk, who shall be paid by the copy-sheet for transcribing what we have prepared, and what of course will exhibit, in its face, many alterations and erasures. With such assistance, we can present to the Legislature every act which has undergone our revision, in apt form, and fair proportions.

We herewith submit "An act concerning entries and grants of land," as the specimen to which we have referred. We request your Excellency to communicate our views to the General Assembly, in such manner as you may deem proper; and we shall receive, with cheerfulness, any suggestion by which our plan may be improved, and the work made more valuable.

With great respect,
Your obedient servants,
JAMES IREDELL,
WILL: H. BATTLE.

RALEIGH, Dec. 3d, 1834.

Document II-40 Joint Select Committee Report, 1835

[About a decade before his election to the governorship of North Carolina,[302] William A. Graham chaired the joint select committee of the general assembly on the subject of *The Revised Statutes*. In the 1835 report of this committee to the general assembly, reprinted below, Graham recommended that more time be given to the commissioners to complete their work. In so recommending, he hit upon important themes on law reform by statutory codification. He called the commissioned revision of the state's public laws a "digest"; he reported that he was highly gratified with the alphabetical arrangement of the titles of the unfinished work of the commissioners; and he noted the motive for the commission of *The Revised Statutes*: that "enlightened Legislation" should not be a voluminous pile of legislative acts, filled with contradictory and obsolete provisions. Graham assured the general assembly that the work of the commissioners would "render a knowledge of his most essential rights accessible to every individual possessed of the rudiments of education." Freedom must be secured by law, Graham mused, but the laws that secure freedom must be intelligible to the people upon whom they operate.]

REPORT

OF THE

JOINT SELECT COMMITTEE,

ON THE SUBJECT OF

THE REVISED STATUTES.

The Joint Select Committee to whom was referred, the Message of his Excellency the Governor, transmitting the Report of the Commissioners appointed to revise and digest the public statute laws, and a resolution of the Senate directing an inquiry into the probable expense of printing and re-enacting the statutes after the revision shall be completed, have attentively considered the same, and **REPORT:**

That from the limited period allowed for the session of the present General Assembly, they deem it inexpedient for this Legislature to attempt the re-enactment of any portion of the digest which has been completed. The magnitude of the task, and the great importance of its correct performance, require that it should be done with the maturest deliberation, and with the fullest opportunity of removing all errors and adding proper amendments. So great has been the consequence attached to similar undertakings in other States of the Union, that special sessions of their legislatures have been held, for the purpose of passing upon the revised statutes alone. Your committee however believe, that it is in the power of this General Assembly greatly to facilitate the labors of their successors upon this subject, and that probably the necessary delay in the final accomplishment of the work, will but add to its accuracy and usefulness. In ordinary legislation, where the subject is in the least degree complicated, it is deemed unsafe to proceed without having printed copies of the bills for the rigid security of every mind, whose approbation is required to the success of a measure proposed. This common precaution would appear to be altogether indispensable, where the whole of the statutes which have been enacted on any particular subject for six centuries past, are to be reviewed, collected, arranged in lucid order, and if necessary amended. By causing the whole of work to be printed in the course of the next year, it will be found ready for the immediate action of the members of the next legislature at the commencement of their session, and a large part of it may undergo the revision to the General Assembly in that early period, which is usually spent in the mere preparation of business.

In regard to the expense of printing, into which your Committee have been instructed to inquire by a resolution of the Senate, they have learned through members of their body appointed for the purpose, that two hundred copies of three hundred octavo pages each, may be procured at the moderate expense of $1 per page, or three hundred dollars for the whole, and so in proportion for any greater number of pages. The entire digest when finished will probably not exceed six hundred pages—so that the printing of the whole number of copies required for the use of the next General Assembly will be less than the compensation of the numbers thereof for a single day. Your committee, therefore, recommend that the portions of the work of the commissioners which have been submitted to the inspection of the Legislature shall be returned to them, and that when they shall have completed the residue, they shall procure two hundred copies of the same to be printed, upon the most economical terms, and deposite [*sic*] them in the office of the Governor for the use of the next General Assembly.

Your committee are of opinion that it would much accellerate [*sic*] the progress of the work, as well as diminish the claims of the commissioners to additional compensation, according to the provisions of the act directing their appointment, should the Legislature authorise the employment of a clerk to assist in transcribing their manuscripts, and preparing them for the press; an appropriation of three hundred dollars will be sufficient to procure one—and it is respectfully suggested that it should be made.

From a cursory examination, which your committee have been able to bestow on the unfinished work of the commissioners, which has been referred to them, they have been highly gratified, both with the plan of the digest which has been adopted and the mode of its execution. The heads, or titles, of the different subjects of statutory enactment, are alphabetically arranged; and all the acts, or parts of acts, now in force and use, pertaining to any particular title, are disposed according to their appropriate connexion, without regard to chronological order, so as to present the whole body of our Legislation on any subject in a single act or chapter. Marginal references are also added, showing the dates of the respective acts thus embodied. A highly useful branch of the labors of the commissioners has been, to prepare additional sections, to reconcile conflicting provisions of different statutes, which they recommend as amendments, for the adoption of the Legislature, where the existing Laws are believed to require such amendments.

Your committee anticipate the greatest benefits to the people of the State, from the completion of the digest of our statute laws, in the manner thus briefly described. Freedom can only exist when secured by law. But it is in vain that laws are enacted and promulged, unless they shall be made intelligible to those upon whom they operate. The legislation of North Carolina, since the year one thousand seven hundred and fifteen, (the date of the earliest colonial statute) is spread over more than two thousand octavo pages, to say nothing of the statutes of England, which are recognized as in force here. So voluminous have the acts become on many titles—so various and contradictory on others—and so much that has been rendered obsolete by the change of government and other circumstances, is still preserved in the statute book, that it is not unfrequently difficult even for the legal profession to determine whether a particular act is in force, or whether it has been repealed: Such confusion and uncertainty in that department of the law, which is of the most common application and capable of constant improvement, are not only embarrassing and inconvenient to the citizen in private life, but are extremely unfavorable to enlightened Legislation. The work of the commissioners, now in an advanced state of preparation, will reduce the whole body of our statute law, both English and American, to a single volume of less than six hundred pages, and present it in such form as to render a knowledge of his most essential rights accessible to every individual possessed of the rudiments of education. When approved by the Legislature, and prepared for publication, the copy-right may be secured to the State; and, it is believed by your committee, that it will afford a complete indemnity, in a merely pecuniary point of view, for the expense incurred in its preparation.

To carry into execution the measures recommended in this report, your committee present the accompanying bill to the consideration of the Legislature.

Respectfully submitted,

WILL. A. GRAHAM, *Chairman.*

Dec. 11*th*, 1835.

Document II-41 Commission Report, 1836

[The commissioners of *The Revised Statutes* here reported to the general assembly the completion of their task. The codification consisted of about 115 acts pulled together from more than 2,000 session laws and British acts. The commissioners recommended that the general assembly publish a second volume for acts concerning charters and boundaries. The commissioners hoped their codification would diffuse a knowledge of the laws, which might aid future assemblies and "which in every community is essential to the security, the happiness and the liberty of the people."]

REPORT

OF THE

COMMISSIONERS,

APPOINTED TO REVISE AND CONSOLIDATE

THE PUBLIC STATUTES,

OF

NORTH CAROLINA.

THE undersigned, appointed under the provisions of an act of the General Assembly, passed in the year one thousand eight hundred and thirty three, Commissioners to revise and consolidate the Public Statute Laws of this State, respectfully report.

That they have completed the task assigned them, and the result of their labors is now submitted to the Legislature. Their revision, including all the Public Acts of our own Legislature and the Statutes of England, believed to be still in force in this State, is comprized in one hundred and fifteen acts, which in obedience to the directions of the last General Assembly have been sent to the Printer appointed for that purpose by the Governor, and have all been printed with the exception of eleven, (which are now in the press) and will accompany this communication. The commissioners have pursued the plan which they indicated to the General Assembly in their report made at the first session after their appointment. They have consolidated in one act, all the Statutes both our own and English, which related to the same subject, pointing out by marginal references, the sources from which each section and part of the act were derived. The Commissioners were restricted, except in one instance, by the law under which they acted, from offering any new law, or from making such alterations as would affect the sense or construction of any of the Statutes. With this restriction they have endeavored carefully to comply, and in a very few instances, where an amendment seemed obviously called for, and was inserted, it has been marked in the margin "proposed as an amendment" or has been left without any marginal reference. They were indeed authorized at their discretion to recommend the repeal of any Statute, and the adoption of such new provisions as such repeal might render necessary. But on reflection, they have deemed the exercise of such a power of too delicate, if not presumptuous a nature, and they have thought it better, with the exceptions above referred to, to leave to the Legislature the suggestion as well as the perfection of such amendments of the Law, as the public interest may require. A list of the acts revised is hereto appended marked A. If the Legislature should adopt this revision with such alterations as their wisdom will suggest, and direct its publication, it is respectfully proposed that the revised acts, should be published in one volume, arranged in alphabetical order according to their heads or titles, with reference to decisions of the Supreme Court, and that these should be prefixed in the same volume, the Constitution of this State, and of the United States, and added in an appendix the Statutes relating to descents, to the probate of wills and granting letters of administration and the probate of deeds and perhaps some others which have not now any prospective operation, but which are the subject of frequent reference in the investigation of claims to real and personal property.

There are many of our public Statutes, which from their very nature were not susceptible of revision and consolidation; such are the charters to the University, to the several Banks of this State, and to the navigation and Rail Road companies, and the Statutes defining the boundaries of the State and of its several counties, and perhaps some other Statutes. Of these the Commissioners recommend the publication in a second volume, of which, being of less general interest, and less frequent reference, a smaller number of copies than of the first volu[m]e will be required. A list of these acts is hereto appended marked B.

A list marked C. is also appended, of such public acts of the General Assembly to be found in the Revised Code, Taylor's Revisal and Pamphlets since that period, as the Commissioners believe to have become obsolete or to have been repealed or superseded by subsequent acts, or to have had their effect. This list is perhaps too comprehensive in its title, because it does not embrace many acts and parts of acts relating to subjects on which a revised Statute has been reported, and when the repeal may be seen by examining the marginal references.

The Commissioners in conclusion will remark, that they are aware the execution of the trust reposed in them required no high degree of ability, but demanded rather patient investigation, care and attention. However faithfully they may have endeavored to apply these qualities, they are fearful that there may exist many defects and imperfections in their work. The difficulty of avoiding these and the labor necessarily employed, may be in some degree estimated from the fact, that the public printed Statute laws of this State, without reference to the British Statutes, consist, of nearly two thousand acts, all of which had to be carefully examined and collated, and the parts still in force to be arranged in proper order and under their appropriate heads. If the present revision should be adopted, the whole Statute Law, including the British Statutes, in force in this State, will be comprised in about one hundred and fifteen acts, some of them very short and none inconveniently long.

The Commissioners will feel a high gratification if they shall have been in any degree instrumental in abridging the labors of future Legislation, or in diffusing more generally a knowledge of the laws, which in every community is essential to the security, the happiness and the liberty of the people.

FREDERIC NASH.
JAS. IREDELL.
WILL. H. BATTLE.

Raleigh, Nov. 28th, 1836.

Document II-42   Revised Statutes, 1837

[A legislative edition[303] of what would become *The Revised Statutes* had printed the full text of 115 acts codified by the commissioners for inspection of a joint select committee of the general assembly. In the legislative edition, chapter numbers and subject headings were yet to be assigned to the acts comprising the codification, and so the acts were not yet arranged alphabetically. Nor had the legislative edition been continuously paginated. It lacked references to pertinent cases of the supreme court; its marginal references mixed subject indicators and history notes;[304] it contained no index; and it included no content for the second volume of the work. It also contained an "Errata and Addenda" of four pages. The committee used the edition, preliminary though it was, to examine the commission's proposals and to then report these proposed acts to the general assembly with whatever amendments it thought proper.

After the work of the joint select committee was completed and passage of the individual acts by the general assembly was secured, the act excerpted below, "An Act Concerning the Revised Statutes," was passed by the general assembly at the session of 1836–'37 and was reprinted as the first chapter of *The Revised Statutes*.[305] According to section 9 of this act, *The Revised Statutes* was to be published in a volume separate from the session laws, arranged alphabetically by subject, studded with marginal references to prior statutes, enhanced by references to the decisions of the state supreme court,[306] and made even more accessible by an index. The codification was to be comprised of the 115 acts listed in the first section of this act, already passed individually by the general assembly, and the "acts of a public nature passed at this session."

While the legislative edition had contained the full text of these 115 acts, *The Revised Statutes* as ultimately published contained eight additional acts. These eight acts were:

- Chapter 1, Revised Statutes (ch. 26, Laws of N.C. 1836–'37)
- Chapter 27, County Boundaries (ch. 3, Laws of N.C. 1836–'37)
- Chapter 61, Internal Improvements (ch. 22 & 36, Laws of N.C. 1836–'37)
- Chapter 67, Draining Swamp Lands (ch. 23, Laws of N.C. 1836–'37)
- Chapter 68, Draining Matamuskeet Lake (ch. 25, Laws of N.C. 1836–'37)
- Chapter 69, Draining Swamp Lands (ch. 24, Laws of N.C. 1836–'37)
- Chapter 77, Names (ch. 15, Laws of N.C. 1836–'37)
- Chapter 93, Public Arms in Arsenals (ch. 34, Laws of N.C. 1836–'37)

Section 14 of the "Act Concerning the Revised Statutes" determined that copies of the published version of the codification would be evidence of the law in the same manner as the originals in the office of the Secretary of State. This topic was revisited in the next session because numerous errors were found in the enrollment which had to be corrected by the Commissioners before publication of *The Revised Statutes*. Under these circumstances, the general assembly enacted a provision that "the printed text of the said Statutes, as published by the said Commissioners, shall be held, deemed, and taken to be the true text of the said Statutes . . . any variance or variances therein from the enrolment [sic] of the said Statutes notwithstanding."[307]]

MISCELLANEOUS.

CHAP. XXVI.

An Act concerning the Revised Statutes.

Be it enacted by the General Assembly of the State of North Carolina, and it is hereby enacted by the authority of the same, That the following acts, passed at the present session of this General Assembly, and known as "the Revised Statutes," shall take effect and go into operation on the first day of January next and not sooner, except those as to which a different provision is expressly made therein, and the acts concerning Courts of Justice, the Militia, the collection and management of the public revenue, the Treasurer of the State and Comptroller, Pilots and pilotage, salaries and fees, which shall take effect immediately, to wit:

1. An act ascertaining the mode of proving book debts.
2. An act concerning entries and grants of land.
3. An act concerning wrecks, and wrecked property.
4. An act concerning the militia of this State.
5. An act concerning public documents.
6. An act concerning the mode of choosing Senators and Representatives in the Congress of the United States.
7. An act concerning bastardy, and prescribing the mode of legitimating bastard children in certain cases.
8. An act concerning divorce and alimony.
9. An act concerning attorneys at law.
10. An act concerning constables.
11. An act providing for the support of the poor.
12. An act concerning bail in civil cases.
13. An act concerning executors and administrators.
14. An act concerning Coroners.
15. An act concerning the Comptroller.
16. An act concerning quarantine, and to prevent the introduction and communication of contageous [sic] diseases.
17. An act concerning the Treasurer of the State.
18. An act to provide for the collection and management of a Revenue for this State.
19. An act concerning religious societies and congregations.
20. An act prescribing what shall be evidence in certain cases.
21. An act to prevent the abatement of suits in certain cases.

22. An act to prevent the destruction of oysters in this State.
23. An act concerning the Secretary of State.
24. An act concerning mad dogs.
25. An act concerning last wills and testaments.
26. An act for the relief of such persons as have been disabled by wounds, or rendered incapable of procuring for themselves and families subsistence, in the militia service of this State, and providing for the widows and orphans of such as have died.
27. An act concerning overseers.
28. An act for restraining the taking of excessive usury.
29. An act providing for the appointment of electors to vote for a President and Vice President of the United States.
30. An act concerning the action of replevin.
31. An act concerning hunting.
32. An act concerning the currency of this State.
33. An act concerning the draining of lands.
34. An act providing for the appointment of notaries.
35. An act concerning corporations.
36. An act to establish a fund for Internal Improvement and to create a board for the management thereof.
37. An act prescribing a mode by which partition of real and personal estates may be made among tenants in common, and in what cases such estates may be sold for a division.
38. An act to reduce into one the several acts concerning pilots and commissioners of navigation.
39. An act concerning the Attorney General and Solicitors for the State.
40. An act concerning strays.
41. An act concerning idiots and lunatics.
42. An act concerning weights and measures.
43. An act authorising attachments to issue for the recovery of debts and directing the proceedings thereon.
44. An act concerning iron and gold mines.
45. An act concerning fences.
46. An act to regulate descents.
47. An act concerning the appointment and duties of a patrol in each county.
48. An act concerning legacies, filial portions and distributive shares of intestate's estates.
49. An act concerning cattle, horses and hogs.
50. An act for the relief of sick and disabled American seamen.
51. An act concerning the repeal of statutes.
52. An act concerning incorporated towns.
53. An act to enable women in certain cases to maintain actions of slander.
54. An act concerning charities.
55. An act for regulating ordinaries.
56. An act concerning the University of North Carolina.

57. An act for the more effectual suppressing of vice and immorality.
58. An act prescribing the mode of recovering against certain officers therein mentioned, and their securities.
59. An act concerning apprentices.
60. An act concerning oaths.
61. An act concerning the Governor and Council of State.
62. An act concerning the improvement of rivers and creeks, and to prevent obstructions to their navigation.
63. An act concerning mills and millers.
64. An act concerning the appointment of guardians and the management of orphans and their estates.
65. An act for the relief of insolvent debtors.
66. An act concerning the Supreme Court.
67. An act concerning Courts of Equity.
69. An act concerning the powers and jurisdiction of Justices of the Peace.
70. An act appointing commissioners to take affidavits.
71. An act to empower the several County Courts to establish fairs in their respective counties.
72. An act declaring what parts of the common law shall be in force in this State.
73. An act prescribing the salaries and fees of the several officers of this State.
74. An act concerning offices.
75. An act concerning the burning of woods.
76. An act concerning the seat of Government and public buildings.
77. An act concerning surety and principal.
78. An act to create a fund for the establishment of common schools.
79. An act providing for the appointment and directing the duties of County Trustees.
80. An act concerning bills, bonds and promissory notes.
81. An act prescribing the mode of subjecting the lands of deceased debtors for the payment of their debts.
82. An act concerning auctions and auctioneers.
83. An act concerning the clerks of the County and Superior Courts.
84. An act concerning deeds and conveyances of lands and slaves, mortgages and powers of attorney, their execution, probate and registration.
85. An act concerning Sheriffs.
86. An act for limiting the time within which actions may be brought, and for quieting the title to lands and slaves, and prescribing the time within which presumption of satisfaction may arise.
87. An act concerning waste.
88. An act concerning gaming.
89. An act concerning the processioning of lauds.
90. An act concerning courts of justice, practice, pleas, and process.
91. An act concerning Registers.
92. An act prescribing the disposition of money remaining in the hands of clerks and sheriffs a certain time.

93. An act concerning court houses, prisons and stocks, and prescribing the appointment and duties of the Treasurer of public buildings.

94. An act concerning the appointment and duties of clerks and masters in equity.

95. An act concerning county revenue and county charges.

96. An act concerning marriage.

97. An act concerning prisoners.

98. An act for the prevention of frauds and fraudulent conveyances.

99. An act concerning estates.

100. An act concerning crimes and punishments.

101. An act concerning executions, and execution sales.

102. An act concerning appeals and proceedings in the nature of appeals.

103. An act concerning the General Assembly of the State of North Carolina.

104. An act concerning the public roads, ferries and bridges in this State.

105. An act concerning slaves and free persons of color.

106. An act concerning forcible entry and detainer.

107. An act concerning writs of quo warranto and mandamus.

108. An act to prohibit the circulation of Bank notes, under five dollars.

109. An act concerning the amendment of process, pleadings and other proceedings at law.

110. An act concerning widows.

111. An act to prevent the taking away of boats, canoes and pettiaugers from landings or elsewhere without leave.

112. An act concerning the public arms.

113. An act concerning proceedings in criminal cases.

114. An act for the better security of personal liberty.

115. An act for establishing public landings and places of inspection, and for the appointment of inspectors and regulation of inspections.

Sec. 2. All acts and parts of acts, passed before the present session of this General Assembly, the subjects whereof are revised and re-enacted in the Revised Statutes, or which are repugnant to the provisions therein contained, and all the statutes of England or Great Britain heretofore in use in this State, are hereby declared to be repealed, and of no force and effect from and after the first day of January next, with the exceptions and limitations hereafter mentioned. . . .

Sec. 9. The Revised Statutes enumerated in the first section of this act, shall not be published in the usual pamphlet form, (except those herein before directed to take effect immediately,) with the other acts of the present session, but shall be published in a separate volume, under the superintendence and direction of two commissioners, to be appointed by the Governor, who, in case of vacancy after the appointment, shall fill the same; who shall procure the same to be done in good style, upon the most economical terms, giving a preference, when the style and terms of printing are equal, to the printers of this State; shall take bond for the faithful performance of the work of those who may undertake the same. They shall be arranged, in the publication, in alphabetical order, according to their heads or titles, with marginal references as reported by the commissioners of revisal, and also with references to the decisions of the Supreme Court upon their subject, and with a full index. In the same volume shall be published the constitution of the United States, and the constitution and bill of rights of this State, and the Mecklenburg declaration of Independence, with a short narrative thereof. There shall also be published in the same volume, the acts of a public nature passed at this session, excluding all acts granting corporate privileges.

Sec. 10. There shall be published, in a second volume, the second charter of Charles the second, to the Lords Proprietors of this State; the Great Deed of Grant from the Lords Proprietors; the Grant from George the second to Earl Granville; and the following acts, to wit: all the acts relating to the boundaries of the State, and its several counties; all acts ceding the lands of this State to the General Government; all acts incorporating banks and rail road, turnpike and navigation companies, which are now in force and use; all acts relative to the incorporation or to the corporate powers of the Trustees of the University; and such other acts, now in force, and not repealed by this act, as the superintendents may in their discretion think proper to place in the said second volume....

Sec. 14. *Be it further enacted*, That the copies of the Revised Statutes, which shall be printed as aforesaid, shall be received as evidence of the law before all tribunals, and in all places, in the same manner, to all intents and purposes, as the originals in the office of the Secretary of State.

[Ratified 23rd January, 1837.]

Former governor James Iredell Jr. served as a commissioner on *The Revised Statutes*, 1837, and as reporter of opinions of the Supreme Court of North Carolina from 1840 to 1852. Photograph of portrait of James Iredell Jr. by William Garl Brown, 1858. (*Credit*: State Archives of North Carolina, Raleigh)

DOCUMENT II-43 REVISED STATUTES' PREFACE, 1837

[In this preface the commissioners acknowledged that *The Revised Statutes* "differ[ed] in its character from any heretofore executed . . ."[308] This codification settled one of the more vexing problems of the early years of the state—the question of which English statutes were in force here. When the general assembly put the codification into operation, it "repeal[ed] all the British acts." The general assembly also repealed all its public acts and thus the laws from prior sessions no longer needed to be consulted for one to know the public laws in force in 1837. These major changes, as well as the over-arching change from a chronologically arranged compilation of acts in force to a subject-arranged codification of positive laws, helped to "contribute in some degree at least, to the object for which they were designed, a simplification of the Statute Law and an extension of its knowledge among the people." One could hardly have expected to find a more Jacksonian sentiment.]

PREFACE.

THE revision and consolidation of the whole public statute law will constitute an important epoch in the legislative history of North Carolina. . . .

At the session of the General Assembly in 1787, it was enacted "That James Iredell be, and he is hereby appointed a commissioner to revise and compile the acts of the General Assemblies of the late Province and present State of North Carolina, and to insert the charter from the crown of Great Britain, &c.—and further, the said commissioner is hereby authorized and directed, in revising and collecting said acts, to leave out all laws repealed or obsolete, all private acts, and all other acts on which no question of property can arise: and further, the said commissioner is hereby required to see the said acts printed in the same order and in the same words in which they now stand, with marginal notes of the contents of each section, a marginal reference, and a copious general index with reference to each act, and the contents of each section." This duty was performed by the commissioner appointed, and the laws so revised printed by Hodge and Wills, at Edenton, in 1789, including the acts of 1788. It was approved in every respect by an act passed in 1791, and has since been commonly known as "Iredell's Revisal." In the year 1792, Francois Xavier Martin, in obedience to a resolution of the General Assembly of the preceding year, published a "Collection of the statutes of the Parliament of England in force in the State of North Carolina," of which work in may only be remarked that it was utterly unworthy of the talents and industry of the distinguished compiler, omitting many important statutes, always in force, and inserting many others, which never were, and never could have been in force, either in the Province or in the State of North Carolina. In the year 1794, also in pursuance of a resolution of the General Assembly of the preceding year, the same gentleman published "A collection of the private acts of the General Assembly, from the year 1715 to the year 1790, inclusive, now in force and use." In 1800, John Haywood, one of the judges of the superior courts of law, published "A Manual of the laws of North Carolina, arranged under distinct heads, in alphabetical order; with references from one head to another when a subject is mentioned in any other part of the book than under the distinct head to which it belongs." This work was a great favorite with the public, and passed through several editions. In 1803, it was resolved by the General Assembly "that Francois Xavier Martin collect and revise the public acts passed since the publication of Judge Iredell's Revisal, to the end of the present session inclusive; which said revisal shall connect the acts passed since Judge Iredell's by notes and remarks, adverting to such as appear to have been virtually repealed, and retaining such as are not expressly so, and cause his said revisal to be printed." This revisal was prepared and published by Mr Martin, and approved by the succeeding legislature. At the session of the General Assembly in 1817, it was enacted, "That a committee of three persons be appointed by joint ballot of both houses, whose duty it shall be to revise and consolidate the public acts, and parts of acts of the General Assembly of this State heretofore passed, or which may be passed before the completion of their work," and also, "That it shall be the duty of said commissioners to enumerate and specify those statutes and parts of statutes of Great Britain, which are in force within this State." The commissioners appointed were John Louis Taylor, chief justice of the supreme court, Henry Potter, judge of the district court of the United States, and Bartlet Yancy, speaker of the senate. The revisal, completed by these gentlemen after the manner of Iredell's revisal, was ordered by the legislature to be published, and was published in 1821, under the superintendence of Judge Potter, the acts of 1820 being included. This work has usually been called "the Revised Code," or the "New Revisal."

In concluding this sketch, the undersigned will offer a brief notice of the revisal now published, which differs in its character from any heretofore executed. At the session of the General Assembly in 1833, it was enacted, "that three commissioners be appointed by the governor of the State to collate, digest and revise, all the public statute laws of this State, commencing with the earliest English statutes now in force, and including those which may be enacted during the present session of this General Assembly; that in the performance of this duty they shall carefully collect and reduce into one act the different acts, and parts of acts, which, from similarity of subject ought, in their judgment, to be so arranged and consolidated, distributing the same under such titles, divisions and sections as they shall think proper, omitting all such acts, and parts of acts before passed as shall have either expired by their own limitation, become obsolete, or been repealed; that in every other respect they shall complete the said revision in such manner as to them shall seem most useful and proper to render said acts more plain and easy to be understood; and that, from time to time they shall lay before the legislature the acts so arranged and revised by them, to be re-enacted, if the legislature shall so determine." This act, though such a measure had long been desired by many intelligent citizens, owed its origin at this period, principally to the exertions of Governor Swain, who, in his annual message to the legislature had earnestly and eloquently urged its importance, and who manifested a deep solicitude for its success.

Soon after the passage of the act, the performance of the important duties which it required, was entrusted to the late Gavin Hogg, Esquire, of the city of Raleigh, in conjunction with the undersigned. At an early period after their appointment, the commissioners held a meeting, in which they made a cursory examination of the acts of assembly, and the British statutes in force in this State, and agreed upon the plan upon which the revisal should be conducted. With these preliminary arrangements, Mr Hogg's connection with the work ceased. Severe and protracted ill health prevented his further discharge of duties, upon the performance of which he had entered with zeal, and which no one was better qualified to perform in a manner creditable to himself and useful to the public. In the winter following, he resigned his commission, and the Hon. Frederic Nash, of Hillsborough, now one of the judges of the superior courts of this State, but then at the bar, was appointed to supply the vacancy. Reports of the plan and progress of the work were made by the commissioners to the governor, and through him to the legislature at its respective sessions in 1834 and 1835. The plan adopted by the commissioners was, in the language of one of their reports, "simply to digest and consolidate into one act, all the various statute laws relating to one subject, occasionally to alter vicious and inadvertent phraseology, and to insert into the body of the statute such new provisions as seemed to them manifestly proper;" and as regarded the British statutes, "to incorporate them in acts distributed according to the subject to which they relate, clothing them in a modern garb." Upon the report made at the session of 1834 no definite action was taken by the legislature, but that submitted at the subsequent session, was referred, together with several revised acts which had accompanied it, to a joint select committee of both houses, who, after having had the subject under consideration, reported that they deemed it inexpedient for the legislature at that session, "to attempt the re-enactment of any portion of the digest which had been completed." They, then, after expressing themselves "from a cursory examination, highly gratified both with the plan of the digest, which had been adopted, and the mode of its execution," recommended that the time for completing the revisal, which in the original act had been limited to two years, should be extended to the first day of December, 1836; that the revised acts which had been submitted by the commissioners should be returned to them, and that when they should have completed the residue, they should procure two hundred copies of the whole to be printed, and have them deposited in the governor's office for the use of the next General Assembly. A bill for that purpose was accordingly introduced, and passed, and at the session of 1836, the whole work was reported to the legislature, and with the report were transmitted the required number of printed copies of each of the revised acts for the use of the members. These acts, with the accompanying report, were referred to a joint select committee of six members from each house, by whom they were examined and reported from time to time, to one or the other of the houses, with such amendments as the committee thought proper to suggest, and were then passed separately, according to the forms usual in passing bills, except that they were not required to be engrossed after passing one house before they were sent to the other. After the revised statutes had been all acted upon by the legislature, an act entitled "An act concerning the Revised Statutes" was passed, which prescribes the time when they shall go into operation, provides for their publication and distribution, repeals all the British acts, and all the acts of our own legislature, the subjects of which had been revised, and directs that when published, the printed copies shall be received as evidence of the law. From this it will be perceived that the work now presented to the public has the very highest character of authenticity and authority.

It remains only for the undersigned to add a few remarks as to the manner in which their duties as superintendents of publication have been discharged. By reference to the ninth and tenth sections of the "Act concerning the Revised Statutes," will be seen the authority under which they were appointed, and the particular duties prescribed them. They have endeavored to comply strictly with the requisitions of that act. How far they have succeeded, it must be for others to determine. As regards the style of execution, and arrangement of the work, it will show for itself. The "Act concerning the Revised Statutes" has been placed as chapter first of the statutes contained in the first volume, and the revised acts themselves follow in alphabetical order. The other public acts, which were passed at the same session, and required to be inserted in the same volume with the revised statutes, have been either incorporated with them or published as separate chapters under the same general title where similarity of subject admitted, or have been placed under distinct heads but still in their proper alphabetical order. In annexing the references to the decisions of the supreme court, it was intended to place the cases referred to, in the margin opposite to the sections to which they related, but it was found that it could not be done without too much encumbering the page, and the references were therefore placed at the end of the respective chapters, but still noting the particular sections which they are designed to elucidate.

In preparing the materials directed to be published in the second volume, the superintendents found some difficulty in ascertaining and determining what acts relating to navigation companies were now "in force and use" so as to require their insertion. They were aware that there were several charters of those companies still in legal existence, but they had reasons to believe that the companies were so near a final extinction from nonuser or abandonment, that it was entirely useless to retain them. As they found that this volume when going to press would not be so large as they anticipated, the superintendents have ventured to insert in an appendix several articles which were deemed not inappropriate to such a work. These articles, comprising among others the great charters of English and American liberty, not already inserted, will, it is hoped, be found neither uninteresting nor uninstructive; and as those of them, which are not entirely new, are not often seen in works easily accessible to the public, it is trusted, that their appearance in their present position will be favorably received.

In the progress of these volumes through the press, one or the other of the superintendents has constantly attended to them, and every sheet has undergone his supervision and correction. With what accuracy this part of their duty has been performed, it is not for them to say. They have anxiously endeavored to have the typographical part of the work perfect, so far as their exertions could contribute towards so desirable an object. But yet from the great desire to have the volumes ready for distribution at as early a day as possible, their publication has been hastened in a manner inconsistent with entire correctness. It is hoped and believed however, that no error will be found, particularly in the body of the work, at all affecting the sense of the passage in which it may occur. It may be proper to mention here that the revised and other public acts contained in the first volume of this work, were regularly ratified in the usual form and signed by Messrs Hugh Waddell, speaker of the senate, and William H. Haywood, Jun., speaker of the house of commons, but the certificate of ratification has not been retained, because as the acts were passed separately, it would have presented a useless repetition.

With these explanations and remarks the "Revised Statutes" are submitted to a generous public, with the hope, that with the corrections and amendments which they received from the legislature and the sanction given to them by that body, they will contribute in some degree at least, to the object for which they were designed, a simplification of the Statute Law and an extension of its knowledge among the people.

JAMES IREDELL.
WILL: H. BATTLE.

Document II-44 Swaim's Preface, 1841

[Benjamin Swaim was known for his treatise, *The North Carolina Executor*; his newspaper, *The Southern Citizen* (published in New Salem in Randolph County); and his monthly law magazine, *The Man of Business*. Swaim's monthly magazine was intended "to render every man his own counselor in matters of ordinary business."[309] Swaim was president of the Manumission Society after 1827.[310] With the subsequent passage of harsh legislation, membership dropped, and the last meeting of the society was held at Marlborough Friends Meetinghouse in 1834, the "faithful attenders at this final session [being] Benj. Swaim, John Leonard and Wm. Raynolds . . ."[311]

The document excerpted below prefaced Swaim's small treatise about executors and administrators, a subject represented by five other documents in this compilation on nineteenth-century law reform in North Carolina.[312] The preface emphasized the author's interest in helping the layman,[313] though the layman was not meant as the exclusive audience of the work. "We have said that this work is intended *principally* to aid the general reader;—so it is. But we hope, as a sort of digest it will be useful to the profession."

Fannie Memory Farmer, in her 1953 article published in the *North Carolina Historical Review*, elaborated on the importance of this theme of assisting the layperson with legal needs. She wrote:

> Other aids included such materials as Benjamin Swaim's magazine, *The Man of Business*, which included much law, with supporting citations. Swaim had every number of the publication scrutinized by a member of the profession in hope of eliminating errors. He said that the purpose of the publication was to set forth the principles of law in easy and familiar style *so that any man with common sense* could ascertain what his legal rights were without the necessity of going to counsel. The advertisement of the magazine stated that the forms alone were worth the price of the subscription. Swaim also edited a book containing forms, statutes, digests of state Supreme Court decisions, and other pertinent information [entitled, *The North-Carolina Justice* (1839)]. When one remembers that he was a lawyer, one is amazed that Swaim was eager to help the common man and to assist him in being his own attorney.[314]

Swaim's faith in the common sense of the common man echoed the philosophy of Archibald Henderson of the prior generation[315] and foreshadowed a sentiment that would drive reformed procedure in North Carolina in the next generation.[316]]

PLAN OF THE WORK.

This book, it is believed, contains a careful collection of all the statute law of the State, now in force, on the subject of Executors and Administrators.—*Ten* chapters of the new "Revised Statutes of North Carolina" are copied entire, making *nine* chapters here; and, for convenient reference, the *number* and *order* of the sections are accurately preserved.

Our 1st chapter contains the 44th chapter of the Revised Statutes of 37 sections, and to each section are added such points of law as are considered to be of most practical utility, collected from the books of best authority on the common law, and from the Reports of the Supreme Court. We then completed this first chapter by adding a series of 22 sections more, arranged under apt heads, making 59 sections in all.

All the necessary and most approved Forms and Precedents, for carrying the subject matter into practical effect, are collected and inserted under their appropriate sections.

This description of the *first* chapter is given as a specimen of the whole: for the same plan is pursued throughout every chapter.

Our 2nd chapter, "Abatement," corresponds to the 2nd chapter of the Revised Statutes; our 3d "Descent of real estate"—to the 38th Revised Statutes. Our 4th "Wills and Testaments"—to the 122d Revised Statutes. Our 5th "Legacies, Fillial portions and Destributive shares"—to the 64th Revised Statutes. Our 6th "Lands of Deceased Debtors"—to the 63d Revised Statutes. Our 7th "Partition"—to the 85th Revised Statutes. Our 8th "Widows"—to the 121st Revised Statutes,—and our 9th "Guardian and Ward—Idiots and Lunatics"—to the 54th and 57th Revised Statutes.

All the alterations in and additions to the Revised Statutes that have been made by the Legislature down to the present time, are carefully inserted in their proper places.

In as much as this work is intended principally to aid the common reader in acquiring the knowledge and the practical application of this, perhaps the most generally important branch of the law,—great pains have been taken to simplify the subject as much as possible. And where technical expressions could not well be avoided, they are explained, either in the body of the work or in the Glossary, so as to be understood.

All possible brevity has been studied; and particularly in the forms,—some of which are taken from the old books, and shortened as much as could safely be done; but many of the forms have never before appeared in print.

We have said that this work is intended *principally* to aid the general reader;—so it is. But we hope, as a sort of digest it will be useful to the profession. In all the points of law herein stated, reference is generally made to the authority; and where no authority is referred to, the reader may understand that the author is responsible for the correctness of the point stated.

ASHEBOROUGH, N. C., *September*, 1841.

Document II-45 Administration of Justice, 1845

[This newspaper article from the *Raleigh North Carolina Standard* agreed with William Eaton Jr.'s preface to his *Book of Practical Forms* that the reality of practice in antebellum North Carolina was "utterly unexampled elsewhere" and did not match the law reflected in the statutes.[317] The writer of the article said, "The truth is, we have never possessed but its [the common law's] most attenuated shadow [in practice and procedure]. We have neither allegation of the plaintiff nor response of the defendant. . . ." The article argued that the rigid system of pleading in England, an essential part of the common law which North Carolina had received, had many advantages: it reduced cost and delay by requiring fewer witnesses; it eliminated surprise at trials; it maintained the distinction between law and fact which prevented the jury from usurping the role of judge; and it properly focused the attention of judge and jury. He hypothesized that emigration had kept the adulterated system prevailing in North Carolina from exploding—that, and the shining example of the top lawyers and judges.

One should not read this article, then, as being pro-codification or anti-common law, the author having asserted that the system of common law pleading is what gave the English common law the "precision and certainty entitling it to rank as a practical science." Rather than attack the common law, the writer sought stricter enforcement of common law pleading as a cost-effective and fair means of reaching judgments that could be reviewed when necessary. Yet the laxness in local practice identified by the author may help to explain the absence of complaint by laypersons, and newly educated lawyers alike, that pleading was a mysterious labyrinth of arbitrary rules designed to give the older members of the profession an advantage. Perhaps due to loose practice in antebellum North Carolina, anyone could be his own lawyer before adoption of *The Code of Civil Procedure* in 1868, so long as the local clerk of court and judge provided the clues to solve a less scholastic sort of mystery—the mystery of unwritten local practice.]

The Administration of Justice in North Carolina.—(No. 4.)

Superior Courts. Next in order are the Superior Courts, in which a Judge educated in the law presides. It is unnecessary to say that any defects we find in this Court are unconnected with its constitution or the character and qualifications of its Judges. As a body they are entitled to encomium and respect, and individuals might be selected worthy of comparison with the Judges of any land. The evils we find exist mostly in the practice rather than in the theory of this Court as established by law, and yet they are those which the present Judges have not established, and for the continuance of which to the present period they cannot justly be held responsible. They exist principally in the mode of presenting issues of fact to the jury, known as pleading. The same exist to even a greater extent in the County Courts. Want of space will prevent our giving to the subject the full examination its importance warrants, and we fear after all the full extent of its importance and of the existing errors can be estimated only by the profession. We regret the less, however, the necessity of brevity, because we feel assured that the opinions we shall advance are those held by the most eminent as well as the most numerous part of the profession.

With the laws of England our ancestors received its system of pleading. The system, indeed, is an essential part of the common law. It is a system of unrivalled excellence, the result of long experience gradually adopted and perfected to fulfil [sic] an unchanging want. Perhaps no human invention was ever more perfectly adapted to its end. It was really what Lord Coke called it, the life and soul of the law; and alone could give it that precision and certainty entitling it to rank as a practical science. It has received and deserved the encomiums of every distinguished lawyer from Coke to Stephens. Its object was the production of an issue by which some single and material fact should be asserted on one side and denied on the other. It is obvious that one or more of these material facts exists in every suit not turning entirely on a question of law, and the affirmance or negation of either of these would decide the controversy between the parties. The production of this issue was accomplished by following or imitating the natural and logical order of parties orally stating a claim and a defence. In the first place the plaintiff makes his complaint: if the defendant admits it and says it does not constitute an injury in law, then nothing remains but for the Judge to decide whether it does or not; if he denies any material fact entering into the complaint, an issue is formed at once for the jury to decide affirmatively or negatively: and so in like manner if the defendant admits the allegations of the plaintiff, but alleges a new fact in justification, which the plaintiff admits or denies in his turn. In this manner, ultimately, the kernel of the controversy is reached, some single and material fact decisive of the whole merits is affirmed and denied.

The advantages of thus narrowing the issue must be obvious. In every cause, by far the greater number of facts constituting a claim or a defence are really not in dispute. Yet, unless the issue be confined to some one or more which are really disputed, witnesses must be in attendance to prove the whole; and if a party fail, from ignorance, accident or surprise, in the full technical proof of any one, no matter how notorious it may be, he fails in his claim or defence. But by thus narrowing the issue, the attendance of numerous witnesses, the greatest source of cost, is dispensed with. The most common cause of delay—their absence when required—is removed. The parties know the precise fact to be decided, and come prepared to try it; the decision of the jury, from their attention being confined to one single contested fact and not dissipated over a multitude, is much more likely to be right. The parties not being deceived or surprised, are much more likely to be satisfied. And should any error occur in the course of the trial, or any misapprehension of the law by the jury, it can be more easily seen and corrected by the Court; and finally, should the jury give a wrong verdict under the influence of improper motives or caprice, the fact will be more obvious. These are some of the inappreciable advantages of a rigid system of pleading.

It is true that for a number of years past considerable relaxation had been allowed in the English practice, from the rigor of this system; but it is equally true that, urged by a strong sense of the evils attending the relaxation, enlightened by experience, and after great deliberation, with the approbation of all the Judges and the vast majority of the eminent of the profession the practice has been brought back in England, by recent acts of Parliament and rules of Court, to all the pristine and theoretical rigor of the system. The beneficial effects of the reform are generally acknowledged. Mr. Chitty enumerates among them "reducing the number of witnesses and the expense of evidence on a trial."—(3 *Gen. Prac.* 427.) And again he says: "Whilst the *abuse* of the plea of non assumpsit or other general issue was permitted, the jury, according to their general view of the *whole* of the plaintiff's or the defendant's case, or even their unjust *prejudice*, used frequently to find their verdict for the plaintiff or defendant, generally without assigning or perhaps being able to assign one adequate reason or ground or stating on what particular point they found. But now, when issues are so much more precise and limited to the existence of one particular fact, a different result must be experienced; and if the jury should find a perverse verdict, contrary to the evidence and the Judges direction, their misconduct can be more readily detected and remedied on a motion for a new trial."—(*Ib. p.* 918.)

This admirable system, one would suppose from an examination of our statute book, was fully enjoyed in North Carolina. It is, as we said, a part of the common law, and the common law has been adopted by express enactment. Moreover, the statute prescribes when declarations and pleas shall be filed and demurers argued, and that an "entire and perfect record" of the proceedings in each suit shall be made. The truth is, we have never possessed but its most attenuated shadow. We have neither allegation of the plaintiff nor response of the defendant. The one does not know before trial what he is sued for, nor the other what defence is set up in his demand. All the witnesses are summoned that can possibly in any event be wanted, and every point going to make up a case or defence is labored before the jury with as much copiousness as if that were the sole point in controversy between the parties. The result is a monstrous accumulation of unnecessary witnesses at enormous cost; repeated continuances and delays; constant surprise at trials, and consequent dissatisfaction; and frequent irreparable error and injustice. The attention of the Court and jury being spread over a vast surface of facts, it is impossible that they should within the brief time allowed for deliberation accurately separate those which are of the essence of the case from those which are entirely irrelevant or merely in aggravation or extenuation, and adequately weigh their respective importance and draw the proper inferences from each. The judgment is much more likely to be confused by the attention being artfully misled to immaterial points, or to become bewildered in a maze of complicated facts. Questions of law and fact become inextricably blended, and the jury usurps of necessity and with impunity the functions of the Court. A case presented in this way is like a ship without a rudder committed to the wind and waves—it is utterly uncertain into what port she may be blown.

We believe the practice prevailing in North Carolina, in this respect, to be utterly unexampled elsewhere. And it cannot fail, on consideration, to strike every one with astonishment how we have been able to get along for a century under a system compared with which the rudest and most aboriginal form of settling disputes, arbitration by neighbors, is vastly superior. It must have originated about those times when a Commissioner from Virginia visited this Province for the purpose of running the boundary, and left it on record that there was not a meeting-house or a clergyman in the country; that fat pork fried in New England rum was the chief delicacy of the table; and that law and physic were both very plenty, very cheap, and very bad in their kind. (*Jour. of* — 1736.)

Another effect of this practice is to deprive parties almost entirely of a most important right secured by statute—the right to a writ of error for error in the record. There being no record there can be of course no apparent error. It would be a disagreeable and unnecessary inquiry as to whether the Bench or the Bar are most responsible for this shameful state of practice. We think it must be admitted, however, that the remedy can only come from the bench. It was, we believe, under a statute not more comprehensive than that which *requires* our Supreme Court to prescribe rules of practice for the Superior Courts, that the English Judges commenced their celebrated reforms. And we may be permitted to say that, in our humble opinion, it would tend more to the solid honor and usefulness of that Court, to *lead* public opinion in this important measure than to delay until public opinion shall have become sufficiently enlightened to urge its wants.

It may not be inappropriate to add a few remarks on the influence of the system and practice we have been discussing, on the character of the bar. Learning and elevated character are essential in the law, not merely because it is the reservoir for the supply of the bench, but because of the direct and important influence it exercises both on the bench and on the community. The bar of North Carolina have always been happily remarkable for these high qualities. Yet it cannot be denied that it must be attributed more to other causes than to any thing in the established system. Perhaps the most effective of these, hitherto operative, have been the influence of the example of some of its most eminent early members, and the absence of that keen competition which exists in more populous communities. Unexampled emigration has checked the population of North Carolina so that it has not doubled in fifty years, and the census shows a smaller proportion of professional persons in it than in any other State in the Union. With the cessation of emigration must come competition. The looseness of the mode of pleading and of conducting trials, the indefinite nature of the questions presented to juries, the general ignorance of juries, in the inferior Courts the ignorance of the Courts themselves, are so many encouragements to ignorance and unworthy conduct in the bar. Doubtless the many shining examples now in the profession will long continue to exert a salutary influence; but who will say, that in time the degrading agents will not have their natural operation? that an useless knowledge will not cease to be cultivated, and the facility of imposing on the ignorance of juries exercising such latitudinous powers, will not give to the art of persuasion an undesirable superiority of attraction over the more difficult and useful study of the principles of law?

Document II-46   Smith's Preface, 1846

[Attorney James Smith admitted in his preface to a treatise on civil practice that "practice in most of the States . . . has departed from any textual rule, and is a matter of tradition merely," but conjectured that "no State is more loose in its practice than [North Carolina]."[318] While nonchalance about technicalities relieved the lay advocate of much disadvantage, Smith thought that disregard of technicalities was a disgrace to the profession. Smith's book was a remedy for the nonchalance and unwrittenness of the state's civil practice—that is, for its "hidden mystery of legal procedure." It was a remedy provided especially for the unapprenticed youthful attorney for use against the seasoned professional. The focus of the author was on the antebellum county courts rather than the superior courts.]

PREFACE.

No apology, but that of necessity, is offered to the public for the appearance of this work. Hitherto, there has been a general complaint made by the members of the bar in North Carolina, on account of the non-existence of a treatise upon the subject of the practice of the law. It is not intended to state that this complaint has been made by the old practitioners, yet among the less experienced attorneys, it has been almost universal. So, it is quite correct to say, that the want of some work purporting to give the existing practice of the court, in which the *desideratum* is mostly located, has been sadly experienced by the bar of this State.

It is well known that the practice in most of the States in the Union has departed from any textual rule, and is a matter of tradition merely; and it is probably true, that no State is more loose in its practice than this. No condemnation is expressed, or even designed, against the courts here or elsewhere, for this kind of practice; for there is nothing without a cause, and if a reduction of stale rules and precepts had not been advisable from the course of events, the practice here would nothing differ from what it is in England, or, perhaps, in some of the States of the Union. All that it is here intended to say is, that since the practice is thus altered by the courts and the profession, and is satisfactory to the people, judging from their acquiescence therein for so long a time without any wish for a change, it is but just and proper that it should be condensed into a convenient system, and handed to those who may be interested in the proceedings of the courts.

After suffering for the usual term of years as a novice and probationer, the author of this work still waited for some member of the bar to take the matter in hand, and relieve the public necessity. But though the wish for a treatise was so common, and often expressed on all sides, still none presumed upon the charity of the citizens of their State so far as to enter upon the undertaking, or had time and opportunity for the important and heavy task before them. It, therefore, seemed to devolve on the author by virtue of the public silence, and hence the present work has been planned and perfected; and, after much labor and expense, borne by the author and proprietor respectively, it makes its appearance, and claims that patronage and support from the intelligent citizens of North Carolina which the wants of the people and the characteristic humanity of the State may be justified in bestowing.

But although the auspices under which this production issues bid so fair, yet a very slight knowledge of human nature serves to foretel [sic] that out of so many who are practitioners, and labor in the profession for a livelihood, there may be some who, having endured the servitude of the novitiate, and are enabled to look back upon that as something in the dim distance of the past, will not only be slow to perceive any peculiar merit in the work, but will anathematize it,—inasmuch as it is measurably intended for the youthful members of the bar, and lets them into the labyrinthian avenues of the existing practice, and places them, with infinite ease to themselves, upon an equal footing with those who have served their apprenticeship.

And if the memory of departed worth permitted, this premonition just alluded to might be further strengthened by insinuations already made partially public, "that it was just that the attorneys who had but entered upon their professional career, should be made to serve their time in the practice, and glean, as they might, the stray thought and wisdom of the superiors." *But such is not the spirit of this age*, and let the sentiment slumber with him who uttered it.

A few may, therefore, arraign the author of this treatise as dealing uncharitably with the older members of the bar, by so largely favoring those who are less experienced; but against such the author is prepared, and thus prepares the public mind.

But as an instance of the sympathy of the aged practitioner has been given, and expectation aroused as to others of a similar character, it cannot be suppressed that the young advocates of this State have been greatly favored with attentions from those who were their elder brethren; and so general and constant has been this devotedness to the furtherance of youthful investigation, that it has become a striking feature in the character of the bar. But because there is so much humanity felt and exhibited in this way, it is surely no reason why it should be forever taxed. A respite is, therefore, offered to those who have demeaned themselves so nobly, and the author, and, no doubt, hundreds of other attorneys, respond with tenderest emotion to the magnanimity which prompted such timely aid.

Again,—there are some who have too much pride of feeling, or are at least too timid to apply to the judges or experienced lawyers at the bar, for the information they need, and therefore, prefer remaining in ignorance as to any particular fact, rather than suffer the mortification attendant upon an exhibition of their weakness—if it can be called a weakness—not to know what there is no means of knowing. And besides this private evidence of folly, how many there are who suffer more during one short term of the court by the advantage those who have been long in the practice have over them simply in matters of mere form and ceremony, than a rich ingathering of profits ever repays them for. This should not be; and if there be a distinction to be drawn between the members of the bar, let it not lie in the ceremony of the practice, but in the manifestations of superior judgment and learning.

Not only so, but how many attorneys come to the bar without any knowledge of the practice at all, being expected by the judges who grant them their license to be only acquainted with the *written* law? The result is easily conjectured; for whilst one cannot file his first declaration, another cannot draw his demurrer to it. So clients, imagining that the license to practice presupposes a thorough knowledge of the law, and that the law and the practice are synonymous terms, and finding so much of what appears real ignorance, neglect such counsellors, and indignantly betake themselves to those who have not half the mind, nor a third of the learning, yet who happen to be acquainted with the hidden mystery of legal procedure.

The evil is, therefore, at once discovered, which it is the partial aim of this volume to remedy, and it is put forth mainly with this view; and this object alone gives the work a claim to public notice if not public favor.

But it will be furthermore perceived, that the work is an auxiliary to the officers of the court, from the chairman down to the clerk; and that no magistrate can be too familiar with its contents, so far as it relates to his functions.

And should the author forbear to suggest, though with becoming diffidence, that the authorities upon which the work is grounded should claim the regard of those who have risen high by their genius and effort? Their numbers and the care with which they have been selected foster the hope.

The work purports to be a system of civil practice, as found existing in the County Courts, and the design has been not to go out of the boundaries it prescribes; and, in fact, to detail only that portion of the practice which is of most common use. In giving the practice of the County Court, however, the most of the proceedings in the Superior Court are also given,—the variance between the conduct of the one and of the other being extremely slight.

With these remarks, the volume issues, and the lenity of the public is asked, so far as an examination of the contents may be concerned; and should it prove auxiliary to the practice in the courts by relieving any in their necessities, the time spent in careful thought over its pages, will find a recompense in the good thus effected by the treatise.

THE AUTHOR.

Document II-47 Nash on the Common Law, 1849

[Associate Judge Frederick Nash became a member of the Supreme Court of North Carolina in 1844. Prior to that, he had served as a code commissioner for *The Revised Statutes* with William H. Battle and James Iredell Jr., and had taught law with John L. Bailey in Hillsborough. Born in 1781, Nash was older than his brethren on the supreme court, which may account for his unwavering confidence in the common law as a system of principles and his view that they admirably fenced in judicial discretion, as expressed in his concurrence in *State v. Cæsar* in June term 1849.]

THE STATE *vs.* CÆSAR, A SLAVE....

NASH, J. I concur with Judge PEARSON in the opinion ...

... But I am called on, not only to abrogate one rule, but, necessarily, to introduce another.... I ask for the authority so to declare.... It does not belong to the bench, but to the halls of legislation.... I see no authority in the Courts of justice, to make the alteration. The evil is not one, which calls upon the Court to abandon their appropriate duty, that of enforcing the law as they find it. The Legislature, and only the Legislature, can alter the law.... This is a new case, and I feel, not only justified, but commanded to adhere to the common law.... Not only do I not see my way clear as a sunbeam, but my path, the moment I desert the well known principles of the common law, is obscured by doubts and uncertainties.... Why should I desert this safe guide, to wander in the mazes of judicial discretion, and that too, in a case of life and death; and which has been correctly designated by this Court, in a recent case, as the worst and most dangerous of tyrannies....

DOCUMENT II–48   PEARSON ON THE COMMON LAW, 1850

[In describing his views on the codification debates of the nineteenth century, Professor Mark Tushnet pointed to the language of appellate judges concerning the common law and cited such cases as *State v. Jowers* from 1850. Tushnet argued:

> The implicit contrast [in the judges' description of the common law] was with a legislative code, which could not readily adapt to the growth of a new class such as that of free blacks. The accuracy of this contrast can of course be questioned ... But that the contrast underlay the opinion is unquestionable.[319]

In *Jowers*, Judge Richmond Pearson described the common law as principled and flexible,[320] and codification as not so.[321]]

THE STATE *vs.* ATLAS JOWERS....

PEARSON, J....

Such a being as a slave or a free negro, did not exist when the ancient common law was in force. But the excellence of that "perfection of reason" consists in the fact, that it is flexible and its principles expand, so as to accommodate it to any new exigence or condition of society, like the bark of a tree, which opens and enlarges itself, according to the growth thereof, always maintaining its own uniformity and consistency.

DOCUMENT II–49   PEARSON ON THE COMMON LAW, 1851

[In *Gaskill v. King* from 1851, Judge Richmond Pearson described common law as a science, by which he meant a liberal discipline having general principles and proceeding by reason.[322] His dissenting opinion contrasted principle and authority.]

ELIJAH GASKILL *v.* WILLIAM C. KING....

PEARSON, J. *dissentiente*....

My idea is, that "law" is not a mere list of decided cases, but a "*liberal science*," based on general principles and correct reasoning. Cases are mere evidences of what the law is; and if a case is found to be unsupported by principle and "the reason of the thing," the Court is no more bound to follow it, than is a jury bound to believe a witness, who is discredited by proof of his bad character, or his demeanor or direct contradiction. In the one, there is a *sworn* witness: in the other, there is a decided case—both are *prima facie* entitled to credit, until the contrary is made to appear.

It is true, law should be "fixed and steady;" but it is also true, it should be "reasonable and right." The latter is the most important; because, without it, the former object cannot be attained. There are two

Frederick Nash served as a commissioner on *The Revised Statutes*, 1837, and assisted in the development of the state's common law during his tenure on the Supreme Court of North Carolina. Photograph of a portrait of Frederick Nash by William Garl Brown, 1888. (*Credit*: State Archives of North Carolina, Raleigh)

extremes—a disregard of authority, which I disclaim; and a blindfolded following of cases, which I also disclaim, as not only absurd, but impossible, (for, suppose a Court, in attempting to follow a case, should "miss the point," which case is then to be followed?) There is a medium, which I try to adhere to—take a comprehensive view of all of the cases from the "year books" down to the present time—has not this middle course been adopted and acted on throughout? Is it not supported by good sense and general practice? Let a case be taken, as settling the law, *prima facie*; but if it is shown, not to be supported by principle and "the reason of the thing," let it be over-ruled—the sooner the better; for, if the error is allowed to spread, it may insinuate itself into so many parts, and become so much ramified, as to make it impossible to eradicate it, without doing more harm than good. But if the seed has not spread too much, pull it up and throw it away.

DOCUMENT II–50 NASH ON LOCAL PRACTICE, 1853

[The looseness of common law practice in North Carolina, as recognized in the *Raleigh North Carolina Standard*,[323] the preface to Smith's *Civil Practice*,[324] and the preface to Eaton's *Book of Practical Forms*,[325] is here acknowledged by the supreme court in its August 1853 opinion in *Patton v. Marr* from its Morganton term of court.]

A. J. PATTON *vs.* WILLIAM MARR. . . .

NASH, C. J. . . .

It cannot be doubted, that according to the authorities cited by the plaintiff's counsel, the return in this case is informal, and under the practice in the English Courts would not be sustained; and we admit that the reasons assigned at the bar are very strong to show that the same strictness should be observed here. Neither in England however, nor here, is there any legislative act directing in what manner a sheriff shall make his return in such a case. In both countries it is a matter of practice adopted by the Courts, and such practice, when sanctioned by time, becomes the law of the Court. In England, whose judicial history reaches back to a very remote period, a strict adherence to forms is required, from which the Courts in this State have, in a great measure, departed. From the circumstances under which our judicial system came into existence, it was soon found that such a departure was necessary. The cumbrous forms sanctioned by time *there*, did not suit the wilderness here, and in consequence, following in the footsteps of those who had gone before them, a system was adopted which, while it recognised the value of placing on record the pleas exhibiting the controversy between the parties, greatly relaxed the rigid adherence to mere matters of form, both in the judicial proceedings of our Superior Courts, and in the acts of our executive officers, in making their returns. Our reports are full of such cases, required alike for the security of suitors and others deriving title under official sales. . . .

DOCUMENT II–51 REVISED CODE'S PREFACE, 1854

[Of the four men associated with the project of re-codifying the public laws of the state in 1854, Romulus Mitchell Saunders, Asa Biggs, William Rodman, and Bartholomew F. Moore,[326] credit went chiefly to Moore and to Biggs for the actual codification and consolidation of the acts of North Carolina.[327] Moore and Rodman supervised and directed the printing and publishing of the code.

The question recurs whether the *Revised Code* of 1854 differed in important respects from *The Revised Statutes* of 1837. The latter codification had broken radically with the past in the treatment of the written law in North Carolina, much as moderate codification had broken with the past in New York in the 1820s. Did our *Revised Code* continue in this genre, or was it rather a transformation to a new outlook or even a retreat to less radical thinking? The preface to the *Revised Code*, reprinted below, offered a response, asserting that the commissioners,

> departed in one respect, very essentially from the course pursued by former commissioners; they not only compiled, and brought together the different acts, and parts of acts on the same subjects; but they consolidated them, by fusing them together, and giving them the character of a single enactment; and as to a great many, and indeed most of the acts, they expunged the verbiage, where it was merely cumbersome and imparted no aid in ascertaining the meaning of the law.

Beyond "fusing" disparate acts on the same subject, the *Revised Code* also enlarged and enhanced the marginal digests of the sections of the acts and moved to the "lead case" method of referring to relevant decisions of the supreme court.]

PREFACE

CONTINUED BY THE COMMISSIONERS OF 1854.

AT the session of the General Assembly, in 1833, it was enacted, that three commissioners should be appointed by the Governor, "to collate, digest, and revise, all the public statute laws of the State," with instructions to reduce into one act, all acts and parts of acts upon the same subject, and distribute the acts thus consolidated, under proper titles, divisions, and sections. For this purpose the late Gavin Hogg, Esq., and Gov. Iredell, with the Hon. William H. Battle, now a judge of the Supreme Court, were appointed. Mr. Hogg, by reason of ill health, soon abandoned the commission; and the vacancy was filled with the Hon. Frederic Nash, now chief justice of the Supreme Court. The plan of revision adopted, was "simply to digest and consolidate into one act, all the various statute laws relating to one subject, occasionally to alter vicious and inadvertent phraseology, and to insert into the body of the statute, such new provisions as seemed to them manifestly proper," and to incorporate with them, such British statutes as were in force.

The work was finally reported to the General Assembly of 1836; and at that session, the acts thus digested, were amended and passed into laws, entitled, "The Revised Statutes," which were comprised wholly in the first volume printed under that title,—the second volume being little else than a collection of charters, and boundaries of counties.

This was a work much demanded, and was favorably received by the public. From the construction, however, put on their powers by the commissioners, very little change was made in the language of the statutes, as they were originally enacted, or last revised. To some extent, and in cases very palpably requiring it, this was done by the legislature of 1836.

In 1850, the General Assembly deeming another revisal of the statutes necessary, empowered the Governor to appoint three commissioners for that purpose, with instructions similar to those prescribed in the act of 1833. The undersigned B. F. Moore, with the Hon. R. M. Saunders, and the Hon. Asa Biggs were appointed; and after some progress in the work, Mr. Saunders resigned. At the ensuing session of the Legislature, Messrs. Biggs and Moore were directed to continue and complete the unfinished work. In its execution, (to use the language of their report to the General Assembly of 1854,) they "departed in one respect, very essentially from the course pursued by former commissioners; they not only compiled, and brought together the different acts, and parts of acts on the same subjects; but they consolidated them, by fusing them together, and giving them the character of a single enactment; and as to a great many, and indeed most of the acts, they expunged the verbiage, where it was merely cumbersome and imparted no aid in ascertaining the meaning of the law."

The laws as revised and reported, with such alterations and amendments as were deemed proper, were passed; and have now become the law of the land, under the title of "The Revised Code of North Carolina."

By virtue of the "act concerning the Revised Code," the undersigned were appointed superintendents of publication. In that act are prescribed their duties. The marginal digests of the sections of the acts as first published, have not been revised for many years past, imperfect and scant as they were. Although a great part of them was the hasty work of the public printer, they had undergone no change, and furnished almost the entire material of the index to the matter contained in the statutes. These digests have been greatly enlarged in number, and most of them were corrected in phrase, by the commissioners of revision; and all have received, at the hands of the undersigned, much additional alteration. The Constitutions of the State, and the United States, they have caused to be printed with a marginal digest, and an index following each instrument.

In regard to the references to the decisions of the Supreme Court, they have felt much embarrassed. These decisions have greatly increased in number since the publication of the Revised Statutes in 1837. To have referred to those only, which directly construed the words of the statutes, would have answered, very imperfectly, the end designed; to have referred to all indirectly connected with the statute, would have been cumbrous. Moreover, in not a few instances, the known purpose of laws having been defeated by judicial decision, (a calamity which sometimes befalls the best considered acts,) an attempt has been made to regain the purpose, by a change, in the Revised Code, of the language which defeated it. In such cases the decision is of little consequence, except, perhaps, to aid the inquiring lawyer to discover, that the case is of no authority against a change of the construction, while it may mislead those who skim the surface of investigation. In such cases, they have not prescribed for themselves any inflexible rule, but have endeavored to refer to all the leading cases connected with each subject, which they thought the practising lawyer would likely be desirous to use. Notwithstanding all the care which the commissioners have been able to use, imperfections will doubtless exist in their work; but having discharged their duty, with faithful purpose and industry, they submit it to the public.

B. F. MOORE,
WILL. B. RODMAN.

Document II-52   Eaton's Preface, 1854

[In his preface to his 1854 book of practical forms, William Eaton Jr.[328] provided several examples of how North Carolina had been injured by the "slovenly manner in which her records are made up." Instead of advising the abandonment of common law pleading and the adoption of a code in the style of New York's practice and procedure, Eaton responded by distributing his expert knowledge in procedure in a book of forms, thus benefitting especially "the junior members of the profession" who would otherwise be beholden to the elder members. Eaton was not the first to notice looseness of local practice and to offer the solution of a treatise for junior members of the bar.[329] Eaton also noted in his preface that changes in practice in England which made the law of England "very different" from that of North Carolina and explained that under such circumstances he had relied upon editions of Chitty and of Stephens published prior to the changes in English procedure.]

PREFACE.

In submitting the present work to the indulgent consideration of the profession, reason and custom require of me to offer a few remarks in reference to its plan, and the purposes which it is intended to accomplish. The object of the author is to present to his professional brethren, in one volume of convenient size, a variety of legal precedents; indeed, almost every form which they will have occasion to use in the ordinary routine of practice. Many of these precedents have been selected from standard works of England, while a very considerable number of them are not to be found in any other book whatever, though of frequent use. The selections are from various sources, the author being careful to get the best, to select those most likely to be needed in this State, and to adapt them, when necessary, to our practice.* The question may be asked, what necessity exists for a new collection of legal precedents, when recourse may be had to the finished productions of Wentworth, Lilly, Tidd, Chitty, Archbold, and others? To this question it is presumed that satisfactory answers may be given. A judicious selection from legal productions like the above, of the forms most likely to be needed here, would of itself be highly useful to the practising lawyer. It will be remembered, too, that many of the English forms require to be somewhat modified, so as to be adapted to our practice, especially since the adoption of the new rules in England,[**] which are not in force in North Carolina, and nearly all of the English works upon the subject of pleading now to be found upon the shelves of the book-stores, or in the lawyer's library, have been published since the adoption of the new rules, and have been written with especial reference to them.

Besides, there are many forms, of constant use in our own Courts, which are not to be found in any book, English or American. In reference to those which are peculiar to our own practice, the junior members of the profession have often experienced great and perplexing difficulties.

It may also be asked, why draw declarations, pleas, &c., for the North Carolina lawyer, when it is notorious that, according to an understanding among members of the bar in the County and Superior Courts, regular pleadings are rarely filed, the writ generally standing in the place of writ and declaration, and a mere memorandum of the grounds of the defence answering the purpose of formal pleas. The usage above referred to does unfortunately prevail in every part of the State. It is a custom deeply to be regretted, one of which is directly repugnant to law, which has contributed to lower the standard of professional skill and proficiency in North Carolina, which has in many respects embarrassed the administration of justice in our own tribunals, and which has caused our records, when copies have been sent abroad, sometimes to be held insufficient, and frequently to be the subject of ridicule. Whenever the Judges of the Supreme Court have alluded to this practice, as they sometimes have had occasion incidentally to do, it has always been in terms of disapprobation; and the author does not believe that there is a single Judge upon the Superior Court Bench, who does not entertain the same opinions upon the subject. The ablest lawyers among us have regretted the practice, and enlightened jurists abroad have been astonished that it could have existed for a single hour in the land of Murphy, Gaston, and Ruffin, and in a State whose judicial decisions have been referred to with respect by Marshall and Kent. The record ought to show distinctly and with certainty the nature of the demand and the grounds of the defence, and present with precision the points to be decided, but a record in this State does not usually accomplish these objects.

A hope is indulged that gentlemen of the bar, impelled by a generous ambition and proper feelings of professional pride, and also by a sense of duty to their clients, the courts and the public, will yet apply the proper corrective to this mischief by their own voluntary action. They certainly have intelligence enough to appreciate the maxim of Coke, "*Ordine placitandi servato, servatur et jus.*" If, however, all hope of reform shall terminate in disappointment, still the forms of regular pleadings contained in this volume will not be void of practical utility. The Act of Assembly creating the Supreme Court requires of the Judges to inspect the whole record, and to render thereon the proper judgment of law, and as appeals were frequently brought to the Supreme Court upon transcripts in which the pleadings were not otherwise set forth than by an abstract or memorandum thereof, so that it was very difficult if not impossible for the Court to comply with the requirements of the law, a rule was adopted at December Term, 1836, that no final judgment should thereafter be entered in any case in that Court until the declaration and other pleadings shall have been fully made up and entered of record. In the case of Runyon v. Anderson, 3 Ired. 586, the appeal was dismissed at June Term, 1843, because no pleadings were sent up, and the parties upon proper notice failed to file them, and the reporter in a note to that case observes that it is the invariable rule of the Supreme Court to enter no judgment at law until the pleadings have been filed. Even in the County and Superior Courts, the rule of practice dispensing with declarations and other formal pleadings has not, so far as my information extends, been understood to apply to actions for slander, libel, and some others. In the course of professional duty it is frequently necessary to have the pleadings full, formal, and accurate, in order that the judgment may be sued upon in another State, and in most if not all of them a record without a declaration, is no record at all. It should be remembered, too, that the want of a declaration may be, and sometimes is objected to by the defendant himself at the appearance term, without regard to the usage among members of the bar. This, however, is rarely done, and is certainly looked upon with some degree of odium.

If the profession shall continue to indulge itself in the present loose practice, they will find in these pages, and at the head of each of the precedents of the defendant's pleadings, the appropriate memoranda of pleas usually adopted among us in the several actions.

By far the greater portion of the precedents in this volume, it is confidently believed, will be of almost constant use to the practising lawyer in this State, even if the present loose system shall continue, and the author most respectfully invites members of the bar, in order that they may be satisfied upon the subject, to examine his table of contents, especially the first page, and the last eight pages which contain a list of the most practically useful forms.

The present is not merely a book of forms and entries but it contains many notes upon the precedents, many practical remarks and suggestions, and copious references to Acts of Assembly, decisions of the Supreme Court, and to standard works, both English and American. After the several pleas, I have been careful to show, from the highest authorities, what may be given in evidence under each. This was deemed necessary, inasmuch as the editions of Chitty and Stephen, now in general use, were written since the adoption of the new rules in England, and set forth the law upon the subject as modified by these rules. The law of England is now very different from that of North Carolina as to what defences are available under the general issue, and what must be specially pleaded, particularly in the action of assumpsit, in which the late reforms have greatly narrowed the scope of the general issue.[***] In setting forth the law upon this important subject, to avoid the least confusion, I have used editions of works which were published anterior to the changes above mentioned, and have generally copied from them so much of the law upon the subject as was deemed appropriate.

I have endeavored in the notes to show in what cases it might be important for the plaintiff to insert a particular count in the declaration, or for the defendant to rely upon a particular defence.

It is proper to state that nearly all the forms of declarations and other pleadings which were prepared by an eminent member of the North Carolina Bar, and which were printed by the editor of the Independent, in 1845, have been inserted in the present collection. They were originally printed in quires, like blank writs, to be filled up as occasion might require, and were prepared with a view to the introduction of regular pleadings in the Courts of this State.

The notes to the precedents drawn by this gentleman have been, with very few exceptions, prepared by myself. In transcribing the above precedents for the press I have sometimes ventured to make slight verbal changes. It has been deemed advisable to fill the blanks in nearly all of the forms contained in this volume, in order to render the subject plainer to beginners.

Peculiar care and attention have been devoted to those forms which no usage among us has, or can dispense with. The precedents of verdicts, judgments, orders, and decrees, have been prepared with great diligence. Upon this head it has been my object to strike a medium between the elaborate forms of the English Courts, and the loose and careless entries which too often disfigure our own records. I have attempted to render the entries upon our records, on which important rights depend, hereafter more formal, precise, accurate, and certain than they have heretofore been, and if this effort shall be attended with success, I shall feel satisfied that some good has been done, both to the profession and the public. The reputation of the State must depend in a considerable degree upon her jurisprudence, and North Carolina has been injured abroad by the slovenly manner in which her records have been made up, notwithstanding she has been blessed with an able, pure, and upright administration of public justice, and has given birth to some of the most learned lawyers and most accomplished advocates in the Union. Our judicial proceedings ought to assume a more technical and businesslike form. Dr. Story truly observed, many years since, that exemplifications of American judgments may pass, nay, do already pass to England, and it ought to be our pride to know that they will not be disgraced under the inspection of the sober benchers of any Inn of Court.[****]

Every patriotic citizen ought to desire that our records may be kept in such style, that exemplifications of them when sent abroad, may reflect no discredit upon the legal tribunals of the State.

In conclusion, the author submits this unpretending volume to the candid examination of the profession, and he hopes that they will not look with undue severity upon his efforts to promote their convenience, and facilitate their labors.

WM. EATON, JR.

* I have occasionally taken the liberty to strike out a few superfluous words from my selected forms.
[**] Regulæ generales of Hilary Term, 1834.
[***] See Appendix to the fifth American Edition of Stephen on Pleading, 56, 57, 58, and 59, as to the present law of England upon these points. As to the former law of England, see Stephen on Pleading, same edition, p. 161, note 20.
[****] Address to the members of the Suffolk Bar, in 1821.

DOCUMENT II–53   BATTLE ON THE COMMON LAW, 1855

[In *Jones v. Ward*, decided at about mid-century, Judge William H. Battle recognized principles of common law above its specific rules and treated English case law as persuasive authority in North Carolina, much as case law from other states would be persuasive, even while admitting that English common law was the source of the state's common law.]

THOMAS JONES vs. TIMOTHY WARD....

BATTLE, J....
In the absence of the authority of any decided case to settle the practice here, we must resort for guides, to the established principles of evidence, and to the adjudications of the country whence our common law is derived....

DOCUMENT II–54   PEARSON ON THE COMMON LAW, 1856

[In his opinion in *Shaw v. Moore* from 1856, Justice Richmond Pearson characterized the common law as a product of reason whose decisions on legal issues can work themselves pure over time as experience with those issues grew.[330]]

H. M. SHAW et al. propounders vs. JOHN A. MOORE et al. caveators....

PEARSON, J....

One excellence of the common law is, that it *works itself pure*, by drawing from the fountain of reason, so that if errors creep into it, upon reasons, which more enlarged views and a higher state of enlightenment, growing out of the extension of commerce and other causes, proves to be fallacious, they may be worked out by subsequent decisions. . . .

DOCUMENT II-55 CANTWELL ON CRIMINAL LAW, 1856

[Attorney Edward Cantwell asserted in his *The North Carolina Magistrate* that North Carolina needed to codify its criminal sentencing laws and reduce the number of its capital crimes. He had great admiration for the Napoleonic codes and great hatred of Bourbon kings; he mentioned stages of civilization and talked of barbaric laws as undermining the integrity of juries who could not rightly enforce those laws in this advanced stage of society; he felt the weight of the rapidly accumulating number of appellate reports and the scarcity of public law libraries; and he noted the inconsistencies and defects of the pertinent criminal statutes in force. In short, Cantwell here provided one of the rare calls to codification found among antebellum documents from North Carolina.[331] Penal reform, like the abolition of slavery, captured the attention of reformers in North Carolina more than did changes in procedure, maybe because the latter was so lax that it was not in and of itself the culprit that blocked the common man from pursuing justice in the courts.

Although Cantwell's book was a mere revision of *Swaim's Justice*—and earlier entries in this compilation tie the name of Swaim to calls for abolition of slavery and for stricter attitudes about civil procedure[332]—the material here excerpted appears to be freshly written by the "reviser," Edward Cantwell.]

SWAIM'S JUSTICE—REVISED.

THE
NORTH CAROLINA MAGISTRATE, . . .

546. The difficulty of administering laws, which date centuries back, and which are intended for a totally different state of society and stage of civilization, of adapting to the wants of the times, the crude and undigested mass of decisions, ordinances, opinions and statutes, which each succeeding year had added to their legislation, and the continual, and, in this condition of the laws, necessary encroachments of the judge, while interpreting the law, upon the proper functions and province of the law-maker; these difficulties, of which one sees in England at this day ample proof, have, [Mr. Sanford] remarks [in a report to the Department of State in the year 1852], caused most of the governments of Europe to introduce order and regularity in this legislative chaos, by reducing to a system in conformity with the wants and condition of the people and the spirit of the age, the vast collection of laws and usages, which had served rather to perplex than to simplify the course of justice. The condition of law in England, in comparison to those States of Europe—France for example, which have codes, shows very strikingly the disadvantages attending the administration of justice in countries which have no *precise written* authority to guide the judge, or to inform the people; the extreme technicality and irregularity of the law, the unnecessary difficulties which attend the obtaining of justice, the expense or tedious length of litigation, the uncertainty of issue, and the delay of decision are well known to all. The business of the judges seems rather to discover not how the evil which has occurred may be remedied, but in what manner it is probable, that in a very different state of society the matter would have been ordered; and their great rule to be, that whatsoever has been done by preceding judges, should be done of course by succeeding judges.

547. By the wisdom of the first Napoleon, the punishment of highway robbery in France without murder, which forms the text of some of Judge Blackstone's most severe strictures, has long since been reduced to the same with that of other misdemeanors, and the clumsy quackery of the Bourbon kings by whom no gradations in guilt were recognized or understood, supplanted by the CODE OF LAWS, the glory of the French people, which being established on principles, undying, unchanging and universal have, after long challenging the admiration and securing the adoption of surrounding nations, carried the fame of their author, and the record of his genius to a country where his eagles never soared, and his victorious legions could not tread.

548. It would be well for the people in North Carolina, seriously to reflect whether notwithstanding all the labour and expense just bestowed upon the new compilation of her statute law, they are not yet to expend more and to learn that legislative wisdom is not displayed by the multiplication of enactments, and especially in the multiplication of penal enactments; that it is far easier to destroy the citizen than to amend the state; small surgical skill indeed may suffice for the business of amputation, but exalted ability, unwearied diligence, unceasing care and learning combined, will hardly save the diseased limb, and restore its wonted grace and beauty. And besides, while doubts so widely prevail upon the right to take life, perhaps it were well to inquire if such severe indefinite and final punishments as yet disgrace our law do not increase, instead of diminishing the number of offenders, and thereby verify the apprehension, that the injured through compassion may forbear to prosecute; juries through compassion, forbear to convict, and forgetting their oaths, either acquit the guilty or mitigate the nature of the offence—whether finally, imitating the example of the continental nations it be not consistent with the public safety, and therefore demanded by our religion, to restrict the punishment of death to crimes of the most malignant type, entirely defined by the plain sense of our own written statute law and affecting the life of the citizen, or the very being of society.

549. Under existing statutes, and independent of the unwritten or common law, the punishment of death is in North Carolina prescribed for not less than eighteen crimes.

(1.) *For the first offence.—*
1. Arson.
2. Bestiality or sodomy.
3. Burglary.
4. Castration.
5. Duelling.
6. Highway robbery.
7. Infanticide.
8. Insurrection.
9. Murder.
10. Obstructing railways.
11. Rape and the attempt to commit it.
12. Stealing free negroes from the State or selling them.
13. Stealing slaves or aiding them to escape.
14. Being accessory before the fact to either of the foregoing.

(2.) *For the second offence.—*
15. Circulating seditious publications.
16. Exciting insurrection.
17. Malicious maiming.
18. Manslaughter.

550. Of these the first fourteen are punishable with death for the first offence, the next four are punishable upon a second conviction; and all are to be returned by the magistrate, for prosecution in the superior courts only. We shall now for his instruction and greater ease, condense in one view, the various sections of the statute law upon each, and accompany it with some account of the unwritten law appertaining thereto, and to take them in their order . . .

631. . . . It is not a little curious and suggestive to remark, that, while even in England itself the whole body of the unwritten and written criminal law of that realm has been digested and compiled into a code of some two hundred and eighty-three pages folio, which, but for the singular opposition and contrariety of the judges would long since have been the law of the land; we of North Carolina are yet to hear of a

similar improvement. Our people seem content, to wade through the vast and alarmingly increased and still accumulating pages of our own and foreign reporters, to ascertain in the plainest cases of guilt, the punishment of our own citizens, but few of whom even in the ranks of professed students can hope in the course of an ordinary lifetime devoted thereto, to master the immense number of treatises and reports in which that information is contained; if indeed the meagre resources of individual fortune and the scarcity of public libraries did not render the mighty task impracticable. So far indeed has the science of law, and especially that branch thereof which includes the definition and punishment of crime, kept pace with the supposed progress of this age that it would not be difficult to name persons of eminence in the profession of law in this State who, regarding certainty of punishment and reasonable intelligibleness in legislation, blended with a proper regard for public morality and human life, as the main purpose of criminal enactments, do not hesitate to express the opinion that in all these particulars, our present statutes are in most respects inconsistent or defective. . . .

William H. Battle served as a commissioner on *The Revised Statutes*, 1837, and as commissioner of the Revisal of 1873; he assisted in the development of the state's common law as a judge on the Supreme Court of North Carolina. Photograph of portrait of William Horn Battle by William Garl Brown, 1859. (*Credit:* State Archives of North Carolina, Raleigh)

Document II-56 Battle on the Common Law, 1864

[Late in the life of North Carolina's statutory supreme court, Judge William H. Battle, in an opinion in *Smith v. N. Carolina R. Co.*, marked off the realms of legislature and supreme court, hesitating to adapt the state's common law of evidence to the changing circumstances of society. The time was the Civil War and the societal change was travel by railroad. Where no established rule of the state's common law of evidence existed, Battle would not venture, leaving it to the general assembly to provide a remedy. Battle justified this reticence both on his understanding of appropriate judicial duty and on a prior instance of judicial reticence which he treated as controlling precedent. Perhaps his view of the court's role in developing the state's common law had come to differ from the view expounded by Chief Justice John Louis Taylor early in the life of North Carolina's statutory supreme court.[333] Perhaps his view differed even from his earlier view in *Jones v. Ward*, where he had urged that for a question of evidence open under the state's common law the court might look to pertinent English adjudications as persuasive authorities, though perhaps even in *Jones*, he might have weighed lightly decisions at *nisi prius*.[334]]

C. D. SMITH v. NORTH CAROLINA RAILROAD COMPANY....

BATTLE, J....

The necessity for admitting a plaintiff as a witness to prove the contents of his trunk in an action against a railroad company or other common carrier, for its loss, is not greater than it was in the case of a book debt; and as in the latter named case the courts felt themselves bound to leave it to the legislature to supply a remedy for the mischief, so we must do in the case now before us. Our duty as a court is, to ascertain in each case that comes before us, what the law is, and then to decide accordingly; and if in the progress of society new circumstances or combinations of circumstances arise, to which there is no principle of the common law applicable, we cannot assume the functions of legislators to devise one. That is the province of the legislature, and we have neither the inclination nor the right to interfere with it....

Document II-57 About the Judges of Our First Supreme Court (1819–1829)

[This memoir by Judge William H. Battle on the life of Chief Justice Leonard Henderson emphasized the traditionalism of the judges of our first supreme court in the 1820s. That court respected the common law as received by our state in 1778 and evidenced a faith that the common law was a systematized and principled unity with historically developed content. The systematic presentation of English judgments and decrees evident in the commentaries and treatises on which these early judges were trained and of American decisions evident in the digests and treatises on which an American science of common law was being built, served as an Enlightenment alternative to Jeremy Bentham's positivistic love affair with codification, albeit a less democratic alternative.

This memoir was cited by the Honorable Robert W. Winston in a talk he gave about the life of Chief Justice Leonard Henderson, Judge Henderson having served as an original member of the supreme court.[335] Judge Winston made the interesting point that Henderson was a thoroughgoing Federalist who saw danger in the teachings of Thomas Jefferson, "who was then teaching that 'laws and institutions should go hand in hand with the advance of the human mind....'"[336] The idealism of Jefferson's position, insofar as it was in fact his, divorced law from tradition, from the whole-cloth of the common law, and from the experience of generations, favoring instead laws imposed from above by "advanced minds," i.e., from those who would one day be known as social scientists. And yet Judge John Hall, another of the original members of the statutory supreme court, also shared Henderson's faith in a systematic common law, even though Hall was a thoroughgoing Jeffersonian.[337]]

MEMOIR OF LEONARD HENDERSON,

LATE CHIEF JUSTICE OF THE SUPREME COURT OF NORTH CAROLINA.

BY HON. WM. H. BATTLE....

... They [Chief Justice John Louis Taylor, Judge John Hall, and Judge Leonard Henderson] were especially desirous to settle for North Carolina a system of law founded upon the common law of England, modified indeed to some extent, to suit the peculiar nature of our institutions, and altered in many respects by legislative enactment. In this attempt they were greatly aided by the arguments of a bar which had no superior, and hardly an equal, in any State of the Union. The truth of this will readily be acknowledged by those who read the names of Archibald Henderson, William Gaston, Thomas Ruffin, Moses Mordecai, Gavin Hogg, Joseph Wilson and Henry Seawell, the last of whom had, about that time, resigned his seat on the bench of the superior court and returned to the bar. Some of these were succeeded a few years later by (among others) Francis L. Hawks, George E. Badger, Thomas P. Devereux, Frederic Nash, Samuel Hillman, William H. Haywood and James Iredell....

DOCUMENT II–58 ABOUT JUDGE JOHN HALL (1767–1833)

[Judge John Hall was a superior court judge who was elected by the general assembly in 1818 as judge of the newly organized supreme court. One of his most notable law students, Mr. William Eaton Jr., wrote the memoir from which this short excerpt is taken. Hall, a member of the old Republican Party of Jefferson, is described as having a rather conservative view of the common law, taking it as a system that promoted stability and certainty in society.]

MEMOIR OF THE HON. JOHN HALL,

LATE ONE OF THE JUDGES OF THE SUPREME COURT OF NORTH CAROLINA.

BY WILLIAM EATON, JR., ESQ.

... He [Judge Hall] did not wish to overrule adjudications and unsettle well established law, in order to indulge a fondness for some darling theory.... He had a just respect for authority, and a deep conviction of the necessity of certainty and stability in our system of jurisprudence....

In political sentiment Judge Hall belonged to the school of Thos. Jefferson, and was a decided and consistent member of the old Republican Party. He had however too correct a sense of the proprieties of his position to be active in political contests, and his heart was entirely free from partisan rancor and violence.... [H]e was ready to give to those who differed from him credit for purity of purpose....

DOCUMENT II–59 ABOUT MR. ARCHIBALD HENDERSON (1768–1822)

[The subject of the sketch here excerpted, attorney Archibald Henderson, was the son of Judge Richard Henderson and brother of Judge Leonard Henderson. Archibald Henderson was born in Granville County, moved to Salisbury, and became a leader of the bar in western North Carolina. He was said to be the most eloquent and successful criminal lawyer in the state. He represented the Salisbury District in Congress, 1799–1803, and the town of Salisbury in the general assembly, 1807–1809, 1814, and 1819–1820. He died October 21, 1822.

The author of the sketch was "Philo Florian," a pseudonym for Archibald DeBow Murphey.[338] Murphey privately reported North Carolina opinions covering terms during 1804–1813, as well as the July Term

1818 (1st and 2nd Murphey), and served as the state's first reporter of decisions for the reorganized supreme court under the Supplemental Act of 1818.[339] He also served as judge of the superior courts 1818–1820[340] and sat for a case on the newly reorganized supreme court in 1820.[341] Murphey has been described as "North Carolina's leading progressive politician in the early nineteenth century."[342]

Murphey's portrait of Henderson touched upon such themes as commitment to common sense in law, politics, and religion, and the rejection of artificial rules, pedantry, and mystery in law.]

Sketch of the Character of Archibald Henderson as a Lawyer....

As he advanced in life, he seemed more and more anxious that the laws should be interpreted and administered by the rules of common sense. He, in a great degree, lost his reverence for artificial rules. He said, the laws were made for the people, and they should be interpreted and administered by rules which they understood, wherever it was practicable: that common sense belonged to the people in a higher degree than to learned men, and that to interpret laws by rules which were at variance with the rules of common sense, necessarily lessened the respect of the people for the laws, induced them to believe that courts and lawyers contrived unintelligible mysteries in the science, merely for the purpose of supporting the profession of lawyers. He said, the rules of pedantry did not suit this country nor this age; that common sense had acquired a dominion in politics and religion, and was fast acquiring an absolute dominion in the law; that judges and lawyers should have the independence and magnanimity to strip off the veil of mystery from every branch of the law, and root out all the remains of a ridiculous pedantry; simplify the science, and make it intelligible, as far as possible, to the understanding of the common people....

PHILO FLORIAN.

Document II-60 About Chief Justice Taylor (1769–1829)

[The argument in a speech attributed to Chief Justice John Louis Taylor, described in the memoir excerpted below, defended the position that the general assembly should allow an elected Jew, Mr. Jacob Henry, to sit as one of its members. In advancing this argument, Taylor showed his acceptance of codification of fundamental public law, such as the state declaration of rights, which protected natural and inalienable rights of the people which ought never be violated. In fact, Taylor accepted a hierarchy of codifications of fundamental law, conceiving of the declaration of rights as prior to and of greater dignity than the constitution that would soon incorporate it.[343] This position subjected potentially conflicting provisions of the constitution itself to the natural and inalienable rights declared in the declaration of rights,[344] in particular, the right of men "to worship Almighty God according to the dictates of their own conscience."[345]

Since the constitution incorporated the declaration of rights,[346] and the declaration of rights contained natural rights that were inalienable and never to be violated, Taylor's argument perhaps denied the power of the people to amend the constitution,[347] even while asserting that constitutional provisions should be read so as not to conflict with declared natural rights. A denial of the power to amend constitutions was not unusual in the early decades of the republic, but would soon thereafter succumb to the rising tide of democracy in American jurisdictions; and, as the centuries passed, would become a misunderstood doctrine.[348] In North Carolina, the power to amend the constitution was exercised in convention in the 1830s, and since that time has been exercised with moderate frequency in this state over both the declaration of rights[349] and the other provisions of the constitution.

Also strange to modern ears was Taylor's narrowing of the definition of "Protestant" to "Anglican" in interpreting a constitution adopted at the late date of 1776,[350] as well as his observation that the sovereign people of the state in the early nineteenth century found offensive the mention of Protestantism—on Taylor's view, Anglicanism—in their constitution.[351] But the fact that Taylor had to compose a speech in defense of Henry shows that public sentiment was not all on Taylor's side. The constitution of 1776 in using "any one Religious Church"[352] in section 34 may have aimed to free worshippers among the differing Protestant denominations from taxation in support of the Anglican church; and its use of "Protestant" in section 32[353] may have meant to exclude from the public civil offices of its government only those persons espousing much older European religious traditions—Judaism, Catholicism, and Islam—or atheists, and not to exclude non-Anglican Protestants.[354]

According to William H. Battle, author of the memoir excerpted below, Taylor cleaved strongly to the doctrine of *stare decisis*. Perhaps his comfort with codification of fundamental public law, then, did not indicate an acceptance of codification of the common law of private rights and remedies.]

MEMOIR OF JOHN LOUIS TAYLOR,

THE FIRST CHIEF JUSTICE OF THE SUPREME COURT OF NORTH CAROLINA.

BY HON. WM. H. BATTLE.

JOHN LOUIS TAYLOR, the first Chief Justice of the Supreme Court of North Carolina, occupied for more than thirty years a distinguished position in the annals of the Judiciary of the State. Very little, however, is now known of his parentage and early history. He was born in London, on the first day of March, 1769, though his parents were Irish. . . .

[Judge Taylor] very early began to take notes of the cases which were decided by himself and his associates; and in the year 1802, gave them to the public in a small volume. . . . In 1814, he published anonymously, the first, and 1816, the second, volume of a work which he styled, "The Carolina Repository . . ." Another volume of Reports containing the decisions of the Supreme Court, under its former organization . . . was subsequently published by him, and is generally known as Taylor's North Carolina Term Reports. . . .

By the General Assembly of 1817, he was appointed, in conjunction with the Hon. Henry Potter, Judge of the United States District Court, for the District of North Carolina, and the Hon. Bartlett Yancey, Speaker of the Senate, "to revise the Statute Laws of the State, and to enumerate and specify those Statutes and parts of Statutes of Great Britain, which were in force in this State." The Revisal was completed by these gentlemen, and was published in 1821, under the superintendance of Judge Potter. Subsequently, Judge Taylor prepared and gave to the public, a continuation of the work on the same plan, which included the acts of 1825, and is known as Taylor's Revisal. He also, about the same time, published a treatise on the duties of Executors and Administrators. . . .

. . . [T]here is a speech which was prepared by [Taylor] and delivered by a member of the House of Commons . . . which still remains to show the elegance of his scholarship, while it attests his ardent love of religious liberty. In the year 1809, Jacob Henry was elected one of the members of the House of Commons, from the county of Carteret. His right to a seat was contested upon the ground that he was a Jew, and as such, that he denied the "divine authority of the New Testament, and refused to take the oath prescribed by law for his qualification." A resolution to vacate his seat being offered by Mr. Mills, one of the members from the county of Rockingham, Mr. Henry rose and spoke as follows: "Though I will not conceal the surprise I felt that the gentleman should have thought proper yesterday to have moved my expulsion from this House, on the alleged ground that I disbelieve in the divine authority of the New Testament, without considering himself bound by those rules of politeness, which, according to my sense of propriety, should have led him to give me some previous intimation of his design; yet, since I am brought to this discussion, I feel prepared to meet the object of his resolution.

"I certainly, Mr. Speaker, know not the design of the Declaration of Rights, made by the people of this State in the year 1776, and one day before the Constitution, if it was not to consecrate certain great and fundamental rights and principles, which even the Constitution cannot impair; for the 44th section of the latter inst[r]ument declares that the Declaration of Rights ought never to be violated on any pretence whatever. If there is any apparent difference between the two instruments, they ought, if possible, to be reconciled; but if there is a final repugnance between them, the Declaration of Rights must be considered paramount; for I believe it is to the Constitution, as the Constitution is to the law; it controls and directs it absolutely and conclusively. If, then, a belief in the Protestant religion is required by the Constitution, to qualify a man for a seat in this House, and such qualification is dispensed with by the Declaration of Rights, the provision of the Constitution must be altogether inoperative; as the language of the Bill of Rights is, "that all men have a natural and inalienable right to worship Almighty God according to the dictates of their own consciences." It is undoubtedly a natural right, and when it is declared to be an inalienable one by the people in their sovereign and original capacity, any attempt to alienate it either by the Constitution, or by law, must be vain and fruitless.

"It is difficult to conceive how such a provision crept into the Constitution, unless it is from the difficulty which the human mind feels in suddenly emancipating itself from fetters by which it has long been enchained; and how adverse it is to the feelings and manners of the people of the present day, every gentleman may satisfy himself by glancing at the religious belief of the persons who fill the various offices in this State. There are Presbyterians, Lutherans, Calvinists, Mennonists, Baptists, Trinitarians and Unitarians. But as far as my observation extends, there are fewer Protestants, in the strict sense of the word used by the Constitution, than of any other persuasion; for I suppose that they meant by it the Protestant religion as established by the law in England. For other persuasions we see houses of worship in almost every part of the State, but very few of the Protestant; so few, indeed that I fear that the people of this State, would, for sometime remain unrepresented in this House, if that clause of the Constitution is supposed to be in force. So far from believing in the truths of the thirty-nine Articles, I will venture to assert that a majority of the people never have read them. . . ."

Of the qualifications of Chief Justice Taylor for the high office which he so long filled, and of his character as a man in the social relations of life, we have an account prepared, soon after his death, by a friend, (supposed to be the late Judge Gaston,) who knew him long and intimately. "How he discharged his duties during the twenty years he administered justice on the circuit, it is impossible that the bar or the community can have forgotten. He was pre-eminently a safe Judge. It was difficult to present a question for his determination, upon which his reading had not stored up, and his retentive memory did not present some analogous case, in which it had been settled by the sages of the law. And with him it was a religious principle to abide by the land-marks, *stare decisis*. In his charges to juries, he was full and perspicuous, and while he left unimpaired their dominion over the question of fact, he never shunned responsibility by evading a distinct expression of opinion on every point of law. His patience was exemplary, and his courtesy universal. Uniting in an extraordinary degree suavity of manners with firmness of purpose—a heart tremblingly alive to every impulse of humanity, with a deep seated and reverential love of justice—the best feelings with an enlightened judgment—he made the law amiable in the sight of the people, inspired affection and respect for its institutions, and gained for its sentences a prompt and cheerful obedience. . . ."

Document II-61 About Mr. George Badger (1795–1866)

[Attorney George Badger was a dominant figure in the legal profession in North Carolina during antebellum days. The discourse in his memory given by Gov. William A. Graham in 1866, excerpted below, contained two points of interest to the study of the changing relation between common law and statute law during the early nineteenth century. One startling point made in passing was the relation of religion to the law and the suggestion that religion, if part of the common law, "might be altered by statute." The notion of "moral science," evident near the end of the excerpt, is also important in characterizing some of the tensions that drove the codification debates, tensions that would erupt near the end of the period here studied with internationally renowned publications by Charles Darwin and later by Sigmund Freud.]

DISCOURSE
IN MEMORY OF THE
LIFE AND CHARACTER
of the
HON. GEO. E. BADGER,
delivered by
WILLIAM A. GRAHAM, of Orange,
(By request of the Bar of Wake County,)
AT RALEIGH, JULY 19TH, 1866.

———

ADDRESS. . . .

———

He attained a high degree of knowledge in every branch of the law; whether in the doctrine of real estate transmitted by Coke, and contemporaries from the days of the Tudors, and before; the modifications introduced by commerce and the higher civilization of more recent times; the supplemental code of equity jurisprudence, invented to eke out the scanty justice of rude Barons and ignorant feudatories, and to apply rules of morality to the affairs of men; or in the criminal law, and the subjects of jurisdiction peculiar to the courts of the United States. And in the altercations of parties through their counsel in writing, which we style pleadings, (designed, by a severe logic, to present their points of disagreement for the decision of courts and juries,) in all these departments, his productions were models, which might safely be transferred to books of precedents for the instruction of his juniors; an adeptness, ascribable, not more to the acuteness of his understanding, than to his accomplishments as an English linguist and critic, causing a false inference, or ungrammatical phrase, to elicit his disapprobation like a false note on the ear of a musician.

These resources were ever at the command of his brethren, and of the court; before which some of his highest efforts were made, in causes in which arguments had been invited, or in which the subject of contest attracted his thoughts from its connexion with his favorite studies, and were delivered to no other auditors save those whose presence was required by duty. On an occasion of this kind, in a case of indictment for blasphemy, the question has been raised whether the Christian religion was a part of the common law, with a suggestion that, if it was, it might be altered by statute, Mr. BADGER volunteered an argument for the cause of religion and sound morality. It so happened, that as he opened his case, a venerable citizen of the State, of great intelligence, entered the court room to speak a word to the reporter, expecting immediately to retire. He was, however, so fascinated with the manner of the speaker, the splendor of his diction, the copiousness of his theological and legal learning, the force and clearness of his arguments and the precision with which they were stated, that he sat down and heard him to the close, observing, as he withdrew, "what folly ever to have made him a Judge; he ought to have been a Bishop.". . .

It was the remark of Lord Bacon that "reading makes a full man, conversation a ready man, and writing an accurate man." Mr. Badger's reading was confined, with the exception of that knowledge of the dead languages, which he had acquired in his youthful studies, to the literature of our own language. With the most approved authors in this he had a familiar acquaintance, and, as already remarked, excelled in his accomplishment as a critic. The field of learning, which next to jurisprudence, he most affected, and perhaps even preferred to that, was moral science. Upon the sublime truths of this science in the conversations of his friends, his remarks and illustrations were often not unworthy of Alexander, Butler or Whately. "In it" (says one of the most intimate of his friends and contemporaries) "the rapidity of his perceptions and the accuracy of his deductions were marvelous. Place before his mind any proposition of moral science, and instantly he carried it out, either to exact truth, most beautifully enunciated, or reduced it to an absurdity." To his acquisitions in the kindred topic of didactic divinity, or theology as a science, only a professional theologian can do justice. . . .

Part III

Code Commission Era

From the beginning of the thirteenth to the middle of the nineteenth century there is no measure in the whole history of our legal system so revolutionary in form as the Judicature Acts in England or the introduction of "code pleading" in New York and the other American states.

—Sir Frederick Pollock

Such cautious progress [in criminal jurisprudence] becomes us also [in] North Carolina, where no effort whatever has been made in any branch of jurisprudence to apply general principles and harmonizing methods. Our statutes in respect to crime are as arbitrary, insolated, and disjointed, each arising upon some particular occasion, as they were a hundred years ago.

—Code Commissioners

The New York system was devised upon a model deemed suitable to a dense, commercial community; and yet it is well known that it was adopted there through an innovating freak of the Legislature of 1848, without consulting the people. . . . This costly, cumbersome, impracticable system which New York is seeking to cast off has been imported into North Carolina where it is tenfold more unsuitable, and where it is already regarded, by nearly everybody, as little short of a public nuisance. . . . The "Code of Civil Procedure" and kindred inventions which we have borrowed from New York, inaugurate a complete revolution in the system of practice and proceeding in Courts, superseding the old common-law methods. Instead of improving the old system, as has been so successfully done in England since 1834, the New York innovators in 1848 destroyed it entirely, and introduced this novelty. Some other States, and finally North Carolina, followed the rash example. . . .

—Senate Committee Members

These acts, with many others [drafted by the Code Commission] form a body of law, the enactment of which will, for at least a century to come, mark an era in our history.

—Code Commissioners

[I]t is admitted by all, that the Constitution and Code—are [Tourgée's].

—Mr. George V. Strong

[My opponents] clung to the old common-law practice and refused to accept the new-fangled Code which the Yankee Colonel Tourgée had brought down from New York and superimposed upon our jurisprudence.

—Judge Robert Watson Winston

Introduction to Code Commission Era

In this third part of *Selected Documents Relating to Law Reform in North Carolina during the Nineteenth Century* are gathered documents chiefly concerning the codification of adjectival law and substantive law through a code commission established by the North Carolina Constitution of 1868. This Code Commission Era runs from the close of the Civil War to the close of Reconstruction.

Early in the period, delegates to the state's 1868 Constitutional Convention radically break with North Carolina's legal tradition by abandoning "common law pleading," merging law and equity jurisdictions, and directing that a code commission be established to adopt "code pleading" and engage in other initiatives. Commissioner Albion W. Tourgée leads the reform effort, he and his fellow commissioners relying on similar codification efforts already accomplished in other jurisdictions and expressing their philosophy of law in sundry reports to the general assembly. Their efforts at codification are controversial, especially among lawyers and judges. The commission is dissolved by constitutional amendment before it can take up with rigor the codification of private substantive common law or offer a revisal of the state's public statutes.

The documents excerpted in this third part of the compilation reveal two fundamental themes raised during the Code Commission Era. Supporters of codification view legislation as a science having universal principles applicable to any jurisdiction, similar to geometry and physics, while detractors generally agree with the universality of divine and natural law but contend that positive law, whether common or statutory, grows from the custom of a people over time, much as the language of a people develops. That is, supporters of codification might agree with the code commissioners that "laws sometimes make a people," while detractors might contend that a people—their "habits, manners, feelings, and opinions"—always make the law, an idea advanced earlier in the century in criticism of *The Fundamental Constitutions of Carolina*. Secondly, codifiers say their efforts bring writtenness, simplicity of expression, and common sense to the law, while detractors claim that codification has in fact killed "chimney corner law" (that is, the people taking care of many of their own legal needs) and has confused and overwhelmed juries in civil cases by introducing a multiplicity of questions of fact.

Document III-1   Laws in Force, October 18, 1865

[Much as the assembly in North Carolina declared which laws were in force after the Cary Rebellion,[355] the Tuscarora War,[356] and the declaration of its independence from Britain,[357] an ordinance of the 1865–'66 constitutional convention declared what laws were in force in North Carolina after the Civil War. The ordinance included in its declaration all state laws compatible with allegiance of citizens to the government of the state and of the United States that were in effect prior to secession or passed during the hostilities—with some exceptions. Presumably this declaration encompassed both the statute laws as reflected in the *Revised Code* of 1854,[358] as amended, and the common laws as declared by the courts.[359]]

AN ORDINANCE DECLARING WHAT LAWS AND ORDINANCES ARE IN FORCE, AND FOR OTHER PURPOSES.

Whereas, Doubts may arise from the late attempt of the State of North-Carolina to secede from the United States, whether any, and what laws have been and are now in force, and what acts done by officers and individuals are valid and obligatory: Now, for the purpose of preventing such doubts about these and other matters hereinafter mentioned:

Be it declared and ordained by the delegates of the people of the State of North-Carolina, in Convention assembled, and it is hereby declared and ordained as follows: 1. All the laws of the State, except as hereinafter is excepted, which on the twentieth day of May, eighteen hundred and sixty-one, were compatible with the allegiance of the citizens of the State to the government of the United States, and not since repealed or modified; and all the laws and ordinances passed since that day, except as hereinafter is excepted, compatible with such allegiance, and not since repealed or modified, and which are consistent with the Constitution of the State and the United States, are hereby declared to have been, at all times since their enactment, and now to be in full force, in like manner, and to the same extent, and not otherwise as if the State had not on that day, nor at any time since, attempted to secede from the government of the United States, and as if no question had been made of the lawful authority of the Convention assembled on that day, or of any General Assembly assembled since that day to enact such laws and ordinances, and all other of said ordinances and laws are hereby declared to have been and to be null and void: *Provided, however*, That nothing herein contained shall be so construed as to prevent the General Assembly from repealing or modifying any of said laws and ordinances hereby ratified, which shall not form a part of the Constitution of the State. . . .

[*Ratified in Convention, this 18th day of October, 1865.*]

EDWIN G. READE, *President.*

JAS. H. MOORE, *Secretary of the Convention.*
R. C. BADGER, *Assistant Secretary.*

DOCUMENT III–2   REPORT ON FREEDMEN'S CODE, JANUARY 22, 1866

[In pursuance of an ordinance of the 1865–'66 Constitutional Convention,[360] William Holden, as provisional governor, appointed three commissioners to compile a "system of laws" concerning the freedmen.[361] Approximately one month before the report of the commissioners was presented to the general assembly, provisional government in North Carolina was discontinued and Holden turned the state seal over to the civil governor, Jonathan Worth. Governor Worth made evident his positions on the rights of previously enslaved persons and on the Freedmen's Bureau in his remarks to the house of commons at its Special Session of 1866, January 18, 1866, where he distinguished social, political, civil, and religious rights:

> While *social* equality with the whites (which prevails no where in the United States, notwithstanding pretences to the contrary in some quarters and among some persons,) is not to be expected, nor is the *elective franchise*, I am fully warranted in saying, there is no disposition to deny to them any of the essential rights of *civil* or *religious* freedom in this State: on the contrary, every day's observation makes it manifest that restraining measures are necessary to prevent pauperism, vagrancy, idleness, and their consequent crimes, in the new phase which our social system presents. And it is important to safety, peace and welfare of society, that the conflicts of systems of law and administration,—the one for the whites and the other for the colored man—(the latter, however, drawing into its jurisdiction every transaction in which a black may be involved,) shall cease among us; and that the great interests of rights, wrongs, and remedies, may be committed to judges and juries of the vicinage, according to ancient English and American usage. It is hoped, therefore, that the President and Congress of the United States may order, as early as possible, the withdrawal from our limits of the Bureau of Freedmen . . .[362]

Former provisional governor Holden, on the other hand, did not contemplate equal civil rights for the freedmen, much less equal political privileges or social equality. Conflict arose, then, when the report and accompanying bills offered by commissioners B. F. Moore, W. S. Mason, and R. S. Donnell proposed an extension of civil rights to the freedmen. Regarding this controversy, historian Samuel Ashe wrote:

> Governor Holden . . . had been bitterly opposed to any enlargement of negro rights. . . . Section 11 of the bill reported by [the commissioners of the Freedmen's Code] allowed "persons of color to bear witness when their right of person or property are concerned." Governor Holden was so averse to conferring privileges upon the negroes that he opposed this proposition with such heat as to secure the defeat of Mr. Moore for

the legislature because he advocated it. This legislation was then accomplished under the leadership of Hon. W. N. H. Smith, afterward chief justice of the State."[363]

The commissioners who compiled the code concerning the freedmen held a view sharply different from Holden's position. They explained in their report to the legislature here excerpted that upon the repeal of slavery the freedmen were governed by whatever laws had governed the free negro in North Carolina, that the free negro had long been held to be a "freeman" under the North Carolina Constitution of 1776, that therefore the same common law existed for both races of freemen, and that statutory deviations from it operated equally on all. In fact, the commissioners observed, "some of the provisions of this bill [for a Freedmen's Code] which seem to confer rights and privileges, were strictly unnecessary; because persons of color were entitled to them without any new enactment." And the commissioners concluded that they "prefer to let the common law apply its flexible rules for human conduct to the new state of things, rather than frame for it rigid, and perhaps misconceived legislation." And yet, the "Black Codes"[364] as initially passed would not in fact secure freedom from all legal discriminations which the logic of the commissioners would permit.]

REPORT OF COMMITTEE,

RALEIGH, *January 22nd*, 1866.

To the Speaker of the House of Commons
  of the General Assembly of North-Carolina:

SIR:—The Committee appointed by the provisional Governor in pursuance of a resolution of the recent Convention "to prepare and report to the Legislature a system of laws upon the subject of freedmen, &c.," herewith present their report, and request that through you, it may be laid before the General Assembly.

Respectfully,

B. F. MOORE,
W. S. MASON,   COMMITTEE.
R. S. DONNELL.

To the Honorable, the General Assembly
  of the State of North-Carolina: . . .

The Committee, in presenting their report, deem it proper that they should explain the course they have pursued; and to some extent, the reasons by which they have been governe[d].

Prior to the emancipation of slaves there had existed, in the State, three classes of population, besides Indians, to-wit: the whites, the slaves, and the free negroes; and for many purposes, there existed a special legislation for each class. Upon the emancipation of the slaves, the laws specially respecting them, ceased to have any force; and that class fell under the laws respecting free negroes: the political and civil condition of all the colored population became that which had already been established for the free negro. It became the duty, therefore, of the Committee to look through the entire body of the laws of the State, for the purpose of ascertaining what part of them governed the free negro, as distinguished from the white man. In performing this duty your Committee have deemed it the more advisable course, (as this species of special legislation was scattered throughout the civil and criminal laws,) to advise the repeal of all laws that specially affected the colored race, and re-enact such as, in their opinion, ought to exist; and also to recommend other and original legislation, when it was deemed expedient. Believing that a brief synopsis of the several sections of the first named bill, and also, of the other bills, would not be unacceptable, they proceed to furnish it: . . .

It has been held, that under our laws, the marriages of slaves by their own mere consent, and simply consented to by their masters, are void; and, as the Legislature is forbidden to legitimate persons born in bastardy, the provision for such legitimation, which was contained in an ordinance offered before, but rejected by the Convention, (because of the adoption of the resolution under which the Committee are now reporting) must be again submitted to that body, or the freedmen now living will all be bastards, and incapable of inheriting from their fathers any estate which he may chance to die possessed of.

It is believed that a marriage merely voidable may be validated by the General Assembly; and that when thus confirmed, all the incidents of ratification follow; one of which is the legitimation of the issue previously born. But, it is more than doubted whether such result follows the enactment of a marriage under section 7. . . .

The Committee observe that in some of the late slaveholding States, much legislation is employed to confer on persons of color the civil rights which belong to white men. In this State very little is necessary; indeed, none beyond a repeal of the laws, which, from time to time, have been introduced, making distinctions between whites and colored persons. And, it may be observed, that some of the provisions of this bill which seem to confer rights and privileges, were strictly unnecessary; because persons of color were entitled to them without any new enactment. But it was deemed better, at this time, to solemnly declare them in a bill drawn to define their civil status.

Many years since it was solemnly decided by the highest Court of the State, and indeed, it has been so regarded, that the term "freemen," (than which none used in the declaration of rights and the Constitution of the State, to describe a citizen, is of higher dignity,) included in its fullest extent, a free negro, whether free in 1776, when the Constitution was framed, or become so since by emancipation. He was, at the beginning of the late unhappy conflict of arms, and is now, included in the term "freeman," as used in that instrument.

This class of our population have never been debarred from owning any species of property, except by one enactment, that of 1861, which forbade them thereafter to own slaves. They have ever been protected from trial for crime, except through presentment by a grand jury, and trial by a petit jury, with all the rights of challenge accorded to white persons. They have ever been allowed trial in the same tribunals where, for like offences, the white man was prosecuted. The same common law which yet prevails so extensively in this State, and regulates, almost entirely, the duties of husband and wife, of parent and child, of guardian and ward, of master and servant, and of master and apprentice, exists alike for both classes. The same power of making contracts, and the same remedies for enforcing them in courts open alike to both, are equally the rights of the one race and the other, without distinction.

In a word, the common law is the law of the State in all matters where it has not been superseded by statute; where it exists, colored and white persons are equally protected under its shield, and exposed to its punishments; and where it is changed by statute, the change operates on all. . . .

Among the most efficient means of accomplishing this object, they deem the protection of every man's property against unauthorized intrusions, trespasses and thefts of the idle and vicious.

In our present demoralized condition there is no species of live stock which escapes the roving robber; and every man is plundered, when the market is convenient, of whatever may be found on his lands, growing or severed, that is valuable for sale.

Wilful trespasses on lands have long been a grievance greatly complained of. The common law did not allow criminal prosecutions for this species of wrong; but the General Assembly have, from time to time, in many instances, departed from this rule in order to afford protection against the lawless idler and insolvent trespasser. In proportion as circumstances may increase the frequency of such wrongs, it will become the legislative power to follow them with appropriate remedies.

The Committee, therefore, report and recommend the passage of the following bills:

1. "A bill to punish persons pursuing horses and other live stock with intent to steal them."
2. "A bill to prevent wilful trespasses on lands and stealing any kind of property therefrom." . . .
3. "A bill more effectually to secure the maintenance of bastard children, and the payment of fines and costs on conviction in criminal cases."

The purpose of this bill is to relieve the County Treasuries; *first*, from the burden of supporting bastard children, which are likely to greatly increase in number, in the midst of a demoralized population.

It is naturally just that the father should support his offspring, whether born in or out of wedlock. No one, if able to work, ought to be allowed to cast his spurious progeny on the charity of the industrious poor, whose toil is stretched to its utmost extent in supporting the public charges and their own virtuous families.

Secondly, From the burden of maintaining, at heavy expense, the judicial tribunals of the land established for the preservation of the public peace against the turbulence and violence of those who, having been the principal instrument of its breaches, seek, when brought to justice, to evade by an idle life, the payment of the costs of suppressing their own disorders.

As yet, no steps have been taken by that authority, which claims exclusive jurisdiction, both civilly and criminally, over all matters that concern the freedmen, to encourage or enforce the marriage of such as, while slaves, were long living together willingly, as man and wife. By the laws of this State the husbands and wives, popularly so called, of a population of 300,000 human beings, are lewdly and la[s]civiously cohabiting together, without any other link of connection than their own free will. They may part when they choose, and select new partners for a day or a month. Among the whites such cases are indictable. If, after the courts shall assume their criminal jurisdiction, the colored people shall still be allowed to continue in the practice of such unlawful connections, without reproof or punishment, they will be in a more demoralized condition, in respect to that relation, which among all civilized human beings, is deemed so sacred, than were free persons of color, or even slaves, before the late epoch of emancipation. The former were not allowed to cohabit without marriage, duly celebrated; and the latter were much restrained from such licentious co-habitation, by the care and prudence of their masters.

If the Freedmen's Bureau will neither turn over to the civil authorities for correction, this species of crime, nor take efficient means, itself, for its correction, it will be impossible to elevate the race by any legislative means yet practiced or devised. No race of mankind can be expected to become exalted in the scale of humanity, whose sexes, without any binding obligation, cohabit promicuously together. Among such a people, chastity can have no name or place; and the performance of parental duties, no encouragement or sanction.

It is much hoped that the Freedmen's Bureau will take the subject into serious consideration. . . .

The Committee are aware that the great and radical changes occasioned by emancipation, in the fixed habits and custom of the people, cannot be truly estimated at once; and therefore, they forbear, as much as possible, to speculate by legislative anticipation, for such changes as may even probably become necessary in the course of time. They deem it the more prudent course to proceed now by new laws, only so far as the way appears to be clear. They prefer to let the common law apply its flexible rules for human conduct to the new state of things, rather than frame for it rigid, and perhaps misconceived legislation. . . .

Respectfully submitted,

B. F. MOORE,
W. S. MASON,
R. S. DONNELL.

Document III-3   Freedmen's Code, March 10, 1866

[The bills for the "Freedmen's Code" of 1866 presented a system of laws upon the subject of the freedmen, as well as a series of companion bills designed to deal with social ills perceived to have been caused by the war and by the repeal of slavery (e.g., acts dealing with seditious language, pursuing of livestock, and vagrancy). The commissioners who reported these bills to the legislature also recommended changes to conform existing statute law to the repeal of slavery. The house took up the nine bills offered by the commissioners in late January 1866.[365] The main bill contained two notorious discriminations: (1) a punishment of death for the assault with intent to commit rape upon a white woman by a black man; and (2) an extension of an imperfect right to bear evidence in controversies at law and in equity.[366] The section recognizing a right to bear evidence carried with it two provisos, one of which delayed its effectiveness "until jurisdiction in matters relating to freedmen shall be fully committed to the courts of this State." This section and its proviso nearly caused the bill to fail.[367] While the bill ultimately passed, both provisos to the section on bearing evidence were repealed by the state convention in June 1866, as was the discrimination in cases of assault with intent to commit rape upon a white woman.[368] Whatever the immediate effect of removal of these discriminations, with passage of North Carolina's Constitution of 1868, the "Black Codes" of 1866 were presumed dead.[369]]

AN ACT CONCERNING NEGROES AND PERSONS OF COLOR OR OF MIXED BLOOD.

SECTION 1. *Be it enacted by the General Assembly of the State of North Carolina, and it is hereby enacted by the authority of the same,* That negroes and their issue, even where one ancestor in each succeeding generation to the fourth inclusive, is white, shall be deemed persons of color.

SEC. 2. *Be it further enacted,* That all persons of color, who are now inhabitants of this State, shall be entitled to the same privileges and subject to the same burthen and disabilities as by the laws of the State were conferred on, or were attached to, free persons of color, prior to the ordinance of emancipation, except as the same may be changed by law.

SEC. 3. *Be it further enacted,* That persons of color shall be entitled to all the privileges of white persons in the mode of prosecuting, defending, continuing, removing and transferring their suits at law and in equity; and, likewise, to the same mode of trial by jury, and all the privileges appertaining thereto. And in all proceedings in equity by or against them, their answer shall have the same force and effect in all respects as the answer of white persons.

SEC. 4. *Be it further enacted,* That in all cases of apprenticeship of persons of color, under chapter five of the Revised Code, the master shall be bound to discharge the same duties to them as to white apprentices, and the words "as are white" in section three, line three, are hereby repealed, and the word "apprentice" shall be read after the word "such." in said line, and the words "if a white person," in the second line of section six are hereby repealed: *Provided, always,* That in the binding out of apprentices of color, the former master of such apprentices, when they shall be regarded as suitable persons by the court, shall be entitled to have such apprentices bound to them in preference to other persons.

SEC. 5. *Be it further enacted,* That in all cases where men and women, both or one of whom were lately slaves and are now emancipated, now cohabit together in the relation of husband and wife, the parties shall be deemed to have been lawfully married as man and wife at the time of the commencement of such cohabitation, although they may not have been married in due form of law. And all persons whose cohabitation is hereby ratified into a state of marriage, shall go before the clerk of the court of pleas and quarter sessions of the county in which they reside, at his office, or before some justice of the peace, and acknowledge the fact of such cohabitation, and the time of its commencement; and the clerk shall enter the same in a book kept for that purpose; and if the acknowledgment be made before a justice of the peace, such justice shall report the same in writing to the clerk of the court of pleas and quarter sessions, and the clerk shall enter the same as though the acknowledgment had been made before him; and such entry shall be deemed *prima facie* evidence of the allegations therein contained. For making such entry and giving a certificate of the same, the clerk shall be entitled to a fee of twenty-five cents, to be paid by the party for whom the services are rendered.

SEC. 6. *Be it further enacted,* That if any of such persons shall fail to go before the clerk of the county court, or some justice of the peace of the county in which they reside, and have their marriage recorded before the first of September, one thousand eight hundred and sixty-six, they shall be deemed guilty of a misdemeanor, and punished at the discretion of the court, and their failure for each month thereafter, shall constitute a separate and distinct offense.

SEC. 7. *Be it further enacted,* That all contracts between any persons whatever, whereof one or more of them shall be a person of color, for the sale or purchase of any horse, mule, ass, jennet, neat cattle, hog, sheep or goat, whatever may be the value of such articles, and all contracts between such persons for any other article or articles of property whatever of the value of ten dollars or more; and all contracts executed or executory between such persons for the payment of money of the value of ten dollars or more, shall be void as to all persons whatever, unless the same be put in writing and signed by the venders or debtors, and witnessed by a white person who can read and write.

SEC. 8. *Be it further enacted,* That marriage between white persons and persons of color shall be void; and every person authorized to solemnize the rites of matrimony, who shall knowingly solemnize the same between such persons; and every clerk of a court who shall knowingly issue license for their marriage, shall be deemed guilty of a misdemeanor, and, moreover, shall pay a penalty of five hundred dollars to any person suing for the same.

SEC. 9. *Be it further enacted,* That persons of color, not otherwise incompetent, shall be capable of bearing evidence in all controversies at law and in equity, where the rights of persons or property of persons of color, shall be put in issue, and would be concluded by the judgment or decree of court; and also in pleas of the State, where the violence, fraud or injury alleged shall be charged to have been done by or to persons of color. In all other civil and criminal cases such evidence shall be deemed inadmissible, unless by consent of the parties of record: *Provided*, That this section shall not go into effect until jurisdiction in matters relating to freedmen shall be fully committed to the courts of this State: *Provided, further*, That no person shall be deemed incompetent to bear testimony in such cases, because of being a party to the record or in interest.

Sec. 10. *Be it further enacted*, That whenever a person of color shall be examined as a witness, the court shall warn the witness to declare the truth.

Sec. 11. *Be it further enacted*, That any person of color, convicted by due course of law, of an assault with an intent to commit rape upon the body of a white female, shall suffer death.

Sec. 12. *Be it further enacted*, That the criminal laws of the State, embracing and affecting a white person, are hereby extended to persons of color, except where it is otherwise provided in this act, and whenever they shall be convicted of any act made criminal, if committed by a white person, they shall be punished in like manner, except in such cases when other and different punishment may be prescribed or allowed by this act.

Sec. 13. *Be it further enacted*, That at the time now provided for the election of wardens of the poor, the justices of the court of pleas and quarter sessions of each county, under the rules and regulations now prescribed, may, in their discretion, elect two distinct and independent court of wardens; one of whom shall act as the wardens of the white poor, and the other as the wardens of the colored poor.

Sec. 14. *Be it further enacted*, That the persons constituting each court shall be qualified as now provided; and the wardens severally, and each court shall have all the powers and authorities now conferred on them, and they and the officers of each court, and all other persons whatever, shall be subject to all the duties, liabilities and penalties imposed on them by chapter eighty-six, of the Revised Code.

Sec. 15. *Be it further enacted*, That the following laws and parts of laws are hereby repealed: First. Certain laws contained in the Revised Code, viz: . . .

[*Ratified this 10th day of March*, 1866.]

Document III-4   Merger of Law and Equity, February 25, 1868

[The provisions in a committee report preserved in the journal entry of the constitutional convention here reprinted were by and large incorporated into the 1868 Constitution. The first section of the committee report eliminated common law pleading and united law and equity, while the second provision demanded that a three-person code commission draft modern rules of practice and procedure.[370] The requirement of section three, that the commissioners shall report a "Code of Law of North-Carolina," was not fulfilled before the commission was dissolved by amendment to the constitution.[371] It is not clear from this journal entry alone whether the convention meant to require only a re-codification of the statute law of the state or demanded also a codification of the common law.[372] An ordinance of the convention would shed more light on the subject.[373]]

TUESDAY, February, 25th, 1868. . . .

PLAN FOR ORGANIZATION OF THE JUDICIAL DEPARTMENT, REPORTED BY THE COMMITTEE ON THAT SUBJECT.

JUDICIAL DEPARTMENT.

Section 1. The distinction between actions at law and suits in equity, and the forms of all such actions and suits shall be abolished, and there shall be in this State but one form of action, for the enforcement or protection of private rights or the redress of private wrongs, which shall be denominated a civil action; and every action prosecuted by the people of the State as a party, against the person charged with a public offence, for the punishment of the same, shall be termed a criminal action. Feigned issues shall also be abolished and the fact at issue tried by order of Court before a jury.

SEC. 2. Three Commissioners shall be appointed by this Convention to report to the General Assembly at its first session after this Constitution shall be adopted by the people, rules of practice and procedure in accordance with the provisions of the foregoing section.

SEC. 3. The same Commissioners shall also report to the General Assembly as soon as practicable, a Code of Law of North-Carolina. The General Assembly shall have power to fill vacancies occurring in this Commission. . . .

Document III–5   Code Commissioners, March 13, 1868

[While the convention's journal entry[374] (and later the constitution's directive[375]) that the commissioners shall report a "Code of Law of North-Carolina"[376] left doubt as to the scope of the required codification, the ordinance reprinted below sheds some light on the question. Section one of this ordinance divided the codification project into two parts: a code of practice and procedure[377] and a code of law. Regarding the code of law, the ordinance directed the commissioners to reduce to writing and systematize the entire body of state law, insofar as that was practicable. That the commissioners must *reduce* all of state law to a *written* form suggested that the convention envisioned codification of law not evidenced by writing (i.e., law evidenced by common law adjudications, rather than by acts of assembly). Indeed, the convention envisioned a code of law in three divisions: (1) political, (2) personal rights and relations of property and obligations, and (3) criminal.[378] In the third division, the commissioners were to define crimes, not simply prescribe punishments, which perhaps suggested codification of the state's many common law crimes. And while the last dozen years of acts of assembly had not yet been systematized into a scientific statutory code, the *Revised Code* having been published in the mid-1850s, the discretion given the commissioners to limit their codification efforts to what was "practicable and expedient" suggested the convention's intent to empower the commissioners to systematize the common law in addition to the recent session laws. Besides, the convention's demand to codify "the whole body of law of the state" was broader than the governor's revolutionary demand of the 1830s to codify "the whole body of our public statute laws,"[379] and presumably intentionally so. Finally, the ordinance required the commissioners to offer the codes of practice and procedure and of law to officials of the judiciary for criticism, which suggested that the peculiar expertise of judges—their experience in the elaboration, clarification, and declaration of the common law—was invoked because the project included codification of the common law.

This ordinance tracked closely a New York statute of 1857 to appoint commissioners to prepare a civil code for that state.[380] The general analysis of the code prepared in compliance with the North Carolina ordinance tracked closely the general analysis prepared by David Dudley Field in execution of the New York statute.[381] The breadth of this analysis, especially the wide scope of its civil code, suggested that the ordinance was read very broadly by North Carolina's code commissioners. Furthermore, the first report of North Carolina's code commissioners[382] copied language from the first report of the New York Commissioners of the Code, stating that "Nothing within the range of government, can exceed in magnitude the task of collecting, condensing and arranging the jurisprudence of a people." This assertion pointed to an ambitious codification project, as the term *jurisprudence* was too broad and too inaccurate to refer only to the public laws passed by the general assembly.[383] In North Carolina, as in its sister state, the code commissioners likely intended to do much more than update the *Revised Code*.[384]]

FRIDAY, MARCH 13TH, 1868. . . .

AN ORDINANCE APPOINTING COMMISSIONERS TO PREPARE A CODE OF PRACTICE AND PROCEDURE IN THE DIFFERENT COURTS OF THE STATE.

SECTION 1. *Be it ordained by the people of North-Carolina in Convention assembled, and it is hereby ordained as follows:* That Victor C. Barringer, A. W. Tourgee and Wm. B. Rodman are hereby appointed

Commissioners, whose duty it shall be to prepare a Code of Practice and Procedure in the different Courts of the State, and to reduce into a written and systematic Code the whole body of law of the State, or such parts thereof as shall seem to them practicable and expedient, and consistent with the provisions of the Constitution.

SEC. 2. *Be it further ordained*, That the Commissioners shall divide the Code of Practice and Procedure into two parts, the one as a Code of Criminal Procedure, with the requisite forms, the other a Code of Civil Procedure, with forms thereof.

SEC. 3. *Be it further ordained*, That the first division of the Code of Law must embrace the laws respecting the government of the State, its civil polity, the functions of its public officers and duties of its citizens. The second must embrace the laws of personal rights and relations of property and obligations. The third shall define crimes and prescribe their punishments.

SEC. 4. *Be it further ordained*, That the Commissioners shall hold their offices for three years; but the General Assembly may continue their term if it shall be deemed necessary.

SEC. 5. *Be it further ordained*, That the Commissioners shall report to the General Assembly at its first session after the adoption of this Constitution a general analysis of the Code projected by them and the progress made by them therein, and shall continue to report at each succeeding session of the General Assembly the progress made to that time.

SEC. 6. *Be it further ordained*, That whenever the Commissioners shall have prepared the Code, or any portion of the same, they shall contract with the printer of the State for printing of the same, and cause the same to be distributed among the Justices of the Supreme Court, Judges of the Superior Courts, and other competent persons, for examination, after which the Commissioners shall re-examine their work and consider such suggestions as may have been made to them. They shall then cause the Code as finally agreed upon by them to be re-printed under the contract as aforesaid and distributed to all the Justices of the Supreme Court, the Judges of the Superior Courts and Clerks of the Superior Courts thirty days before being presented to the General Assembly; and the Penal Code in like manner to be distributed to the Solicitors of the State.

SEC. 7. *Be it further ordained*, That the Commissioners shall from time to time specify such amendments, alterations and revision of the law as to them may seem necessary to carry into effect the provisions of the Constitution, and report the same to the General Assembly.

SEC. 8. *Be it further ordained*, That each of said Commissioners shall receive a salary of two hundred dollars per month, while actually engaged in the performance of his duties as such. A suitable room in the capital [*sic*] shall be assigned to said Commissioners as an office, and the necessary printing and stationery allowed the same.

SEC. 9. *Be it further ordained*, That this ordinance shall be in force from and after its ratification. . . .

DOCUMENT III-6 CONSTITUTION, APRIL 21–23, 1868

[Unlike the Revolutionary drafters of the North Carolina Constitution of 1776, the people in convention in 1868 divided the Reconstruction constitution into articles, three of which reflected the major separation of powers—legislative, executive, and judicial. It was in the judicial article that the people placed the code commission. Given the constitutional merger of law and equity and the replacement of traditional practice and procedure with new civil and criminal actions, this placement made sense. And perhaps the placement of the code commission in the judicial article suggested that the provision for a "code of law" would displace the judicial product, i.e., the substance of the common law. The judicial article also declared the laws of the state to be in force insofar as not repugnant to the state constitution or the constitution and laws of the United States.]

CONSTITUTION OF THE STATE OF NORTH-CAROLINA, TOGETHER WITH THE ORDINANCES AND RESOLUTIONS OF THE CONSTITUTIONAL CONVENTION,

Assembled in the City of Raleigh, Jan. 14th, 1868....

ARTICLE IV.

JUDICIAL DEPARTMENT.

SECTION 1. The distinction between actions at law and suits in equity, and the forms of all such actions and suits shall be abolished, and there shall be in this State but one form of action, for the enforcement or protection of private rights or the redress of private wrongs, which shall be denominated a civil action; and every action prosecuted by the people of the State as a party, against a person charged with a public offence, for the punishment of the same, shall be termed a criminal action....

SEC. 2. Three Commissioners shall be appointed by this Convention to report to the General Assembly at its first session after this Constitution shall be adopted by the people, rules of practice and procedure in accordance with the provisions of the foregoing section, and the Convention shall provide for the commissioners a reasonable compensation.

SEC. 3. The same Commissioners shall also report to the General Assembly as soon as practicable, a code of the law of North-Carolina. The Governor shall have power to fill all vacancies occurring in this Commission....

SEC. 10. The Supreme Court shall have jurisdiction to review, upon appeal, any decision of the courts below, upon any matter of law or legal inference; but no issue of fact shall be tried before this court: and the court shall have the power to issue any remedial writs necessary to give it a general supervision and control of the inferior courts....

SEC. 24. The laws of North-Carolina, not repugnant to this Constitution, or to the Constitution and laws of the United States, shall be in force until lawfully altered....

SEC. 26. The Justices of the Supreme Court shall be elected by the qualified voters of the State, as is provided for the election of members of the General Assembly. They shall hold their offices for eight years....

DOCUMENT III-7 RODMAN TO HOLDEN, MAY 5, 1868

[In this letter to Gov. William W. Holden, Justice William B. Rodman accepted the duties of a code commissioner only to the extent of contributing to a code of practice, presumably of both civil and criminal practice, explaining that time hardly permitted him even that endeavor. Rodman anticipated clarification of *The Code of Civil Procedure* as the courts gained experience with the new practice, rather than a constant duty of amendment devolving on the general assembly or that duty being denied altogether on the ground that the practice code had resulted from so much experience (in other jurisdictions) that no more pertinent experience was expected to affect it.]

Washington 5 May 1868

My dear Sir....

I shall be unable properly to attend to the duties of Code Commissioner—beyond the preparation with the others of a Code of practice & procedure which may serve until the experience of our Courts enable them to amend it. I hope you will consider the matter of the appointment of some proper person to succeed me, after that much is done, when I shall send you a formal resignation. Indeed I can hardly afford the time and labor necessary for the preparation of the practice part of the Code, but so many of the profession urge me to undertake that—that I mean to attempt it if possible.

> Very truly
> Yours &c
> Will B. Rodman

Hon. W. W. Holden

William B. Rodman served as a commissioner on *The Revised Statutes*, 1837, and as a code commissioner during Reconstruction; he also served as a justice on the Supreme Court of North Carolina from 1868 to 1878. Photograph of portrait of William B. Rodman. (*Credit*: State Archives of North Carolina, Raleigh)

DOCUMENT III–8   TOURGÉE TO RODMAN, JUNE 8, 1868

[Commissioner Albion Tourgée suggested in this personal letter to co-commissioner William B. Rodman that North Carolina would not rely solely on the code of practice of New York in drafting its code of civil procedure.]

Greensboro NC
June 8th 1868

Hon. W^m. B Rodman:

Dear Sir: . . .

I have the opinion that it would be expedient for us to organize immediately and communicate with the officials of the various states which are working under Code Procedure, and get copies of their codes &c &c. . . .

Yours Respectfully

A. W. Tourgee

Document III–9   Field to Tourgée, 1868

[There is a strong tie between the work of North Carolina's code commission and the procedural codification that was accomplished in New York, as evidenced by this letter of 1868 from Mr. David Dudley Field to Commissioner Albion W. Tourgée, reporting the shipment of the codes of procedure of New York to the commissioners. Tourgée and Field would continue to exchange letters over the coming decades.[385]]

New York City [Oct.] 20/68

Dear Sir,

. . . I send you several volumes of law Codes— . . . for yourself [*illegible*], & [*illegible*] to your colleagues. . . . [T]his book of laws is preceded by the draft of an act, which it would [*illegible*] to laws passed, is not to obviate any difficulty about pleading with the Code.

It will give me pleasure to hear from you again and particularly on the subject.

This Book of laws would [*illegible*] the Code much reason acceptable to your bench & bar, than if they came [*illegible*] to frame their case pleading codes as Law systems.

Very truly,
David Dudley Field

Document III–10   First Report of the Code Commissioners, July 15, 1868

[In their first report to the general assembly, the commissioners stressed that they were tasked with arranging the jurisprudence of a people, which was a broad and important task: all sound morals, not to mention civilization itself, they said, depended on these rules of action prescribed by the state for the conduct of its citizens.

In this report there was a lengthy quotation outlining the death of feudalism, monarchism, and the inalienability of real property, this quotation being lifted from a similar report submitted to the legislature of New York in 1858 by the commissioners of its code.[386] Also borrowed from the New York report was the general analysis of its code. This analysis was broken into pieces by North Carolina's commissioners, each offering a bare outline of its area of law, as such: General Analysis of the Political Code; General Analysis of the Civil Code; and General Analysis of the Penal Code.[387] In this way, the commissioners complied with section five of the ordinance of convention.[388]

A major theme in debate about codification was the delusion of some positivistic proponents that they might write laws appropriate for enactment by any legislature. The principles of legislation, it was suggested, were as universal as the principles of geometry and mechanics. Thus, an outline of the law of the State of New York would be of great use to the legislature of North Carolina, not because each was an American state with a common history (if one were willing to judge from a distance), but because each legislature wished to follow the correct principles of legislation. Codifiers, then, could be codifiers for the world.]

Office Commissioners of the Code,
Raleigh, July 15th, 1868.

To the General Assembly of North Carolina:

The Commissioners appointed by the Act of March 13th, 1868, to "prepare a Code of Practice and Procedure in the different Courts of the State, and to reduce into a written and systematic code the whole body of the law of the State," and who are required by section 5, of said act to "report to the General Assembly, at its first session, a general analysis of the Code projected by them, and the progress made by them therein," beg leave to submit their first

REPORT.

Immediately upon the ratification of the Constitution, the Commissioners began their labors. It is known to the General Assembly that the labor imposed upon the Commission is one of the greatest difficulty and responsibility. Nothing within the range of government, can exceed in magnitude the task of collecting, condensing and arranging the jurisprudence of a people. The structure of government and society, and all their complex relations are comprehended within it. Public order, sound morals, all advancement in the arts of civilization, and all growth in true prosperity, are dependent, in a great degree, upon those rules of action, which the state prescribes for the conduct of its citizens.

These difficulties are increased by two considerations:

1. The present state of the law, and
2. The present state of society.

Our language cannot furnish a better picture of the present condition of our law, than the words of the first codifier of the common law:

"Our law is the product of ten centuries, most of them filled with tumult and disorder; it is compounded of many incongruous elements, Saxon and Norman customs. Feudal and Roman law, provincial usages, and the decisions of various and disagreeing tribunals. We have Equity law, Admirality [*sic*] law, Common law, as the law of marriage and succession, and two kinds of common law, one, contradistinguished from Statute, and the other, from Equity. Society has undergone an entire transformation. The Feudal system has fallen to pieces, monarchical institutions have given place to republican; land, from being almost inalienable, has become an article of daily and hourly traffic, and commerce, once so narrow and timid, embraces the world. Personal rights and personal property have assumed an importance never before known; the numberless questions arising from modern enterprise, travel, emigration and the expansion of industry and commerce have developed new departments of jurisprudence; while the multiplication of courts required by the necessities of an increased population, and a traffic constantly augmenting, has produced a mass of adjudications, painful for the student to contemplate and often difficult if not impossible to reconcile. Thus we have arrived at the period of which the Roman historian, complained so justly, when "the infinite variety of laws and legal opinions had filled many thousand volumes, which no fortune could purchase and no capacity could digest."

The changes which the last eight years have wrought in the fundamental relations of society, blotting out entirely one of the great classes of personal relations—that of master and slave—opening the ears of justice to those who were before dumb in her presence, and giving parity of right, authority and remedy, to the highest and lowliest; breaking down the barriers of the jury-box, and permitting the landless citizen and the man of African descent to come within its bounds, opening the forum, the bar and the bench, to the honorable competition of the colored man—all these mighty changes in the relations of the great component elements of society, demand equivalent changes in the laws and render the work both of the Legislator and the codifier, one of extreme difficulty and delicacy. The Commissioners are determined to perform their portion of it, with conscientious carefulness, neglecting no pains, and refusing no aid, which will tend to secure as perfect a compilation and revision, as circumstances will permit.

GENERAL DIVISION OF LABOR.

In considering the duties of the Commissioners, it was found that they were comprehended under seven distinct sub-divisions as follows:

I. A Code of Civil Practice and Procedure in the several Courts of the State.

II. A Code of Criminal Practice and Procedure, in the several Courts of the State.

III. A Political Code.
IV. A Civil Code.
V. A Penal Code.
VI. Suggestion of alterations, amendments and revisions of laws necessary to carry into effect the Provisions of the Constitution.
VII. A General Analysis of all the Codes.

THE GENERAL ANALYSIS.

The general Analysis of Codes, herewith presented, is not expected to be in all respects complete or exhaustive. It would be almost impossible to present an accurate analysis of this work previous to its completion. The one presented will, however, indicate the general plan and scope of the Code projected by the Commissioners, and contemplated in the act of appointment. Such variations will be made from this plan as further time, and progress, may show to be expedient. The analysis now submitted, is complete as to all the Codes, except the Code of Penal Procedure, which will be offered at some time during the session, if possible.

ALTERATIONS, AMENDMENTS, &C.

Under this head, the Commissioners will present to the General Assembly, from time to time, such portions of the general Code, as they may deem most important, and be able to complete. Those already prepared, and only waiting to be printed, consist of the powers and duties of Clerks of the Superior Courts, of County Commissioners, of the Superior Court Clerk as Probate Judge, General Elections, the powers and duties of Legislative and Executive officers, the passage of Private Acts, Testimony in Legislative Proceedings.

NECESSITY FOR THESE PROVISIONS.

The Constitution, providing, as it does, for great and numerous changes in the organization of counties, immediate provisions must, of course, be made for the transaction of county business and the holding of elections. In preparing this, every means has been taken by the Commissioners to secure the most perfect system compatible with our situation. The laws of almost every State have been examined, and whatever seemed most simple and expedient, has been selected to become a part of our organization. It was considered, as indeed is well known to have been the intention of the Constitutional Convention, that the very object of establishing the Board of County Commissioners, and extending the jurisdiction of Justices of the Peace, and conferring probate powers upon the Clerks of Superior Courts, was to separate the Judicial and Legislative functions of the County Court, the latter being conferred upon the Board of Commissioners, and the former upon the Justices and Clerks. It was considered too, that the duties of County Commissioners were strictly defined by section two, Article VII, of the Constitution, and that the power of the Legislature extends only, to prescribing the manner in which those duties should be performed. No extension of those duties, therefore, has been attempted.

THE CODE OF CIVIL PROCEDURE.

It was deemed necessary to provide at once, certain portions of this Code, in order that Justice might not be delayed, and that parties might have adequate remedies in all cases. It will be submitted in detached portions, as rapidly as possible. It is the desire of the Commissioners to complete it before the adjournment of the General Assembly. During the consideration of portions of the Code presented by them, the Commissioners will be pleased to offer any explanation which may be desired in regard to the same.

Hoping that by earnest and united effort, order may be brought out of disorder, and confusion give way to certainty in our laws, we remain,

With the utmost respect,
Your obedient servants,

W. B. RODMAN,
V. C. BARRINGER,   *Commissioners.*
A. W. TOURGEE,

Secretary.

Document III-11 The Judicial System, July 29, 1868

[The author of this newspaper article in the *Wilmington Daily Journal* from July 1868 broadly complained that codification would sweep away the slow work of generations; he also specifically derided the abolition of the antebellum county courts. The writer suggested that simplification of legal procedure served the needs of the freedmen and Northerners.]

The New Judicial System—The Commission on "Rules of Practice and Procedure"—The Recent "Corporation Act."

Messrs. Editors:—Upon the adoption of the "new Constitution" the County Courts and the Superior Courts, as regulated under the old *regime*, ceased to exist, and we are now, in fact, without State Courts of any description, save, perhaps, Magistrates Courts.

The late Convention appointed three Commissioners to report to the present General Assembly "rules of practice and procedure" adapted to the changes in our judicial system contemplated by the new Constitution.

The Commissioners entered, of course, on their labors as soon as it was ascertained that the Constitution had been adopted by a vote of the people. The wiseacres of the late Convention declared that, in abolishing all distinctions between actions at law and equity, and in reducing all the old forms of actions to one "which shall be denominated a civil action," they had succeeded in simplifying our legal proceedings. Their purpose evidently was to do away with the necessity of legal learning, so that negroes and carpet-baggers might be qualified to come to the bar, or sit upon the bench.

The rules of practice and procedure must, of course, be as simple as the judicial system of which they are to form a part.—The Commissioners have had now three months to perform their work. Why, then, are we left to grope in darkness without any such "rules," without any guide as to the form of action, and without any knowledge even of the return day of a writ? If the old forms of action ceased to exist with the adoption of the new Constitution, there is not a lawyer in North Carolina who knows to-day the proper form of a writ or of any other process. What have the Commissioners been doing since the adoption of the new Constitution?

Radicalism has always an eye to the "main chance," and the members of the party are making the most of their present opportunities for public plunder. The "new Constitution" declares that "no person shall hold more than one public office under the State at the same time," but provides that "Commissioners appointed for special purposes, shall not be considered officers within the meaning of this section." This proviso, if I mistake not, was introduced by one of the Commissioners himself, with a view, doubtless, to his own case. So that the members of this Commission not only draw their salaries as Judges, but $200 a month each, besides, as Commissioners. Under these circumstances we must expect that, consistently with Radical principles, it will require some time longer to hatch the "rules of practice and procedure."

Our former Judicial system was the growth of years, and was admirably adapted to the situation and wants of our people. Every attempted inroad had been rejected by former Legislatures and Conventions, but a few men—wretched adventurers—without prestige, without character, without learning, banned from all respectable society, and finding fellowship only with negroes, overturned, in an hour, the work of generations. We know very well that these men could never have disgraced the halls of the Capitol as legislators save for the enfranchisement of our former slaves; but how white men—North Carolinians—could be induced to follow in the Legislature the lead of characterless vagabonds, in destroying the time-honored institutions of their native State, is one of those mysterious phenomena of history which can be accounted for only on the principle "whom the Gods wish to destroy they first make mad."

Nothing more inconvenient or unsuitable could have been devised than the abolition of the County Courts, and the substitution of two Superior Courts in the year for every county, each Court with a session of *two weeks*. The General Assembly may, indeed, provide for more than two Courts in the year for each county, but this is almost impossible with *two weeks* to each Court, which the new Constitution requires. In some districts three Courts in the year, in each county, would keep the Judges on the Circuit *forty-eight* weeks, making only four weeks in the year for vacation. A more senseless fundamental enactment cannot elsewhere be found. The Legislature cannot remedy the evil; this can be effected only through a change in the Constitution.

It is to be presumed that the Governor will soon try his hand on the removal of your municipal officers. Well, you have good lawyers in your city, and why not have recourse to the Court? But alas, what can be expected from a bench, the incumbents whereof, with a few ex[c]eptions, were elected as the c[r]eatures of the party which perpetrates the outrage. CIVIS.

DOCUMENT III-12 PEARSON TO RODMAN, AUGUST 6, 1868

[In this letter to Justice William Rodman, perhaps from August 1868, Chief Justice Richmond Pearson argued that if all principles of practice and procedure could be codified, then the task of construing them would be more difficult than the task of announcing them had been. Pearson asked, Why not maintain the principles of North Carolina's common law and equity decisions as a foundation for the commission's work, modifying these principles as new conditions required?]

Richmond Hill August 6th [1868?]

My Dear Sir.

I read your favor of the 26th inst. & the papers referred to me yesterday.

I return "the Code of Civil Procedure[.]" You will see that I have used my pencil very freely—These are some off hand suggestions occurring as I read & [should?] be treated as such.

I think the commissioners are happy in making the general analisis, & if it be carried out well, they will deserve the thanks of their country.

It is impossible to reduce to a code of *lex scripta*, all of the principles of the common Law, & equity—including rules of evidence &c &c—so as to make the duty of the courts a mere matter of construction & if possible, The difficulty of construction would be greater than the task of announcing principles, which have been so well settled as those of the common Law & equity as heretofore disclosed by our courts. So I hope you will not attempt to abolish the common law—under which I include equity—but will consider your task performed by making a code, setting out such modifications of the common Law & the statutes, as our new condition calls for—which is all that in my opinion the constitution requires, having the common Law, as heretofore in force & in use in this State, as a substratum or foundation, on which the superstructure rests. It is unwise to attempt too many changes, especially in the present condition of our country—when a strong party is threatening to upset every thing, even at the risk of another civil war— The changes in our court system & county organizations is enough for the present— bear this in mind—

In regard to the clerkships—I have a gentleman in view, every way competent—so we had better not make up our conclusions untill we meet in January. Provided the "Nullifiers" permit us to do so.

My respects to your [*illegible*].

Yours truly,
R. M. Pearson

DOCUMENT III-13 THE CODE COMMISSION, AUGUST 8, 1868

[This newspaper article of August 1868 from the *Raleigh Daily Sentinel* evidenced contempt for both the code commissioners and for their codifications. As to the latter, the author said that the numerous bills offered to the general assembly by the commission "seem to be mere copies of Legislative acts at the North, without regard to fitness and adaptation"; "[t]he changes proposed . . . are not only fundamental and radical, but . . . vexatious and expensive"; and "the people, in order to understand the simplest matters of process in the Courts, must go to the lawyers for information." As to the former, the writer said that "this entire system of changes has been made so offensive by the character of the men who have succeeded in imposing them upon us. . . ."]

THE CODE COMMISSION.

This Commission seems to have been industriously, (at least,) at work. It is composed of Judge Rodman, Mr. V. C. Barringer, and *"Judge"* Tourgee. The number of bills already presented by this Board is very large, and they seem to be mere copies of Legislative acts at the North, without regard to fitness and adaptation. The General Assembly has come to regard this Board as its lever power, which does the thinking for it, and seems inclined to adopt the bills prepared by the Board, without proper reflection. Indeed, to a great extent, this is the character of *all* the important legislation. What is determined in caucus is rushed through under the power of the gag law, i. e. the previous question,—a thing heretofore unknown in North Carolina legislation.

Some of the bills are either incorrectly printed or drawn up, as we discover important omissions, which, in the hurry of legislation,—in fact the neglect to read the bills,—will make serious jargon of the laws.

The changes proposed in our Court practice, and in our entire municipal government, are not only fundamental and radical, but must be so provoking to the people, vexatious and expensive, that we have no idea they will long bear them. Such radical changes in the customs, habits of thought and practice of a people, can only be effected in a generation. That native citizens of any sense, whatever, should have submitted in the Convention to such changes as these, simply upon the urgent recommendation of a set of carpet-baggers, without either intelligence or *prestige* of any kind to commend them, except that these plans were doing well in such States as New York and Ohio, is most remarkable. There never was anything like it before. Tourgee, in the Convention, was an over-match for Mr. Rodman, and every lawyer or native citizen in it. We have not heard of a single native who *approved* them, who had considered, for a moment, the enormous, expensive and vexatious changes proposed, and yet, Tourgee, by a little stubborn persistence in his course, brought over a large majority of the Convention to his wishes.

Every lawyer in the State, old and young, must forget a good deal that he has learned, and plunge at once into the study of the Code of Procedure in the practice of the Courts; and the people, in order to understand the simplest matters of process in the Courts, must go to the lawyers for information. These things will prove so vexatious to our plain people, that the authors and supporters of them may look for general and bitter execration, as well as utter contempt, from the people. Moreover, these changes cost enormously, and will prove a serious drawback. Within five years from to-day, the people will call a Convention in North Carolina to wipe out this entire system of changes, which have been made so offensive by the character of the men who have succeeded in imposing them upon us, and which will be vastly more so by the experience of that period, and will return to our old systems and usages, with such modifications as good sense may dictate. No man of sense, who has lived in North Carolina for five years, can suppose, for a moment, that such a system, as has been introduced by these carpet baggers, is at all adapted to this State or will be borne long by our people.

We have examined several of the bills prepared by the Commission, and find them lacking in that simplicity and perspicuity which are so necessary. The bill providing for registration, &c., should be called a bill to prevent the good citizens of North Carolina from registering and voting. If any law should be simple and made easy of accommodation to the general sense and wishes of the people, it should be this, and yet the Code Commission have prepared a bill of twenty-four pages. It provides for all registration to be done *in one day*, requires registration every two years, adopts an exceedingly expensive system of records, &c., and makes no provision, whatever, for inspectors and judges of opposing parties to detect frauds. In our sparsely settled country, registration is wholly unnecessary. The best protection to the polls is to require all voters, at all ages, to pay not what has heretofore been called a poll tax, but a poll tax in fact, *a tax for the privilege of voting*,—the poll keepers being required to demand the receipt of the tax collector that, it has been paid by the voter, before voting.—This simple method in our State, with such instructions to the tax assessors and collectors as are necessary, would do far better than the complicated and expensive mode prepared or copied from the New York system by the Commissioners. The books necessary to prepare for registration will cost at least $100 for each county.

Serious objections will be found to almost every bill we have seen.

Document III–14 Tourgée and the Code Commission, August 13, 1868

[In this news correspondence of August 1868 from the *Wilmington Daily Journal*, Commissioner Albion W. Tourgée was depicted as an evil force and his code commission described as a nuisance.]

OUR RALEIGH CORRESPONDENCE....

RALEIGH, AUGUST 11, 1868. . . .

Speaking of the Code Commission, it is almost universally voted a nuisance. Its Code of procedure is ridiculed, as well as deplored, by intelligent lawyers, while the various bills which are reported from it bear the impress of crudity and mean partisanship. Rodman is a good lawyer, but he succumbs to Tourgee, who is powerful for evil, while Barringer is so prostrated physically as to have but little mental energy. Tourgee, it is well known, is the author of old Welker's standing army bill.—It is really surprising to witness the extent of his (Tourgee's) influence, considering that less is known of him than of any other of the Yankee adventurers. Generally, a little inquiry and investigation has disclosed something as to the antecedents or whereabouts of other carpet-baggers. But no one has ever, that I have heard, been able to ascertain anything, as to Tourgee's history or the place of his nativity. A man who is, himself, so reticent about these things, must have something in the past to *fear* being brought to light. . . .

Document III–15 C.C.P. Preface, August 25, 1868

[The preface to *The Code of Civil Procedure*, here reprinted, reveals the hastiness in which North Carolina's provisions for code pleading were prepared for publication, and the anticipation already of their thorough revision and amendment.]

PREFACE.

In submitting that portion of the Code of Civil Procedure which has been prepared and adopted, to the profession and the people of the State, the Commissioners, recognizing and regretting its deficiencies, beg leave only to call attention to the very brief time which has been occupied in its preparation and publication. By the conditions imposed by the Constitution and Act of Appointment,[389] the Commissioners were compelled to report a Code of Civil Procedure as well as a General Analysis of the Codes projected by them, to the first session of the General Assembly. In addition to the duties, thus imposed, they were requested, by resolution of one or both Houses of the General Assembly, during the late session, to prepare several bills upon subjects connected with necessary amendment of our laws, to adapt the new machinery of the State Government to its work.

The actual work of preparation of the Code can hardly be said to have commenced until the inauguration of the State Government, July 3rd, 1868. Since that time, the Commissioners have not only prepared and published the present volume, but have prepared and submitted nearly as much more, for the consideration of the General Assembly. The necessity for this haste no one regrets more keenly than the

Commissioners, yet they hope it will not be without good, in its final results, as it will render possible a complete and thorough revision and amendment of the Code of Civil Procedure, before the final publication of the Codes projected by the Commission. It is hoped that the entire Bench and Bar of the State, will unite with the Commissioners in endeavoring to perfect and harmonize the system of Procedure now introduced, and made necessary by the Constitution, by forwarding to them such amendments as may occur to them, in practice under it, as necessary or valuable. Having fulfilled the conditions of the Constitution in regard to the work which was required to be reported to the first session, we can assure the profession that no pains will be spared to make the future work of the Commission as complete as time and assiduous labor can render it.

It is expected that the volume will be in the hands of the profession and the officers of the courts by the first of September, or in less than ninety days from the time its preparation was commenced.

The Ordinance of the Convention of 1865 and 1866, in regard to the jurisdiction of the courts, amended by the Convention of 1868, is for the first time published in its amended form, in this volume, for the convenience of public officers and parties interested.

THE COMMISSIONERS.

Raleigh, August 25th, 1868.

Document III–16 Second Report of the Code Commissioners, August 31, 1868

[According to North Carolina's code commissioners in this, their second report, neighbors in all countries resolved disputes essentially by summons, complaint, and answer, because these aspects of procedure were "fixed in justice." Yet, other aspects of procedure, they observed, were purely arbitrary, such as the nature of the summons. The commissioners based their codification of these arbitrary things on the "Code of New York," just as North Carolina's constitutional convention, in abolishing the forms of action—that abolition which created the need for this procedural code—had "adopted the language of the law of New York."]

Office of Commissioners of Code,
Raleigh, August 31st, 1868.

To the General Assembly of the State of North Carolina:

The Commissioners appointed by the Constitutional Convention, to prepare among other things, a Code of Practice and Procedure in civil actions for the courts of this State, respectfully present the concluding portion of that Code with the exception of certain detailed regulations for what are called "Special Proceedings," including:

1. Application for year's provision of a widow.
2. The laying off of dower.
3. Partition of real and personal property.
4. Foreclosure of mortgage.
5. Habeas Corpus.
6. Mandamus.
7. Laying off property exempt from execution.
8. Ejectment for the recovery of real estate.
9. Proceedings in contempt.
10. Proceedings on impeachment.

As they understand the law of New York, these proceedings are only generally, and not fully, provided for in its Code of Procedure, but are regulated at least in part, by certain statutes contained in the second volume of their Revised Statutes.

Proceedings in these cases, are accordingly left by your Commissioners for the present, to be governed by the existing Statutes, as far as may be consistently with the provisions of the Code of Civil Procedure.

The Commissioners ask leave to submit a few observations respecting the circumstances under which their work has been performed, and the manner of its performance.

The Constitution required that they should present such a Code to the Legislature at its present session; it contemplated the abolition, as soon as such a Code could be prepared, of all existing forms of actions, and of all distinctions between actions at law and suits in Equity; Courts of Equity were immediately abolished by the Constitution. The Commissioners felt the necessity of diligence and even of a degree of haste incompatible with the perfection which might reasonably be expected from a longer time for consideration and review. They commenced their labors as soon as they had any assurance that the Constitution would become the law of the State, and in two months have prepared and presented to your body:

1. An Analysis of the entire Code of the State.
2. A bill for the government of counties.
3. A bill defining the powers and duties of Clerk's of the Superior Courts as Judges of Probate.
4. A bill concerning the Jurisdiction of Justices of the Peace.
5. A Code of Civil Procedure for the Superior Courts.

Besides many others on subjects of great importance, requiring both research and reflection, but upon which members of your body thought early legislation necessary for the public good. Some idea may be formed of the diligence with which the Commissioners have labored, when it is considered that nearly five years elapsed between the appointment of the Commissioners to prepare the Revised Code, and its publication. In reference to the Code of Practice, so great has been their sense of the necessity for promptly providing rules for the guidance of the newly created Courts, that they have ventured to present it to you in piece meal, without reserving to themselves any opportunity for reviewing it *as a whole*.

Under such circumstances, it is inevitable that imperfections will be found, which such a review would have readily disclosed. We feel authorized, therefore, to ask a generous criticism of our labors from you, as well as from the profession, which because it is best able to appreciate the difficulties of the task, is always disposed to regard in a kindly spirit, every effort directed in good faith to improve the administration of justice.

As the Constitution adopted the language of the law of New York in its provisions for abolishing the distinction in the forms of actions; and as the Code of that State was the first adopted, and has been the model on which those of many other States have been since framed, the Commissioners did not hesitate to take the Code of New York as the basis of that to be prepared for this State, with such modifications as the differing circumstances of the two States might make expedient.

In general, they have endeavored to make such changes only as were absolutely commanded or clearly implied in the words of the Constitution, or as were manifestly proper. To point out the changes in detail, would occupy too much of your time.

The Code we present, forms as nearly as was possible under the circumstances in which it has been prepared, a consistent whole; there is scarce any part which can be altered without involving alteration in some or numerous others. We therefore invite your honorable body to pass it as it is, and leave to experience, to expose the places which require amendment. The Code of New York was adopted in 1848 as it come from the hands of the Commissioners, and has ever since been undergoing amendments, suggested by experience, and so framed by the most able lawyers, as to fit in and harmonize with the other parts.

All can understand the value to a people, of a Code of laws, embodying and regulating according to justice and reason, the rights and duties of men in all the varying relations of life and business; but none but those whose profession makes them necessarily familliar [*sic*] with the modes of applying those principles to actual transactions, can appreciate that the machinery for such application is as essential to justice as is the recognition of its principles.

In every Code for the administration of law, much is fixed by the laws of the human mind, and is, therefore, essentially alike in the practices of all countries; while much also is purely arbitrary, and depends for its wisdom, on the habits and condition of the people to whom it is applied.

For example: every man who has a complaint against his neighbor, for which he seeks redress, must first summon the supposed wrong-doer before some Judge, and must inform him of the grounds of the complaint, and the defendant must have an opportunity to answer.

These things are fixed in justice, and are to be found in the practice of all countries. But what shall be the nature of the summons,—whether or not the defendant shall be arrested and held to bail, the time of notice, the manner of service, and a vast number of other details which it is indispensable for the convenience of all parties shall be prescribed by some fixed and certain law, are purely arbitrary, and are scarcely ever the same in any two States. It is not so important what they are, as that they should be fixed and clear and known, and conformable to the business usages of a people, their grade of culture and facilities for mutual intercourse.

We make these general observations to show the views which have guided us in the preparation of this Code, confident, that whatever may be the skill with which we have applied them, the views themselves will be received by all, as true.

Detailed regulations for what are called "Special Proceedings" are not urgent, they being sufficiently provided for, at present, by the Code, and by the existing laws; we do not propose, therefore, to present those at this session of the Legislature.

Very respectfully,

WM. B. RODMAN,
A. W. TOURGEE,
V. C. BARRINGER.

Document III-17 Pearson to Rodman, September 24, 1868

[The letter transcribed below to Justice William B. Rodman from Chief Justice Richmond M. Pearson revealed Pearson's opinion about codification of the common law of homicide.[390] In an erudite pose—Pearson was the greatest teacher of law in nineteenth-century North Carolina—which referenced Sir Edward Coke (1552–1634), John Locke (1632–1704), and Sir Matthew Hale (1605–1676), Pearson objected that codification of the law of homicide was "impossible."

His reference to Locke perhaps blurred the question of the scope of codification that Pearson thought the code commissioners meant to engage, since *The Fundamental Constitutions of Carolina*,[391] a work that Locke was thought to have contributed, was chiefly a political code and not a codification of the entire common law. On the other hand, nineteenth-century critics of the codification movement often cited Carolina's misfortune, describing *The Fundamental Constitutions of Carolina* as a "code":

> The subject of codification is beginning to excite a strong interest in our country. . . . Among us, the *codification* proposed is simply *revision* and *redaction*,—the reduction of a portion of the vast mass of decided cases (*Jurisprudence des arrets*) to a written text,—thus establishing, as it were, a *stratum* of written law, which will give firmness and solidity to that portion which remains *unwritten*. By such a course, it seems to me that we, in a great degree, avoid the evils pointed out by Savigny and the Historical School. We still preserve the historical features of the law, not presuming to frame a *new* system from *new* materials without consulting the previous customs, habits, and history of the country. The error of Jeremy Bentham and of John Locke was in supposing that they, in their closets, could frame *de novo* a code for a people. Locke prepared a code, a century ago, for one of the North American colonies, which proved a signal failure. . . .[392]

Not only was Pearson's reference to Locke arguably imperfect, but his reference to Coke perhaps understated the good intentions of codifiers. The maxim Pearson cited was this:

> . . . for as by the authoritie of *Littleton, discretio est discernere per legem, quid sit justum*, that is, to discerne by the right line of law, and not by the crooked cord of private opinion, which the vulgar call discretion. . . .[393]

But this maxim suggested that a strong body of precedent would control arbitrariness in judging, which was a goal of both classic common law adjudication and of codification. Pearson's point, it seems, was that codification would fail to attain its goal, an inflexible "statute code" making the law less certain, its inflexibility not repairable by judges resorting to their "good sense" in interpreting it. While Pearson's point may be conceded, it is not clear from the oblique reference in this letter that Rodman advocated the adoption of an inflexible "statute code" or that by "good sense" he meant anything less than applying reasoned judgment in cases clearly distinguishable from nearby precedents, even if commissioners Tourgée and Barringer did so advocate. Rodman may have meant for the commissioners to write a code with the authority of a modern restatement of the law, leaving courts free to develop and to distinguish applications of principle declared in the code.[394] If so, Rodman's position approached the point of view of Pearson himself, who conceded the usefulness of the less rigid "codes" of Coke and Hale. The codes of the latter gentlemen to which Pearson referred were presumably their seventeenth-century treatises, much along the lines of what Blackstone would elaborate for post-Revolution England in the latter half of the eighteenth century. In other words, Pearson might tolerate a codification of the common law only if it were as distant as possible from the codes which Bentham had proposed earlier in the century.]

Richmond Hill, Sept. 24th 1868
My Dear Sir—

The specimen sent—of an attempt to codify "the law of homicide," confirms my impression that the thing is impossible & the result will be to make the law more uncertain than it is. Coke, Locke, Hale: Each man codified the law but their codes were not rigid and could be made by the courts to yield to better evidence of what the law is—a statute code will have no flexibility, & the judges will be driven to printed construction, of which the New York case referred to, an instance. I see you rely on "the reserved force, of the common law—or good sense." For mercy sake don't leave it to good sense—whose sense? That is a discreet judge! So in the words of Coke, we shall have "the crooked end of one man's opinions, instead of the straight line of the law, which is not the opinion of one but of many men put together" and its [*two illegible words*] by the experience of ages.

It is true, the abolition of Slavery—change of punishments &c. &c., render it necessary to revise our present code—cannot you induce Tourgee & Barringer to be content with a change of this kind, at least for the present, the Legislature would no doubt fall with it, if recommended by the commissioners. I do assure you, this is not an auspicious time for making radical changes in the Laws; sufficient for the day are the changes, which the new order of things make necessary in the constitution, the offices of the government, & mode of judicial procedure.

My Letter was meant for the peace-loving conservatives, I think with you it is producing the effect intended. The pains taken by the Nullifiers to keep it from circulation, the [*illegible*] comments giving only gathered extracts; & the personal [*illegible*] hurled at me, show how they [*illegible*] it. If the freedman stand firm, I have no doubts as to the result, but there is a sure purpose on that part of the line, & no pain should be spared to support it.

I return the papers as reprinted. I will [*two illegible words*] aid all I can, but it requires time. When the justices meet next January we can advise [*illegible*]. Please send the 1st Rep. "Code of procedure" I have none & wish to lecture my students on it.

[*illegible*] R. M. Pearson

Document III–18 The Code Commission, November 6, 1868

[This newspaper editorial in the *Raleigh Daily Sentinel* from late in 1868 suggested that the code commission had moderated excesses of the general assembly but had done little good for the judiciary.]

STATE AFFAIRS. . . .

But it is especially in the character of the Judiciary and the Legislature, that this incompetency and inefficiency will appear most glaring. Without the aid of the one or two sensible lawyers on the Code

Commission, whose legal ability and originality of thought, however, have not been very apparent in what they have already done, and intelligent Conservative or Democratic members of the body, it is hardly conceivable to what lengths in bad legislation the present General Assembly would not reach. Its extravagance has already passed all bounds of propriety, honesty or reason. It is really apprehended that, without some additional check upon it, within the two years yet to come, for which they were elected, they will so utterly bankrupt the State, that every man will have to become a *carpet bagger*, to reduce all his means to greenbacks or government bonds, so that his resources can be kept ready packed up at any moment, to be off when the crash comes, rather than be the possessor of any real property upon which the tax-gatherer can gorge.

The character of our State Judiciary has been so completely metamorphosed by the change, that men will seriously hesitate whether to resort to the Courts for the protection of life, liberty or property, or take their chances in a rough and tumble scrimmage with their neighbors in the defence of either. . . .

Richmond M. Pearson served as chief justice of the Supreme Court of North Carolina both before and after the Civil War. Photograph of a portrait of Richmond M. Pearson. (*Credit*: State Archives of North Carolina, Raleigh)

Document III–19 The Code Commission, December 9, 1868

[This newspaper editorial in the *Raleigh Daily Sentinel* from late in 1868 suggested that the code commission did little work that was original or adapted to the needs of North Carolina, and that it should be abolished.]

THE CODE COMMISSION.

We understand that Judge Rodman and Mr. V. C. Barringer are here, *at work* on the "Code." They get $200 per month, each, and for what? Why simply to cut up a *printed copy* of the *New York Code* and adapt it, *in name*, to North Carolina!—What a shame that the people should be so robbed!

We wonder that the plain, home-spun "radikils" in the Legislature can stand such barefaced imposition. Tourgee will be along, as soon as his Courts are over, and then the State will pay $600 per month, and for clerk-hire and fuel and lights, to the "Code Commission." And we will venture to assert, that "Judges" Rodman and Tourgee will draw, in addition to their $200 per month as "Code Commissioners," their regular salaries as "Judges." See if they don't.

We call upon members of the Legislature to see how this is, and let the people know how their hard earnings go. The "Code Commission" is a nuisance and ought to be abolished forthwith. But the Radical majority in the House refused even to *entertain* the resolution of enquiry, introduced by Mr. Malone, as to the *power* of the Legislature to discontinue it![395] So we go.

Document III–20 The Code Commission, December 18, 1868

[This diatribe against the code commission, published in the *Raleigh Daily Sentinel* in December 1868, hoped for a quick restoration of the old system of pleading and practice.]

MISMANAGEMENT AND INCOMPETENCY. . . .

Nor are the judicial matters of the State likely to fare any better. The labors of the Code Commission seem to be manipulated by surgeons better acquainted with the broad-axe and the cross-cut-saw, than the polished steel employed by skillful practitioners. They can cut roughly or chop the body of the law in pieces, but are incapable of bringing the joints together, arranging the nerves, muscles and vital parts, putting on the skin and making the dry bones to live.

The Code Commission have asked counsel of the learned members of the Bar now in this City, and a meeting was held in the Capitol, on Wednesday afternoon, to obtain their suggestions as to the best mode of putting into operation the machinery of the new Civil Code in this State. What will grow out of it we shall see. It is evident that the Commission are at their wit's end. For months, they have been setting up men of straw, one day, to knock them down the next. Professional men of real legal learning can doubtless arrange this Code, which has been tried in New York for twenty or thirty years, and yet, to this day, is not understood by many lawyers of that State, except those of more than ordinary skill,—but how long will it take *the people* of North Carolina to become sufficiently familiar with it to understand and appreciate it? If the people will find it so difficult of comprehension, will become so chary of its mazes and uncertainty as to avoid an appeal to law, when it is possible to do so, it may be of value to them, but we are sure that nine-tenths of the people will prefer the *old* to the *new* way, and the speedy restoration of our former *cheaper* and *safer* system.

Document III–21 The Code Commission, December 19, 1868

[This newspaper editorial in the *Raleigh Daily Sentinel* from late 1868 against the code commission shed no new light on codification, but showed how greatly the movement was detested.]

"THE CODE."

As announced, on yesterday, quite a number of legal gentlemen assembled in the Senate Chamber, on Wednesday evening last, to consider the "Code." We learn further, that it was discussed and "*cussed,*" and that nobody approved of it. It seems to satisfy nobody but the "Code Commissioners," "Judges" Rodman and Tourgee and Mr. Victor C. Barringer, and they go for it, because they get $600 per month, besides fuel, lights, and incidentals, for cutting up a copy of the New York Code and adapting it, in name and date, to poor old North Carolina.

We learn that the objections to "the Code," pointed out in the meeting to which we refer, were endless and serious. Nothing definite, however, was done, further than the appointment of a Committee to report, after mature consideration, what changes can and ought to be made, to an adjourned meeting, on the 7th. January.

We predict that "Judges" Rodman and Tourgee and Mr. Barringer will raise the hue and cry that the "rebels" are rising, that "The Code" is in danger, and "loilty," too, and that nothing will come of this Committee and meeting of and for reform, though "Lt. Gov." Caldwell and "Judge" Cloud, and other Radical lights, were present and participated in the meeting. It won't do to displace this "loil" Code Commission; the State cannot do without the legal light of "Judges" Rodman and Tourgee, and Mr. Barringer; *they* must be continued at whatever cost of money or judicial confusion and darkness that may come upon and cover this "rebellious" and down-trodden "disloil" people. This is, indeed, an age of Radicalism and "carpet-bagism!" And, as a result, the people are *happy* and *prosperous!* Their faces are glad; their barns are full; their fortunes are multiplying and their hopes are high? Aye, and in truth, their condition is intolerable! Intolerable, that is it!

Document III–22   Schenck's Diary, December 23, 1868

[In this diary entry, attorney David Schenck joined his profession in cussing the "New Code."]

"New Code"—other iniquities
December 23, 1868

The shifting scenes of these eventful times change so often and assume such varied shape that it requires too much space and labor to depict them here_ I have been industriously and laboriously engaged in my office, my professiona[l] business being largely on the increase, and the entire change in our Remedies as prescribed by our "New Code" greatly deranges our practice and increases our labor_ It is one of the most annoying of all the Yankee Curses, which Radicalism has inflicted on us; but like negro equality, and political and official prostitution we must bear it until the "dear people" learn its evils by experience, which ought to be seen by common sense_ It has put the whole profession to saying "Cuss words" and a thousand amendments have been and are being offered to it_ It is only making "Confusion worse confounded"— . . .

Document III–23   Meeting of Bench and Bar, December 24, 1868

[This newspaper article in the *Greensboro Patriot and Times*, from December 1868, is about a meeting of the bench and bar regarding *The Code of Civil Procedure*. The article reported the appointment of eight lawyers to study what amendments to the code would be beneficial.]

A MEETING OF THE BENCH AND BAR OF NORTH CAROLINA.

In accordance with previous notice, a considerable number of the Judges and Attorneys of the State met in the Senate Chamber at 2 o'clock P. M., of the 16th instant.

On motion of J. M. McCorkle, Esq., the Hon. Tod R. Caldwell was appointed Chairman, and on motion of Judge Cloud, J. M. McCorkle, Esq., was appointed Secretary.

Judge Cloud stated that the object of the meeting was to interchange opinions with the Code Commissioners, and to make such suggestion in regard to changing the Code of Civil Procedure, as was deemed necessary. He also called the attention of the meeting to several sections of the Code, which, in his opinion, required amendment, and concluded by offering the following resolution:

Resolved, That when this meeting adjourn, it will adjourn to meet on the 7th of January next, and that the chairman appoint eight members of the Bench and Bar of the State, who are requested to report to said meeting, what beneficial amendments, not inconsistent with the Constitution, can be made to the Code of Civil Procedure.

An interesting discussion followed, which was participated in by Judges W. B. Rodman, J. W. Osborne and J. M. Cloud, and V. C. Barringer, Wm. M. Robbins, L. P. Olds and J. M. McCorkle, Esquires.

The resolution was unanimously adopted when the Chairman appointed the following gentlemen as members of said Committee to wit: Chief Justice Pearson, Justices Reade and Dick, Hons. W. H. Battle, B. F. Moore, A. S. Merrimon, and S. F. Phillips and W. H. Bailey, Esquire.

An interesting and able communication was read from Chief Justice Pearson, which on motion of Judge Mitchell was referred to the above Committee.

W. M. Robbins, Esq., introduced the following resolution which was adopted to-wit:

Resolved, That the members of the legal profession of North Carolina be requested to communicate such views as they may think useful in reference to the amendment of the Code of Civil Procedure to the Chairman on that subject appointed by this meeting.

On motion the Secretary was requested to furnish a copy of the proceedings of this meeting to the *Standard* and *Sentinel* for publication, and that the other newspapers of the State be requested to copy.

On motion the meeting adjourned till the 7th day of January next.

    T. R. Caldwell, *President.*
J. M. McCorkle, *Secretary.*

From the above it will be seen that even Radicals are disgusted with the New York "Code of Civil Procedure" so recently palmed off upon this State by the Code Commissioners—Judges Tourgee & Co. This code has cost too much to be so soon discarded—either keep the code or employ more brains on the next one, is our advice.

Document III–24 Suspension of Provisions on Contract, 1869

[Perhaps the biggest objection to the vast change in civil procedure in 1868 was the increased efficiency of the administration of justice, especially where the clerk was the court and the court was always available. Stay laws obviated the objection. These laws failed the test of constitutionality, though, so the legislature suspended parts of *The Code of Civil Procedure.* The publisher's notice to the second edition of the *Handbook for County Officers,* excerpted below, mentions not only this objection to the efficiency of the new civil procedure, but also manages to touch upon a theme in support of codification of procedure: systemization of the law for the benefit of the non-professional reader.]

Publishers' Notice.

The favor with which the first edition of our Hand-Book, (issued at the request of members of the General Assembly,) was received, induces the Publishers to perfect it as far as possible, and give to the public an edition, containing all the additions, amendments and modifications of the law, as adopted at the last session of the General Assembly. The first edition was soon exhausted; and the demand now, since the recent elections, for a manual to supply the wants of the newly elected officers, imperatively calls for an enlarged and amended book, in text, and also in the forms. This want, the Publishers flatter themselves they have supplied, so far as the present transition state of the law will admit, having spared neither expense nor trouble in the compilation.

Our Supreme Court, at January Term, 1869, having decided the Ordinance of the Convention of March, 1868, familiarly known as the "Stay Law," to be unconstitutional, the General Assembly, in order to obviate the distress which would have inevitably followed the summary collections of debts as provided for in the Code of Civil Procedure, suspended many provisions of that Code in relation to suits on contracts, until the 1st of January, 1871. These temporary modifications are contained in the present edition, together with the last Acts relating to the several county officers and county police. With the full and exhaustive index contained in the work now offered to the public, these additions and alterations may be easily marked and compared, so that the publication of those things which may not be law *now* (nor until after the 1st January, 1871,) may be easily distinguished from those enactments designed to meet a temporary emergency. Until, however, the laws are systematically codified, no manual for the use of non-professional readers can be possibly complete. It is the design of the Publishers, when the Commissioners appointed to revise the Code have completed their labors, to issue an edition which will be full, satisfactory and complete, answering the demands of officers and business men generally. In the meantime, if the material alterations in the law justifies it, a supplement to this edition will be issued, the cheapest and most effectual method of keeping the public advised of the changes and modifications of the laws.

This edition, the Publishers have placed within the reach of every man, who desires to administer the duties of his office with legal and effectual justice. If a Magistrate, through passion, ignorance of authority or absurdity, mistake the limits of his power, or his duties, he will be the object of contempt from his inferiors, and of merited censure from the power that appointed him, and to whom he is accountable for official misconduct.

Document III–25   Meeting of Bench and Bar, January 8, 1869

[The committee of eight lawyers appointed on December 24, 1868, to consider changes to *The Code of Civil Procedure*[396] met in Raleigh on January 8, 1869, one day late. The short newspaper report of that date from the *Raleigh North Carolina Standard*, reprinted below, suggested that all went well at the meeting, the code not sustaining any fatal blow.]

The Meeting of the Bench and Bar.

A large and interesting meeting of judges and members of the bar was held in the Senate Chamber on yesterday afternoon for the consideration of the Code of Civil Procedure. Lieut. Gov. Caldwell presided, and W. L. Bailey, Esq., acted as Secretary. Many able speeches were made by Judges Cloud, Battle, Pearson, Rodman, Read, Tourgee, Barringer, Jones and others. The discussion was conducted in an amiable spirit, and the conclusion generally arrived at seemed to be that the new Code, though defective in some of its parts, was not liable to any criticism upon its intrinsic value.

Document III–26   Superior Courts and Clerks, January 25, 1869

[This newspaper article in the *Raleigh North Carolina Standard* from early 1869 questioned the value of the jurisdiction of the clerk of court and explained how the modification by *The Code of Civil Procedure* of when executions were returnable affected the traditional financing of agriculture, which he described as "the settled policy of the State," and which he said the code "breach[ed]." Dealings in North Carolina, he said, must account for "seed time and harvest."]

OUR COURTS.

For the Standard.

To the Code Commissioners—Superior Courts.
No. 6. . . .

Of what avail is the constitutional dogma, that "the courts shall always be open," if the remoteness of the Judge or his inaccessibility, makes the provision of little service to any but *neighborhood* suitors? If three terms of the Superior Courts should be established, if "not always open," they certainly would be, for practical purposes, *oftener* "open," than they now are, under the benignant platitude of "always open."

What the people want is, not enticing words which give no substantial or only partial relief, but they want the Judge brought, at stated times and short intervals, within their easy reach, so that they may know, when and where to find him, but find him without traversing half the State and then perhaps not find him at home.

I am convinced, therefore, that the people would receive a more equal and beneficial administration of the laws, by abolishing the clerks' jurisdiction, and whether abolished or not, by holding three terms of the Superior Courts, at intervals of four months, and making process returnable, to these terms and conforming, as far as possible, to the old practice and usages. This view is reinforced by a brief consideration of the law of "*executions*" under the new Code, which is certainly not in harmony with the "relief laws" which appear to be the peculiar policy of the times. All executions are now made returnable in *sixty days*, instead of, to the next *term of the Court*, as of old. Why this sharp and sudden remedy? Why this *dash* upon the fortifications of the relief laws?

It fills the heart of the debtor with consternation and dismay! It stabs him under the fifth rib, and is a "mortal dissection of his whole anatomy!" Unintentional, of course, for I well knew the benevolent feelings of the commissioners; yet it is a *breach* of what seems to be the settled policy of the State.

What is the daily life and history of our population? In the spring time they sow, and then anxiously watch and wait upon the young and tender plant. They plow and hoe the growing crop. They look up to Heaven for the rain in due season, and if it fails, their hearts are saddened, for their children will want bread. When the genial shower gladdens the drooping corn, their hearts expand with gratitude and cheerfulness, because they know their children shall not suffer the pangs of hunger. So, from spring to autumn they toil with patience and anxiety, and finally the husbandmen are rewarded by gathering in the harvest of their labor.

Such is the life of the people of this State.

Their general dealings are made with reference to "seed time and harvest," and their ability to meet their liabilities, are measured by the same standard of their *yearly* harvests. Our old laws were conformed to the life and habits of our people, and executions were made returnable, as far as possible, in accordance with the agricultural pursuits of our population.

Now, however, no one knows when a judgment will be taken or execution levied upon his property. He plants in April, and in June his horse is taken from the plow by the sheriff, and his crop is lost.

I am no advocate of stay-laws, repudiation laws, or bankrupt laws, and am the advocate of the inviolability of contracts. But when laws are made to enforce rights, they should be so made as to secure the end aimed at, with as little violence and injury as possible to the pursuits and habits of the people. . . .

SOMERS.

Document III–27   Practice of Law, February 15, 1869

[Now, in the year 2024, folks resist the judgments of the North Carolina Board of Law Examiners on character and fitness to practice law[397] and acquiesce more readily in the requirement of an examination which tests technical skill in basic legal subjects. There was a year, though, when the philosophy of the state was quite the inverse: good moral character and only good moral character was the accepted requirement for a license to practice law. An act of assembly from February 1869, excerpted below, found its origin in the following resolution of the Constitutional Convention of 1868:[398]

> The following preamble and resolution presented by Mr. Forkner, was taken up, and,
> On motion, was adopted:
> WHEREAS, This Convention has passed an ordinance allowing men of legal profession, of a good moral character, by exhibiting a certificate granted by the Courts of other States, to the bar in the Courts of North-Carolina; and whereas, many of the States requiring nothing more than the establishment of a good moral character, to admit men to the bar; and that citizens of this State should be on equality with those of other States; therefore,

Be it resolved, That the Committee on the Judiciary be instructed to report an ordinance or clause for the Constitution, which will allow citizens of North-Carolina to practice, and plead law in the Courts of the State by establishing a good moral character and paying necessary fees.

The act of assembly of 1869 abiding this resolution was repealed in 1870,[399] the provisions which had been in effect under the *Revised Code* of 1854, chapter 9, "Attorneys at Law," being re-enacted.]

CHAPTER XLVI.

AN ACT TO ALLOW CITIZENS OF NORTH CAROLINA TO PRACTICE IN THE COURTS OF THE STATE

Section 1. *The General Assembly of North Carolina do enact,* That any citizen of this State, by establishing a good moral character, and paying a license tax of twenty dollars, shall be allowed to practice law in the courts of North Carolina.

Sec. 2. All taxes arising under the provisions of this act shall be paid over to the Sheriff or Tax Collector of the County in which the applicant for said license shall reside, for the benefit of the County.

Sec. 3. That it shall be the duty of the Judge of the Superior Court of the District in which application is made to him to practice law in the Courts of this State to grant the same, when the foregoing provision of this act is complied with.

Sec. 4. That this act shall be in force from and after its ratification.

Ratified the 15th day of February, A. D. 1869.

Document III–28 Schenck's Diary, March 8, 1869

[Attorney David Schenck reported in early 1869 a good side to adopting *The Code of Civil Procedure* in North Carolina: it increased his business by depriving the people of their traditional practice of "chimney corner law."]

New Code—Fish Pond—Children &c
March 8th, 1869

The "New Code of Civil Procedure" adopted by us from the New York Practice has worked a perfect revolution in our practice and procedure_ It has thrown immense labor on the profession and put us to considerable expense for Books and Stationary_ Were it not for the assistance of my young friend Beverly Cobb I could scarcely get along these days with the writing required_ But one good effect is to drown out all the hangers on at the bar_ they Cant buy books or learn the practice being too lazy or too stupid_ It has also increased our fees and thrown all the business into lawyers['] hands because the people cannot get along with "chimney corner law" as in old times.

Upon the whole though clinging with veneration to our old Common law system as the foundation of right and the perfection of reason, I have no reason professionally to complain_ It has worked well for me so far_ . . .

Document III–29 Report of the Code Commissioners, March 20, 1869

[In this, their third report to the general assembly, printed in the *Raleigh North Carolina Standard*, the code commissioners took the offensive posture that it was time to leave behind North Carolina's traditional agrarian dealings and adapt to the bustling business of the nineteenth century. Not surprisingly, the commissioners argued that it was "the Code, with its speedy and efficient remedies" that would strengthen the people's habits of "promptness and punctuality." As if this foreign standard of judgment were not offensive enough, the commissioners emphasized it by emblazoning its report with the very principle that has made all efforts at codification anathema: "It is a mistake that people always make laws. The laws sometimes make a people." Codifiers, then, were reformers, reformers out to make a people.[400] North Carolina was ripe for progressive change, the commissioners pedantically prated, because its people lived "[i]n a juncture of affairs . . . where society is ready to receive new impressions." No matter that that society was a torn, impoverished, and defeated country, and that the juncture was Reconstruction, better known in North Carolina for its resentments, rebellions, riots, and regressions than for its acquiescence in modernity. Ultimately, though, all this effrontery by the commissioners was just a bit of self-defense that allowed them to reiterate their driving goal: to apply general principles and harmonizing methods in order to achieve a rational and consistent system for all law, beginning with a scientific arrangement of civil procedure.]

Report of the Code Commissioners, Session of 1868–'9.

OFFICE CODE COMMISSIONERS,
Raleigh, N.C., March 20, 1869.

To the General Assembly of North Carolina:
GENTLEMEN: The ordinance of appointment, creating the Code Commission, directs the Commissioners to report, at each session of the General Assembly, the progress made to that time.

We append herewith a list of the bills, by their titles, prepared and submitted by us during the present session.

These bills, it will be observed, embrace a great variety of subjects and cover a wide ground. Taken with what was presented at the special session, 1868, they displace not less, perhaps, than three-fourths of the Revised Code.

The Code of Civil Procedure has now been before the public for several months, and has been put to some test in the Courts. It is too early, we admit, to pass upon its merits or defects as a practical system. We have not been surprised to find that a scheme of remedial justice so novel to our former methods has been frequently ill understood, or not understood at all. This is quite natural. But it has not been as general as we were led, from precedent conditions of the human mind, to anticipate. We have received from the Bench and Bar of the State, in divers ways, suggestions for the amendment of the Code in matters of detail. From no quarter has a single mature suggestion reached us, which proposed a radical alteration that could consist well, or, indeed, consist at all, with the imperative innovations of the organic law. We note this singular fact, because it indicates a not less singular era in our history. Our people have taken fast hold of the idea that some legal reform is necessary. Silently, and, it may be, unconsciously this conviction has found its way to our business and our bosoms. It is generally acknowledged that legal development must keep step with commercial and industrial development. Hence the objection to the Code so much pressed at first, that it is unsuited to our habits, is daily losing force; because our habits themselves are in a formative state. And why may not the Code, with its speedy and efficient remedies, strengthen and confirm our habits of promptness and punctuality, confessedly much weakened by the legislation of the last ten years? It is a mistake that people always make laws. The laws sometimes make a people. In a juncture of affairs, like ours, where society is ready to receive new impressions, the duty is important early to secure and settle the basis of a prompt and uniform administration of justice between man and man. To the plastic hand of the courts and of future legislation, we must look to build up and fitly join together the structure. Such a basis we have in the Code of Civil Procedure which is rapidly becoming the national system in America.

The generous criticism which we invited as well as our own mature reflection, has revealed several deficiencies and imperfections in the Code of Civil Procedure. These we have endeavored to correct and supply, as we will continue to do from time to time.

To bring the body of our civil and political law, including appropriate modes of proceeding therein, into harmony with the organic changes of the Constitution and the existing judicial order of the State, seemed to us to be a concern of prime importance. Until this is done, there must be ceaseless confusion in our courts, and, frequently, if not a denial of right, a mistake of remedy, which will amount to an expensive delay of right. To this end, therefore, we have hitherto chiefly directed our labors, as an inspection of the appended list of bills will show. Those bills, should they all become laws, will reach, it is believed, nearly every case where any serious question can exist either as to the tribunal of relief, or the mode of relief. We have not been ambitious of using the liberty accorded us by the Act of Appointment "to specify from time to time such amendments, alterations and revisions of the law as may [d]eem necessary." We have sought rather to depart as little as possible from the "old paths, which is the good way," either in the substance or in the language of the Statutes, except where it was clear to us that both could be improved. Our aim has been, from the beginning, to fashion our work on a consistent plan of construction, with a view to the ultimate result of our labors—a complete Code of the law of the State.

On the Penal Code we have attempted but little. We have brought Criminal Procedure up to the finding of the indictment; and we have shortly provided for the criminal jurisdiction conferred, or contemplated to be conferred, in thirty-third Section, Article IV, of the Constitution, upon Justices of the Peace. Here we have paused. A word of explanation for this course may not be out of place.

The subject of criminal jurisprudence is one of vast breadth and importance. Its administration touches the very quick of human rights. Its scientific arrangement has always been attended with peculiar difficulty. We are aware that this is not the common notion. The popular imagination, which infects the profession also, is, that criminal law is extremely simple as compared with the laws relating to property. The truth, rather, is, that this branch of jurisprudence, though of necessity the earliest in development, is the latest to be reduced to a rational and consistent system. We have not space to discuss the philosophical grounds of the distinction here pointed out. It is sufficient to appeal to universal fact. Roman civil law has always been admired as much for its systematic expression as for the wisdom of its maxims. Roman criminal law has never been any thing but rude and barbaric, without method and without mercy. The Continental States have had, many of them, for generations a code of municipal law more regular in structure and sy[m]metrical in form than any thing that we, who are apprentices to the common law, meet with even at this day in that famous system. But none of them made any advance in codifying their law of crimes till our century. France led the way. She perfected her *Code Penal* in 1812. The other nations followed in close order: Sardinia in 1839; Russia in 1846; Spain in 1848; Prussia in 1851; Austria in 1852. The abundant labors for thirty years of the Criminal Law Commissioners produced the Consolidated Statutes of 1861, which embody the present penal legislation of England. Criminal codification has not met with much favor in our American States; at least, not much has been attempted. Georgia and New York have accomplished most in that direction; though the projected Code of the latter State has not yet been adopted by her Legislature.

The foregoing sketch shows with what tardy steps the nations have advanced to the revision of their criminal justice. Such cautious progress becomes us also in North Carolina, where no effort whatever has been made in any branch of jurisprudence to apply general principles and harmonizing methods. Our statutes in respect to crime are as arbitrary, insolated, and disjointed, each arising upon some particular occasion, as they were an hundred years ago. The Commissioners purpose, however, to prepare a plan of revision, which they hope to distribute among the judges and the profession, during the course of the summer, for their suggestions, as directed in the sixth section of the Ordinance of Appointment. And the plan, after re-examination by the Commissioners, will be laid before the General Assembly at the next session.

We have the honor to be, gentlemen, with great respect, &c.

VICTOR C. BARRINGER,
WILLIAM B. RODMAN,
ALBION W. TOURGEE,

Code Commissioners.

APPENDIX

Of Bills Submitted by the Code Commission,
At Session, 1868–'9.

1. A bill to amend the Code of Civil Procedure in several of its sections.
2. A bill to make certain amendments in the Code of Civil Procedure.
3. A bill to amend Title XX Code of Civil Procedure and to ratify stay of execution by justices of the peace in certain cases.
4. A bill to amend Title XXI Code of Civil Procedure relating to fees.
5. A bill to add another section, to be marked Section 460*a* to Chapter VII, Title XIX Code of Civil Procedure.
6. A bill to prevent the taking of illegal fees under Title XVII of the Code of Civil Procedure, and to extend the time allowed in Section 406 of said Title.
7. A bill containing amendments of detail in the Code of Civil procedure.
8. A bill to amend certain sections of the Code of Civil Procedure and to repeal certain sections of the Revised Code.
9. A bill to cure certain irregularities in the mode of commencing certain actions, and to amend certain sections of the Code of Civil Procedure.
10. A bill to amend Sections 73, 76 and 77 of the Code of Civil Procedure.
11. A bill to impose a tax on successions to real and personal estates, and to provide for its collection.
12. A bill to provide for the collection of taxes by the State and by the several counties of the State, on property, polls and incomes.
13. A bill to impose taxes on trades, professions and franchises, and provide for their collection.
14. A bill in relation to landlord and tenant.
15. A bill providing for the laying off the several counties of the State into Townships.
16. A bill to establish the days and places for selling real property under execution.
17. A bill to regulate proceedings upon impeachment.
18. A bill to regulate proceedings upon writs of *Habeas Corpus*.
19. A bill to provide forms in civil proceedings before Justices of the Peace.
20. A bill to provide a procedure in special proceedings generally, and in applications for widow's year provisions and in dower.
21. A bill to amend an act entitled "an act to provide for the employment of convicts and the erection of a Penitentiary," ratified the 24th August, 1868
22. A bill to establish in the office of the Secretary of State, a Bureau of Statistics, Immigration and Agriculture.
23. A bill to create a mechanic's and laborer's lien law.
24. A bill concerning the settlement of the estates of deceased persons.
25. A bill relating to division fences.
26. A bill to provide for holding special terms of the Superior Courts.
27. A bill to provide a proceeding in cases of bastardy.
28. A bill to regulate proceedings in the legitimation of bastard children.
29. A bill relating to special procedure in cases of mills.
30. A bill to provide a trial jury for second week of the terms of the Superior Courts.

31. A bill to lay off homestead and personal property exemption.

32. A bill to amend chapter forty (40) Revised Code, respecting the draining and damming of low-lands.

33. A bill to amend chapter forty-eight (48) Revised Code entitled "Fences."

34. A bill to regulate proceedings in the partition and sale of real and personal property.

35. A bill in relation to proceedings in contempt.

36. A bill concerning Townships.

37. A bill concerning the powers and duties of State officers.

38. A bill to prescribe the power and duty of the Governor in respect to fugitives from justice.

39. A bill to amend and consolidate the several Acts of the General Assembly of this State for the organization and government of the University, and for other purposes Prepared at the request of the trustees.

40. A bill to declare persons of color competent to testify in all cases.

41. A bill in relation to punishments.

42. A bill concerning guardian and ward.

43. A bill respecting the County Treasurers.

44. A bill concerning criminal procedure and criminal jurisdiction of justices of the peace.

45. A bill concerning the estates of insolvent and imprisoned debtors.

46. A bill concerning an entry-taker.

Document III-30 Rodman to Tourgée, July 21, 1869

[In this note to Commissioner Albion W. Tourgée, Commissioner William Rodman suggested that the Supreme Court of North Carolina opposed codification of civil procedure, but that the general assembly might support it. Perhaps Rodman meant that the legislature might clarify language which had led to perverse interpretations of the code by the court.]

Raleigh 21 July 69

My dear Sir

I have done my best in McAdoo v. Benbow [63 N.C. 461 (June Term, 1869) (Rodman, J., *dissentiente*)]—and I don't quite know whether the Code will go down beneath the dark waters or not. Pearson is against it & I fear the rest all are. I think (of course) I have the best of the argument. Our hope is in the Legislature. I will write you about it some things in the Code whenever I get time after getting home.

Yours truly
Will. B. Rodman

Hon. A. W. Tourgee Esq.

Document III-31 Barringer to Rodman, November 15, 1869

[Commissioner Victor Barringer drafted the bill for a penal code in North Carolina, relying chiefly on North Carolina common law and on treatises for the definitions of crimes. In addition to the letter excerpted below from Barringer to Commissioner William B. Rodman, there exists another one on the same subject where he informs Commissioner Albion W. Tourgée that, "As to our work, I have got a considerable part of the Penal Code prepared...."[401]]

Concord, N.C.
Novr. 15 '69

Dear Judge:

I go to Raleigh tonight. I will put my material to press, but not send it out till you can revise. I have taken generally our own criminal law, with few additions. My definitions of offences are taken from the standard text-books, rather than from the New York Code.

As to the Act for settlement of estates of deceased persons, our bar generally consider it to apply to administrations already granted, and prefer that it should be so. Our settlements have proceeded upon that idea since last July: and the country is rapidly adjusting itself to settlements on that basis. Would not an Act of the Kind you speak of, only confuse things afresh? Had we not better let it alone, except in those instances where parties choose to make the question before the Courts: the law as it stands will hasten old settlements, and this is very desirable.

Yours &c.
V. C. B.

Document III–32   Bill for a Penal Code, 1869

[The first part of a draft penal code was submitted to the general assembly by the code commissioners in late 1869 or early 1870. Apparently, Commissioner Victor C. Barringer had compiled it.[402] The judiciary committee of the general assembly postponed consideration of the bill until the following session,[403] and no evidence of consideration of the penal code is found again in the legislative record during the Code Commission Era.

Had the bill for a penal code passed into law, it would have codified a portion of the public law of the state. Criminal law is public law[404] in the sense that it consists of "rules which may be necessary for the protection of the State" and consists also of punishments, "the only object of [which] is to protect society," according to the preamble to the bill reprinted below. Codification of public law was less controversial in the nineteenth century than codification of private law (what today we would call the law of property, contract, and tort).[405] The code commissioners did not attempt to codify those portions of the common law understood to be private law.

Like property, contract, and tort law, criminal law is substantive law, as opposed to procedural law. The bill for a penal code was the only major portion of substantive common law that the code commissioners attempted to codify.[406] In procedural law, on the other hand, the code commissioners enjoyed some success at the general assembly with their codes of criminal[407] and civil procedure.[408] Of course, the state constitution of 1868 had abrogated common law procedure,[409] so the commissioners had every prospect of success in adopting procedural codes.

Just as the code commissioners had leaned upon codification in New York for their procedural codes, so they leaned upon New York law in drafting a penal code. Comments in North Carolina's first part of a bill for a penal code reveal this reliance, for instance, in the restriction on the definition of blasphemy, reprinted below, and in the citation of decisions concerning perjury gathered by the New York commissioners.[410] The influence of Edward Livingston's penal law for Louisiana was clear as well, the preamble for Livingston's work being largely incorporated in the North Carolina bill.[411] Despite this reliance by the code commissioners on key nineteenth-century reformers of the common law of crimes, the comments to the bill for a penal code frequently referenced the traditional law of North Carolina as reflected in the criminal law provisions of the state's *Revised Code* of 1854[412] and in treatises on the common law, such as Coke's *Institutes of the Laws of England* and Blackstone's *Commentaries on the Laws of England*.[413] Ironically, Commissioner Barringer even admitted to eschewing the definitions of crimes offered by the New York commissioners in favor of definitions found in standard textbooks, by which he seems to have meant sources like *Bishop on Criminal Law*, used perhaps to update English common law with the common law as it was developing in the American states.[414]

The preamble to the bill for a penal code, reprinted below, typifies the principles of codifiers in nineteenth-century America. The penal code will remove doubts about the applicability of the common law in North Carolina, it will abrogate references to the law of other nations in the definitions of offenses, it will achieve writtenness of law in plain language, technical terms being clearly defined, and it will promote "consistency in legislation and uniformity in the interpretation of laws." More specifically, the penal code would have abolished all common law offenses and have substituted statutory crimes. The chief change in policy introduced by the penal code would have been the rejection of vengeance as a theory of punishment.[415]

While law reform in the nineteenth century evidenced a strong preference for plain, clear, published criminal laws written by democratically responsible authority over the traditional common law of crimes, Commissioner Barringer's array of crimes included in the bill for a penal code did not break dramatically with tradition.[416] Offenses in the bill included blasphemy, abortion, and the crime against nature, all of which law reformers would challenge dramatically in the twentieth century. These crimes, along with preliminary provisions and the preamble to the bill for a penal code (first part), are excerpted below.[417]]

THE PENAL CODE,
OF THE
STATE OF NORTH CAROLINA.

PART I.

AN ACT TO ESTABLISH A PENAL CODE.

THE PENAL CODE.

PREAMBLE.

WHEREAS, Changes are required by the alteration of circumstances and amendments by the imperfection of all known institutions, and since laws ought never to be changed, but with deliberation and due consideration of the reasons on which they were founded; it is therefore, proper, in the formation of new laws, to state clearly, the motives for making them, and the principles by which the framers were governed in their enactment. Without a knowledge of these, future legislatures cannot properly perform the task of amendment so as to produce consistency in legislation, and uniformity in the interpretation of laws.

For these reasons the General Assembly of North Carolina declare that their object and intention in establishing a Penal Code, are as follows:

I. To remove doubts as to the authority of any parts of the Common Law, in the definition, punishment, or prosecution of any offences in this State;

II. To embody into one law such of the various prohibitions of existing statu[t]es as are proper to be retained in a Penal Code, and enact such others as may be necessary or requisite at the present time;

III. To abrogate the reference, which now exists, to the law of another nation, for the definition of offences;

IV. To collect into a written Code and express in plain language, all the rules which may be necessary for the protection of the State, and of the person, property and reputation of individuals, so that no one need be ignorant of that which the law prohibits, and which it concerns every one to know;

V. To change the present penal laws, in all those points in which they contravene the following fundamental principles, viz:

1st. Veng[e]ance is unknown to the law. The only object of punishment is to protect society. It should operate, *firstly*, on the offender, to deprive him of the present means, and of future inclination, to repeat the offence; and *secondly*, on the rest of community so as to deter them from the contravention of the laws, by example. Punishments should be never greater than may be necessary to secure these ends.

2nd. Punishments should, so far as possible, be of such a nature, that they may be remitted, and (so far as practicable) compensated, in cases where the injustice of the sentence becomes apparent:

3rd. Where guilt is ascertained, the punishment should be speedy:

4th. Penal laws should be written in plain language, clearly expressed, so that they may neither be misunderstood nor perverted—so that they may be easily understood and remembered, and all technical terms that they contain should be clearly defined.

VI. TO PROVIDE THAT NO MAN MAY BE PUNISHED FOR ANY ACT OR OMISSION WHICH IS NOT IN EXPRESS TERMS DEFINED AND FORBIDDEN BY THE LAW OF THE STATE.

NOTE BY THE COMMISSIONERS.—The foregoing preamble is adopted chiefly from the Code prepared by Hon. Edward Livingstone, of Louisiana. The Commissioners are fully convinced that no ability which they could command, could clothe these noble sentiments in more simple, appropriate or beautiful language.

PRELIMINARY PROVISIONS . . .

The General Assembly of North Carolina do, therefore, enact as follows:

§1. This Act shall be known as the PENAL CODE OF THE STATE OF NORTH CAROLINA.

§2. No act or omission commenced after the day on which this Code shall take effect as a law, shall be deemed criminal or punishable except as proscribed or authorized by this Code or by some of the Statutes which are specified in section — as continuing in force. Any act or omission commenced prior to that day may be inquired of, prosecuted and punished in the same manner as if this Code had not been passed.

Offenses abolished.—This section abolishes all common law offenses and makes all crimes statutory. The Ordinance appointing the Commissioners prescribes that the Penal Code shall "define crimes and prescribe their punishment." By far the greater number of crimes had become statutory previously, and the only result of this provision is to extend the same principal [*sic*] to all crimes, viz: That the State shall not punish as criminal *any act which her published laws do not distinctly declare to be so*. Objection is frequently made to the abolition of common law offenses, and the substitution of statutory ones. Yet those offenses have become reduced to a code as inflexible as any which can be created. The only difference being that they are now announced in a form, which though recognized and binding upon the Courts, has not received the *imprimatur* of the State, but rather that of legal theorists and foreign judges—while the Penal Code would define all offenses by statute. . . .

TITL[E] III.
OF CRIMES AGAINST RELIGION AND CONSCIENCE. . . .

§33. Blasphemy consists in wantonly uttering or publishing words contumelious reproach or profane ridicule upon God, Jesus Christ, the Holy Ghost, the Holy Scriptures or the Christian religion.

§34. If it appears beyond a reasonable doubt that the words complained of were used in the course of serious discussion, and with intent to make known or recommend opinions entertained by the accused, such words are not blasphemy.

A restriction upon the definition of blasphemy, which is intended to prevent the law being made the instrument of religious persecution. The favor which the law shows towards liberty of speech, and the free discussion of religious opinions, forbids that the sincere expression of belief however erroneous, should be embarrassed by the penalty of blasphemy.—R. P. C. of N. Y. . . .

TITLE X.
OF CRIMES AGAINST THE PERSON AND AGAINST PUBLIC DECENCY AND GOOD MORALS....

CHAPTER III.
ABORTION AND CONCEALING DEATH OF INFANT.

...

§332. Every person who provides, supplies or administers to any woman, whether pregnant or not, or prescribes for any such woman, or advises or procures any such woman to take any medicine, drug or substance, or uses or employs any instrument or other means whatever, with intent thereby to procure the miscarriage of such woman, unless the same is necessary to preserve her life, is punishable by imprisonment in a State prison not exceeding three years or in a county jail not exceeding one year.

Founded on Rev. Code, Ch. 34, Sec. 24, 25; Vict. Ch. 100, Sec. 91.

§333. Every woman who solicits of any person any medicine, drug or substance whatever, and takes the same, or who submits to any operation or to the use of any means whatever with intent thereby to procure a miscarriage unless the same is necessary to preserve her life, is punishable by imprisonment in a county jail not exceeding one year, or by a fine not exceeding one thousand dollars or by both.

The offense of killing an unborn quick child is covered by Secs. 242, 243 under the title homicide....

CHAPTER V.
BIGAMY, INCEST AND THE CRIME AGAINST NATURE.

...

§341. Every person who is guilty of the detestable and abominable crime against, nature committed with mankind or with any animal, is punishable by imprisonment in a state prison not exceeding ten years.

342. Any sexual penetration, however slight, is sufficient to complete the crime against nature....

Document III-33 Call for Convention, 1869–1870

[One interesting aspect of the legislative report providing for the calling of a state convention, excerpted below, is how firmly it related the codification of procedural law to the movement for a new moral science dependent upon a leveling sentiment that rejected the wisdom of the past. The report quoted an 1857 opinion of the United States Supreme Court which condemned the codifiers as sciolists:

> This [common law] system, matured by the wisdom of ages, founded on principles of truth and sound reason, has been ruthlessly abolished in many of our States, who have rashly substituted in its place *the suggestions of sciolists, who invent new codes and systems of pleading to order*. But this attempt to abolish all species, and establish a single genus, is found to be beyond the power of legislative omnipotence. They cannot compel the human mind not to distinguish between things that differ. The distinction between the different forms of actions for different wrongs, requiring different remedies, lies in the nature of things; it is absolutely inseparable from the correct administration of justice in common-law courts.[418]

In his classic treatise from 1865, *The American Republic*, Orestes Augustus Brownson contrasted contemporary politicians, who were mere sciolists in his view, with the founders of our nation, who he thought were true statesmen.[419]]

REPORT OF THE SPECIAL COMMITTEE ON THE SENATE BILL TO PROVIDE FOR CALLING A STATE CONVENTION.

To the Senate of North Carolina:

The undersigned, members of the Special Committee, to whom was referred the Senate bill entitled "An act to provide for calling a Convention of the people of North Carolina," would respectfully recommend a favorable consideration of said bill by the General Assembly. A notice of some of the reasons therefor[e] will not be deemed inappropriate.

The circumstances under which our present State Constitution was formed and adopted were such that serious errors and imperfections were almost unavoidable. It was in a time of change and revolution, of social and political chaos, of conflicting interests and opinions, and of general depression and demoralization. Troublesome questions respecting our Federal relations and the rights of the races,—questions now settled,—then convulsed the public mind. The situation was peculiarly unfavorable to the exercise of that sober wisdom so needful in framing a permanent organic law for a great State.

Our changed social condition, as well as the requirements of Congress, made it obligatory on us to alter and remodel some of our old forms, admit new ideas, infuse a new spirit and somewhat modify our ancient customs and usages. This fact we all recognized; and all would have been satisfactory, if the framers of our new system had simply made such changes in our old polity as were necessitated by our social revolution and by the enactments of Congress. Then the sturdy old North Carolina character and individuality would have been preserved; and being reinvigorated, refreshed, and made alive, would have begun a noble developement [sic] under new auspices.

But the spirit of innovation carried our Constitution-makers far beyond the necessities of the time and the wishes and requirements of the Federal authorities. Instead of pruning off dead branches, and grafting fresh scions on, they uprooted the tree and planted another in its place. Instead of modifying our system, they destroyed it and imported a wholly novel one. Our present system is not native and indigenous; it is exotic. It is not the product of the staid, sober, sterling North Carolina mind; it is the invention of experimenters not well acquainted with the genius of our people. Under it we shall never develope [sic], as we ought to do, into a grand, vigorous new North Carolina, but into an awkward caricature and feeble imitation of other State models. Our growth, like that of a transplanted tree, will be unhealthy, ungraceful, and unfruitful.

A very large portion of our citizens, who voted to ratify our present Constitution, did not approve many of its prominent features. But we were in an anomalous and disagreeable position. A restoration of the State to the Union, and relief from the yoke of military government, were ardently longed for. These happy results were expected to follow a ratification of the Constitution; so shutting their eyes to its faults, stopping their ears to objections, and preferring *any* form of civil government to military, the majority voted to ratify it, with the general expectation and intention of having it amended soon. The necessity of its amendment is now apparent to a very great majority of the people, without respect to party or race. They desire a constitution more in conformity with their circumstances and their true spirit and character. The people of North Carolina have always been distinguished for the simplicity of their tastes, their frugality and economy, their honesty and integrity, their scorn of empty pretension, and their sturdy independence. They ought to have a system of internal government in accord with these characteristics; and this they will have, if they are permitted to come together and make a government for themselves, the true type and embodiment of their own genius, instead of having a government made for them.

It is due our people to declare, and important for our fellow-citizens of the whole Union to understand, that the desire to amend our Constitution proceeds from no purpose or design to annul or abolish those of its features which guarantee the inviolability of the Union, the equal rights of the races, or any of the other legitimate results of the recent war, as embodied in the Congressional plan of reconstruction. All these are regarded here as settled questions. The purpose is only to make such amendments as will secure to the State a system of internal administration that will be simpler, cheaper, more suitable to our situation, and more efficient in promoting the public peace, dispensing public justice, and advancing the material interests of the State.

The grandest mistake in our existing Constitution, and that which of itself would warrant the call of a Convention to remedy it, is the change it has made in our Judicial system. An effective method for dealing out cheap and impartial justice is the very soul of a government. This we once had in North Carolina. But that splendid temple in which such men as Gaston and Ruffin ministered as high priests is in ruins. The people remember and long for it again, like the captive Jews longed for their ruined sanctuary. Shall it not be rebuilt? From all the land comes up the response—It shall!

Our present Judicial system is a servile copy of that of New York, a State less like ours than almost any other in the Union. New York is densely populated, North Carolina sparsely. New York is full of large towns and cities, and her people are extensively engaged in commercial and maritime pursuits. North Carolina is an agricultural State with a rural people. The New York system was devised upon a model deemed suitable to a dense, commercial community; and yet it is well known that it was adopted there through an innovating freak of the Legislature of 1848, without consulting the people, who, if they had understood its true character before it was fixed upon them, would probably have frowned upon it. Many alterations have been found needful in it there; still there is great dissatisfaction with it, and the desire for its total abolishment and a return to the old ways is becoming very general. This costly, cumbersome, impracticable system which New York is seeking to cast off has been imported into North Carolina where it is tenfold more unsuitable, and where it is already regarded, by nearly everybody, as little short of a public nuisance.

The "Code of Civil Procedure" and kindred inventions which we have borrowed from New York, inaugurate a complete revolution in the system of practice and proceeding in Courts, superceding the old common-law methods. Instead of improving the old system, as has been so successfully done in England since 1834, the New York innovators in 1848 destroyed it entirely, and introduced this novelty. Some other States, and finally North Carolina, followed the rash example. Upon the workings of this "Code" in New York, an able treatise was published two years ago by W. H. Greene, of Buffalo, to which inquirers are referred for a description of the enormous confusion which has resulted from it. It would have been abolished there long since but for the fact that the great increase of fees and charges under it has interested so many officials in its perpetuation. This is a strong reason why we should abolish it at once, before it becomes a fixture here through its very evils in opening up avenues to peculation and extortion.

Upon this important subject of the folly of casting aside the common-law forms and substituting novel "Codes" like this, the Supreme Court of the United States has often spoken in strong terms. It is inconvenient to make extensive quotations from its reports, but the Senate will pardon an extract from the opinion of that Court in the case of *McFaul v. Ramsey*, (20 Howard, 523,) a case coming up from Iowa, a State which has a "Code" very much like our new one. The Supreme Court says:

"The Common Law, which wisely commits the decision of questions of law to a Court supposed to be learned in the law, and the decisions of questions of fact to a jury, necessarily requires that the controversy, before being submitted to the tribunal having jurisdiction of it, should be reduced to one or more integral propositions of law or fact; hence it is necessary that the parties should frame their allegations to support respectively the demand or the defence into certain writings called pleadings. * * * * The end proposed is to bring the matter of litigation to one or more points, simple and unambiguous. At one time the excessive accuracy required the subtlety of distinctions, * * * The introduction of cumbrous forms * * * had brought the system of special pleading into disrepute. * * * But in modern times it has been trimmed of its excrescences, and the pleadings in every form of common-law action have been reduced to simple, clear and unambiguous forms. * * * This system, matured by the wisdom of ages, founded on principles of truth and sound reason, has been ruthlessly abolished in many of our States, who have *rashly* substituted in its place *the suggestions of sciolists, who invent codes and systems of pleadings to order*. But this attempt to abolish all species and establish a single genus is found to be beyond the power of legislative omnipotence. They cannot compel the human mind not to distinguish between things that differ. The distinction between the two forms of action for two different wrongs, requiring different remedies, lies in the nature of things; it is absolutely inseparable from the correct administration of justice in common law courts.

"The result of these *experiments* * * * has been to destroy the certainty and simplicity of all pleadings, and introduce on the record an endless wrangle in writing, perplexing to the court, delaying and impeding the administration of justice. In the case of *Randon vs. Toby*, 11 Howard, 517, * * * a simple action on a promissory note, the pleadings of which, according to common law forms, would not have occupied a page, they were extended to over twenty pages, requiring a two years wrangle * * * before an issue could be formed. * * * In the case of *Bennett vs. Butterworth*, 11 Howard, 667. * * * The court was unable to discover from the pleadings the nature of the action or of the remedy sought. It might, with equal probability, be called an action of debt, or detinue, or replevin, or trover, or trespass, or a bill in chancery. The jury and the court below seemed to have labored under the same perplexity, as the *verdict* was for $1200, and the *judgment* was for *four negroes*. * * * This court has endeavored to impress the minds of the judges of the District and Circuit Courts of the United States, with the impropriety of permitting these *experimental codes* of pleading and practice to be *inflicted* upon them. In the last mentioned case the Chief Justice, in delivering the opinion of this court, says: 'The Constitution of the United States has recognized the distinction between law and equity, and it *must* be observed in the Federal Courts.'

"In the States where the courts of the United States administer the common law, they cannot adopt these *novel inventions*. * * * We have made these remarks in order that the bar and courts of the United States may make their records conform to these views, and not call upon us to construe new codes and hear special demurrers and pleadings, which are not required to conform to any system founded on reason and experience."

These weighty words from the Supreme Judiciary of the Union are commended to those who reverence profound wisdom and experience, speaking in harmony with the sanctions of the Federal Constitution itself. Shall we in North Carolina listen to these words and root out this new "Code;" or shall we still be led by the nose by one or two freshly imported innovators far more remarkable for *pertinacity* and *self-assertion* than for *sound sense* or *legal learning*?

The cost of litigation under this "Code" is hugely increased. Formerly a case in a Justice's jurisdiction cost *forty cents*, now *two* to *five dollars*, perhaps more. In the Superior Courts it is increased in like manner. Fees are doubled and quadrupled in all directions. It is impossible to give details. They are found on nearly every page of the "Code." Some ado has been made about the abolishment of the little old *four* dollar fee of attorneys, and behold, a *fifteen* dollar fee for attorneys is snugly inserted under another name! The people are entitled to know such things, and they must. The purpose, it is argued, of the great admitted increase in costs is to keep down litigation. This really means that instead of granting the people cheap justice, we must frighten them away from the courts by the fear of ruin through the costs and charges wantonly imposed. Noble idea! worthy of the "sciolist who invent codes to order!" But all experience shows that litigation is greatly multiplied by such "Codes." A distinguished lawyer, once on our Supreme bench, points to the telling fact that all the decisions, upon *technicalities* strictly, rendered by the Supreme Court of North Carolina in the past seventy-five years, would not fill two volumes, while the same class of decisions in New York, in the last twenty years, would fill fifty volumes. That needs no comment.

Another great error in our judicial system, not yet fully realized here, but profoundly felt in New York and recently changed there, is the shortness of the official terms of the Judges and no prohibition against their being re-elected. A judge for life or a very long term is inspired by the dignity of his vocation, the glory of the ermine, and the ambition to leave after him an honorable fame as a pure, able and learned jurist. These are noble motives and influences, and they have made our judiciary resplendent in the past. But elect your judges for short terms, make them the playthings of the popular breath, and you drag them down from the pinnacle where justice sits robed in eternal sunshine, into the fog of passion and prejudice, if not corruption. You, in a manner, compel them to be politicians and therefore partisans, and expose them to evil influences without number. Some will stand firm and remain pure; some will become corrupt, but *all* will be suspected. Those who *deserve* public confidence, will often fail to command it; for multitudes will suspect others of yielding to temptations which themselves would not resist. And popular distrust of the judiciary is an evil only less than a corrupt judiciary itself. Instances are not wanting in North Carolina at this moment to prove this truth. Men forsaking the courts and taking the law into their own hands; private and neighborhood feuds, outrages and violence agitating this Assembly and disturbing the peace of the State, all proceeding from a want of confidence in some of our judicial officers, and this perhaps undeserved. The fault is not so much in the officers, it is in the system, and the evil can only be eradicated by amending our Constitution and returning to our old plan of appointing Judges for life. Perhaps very long terms might do, with ineligibility afterwards.

The expense of the present Judicial system is much greater than that of the old one. Then we had eight Superior, and three Supreme Judges, and their salaries amounted to $23,100. The whole Department of the Judiciary cost less than $30,000 a year. Now we have twelve Superior, and five Supreme Judges, whose salaries amount to $42,500; though the individual salaries of the Supreme Judges stand at the old figure, and are relatively less than those of any other officers. The public Treasurer (see his Report of Feb, 8th 1870) estimates the whole cost of this Department for the current fiscal year at $54,000. Here then, in this Department, is an *increase* of $24,000, or more, over the former expense. How many children would this educate who will die in ignorance for the want of it?

But it is said these additional judges are needed because the county courts are no more. But the County Courts cost little for salaries or fees of officers. They dealt out substantial justice in a plain and simple way. They educated the people in the most common and practical parts of the administration of the law, and gave even illiterate men much useful knowledge of legal forms and proceedings. They were emphatically the people's courts, and the people want them back again. With some slight improvements, no more useful tribunals ever existed in any country. Among other excellences, they constituted the cheapest and most honest system of county government ever devised. Moreover, the great mass of business pertaining to the administration and settlement of estates, to guardianships, to the probate of wills, and the many kindred subjects, was done by these courts, in the easiest and simplest manner, and at very small cost.

Under the present system, exceedingly cumbrous proceedings and forms are required in this latter class of business, so that taking out letters of administration is as troublesome as a superanuated suit in Equity; and the whole matter of estates, wills, deeds, guardianships, partition, dower, and numberless other things, are thrown on the hands of the Superior Court Clerk; and if the *innovators* could have full sway, he would also decide most of the cases in the Superior Court itself. But this last idea is temporarily checked. Nevertheless, as it is, this clerk's office is the grand receptacle of miscellanies,—a curiosity shop,—a farmer's old barrel into which all kinds of plantation tools and old irons and trinkets are tumbled pell-mell. No one man can properly discharge such a variety of duties, in addition to his appropriate duty as Clerk of the Court; and endless confusion will soon show itself in this quarter.

The cost here, in the way of fees and charges, is also immense. This Assembly has just passed an Act making the Superior Court Clerk of one County a salaried officer with a salary of $5000; for the reason, as was stated on this floor, that the said clerk was receiving in fees an unknown number of thousands—perhaps *twenty* thousand dollars a year. Are the people to endure a system by which ten, fifteen, or twenty thousand dollars of fees are annually paid to a single County officer? You give a Clerk a salary of $5000, equal to that of the Governor; but you do not thereby stop the extra amount of fees from coming into his office out of the people's pockets.

From the statements made here while that bill was under debate, it is certain that the eighty-nine Clerks of the Superior Courts receive, on an average, $4000 a year each; making, for the whole State, the vast sum of $356,000 annually for this one class of officers. In old times it was scarcely one third as much; and after duly allowing for the former expense of transacting the *extra* work now thrown on these clerks, which used to be done very cheaply by the county courts and otherwise, it is safe to say that the *business now* transacted in the offices of the Superior Court Clerks costs the people at least $150,000 a year more than the very same matters cost under the old system. True, this is not paid as taxes; but it is paid as fees and charges; and where is the difference! It comes out of the people and forms a part of their burdens.

If we look into the Executive Department, we find several new offices, and a great increase in salaries; so that the cost of this Department for salaries of officers and clerks is nearly three times as great as formerly. The estimates for this Department, during the current fiscal year are placed at $45,500, by the Public Treasurer. (See his Report of Feb. 8, 1870.) This is an *increase* of $25,000, or more, over the former expense. And then besides this, there is the swarm of subordinates about the offices and the Capitol and the Capitol grounds, doing nothing or worse than nothing, but costing an immense amount of money; who can tell how much!

How is it in the Legislative Department? The General Assembly meets twice as often as formerly, its mileage and *per diem* are twice as large; and it sits twice as long. The old General Assembly used to cost about $60,000 biennially, or $30,000 a year. The present Assembly has *now* sat altogether nearly *nine* continuous months. According to the aforesaid Report of Treasurer Jenkins, this Assembly has cost the State, since October 1st, 1868, the startling sum of $288,599.73, and besides this the State owes us now for the last month. This does not include the expense of our first, or Summer Session of 1868. The Treasurer (see his Report) estimates the expense of the Legislative Department, for this current fiscal year alone at $173,700. This is an *increase* in the annual expense of this Department, over that of old times, of $143,000, or more.

Besides all this, there is the expense of the Asylums, of elections, of "contingencies," &c., &c., most of these costing immensely over former figures. A reference to the aforesaid Report of the Treasurer will show that the annual cost of the *State* government proper, without paying any interest on our debt, is at least $300,000 more than under the old system. Look at the following overwhelming figures showing the money used by the present State government since it began in July, 1868; viz:

Surplus in Treasury, July 1, 1868,	$ 42,164 31
Ordinary State Tax for 1868, (See Report,)	250,726 19
Proceeds of Dividend on N. C. Railroad,	117,600 00
General Fund Tax for 1869, (See Report,)	485,000 00
Deficit now (about)	260,000 00
Total general fund receipts,	$1,155,490 00
Deduct amount paid as interest on our old debt October 1, 1868,	111,153 00
Balance,	$1,044,337 50

The above figures are taken from the Reports of the Treasury itself, and are indisputably correct. And the aforesaid *balance* of $1,044,337 50 shows the sum which has been expended and incurred, merely in carrying on the machinery of the *State* government *proper* since July 1, 1868, less than twenty months, or one year and two-thirds of another. This is equal to $626,600 per year. In 1859 the State government cost $212,385 78. (See Report of D. W. Courts, Treasurer.) In 1860 it cost considerably less, as the Assembly did not meet in that fiscal year. (See [R]eport of C. H. Brogden, Comptroller.) After making all possible allowances, it is certain that we do not exaggerate when we set down the *increase* in cost of *State* government under $250,000 a year more than formerly, the present system at $300,000 a year.

The Treasurer tells us the deficit will amount to $300,000 by the first of April. He knows not how to raise funds to meet it. Nobody will loan him any thing. He therefore asks us to levy an early crop of spring taxes, 20 cents on the $100, to be collected by April 15th, 1870. He also proposes an *extra* tax to build the Penitentiary and support the Asylums, to be payable July 15th, 1870, and the tax payer to be charged interest of *one per cent*. for the first month, and *two per cent*. a month afterwards on his tax while it remains unpaid, after July 15th. He also asks us to instruct the Board of Education to loan its moneys to the State; and recommends that the opening of the public schools be postponed. (See his report, Feb. 8, 1870.) These extraordinary propositions show the desperate straits we are in. They truly indicate panic and despair. We thought taxes, and heavy ones, once a year were bad enough. But here is a Spring tax, and a Summer tax, besides the regular Fall tax.

We need a Convention to stop this wild career towards beggary and utter ruin. The way to do it is to amend the Constitution so as to limit salaries and expenses to a *low figure*; limit also *per diem* of the Assembly to *three* or *four* dollars; mileage to five or ten cents; limit the duration of Legislative sessions, and have fewer of them. As it is, the laws are changed so often the people are kept in utter uncertainty and confusion on this subject. It is sometimes objected that a Convention will cost a great deal. But Senators can easily see, from the above figures, that a Convention, by altering our system so as to reduce salaries and expenditures, would in one year save to the State enough to pay for its own cost three times over.

Let us glance briefly at County and Township matters. Authentic information from one county, about an average one, shows that its Board of Commissioners and other officers cost $3,500 a year; in the same County the old County Courts, doing more work and doing it better, used to cost $1,500, a difference of $2,000 against the new system. Leaving out all other items in the County governments, the above ratio gives an *increase* of $179,000 annual expense in the eighty-nine Counties. As for the *Townships*, there are over seven hundred of them in the State, and the expense of *governing* each may be safely estimated at not less than $200 a year. Put down the aggregate at $140,000, and this is entirely a new expense.

We need a Convention to take proper steps in regard to the State debt. The hopeless tangle we are in on that subject needs no comment.

We need a Convention to amend the Constitution so as to prohibit one person from holding two or more offices at once, a thing only partially prohibited now, and which threatens to grow into a great evil. Many persons are holding a Federal office and a State office also.

We need more stringent guarantees against improvident appropriations of the public money and pledging of the State's credit.

We need clearer and stronger restrictions and limitations upon the rate of taxation, and an uprooting of the present system of special State and County taxes, by which device all barriers are overleaped and the people taxed *ad libitum*.

We need a decrease in the number of offices. The great variety and multiplicity of these not only cost insufferably, but beget a fondness for office-holding, which is growing into a species of insanity all over the country.

But it is impossible to mention *all* the obviously useful and important amendments needed in our present system. We think this report points out a number which are essential; such are the reform of the present Judicial system, and the abolishment of its pendant—the "Code"; the simplifying of the duties of Superior Court Clerks; the restoration of the County Courts; the remodeling of the county governments, and other matters suggested above. A general reform is needed in *all* departments, with a view to greater *economy:* so that we may perfect our School system, and convert the hundreds of thousands of dollars now wasted on useless officials into a fund for the advancement of the sacred cause of Education.

The estimates and figures embodied in this report, which by no means embrace all the items of expenditure, and which we have tried to set forth without exaggeration, when brought together show the following *increase* of annual expenses, costs, fees and taxes for merely carrying on the *State* and *County governments* on the present plan, to wit:

State government, increased cost,	$300,000
Business done in Superior Court Clerk's office, increased cost,	150,000
County Commissioners, &c., extra cost,	179,000
Township governments, new expense,	140,000
Total *increase*,	$769,000

Such is the vast amount uselessly spent in various ways, and therefore *wasted*, annually, under the present system of internal government in North Carolina. Do we not need a change?

No wonder the State is bankrupt. No wonder the treasury is empty, though a heavy tax has just come in. No wonder the inmates of our Asylums are in danger of actual want. The people groan under their burdens. The Assembly imposes taxes for the State; the County Boards levy taxes; the Township Boards levy taxes. Everybody and everything is taxed, and money pours into the public coffers; but it will scarcely lodge there over night. *Seven hundred and sixty-nine thousand dollars needless increase of annual pay to officials*, while the children of both races are growing up ignorant, untutored; thousands of precious intellectual diamonds destined never to be polished, and the State government only giving them the poor pittance of *fifty cents* a piece annually to get an education with, and the school-houses to build, too!

The people demand a change. Without regard to party or race they demand it. We ought to hear and heed their voice. We cannot, if we would, quench the mighty spirit which is awaking like a ground-swell in the hearts of the masses. We might as well try to imprison a volcano under a half-bushel, or quiet an earthquake with a cradle song. Let us then grant the people the most effectual remedy for the evils they complain of by calling a Convention to change the present system, and remodel it upon sound principles.

The undersigned would not close this report without earnestly calling upon all sober, thoughtful and moderate men in this Assembly, and outside of it, to unite together. The people are weary of extremes. The time has come, and the hour has struck when men who love North Carolina more than they love *any* party, must strike hands in token of concord, and stand shoulder to shoulder. This is undoubtedly the spirit of the people. Let us respond to it and show ourselves statesmen and not more partisan bigots and fanatics. Let us search and see if we cannot find some solid ground on which all *true North Carolinians* can rally to redeem the State, and start her out on a new career of prosperity and glory, transcending all the past. We have been chastened by misfortune. We are in profound difficulties now. Let us learn wisdom from these lessons and begin a new era. And as the first step in this path, let us allow the people of the State to assemble together in Convention to frame for themselves a true North Carolina government.

In conclusion, it is proper to add that though plainness and candor have been used in this report, nothing has been said with any purpose to wound the pride or prejudices of any true North Carolinian, either native or adopted. Begging that any seeming warmth may be set down to the account of honest zeal and sincere conviction, this report is

Most respectfully submitted,

WM. M. ROBBINS, Ch'mn.
C. T. MURPHY.

Document III–34 Pearson on Judicial Legislation, 1870

[Late in his judicial career, Chief Justice Richmond M. Pearson argued in *Tate v. Powe* for the role of the courts in application of rules of practice and procedure. This role for the state's courts in adjectival rulemaking would become a refrain of critics throughout the twentieth century, one reasserted in this compilation in its very last document—an essay by Dean Roscoe Pound in 1958.[420]]

L. A. TATE *v.* W. E. POWE and others. . . .

PEARSON, C. J. . . .

Judicial legislation in regard to practice and procedure, is a necessity. The many little "odds and ends" that the diversity in our way of living and talking presents, cannot be picked up and fastened by Statutes; such things must be confided to the Courts.

We might have expected that this Statute, emanating from the Code Commissioners, would have marked the dividing line between civil actions and special proceedings. But it is not so, for the reason, as may be presumed, it was a perplexing subject, fit to be left to *judicial legislation*. The questions occur every day: the mode of procedure is one of instant pressing necessity, and this Court must assume the task of making the dividing line. . . .

Document III–35 Commissioners' Response, January 25, 1870

[A senate resolution challenged the code commissioners to account for their time. The commissioners responded by previewing their next report, providing enough information "as may be pertinent to the *inquiry* contained in the foregoing resolutions." Among other endeavors, the commissioners said they had nearly completed the remainder of the Penal Code[421] as well as a Code of Criminal Procedure.[422] They also reported having diligently followed the direction of the ordinance[423] not only to revise and compile the laws, but additionally "to reduce the whole body of our law into a 'systematic code,'" which was a much more onerous task. It was not made perfectly clear, though, whether the commissioners still intended to codify the common law or would henceforth focus on statute laws by updating the *Revised Code* of 1854. On top of their normal duties, the commissioners reported that they had engaged in bill drafting for the general assembly.]

OFFICE CODE COMMISSIONERS,
Raleigh N. C., Jan. 25, 1870.

To the Honorable the
    Senate of North Carolina:

The Commissioners of the Code have the honor to state that they are this day in receipt of a copy of the following resolutions of your honorable body:

Senate Resolutions in relation to the Code Commissioners.

Resolved by the Senate, That Victor C. Barringer, William B. Rodman, and A. W. Tourgee, Code Commissioners, be and they are respectfully and respectively requested and each for himself, in a separate report, to report to the Senate without delay, what time they have been each actually engaged in the performance of his duties as such Commissioners aforesaid.

Resolved, That said Commissioners are respectfully requested to make their report in accordance with the words used in Section eight, Chapter forty-one, of an ordinance of the State Convention, ratified the 13 day of March, A. D. 1868.

Resolved, That the Clerk of the Senate be requested and directed to forward copies of these resolutions to each of said Commissioners immediately after their adoption.

Passed this 9th day of December, A. D. 1869.

TOD R. CALDWELL,
President of Senate.

STATE OF NORTH CAROLINA,
Office Secretary of State.
Raleigh, January, 21, 1870.

I, Henry J. Menninger, Secretary, of State, do hereby certify that the foregoing is a true copy of the original resolutions on file in this office.

H. J. MENNINGER,
Secretary of State.

[Seal.]

In response to these resolutions, Victor C. Barringer, Wm. B. Rodman and Albion W. Tourgee, Commissioners of the Code, jointly and severally, and in the words of the resolutions—"respectfully, respectively and each for himself"—make answer as follows:

That by the Ordinance of the State Convention of 1868, under which they act as such Commissioners, they are required to make report of their work and their progress therein to each session of the General Assembly—a duty which they have heretofore strictly performed, and which they by no means intend to neglect during the present session. For the information of your honorable body, however, they are willing to anticipate so much of said report as may be pertinent to the inquiry contained in the foregoing resolutions.

They have, therefore, the honor to inform your honorable body that they have been actually engaged in the performance of their duties as Commissioners of the Code, from the adoption of the Constitution of 1868, until the present moment; that the work has been at no time intermitted, given over, neglected, or abandoned by all or any of them during that time; that owing to the peculiar nature of the work assigned them, it has required not only an extensive and cautious examination of the laws and decisions of our own State, but also of the laws, codes, and text-writers of other States and nations,—which has been constantly in progress; that in the preparation of the Penal Code, and Code of Criminal Procedure, now nearly ready for your consideration, every available authority has been consulted, and members of the commission have, at their own personal expense, procured the latest revisions and amendments from other States and countries, and carefully compared, for the purpose of laying the whole matter, in as complete a form as possible before the General Assembly; that in addition to these duties, the Ordinance of Authorization, imposing upon us to suggest amendments and alterations of the laws existing, has devolved upon the Commission an immense amount of labor, owing to the peculiar circumstances which have surrounded our State government since our appointment, and the changes made necessary by our new Constitution; that whenever we have found any evil in the operation of our law, or defect in its provisions, we have suggested such remedy as we could best devise; that whenever the Assembly, or either house of the Assembly, has requested, as in very many instances they have requested the preparation of any particular bill, the same has been prepared with all possible dispatch and care; that we have, also, at the request of any member of either house, prepared such bills as they suggested or required, provided they were such as we deemed of general public utility, and not of a partizan character.

Such is the nature of our duties, that it is impossible to act in their performance conjointly, to any great extent. That being ready to take up the preparation of any part of the Code, and its general plan agreed upon, the same is parcelled off, a portion to each, by whom it is separately prepared. His separate work is then submitted to the other members of the Commission, considered and revised by them, and the result of their labors submitted for the consideration of the Assembly.

It will thus be seen, that but a small portion of our labor is of a merely manual character, and that the idea, which seems to prevail to some extent, that it must be all transacted at stated sessions of the Commission, is entirely erroneous. That, on the contrary, each member is, as it were, a sub-committee, which prepares work for revision and adoption by the whole Committee,—and whose labor is constantly in progress.

The Commissioners would beg leave to call to your attention the fact, that a greater portion of the public laws of the last session of the Assembly were prepared by them, and that at the close of the session, as also of the preceding session, there were still remaining untouched upon your calendar, a large number of most important bills which we had prepared, whose adoption was necessary to the harmonious operation of our laws, and which should now be taken up and adopted, or others in their stead.

The Commissioners would also suggest to your honorable body, that the duties imposed upon them by the Constitution and the Ordinance of Authorization, are of a much more onerous nature than a mere compilation and revision of the laws. In addition to such compilation, they are directed to reduce the whole body of our law into a "systematic code." It contemplates and demands an entire change in the mode of arrangement, form, and system of our laws, as well as such changes which the nature of contemporaneous events, and the marvellous changes of the past decade may render necessary and proper. To this attempt at systematic and scientific arrangement and revision, the Commissioners have applied themselves with the most unremitting diligence.

The Commissioners would also call to the attention of your honorable body the fact that all previous commissions in this State have been for the mere purpose of compilation and revisal of the previously enacted statutes. The revisal of 1833, occupied three years in its preparation. In 1850, another revisal having become necessary, a Commission was appointed for the purpose of digesting and compiling the statutes which had been passed since 1836, fourteen years. They completed their labors in 1856, requiring five years for their performance. Upon the present Commission has fallen the labor of compiling the statutes enacted since 1856, the date of adoption of the Revised Code—a period of time nearly as long as that covered by the labors of the Commission of 1850, with annual, instead of biennial, sessions of the General Assembly, and embracing the most stormy period, and the most violent and radical changes, in legislation, manners, customs, political rights and social relations, which has ever been known in any State or nation whose laws are derived from an English stock. They would have you note that during this period of our national *renaissance* there has been—

I. A civil war, unparalleled in magnitude and duration by any which has occurred in the previous history of our Anglo-saxon race. One government has been overthrown in our midst and another built up. One system of laws swept away and another substituted; one allegiance broken down and another established. After four eventful years, when the changes attending this colossal revolution, had interpermeated every relation of life, and extended to even the humblest and meanest citizen of the State, there came another change, equally great, equally violent, and the previously existing government was re-established.

II. In this period there has also occurred the most astounding social revolution which has ever been in any State or nation. In the twinkling of an eye, all the relations which one-third of our people sustained to the remaining portion was changed, a servile class was made free, chattels real were made citizens. Slavery, the relations and ideas of which had interpermeated and modified every department of our State government, every branch of our law, and all the habits and customs of our people, was swept away. All its footsteps in our judicature have to be obliterated, and the learning which it had engendered laid aside and forgotten.

III. Military government has also existed here; and the extraordinary legislation of the past few years, known as the "Reconstruction Acts of Congress," have required the adoption of unusual measures for their administration.

IV. During this period there have also been three State Conventions, and two entirely new Constitutions, with numerous suggested amendments to the old.

By all these changes of government, of law, of administration, of customs, of social and political relations, all modifying and affecting the character of our laws, the work of digesting, pruning, compiling, and harmonizing the conflicting laws and decisions of the past fourteen years, is rendered peculiarly difficult and tedious.

In the performance of these various and onerous duties the Commissioners have been engaged without intermission or delay from the time of their appointment until the present, with such diligence and capacity as they could command.

All of which is respectfully submitted.

VICTOR C. BARRINGER,
WM. B. RODMAN,
ALBION W. TOURGEE,
Com. of the Code.

Document III–36 Report of the Code Commissioners, March 1870

[The commissioners in this, their fourth report, explained that constitutional change, not the caprice of the commissioners, required legislation which (1) established a code of practice and procedure, (2) reworked the law of crimes and punishments, (3) defined the duties of new public offices, (4) addressed the law of private and municipal corporations, and (5) elaborated the ramifications of change in the law of women's property. The implication of this explanation is that only the scope of codification of the common law—that is, the extent to which private substantive law should be codified—was left to the discretion of the code commission.

With this fourth report, the commissioners offered no significant amendment to *The Code of Civil Procedure* because its improvement, they said, was "much better performed by the Courts than it is likely to be by the Legislature."[424] It is not clear what the commissioners meant here. Did they refer merely to interpretation of statutory language by the courts? Did they imagine that the courts or bar would lobby the legislature for appropriate change? Did they think the courts might supplement the code by rules of court? Or did they mean to suggest the purely declaratory nature of adjectival codes? It is possible that the commissioners meant none of the above, but merely aimed to give as little ammunition as possible to their critics of the ineffectiveness of legislative codification, ammunition that would be abundant if constant statutory amendment to *The Code of Civil Procedure* were necessary here, as it had been in New York.[425]

The commissioners did submit to the general assembly a code of crimes and punishments and a code of criminal procedure. As to the former code, they recommended it not be adopted this session, while the latter code they recommended for prompt adoption, probably because it was chiefly a digest of the statutes and precedents on criminal procedure then existing. The commissioners reminded the general assembly that their draft bill on the duties of the various public officers had already passed into law and reported that they planned to submit draft legislation on corporation law and on the laws regarding married women. Furthermore, the commissioners intended to offer a draft bill on the laws respecting internal improvements in which the state had an interest, which they were directed to prepare by a resolution from the prior legislative session.

While all this reporting by the commissioners was factual and defensive, they did here interlace notice of a stunning retreat: the commissioners revealed that they would close their labors after they submitted to the legislature a codification of the whole *statute* law of the state. That is to say, they no longer expressed an intention to codify the entire body of common law, as their general analysis from their first report to the general assembly had suggested.[426] Apparently, the effort at full codification of the common law was no longer "practicable and expedient,"[427] at least not politically practicable and expedient.]

REPORT OF THE CODE COMMISSIONERS.

RALEIGH, March 12th, 1870.

To the HON. TOD R. CALDWELL,
  Lieutenant Governor and President of the Senate:

SIR: The Commissioners of the Code have the honor to report to the General Assembly that they have nearly reached the end of the labors which were imposed on them by the Convention of 1868.

The constitution adopted by the people in that year made radical changes in the fundamental law in some most important particulars.

1. It abolished courts of equity, and all difference in the forms of actions.
2. It prohibited the old and introduced a new system of punishment.
3. It created a number of public officers whose duties had to be defined.
4. It required that corporations, both municipal and private, should, except in peculiar cases, be chartered by general laws.
5. It essentially altered the common law relations of husband and wife, by making all the property of the wife separate.

Such comprehensive changes in accustomed law have rarely been enacted in so short a time. Some of them at least may be justified upon the ground that a great revolution had occurred, as a result of which society stood on a new basis and required different laws from those which were appropriate to the stage which had perished. Others must stand upon their intrinsic merits. What these are it is no part of our duty to decide; time alone can give a positive answer. For the changes made by the constitution the Commissioners are no wise responsible; we took them as accomplished facts; and our duty was as skillfully and as prudently as we could to bring the law of the State into harmony with them. It was evident that until that was done, there would exist an anarchy and confusion of private rights scarcely compatible with peace and order and incompatible with public happiness or prosperity. The old system of procedure in civil actions was abolished; and until a new one was supplied, there were no means by which a private controversy could be determined, or an acknowledged right enforced; the State was practically without law.

Sensible of the danger arising from this state of things, in a very few months the Commissioners presented to the General Assembly a Code of Civil Procedure which met your sanction. It was, we humbly conceive, the best that could have been framed in obedience to the constitution. At first this code was unacceptable to the bench and to the bar, as all changes must be, but we believe it has gained in the favor of both. For over eighteen months justice has been administered under it in civil actions without complaint. While we ourselves candidly admit its imperfections in some respects, we think its greatest enemies will admit that it has some merits over the former system. However, whatever may be the merits or demerits of the new system, all calm men must admit that a return to the old is impossible. The only resource is to improve and amend the new. We believe that duty can now be much better performed by the Courts than it is likely to be by the Legislature, and therefore, with the exceptions of some corrections of misprints and clerical mistakes, we have not presented to the honorable General Assembly any proposals for a substantial amendment of the Code of Civil Procedure.

As an essential complement to the changes made by the Constitution, we have presented to your honorable body at this session a Code of Crimes and Punishments. The subject is one of great importance; the lives of men may depend on a phrase. We have given it great consideration, but in view of its importance we do not recommend to your honorable body its adoption at the present session. We prefer that it shall await the quiet and repeated consideration of those best competent to pass on its merits.

We have also at this session submitted a Code of Criminal Procedure. Generally, it is a mere digest of the present law as shown by our statutes or decisions; the few changes made in the present law we think important. We recommend the early passage of this most important statute. We have submitted it to the bar of the State and so far have received a criticism upon one point only, viz: the authority of the Solicitor to enter a *nol. pros.* The Solicitors desire to retain the authority. The opinion of the bench and the bar is against them, and confirms our proposition in that Code. We have therefore to ask the consideration of your honorable body to that Code, and we think we are justified in saying it meets the approval of all competent judges.

The bill which we prepared regulating the duties of the various public officers throughout the State, met your approbation and is a part of our law.

These acts, with many others, such as those concerning the settlement of the estates of deceased persons, guardian and ward, landlord and tenant, fences, draining low land, &c., prescribing just rules and convenient modes of procedure in all these important subjects, form a body of law, the enactment of which will, for at least a century to come, mark an era in our history. We may be permitted to believe that this body of law, by the certainty and economy it has introduced into the administration of justice, has saved, and will save, millions of dollars which would otherwise have been spent in unnecessary legislation, and will go far to compensate the people of North Carolina for all their losses of property in the late disastrous war. This General Assembly may appeal to those statutes as a vindication from any charges that may be made against it because of prolonged and expensive sessions.

It is said of a certain obscure and badly drawn English statute (of frauds,) that every line of it has cost the people of England a million of pounds in getting it interpreted by the courts. If this General Assembly had done nothing else but to enact those statutes, we feel at liberty to say that in our opinion, the work would have been worth the whole cost of your sessions. It will be a source of pride to you, in which we may be permitted to share, that your names are forever connected with such just and useful legislation.

But two of the great subjects embraced within our duties remain untouched; a general corporation law, and one defining the powers of married women over their separate property. Besides that the Constitution positively commands the first, its necessity is obvious. Much of the time of the General Assembly at every session is occupied, at vast expense to the people, in considering special acts relating to private or other corporations, which would be saved by a general act. As to the second subject, probably few have as yet realized the dangerous uncertainty and confusion of the law at present affecting it. No one can say, with certainty, what contracts a wife may or may not make, nor how far her husband may be bound by her acts. We propose to present, for your consideration at your next meeting, bills on these two important subjects. We shall also have ready then, to submit to you, the complete compilation of all the laws respecting internal improvements, in which the State has an interest, which we were directed to prepare by a resolution passed at your last session, but which, unfortunately, did not come to our knowledge until too late to prepare it for your present session. We shall also submit to you, at that time, a codification of the whole statute law of the State, arranged in convenient form for reference, and making a single volume about the size of the Revised Code. When this shall be done our labors will have finished.

We remain, very respectfully,

Your obedient servants,

WILL. B. RODMAN,
V. C. BARRINGER,
A. W. TOURGEE.

Document III-37 New Code Commissioner, July 30, 1870

[This newspaper blurb from the *Raleigh Daily Sentinel* referred to an act of the legislature that had been misplaced, which would have abolished the code commission. The blurb also reported Gov. William Holden's proposal to replace Victor Barringer with Chief Justice Pearson on the code commission.]

NEW CODE COMMISSIONER.

It may not be uninteresting to the public just at this time, to know, as we learn, that Chief Justice Pearson has received at the hands of his Excellency, Gov. Holden, the appointment of Code Commissioner, *vice* Victor C. Barringer, who resigned to accept a better paying place. The pay is $2,500 a year, and he gets $2,500 also as Chief Justice, so that he holds two offices as does Mr. Justice Rodman, and, each takes from the Treasury $5,000 a year. We have no comments to make upon any view of the matter at this time.

But we will add this: The Legislature passed an act abolishing this Code Commission, *and in the hurry of business at the close of the session, the act passed got lost by the indiscretion of somebody!* That is well known here and to members of the Legislature. This fact being true, we can't understand how any one having a proper self-respect or tolerable regard for legislative sanction *can continue* on the Commission much less *go on it*.

Document III–38 Bill Dissolving Code Commission, September 29, 1870

[This newspaper article from the *Raleigh Daily Sentinel* referred to legislation that would have asked the people of the state to dissolve the code commission, but which was "lost" prior to ratification. The writer also alleged that lawyers cannot advise clients due to the difficult questions arising under the code in very simple matters—"matters which ought to be generally understood by the people." That common law pleading in debt and in antebellum probate matters was better understood by the non-professional than comparable code pleading was condemnation indeed.]

CIVIL CODE COMMISSION.

The appointment and continuance of this Commission is an iniquity and a crime against the people of the State, which ought to be punished without benefit of clergy. The classes of the people against it, led the General Assembly at its repentant and last session to pass a law, dissolving the Commission at once, but by some piece of legerdemain, used in more cases than one, by interested parties upon the engrossing committees or the clerks and attaches of that body; the bill after passing through all the various stages of legislation, failed to be ratified, because it *could not be found*. Who lost that bill? Does Judge Tourgee know anything about it?

So far as we are informed of the labor of this Commission, it has been chiefly confined to the simple copying the New York Code, with certain changes to adapt it as nearly as possible to our present circumstances. This has not employed, to any extent, but one of its members, requiring the two others to revise and amend his work. But it has been so bunglingly prepared, that what one session of the Legislature would adopt was found to fit so badly, it had to be amended or repealed at a subsequent session. And now, except among that class of lawyers whose business has been large and very general, it will be found that those who have not given the closest possible attention to it, cannot give the necessary advice to clients. Almost every day the most difficult questions are arising under this Code, in matters which ought to be generally understood by the people.—And there is no end to this. New York has been trying this Code for more than twenty years and her best legal talent feel that they have not begun to touch bottom yet, in settling the endless difficulties which are constantly occurring.

This iniquity is not only enormously expensive requiring a heavy salary for three men, which has been enjoyed by two Judges, receiving stated salaries besides, and a very heavy expenditure for printing &c. but it provides for a most onerous and unusual tax upon every man who goes to law for any purpose, and produces greater doubt and difficulty in the minds of the people as to the "uncertainties of the law." The processes for action in debt, for matters of probate, for guardians, executions, administrations, &c. ought to be very simple, easy and cheap. Under our old system, the people generally understood these matters, but now it is difficult for the people to understand them. Let the whole thing be quelched as soon as possible. The people demand a return and a speedy one to our old Court system and laws, as cheaper, more prompt and far more satisfactory.—The $20,000 which this Commission and Code have cost the State, besides the heavy costs to the people in fees &c. has been worse than thrown away, and belongs to the category of corruption and stealage foisted upon us by Radical carpet baggers and scalawags.

Document III–39 Report of the Code Commissioners, November 1870

[In this, their fifth report, the code commissioners pointed out that "fundamental law COMMANDS a CODE to be prepared, and also COMMANDS that a commission to effect that object be created." In other words, the commission had not pitted its will against the legislative will; rather, the legislative discomfort with the abandonment of common law pleading and other proposed forays in codification pitted the political will of the general assembly against the fundamental will of the people in convention. One of the disadvantages of a written constitution, then, is that commands can be written into it—commands perhaps wildly out of tune with the historical ideals of a community (but perhaps in tune with the self-serving whims of demagogues) which could not have succeeded in clothing themselves as fundamental law under an English-style customary constitution. But having succeeded in North Carolina during the fervor for re-admittance of the state into the federal union, the arbitrary command for codification quickly drove the general assembly to ask the people to reconsider their will. The legislation to amend the constitution in order to dissolve the code commission, though, was misplaced according to newspaper reports published as early as July 30, 1870[428] and was not quickly found, and so the code commission continued, though not without disruption. Commissioner Victor Barringer resigned. Chief Justice Pearson declined an offer to serve in Barringer's place.[429] But then W. H. Bailey accepted the offer. Furthermore, Commissioner Albion W. Tourgée resigned and no one was appointed to replace him.[430] Thus, only Commissioners Bailey and Rodman reported.

In this report the commissioners acknowledged that *The Code of Civil Procedure* for North Carolina was hastily prepared. They bragged, though, that this code was modelled on the law of New York, "one of the most intelligent commercial and enlightened States of the Union," whose code of civil procedure was "a system of practice and procedure adapted to its high state of cultivation." The impetus for this code in New York, the commissioners here reported, was attributed to "the HON. CHARLES O'CONNOR, one of the most gifted lawyers of America," and its implementation was entrusted to "the fostering oversight of DAVID DUDLEY FIELD, Esq., one of the most learned and scientific, as well as talented lawyers, that our country has produced." Furthermore, the commissioners reported, a code of practice and procedure differed from a code of general principles of jurisprudence in some way that would make its importation from New York less offensive. With these apologies and excuses, the commissioners here presented to the general assembly a "new CODE" of civil practice and procedure meant to cure the defects of the code passed in 1868.[431] The commissioners expressed their indebtedness for some of its ideas to "the Report of the Commissioners appointed by Parliament to codify the English law."]

REPORT OF THE CODE COMMISSIONERS.

———

OFFICE OF CODE COMMISSIONERS,
RALEIGH, N. C., November, 1870.

To the Honorable the General Assembly
of the State of North Carolina:

GENTLEMEN: The time allowed to the Commission by the Convention to prepare and submit a CODE OF PRACTICE AND PROCEDURE was so limited, and the changes made by the Constitution itself so radical and far-reaching, that the opposition is not to be wondered at; the complete uprooting of an old system, grown grey with years, and by long use become greatly endeared to nearly the entire body of the profession, would naturally have engendered a strenuous opposition to any CODE providing for a novel made [*sic*] of practice; and the imperfections of the one prepared two years ago were unavoidable, though they furnished food for criticism and fed the flame of prejudgment.

A meeting of the Bar was called and held in Raleigh, (in which was represented a large portion of its first talent,) to discuss the Code and interchange views as to such of its objectionable features as were without the scope of constitutional requirements.

At that meeting, it was conceded on all hands that the constitutional abolition of the distinction between the forms of actions at law and suits in equity, and the provision for the Superior Courts remaining open at all times, would, *proprio vigore*, have necessitated a new CODE; that the former practice could not be applied by the Courts to meet the emergency created by the Constitution, and it seemed also to have been conceded that the codification enjoined by the Constitution could be most easily, economically and speedily effected through the machinery of a Commission.

However this may be, the Constitution had provided by sec. 2 of Art. IV for such a Commission to be appointed by the Convention which framed the instrument, and three gentlemen were accordingly appointed. So it will be observed that the fundamental law COMMANDS a CODE to be prepared, and also COMMANDS that a commission to effect that object be created.

Owing to the short time allowed them to prepare a CODE OF PRACTICE AND PROCEDURE, it was, perhaps, not impertinent for the Commission to examine the CODE of different States and select some one as a standard and a guide. They selected, with that view, the CODE of New York—the first State to advance the idea of a CODE system, and whose Legislature had for twenty years pruned and trimmed the original act, until, by the almost complete cesser of legislative amendments, it had provided for one of the most intelligent commercial and enlightened States of the Union, a system of practice and procedure adapted to its high state of cultivation.

The Commission did not impliedly admit our inferiority, by conceding that a system suited to the highest civilization would be unsuitable to ourselves; and, in adopting the New York CODE as the basis of their own labors, conceived that they were but following the example of wise law-givers in all ages, in studying for imitation and use the laws of the most enlightened nations.

The Commission were the more inclined to take this course, as the scheme of a CODE had received its first impulse in the New York Convention from the HON. CHARLES O'CONNOR, one of the most gifted lawyers of America, and was perfected under the fostering oversight of DAVID DUDLEY FIELD, Esq., one of the most learned and scientific, as well as talented lawyers, that our country has produced.

It seemed to the Commission that any well-digested CODE system of *practice and procedure* could not need much elimination, and therein differed from a CODE embodying the general principles of jurisprudence. The Commission could not allow the general sentiment that a CODE practice was unsuitable to the habits, dispositions or conditions of our people, to influence their action, because the people themselves, in Convention, had declared that *it was not*, and had enjoined its adoption.

Immediately after the passage and distribution of the CODE OF CIVIL PROCEDURE, many persons, (including gentlemen of the Bar,) gave currency to the idea that it had enacted a revolution in our system of jurisprudence. This was a superficial view, as any intelligent and candid student will admit; for there can be found but one principle of jurisprudence changed by the CODE. At the meeting of the Bar there were but few objections stated, and all of them have been remedied by subsequent legislation, or by the CODE we have prepared and propose to present to your body for action in a few days.

In addition to the objections alluded to, the Commission has endeavored to ascertain every other objection that might be suggested, and have received from divers lawyers and laymen specific objections. To these the Commission has yielded a patient hearing and investigation, and in the *great majority of instances* have, in the CODE to be shortly submitted, incorporated the same by such emendations, alterations and additions as were necessary to effect that end.

In doing this, we have in some instances been convinced of the practical merits of the proposed alterations, by the reason of the thing; in some by practical illustrations of the inconvenience of the former provision; and in many we have yielded our doubts as to the practical workings of proposed changes in deference to the nearly unanimous sentiment of the Bar.

It would be impossible and out of place to call your attention to the various changes made in the CODE by the new CODE so soon to be presented; but it is perhaps meet that we should allude to the most important changes, and may say in advance that in some respects we are indebted for our ideas to the Report of the Commissioners appointed by Parliament to codify the English law. We have provided that

ORIGINAL ATTACHMENT

shall constitute a separate and distinct action, and have conformed the practice in most respects to that which formerly prevailed.

EJECTMENT.

We have, while not treating this as a special Proceeding, provided for it as an independent action; and in doing so have followed in a great measure the mode suggested by the English Code Commissioners.

RULE DAYS.

We have provided for the establishment of rule days on which the pleadings and issues can be made up, and thereby save the time usually consumed in such matters in term time to the people. But while rule days are to be established, yet it is left to the option of the plaintiff whether he will make his summons returnable to a rule day or to term.

UNIFORMITY.

In consequence of the decision declaring the Acts commonly called the "stay law" unconstitutional, we have stricken out all distinctions as to the mode of procedure between one and another class of debts, and apply the CODE practice to every action.

COSTS AND FEES.

Owing to the great complaint made by attorneys and people on account of exorbitant fees, we think that the fees must be too high, and in deference to the attorneys we have restored the fee bill and allow them only four dollars, except in the Supreme Court, where we fix the fee at ten. It will be remembered that under the name of *indemnity to the successful litigant*, the attorneys have been receiving from $10 to $15 in the Superior Courts and $30 in the Supreme. The reduction is made at the urgent and almost clamorous demand for a general reduction by the attorneys, and it is to be hoped their self-sacrificing spirit in this behalf will be duly appreciated by a grateful public. We have provided for the abolition of mileage to sheriffs and other officers, and reduced their fees very nearly to the old standard.

CLERKS.

We have greatly curtailed the fees of Clerks, and provided for a maximum sum in any case. We deem this necessary to provide against the tendency to extortion.

JUSTICES.

We have abolished the fees of Justices of the Peace altogether, except for taking depositions.

CONSTABLES.

We have provided for them the same fees as prescribed by the Revised Code.

COUNTY COMMISSIONERS.

The great complaint made from various sources against this class of officers has induced us to make this an honorary office by abolishing all fees and mileage.

In short we have endeavored in compliance with the loud complaint on all sides in the matter of fees to restore the *status quo ante bellum*.

JUSTICES OF THE PEACE.

We have nearly restored in Justices' courts the practice as it existed under the old system.

As jury trial was provided for by the Constitution, Sec. 33, Art. IV., we have been compelled to retain that feature of the new system, but think that by a provision touching the waiver of jury trial it will be but rarely demanded.

There are many other changes scattered through the CODE, as we have revised it, which we think will commend themselves to the better judgment of calm and impartial minds.

We respectfully ask, in all fairness, that the odium of Constitutional requirements be not put upon our shoulders, but that as our people are compelled to have a CODE, and we are the persons designated by law to prepare it, you will give to the new one proposed that dispassionate examination and impartial judgement which is expected from *you* as Legislators toward *it* as a proposed law.

We have the honor, gentlemen, to subscribe ourselves,

Very respectfully,
Your obedient servants.

W. H. BAILEY,
W. B. RODMAN.

N. B.—Judge Tourgee had resigned his place on the commission before this Report was prepared and his successor had not been commissioned.

Document III-40   Report of the Code Commissioners, December 18, 1870

[The report of the code commissioners here excerpted—perhaps its sixth report—evidenced some anomalies.[432] For instance, it claimed to submit to the legislature a bill for a code of criminal procedure. Yet, the first four chapters of that code had become law shortly after the third report was submitted in March 1869;[433] additional chapters were submitted to the legislature shortly after the "commission response;"[434] and consideration of these additional chapters was postponed until "next session" by the senate judiciary committee on March 17, 1870. Perhaps these additional chapters to the code of criminal procedure were resubmitted to the general assembly by the commission with this sixth report. This conjecture was supported by Commissioner William Rodman's explanation in this report that Commissioner Bailey had seen the bill before being named commissioner. Another slight anomaly was that this sixth report spoke of a new code of civil procedure, as had the fifth report, even though there was evidence that this new code of civil procedure had been submitted to the legislature on December 14, 1870, four days prior to the date appearing on this sixth report. On the other hand, a review of the journals of the general assembly showed that a report of the code commissioners was offered to the general assembly and rejected by that body on January 20, 1871.[435] The report excerpted below, dated December 18, 1870, perhaps answered to that journal entry.

The failure of the commissioners to resubmit the penal code with this report suggested that even the hope of codification of public substantive law had been abandoned by them, their efforts toward a complete codification of private substantive law having been dropped much earlier in 1870. The commissioners also failed to submit with this report a bill on municipal corporations and a bill on internal improvements, both promised in prior reports, and failed to provide in the new code any procedure in the Court of Probate or before the justices of the peace. Still, the commissioners accompanied their report with bills on the property of married women and on non-municipal corporations, both subjects answering mandates introduced in the 1868 Constitution and promised in prior reports. The commissioners also noted that they would update the *Revised Code* of 1854 at some time after these other important bills had passed into law, even if the statutory codification would have to be undertaken merely as a labor of love.]

Raleigh December 18, 1870

To the Honorable the Speaker of the House of Representatives of North Carolina:
  Sir:
  The undersigned Commissioners of the Code have the honor to submit for the consideration of the Legislature:

1. An amended Code of Procedure in Civil Cases
2. A Code of Procedure in Criminal Cases

3. An Act relating to Marriage and Divorce

4. An Act relating to Corporations non-municipal.

We hope to be able to present to you at an early date, a complete substitute for the Revised Code of 1856. It will be manifest however that it will be impossible to put the whole statute law of the State into a compact form until, the several acts presented to the Legislature shall have been acted on by them.

In respect to the several bills above mentioned we desire to submit some explanations,

1 <u>As to the Amended Code of Civil Procedure.</u>
The present Code which was created in August 1868 was prepared by the Commissioners with a degree of haste which the circumstances made absolutely necessary. The Constitution adopted in June 1868 abolished the pre-existing Courts and provided new ones; it {was} required also by an ordinance of the Convention, and not less imperatively by public convenience, that the Commissioners should present to the General Assembly ~~before the~~ at their first session after the adoption of the Constitution, a Code of Practice and Procedure for the newly created Courts. We can truthfully say, that no body of men was ever called upon to do such a work in so short a time. The circumstances left to the Commissioners no choice: the language of the Constitution directed their attention to the Code of New York, and ~~with~~ by constant and assiduous labor they presented to the Legislature in about two months after its meeting, the Code of New York altered and adapted as far as it appeared to them the ~~different~~ {differing} conditions of society in this State required, and the language of the Constitution permitted. No one could be more sensible than the Commissioners that under such circumstances, where the pressure of time allowed so little opportunity for considerate judgment, their work must necessarily be imperfect in many respects. It was presented to the Legislature with the ~~expectation that it would thereafter undergo many amendments~~ consciousness that it had many defects, ~~and with the expectation that~~ {which} a brief time would clearly reveal, ~~there~~ and, with the expectation that it would soon undergo a thorough revision and amendment.

When the Commissioners reflect that no Code ~~of such~~ embracing such an extent of change has ever been presented within so short a time as has elapsed since their appointment they cannot accuse themselves of any want of diligence. The Code of Justinian was about three years in preparation, and its want of method betrays the haste of its preparation; t{T}he Code Napoleon took at least five years notwithstanding the impetuous energy of its nominal author; the Code of New York (a skeleton of what it now is) required over five years; five years elapsed between the appointment of the Commissioners to prepare the Revised Code of N. Ca. and its report to the Legislature; for more than thirty years England has had several bodies of Code Commissioners and their labors have not yet been completed.

The undersigned now present to your honorable body that revised and amended system of procedure which meets their deliberate judgment. Upon the publication of the Code of 1868 the Commissioners sought the frank opinions of the public generally and especially of the Bench and Bar. Every suggestion has been listened to, and carefully considered. Numerous changes have been made, {all} in accordance with these opinions; every point has been abandoned to which it seemed that a fair and reasonable objection could be brought. The undersigned would like to explain here in detail the several changes which they have made, but they fear, {that} such a discussion would be out of place, and therefore refer professional readers to the amended Code itself. We respectfully desire that the Legislature will have it printed, for ~~the use of~~ {its own use and} that ~~body and~~ of the legal profession generally; and we would suggest that the superintendence of the printing be committed to one of the undersigned, who will prepare a necessary index.

We submit that <u>under the circumstances existing or likely to exist, some</u> law of procedure is indispensable to the administration of the law: without it justice cannot be administered with {the} certainty which is

one of the essential elements of a good government. We believe the Code we have now the honor to submit will more nearly meet the wishes of the people and of the legal profession than any that can be prepared within an indefinite time, and we therefore submit it to the candid judgment of your honorable body. {The Code now presented does not contain any provisions relating to the Procedure in the Court of Probate, or before Justices}
2 ~~The Code of Procedure in Criminal Cases.~~

~~Will. B. Rodman~~
~~W. H. Bailey~~

2 ~~The Code of Criminal Procedure.~~
of the Peace. The portions of the Code relating to those subjects, will be shortly submitted to you.

We have the honor to be
very respectfully,
Yours &c
Will. B. Rodman
W. H. Bailey

After the appointment of Mr Bailey as Code Commissioner the undersigned (W. B. Rodman) met him in Raleigh and I exhibited to and discussed with him, the Code of Civil Procedure, which has been spoken of in our joint report; he suggested several amendments to my original draught, which we discussed, and mostly adopted, and the Code as now presented was approved by both of us. {Although} Judge Tourgee ~~although~~ {was} then a member of the Commission, {we regret that} we did not have an opportunity of consulting with him.

Mr Bailey as a member of the bar had previously seen a copy of my {proposed} Code of Criminal Procedure, and I then read to him my proposed acts concerning marriage and divorce, and corporations, but he had no time to give them a serious consideration. Consequently {for} the following remarks on those acts, I alone am responsible.

2 The Code of Criminal Procedure.

It seems to me that every lawyer must admit the convenience and propriety of a code of procedure in criminal cases. The object of every criminal action, is, of course, to determine the guilt or innocence of the accused. The procedure for such a determination may most influentially affect the result. If the Judge commits an error, it will surely affect the prisoner for ~~good~~ {his} good or ill. If the case should come (as it generally will) before an appellate court, it will surely be unfortunate (to say the least) that a fair verdict should be set aside for any defect of form. That such is often the case, all of us know. To avoid this;—to inform the Court, the bar, and the prisoner, of the forms of procedure, a Codification of the law on that subject, is at least desirable. A law on it exists: it is to be found {scattered} in treatises of common law writers (such as Hale, Foster, Chitty, Russell &c) {and in our statutes} and the decisions of ~~our Supreme~~ {many} Courts; Certainly it will be a great convenience to all: to the Court, the bar, and the prisoner, to put this law—uncertain, if for no other reason than because it is spread over so many volumes many of which are inaccessible,—into a compact shape in which it will be accessible to all.

After these general remarks on the convenience of a Code of Criminal Procedure, I think I may without immodesty commend what I have now the honor to present; because ~~I have~~ in preparing it, I have not aimed at any improvement or alteration of the existing law, but have taken it as I found it laid down, especially in the Reports to the English Parliament of the Criminal law Commissioners (which I procured from London) and our own Reports and Statutes. My work is purely a Codification,—there is no change attempted except in a few unimportant matters of practice, where some regulation was indispensable.

3 <u>An act relating to marriage and divorce.</u>
The most important portions of this act are those which ~~enact the~~ undertake to define the effect of marriage on the property of the parties to it; and the rights of married women to contract and be contracted with. The Constitution provides that all the property of ~~married~~ women shall ~~be~~ after marriage remain their separate estate. (Art. X. sect. 6.) The magnitude of this change in our law has ~~ev~~ scarcely been yet appreciated even by the legal profession. Its consequences have not been studied; but on a little reflection it will be manifest that many questions must soon arise, which in the present state of the law, it will puzzle the Courts to decide. ~~It seems to me therefore better that the Legislature~~ If there be no legislation upon it the Courts must in time by a course of decisions frame a system of law to meet the emergencies: but possibly that system may not be what the Legislature would approve, and certainly its production would be both tedious and costly. It seems to me therefore indispensable that the Legislature should at once supply the want, and provide for the cases that will certainly arise. In framing the bill which is submitted, I ~~I~~ could find no ~~ga~~ precedent in the legislation of any State which I could ~~safely follow~~ implicitly follow: but for most of the ideas I am indebted to the legislation of Alabama and Louisiana. It is with much diffidence therefore that I submit this portion of ~~my~~ my work, and I ask for it a careful examination by the Legislature.

4 <u>An Act respecting Corporations non municipal.</u>
The Revised Code (Ch. 26. Sect. 14 <u>et seq.</u>) contains provisions under which corporations for ~~certain~~ purposes of benevolence, mining or manufacturing, could be formed without a special act of the Legislature. Notwithstanding this, the Acts of the Legislature ever since abound with special Acts of incorporation. The Constitution of 1868 forbids the creation of private corporations except under a general law; it was a most useful provision, but unfortunately it contained an exception, under cover of which the Legislatures which succeeded it, have nullified ~~that~~ its value. Every volume of our laws since 1868 has been full of special acts ~~of~~ {for the} incorporation of companies, which might just as well have been effected under the general law. Whether these will avail I do not undertake to say. But it is certain, that ~~these~~ the passage of these special acts has cost the people of the State hundreds of thousands of dollars. If each day of a <u>session</u> of the General Assembly costs $1000,—the cost of each of those acts may be estimated at, at least that sum. It is an abuse that ought to be arrested if possible.

As long as ~~the~~ Ch. 26. of the Rev. Code, remains the only law under which Corporations can be formed without special legislation, there will be some excuse ~~for~~ in some cases not covered by that act for an application to the Legislature. This Bill is intended to reach all cases, and remove any such excuse; and the people must rely upon the firmness and virtue of the Legislature hereafter, to entertain no bill for a private corporation.

It will be observed by all who read the proposed bill that it contains provisions against the monopoly of the soil of the State by Corporations. These provisions are not untimely. In every country in Europe, great corporations, Ecclesiastical or other, have been disposed to monopolize the soil, to the detriment of the laborer. Long ago in England the Statute of <u>Mortmain</u> was found necessary. The Legislature of N. Ca. in several instances has violated this <u>salutary</u> principle, and unless the practice be speedily arrested, there is danger that still larger portions of the <u>soil</u> of our State will be put in the hands of corporations and out of the possibility of acquisition by ~~p~~ individuals.

~~The pers~~

In conclusion, I have seen that one branch of the Legislature has taken away all pay from the Code Commissioners. However disputable the right of the Legislature in that respect may be, I will not dispute it. From the first the preparation of a Code for N. Ca. has been with me (and I beleive it has with my associates) a labor of love. We felt an honorable ambition to associate our names with great and durable improvements of the law, and I may say under the circumstances without impropriety, that many of the ~~acts that~~ enactments which have already been found valuable, and will be hereafter still more highly . . .

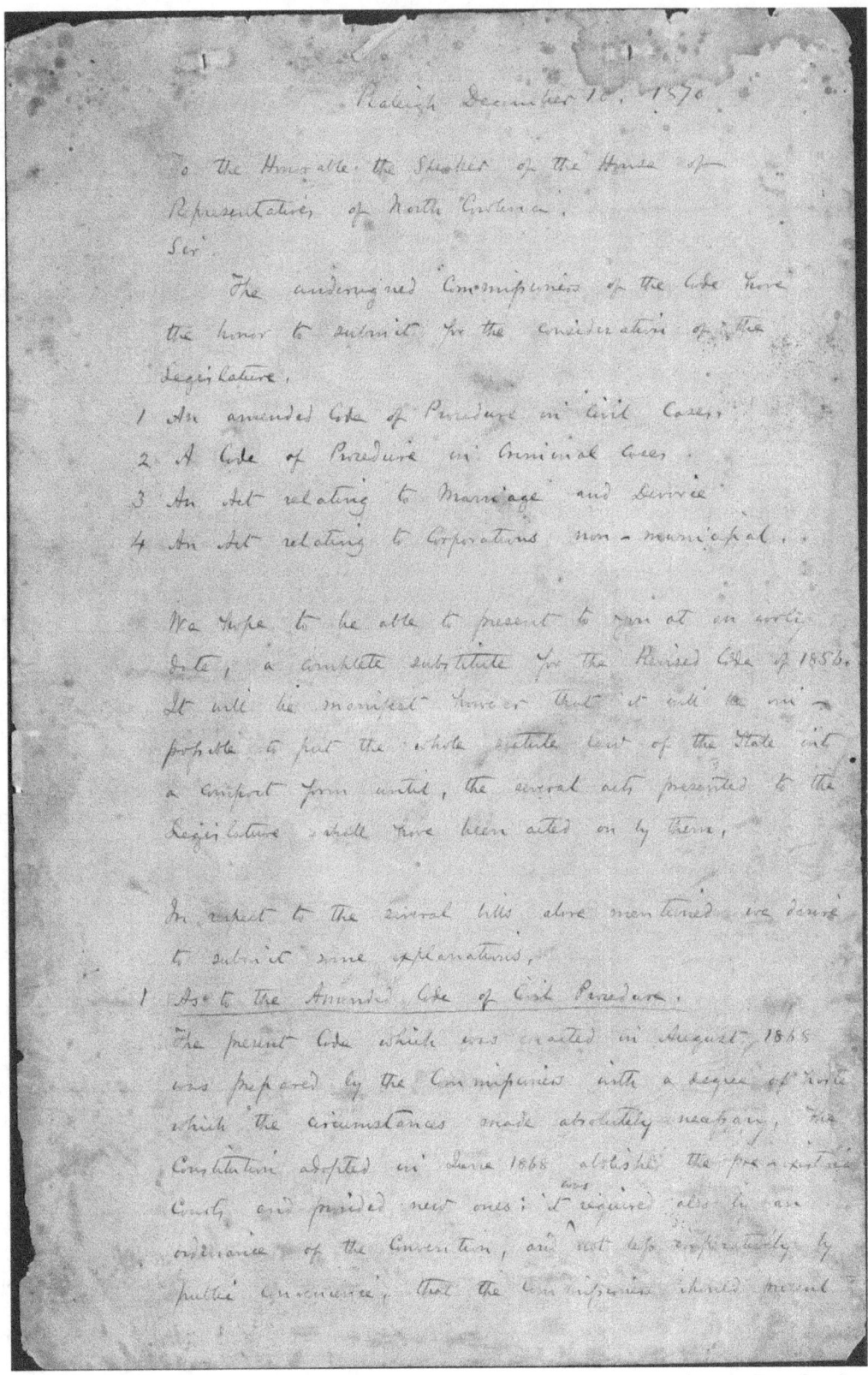

First page of handwritten report of code commissioners from December 1870. (*Credit*: East Carolina Manuscript Collection. J. Y. Joyner Library, East Carolina University. Greenville, N.C.)

Document III-41 Law Library of the Supreme Court Separated, 1871

[Insofar as supporters of codification complained about the difficulty of determining what American law is without expensive, time-consuming training, an accessible collection of legal materials might alleviate the difficulty. In other words, the library[436] was a "meta-response" to the problem of inaccessibility of law in common law jurisdictions. Publication and distribution of appellate decisions and session laws at public expense assured that primary law did not reside only in the memory or private collections of elite experts, while digests, statutory codifications, practitioner's manuals, and academic treatises helped both the experienced lawyer and the layperson find and understand the primary law. At the meta-level, a classified law library provided to the expert and inexpert citizen alike a laboratory of these primary and secondary materials. Such was the law library of the supreme court, separated from the state's public library in 1871 and placed under the control of the court. A law library was less necessary, of course, on the theory of the more zealous codifiers, who maintained that the scientific organization and simplification of the law through codification would reduce its evidences to such a point that any man could afford to purchase and house its volumes, eliminating the need for extensive collections of materials.]

CHAPTER LXX.

AN ACT IN RELATION TO THE PUBLIC LIBRARY.

Section 1. *The General Assembly of North Carolina do enact*, . . .

Sec. 3. That it shall be the duty of the clerk of the supreme court to take charge of the law library of the supreme court, under such rules and regulations as the justices of said court may prescribe. . . .

Ratified the 15th day of February, A. D. 1871.

Document III-42 Caldwell to Graham, March 7, 1871

[Former North Carolina representative and delegate to the state constitutional convention of 1868, David Franklin Caldwell of Guilford County—a strong Unionist and anti-secessionist before the Civil War—informed his friend, former governor William A. Graham, in 1871 that he would not practice law while *The Code of Civil Procedure* was in effect. He accused the "Radical Judges," particularly Judge Albion W. Tourgée, of "partial rascality and fraud," having evidence of their misdeeds sent to Graham.]

> Washington Street,
> Greensboro', N.C.,
> March 7, 1871.

I have not attempted to practice law since the new Yanke code went into opperation, nor do I intend to do so while it remains in opperation. Consequently I rented my office to a Radical magistrate, but I keep my [board] and library in it, and I have seen much that has transpired in his Court. And never before have I seen such proceedings in the way of taking bail. I have seen negroes who were caught while in the store thay had broken into, others for highway Robbery, and for other high offences, bailed out on bonds for $50., with negrow securities that are notoriously insolvent &c. Of course scoundrulls all failed to appear—and that was the last of the matter, and even when Revenue officers become bail and the parties failed to appear, not a cent of the bond was ever collected, or will be. I have been the cause of having letters written to Caswell, Alamance, etc., requesting the clerks to send you a certified coppy of all the criminal cases on those dockets, of what race, what charged, and how disposed off. This record, if fairly gotten up, will speak louder than seven peals of tundur, and louder still if the politics of these criminals was made known.

Pardon me, will you, for the interest I take in this matter, for venturing to suggest to you to examine closely as you possibly can J. R. Bulla, as to the amount of compromises, nonsuits, nolprossing, he has entered, and the number of convictions he has made, etc., and Judge Tourgee as to the new Trials, and how and what has been the only sentence he can inflict on rogues. You may think me very presumptious, and no doubt will, for venturing to call these things in this hurrid manner to your attention, but, my dear Sir, much as you may have seen, heard, or know of the workings of radicalism, I feel confident you have seen, heard, or know but little of the extent of this partial rascality and fraud that has and is still practiced on the part of the Radical Judges, Solicitors, Magistrates, and other officers in this State. They have and are in my humble opinion doing more to corrupt the people and encourage *Thieves and roguery* than did the notorious Jonathan Wild. And I hope that the prosecutors of Holden will spare neither time or expence to ventilate as much of the proceedings of Tourgee and Bulla as possible; it is due to truth, justice, and the people of this section of N. Carolina, and may God help you to do those notorious disturbers of the peace & leaders of faction *Justice*. If this could be done, then they would be comparatively harmless, and gradually die an infamous death. I wish to call your espec[i]al attention to the perils that are at the present moment threatening the existance of the N.C. Rail Road. So sure as you live, the Baltimore and Ohio Rail Road will proceed at once to organize and build the Danville and Coal Field Rail Road from Danville to Statesville. This will give a rout some 50 miles shorter, from Charlotte to Lynchburg, Alexandria, Washington, Philadelphia or New York than any and all other routs passing through N.C. without any break of bulk or change of guage or bag[g]age to any point North of Statesville. This will, under existing arangements, on the N.C. Rail Road, simply destroy it—and that to a moral certainty. Of course I cannot enter into a lengthened argument to prove this assertion in a letter. Yet I assert once for all, such will be the fact, and the only way to prevent this result will be to give the P. C. R. Road a fair chance to compeat with the B. & O. Road. If the proper steps are taken, they can be strained up to give a liberal price for the N.C. Road, in part, or the whole of it. And pardon me for again presuming to say that I think you ought to look to this matter carefully. I have long had about $5,000., most of which cost me dollar for dollar, and I can't now afford to be swindled out of it by narrow minded and bigoted legislation.

Document III-43 Supreme Court Reporter Abolished, 1872

[In an act of 1872, reprinted below, the legislature abolished the office of Supreme Court reporter,[437] apparently held at the time by J. M. McCorkle, and transferred the duties, fees, and emoluments of reporting the court's opinions to the attorney general.[438] The act did not record the evil which this legislation remedied. Decades later, Chief Justice Walter Clark suggested a legislative motive for the abolition of this judicial office: in order to reduce labor costs, while increasing profit, the reporters had been printing the records and briefs of counsel too fully.[439] The office of reporter was re-established in 1893, during the tenure of Chief Justice James E. Shepard, shortly before Associate Justice Walter Clark began his work on the reprints of the *North Carolina Reports*.[440]]

CHAPTER CXII.

AN ACT TO ABOLISH THE OFFICE OF SUPREME COURT REPORTER AND FOR OTHER PURPOSES.

Section 1. *The General Assembly of North Carolina do enact*, That so much of section twenty-three, chapter thirty-three, of the revised code as requires the judges of the supreme court to appoint a reporter of the decisions of said court be and the same is hereby repealed.

Sec. 2. That the office of reporter of the decisions of the supreme court is hereby abolished, and it shall be the duty of the attorney general of the state to report said decisions and to discharge all other duties which are now required by law to be performed by the supreme court reporter, for which he shall receive all the fees, emoluments, &c., now allowed by law to said reporter for the duties now performed by him.

Sec. 3. That this act shall be in force from and after its ratification.

Ratified the 8th day of February, A. D. 1872.

Document III-44 Battle's Report on Revisal, 1872

[In his revisal published in 1873, William H. Battle, a former commissioner of *The Revised Statutes* of 1837, presented the state's first full codification of its statute law since before the Civil War.[441] The commissioning act required Battle to collate, digest, and compile all the public statute laws of the state in force or in use. Battle, of course, read this injunction in light of a provision of the state's Reconstruction constitution in article 4, section 24, which had declared, according to Battle, the *Revised Code* of 1854 and subsequent legislation to be in force except insofar as repugnant to the state or federal constitution.[442] In his report on his revisal, Battle noted that in deciding "what former laws . . . remain still in force and use, [I have] often been sorely perplexed." His work suffered not only from these grave difficulties of determining the continued efficacy of antebellum statutes under a radically different post-bellum constitution, but also from a pair of procedural infirmities: the general assembly did not enact *Battle's Revisal* as one statute, as it had done for prior revisals of the state's public laws, and the general assembly did not repeal all acts not contained therein.[443]]

REPORT OF WILL. H. BATTLE.

Raleigh, Nov. 18th, 1872.

To His Excellency, Tod R. Caldwell, *Governor, &c.*

Sir: By an act of the General Assembly, entitled "An act to provide a compilation of the public statutes," the undersigned was appointed a commissioner "to collate, digest and compile all the statute laws of the State now in force or in use, including those which may be enacted by this General Assembly, distributing them under such titles, divisions and sections as he may think most convenient and proper to render the said acts more plain and easy to be understood."

The undersigned, soon after the passage of this act, which was ratified the 12th day of February, 1872, entered upon the performance of the important duties which it imposed. His first care was the selection of such a plan for his compilation as would accomplish the object of making the laws "more plain and easy to be understood." After due reflection, he concluded to select the plan which was first adopted in the preparation of the Revised Statutes of 1836, and was afterwards followed in the Revised Code of 1856. This arrangement was recommended, as well by its intrinsic merits, as by the fact that it has been long known to, and approved of by the profession and the public. All the statutes relating to the same subject are brought together and included in one chapter, which is sub-divided into sections. Then the various chapters are arranged in alphabetical order, according to the nature of the subject matter. Among these chapters is placed, in its proper order, the "Code of Civil Procedure." The various enactments composing that code are parts of the public statute laws of the State now in force and use, which are required to be digested and compiled. The amendments which subsequent legislation has made to this code, have been embraced in it, but in doing this the original divisions and sections have been retained. This was rendered necessary to prevent confusion in the references to the decisions of the Supreme Court to such sections as have been the subject of judicial construction. Where additional sections are inserted they are distinguished by a repetition of the number of the section which they follow, and annexing the letters of the alphabet, e. g. 11a, 11b, 11c, &c. In looking over the chapter, (Code of Civil Procedure,) it will be seen that several of the subjects which formed a part of it as originally published, are arranged in separate and distinct chapters; such, for instance, are those concerning apprentices, executors and administrators, guardian and ward, wills and testaments, &c. They do not properly belong to a "Code of Civil Procedure," and in excluding them from it, the undersigned has followed the course pursued by His Honor Judge Rodman, in the new Code of Civil Procedure, which he prepared and submitted to the last General Assembly, but which, though reported upon favorably by the Judiciary Committee of the House of Representatives, was not adopted by any legislative action.

In preparing this compilation, the undersigned met with many and serious difficulties. The 24th section of the 4th Article of the constitution declares "that the laws of North Carolina, not repugnant to this constitution, or to the constitution and laws of the United States, shall be in force until lawfully altered." This provision of the constitution recognizes, as being in force, the whole of the Revised Code, and all the subsequent acts of the Legislature up to the time of its adoption, except such parts as were abrogated by their repugnancy to the new constitution of the State, to the constitution and laws of the United States, or have been varied, modified, altered or repealed by subsequent legislation. Such being the case, the Revised Code has been taken as the basis of this revisal, and that and other public statutes, passed prior to the adoption of the new constitution, have been retained unless expressly or impliedly repealed in whole or in part by statutes which have since been enacted. In deciding, as it has been the duty of the undersigned to do, what former laws and parts of laws have been repealed, and what remain still in force and use, he has often been sorely perplexed. The delicacy and difficulty of his situation can well be appreciated by those who have been engaged in either the practice or the administration of the law.

The second section of the statute, under which he is acting, requires of the undersigned to have his revisal prepared in time to be submitted to the present General Assembly, and that it should be accompanied by such notes and references to the sections that have been the subject of judicial decision, fixing the construction of such statutes with a full index in order that the same may be in readiness for publication as soon as the Legislature shall order and direct. A diligent application to the task required of him has enabled the undersigned, with the aid of a clerk whom he found it necessary to employ, to complete the revisal which he now submits to the General Assembly. But the preparation of the required notes, references and index has not yet been made, because it seemed to him that they must necessarily be delayed until the work has been approved and adopted by the Legislature and its publication been ordered by that body. Such was the course pursued with both the Revised Statutes and the Revised Code, and indeed it is the only course of which such a work admits.

In submitting this result of his labors, through you to the General Assembly, the undersigned indulges the hope that he has accomplished the main purpose for which he was appointed, that is, to place the whole body of our public statute laws in such a form as to make them, when published, "more plain and easy to be understood."

Respectfully submitted.

WILL. H. BATTLE.

Document III-45 Constitutional Amendment Dissolving Code Commission, 1873

[This act of 1873 sought an amendment to the Constitution of North Carolina to eliminate the code commission.[444] The people overwhelmingly approved it.[445]]

CHAPTER LXXXVII.

AN ACT TO ALTER THE CONSTITUTION OF NORTH CAROLINA

IN RELATION TO CODE COMMISSION.

Whereas, At the session of the last General Assembly, begun and held at Raleigh, on the third Monday of November, in the year of our Lord one thousand eight hundred and seventy-one, a bill entitled, "A bill to alter the Constitution of North Carolina," was read three times in each House of said General Assembly, and agreed to by three-fifths of the whole number of members of each House respectively; *and whereas,* The bill so agreed to has been duly published six months previous to the election of the members of this present General Assembly, as required by section two, article thirteen of the Constitution; and it is the intention of this bill to agree to the alteration proposed by the last General Assembly in the bill aforesaid,

The General Assembly of North Carolina do enact, (two-thirds of the whole representation in each House of the General Assembly concurring,) That the Constitution of this State be altered as follows, to-wit:

Strike out sections two and three of the fourth article, being the provisions which refer to the appointment and duties of the code commissioners.

Ratified the 24th day of February, 1873.

DOCUMENT III-46 CONSTITUTIONAL AMENDMENT ON PROCEDURE, 1875

[Although the people had already disbanded the code commission and had abandoned the notion of completely codifying private substantive law, the 1875 convention constitutionalized a legislative role in the development of "methods of proceeding" in the courts of the state below the supreme court. Presumably, the expression, "methods of proceeding," in this 1875 ordinance carried the same denotation as "practice and procedure" had carried in the first two sections of the ordinance of March 13, 1868,[446] and therefore included within its purview civil and criminal procedure.[447] And yet the 1875 ordinance differed from the 1868 ordinance by commanding the legislature to regulate methods of proceeding "when necessary."[448] Apparently, *The Code of Civil Procedure* and that part of the codification of criminal procedure that had passed into law were necessary, as they remained in force.

This apparent restriction on legislative involvement to situations of necessity may have indicated a retreat from *a priori* legislative control to the traditional legislative role of either declaring common law rules[449] or legislating in derogation of them with the understanding that the courts would read derogatory statutes narrowly and within the framework of an already existing common law. Such a retreat might have rested on the premise that the methods of proceeding in trial courts were necessary means to the exercise of the sacrosanct judicial power (i.e., trying cases, rendering judgment, pronouncing sentence), the constitutional authorization of limited legislative interference in these methods serving only as a check and balance to that inherent power. This interpretation linking methods of proceeding to inherent judicial power makes sense given other new language found in the same provision of article IV of the state constitution: "The General Assembly shall have no power to deprive the Judicial Department of any power or jurisdiction which rightfully pertains to it, as a co-ordinate department of the government. . . ." Alternatively, the restriction of legislative power to situations of necessity may have rested on the understanding that the statutory methods of proceeding already in place were adequate and that stability in these methods was prized enough to warrant cabining legislative experimentation.]

CHAPTER XVII.

AN ORDINANCE TO ABROGATE AND ANNUL SECTIONS FIFTEEN, SIXTEEN AND SEVENTEEN, OF ARTICLE FOUR, OF THE CONSTITUTION.

The people of North Carolina in Convention assembled do ordain, That sections fifteen, sixteen and seventeen, of article four, of the Constitution be abrogated and annulled, and the following substituted therefor:

SECTION —. The General Assembly shall have no power to deprive the Judicial Department of any power or jurisdiction which rightfully pertains to it, as a co-ordinate department of the government; but the General Assembly shall allot and distribute that portion of this power and jurisdiction, which does not pertain to the Supreme Court, among the other courts prescribed in this Constitution, or which may be established by law, in such manner as it may deem best; provide also a proper system of appeals, and regulate by law, when necessary, the methods of proceeding in the exercise of their powers, of all the Courts below the Supreme Court, so far as the same may be done without conflict with other provisions of this Constitution.

Read three times and ratified in open Convention, this 6th day of October, 1875.

E. RANSOM,
President of Convention.

JOHNSTONE JONES, Secretary.
W. M. HARDY, Assistant Secretary.

Albion W. Tourgée served on the code commission beginning in 1868 and as a superior court judge during Reconstruction. Photograph of a portrait of Albion W. Tourgée. (*Credit*: State Archives of North Carolina, Raleigh)

Document III–47 Tourgée's Notes, 1878

[The year before he abandoned his adopted state of North Carolina, the father of code pleading in the state, Albion Winegar Tourgée, compiled a digest-treatise "designed for the special use of the legal profession" whose "object is to enable the professional reader more easily, quickly and certainly to ascertain what is the law in regard to practice in Civil Actions and Special Proceedings." The production of such a for-profit work by Tourgée, entitled *The Code of Civil Procedure of North Carolina, with Notes and Decisions*, is among the richest ironies in the 360 years of North Carolina legal history. Whether it was the desire for a readable organization of the text of the code and its amendments, for references to the many difficult appellate decisions construing it, or for the privileged insights of its principal drafter which motivated the compiler to produce this work is of little consequence: Tourgée, like codifiers before him, had billed his code of civil procedure as a tool that would speak transparently to an audience of non-professionals[450] in a way that common law pleading, with its many forms of action,[451] could not speak. In the first note to this digest-treatise, Tourgée boasted of the simplicity and rationality of the code as initially adopted in North Carolina:

> One purpose which the writer hopes may be subserved by the publication of this volume, will be to narrow the attention of the bar and the courts to the Code of Procedure *as it is*—a statute by no means perfect, but constituting, as the writer believes, the germ of the simplest, completest and most rational judicial procedure ever known.

And in the preface to his digest-treatise, Tourgée wrote of the appeal of the code to the common reason of the people:

Its [the Code system's] clear, distinct and logical system of pleading, the abolition of feigned issues and the abolition of the distinctions between actions at law and suits in equity, appeal too strongly to common reason not to receive the hearty endorsement of a people very much inclined to think for themselves, in matters affecting their personal interest.

The production and sale of this work belied these advertisements. Apparently, code pleading still required professional pleaders—and professional pleaders armed with privately published how-to books, at that. Code pleading, it seems, required as artificial a reason as had common law pleading.

But in the view of Tourgée and other law reformers, this innocent faith in the transparency and simplicity of code pleading served a good purpose, even if the purpose was not to make every man a lawyer in his own cause or every lawyer a competent pleader. Code pleading buried the scholastic reasoning of common law and promoted common sense. It required language that was "*ordinary* instead of *technical*" and "*concise* instead of *formal*"; it set out "*facts* instead of *conclusions*"; it developed "the *true nature* of the action instead of a prescribed fiction"; and it alleged facts *separately* (allowing *specific* denial), instead of averring them *connectedly* (requiring *inferential* denial). More fundamentally, it demanded that courts construe pleadings differently than they had under common law pleading: "At common law everything was construed most strongly against the pleader," while under code pleading the court "liberally construed" the pleadings "to promote 'substantial justice between the parties.'"

By relieving litigant's counsel of the need to reason and of the skeptical eye of the judge, code pleading promoted litigation, even if it still required that a lawyer-clerk dot "I"s and cross "T"s per the wisdom of commercial manuals. And code pleading promoted such litigation just as it undermined the effectiveness of the civil jury, that great bulwark of private property in North Carolina.[452] Instead of a single issue of fact going to the jury in civil actions seeking remedies that had been recognized by the common law, multiple issues in a case might now go to these lay persons;[453] and in North Carolina, the many issues of fact in actions seeking equitable remedies, too, would go to the jury.[454]

Just as Tourgée's code of civil procedure relied heavily upon David Dudley Field's work in New York, so his digest-treatise relied upon greater minds—in this case, the work of Professor John Norton Pomeroy.[455] Excerpted below are the preface to Tourgée's work and the notes of substance.]

PREFACE.

The test of practical utility is the only one which should be applied to a work in any manner designed for the special use of the legal profession. The object of this volume is to enable the professional reader more easily, quickly and certainly to ascertain what is the law in regard to practice in Civil Actions and Special Proceedings. For this purpose, the amendments which have been made to the Code of Civil Procedure have been carefully collated and, where it has been possible to do so without material change, incorporated in the text, with proper references to the amending acts. Where this was not practicable, they have been inserted as additional sections, in the most fitting relations.

The decisions of the Supreme Court upon the various sections and modifying and amending acts have also been carefully digested and arranged for immediate reference.

It was not intended to have the character of a treatise, though a few notes have been introduced. The decisions upon our Code are not yet sufficiently numerous to allow the details of the system to be filled out by analysis of the cases, and the writer was not vain enough to suppose that his own opinions could supply the lack of data in our Reports.

The decisions of other States have been referred to in but few instances. The early announced intention of our Supreme Court to regard the decisions of no other State as authority upon matters of practice, has been very closely adhered to, and the result is, that the North Carolina practitioner is almost without a guide in such matters, unless the very point in question can be found in the volumes of the Reports. It is in a clear and distinct arrangement of the law, specific reference to the amending statutes and the means it affords for an easy and exhaustive consideration of the authorities bearing upon each section which has been adjudicated, that the chief value of the work will be found to lie.

Great care has been taken to secure fullness and accuracy in citation. A few errors have been discovered in citation, and one or two unimportant ones in phraseology of amending laws. There are some typographical errors, which will not be likely to mislead the reader, though they are somewhat annoying to the writer, as our own short-comings usually are.

The list of cases is believed to be entirely accurate, and any error of citation which may be found in the body of the work, may be easily remedied by reference thereto. As the decisions affecting the Code are all contained in the numbered volumes of the Reports, the abbreviations "N. C. R." have been omitted and only the number of the volume given both in the citations and the list.

Special Proceedings—except Divorce, which I think has quite lost that specific character and become a civil action, pure and simple—are included as being so intimately connected with the practice controlled by the Code and its amendatory legislation, that any work which sought to present the one, would be fatally defective unless accompanied by the other.

To this has been added also, the rules of the Supreme Court since 1868, many of which are of very great importance in the practice, and worthy of far more careful consideration than they have generally received from the profession.

A collection of decisions affecting the various sections of the Constitution of 1868, with a brief statement of the subject of each section is also appended. This collection is not claimed to be absolutely complete, though it is thought very few cases bearing upon constitutional questions will be found which are not there cited. It had been found of great convenience in my own practice, and was published at the earnest request of friends who had observed its advantages.

The index is to the text alone, and no pains have been spared to make it full and complete. Every section has been thoroughly cross-indexed, and, as far as possible, re-reference avoided. Convenience, readiness and certainty in the use of the volume as a means of ascertaining what *is* the law, have been kept constantly in view, and all other considerations have been steadily subordinated to them.

I desire to express my thanks to the publisher for the care which he has taken to give the volume a becoming appearance, and the patience with which he has submitted to the numerous changes, which a desire for exhaustive accuracy prompted.

That the Code system, as it is termed, is to be the procedure of the future, there is no doubt. Both reason and experience point to that result. That there are evils attending the abandonment of the old system and the adoption of the new, no one can doubt. That the circumstances under which it was adopted in this State have placed it under the interdict of prejudice from the outset, every one will admit, and it must also, I think, be admitted that even under this great disadvantage, it has secured a permanent foothold not to be disturbed either by legislation or construction. Its clear, distinct and logical system of pleading, the abolition of feigned issues and the abolition of the distinctions between actions at law and suits in equity, appeal too strongly to common reason not to receive the hearty endorsement of a people very much inclined to think for themselves, in matters affecting their personal interest. It is believed that the Code, also, is fast overcoming the prejudice with which it was at first received by the profession, as its merits and advantages are more fully apprehended and better appreciated by them.

My thanks are due for the kindly co-operation and encouragement of many of the members of the bar in the preparation of this work. It is my hope that they may not be disappointed in the prognostications they have made in regard to its usefulness, but that it may prove to be of value to the profession of the State, and lead to a closer study and better appreciation of that system which now prevails in a majority of the States and Territories of this Union, and which has recently dispossessed the Common Law procedure in the English Courts, where it was cradled.

ALBION W. TOURGEE.

Raleigh, N. C., Feb. 25, 1878. . . .

[THE CODE OF CIVIL PROCEDURE. Comment appended to the title of the book.]

[d]The acts constituting the Code of Civil Procedure embraced all that was contained in the volume published under the supervision of the Code Commission in 1868, and entitled "The Code of Civil Procedure," to the close of Title XVIII, Sec. 416, page 153 of that volume, except Title II and Chapter VIII of Title VIII.

This has, very properly, been decided by the court, to be one act. The other acts included in that volume, were directed to be published with it, but the writer of this note is alone responsible for the arrangement of the various acts directed to be published by the Act of August 24th, 1868, and designated as Title XXII of that volume. That the insertion of Title II and Chapter VIII of Title VIII, in those places, was a mistake, and has tended to mar the harmony and obscure the meaning of the Code, he is free to admit. It is, perhaps, to be regretted that Judge Battle's Revisal perpetuated this error. It was, at first, intended that only the original act, with the amendments which have since been made, should be presented in this volume. As, however, these acts have come, by long association with the Code, to be regarded by the profession generally as a part of it, and the legislation in regard to those subjects would naturally be sought there, the author, in accordance with his fixed purpose to make the work useful to the practitioner by every means in his power, has determined to embrace them in this volume, as well as a part of the XIIth Title, which has been repealed, marking the distinction, however, by the use of a different type for the text of those portions. The sections of the Revised Code and other antecedent statutes introduced in Battle's Revisal, as supernumerary sections of the Code, will be omitted as being even less proper to be considered a part of that act, than the chapters already mentioned. In many instances, however, where they are evidently of interest, as being in *pari materia*, with the portions of the Code to which they were attached in the Revisal, they will be printed in a different type and under their appropriate titles. The attempted commingling of the provisions of the Revised Code and other statutes with the Code of Procedure, has tended not a little to produce a confused and indefinite idea of the provisions and character of the latter act, both in the minds of the profession and on the bench.

One purpose which the writer hopes may be subserved by the publication of this volume, will be to narrow the attention of the bar and the courts to the Code of Procedure *as it is*—a statute by no means perfect, but constituting, as the writer believes, the germ of the simplest, completest and most rational judicial procedure ever known. Its power of symetrical development is not the least of its valuable features. A word, added here or eliminated there, a sentence appended to a section, or a section to a chapter, as the result of a careful scrutiny of its workings, will soon constitute it a system of statutory procedure which shall perfectly subserve the wants of the people, and develope [*sic*] the best qualities of the legal profession. Many of the amendments already made to the Code are of this character. Others are not. Time and care are required to complete its outlines. It is hoped that this volume will lead to, and aid in, such discriminating study of the Code, as to secure its proper amendment and perfection. . . .

[**§ 5.—Criminal Action.** Comment discussing State *v.* Simons, 68 N.C. 378 (1873) (Boyden, J.).]

ᵈThe language of this decision, that the terms "Criminal Action" and "Indictment," are now synonymous, seems hardly to be supported by the reasoning of the learned Justice delivering the opinion. In order to arrive at this conclusion, it becomes necessary to use the term *indictment* in the broad secondary sense of a prosecution, rather than in the narrower sense of a bill found by a grand jury. That this secondary sense is sometimes employed is quite true, but it is not strictly correct. It is merely by a figure of speech that the indictment—the formal charge—is used for the entire prosecution. The strictly legal sense, that of "a written accusation preferred by a grand jury" would seem to be the force of this term in the constitution. "All *indictments which have been found.*" Sec. 9, Art. XIV: "No person shall be put to answer any *criminal charge* but by *indictment*, &c." Art. I, Sec. 12, are both susceptible of a construction fully in accord with this decision, without varying the ordinary force of this term. In both instances, the word is obviously used in its narrower and more correct significance. So that it would be more accurate to say, that the term "*indictment*" is used therein to designate the *charge* which is preferred by a grand jury against the defendant in a "*criminal action.*" By this construction the term "criminal action" is used, as it was no doubt intended, to designate the entire proceeding against a person charged with crime, while the term "indictment" applies only to a single step in that proceeding. This view seems to be rendered necessary by the definition of criminal action in Sec. 1, Art. IV, taken in connection with §§ 6 and 7 of the C. C. P. Indictment has never been used as applicable to the cases included under § 7. It was evidently not the purpose of the Constitution or the Code, to change the method of proceeding against persons charged with crime. Such prosecution was still to be by *means of an indictment*, but the whole proceeding was to be "denominated a criminal action." It would still be proper to use either the words "Criminal Action" or "Indictment" in the title of the charge presented by the grand jury, not because they are synonymous, but because one includes the other. Indictment sustains the same relation to a criminal action, that complaint does to a civil action. It is the pleading by which the defendant is charged.

[§ 6.—**Civil Action.** Comment contrasting civil actions and special proceedings.]

a"CIVIL ACTION"—"SPECIAL PROCEEDING."

What is a "civil action" and what a "special proceeding" is a question which seems to have proved very troublesome to the courts. Yet the difficulty is more fanciful than real. Its only importance arises from the fact that, in some unimportant particulars, the procedure in the latter differs from that prescribed in the former. Three attempts at a definition or construction of the term "civil action" appear in our reports. One by Pearson, C. J., in *Tate* v. *Powe* as cited above, one by Judge Battle as *amicus curæ* in the same case, and one by Justice Rodman, in *Woodly* v. *Gilliam, supra*. The rule laid down by the Chief Justice is in these words:

"Any proceeding that under the old mode was commenced by a *capias ad respondendum*, including ejectment, or by a bill in equity for relief, is a civil action; any proceeding that under the old mode may be commenced by petition, or motion upon notice, is a "special proceeding."

Judge Battle *suggested*, that "whenever the proceeding *may be ex parte*, it is a Special Proceeding."

Justice Rodman says—"I think those actions are special proceedings, in which *existing statutes*, direct a procedure different from the ordinary."

It is somewhat remarkable that neither of these learned men seems to have been quite satisfied with the distinction he had himself drawn. Judge Battle, says the report, "concluded that *his* was not the true line"; the Chief Justice in his decision admits that the distinction drawn by him is "merely arbitrary" and intimates that it was done more to settle a question which was troublesome, than because the court believed it correct; and Justice Rodman gives his view as an explanation of his having assented to the decision on *Tate* v. *Powe*.

Besides the fact that the rule in *Tate* v. *Powe* is merely arbitrary, as suggested by the Chief Justice, it is open to the following serious objections:

1. It is based on the assumption that the Constitution, in this respect, was framed in contemplation of the laws previously in force, when, by its express provisions, "the forms of all actions at law and suits in equity," then and theretofore existing were *abolished*. It is as unreasonable to seek for the line of demarcation between civil actions and special proceedings in the *Natura Brevium*, as it would be to attempt to separate legal from equitable defences, under the Code.
2. It presupposes the minutest knowledge of the intricacies and artificial subtleties of the common law system, as a condition precedent to a comprehension of the fundamental distinctions, of a system whose professed object is the utter abolition of those distinctions. One of the very objects of the Code was to obviate the necessity of mastering the artificial subtleties of actions at law, but this definition would render it necessary that one should be a perfect master of its ins and outs, before he could understand the initial provisions of the Code. It is tying to the new system the corpse of the old. It preserves all the evils of the old system with none of its advantages. "This idea[,"] says Judge Swann in his *Pleadings and Precedents*, ["]of subordinating the Code system to any other system is in every way mischievous. The Code abolishes the common law system and adopts a new one."
3. It is not only "judicial legislation," as the Chief Justice admits it to be, but in direct repugnance to the express provisions, both of the Constitution and the Code.

Statutory definitions of "Civil Action."—It seems to have escaped the attention of the court that, while the term "civil action," as used in the Constitution, has a meaning which is defined with great precision in that instrument itself, and the same term when used in the Code of Procedure is therein defined with equal care and certainty, that the "civil action" of the Constitution is an entirely *different* thing from the "civil action" of the Code. To attempt to harmonize them is futile. They are not, and could not have been intended to be, identical, and it is by no means necessary that they should correspond. Each has a distinct and separate purpose to perform. They happen to be identical in name but one might as well try to put a *beer quart* in a *wine measure* of that denomination, as to superimpose the "civil action" of the Constitution upon the "civil action" of the Code, with the expectation that their parts will coincide.

Constitutional Definition.—§ 1. Article IV of the Constitution defines a Civil Action, as follows: "There shall be in this State but one form of action, for—

(*a*) The enforcement of private rights, or,

(*b*) The protection of private rights, or,

(*c*) The redress of private wrongs,

which *shall be denominated a civil action.*" It will be seen that this definition includes every application, for any remedy or relief, which any private person can possibly make, in his own behalf, to a court of justice.

Every proceeding instituted for the advantage or relief of a private party, in any court, whether adversary or *ex parte*, *must* fall under one or more of the elements of the definition. It is not possible to imagine any controversy or proceeding in regard to private rights or wrongs, which is not included in this category—so that the "civil action" of the Constitution includes every action or proceeding that a private person can bring, or have need to bring, in any court of the State.

The Reason.—This definition is made thus broad for a reason which is perfectly evident, when we consider the previous portion of the same section—which abolishes—

(*a*) The distinction between actions at law and suits in equity,

(*b*) The forms of all *such* actions,

(*c*) The forms of all *such* suits.

The purpose was to utterly wipe out and annul all forms of civil proceeding—all means for the ascertainment and adjudication of private rights—and to substitute in the place of all that had been theretofore, "*one form of action*" under which all civil remedies might be sought and obtained in the courts of this State.

This definition was never intended to apply only to causes of action of which the Superior Court has jurisdiction, any more than to actions in the Courts of Justices of the Peace, or Probate Courts. It was not intended simply to mark the line which separates the jurisdiction of the courts. It is as universal as words can make it and leaves no room for construction. It does not appeal to any obsolete forms or obliterated distinctions to ascertain the limits of the term "civil action," but only inquires, "What purpose is it designed to subserve?" If a private one, then it is *civil action*.

The Code Definition.—By careful consideration of the first six sections of the Code, the following definition of a civil action is eliminated:

A civil action is—

(*a*) An ordinary proceeding in a court of justice,

(*b*) by which one party prosecutes another party,

(*c*) for the enforcement of a private right, or,

(*d*) the protection of a private right, or,

(*e*) the redress of a private wrong.

It will be seen that the last three of these elements by which a civil action is to be distinguished, are identically those of the constitutional definition.

The two first, to-wit: "an *ordinary* proceeding in a court of justice by which *one party prosecutes another*" have been superadded to the constitutional definition.

The suggestion of Judge Battle in *Tate* v. *Powe* is in strict conformity with this definition. A proceeding which *may* be *ex parte*, *cannot* be a civil action under the definition given in the Code.

The Cause of these Differences.—The reason of this difference between the Code definition and that found in the Constitution is this. The section of the Constitution which has been referred to, was taken originally from a code in which it occupied the same relative position as does Section 12 in ours. That is, it followed the definition of civil action, and was designed mainly to negative the idea that the civil action was an additional remedy—a new form of action added to the common law and equity forms, already extant, but not inconsistent with them. In our case, however, it was separated from this relation and put in the

Constitution as the root of the Code system. As such it precedes and dominates the classification of the Code and can neither be avoided by construction nor legislated out of its imperative significance either by the Legislature or by the Court.

The Effect of this Difference.—Altogether unconsciously, the logical instincts of the profession have led both the bar and the bench to give the fullest effect to both of these definitions, in the spheres they were respectively designed to control. Every action or proceeding by which a *private* right is to be vindicated or *private* wrong redressed, in any court of the State, is today, a civil action according to the constitutional definition.

There is but *one* form of action in use to accomplish such an end. By "form of action" is not meant mere identity in the form of the summons or in the time, when, or place where, the same is returnable. The form of action, at the common law, affected not only the writ but the declaration, the plea and the judgment. In other words, the form of action depended on the declaration which could be met only by certain specified pleas and allowed only a specific judgment to be pronounced. There were many "forms of action" at common law. In equity there was but one "form of action." Under the operation of the Constitution we have now but one form of action whether in the Courts of Justices of the Peace, Probate, or Superior Courts; whether in adversary or *ex parte* proceedings; whether as regards legal or equitable rights. That form of action, briefly stated is, that the party applying for relief, having made the proper parties, and set forth the facts which constitute his cause of action, in ordinary and concise language, and made due proof thereof, may receive any relief within the verge of the court's jurisdiction, to which those facts show him to be entitled, without regard to the prayer of his complaint or the remedy which he sought to obtain or believed himself entitled to receive.

Thus, effect has been given to the definition embodied in the Constitution.

The civil action of the Code has also been universally recognized as meaning the necessarily adversary actions cognizable by the Superior Courts,—those "in which one party prosecutes another party," according to the terms of that definition. Without having been distinctly stated hitherto, it has been tacitly admitted that the "civil action," as defined in the Constitution is one thing, and the "civil action" as defined in the Code is quite another thing.

Special Proceedings.—Are special proceedings, then violative of the Constitution? In *name* they certainly are. The Constitution expressly declares that every proceeding, to establish private right or redress private wrong "*shall be denominated a civil action.*" This was purposely and wisely done. In the law *names* easily become things. There is little doubt that there was, at first, but one form of action at common law, but the habit of calling certain frequently used and approved forms of declaration by specific names, finally established them as distinct and separate, technical forms of action. To prevent this and to preserve the great principle of *one form of action*, the Constitution prescribed also, that it should have but one name wherever found, because identity of name is a most potent instrumentality for securing identity of character.

In spirit, as already observed, the Special Proceedings have not been violative, to any considerable degree, of the Constitution. The oneness of form has been well preserved in nearly all of them. In general, the party seeking relief must make the necessary parties by summons, state his cause of action so that its substance may be readily gathered; his adversary may deny his facts by answer or his law by demurrer, and he may have either equitable or legal relief according to his merits and without regard to his prayer. In effect, and according to the practice of the courts, the suggestion of Mr. Justice Rodman, in *Woodley* v. *Gilliam* is the true distinction between the "Civil Action" of the Code and "Special Proceedings." "Those *actions*,["] says he, (evidently referring to the *constitutional* classification of civil actions[),"] are Special Proceedings, in which *existing* statutes direct a procedure different from the ordinary." In other words, as I understand the learned Justice, to say,—the legislature has taken a portion of the actions defined by the Constitution as "civil actions," and made them "Civil Actions" under the Code. It has taken others of the constitutional class "civil action" and made *them* Special Proceedings, still preserving identity of form and using the term Special Proceeding, simply to distinguish certain specific classes whose procedure varies in some unimportant particulars from others.

I cannot refrain from again calling the attention of the profession, in this State, to the very admirable discussion of the Civil Action, given by Mr. Pomeroy in his excellent work entitled "Remedies and Remedial Rights." This is the only systematic work upon the Reformed Procedure, and it is not too high praise to say that no one can obtain a full knowledge of that system, in no manner so easily and well, as by the study of the work....

[**§ 12—Distinctions between Actions at Law and Suits in Equity abolished—Civil Action prescribed.**
Comment discussing Bitting *v.* Thaxton, 72 N.C. 541 (1875) (Reade, J.).]

*b*The abolition of that peculiar antinomy, law and equity, is the central idea of the Reformed Procedure. That it ever had any foundation in reason no one can even pretend. It was the result of accident, and as absurd in its primary idea, as the distinctions between the different actions at law or the feigned issues by which their defects were sought to be remedied or evaded by the courts. Logically, there is no reason why the rights known as equitable should be administered in a different forum or under different forms from those denominated legal. Why a suitor should be denied a right in one court and allowed it in another upon the same state of facts, is susceptible of no more sensible explanation than the mere statement that one was a court of law and the other a court of equity. This absurdity is susceptible of no better exemplification than the fact that no human subtlety has been able to eliminate a definition of equity, as the term has hitherto been used in our legal nomenclature. Mr. Story, in his Equity Jurisprudence, after having carefully considered all the previous attempts and disclosed the defects of each, concludes that no more accurate one can be given than that *"an equitable right is one which may be enforced in a Court of Equity!"* As a definition this is about as satisfactory as to say that an American citizen is a citizen of America.

As a practical fact, however, the abolition of these distinctions has given rise to many nice and difficult questions. Fortunately for the profession and the future development of the Code in this State, our Supreme Court have not indulged in the finespun theories as to the effect and intention of this provision, which have prevailed in other States immediately after the adoption of the reformed procedure. While manifesting the fullest purpose to carry out its provisions in their true spirit, they have not been fruitful in general treatises upon it. There are some questions which have provoked very much discussion in other States, which have hardly been mooted here, either at the bar or upon the bench. The discussions in regard to the forms of actions and the abolition of distinctions between them are few and somewhat meager in our Reports. Perhaps one reason of this may be the early announced determination of the Court to administer the Code strictly according to its spirit and intent as their own reason and judgment might dictate, without regarding the decisions of other States as authority in its construction. In nearly all respects their general views have been in striking harmony, however, with what has been established as correct, after much variance and discussion, in other States.

No attempt has been made to assimilate the civil action of the Code to actions at law, or to superimpose upon it the forms or rules of pleadings which prevailed in such actions, except in one or two cases, in which it has been intimated, apparently without much deliberation, that the common law rules of pleading still apply. See §91 *note*, and the cases there cited.

The distinction between suits in equity and the forms of such suits, and the civil action has not been so clearly drawn as is desirable. The court seem to have adopted the view that the civil action was an extension of equity procedure, and have been governed in almost all their decisions by the analogies to be drawn therefrom. As, however, they have logically construed the contemporaneous provisions of the Constitution, as providing but one mode of trial, the objections to this view are much less than they would otherwise have been.

In the making of parties, the pronouncing of several judgments between them, whether plaintiffs or defendants, the interpleading of persons not parties of record, the joinder of legal and equitable causes of action or defences and in a just apprehension of the nature and office of the counterclaim, the decisions of this State may challenge comparison with those of any other in a fair, manly and logical application, and clear exposition, of the true principles of the reformed procedure. In no other which has fallen under my observation has there been such an absence of evasive subtlety or so little attempt to wrest its provisions from the plain purpose of the law-makers. Taking the Code as clearly intended to be a new system of procedure, they have applied its provisions, in the main, without regard to the speculations of others and with a remarkable freedom from the bias arising from previous professional study and experience.

Perhaps the liberality and breadth of view with which they have construed the Code have led them to overestimate what they have termed the "liberality of the method of procedure now in force," and to permit a laxity of pleading and encourage a facility of amendment, without noting the fact that the Code, while liberal in allowing amendment, is rigorously careful in allowing such amendment *only upon terms*. Only two instances, I think, are to be found in which error, inadvertence or mistake can be remedied, except upon terms. The Code was not designed to encourage laxity but accuracy. It does not favor negligence but promotes vigilance. The circumstances under which it went into operation here—the Constitution taking effect on the 3d of July, 1868, and the Code on the 24th of August of the same year—gave the bench and bar but little opportunity to familiarize themselves with its provisions before they were called upon to put it in practice. This, undoubtedly, laid the foundation of that habit of indulging error and condoning negligence which has marked our practice. That this will gradually disappear is nearly certain. As the details of practice become more generally understood by the profession, they will naturally insist upon a more strict compliance with them.

It is somewhat remarkable that the court, by construing our constitutional provisions so as to make a jury trial in all actions a matter of right, seems likely to have overcome the only impediment hitherto unsurmounted in the development of the civil action. Mr. Pomeroy says: "*Remedies and Remedial Rights*, § 64.—Absolute unity in the judicial methods by which remedies are to be obtained, is practically impossible so long as the jury trial is required in certain classes of causes and dispensed with in others. In respect to all other features the theoretical unity is attainable."

He intimates also, that this is only to be effected by restricting the right of trial by jury to criminal actions. Our courts have avoided this difficulty and without serious inconvenience, especially such inconvenience as was for a time apprehended, by extending the jury trial to all actions. This is an entirely new step, though a strictly logical one, in the developemente [*sic*] of the unified action which was rendered possible only by the peculiar provisions of our Constitution in regard to jury trial, taken in connection with the section now under consideration. . . .

[**§ 58.—Infants, &c., to sue by guardian or next friend.** Comment regarding infants as parties.]

[a]One of the earliest objections made to the Code of Procedure, was in regard to the provisions for making infants parties. That those proceedings were somewhat cumbrous and minute, is very true, but it may be fairly doubted whether the amendment soon after made and resulting finally in the above section, is any improvement upon the former system. It should be the policy of the law to guard *with the utmost vigilance* the rights of parties under such disabilities, and the very expeditious method now in use, while very convenient for the party opposed, and especially saving of trouble and labor to his attorney, leaves the interests of the infant without any reasonable chance of being ascertained or defended. A guardian *pendente lite* is usually appointed on account of his convenience to the court, and not on account of his relations with the infant or interest he may have in sustaining any claim of right which may exist in his behalf. In very many cases, perhaps, the friends and relations may not even be aware of the action until after judgment has been rendered against the person under disability.

The former method had the merit of erring on the side of too much vigilance, if at all. The utmost publicity was given to the proceeding. It was almost impossible that the relations and friends should not be informed of the action before the time for answer arrived. The infant himself, if above the age of fourteen, was required to be served with a copy of summons against him and allowed a voice in the selection of a guardian to represent his interests. Every conceivable precaution was adopted to prevent the machinery of the law being used to the disadvantage of the party under disability.

The present law invites, by the facility with which it permits infants to be made parties, the grossest imposition. It is no answer to this objection to say that such cases do not often occur, even if that could be established as a fact. Men are but men, and such is their frailty that every avenue for evil should be closed against them, so far as the same may be done by legal enactment. Such care adds something to the labor of the profession, which they ought to be willing to endure for the public good, and also, something to the cost of proceedings, which such parties might well afford to pay for the increased safety it would afford. This amendment has been thought by some obnoxious to the objection of being "lawyer's law," that is, an enactment designed more to promote the ease and comfort of the profession than to secure the rights of the parties in whose behalf it purports to have been enacted.

It has been suggested that some protection would be given to the rights of those under disability by requiring the guardian *ad litem*, before doing any act as such, to take and subscribe an oath that he will diligently and faithfully conduct the defence and in all things protect the rights of his temporary ward as if they were his own. This suggestion seems worthy of attention. Something should be done to give greater security to the interests of this class of persons. . . .

[**§ 61.—Who to be defendants.** Comment discussing Colgrove v. Koonce, 76 N.C. 363 (1877) (Pearson, C. J.).]

*d*This decision would seem to be in conflict with the principle of the preceding ones, and it is not easy to see the distinction the court draws. The language of the section is very broad and, apparently, of no doubtful significance.

There are three classes who may be made parties defendant:

1. Any one having or claiming an interest in the controversy adverse to the plaintiff;
2. Any one who is a necessary party to its complete determination;
3. The landlord with his tenant in actions for realty.

And one class who may be made either plaintiffs or defendants, to-wit:

1. Any person claiming title or right of possession to real estate.

It would seem that the question intended to be tried was, "Who is entitled to the possession of the land in dispute?" and that the design was to have this question settled in one action, instead of allowing A to fight it out with B, and afterwards have a like controversy over the same matter with C. . . .

[**§ 62.—Parties to be joined, &c.** Comment under § 62, discussing Von Glahn v. DeRossett, 76 N.C. 292 (1877) (Pearson, C. J.)]

*e*The principle of this case has been much questioned at the bar. The decision is put by Pearson C. J., who delivers the opinion, upon the ground that "much obscurity and confusion will result from a severance in the mode of defence," in such cases and gives this illustration:

"If the demurrer of the defendant A. be disposed of that will decide the merits of the case and the defendants B. and C. will not have had an opportunity of being heard by counsel. If the demurrer should be overruled the case will be in effect decided against them and if it be sustained the complaint will be dismissed as to A. and they will be left in an anomalous condition."

I confess myself unable to see the force, either of the reason or the illustration given. Indeed, the decision itself seems to me utterly impracticable and at war with every principle of the code practice. It is quite conceivable that there might be a ground of demurrer good as to one defendant and not as to others.

But even if that were not possible, every defendant has a *right*, either to demur or answer, as he may be advised, (§ 94.) One might wish to answer and another to demur. Which should control in such a case? Will the court say to one you shall not *demur*, or to the other you shall not *answer*? The court has as much right to compel the one to yield as the other, and no sort of right to deprive either of any plea he may desire to interpose betwixt himself and any threatened liability. It is suggested that the overruling of the demurrer would be in effect, deciding the case against the other defendants, and if sustained leave them in an anomalous condition. I cannot see how. Suppose the demurrer to be that the complaint does not state a cause of action. Then the action falls as to all, if it is sustained. Suppose it should be overruled; then the party interposing it has a right to answer over if it was interposed in good faith. The court try to avoid an imaginary difficulty by overruling the demurrer and saving the equity, as they say.

Such a course is not only open to the objection of, perhaps, submitting the party to unnecessary costs and trouble, but would seem to be in direct conflict with §222 of the Code which appears to have been designed to meet just such a contingency. "Issues of law and fact may arise upon different parts of the pleadings in the same action. In such cases the issues of law must be tried first, unless the court otherwise direct."

The evident purpose of this section is to avoid whenever possible the expense of a trial of the issue of fact and is peculiarly valuable in our State where every case may have a jury trial.

Some of the judges on the circuit have endeavored to apply this case to actions against the obligors upon ordinary bonds. Such are evidently *joint and several* obligors who may be sued either jointly or separately as provided in §63. The court has, however, decided that the stockholders of such banks are *joint but not several* obligors, so that the decision could have no application to obligors upon joint and several bonds, being based solely upon the inseparability of the defendant's interests. . . .

[**§ 69.—Change of place of trial.** Comment under sub-section 2, "When the convenience of witnesses . . ."]

"The power of the court over the place of trial is materially extended by this section. A very broad and just discretion over the removal of causes, is vested in the Superior Court which, if freely exercised, could not fail to be advantageous to the administration of justice in the State. Under the former practice two things must concur to enable a Judge to remove a cause from one county to another:

1. One of the parties must apply for such removal:
2. Such party must show by affidavit a well founded belief that he would not obtain justice in the county where the cause was pending.

Beyond these narrow limits the court had no power of removal. This section provides that the court may change the place of trial.

1. When the action has been brought in the wrong county;
2. When the convenience of witnesses would be subserved thereby;
3. When the ends of justice would be promoted.

The first of these provisions is peculiarly illustrative of the spirit of the Code to aid the applicant for remedial justice by disregarding any error which does not affect the substantial rights of the adverse party. So if an action is brought to the wrong county and the defendant does not demand in writing, that it be removed to the proper one, before the time for answer expires, he can make no further objection to the place of trial. If he does make such a demand the court will order its removal, imposing such terms as may be just, which ought never to be less than the costs accrued up to that time and the cost of removal. In most cases it should be more as the defendant is put to unnecessary trouble and the rule which is applied in some of the districts to demurrers which are overruled, viz: that the party may answer upon the payment of costs, including an attorney's fee, might well be extended to these cases.

The second is also, an entirely new provision but an eminently just and proper one. If all or nearly all the witnesses live in another county it is very proper that the trial should be had in that county unless there be some valid objection to such course.

The third provision is inclusive of the former practice. The promotion of public justice evidently extends, not only to the protection of the rights of a party who may conceive himself unlikely to obtain a fair trial, but also, very many other considerations—such as the crowded state of the dockets in one county and the reverse in another. This section gives to the Judge power, on an application of a party, of the witnesses or of his own motion, when the facts appear, to change the place of trial, not as a matter of right to the parties but in his discretion as having due regard to *public justice* and *public right*.

This section seems to have almost entirely escaped the attention of the bar. During six years upon the bench of the seventh district, I never heard a single application based upon it, and am now unable to find that the Supreme Court has ever considered it in contrast with the former practice.

So far as I have observed removals have hitherto been governed solely by the practice under sections 115, 116, Chapter 31, Revised Code, except in some few cases where they have been brought to the wrong county. . . .

TITLE VIII.

OF THE PLEADINGS IN CIVIL ACTION.

Chapter   I. Of the Complaint.
Chapter   II. The Demurrer.
Chapter III. The Answer.
Chapter   IV. The Reply.
Chapter   V. Duties and powers of the Clerk of the Superior Court
              in relation to the pleadings, and in collateral matters.
Chapter   VI. General rules of pleadings.
Chapter VII. Mistakes in pleadings and amendments.
Chapter VIII. Of the qualification and general duties of Clerks of the
              Superior Courts.

CHAPTER I.

OF THE COMPLAINT.

Sec. 91. Forms of pleading.
    92. Complaint.
Sec. 93. Complaint, what to contain.

§ 91.—Forms of pleading.

All the forms of pleading heretofore existing are abolished; and hereafter, the forms of pleading in civil actions in courts of record, and the rules by which the sufficiency of the pleadings is to be determined, are those prescribed by this Code.

The rules of pleading and construction at the common law have not been abrogated. The essential principles remain, and have only been modified as to technicalities and matters of form. Parsley v. Nicholson, 65—207.a

Contra, Moore v. Edmiston, 70—510, see opinion cited in full under § 128.

---

a The language of Mr. Justice Dick, in this decision, is much broader than the question before him required that he should use and, while it has been several times formally cited and approved by the court, it has, by no means, received their practical sanction. (See the opinion of Rynum, J., cited in full under § 128.) In effect, their decisions have been in direct conflict with it. It has afforded, however, one of those delusive formulas, which are so often the source of actual error. This formula has become a favorite at the bar, where it is often used with as little appreciation of its real import, as it must have been by the learned justice in this case.

The language of the Code is explicit that not only the forms of pleadings at common law are abolished, but also, that the rules by which the sufficiency of pleadings are determined, shall be those prescribed in the Code itself.

The common law rules of pleading.—In actions at law the rules of pleading were designed simply to elaborate, in technical language, a com-

---

In his annotated treatise concerning the *Code of Civil Procedure*, Albion W. Tourgée sometimes criticized opinions of the Supreme Court of North Carolina. Page 75 of *The Code of Civil Procedure of North Carolina, with Notes and Decisions*, by Albion W. Tourgée scanned at the North Carolina Supreme Court Library (*Credit*: The Compilers)

[**§ 91.—Forms of pleading.** Comment discussing Parseley *v.* Nicholson, 65 N.C. 207 (1871) (Dick, J.).]

"The language of Mr. Justice Dick, in this decision [stating that rules of pleading and construction at the common law have not been abrogated by the Code practice, their principles only being modified as to technicalities and matters of form], is much broader than the question before him required that he should use and, while it has been several times formally cited and approved by the court, it has, by no means, received their practical sanction. (See the opinion of Bynum, J., cited in full under § 128.) In effect, their decisions have been in direct conflict with it. It has afforded, however, one of those delusive formulas, which are so often the source of actual error. This formula has become a favorite at the bar, where it is often used with as little appreciation of its real import, as it must have been by the learned justice in this case.

The language of the Code is explicit that not only the forms of pleadings at common law are abolished, but also, that the rules by which the sufficiency of pleadings are determined, shall be those prescribed in the Code itself.

The common law rules of pleading.—In actions at law the rules of pleading were designed simply to elaborate, in technical language, a conclusion of law. It did not aim at a simple statement of the facts constituting the basis of the right to sue, in each particular case, but an allegation of legal effects. Except in one or two of the actions at law there was no attempt at stating the actual facts on which the action was based, in the declaration. Very frequently the allegations of the pleading were utterly at variance with the facts on which the plaintiff rested his right of recovery. In none of them, did he narrate the actual transactions between the plaintiff and defendant, but stated rather, what he conceived to be the *legal effects* of those transactions.

So too, the issue in an action at law was usually one of legal inference, and not of fact. Whether the conclusion set out in the declaration was true or false was the question for decision in such action and the issue was a compound one of law and fact.

It is true, the issue might be one of fact alone, but it was rarely so presented in the pleadings. Thus, in an action upon a promissory note or simple contract to pay money the chief averment, of the declaration was that the defendant promised to pay, and the defendant for plea averred, under the general denial, that he did not *promise*, which might mean that he did not make such contract, that he was an infant and unable to contract, that he was under duress at the time he made it, or that he had performed it or that its breach was compromised. In short, almost every fact which could bar a recovery was embraced in common law pleading, by a denial of the legal conclusion that he had *promised*.

Under the Code, however, *facts only* are to be alleged in the complaint and these must be met either (1) by a specific denial of all, or, (2) by an admission of some and a denial of other *material* facts, or (3) by an averment of other facts, or (4) by the allegation that such facts do not constitute a cause of action or some legal reason why they do not suffice to fix the defendant with liability in the premises.

The object of common law pleading was to develope [*sic*] some one question and agree upon this question as the point to be decided in the case. The Code requires a narrative of the facts constituting the plaintiff's cause of action—the facts on which his right to relief arises—and the admission or denial of those facts by the defendant, leaving the law to be applied, and the relief to be determined, by the court.

That systems so utterly diverse in their character and purposes should be governed by the same rules, is too plainly impossible to be seriously claimed by any one who will for a moment consider their distinctive characters.

Again, the rules of pleading at the common law, were dependent upon, and controlled by, the form of the action itself, which is specifically abolished. Thus, if the plaintiff sued in *debt*, the facts constituting the cause of action were required to be stated, and the judgment must be rendered in a particular form. If he sued in *assumpsit*, on the same contract, the pleading was entirely different and the judgment in another form. So nice was the distinction that if, suing in *debt*, the plaintiff alleged that the defendant "promised" to pay, it was bad, but if he said he "agreed" to pay it was good; while in *assumpsit*, on the same contract, if he said he "*agreed*" to pay it was bad, but good if he said he "promised" to pay.

In accordance with this view, and as if still further to negative the principle enunciated in *Parseley* v. *Nicholson*, the section of the Code now under consideration expressly provides, that "the rules by which the sufficiency of the pleadings is to be determined, *are those prescribed by this Code.*"

Rules of pleading prescribed by the Code.

The general rules of the Code as to pleadings are:
1. That they shall be in plain and ordinary language, (§§ 91, 100, 105);
2. That they shall be concise and without unnecessary repetition, (§§ 91, 100, 120);
3. That they shall state *the facts* which constitute the cause of action or defence, (§§ 91, 100, 102, 105);
4. That they shall show the *precise* nature of the cause of action or defence, (§ 120);
5. They must state facts sufficient to constitute a cause of action or defence, (§§ 91, 100, 102, 105);
6. As to form, each cause of action and defence and each material allegation, (§§ 91, 102) shall be separately stated and numbered;
7. As to construction, that they shall be liberally construed with a view to promote substantial justice between the parties, (§ 119.)

Every one of these rules is in direct conflict with every principle of common law pleading. The language is required to be *ordinary* instead of *technical*; *concise* instead of *formal*; to set forth *facts* instead of *conclusions*; to develope [sic] the *true nature* of the action instead of a prescribed fiction; that these facts shall be *separately* alleged, in order that they may be *specifically* denied, instead of being *connectedly* averred and only *inferentially* denied. In addition to these rules antagonistic to the entire system of common law pleading, the very basis principle by which pleadings at law were to be construed, is expressly reversed by the enactment of its converse. At common law everything was construed most strongly against the pleader. This was the very life of the system. But for this principle the law would long since have been absorbed by equity. Not only did it require a rigid adherence to its technical forms, but it made every presumption against the suitor who sought its aid. It held every one to be wrong who could by possible construction be deemed to be in error. It required language to be used in an unusual sense and then assumed that the party using it, employed it in another.

Instead of this procrustean rule, the Code provides that even the *ordinary* language prescribed for use in the pleadings, "shall be *liberally* construed—"not in favor of the pleader or his opponent nor yet against either—but to promote "substantial justice between the parties." This rule is emphasized by other kindred provisions such as §§ 128 and 129, which provide that "variances between pleading and proofs" shall be disregarded unless material, and shall not be deemed material, "unless they shall actually have misled the adverse party to *his prejudice*;" and also, § 135 which provides "that the court shall, at all times, disregard any defect, which does not affect a substantial right of the adverse party."

But, as if to make assurance doubly sure, and exclude every possibility for a doubt as to the force of these and other, like provisions of the Code, a rule is prescribed for *their* construction also. Section three hundred and ninety-one (§ 391) provides that "The rule of the common law, that statutes in derogation of that law are to be strictly construed, has no application to this Code."

So that, not only are the rules of pleading prescribed by the Code utterly subversive of the principles of common law pleading, abrogating and destroying their force and effect by unavoidable implication, but those rules themselves are to be liberally and beneficially construed. This view of the matter has been generally overlooked. None of the writers upon Code practice seem to have considered it. This provision has frequently been cited as applying to the construction of other parts of the Code, but never before, that I am aware of, invoked in aid of the system of Code pleading. Its application to that subject, however, is very evident.

The Code, therefore, provides (1) That the rules by which pleadings under it shall be construed, are those prescribed by itself, thus excluding by the clearest inference, the common law principles of pleading; (2) That certain specific rules shall be applied, which rules are inconsistent with the common law rules; (3) That the rules themselves shall be liberally construed in order that no loophole should remain by which the courts might limit their application by strict construction, and so, in effect, re-establish the common law system. . . .

[**§ 95.—When defendant may demur.** Comment under sub-division 1., "That the court has no jurisdiction . . . ," discussing Flack *v.* Dawson, 69 N.C. 42 (1873) (Rodman, J.).]

*a*The language of Mr. Justice Rodman, in this case, is somewhat remarkable in its character and tends to produce confusion and uncertainty, rather than to enlighten the mind of the reader. Instead of using the nomenclature of the Code, as he was bound to do in deciding a case under it, he uses persistently and inaccurately the term plea, sometimes as a synonym for answer and sometimes, as it would seem, in a sense broad enough to include all pleading on the part of the defendant.

There is no such thing as a "plea" under the Code, and as used at common law, it is not synonymous with either "answer" or "demurrer" the *only* "pleadings" of the defendant under the Code. He speaks of "sham pleas," instead of "sham and irrelevant answers and defences," as they are designated by the Code.

"The want of jurisdiction," he says, "is not the subject of a '*plea*' at all," yet it [is] one of the very grounds of objection to the complaint which § 93 expressly provides may be taken by *answer*, if it does not appear on the face of the complaint. The confusion which has been produced by the language of this decision has been very great, and is far less excusable in the learned justice than it would be in any of his associates, since, as one of the compilers of the Code, he was necessarily familiar with its provisions, and should have been careful to preserve its distinctions. The use of common law terms as applicable to the Code pleadings, can only be productive of uncertainty both as to what was, at the common law, and what is, under the reformed procedure. . . .

[**§ 96.—Demurrer must specify grounds of objection.** Comment discussing Love *v.* Commissioners of Chatham Co., 64 N.C. 706 (1870) (Pearson, C. J.).]

*a*I think the view announced in this case and, which has been several times repeated more or less explicit[l]y, is somewhat too broad. Indeed, the weight of authority and judgment of other courts upon exactly the same phraseology, seems to be against the doctrine enunciated in this case. Section 96 requires that the demurrer "shall distinctly specify the grounds of objection;" so that the first inquiry is what is meant by the term "grounds of objection to the complaint." The preceding section specifically enunciates six "objections to the complaint," which may be taken advantage of by demurrer; section 98 provides that such "objection" may, in certain cases, be taken by answer, and section 99 provides that if not taken by demurrer or answer "such objection" shall be waived. Comparing these, it would seem that "the ground of objection" was most probably intended to mean the grounds of demurrer set forth in section 95, and that the design of this section was to require the pleader to state specifically upon which of the demurrable objections he relied, rather than to compel him to state the reason or argument, upon which his objection is based. The distinction will, perhaps, more fully appear from an illustration. Under the present ruling a demurrer which simply stated that "it appeared from the complaint, that the plaintiff had not the legal capacity to sue," would be bad. So to[o], one stating merely, that "it appeared from the complaint that the court had no jurisdiction of the subject-matter of the action;" while if to the first was added, "because he was not twenty-one years old at the time the summons was issued," and to the second "because the sum claimed is under two hundred dollars and is due by contract," they would both be good. Yet, in both these cases, the *ground of objection*, is distinctly stated in the form first given, and the words added in the latter form, are simply the *reasons* why the objection is taken. But this is still more apparent when we come to consider two classes, which arise under the sixth paragraph of section 95, viz:

(1.) When some fact, material to the cause of action is not stated in the complaint, as in Leak *v.* Comm'rs of Richmond County, cited under §95, sub. 6, *ante*, in which it was not alleged that a majority of the justices of the county court were present, when an act was done requiring such majority, the validity of which was necessary to a recovery by the plaintiff;

(2.) When the facts, however fully stated, do not and cannot constitute a cause of action, as was the case in Powell *v.* Allen, where the plaintiffs supposed themselves entitled to partition upon the death of two of the three tenants in common for life whose remaindermen they were, cited under § 95.

In the former case it is not so illogical to require a specification, since the omission can be clearly stated and it is perhaps proper to require it, in order that the plaintiff's attention may be called to the specific defect. The pleader can say it is insufficient because it fails to set out any particular named fact which is necessary to complete the cause of action. In the latter case, however, it matters not what may be added to the general formula, "that the complaint does not state facts sufficient to constitute a cause of action," it is simply tautology—a repetition of the same thought in different words. It does not make the denial of the claim that "two and two make *five*" any more specific to add to such denial the equivalent assertion, "because they do make four." In regard to such cases, the ruling that the ground of objection given in § 95, is insufficient is certainly illogical. The farthest extent to which such a rule can reasonably be carried, is to say, that in cases where the statement of the cause of action is *formally* defective, that is, that the statement of some material fact has been omitted, the defect must be specified. From a careful comparison of the cases decided in other States, it appears that the generally accepted doctrine of their courts is—

(1.) That the special demurrer at common law is wholly discarded from the Code system, and its office and functions are subserved by a motion under section 104 to strike out "sham and irrelevant answers and defences," or under section 120, providing for amendment where the pleading is "so indefinite or uncertain that the precise nature of the charge or defence is not apparent," or under § 218 providing for judgment on "frivolous answers and demurrers."

(2.) That it is universally held that a demurrer upon the first and sixth grounds, as to jurisdiction and that the facts stated do not constitute a cause of action, stated in the language of those sub-divisions, is sufficient. With regard to the other grounds of demurrer, some courts hold that the demurrer should be more specific than the language of the sub-division under which it falls, but the general practice is that such allegation is sufficient.

(3.) That if the demurrer states but one ground of objection to the complaint, all other demurrable objections are deemed to be waived.

(4.) That a demurrer interposed to a complaint which contains more than one cause of action without specifying to which it applies, will be overruled if either is good.

The practice and the reasons for it, in regard to general and special demurrers, are well stated in an extract from Mr. Pomeroy's work, referring particularly to § 105, *post*.

"Under the common law system of procedure, the questions of substance in the defendants pleas, if the objection appeared on their face, were raised by a general demurrer, while those of form were raised by a 'special demurrer.' The reformed procedure retains the general demurrer for the same purpose which it subserved at the common law. Where the answer, as in some States, or the new matter in the answer, as in others, does not state facts constituting a defence, or counter-claim, or set-off, as the case may be, a demurrer, or the ground of insufficiency, is the proper mode of raising and presenting the question for decision to the court. Special demurrers, however, are utterly abolished. If the defect is one merely of form; if the denials, for example,—although sufficiently addressed to the plaintiff's allegations to indicate the intended issues,—are so formally defective that it is a question whether the denial or denials attempted to be made do in fact accomplish the purpose for which they were designed; or, if the averments of new matter in some sort embrace or refer to facts which, if properly pleaded, would amount to a defence or counter-claim, but are stated in such an uncertain, ambiguous, inferential manner, that it is a question whether they can avail to the defendant,—in such cases it is settled that the demurrer is not the proper mode of reaching the defect.

Instead of the special demurrer, the codes have substituted the motion to make the pleading more definite and certain. If no such motion is made, and the plaintiff goes to trial upon the answer as it stands, he will not be suffered to raise the objection there for the first time, and to exclude evidence of the defence or counter-claim on the ground that it is informally pleaded." *Pomeroy's Rights and Remedies*, § 596.

See, also, Swann's Pleadings and Precedents, page 233, *et seq.*[456] . . .

[**§ 100.—Answer, what to contain.** Comment discussing Flack *v.* Dawson, 69 N.C. 42 (1873) (Rodman, J.).]

*a*The logical difference between an answer which says, "no allegation of the complaint is true," or "every allegation of the complaint is untrue," and one which avers that "the first allegation of the complaint is not true," &c., repeating the denial as many times as there are allegations in the complaint, is not easily perceptible. *Why* it does not constitute "a general or specific denial of each material allegation of the complaint, to say that *not one of them is true*, the decision leaves us to determine as we may. It seems to me that none can be given—that the one denial is as complete and perfect as the other, and that to require such denial to be placed in a specific form, correlative with the numbered allegations of the complaint, is somewhat repugnant to the spirit of a Code which seeks to discard form in favor of substance. As to the denial of "a *material part* of an allegation," it would seem as if the judge's mind, running as it evidently was upon the old practice, had failed to draw the distinction between the connected allegation of a cause of action, at common law and a specific allegation of fact, under the Code. If the pleadings are properly drawn, it is submitted, that there can be no denial of a *material part* of an allegation, where "each material allegation" of fact is required to be "distinctly stated and numbered."

A writer of great clearness and accuracy of thought, in commenting upon an identical section in the Code of Ohio, says:

"The answer, when it controverts the allegations of the petition, (complaint) may deny generally each and every allegation of the petition or may specifically deny all, or one or more, of the *material* allegations of the petition. If the defendant denies the truth of each and all the allegations of the petition, he may say so, without setting forth in his answer, in negative form, the allegations so denied; and this is called a general denial.

Effect must be given to the words of the Code, "each allegation," and no evasive or ambiguous language, through which the conscience of the defendant might escape, will be tolerated by the court. And the reason why the courts are thus sensitive to evasion in regard to a denial, general or specific, is, that if suitors are compelled to answer squarely to the facts, it avoids unnecessary consumption of time on trial, and brings into the issue such facts only as are really controverted.

The Code allows for the sake of brevity only, a general denial. It must be so drawn as to deny each and all the facts alleged as a cause of action, so that the defendant will understand by it, that he is in effect saying the same as if he specifically denied the whole series of allegations and facts contained in the petition.

A general denial of each "*material*" allegation of the petition is deemed an evasion and bad in form. The difference, however, between the form of the denial and its legal effect, must not be confounded. A general denial must, in form, controvert each and every allegation of the petition. The legal effect of such a general denial, is to controvert each and every *material* allegation of the petition. This legal effect it is the province of the court to determine when the issue is tried, and the defendant has neither the capacity or the right to anticipate it."—*Swan's Pleadings and Precedents*, page 243, et seq. . . .

[§ 125.—**Answer in such cases.** Comment discussing Moore v. Edmiston, 70 N.C. 510 (1874) (Bynum, J.).]

[b]Nothing could better illustrate the spirit and purpose of the Code, than this case. The complaint is at once perceived to be fatally defective under the common-law rules, and the mind of the pleader trained exclusively under that system, jumps, almost instinctively, to the conclusion that it is insufficient under the Code. There is no doubt that the same facts must be denied and the same averments made, in order to set up the pleas of justification and of the statute of limitations, under the Code as at the common law, but the question is as to what *constitutes* such denials and averments. Under the common-law rule where every intendment was taken against the pleader this answer could not stand, *because* it is *possible* to construe the words evasively or as having another or no definite meaning. The defences are insufficiently alleged, when tried by that rule, *because*, with the most unfavorable construction the one does not aver beyond possibility of question, the truth of the words charged; nor the other declare beyond all room for doubt, that the time limited for the bringing of such actions, had expired before the summons in the case was issued.

Yet, under the rules of the Code, its sufficiency is at once apparent. "Ordinary language" to be "liberally construed in furtherance of substantial justice," is the touchstone which it requires us to apply. Judged by this rule, what is the plain import of the answer? What would we understand by such an averment written or printed in a matter not connected with pleading? What would we take such language to mean in the ordinary intercourse of man with man, in all matters unconnected with courts? What must the plaintiff have understood the answer to mean, using this rule to guide his judgment? Applying this rule, it is at once evident that the plaintiff could not have understood the defendant to intend to do otherwise than set up these pleas. In regard to the time at which the language charged was uttered, the words of the answer would be utterly meaningless unless its intention was to set up the objection of the statute of limitations, which it was apparently intended to do.

This appeal was the reasonable fruit of the doctrine announced, without due deliberation by the court, in *Parseley* v. *Nicholson* and *Oates* v. *Gray*, (see *ante*, § 91, cases and notes,) in which it was held that the *principles of common law pleadings and construction were not abrogated, but only their forms;* and that these principles and "the same certainty of allegation" were applicable to the civil action. I have before pointed out the distinction between "the same certainty" under the common law principle of adverse intendment, and the Code principle of ordinary language, construed in furtherance of justice. See note under § 91, *ante*. . . .

[**§ 126.—What causes of action may be joined in the same complaint.** Comment and cross-references under subdivision 1., "The same transaction . . . ;" discussing N.C. Land Co. *v.* Beatty and Bennett, 69 N.C. 329 (1873) (Rodman, J.).]

"This subdivision of this section, is without doubt one of the most difficult provisions of the Code, to construe generally, and it is entirely safe to say that the reasoning of the court in this case, falls far short of a satisfactory analysis of its language or a general elimination of its import. Without questioning the accuracy of the decision in this case, I desire to consider, briefly the reasoning of the decision and the import of this provision. In so doing I shall make free use of the very excellent analysis of this provision given by Mr. Pomeroy, § 465 *et seq.*, of his *Rights and Remedies*.

There are three terms which are to be construed before we can arrive at the real purport of the clause, or determine the classes of actions to which it applies, viz: "transactions," "subject of action," and "connected with." Of these terms, "transaction" is defined to be ["]the act of transacting or conducting any business." It differs from event or action, by its element of mutuality and its power of representing a continued series of act having some common feature or purpose. A transaction is a thing done, by two or more, and may be made up of numerous independent acts, which may or may not be simultaneous, but which have some common element or purpose, which gives to the collective acts the idea of unity.

"Subject of action" has evidently been very frequently confounded by our court, with the "cause of action," and sometimes with the "object of the action." It must be evident from a consideration of the entire section, that it cannot be synonymous with either of them, and that it refers chiefly, to the material matters, the title or possession of which, is the subject of controversy. It is almost, if not quite synonymous with the ["]subject-matter of the action," of the old practice; meaning the material object, some relation of which, is sought to be affected by the controversy.

These two definitions are not only consistent but serve to aid us in determining the force of the other term—"connected with." Several "transactions" may be "connected" with one "subject of action." Or, in other words, several series of mutual or correlative acts, may attach to, or have reference to, one material object, the ownership or possession of which may be the purpose or object of the controversy. As, for instance, suppose A to make a mortgage by parole to B, by purchasing from him a horse to become his own upon payment of the purchase money: Afterwards A sells his interest in the horse to C, after the animal has received serious injury, not disclosing the claim of B, and C executes a mortgage upon the animal to D, not surrendering possession. In an action by B to obtain possession of his property, the horse would be the *subject* of the action, and B's *reserved title*, together with *the failure of A to pay the purchase money*, the "cause of action." The purchase of the horse by A would be one *transaction*, the sale to C another, and his mortgage to D, a third; all "connected with" the subject of the action, and their various rights liable to adjudication in one action, in consequence of this relation. In aid of this view, is the fact that the Code provides for mutual judgments between plaintiffs or defendants, allows the interpleader of any party having an interest in the controversy, provides that all parties having like interests in the subject of the action *must* be made plaintiffs, and that all who have an adverse interest may be made defendants, or may make themselves defendants. In short, makes ample provision for the complete adjustment of just such intricate questions of right in regard to a particular subject, as might arise in the case used as an example. It is true, that all these arise out of several contracts, but they are not mutual or connected contracts, except so far as they all relate to the subject of the action, to-wit, the horse. But why not, for the same reason, the tort arising from the damage of the horse while in A's possession?

The learned justice who delivers the opinion of the court, in this case, says: "It cannot be possible that all these numerous actions, between different parties and having no connection, except that the subject of all is the same horse, can be united."

Yet, why not, if we lay aside the common law restriction of actions? Is there any reason why all claims to the same property should not be decided in one action, by making the proper parties, as well as allow A and B to decide their controversy, and then let the other conflicting interests be decided in other actions? The whole scope and tendency of the Code is to decide all possible conflicting interests in one action. There is no more reason why a cause of action for fraud in the warranty of a horse, and one for breach of contract in the trade in which the warranty was made should not be joined, than there is why two dissimilar contracts, should not be united in one complaint, if the tort and the contract arise out of the same transaction, or affect the same thing which must be the subject of the action.

It may be difficult, in many instances, to determine when causes of action arise out of the *same transaction* or when they arise from transactions connected with the same subject of action: and on account of this difficulty the line is not attempted to be drawn with great accuracy, and very much is left to the discretion of the court in each particular case. At the same time, while the line is thus left open to construction, a court should be very careful about declaring causes of action to be improperly joined, especially when they are between the same parties, or where the only effect of such declaration must be to multiply suits.

See, in connection with this subject, §§ 60, 61, 62 and 91, *ante*, with notes and cases thereunder. . . .

[§ 128.—**Material variance.** Comment discussing Moore *v.* Edmiston, 70 N.C. 510 (1874) (Bynum, J.).]

"The opinion, in this case, is such a masterly exposition of the underlying principles of Code pleading, and is stated with such admirable clearness and force, that it is here cited in full.

In an action of slander, the defendant had answered that he admitted uttering the words charged, but did not speak them from malice, but was informed and believed that they were substantially true. He further stated the sources of his previous information, but did not allege in direct and unmistakable terms that the statements charged were true. He also answered, that he did not admit that the alleged slanderous words were uttered within six months before suit brought. Bynum, J., delivering the opinion of the court, says:

"The subtle science of pleading heretofore in use, is not merely relaxed, but abolished by the Code, and the forms of pleading in civil actions, and the rules, by which their sufficiency is to be determined, are those prescribed in the Code. (§ 91.) The new system thus inaugurated, is such that few, if any, of the ancient rules are now applicable.

All that is required of the plaintiff, is a plain and concise statement of the facts constituting the cause of action; and of the defendant, a general or specific denial of each material allegation of the complaint, not controverted in the answer, (§ 100.)

In order that all technical objections may be avoided, and the parties brought to a speedy trial upon the merits, section 119 provides, that the allegations of each pleading shall be liberally construed with a view to substantial justice between the parties. But to obviate all diverse constructions, which the ingenuity of counsel might give to the pleadings, to the embarrassment of the court and jury, and the delay and obstruction of the course of justice, section 120 provides, that when the allegations of a pleading are so indefinite or uncertain that the precise nature of the charge or defence, is not apparent, the court may require the pleading to be made definite and certain by amendment. Sections 128 to 136 point out how amendments shall be made, the obvious purpose being that parties shall apply to the court, in apt time, prior to the trial, to amend the pleadings in all the particulars objected to, and that they may not be allowed, at the trial, to spring objections to the form or effect of the charge or defence.

So intent were the framers of the Code, to discard all technical forms, that by section 135, it is declared, that "the court and the judge thereof, *shall*, in every stage of the action, disregard any error or defect in the pleadings or proceedings, which shall not affect the substantial right of the adverse party; and no judgment shall be reversed or affected by reason of such error or defect."

And then, by a sweeping curative supplement to this most liberal system of pleading, section 132 confers upon the court the power, both before and after judgment, to make almost any conceivable amendment, so as to conform the pleading to the facts proved.

Applying to the case before us, these new rules of pleading, we conclude that the pleadings and the issues made by them, were so reasonably certain and understood by the parties, that their substantial rights were tried. That according to the Code, the answer of the defendant amounted to the plea of justification, and of the statute of limitations.

If the exceptions taken, and so ably argued by the counsel of the plaintiff, were to be decided according to the intricate system of pleading in the books, we might concur in the reasoning and authorities adduced, but we hold that they have no application here, for the reasons before stated." . . .

[**§ 130.—A failure of proof—when.** Comment discussing Shelton *v.* Davis, 69 N.C. 324 (1873) (Pearson, C. J.).]

*a*See the cases cited under the two preceding sections. This provision was intended to embrace just such cases as are included by the illustration of the Chief Justice, in *Shelton* v. *Davis* cited above. It is designed to prevent a party from suing for a "*horse*," and recovering a "*cow*" by defining, what shall be deemed a variance, and thereby restricting the power of amendment, which is conferred by §§ 128 and 129. The following are the rules established in regard to variance and failure of proof by these sections.

1. In case of an immaterial variance the judge may—
   (*a*) Order issues to be found in accordance with the evidence; or,
   (*b*) Direct the pleadings to be at once amended, *without costs*.
2. No variance shall be deemed material, unless it shall (*a*) have misled the adverse party, (*b*) to his prejudice: and in such case, the judge may order the pleading to be amended *upon terms*.

The distinction between *material* and *immaterial* variance, is thus sharply drawn, yet without the application of any technical rules. There are but two questions for a court to ask in deciding whether a variance is material, and these it *must* ask and decide.

(*a*) Has the adverse party been misled?
(*b*) If so, has it been to his prejudice, in maintaining his action on the merits?

It will be noted, that both of these are questions of fact, and not of construction. No inquiry is made, as to whether the adverse party *ought* to have been misled by the defective pleading, but whether he *was* misled; not whether he *might* have been prejudiced, but whether he actually *has been* prejudiced, by the variance. Upon these questions of fact, the judge may hear testimony, and in all cases where there is any room for doubt, should require affidavits upon the facts of surprise and prejudice. Indeed, § 128 specifically requires that such fact "shall be *proved*, to the satisfaction of the court." The principle is the same as that discussed in *Garrett* v. *Trotter*, in which the answer of the defendant showed that, as a matter of fact, he had not been misled by what he afterwards alleged to be a defect of the complaint, since he answered just as he would have done had he been defending such against a cause of action properly set up. In such case, however great the variance, it must not be deemed material, since the adverse party understood the facts to be alleged as they *should have been*, or *according to the proof*, and not *according to the pleading*.

In case the court shall decide, after such inquiry as to the fact, that the adverse party has been misled by the defective statement of a pleading, and has thereby been prejudiced, he may allow the pleading "to be amended *upon such terms as may be just.*" In case it shall be decided that the adverse party has *either* not been misled, or not been prejudiced, if he was misled, he "may allow the pleading to be amended *without costs.*"

This distinction is not only just, but it gives to the judges a very much needed power, and at the same time restricts their discretion within bounds which prevent its becoming oppressive. Where the variance has not misled or prejudiced the adverse party, the court *may either* submit issues or allow amendment *without costs*, but has *no power* to attach terms to such amendments. On the other hand, if the other party *has* been misled and prejudiced, the court can *only* allow amendment upon terms, and has only a discretion to say what terms are just; and upon this question also, the court may hear evidence and usually should do so.

If this distinction is carefully observed by the courts, material variances will soon become rare. Hitherto, there has generally been too little inquiry as to the effect of variance; and also, too little distinction in the penalty imposed, as a condition precedent to amendment. The Code excuses immaterial variances or imposes, at the farthest, no greater penalty than delay, but it gives the court almost unlimited power to protect its suitors from the negligence of other suitors, or the incapacity or slothfulness of counsel, by the imposition of terms.

Lest, however, this should not prove sufficient in this direction, the power of the court is limited in the construction of the term "*variance.*" It does *not* provide that a man may sue for a "*horse*" and recover a "*cow*" by simply changing "horse" to "cow" in his complaint. On the contrary, it provides that where the cause of action alleged, "is unproved in its entire scope, and not in *some particulars only,*" it shall not be counted a variance, but *shall* be held to be "a failure of proof," for which the court has *no power to give any remedy*. This view is greatly strengthened, by the careful exception made to the power of amendment, by the last clause of § 132, by which the power to conform the pleading to the facts proved, is expressly limited to cases in which the amendment "does not change substantially the claim or defence." So that the three classes are thus graded.

1. In case of *immaterial* variance, amendment may be made and rights saved, *without* terms.
2. In case of *material* variance, amendment may be made and rights preserved, *upon* terms.
3. In case of *failure of proof,* amendment *cannot be made at all,* but judgment must run against the party so grossly offending, without any saving of rights or advantage to be derived from his action or defence. . . .

[**§ 161.—Bail, how exonerated.** Comment discussing Sedberry v. Carver, 77 N.C. 319 (1877) (Bynum, J.).]

*"*The closing sentence of this opinion, expressly limits its application, to the points numbered 1 and 2, in the above synopsis. The language of the others is so strong, however, that they must be considered, at least as very positive *dicta*. Regarding them as such, it seems that the court construe the statute as applying only in case of *perpetual* imprisonment *within* the State; or imprisonment *without* the State, for a term existing at the time of execution against the person of the defendant, and continuing till final judgment against his bail.

This is a very great restriction of the terms of the statute. That the imprisonment intended to be prescribed as relieving the bail, is on criminal process only, and may be either in the penitentiary or county jail, there can be no doubt; and also, that the imprisonment must be for a term, *existing at the time of execution against the body of the defendant*.

That the imprisonment need be perpetual, or for a term extending beyond such issue of execution, does not seem to be consistent, either with the terms of the statute, or with the reasons given, in the opinion.

The statute provides that, on the occurrence of either of four contingencies, the bail shall be exonerated, to-wit: (1) the death, or (2) imprisonment in a State prison; or (3) the surrender, of the defendant; or (4) his discharge from the obligation to surrender himself. These provisions are just as much a part of the undertaking, as the obligation to produce the defendant when required. They are specific limitations of the risk which the bail assumes. The reason of them is obvious. The surrender of the defendant or the discharge of his liability fulfil[l]s the conditions of the undertaking, and the obligors thereon are discharged, of course, thereby. Its purpose has been accomplished, in either of these events. Death renders its fulfil[l]ment impossible, and so, in like manner, does imprisonment on a criminal charge, at the time of the execution against his person, which is "the process issued to enforce the judgment," specified in § 157.

If, at this time, the State has the defendant imprisoned, he is as much beyond the control of the bail as if dead. The learned Justice suggests that the bail or the plaintiff might request the court to order his detention at the expiration of his term. It may be fairly doubted whether the court would have any such power. The plaintiff might, it is true, cause his arrest immediately thereafter, and his right to do so is expressly preserved by statute, but the bail is relieved by the fact that it is *utterly impossible* for him to produce the body of the defendant *when* required to do so, and that by no default of his.

It must be remembered too that the bail can only be proceeded against by *action*, and that any defence which was good at the time he became liable in an action must continue thereafter; so, that a release from custody, of the defendant, after that time, cannot re-obligate the bail. Having been exonerated by the imprisonment at the time of the issue of execution, he cannot again be made liable. It is true, the bail may deliver the defendant in exoneration of themselves, "at any time before final judgment" against them, but this does not require them to do so, when the defendant was in custody of the State at the time of the execution against his body, which is in the nature of a demand upon the bail. This is only a privilege, which is granted to the bail, by which they may escape liability existing at the commencement of the action, by the performance of the condition of the undertaking, afterwards.

Even when liable under *scire facias* this fact being pleaded in return thereto operated as a release of the bail, and upon that plea being sustained the judge was authorized to direct the detention of the prisoner, and *not otherwise*. The abolition of that writ and the proceeding against bail "*by action only*," may not have affected the power of the judge to direct the detention of the defendant on the expiration of his criminal sentence, to answer the civil execution against his person, but it certainly does not make it incumbent on the bail to become the actors and move for such detention. The plaintiff may, perhaps, do so; though why he should when he may just as easily have his execution in the hands of the officer, who has him in charge, as a special order of the court, I cannot see. Formerly, the custodian of criminals and debtors under arrest, was always the same. Now, the warden of the penitentiary is expressly prohibited from detaining any persons except certain specified classes; and is directed by statute to release them on the expiration of the sentence for which they are committed to his custody. He is not an officer of the court nor under its control or direction. While the court might direct the sheriff to detain one in his custody to answer a civil execution, could it, in like manner, direct the warden of the penitentiary to hold him, until the plaintiff should see fit to issue his execution and have it served? If so, during what time would he direct his detention? . . .

[§ 187.—**Notice and affidavit, when and where to be filed.** Comment discussing Boyleston Ins. Co. *v.* Davis, 74 N.C. 78 (1876) (Pearson, C. J.).]

"This decision is placed upon the ground that the provision of the Revised Code, Chapter 98, allowing summary judgments to be taken in actions of *Replevin*, is not inconsistent with the provisions of the Code of Procedure. In support of this, the principle in *Clerk's Office* v. *Huffsteller*, 67—449, in regard to judgment upon undertaking, on appeal is cited.

The opinions, in both cases, are characterized by all the force and subtlety for which the learned Chief Justice (Pearson) is so justly celebrated. They are based, however, entirely on two hypotheses:

1. That the Code of Procedure has made no provision for recovery, in such cases; and
2. That the provisions of the Revised Code, in reference to summary judgment against the bail, are not repugnant to the provisions of the Code.

Both of these propositions appear to me, to be at least doubtful, in their application to the undertaking in claim and delivery.

The forms of actions existing at the adoption of the Constitution of 1868, were abolished by that instrument, and a civil action substituted. As before shown (§6, *ante*, note), the "form of action" includes not only the writ, but the declaration, pleas and the judgment following thereon. The judgment, in *Replevin*, was as much a part of the *form* of that action, as the writ or declaration, and when the Revised Code, provided for a judgment against the sureties, without a hearing, it became *a part of that form of action*. It could not be invoked in any other. It was not a power inherent in the court, but a power granted by specific enactment, *as an incident of the action of Replevin*. The form, the machinery, the distinguishing characteristics of that action, as a means of asserting rights or obtaining remedies, are utterly abolished. The rights, themselves, and the remedies which it afforded the suitor, i. e., restitution and recompense—still exist. They are not a part of *the form of action*, but its object or purpose. The method of accomplishing the results aimed at by that action, are, however, utterly changed.

So far as regards undertakings on appeal, there are two important particulars, in which they may be distinguished from the cases now under consideration:

1. The granting of summary judgments on them was not a part of the *form of any action*. It was an universal rule, applying as well in one form of action as in another.
2. As is remarked by the court, in *Huffsteller's case*, they are not contracts with the appellee or with any other person, but general undertakings which may, perhaps, be considered as in the nature of confessions of judgment. This view is greatly strengthened by observing how unreservedly the appellant, is

required to submit himself, in all respects, to the order of the appellate court, by the various provision of §§ 303 to 312, before execution will be stayed. In such case the rights of the parties are presumed to have been settled by the decision below. In case of undertakings in provisional remedies, however, these rights are altogether unadjusted, and the claimant and his sureties contract, *specifically with the other claimant*. In such contract, they assume only liabilities, which are subject to set-off and defence, as are other private contracts. They constitute private rights and their breaches, private wrongs, which are to be asserted and redressed, by a civil action only.

In support of this view, may be noted, the fact, that, in the case of arrest and bail, it is provided expressly, that the "bail may be proceeded against by action only," (§ 160). This provision is made still more important in considering this question, by fact which does not seem to have been adverted to by the court, to-wit: that the undertaking, under sub-section 3 of § 149, is "to the same effect as that provided by § 181," (§ 158—3). This requires the return of property or its value, as in case of claim and delivery, and yet it can only be proceeded on by an action. The evident purpose of this provision was to allow the bail to set-off any counter-claim, they might have against the defendant, in the action he might bring, which they would be prevented from doing, in case of a summary judgment,—at least unless their claim had been already reduced to judgment, and even then it could, probably, be defeated by assignment, as it would only attach by order of the court. That the defendant *may* proceed by *action* is undoubted. Indeed, such is the decision, in *Woody* v. *Jordan*, 69—189. The Code provides that remedy, and such action must, of course, permit all the defences, which apply to any other private contract; and it is consistent with the strictest justice that such should be the case.

This view is, also, sustained by the fact that §§ 233, 234 and 235, provide, with great particularity, for verdicts and the assessment of damages, in actions to recover personal property; and § 251 provides with equal distinctness, for the judgment in all such cases. In neither of them is there the remotest allusion to a *summary judgment against bail*.

This silence, taken with the fact that another remedy is afforded—which is not the case in undertakings on appeal; that an undertaking of precisely the same import and for the same purpose, whose form is only ascertained by reference to the section prescribing the undertaking in claim and delivery, is to be proceeded against *by action only;* and the fact that this summary judgment was undoubtedly one of the differential features of the action of judgment was undoubtedly one of the differential features of the action of *Replevin*, as regulated by the Revised Code, and as such was abolished by the Constitution, lead me to doubt whether the decision ought to be followed. . . .

[**§ 188.a—What judge may grant injunction.** Comment about an amendment to the code.]

[a]The Act of 1876–'77, Chapter 223, which is here given as §§ 188*a* and 188*b*, was evidently passed with immediate reference to certain orders which had been made in regard to the receivership of certain railroads but a short time before the passage of the act. From a careful consideration of its provisions, I am convinced that a plentiful harvest of jurisdictional questions may be expected from it. Who has the right to issue injunctions and who to hear motions to dissolve? Who may issue orders of restraint and before whom they shall be returnable? Whether two judges may have jurisdiction in one district at the same time? How it is to be determined who will be "in the district" twenty days after the application? What will be the effect of a return before the wrong judge—i. e., if he has not jurisdiction to *hear*, has he for any purpose whatever? Who is "the judge of an adjoining district;" that is, is it the one resident there or the one holding court there, or does the same uncertainty arise here again? When an order to show cause and restraint in the meantime, is granted, can it be made returnable at large; that is, before any judge authorized by law to hear it, at a certain time and place? If so, and it should be heard by the wrong one, what would be the effect on the order? What will be the effect of the statute upon the enforcement of the order? Suppose an order of restraint issue to-day, the judge leaves the district to-morrow and another comes. The defendant disobeys the order. Who can punish the contempt?

These are a few of the questions which this new statute raises. Hitherto, the State has been fortunate in having few jurisdictional issues raised. Perhaps there has never been an instance before, of a system of courts superseded by another system, in which so few questions of this character arose as in this State. Our present system of courts, by its extreme simplicity and the readiness by which transfers are made, almost entirely avoids them. This statute, however, must make their recurrence frequent. A suitor who seeks an injunction hereafter, will be likely to be as uncertain as to the result as the man who writes his own will. In every case of importance it will require the judgment of the highest court to determine the jurisdiction of the provisional remedy of injunction and appointment of receiver, while the jurisdiction of the action to which it is incidental is determinable in an instant. It is noticeable that the jurisdiction of other provisional remedies is not expressly modified by the act, being left as it was before, or only to be *guessed* out from implication. . . .

[**§ 191.—Injunction after answer.** Comment about injunctions after the abolition of equity procedure.]

"The practice in regard to injunctions has fallen into some obscurity, chiefly it would seem from an inaccuracy in the use of terms, or rather a failure to use the language of the Code, especially by the reporters.

The cases in which a temporary injunction by order may be obtained, are stated, in the Code, with as much particularity, perhaps, as the nature of the subject-matter will permit. The three classes specified are—
1. When the prevention of some particular act, is a part of the ultimate remedy sought.
2. When, during litigation in regard to specific property, the defendant is likely to perform some act injurious to the plaintiff's alleged rights in *the subject of the action*.
3. When the defendant is about to remove or dispose of his property, with intent to defraud creditors.

It will be observed that the last of these three classes, is the broadest of the provisions of the Code, which afford a safe-guard against the concealment or removal of property, with an intent to defraud the creditor. Under § 149, sub-sections 3, 4 and 5, the defendant may be arrested, if he has concealed, disposed of or removed or is about to conceal, remove or dispose of his property with such fraudulent intent. And under § 197, an attachment may issue to take his property, on like grounds. This section adds, however, another element, to-wit: "if it shall appear that the defendant *threatens* to remove" &c.

The question has arisen in some States, whether two or all of these provisional remedies may be employed by the plaintiff, in the same action, and there seems to be no good reason why they should not. One is designed to hold the body of the defendant to answer the plaintiff's execution against it, should he obtain one; another to hold his property for a like purpose; and the third to prevent an act which might impair the value of his judgment should he recover.

Another, interesting question, which has been mooted in other States, is as to whether a defendant, who sets up a counter-claim against a plaintiff is entitled to an injunction under the provisions of this chapter, *in the action brought against him*. The case does not seem to have arisen before our Supreme Court and the cases provided for, all specify acts of the defendant, as the grounds of this remedy. There has been one instance, at least, of a defendant claiming an affirmative relief having obtained an injunction order against the plaintiff, under the second sub-division of this section; but the judge who granted it has never yet been able fully to satisfy himself whether his action was correct or not. There seems to be no *reason* why such a party should be driven to another action to obtain injunctive relief in regard to the *subject* of one already pending.

The language of some of our decisions and of many of the reporter's notes, would seem to indicate the idea that the former practice, in regard to injunctions was yet in force, in one important particular, towit: That, *if, on the coming in of the answer, the equity of the complaint is fully denied*, the injunction must be dissolved.

This was a rule of the court of equity, which grew out of the nature and jurisdiction of that tribunal. The very purpose of its procedure, in, perhaps, a majority of cases, was to probe the conscience of the defendant and a very great—in other circumstances it would be deemed an undue importance,—was attached to his answer as being a response to the plaintiff's interrogatories, in the only tribunal in which either could be heard in his own behalf. So great was its authority that, in many cases, that tribunal would hear "no evidence variant from the allegations of the answer." This odor of verity which surrounded the answer in equity has been removed.
1. By the abolition of equity procedure, the forms of which are abolished by the Constitution, and whose rules for the construction of pleadings are also abolished, both affirmatively and by unavoidable inference, by § 91, of the Code as well, and to the same extent, as those of actions at law; and
2. By the removal of all disqualification of parties to testify in their own behalf; and

3. By the fact that this chapter prescribes, without any exception, the procedure, in all cases, where the aid of the injunction order, is invoked as a provisional remedy. By its provisions, certain specific rules are prescribed, which for simplicity and completeness, cannot be excelled, stating as they do, with the utmost exactness, in what manner, injunctions may be obtained and vacated. They are—

1. The plaintiff *must* apply by *affidavit*, and *may* do so (*a*) without notice, or (*b*) upon notice, to the adverse party.
2. If the application is made without notice, the judge may either, (*a*) grant the injunction on the plaintiff's affidavits, or (*b*) grant an order to show cause and, in the meantime, restrain the defendant.
3. *If the order be made without notice*, the defendant may, at any time before trial, move upon notice to vacate either (*a*) on the plaintiff's affidavits, or (*b*) he may file counter-affidavits in opposition thereto.
4. If the defendant move on affidavits, the plaintiff may file other affidavits in reply.
5. The express permission to the defendant to move to vacate *upon notice*, at any time before trial, when the injunction has been granted *without notice*, is a clear negation of the right to make that motion, when it was granted *upon notice* or *after an order to show cause*.
6. As a consequence of these, it follows, that when the defendant has once moved to vacate, he cannot move again, before the trial, since the matter is then *res adjudicata*.

It will be noted that there is no reference, in the entire chapter, to the *answer*, except as an affidavit, and no reference to the *complaint*, except in sub-division 1 of §189, where it is mentioned, not as a part of the papers in the provisional remedy, but as showing to the court what is the subject-matter of the action.

The injunction is granted on only affidavit. The complaint need not be verified any more than in other actions, and the facts entitling the plaintiff to the provisional remedy need not be set out in the complaint at all. Indeed, in all cases, except those arising under the first subdivision of §189, it is *bad pleading* if they do so appear, and they should be stricken out on motion under § 120. Even under the first sub-division, in very many cases, it is best that they should not be embraced in the complaint, since it is the *imminence* of the injurious acts which entitles him to ask for the *provisional* remedy, while the mere *power to injure, though not even apprehended*, might entitle him to injunctive relief in the final judgment.

The habit of using the verified complaint as an affidavit in an application for injunction, has grown up under the indulgence of the court, though Rodman, J., very clearly pointed out its deleterious effect on the pleadings in *Crump* v. *Mims*, 64—767, and prescribed the proper practice. See note under § 136.

So, too, the verified answer has been allowed to be used as an affidavit, *but there is no such thing, under the Code, as a motion to vacate an injunction, upon the coming in of the answer.* It may be made before that time, or afterwards—"at any time before the trial." Neither are the contents of the answer a matter of any moment in most cases, upon such hearing. Indeed, under the second and third sub-divisions of the section, they can *never be*, for the facts which entitle the plaintiff to injunction under either of them, are entirely independent of the *cause of action* or defence, are outside of the controversy. A sues B on his promissory note. B denies the debt, or answers that he has paid it. A files affidavits showing that B "is about to dispose of his property to defraud his creditors." This entitles him to an injunction, but what place has this allegation in his complaint or its denial in B's answer[?] It is no part of the subject of his action or of B's defence. Whether it be true or false, is a matter entirely foreign to his right of recovery in the action. If the complaint or answer are used in obtaining or vacating an injunction, they must be used *as affidavits merely*, and if the answer is so used, the plaintiff has a right to file counter-affidavits in reply.

The test as to whether the injunction should stand, is not, properly, the inquiry whether the answer denies the plaintiff's equity or not, but the effect of the facts which the judge shall find upon the affidavits and counter-affidavits of the parties. It is true, that if only the plaintiff's and defendant's affidavits were before him, and the latter denied fully and explicitly the averments of the former, the court would, in most cases, *perhaps*, in all, dissolve the injunction, because such an unusual remedy should not be granted or continued except upon a clear preponderance of testimony in the plaintiff's favor. This was undoubtedly the reason of the old equity rule, where only the two parties were heard. Then, if the defendant *denied* the plaintiff's equity, the injunction was dissolved until the hearing. Now, the plaintiff may file sufficient counter-affidavits, to establish in the mind of the judge a belief that every *allegation of the answer* is false, in which case, it becomes his duty to continue the injunction until the time of trial.

For the same reason, that this is a purely incidental proceeding, and not of the substance of the action, a motion to vacate, cannot be properly made at the term, without notice, unless it is a term at which the action is triable and even then, the plaintiff would be entitled to a reasonable time to file counter-affidavits, according to the clear intendment of all the decisions. . . .

[§ 219.—**The different kinds of issues.** Comment discussing Keener *v.* Finger, 70 N.C. 35 (1874) (Pearson, C. J.) (Rodman, J., dissenting).]

*ᵃ*This was a case of exceptions to an account taken by a referee, turning upon the power of the Supreme Court to review his findings of fact, which it was held that the court could not do, they constituting *issues of fact*, upon which a trial by jury might be demanded in the Superior Court.

Rodman, J., filed a very elaborate dissenting opinion in this case, upon the distinction between *issues* of fact and *questions* of fact, adopting and illustrating very forcibly the doctrine, which the court seem previously to have been inclined to hold, that "issues of fact" are only such as are *made by the pleadings*, and "questions of fact" such as arise incidentally in the course of the action, but are not presented by the pleading. The same views are, also, very fully stated in his dissenting opinion in *Green* v. *Castleberry*, decided at the same term (70—20).

So far as the question, presented by this case, is concerned, to-wit: the jurisdiction of the Supreme Court to review issues of fact; this distinction is now, perhaps, immaterial under the amended Constitution. As bearing upon the mode of trial in the Superior Court, this class of cases is of great importance; but the questions presented are so intricate that it is impossible fairly to represent the decisions by a syllabus in each case. They consist of two classes:

1. Those in which matters of fact are presented by exceptions in references to take accounts, or to determine questions not specifically raised by the pleadings, but incident, either to the trial, to some provisional remedy, invoked during the course of the action, to the determination of damages, or the amount of a party's liability after judgment against him.
2. The findings of fact by referees, in cases of compulsory reference.

In regard to both of these classes, the decisions of the court, for a considerable time after the adoption of the Code, inclined to the doctrine that they might be decided by the court without the intervention of a jury, but the contrary view has been steadily held in regard to both, since the seventieth volume of our reports. At that term, January, 1874, two cases were decided, which have since been regarded as settling the law upon this subject, viz: *Keener* v. *Finger*, 70—35, as to the first, and *Green* v. *Castleberry*, 70—20, as to the second of these classes. In regard to the latter, it is now considered as settled by the provision of the Constitution in regard to jury trials, other than the one limiting the jurisdiction of the Supreme Court, which has been abolished. Especially, by Section 13 of Article IV, taken in connection with Section 19 of Article I of the Constitution, which are, very properly, construed to give a jury trial upon all issues of fact. This view is, I think, generally concurred in by the profession.

In regard to the former class, Mr. Justice Rodman has stoutly contended against the opinion of the other members of the court, that the right of trial by jury is not extended to such cases, by the provisions of the Constitution above referred to, upon the ground that they do not constitute *issues of fact*, but *questions of fact*, and his reasoning upon the question, it must be confessed, is very cogent. Indeed, it seems to me unanswerable. How far it may be considered an open question, since the amendment of Section 10 of Article IV, of the Constitution of 1868, it is difficult to determine; but it is well to note that the court were at first inclined to construe the term "issues of fact," used in that section, to include matters of fact arising upon the decisions of motions, as for a new trial under Section 133 of the Code, which view was afterwards greatly modified, if not entirely abandoned, by the court. Or, perhaps, it would be more correct, to say that the tendency of the earlier decisions of the court upon the import of the term "issues of fact" in that section, was to make it include, not only the decision of the facts upon which the judge's decision in the court below was based, but also the conclusion which he drew therefrom, and that this doctrine has been modified by accepting the judge's findings of the facts, as final, but holding the legal inference therefrom to be reviewable. No clear appreciation of the status of the question presented by the first class of coses [sic] can be obtained, however, except by a careful comparison of all the cases affecting both.

These cases are cited under the different sections of this chapter, being arranged under those to which they appear to be each most nearly germane. Nearly all of these embrace, however, more or less of elaborate discussions of the general question.

The view of Mr. Justice Rodman, is unquestionably, that which has been adopted in New York and most other States having the Code practice. The provisions of this chapter are taken without modification from the Code of New York, and have been adopted, without alteration in a majority of the other Code States. As has before been remarked, however, in the note to § 6, *ante*, our Code must, in its construction, be greatly modified, by the peculiar provisions of our Constitution.

The first section of the fourth Article, has a very different force, upon the Code provisions as to the "Civil Action," from what it would have had as [a] simple section of the Code itself. The same is true of section 13 of the same Article. This section provides, that, "In all *issues of fact* joined in *any court*, the defendant may *waive the right*, to have the same *determined by a jury;* in which case the finding of the judge, upon the facts shall have the force and effect of a verdict of a jury."

The kindred provision, in New York, is "The right of trial by jury, in all cases in which it has been *heretofore* used, shall remain inviolate forever; but *may be waived* by the parties *in all civil cases*." In California and Oregon the same provision exists. In Indiana, "The right of trial by jury shall remain inviolate." In Iowa, Kansas, Minnesota, Missouri, Nebraska, Nevada, Ohio, Kentucky and Wisconsin it is substantially the same. In Michigan, the constitution provides that "the right of trial by jury shall remain, but, in all civil cases, shall be deemed waived unless demanded by one of the parties, in such manner as may be prescribed by law."

The constitutions of the other Code States are not accessible at this time; but they are believed to be of a similar import. In all of these it will be observed, that the provision is reflexive in its character. Its function is merely preservative of the former status. It "shall *remain inviolate*," or "in all cases in which it *has been heretofore used*," and similar phrases, are susceptible of no other construction, than that the right is to be restricted thereafter as theretofore. These provisions are very nearly identical in force, with section 18 of our Bill of Rights which declares, that "In all *controversies at law* respecting property, the *ancient* mode of trial by jury, * * ought to remain sacred and inviolable."

Section 13 of the fourth Article is believed to be peculiar to our constitution. At least, I have not been able to find one at all similar to it in any other. It is, no doubt, a positive *extension* of the right of trial by jury. Its enactment in conjunction with the 18th section of the Bill of Rights, and the very striking difference in their language, seems to exclude the idea of Mr. Justice Rodman, so far as "issues of fact" are concerned. It cannot be construed as extending only to what were actions at law, for its language is sharply contrasted with the other section, which had been frequently construed, as abundantly sufficient for that purpose. The legalization of the waiver "in all issues of fact," is as clear a recognition of that right "in all issues of fact," as can be given by language not expressly declarative of that fact.

Not only is the distinction between "issues of fact" and "questions of fact," strictly correct in reason and upon precedent, but the provisions of this chapter give a legislative construction of the former term, which cannot be made to include the latter. The reasoning by which he seeks to limit the *right* to a jury trial by excluding cases in which a *compulsory* reference is ordered, seems to me fatally defective. Indeed, it is little more than an attempt to override an explicit grant of right by an argument *ab inconvenienti*, which would apply quite as strongly to some of the issues, which were triable before a jury at law, as to the taking of an account.

In *Gragg* v. *Wagoner*, 77—246, an interesting question is raised, which, through [sic] not decided, may bear upon the future construction of this section. An equitable defence was set up in an action in the nature of *covenant* at the common law, and issues thereon tried by a jury. Whether under the Constitution as amended, Article IV, Section 8, the court can review the *findings of fact by a jury*, is the very delicate question presented, but not determined by the court. Under the old equity practice the court could review the findings by the *judge* below, in regard to facts. They might also refer issues to a jury, whose finding, they were not bound to follow, but might modify or reverse. In those cases, however, there was no constitutional right to a trial by jury. Now, there is, and such provision would seem to be altogether useless if the court may review and reverse the decision of the jury. The peculiar care with which this right has always been preserved, and the tenacity with which all extensions of the privilege have been maintained, lead to the belief that the proper construction of this amendment will be held to be, that the court only has power to review such findings of fact, as the *judge* below has the power to make. This would allow a review of the facts found, in all cases of reference by compulsion, and where the contrary was not specified, of references by consent, as well as in cases of exceptions to the report of a referee appointed to take an account. That such may have been the purpose of the amendment, may very well be inferred from the hitherto, unsettled, or at least unsatisfactory, state of the decisions upon this question. That the constitution should, as it unquestionably does, guarantee a jury trial, upon all "*issues of fact*," and then allow their findings to be modified and overturned, upon a necessarily incomplete statement of the evidence before them, without even the sworn statement of a single witness, but only the case as made up by the judge, who presided at the trial below, seems somewhat absurd and untenable. Surely no court should review the decision of a tribunal specially empowered to try such issues, upon such testimony.

It seems highly probable, therefore, that the result of this amendment may be to reverse *Keener* v. *Finger*, and the cases which have followed that decision, but it is hardly probable that the principle of *Green* v. *Castleberry*, will be disturbed or that the amendment will be held to apply to issues actually tried by a jury, except those which a judge may submit, for his own enlightenment or which may be referred by consent under § 225 and 244....

[**§ 236.—Entry of the verdict. Motion for new trial on judge's minutes.** Comment discussing Quincey *v.* Perkins, 76 N.C. 295 (1877) (Rodman, J.).]

a"The clear distinction between motions for a new trial under this section and under § 133, is that motions, under this section, *must* be for cause appearing "*on the judge's minutes*;" while, in the cases, embraced by § 133, the grounds, alleged for a new trial, are either entirely extraneous to the course of the trial, or their application can only be shown by evidence, requiring the presentation of affidavits, as a failure to subpœna witnesses, whose materiality was unknown, or any of the numerous matters of surprise or excusable neglect, which may entitle a party to a new hearing. It would greatly tend to regularity and distinctness, if this difference were carefully preserved, and motions for a new trial were entitled "Motion for a new trial on the Judge's Minutes" or "Motion for a new trial for surprise, excusable neglect," &c., and very greatly facilitate reference to the cases decided.

As to the method of making exceptions, there does not seem to have been any adjudication by the Supreme Court, and no rule has been promulgated. The practice varies greatly with different judges, and is fruitful of much misunderstanding at the bar. If the statement of the exception is deferred until the close of the trial or some days afterward, as is frequently the case, it is almost sure to lead to disagreement. There is little doubt that a party may require his exceptions to be made up at the time, and such should be an explicit rule, as it would result in a saving of time, and securing greater certainty in the statement of the grounds of appeal. There is no part of our practice which more clearly requires the exercise of the power vested in the Supreme Court to make rules of practice....

[**§ 264.—Order for discovery of property, examination of judgment debtor, &c.** Comment under subdivision 5., "No person shall, on examination . . . ," discussing Winslow *v.* Com'rs of Perquimans Co., 64 N.C. 218 (1870) (Rodman, J.) (Dick, J., dissenting).]

a"It is very strange that the attention of the court has never been called, in any of this class of cases, to the very broad and comprehensive provisions of § 257, by which every judgment which requires the performance of any particular act on the part of the person against whom it is rendered, becomes self-executing, like the the [*sic*] order in *mandamus*, and may be enforced by a contempt. It is evident that there was no necessity for any distinction or variation of the civil action in those cases formerly remedied by *mandamus* until the Act of 1868–'69, requiring summons to be returned to the term. The judgment, in the civil action, may reach every remedy administered either at law or in equity under the former system. Proceedings, in *mandamus*, are now regulated in some respects by the Act of 1871–'72, Chapter 75.

In other respects, it seems to be the later inclination of the court, to hold that they are governed by the law and practice existing before the Code. After a very careful study of this question in several important cases, I incline to the opinion that the earlier view of the court was the correct one, and that proceedings, in *mandamus*, are properly governed by the Code, except where modified by the Act of 1871–'72, Chapter 75.

The only difference of any moment is, that by following the Code many of the immaterial niceties of the common-law practice, in such cases, are avoided, and all the substantial benefits secured with equal certainty. For instance, instead of taking what was termed a peremptory *mandamus* against a board of county commissioners, requiring them to levy a tax to pay a debt ascertained by judgment, and make their return thereunder, it seems to me quite sufficient and much more convenient, to take a judgment commanding the acts required, and if they be not performed within the time limited to move for attachment for a contempt under section 257....

[TITLE XI. OF THE EXECUTION OF THE JUDGMENT IN CIVIL CASES. Comment under CHAPTER IV. PROCEEDINGS TO LAY OFF EXEMPTIONS UNDER EXECUTION.]

*a*The subject-matter of this chapter, as well as that of the act which constitutes the second chapter of this Title, although not a part of the Code, as originally drawn and enacted, are so obviously kindred to the subject of this Title, and so closely connected with the procedure in civil actions in the Superior Courts, that any volume purporting to give even an outline of that procedure would be inexcusably defective without them. It was my first intention to have published these acts, as appendixes of the Code; but a desire for logical harmony of arrangement, induced me to adopt the present arrangement, as more in consonance with my design of presenting a systematic view of the procedure. By this means, all the proceedings under an execution are grouped together, and impress themselves on the mind of the officer, the practitioner or the student, much more distinctly and with clearer apprehension of their purport, it is believed, than if they were separated from each other. It is thought too, that such an arrangement will greatly facilitate reference to their provisions. That portion of the act referring to the allotment of the homestead, upon voluntary petition of the owner, together with the forms prescribed by statute, is published in this volume under the head of "Allotment of exemptions upon voluntary petition," in order that it may not be necessary to consult another volume in order to examine the context....

[TITLE XII. OF THE COSTS IN CIVIL ACTIONS. Comment explaining that this title has been repealed, perhaps inadvertently.]

*a*This title was repealed without any saving clause, by Section 16 of Chapter 139 of the Acts of 1870–'71, but, as will be seen, different portions of it have been amended since the repeal. I cannot think that it was the intention of the legislature to repeal the very excellent general provisions which it contains in regard to the manner in which costs shall be assessed, and in what cases.

So great is the necessity for these provisions that within a very short time, they have been cited in two instances, by legal gentlemen of considerable prominence upon the circuit, and while these pages are going through the press, have been informed, that one of its sections has been cited as authority in a brief offered in a matter now pending. These facts show how important are its provisions. The legislature, no doubt, intended to repeal the *specific fees allowed* by it, but it is more than probable that the repeal of the general powers, and limitations of discretion in the taxation of costs, were included in the repeal by an oversight, not at all unusual in legislative proceedings. Under the common law procedure, such provisions were scarcely necessary from the nature of the actions cognizable in those courts; but the enlarged powers conferred upon them, and the necessity of making their judgments definitive of all the rights of the parties to the actions, demand a larger power and the more extended discretion, which was conferred by the provisions of this chapter.

With these views, after careful consideration, and consultation with leading members of the profession, it has been decided to reprint the general sections of the chapter in another type, so as to be readily distinguishable from the unrepealed text of the Code, in the hope, among other things, that it may be called to the attention of the legislature, and re-enacted. . . .

[**§ 285.—Referees' fees.** Comment discussing Wall *v.* Covington, 76 N.C. 150 (1877) (Bynum, J.).]

*a*It will be observed that, in this case, the Supreme Court construe several sections of this title as if it were still in force. The action appears to have been tried in 1876. It *may be* that the services were rendered before the repeal of the law in 1871, though it is hardly probable. The court seem to have overlooked the fact that the entire title was repealed, or at least make no reference to that fact, though it has been alluded to in another case. This fact shows the prime importance of these provisions and the very great necessity for their substantial re-enactment. . . .

[TITLE XIV. OF THE MISCELLANEOUS PROCEEDINGS IN CIVIL ACTIONS AND GENERAL PROVISIONS. Comment under CHAPTER I. SUBMITTING A CONTROVERSY WITHOUT ACTION.]

*a*I do not find any discussion of interest, regarding the procedure in submitting a controversy without action, and therefore, only cite the cases, which I have found in which this valuable provision has been resorted to as a means for the ascertainment of right. . . .

[**§ 320.—Form of summons.** Comment discussing impact of the "Act suspending the Code."]

*a*QUÆRE.—Does the "Act suspending the Code" operate to change the form or return day of the summons provided by this section? It is evident, from the language of the subsequent sections, that this proceeding is regarded by the Code, as something distinct from *an action*—a special proceeding, regulated by this chapter, and only as provided therein, governed by the other provisions of the Code. . . .

[**§ 343.—Parties to actions and special proceedings may be examined as witnesses on their behalf, except in certain cases.** Comment inserted in text prior to section 343.*i*—**Examination by commission.** Discusses the inclusion of these sections concerning evidence from the Revised Code.]

The following sections from the Revised Code being the only specific provisions now in force, in regard to the taking of depositions, are reprinted here for convenience. They are very imperfect and have made necessary, in most districts, specific rules upon the subject. This is very objectionable, since it renders the administration of justice variant in different parts of the State and makes the law almost impossible to be ascertained. Some complete and general system should be adopted, by means of which uniformity of practice may be secured. This statute, also, was adapted to a period when the means of communication between different points were much less perfect than they now are, and consequently requires too long a notice to be given. The same numbers have been preserved as were adopted in Battle's Revisal, though the other additional sections given there are omitted. . . .

Document III-48   Rodman to Tourgée, January 8, 1878

[Before leaving North Carolina for good, Albion W. Tourgée published an annotated version of *The Code of Civil Procedure* as amended,[457] which would be continued, years later, by Chief Justice Walter Clark.[458] In the letter transcribed below, former co-commissioner William B. Rodman acknowledged Tourgée's accomplishment.]

Raleigh 8 Jany 1878

Hon. A. W. Tourgée
My Dear Sir

I have examined with some care your Code of Civil Procedure with notes and decisions, though not with as much ~~care~~ as I propose to use. I have no doubt it will be extremely useful both to the practising lawyers, and to Judges, and to all who wish to study our system of practice and procedure. To all these it will save much labor, and ~~{perhaps}~~ give ideas which might not otherwise occur to them.

respectfully
Yours &c
Will. B. Rodman
As[sociate]. Just. of Sup. Co. of N. C.

Document III-49   Phillips about Tourgée, July 18, 1878

[Samuel F. Phillips was the reporter for the Supreme Court of North Carolina after the Civil War and then served as United States Solicitor General. He is also remembered for having assisted Albion W. Tourgée, former code commissioner and judge in North Carolina, in the famous case of *Plessy v. Ferguson* at the Supreme Court of the United States.[459] Phillips almost served on the state code commission during Reconstruction instead of Tourgée, as evidenced by this journal entry of the constitutional convention:

Mr. Heaton called up the ordinance in relation to Code Commissioners, which was read.

Mr. Dowd moved to strike out "A. W. Tourgée," from the names of Code Commissioners and insert "S. F. Phillips, of Orange County." . . .

The motion was lost.[460]

Phillips once described *The Code of Civil Procedure* as "a modern scientific system for administering justice," imagining such a description to be complimentary.[461] Apparently, he corresponded with Tourgée on occasion,[462] and once wrote a very flattering description of Tourgée, which is reprinted below.]

Washington, D.C.
July 18, 1878

I have known the Honorable A. W. Tourgee, of Greensboro North Carolina, for the last ten years, during most of which time he was one of the Judges of The Superior Courts of that State. For several years I practised law in the Courts over which he presided. I take pleasure in saying that he is a man of extensive culture, of extra-ordinary intellectual gifts,—a just and fearless Judge, & a public spirited citizen, with the courage of his opinions.

I regret his determination to leave this State, as I believe that he has done more—in a political way—for it than any other person now living therein.

Upon the whole I have never seen a better visionary Judge preside. His radical views of society have seemed to me to be the very medicine required for the Conservative Community in which I have seen him. I say this without ever having wished to see this State~~d~~ entirely <u>tuned</u> to being <u>such</u>.

S. F. Phillips

Document III-50   About Mr. Lucien Holmes (1797–1871)

[An address preserved in the *North Carolina Reports* had described Mr. Lucien Holmes[463] as a lawyer who had "drunk deep at the well of the common law."[464] And a sketch of his life by Oliver H. Allen printed in the proceedings of the state bar association from 1920, excerpted below, confirmed this assessment. Not surprisingly, then, Holmes "detested the Code practice."]

ADDRESS OF JUDGE OLIVER H. ALLEN....

MY RECOLLECTIONS OF THE BENCH AND BAR

The Bench...

The Bar...

Mr. Lucien Holmes, a brother of Governor Holmes, was at the head of the Sampson bar when I first knew it, soon after the war. He was a man of strong character, violent in his condemnation of wrong. He believed in the common law and detested the Code practice....

Samuel Phillips was reporter of opinions of the Supreme Court of North Carolina from 1866 to 1870, and a close friend of Code Commissioner Albion W. Tourgée. Photograph of a portrait of Samuel Phillips. (*Credit*: State Archives of North Carolina, Raleigh)

Document III–51 About Judge Mitchell (1800–1876)

[Anderson Mitchell served as a trial court judge in the provisional government just after the Civil War and in 1868 was elected by the people to the superior court bench, a position in which he served until 1875. As former Chief Justice David Furches recounted in 1905, in the excerpt below, Mitchell did not like code practice and simply refused to study it.]

JUDGE ANDERSON MITCHELL.

By D. M. Furches. . . .

There was a strong Bar in his [Judge Mitchell's] district at that time. Such men as J. M. Clement, J. F. Graves, Jos. Dobson, R. F. Armfield, W. P. Caldwell, R. A. McLaughlin, M. L. McCorkle, Geo. N. Folk, Col. B. S. Gaither, Judge A. C. Avery, and others. Mr. Boyden, J. M. McCorkle, and others who did not live in his district, attended his Courts. The old style of the lawyers traveling the circuit with the Judge was still kept up.

They were called the Circuit Court lawyers, and traveled with the Judge from county to county. These trips were rough, but usually pleasant, as well as profitable. An old lawyer has told me that it was the most pleasant part of his professional life. But those days are gone to return no more—practice has now become localized.

The Judge did not like the Code practice and would not study it, which sometimes caused a little amusement in Court.

Wilkes county had become very much in debt and its paper floated around at great discount. Everybody was annoyed with persons wanting to sell "county claims," and even the Judge had been troubled in this way. One day Q. F. Neal, Esq., a most excellent gentleman and a good lawyer, though rather timid, rose to ask permission to file a "counter claim" in a case he had. The Judge was not familiar with the word "counter" in the practice of law, and understood the Major to ask permission to file a "county claim," and it made him furious, and he promptly refused the motion, rebuking the attorney, saying, "Major Neal, do you think I can take up the time of this Court in settling the claims of Wilkes county?" Some member of the Bar discovering the mistake and the confusion of Major Neal, came to his relief, explained the matter to the Judge, that it was a new mode of pleading under the Code, when he at once called up the Major, allowed his motion and apologized for the manner in which he had addressed him. . . .

Document III–52 About Chief Justice Pearson (1805–1878)

[On Justice Robert P. Dick's view, Chief Justice Richmond M. Pearson "did" judicial legislation only when the common law had not provided an adequate remedy for a wrong. This "liberalism," said Dick, resembled the revered Lord Mansfield's enlightened approach toward the common law. One must remember, though, that long before either Dick or Pearson was reading law, Mansfield's methodology had elicited two quite contrary reactions among lawyers. Mansfield's liberties with the common law inspired Jeremy Bentham to reject its content and procedure in favor of a scientifically rational codification of law, a system he happily offered to provide to the governor of North Carolina.[465] Those same liberties by Mansfield did nothing to dissuade Sir William Blackstone, his contemporary, from presenting a rational synthesis of the English common law along its moral and historical contours, his four-volume *Commentaries on the Laws of England* serving as the foundation for legal education in North Carolina for the next 165 years. While Justice Dick disparaged positive legislation and codification in his remarks from 1881 about Chief Justice Pearson, excerpted below, his jurisprudential presumptions were not terribly reactionary. Rather, Dick embraced progress in the moral science of the common law without outright rejection of its emphasis on judgment by resolution of concrete cases. "In this enlightened age," he remarked, "when the human mind is so greatly enlarging the domains of science, art and literature, we are neither surprised [nor] much disturbed at the expansion which judicial decisions are giving to the noble science of jurisprudence."]

ADDRESS

—ON—

THE LIFE AND CHARACTER

—OF—

CHIEF JUSTICE PEARSON.

LADIES AND GENTLEMEN,— ...

In 1848 [Pearson] was elected by the Legislature as an Associate Judge of the Supreme Court [of North Carolina], and here he entered upon the field of his future usefulness, greatness and permanent fame. He was brought into contact with Chief Justice Ruffin and Judge Nash, two as able and incorruptible judges as ever presided over any judicial tribunal, and he was soon regarded as their equal in ability, integrity and common law learning. He recognized the exalted merit of Chief Justice Ruffin as a great chancellor, and at once began to devote himself to the study of the enlightened and highly cultivated system of chancery jurisprudence. In a few years he had so completely mastered the subject and become so much interested in the study that he commenced preparing a treatise on equity, and would have completed the same but for the publication of Mr. Adams, which covered the ground and the arrangement which he proposed to adopt. ...

He was sometimes charged with too much fondness for "judicial legislation." He considered legal questions with mature reflection and reasoned from well established principles, and if "the reason of the thing" was adverse to the authorities cited, he sometimes disregarded the narrow boundary of precedents and technical authority in administering substantial justice. He regarded the common law as being like other liberal sciences, capable of growth and expansion to meet the more enlightened spirit and novel wants developed in the moral and intellectual progress of civilization. In one of his opinions he compared the common law to the bark of the oak, which imperceptibly expands to give room for the exogenous growth of the tree, as it sends its roots deeper into the subsoil and among the rocks, to prepare to withstand the storms and to extend its branches graceful with foliage, affording healthful and refreshing shades.

Chief Justice Pearson never did any judicial legislation that caused injustice and wrong to individuals or society, and he never departed from the rules of law if they could by any reasonable construction and application be made subservient to the administration of substantial equity and right. He only modified to some extent the rigid rules of the common law by applying the more liberal and enlightened principles of equity jurisprudence which declare that every legal right should have an *adequate* remedy.

He was controlled by the same liberal and enlightened spirit which influenced Lord Mansfield ... who did so much to ameliorate the rigid rules of the old common law by adapting them to the wants of an expanding commerce and the necessities of an age of rapid development and enlightened progress. The innovating opinions of Lord Mansfield, although much censured at the time, have been approved by the experience and fully adopted by the enlightened judgment of posterity, and he is now universally regarded as one of "the great lights of the law."

In this enlightened age, when the human mind is so greatly enlarging the domains of science, art and literature, we are neither surprised or much disturbed at the expansion which judicial decisions are giving to the noble science of jurisprudence. When we look back over the history and progress of the common law we can readily perceive that it is not a system built up by positive legislation, but in a great degree consists of the dictates of natural justice and cultivated reason applied to particular cases by the enlightened judgment of eminent jurists, who, being familiar with the laws of past ages, and discovering their defects, injustice and inconveniences, which cannot be easily and speedily reformed by positive legislation, apply the proper supplements and remedies to meet the circumstances and necessities of existing conditions of society. This capability of the ready expansion of its own inherent principles, and the facility with which it receives and assimilates to its own substance, the excellencies of other systems of law, are distinguishing features of the common law....

... He was an old line Whig and he was sometimes called a Federalist, as he so firmly believed in the constitutional supremacy of the general government, was such a decided friend of the Union, and was so much opposed to the doctrines of secession and nullification.... He honestly believed that he adhered to the sound, liberal and patriotic principles of the old Whig party, and he was not able to fully understand how he became dissevered from his old Whig friends of former years....

Upon entering [in 1868] upon the duties of Chief Justice under the newly formed State government he was surrounded with many embarrassments and was called upon to consider and determine many cases of "new impressions" presenting difficult and perplexing legal questions growing out of the late war and the reconstruction measures which followed. The abolition of slave property, which had before constituted a large part of the wealth of the State, embarrassed our railway improvements, broke our State banks, disorganized our labor system and industrial interests, and brought a large number of our most enterprizing, intelligent and energetic citizens into bankruptcy. These adverse circumstances gave rise to a large amount of business in the courts from novel sources of litigation. Numerous remedial statutes and ordinances were enacted in legislatures and conventions which made great innovations and radical changes in our old system of government, many of which were ill-considered and unwise and had to be frequently amended or repealed. The system of pleading and procedure in the courts which had been derived from the common law, and had been shaped, moulded and regulated by the experience and judicial wisdom of ages, were suddenly swept away and a new system of civil procedure established for the administration of justice. The difficulties and embarrassments which surrounded the courts in this transition and revolutionary period were greatly increased by the bitter partizan contests which divided and estranged our people. The courts and judges were the subjects of constant denunciation in a part of the public press and on the excited hustings. Many members of the bar of high position and influence, who in former times had been strong friends of the Bench, in the heat of party animosity and under the exasperation of defeat, pronounced a judgment of condemnation against the Justices of the Supreme Court upon the unjust statements of a party press before the condemned had any opportunity of explanation and defense....

Soon after Chief Justice Pearson was elected a Superior Court Judge he opened a law school at Mocksville...

In 1847 he removed to Richmond Hill, in Surry county...

At Richmond Hill the law school was very prosperous. I have heard him say that he had instructed more than a thousand law students, who are scattered throughout the State and nation. He had great skill in the art of communicating knowledge, and by his cheerful and paternal manners he won the respect, confidence and affection of "his boys." He had no strictly scientific arrangement or definite scholastic system of education, but he communicated instruction by frequent examination, on the text-books accompanied by familiar conversational lectures, and like the great philosopher of Athens he never reduced any of his lectures to writing....

Document III-53   About Mr. Joseph Wilson (1810–1884)

[One of the more interesting questions raised by the codification of civil procedure in North Carolina was its impact on the role of the jury. Mr. Joseph Harvey Wilson, the subject of the eulogy by Judge Francis I. Osborne preserved in the *North Carolina Reports* from 1915, and excerpted below, "preferred the single issue [under common law practice] to the multiplication thereof [under code practice], and thought the more numerous issues were calculated to confuse rather than enlighten the jury...." This confusion was worse confounded when we remember Judge Albion W. Tourgée's conclusion that the state supreme court had construed North Carolina's Reconstruction constitution to secure a jury trial in all actions, civil and criminal.[466]]

PRESENTATION OF THE PORTRAIT

OF

MR. JOSEPH HARVEY WILSON

TO THE

SUPREME COURT OF NORTH CAROLINA

BY

JUDGE FRANCIS I. OSBORNE

21 APRIL, 1914

Judge OSBORNE said: . . .

In the busiest period of his life, if not the most important, there occurred the well known revolution in our practice and pleading. In 1868 the Code was adopted, abolishing the distinction between actions at law and suits in equity, and establishing one form of action. It was almost impossible for us who have been bred under the new forms of pleading to understand with what difficulty those older lawyers who had spent their lives in the study of Chitty and Stephens, and filing bills and answers in equity thereto, could reconcile themselves to the new order of things. It seemed to them that they had to forget all the old paths they had trod, and blaze out a new way in a barren wilderness of legal thought without a guide.

To Mr. Wilson's credit be it said, though he preferred the single issue to the multiplication thereof, and thought the more numerous issues were calculated to confuse rather than enlighten the jury, and really was devoted to the old equity practice, he did not despair of fully understanding the new. Being so well versed in the science of good pleading which the old law contained, he brought his knowledge of the old to shed light on the new practice, and soon became a master thereof. . . .

DOCUMENT III–54 ABOUT JUDGE MANNING (1830–1899)

[Professor John Manning re-established the law school at the University of North Carolina soon after Reconstruction. He sought to raise the standard of the bar, which he thought had languished after the Civil War. He found time and patience to adjust to the strange novelty of code pleading, and he served as a commissioner for the 1883 codification of North Carolina's statute law, but his heart remained with Sir William Blackstone's view of the English common law. Like Professor Samuel Mordecai at Trinity College (later Duke School of Law), Manning began a systematic commentary on Blackstone's work from a North Carolina perspective, one volume of which was published posthumously.[467] According to Justice William J. Adams in the excerpt reprinted below, Professor Manning "exhorted his students to a study of the philosophy of law, and admonished them likewise in the philosophy of their personal and professional conduct."]

THE LIFE AND INFLUENCE OF JOHN MANNING

WILLIAM J. ADAMS

ASSOCIATE JUSTICE OF THE NORTH CAROLINA SUPREME COURT . . .

. . . Beginning his practice many years prior to the abolition of the distinctions between actions at law and suits in equity he pondered, not only the principles of substantive law as taught by Coke and

Blackstone, but remedies and forms of pleading as developed by Chitty and Stephen. Hence it is easy to see that transition from the old procedure to the new required mental readjustment; but one can hardly appreciate the difficulty experienced by the ante-bellum lawyers in actually applying the novelties of the Code of Civil Procedure. Many of them concluded in the words of one who referred to another subject, "It will be harder alchemy than Lullius ever knew to sublimate any good use out of such an invention." But Mr. Manning adjusted himself to the change. His surroundings were propitious. He had time for reflection and the advantage derived from association with thoughtful men who were studiously endeavoring to assimilate the new practice and procedure.

For the demands alike of the office and the forum he was thoroughly furnished by nature and training. He was qualified for achievement by the texture of his mind, by his power of concentration and his capacity for research, by his personality, his purpose, and his conscience. He treated the law, not as a "wilderness of single instances," but as a branch of systematized knowledge. He traced the development of the common law and reflected upon its history. He found the study of its obsolete forms and its antiquated "rights" not without profit. He did not scorn to bestow profound thought upon such subjects as the feudal system and ancient as well as modern legal tenures, though he knew that almost every vestige of the old feudal land law had disappeared. While he did not care to

"—keep an ancient form
Through which the spirit breathes no more,"

he had no fear of "losing his memory by reading tombstones."

For the wholesome traditions of the bar he had profound respect. He could tolerate Mr. Bumble's assertion that "the law is a ass, a idiot" only in case it "supposed" that which it never supposes; and his exalted conception of ethics was a sharp condemnation of Charles Macklin's aspersion, "The Law is a sort of hocus-pocus science, that smiles in yer face while it picks yer pocket." . . .

The conditions under which Dr. Manning took control of the Department of Law were not auspicious. The venture, in the words of Dr. Battle, "required faith and pluck of a high order." There was no appropriation for the school; no salary for the teacher. Fees from his students and from his clients were the only source of remuneration. But he was confident. His first class numbered seven students; his last approximately ninety.

Since the death of Judge Pearson there had been in the State only two or three schools of law. The standard of admittance to the bar was not high. The State had recently emerged from the era of Reconstruction, and the profession was not yet immune from the contagion of that direful legislation which authorized the delivery of a license to any applicant who was willing to pay for it with a double eagle. Mr. Manning sought to raise the standard. He stressed the necessity of laying a foundation deep and broad. He taught the law as a science; he avowed its adaptability to the changes wrought by every forward movement; with prophetic vision he foresaw striking advances; legal reforms; changes in the law, in social life, in industry and science; he exhorted his students to a study of the philosophy of law, and admonished them likewise in the philosophy of their personal and professional conduct. Blackstone's *Commentaries* was one of his textbooks. He was not ignorant of the assault under which this work was languishing or of this celebrated jurist's alleged want of qualification for the arduous task of explaining the reasons, the merits, and the defects of the law; but he was convinced that as an expositor of the English law and its doctrines Blackstone had not been surpassed. Moreover, it was thought, the publication of the *Commentaries* had served as a useful agency in engrafting the common law upon the jurisprudence of this country. Indeed, it has been said, "For more than a century practically every American lawyer received at least his first impression of law from Blackstone and through him came into a consciousness of heirship to the great traditions of the English Common Law." It detracts nothing from Mr. Manning's thoroughness to admit that the modern methods of teaching law, made most prominent within the last quarter of a century, direct the student not so much to the text books as to the original sources for the attainment of proficiency in his investigations. It was Dr. Manning's purpose to prepare a series of works with a view to adapting Blackstone to modern needs. His *Commentaries on the First Book of Blackstone* was published after his death and gave evidence of the high character of the work he was fitted to do.

... He looked upon the Federal Constitution, with the implied powers it gave to the Federal Government, as the supreme law of the land; and upon the Constitution of North Carolina as the State's organic law, subordinate only to the fundamental law of the nation. The notion of congressional review of the decisions of the Supreme Court of the United States would have impressed him as utterly chimerical; the proposal to recall judicial decisions by plebicite as the first step toward revolution. If he thought of law as the basis of government he regarded the object of government the maintenance of ordered law. Upon this foundation he rested his theory of law and government; and in the exposition of his theory he inspired his students with a keen desire to perceive and to respect the demands of the law as a progressive and expanding science....

Document III-55 About Judge Tourgée (1838–1905)

[According to Major John Graham in an address to the bar association in 1918, Superior Court Judge Albion W. Tourgée had cared little about the history of North Carolina. Tourgée had not been born or raised in North Carolina, nor had he ended his days in the state. But before fleeing for western and northern states, he had managed to undermine North Carolina's constitutional and common law inheritance by his work in the state constitutional convention and on the code commission.]

Major John W. Graham, of the Hillsboro Bar, then addressed the meeting as follows:

SOME EVENTS IN MY LIFE ...

... This Convention, as is well known, met in Raleigh in January, 1868. Col. W. B. Rodman, who afterwards for ten years was a member of our Supreme Court, was easily the most distinguished lawyer in the body. While I differed from his view, that it was best to acquiesce in an overruling power, civil and military, which we could not resist, I acknowledge the sincerity of his purpose to make the best of circumstances and get a restoration of State government. I wish his pictorial sketches of many of the members could have been preserved. Of the members, A. W. Tourgee, who became a Judge of the Superior Court for six years, was among the most active, and with others, who knew little, and cared less, about the past history of the State, anxious to make a clean sweep of our past system of laws and practice and give us a constitution taken here and there from other parts of the country. At the July meeting of the Legislature, elected at the time of the ratification of the Constitution in May, ... I was elected Senator from Orange.... From 1868 to 1876, inclusive, we had annual sessions of the Legislature....

With the year 1874 ended the judicial career of Hon. Albion W. Tourgee, one of the carpetbaggers, who had come South on what he describes in one of his novels as "The Fool's Errand." After the opening of the courts in 1875, he was doubtful whether he would be permitted to practice before Hon. John Kerr, who had succeeded him as Judge, but the latter stated that he could not allow the record to show that a person had presided as Judge who had never received license to practice law in the courts of the State. Chapter 46, Laws 1868-9, which put applicants to practice law and to keep a bar on the same footing for license, "$20 and proof of moral character," had been repealed by chapter 120, Laws 1870-1, ratified March 11, 1871....

Part IV

Applied Democracy

It would be a great pleasure to see all the codes prepared for New York adopted in North Carolina. You seem to be the very man to take the lead as law-reformer in your State.

—David Dudley Field, Esq. to Justice Walter Clark

The codification of the laws in the sense of embodying in one statute the entire body of the law as in the Codes of those States where the Civil law forms the basis of the jurisprudence, is hardly practicable at this time.

—Colonel John W. Hinsdale

Generally speaking, however, I feel quite sure that the time has not come when we should attempt an entire codification of the unwritten or Common Law of our State.

—Chief Justice James E. Shepherd

A very high authority has added materially to the complexity of the subject by declaring that the "lex non scripta" is law not written by the authority of law. Could confusion itself be worse confounding? If we keep on improving our definitions in this manner—and this is by a noted American judge—we shall soon have some conceited legal sensationalist asserting that the Common Law is unlawful law.

—Commissioner Albion W. Tourgée

All the laws should be burned every thirty years.

—Attributed to Chief Justice Walter Clark

We must some day come to the remedy which was adopted by Justinian and Napoleon in their Codes and which obtains in all the continental countries of Europe. We must codify our laws.

—Chief Justice Walter Clark

Demand for socialization of law, in the United States, has come almost wholly, if not entirely, from the city. . . .

—Dean Roscoe Pound

What was revolutionary was rather the expectation of the legislative law reformers of 1848 and thereafter to make everything over by minutely detailed codes.

—Dean Roscoe Pound

INTRODUCTION TO APPLIED DEMOCRACY

In this fourth part of *Selected Documents Relating to Law Reform in North Carolina during the Nineteenth Century* are gathered documents from the period of Applied Democracy in North Carolina. This period typically is said to run from 1880 to 1914, but for purposes of this compilation, the period is treated as extending through the deaths of Chief Justice Walter Clark and Dean Samuel Mordecai in the 1920s. Excerpts from two additional documents, one from the 1930s and one from the 1950s, both of which look back to this period of Applied Democracy, close out the compilation. We include these post-nineteenth-century documents only to shed light on nineteenth-century law reform, though we acknowledge that some ideas expressed in these documents, like the relation of law to efficiency and the slow walk to general statute, will gain great importance in twentieth-century law reform.

At the period's beginning, the code commission has only recently been disbanded and one of its commissioners, Albion W. Tourgée, run out of the state. In the decades that follow, Chief Justice Walter Clark agitates for further reform in the administration of law. Eloquent opponents of his initiatives include Judge Robert Winston and Dean Samuel Mordecai. Near the end of the period, constitutional change has put the general assembly more firmly on the track of legislating by general statute in displacement of the common law.

Documents in this fourth part of the compilation emphasize the theme of the disruption of the common law tradition by reform through legislative codification. University of North Carolina president Kemp P. Battle reminds his listeners that good government is by slow growths, like the common law, not by metaphysical imposition, like the early "code" known as *The Fundamental Constitutions of Carolina*. Dean John Manning teaches that common law rests upon customs prevailing among a people and declared by their courts, while statutory deviation from custom must be proclaimed, as these deviations reside outside the consciousness of the people. Chief Justice Shepherd observes that the great principles of justice and equity are found in the state's common law, not in its statute law. Even former code commissioner Albion Tourgée acknowledges in a late essay that the strength of the common law is its link to the common life of the people. And Tourgée admits that *The Code of Civil Procedure* adopted in 1868 "substitute[s] for a half dozen forms of action, an infinity of inconclusive motions." Both Tourgée and Chief Justice Walter Clark, editors of handbooks on that code, must also admit that codification has caused an increase in reported appellate opinions that weigh down law libraries. Even Judge Winston, a conservative moving toward moderation, complains that the legislature regulates court procedure in too much detail in its codes. And Clark assesses court procedure under the code in North Carolina at the turn of the century as inefficient and obsolete. Given these admissions and complaints, how save the ideals of writtenness of law in simple language, common sense, and practicality once espoused by the nineteenth-century proponents of procedural codification? The solution offered on the national stage by Dean Roscoe Pound, and parroted locally by Winston, is for the legislature to return responsibility for details of court procedure to the courts, allowing the expert specialist—the judge—to legislate by court rule.

DOCUMENT IV–1   NORTH CAROLINA SUPREME COURT LIBRARY, 1883

[University of North Carolina president Kemp Battle's "Address on the History of the Supreme Court" tied the institution of the law library to access to sound law,[468] perhaps implying that law is a science and the law library its laboratory. The following act of 1883 formally separated the library of the supreme court from its administration by the clerk of the supreme court, who had responsibility for the court's library since the law books had been separated from the collection of the state library a dozen years earlier.[469]]

CHAPTER 100.

An act to authorize and empower the trustees of the Supreme Court library to appoint a librarian and for other purposes.

The General Assembly of North Carolina do enact:
SECTION 1. That the justices of the supreme court and their respective successors in office, be and they are hereby appointed trustees of the supreme court library, and all moneys appropriated for its increase shall be paid out under their direction and supervision. The justices aforesaid shall have charge of the court library and may, in their discretion, employ a librarian, who shall perform his duties under such rules and regulations, and shall receive such compensation as may be prescribed by such trustees.

SEC. 2. That the said trustees of the supreme court library are hereby authorized to employ such person as may be by them appointed or selected to act as librarian for the supreme court at a salary not to exceed the sum of three hundred dollars per annum. . . .

DOCUMENT IV–2   COMMISSION REPORT ON *THE CODE*, 1883

[Commissioner William T. Dortch and his co-commissioners, John Manning and John S. Henderson, here reported their completion of a fully annotated code of the general laws of the State of North Carolina in 1883, the first true code approved by the general assembly since the *Revised Code* of 1854.[470]]

REPORT OF COMMISSIONERS.

To the General Assembly:
The undersigned, Commissioners appointed to revise and consolidate the public statutes, pursuant to chapters one hundred and forty-five and three hundred and fifteen, of the laws of the year one thousand eight hundred and eighty-one, herewith submit the result of their labors, in the form of a bill to be entitled "An act for revising and consolidating the public and general statutes of the state of North Carolina, to be known as THE CODE."

The Commissioners have devoted to this work an immense amount of time and labor, and have barely been enabled to get the said bill ready for the action and consideration of the General Assembly, at its present session. The printing has just been completed. The *errata* and corrections will be found noted in the pages preceding the title of the said bill.

It has been found impossible, within the limited time at the disposal of the Commissioners, between the date of the final printing and the meeting of the General Assembly, to prepare such an index as the law requires. But a temporary index has been printed for the use of the members. This index is not upon the plan determined upon by the Commissioners, and for the reason given is necessarily imperfect and incomplete. It will, however, be found useful to the members of the General Assembly, and will somewhat lessen their labors. A full alphabetical index will be prepared for the whole work after the General Assembly shall have duly considered and enacted the proposed Code.

The Commissioners recommend that they be authorized to include in the said Code, such general acts as may be enacted by the General Assembly at its present session, and that they may also be authorized to re-number and transpose the sections and head-notes of the Code, if deemed expedient, before the book shall be published.

The references to the statutes and to the decisions will be found noted on the margin of, and under, each section. These references, if not altogether complete, will be found to be very full. They will be made much more numerous before the Code is ready for the use of the public, and it is the purpose of the Commissioners to bring down the references to the decisions to the very date of publication.

The Commissioners have performed the duties devolving upon them in relation to the Constitutions of the State and of the United States, and to certain acts of Congress; but have not caused them to be printed with the proposed Code, because they considered such printing at this time to be an unnecessary expense to the State. The said Constitutions and acts, with full references to the decisions, will be bound up with the Code when finally published.

WILLIAM T. DORTCH,
JOHN MANNING,
JOHN S. HENDERSON.

January 3, 1883.

Document IV–3   Clark's Preface, 1884

[A reference work published in 1884 by Walter Clark digested cases about reform procedure in North Carolina. Although Clark failed to acknowledge any debt to authors of prior reference treatises, his work followed closely upon a book by Albion Tourgée, the latter book distinguishing itself by its character as a treatise due to its long, clarifying notes.[471] Clark's short preface to his work, here excerpted, managed to skim across some key points in his outlook on life and on the legal profession. For instance, having abandoned the common law tradition for an entirely new system of procedure—one that appealed to simplicity, common sense, and New York's same system, but which nonetheless required construction in numerous adjudications before the Supreme Court of North Carolina—the state's future progress now admittedly depended on the procedural decisions made in the (immediate) past. Apparently, Clark saw no irony in his admission of the importance of the past on the future. He remarked instead on his laborious research and on his unstinted labor in making the court's (immediate past) progress accessible to the profession (but, apparently, not to the layperson). He hoped that his working tool would save labor for others, a debt all lawyers owe to the profession according to the modern empiricist and founder of British codification, Sir Francis Bacon.[472]]

PREFACE.

To the Profession:

This work lays claim to no originality. It had its origin in the necessities of the writer for a ready reference to the adjudications of our court of last resort on questions of practice. These adjudications were necessarily numerous, as they are constructions placed by the court upon an entirely new system of procedure, laying down the successive steps taken and the lines upon which future progress is to be made. They are scattered through twenty-six volumes of reports, and not accessible without much research.

This volume, therefore, is intended as a workingtool, a LABOR-SAVER to a hard working profession. If it has the effect of lightening their labors, the compiler will feel repaid. He will also feel that he has, in his humble way, paid that debt which Lord Bacon says that every lawyer owes his profession.

That there are typographical errors in the work was hardly to be entirely avoided, considering the large number of names and figures used. They have been numerous enough to vex the writer, but it is trusted that the ready intelligence of the practicing lawyer will in no instance be mislead [*sic*] by them. That there are omissions and errors of a more serious nature, it is probable that the use of the work may discover. Labor has not been stinted to make the work complete and accurate, and where there are shortcomings, not "of form, but substance," reliance is placed upon the forbearance and charity of the Profession.

WALTER CLARK.

Raleigh, N. C., Feb. 20, 1884.

Document IV–4   Battle's History, 1889

[In his 1889 speech about the history of the Supreme Court of North Carolina, excerpted below, University of North Carolina president Kemp P. Battle recorded lessons about law reform gleaned from the state's history: all good governments are slow growths, not metaphysical impositions; only research into the law can make appellate opinions certain and professionally acceptable; and only official, written, accessible appellate opinions are tolerable once an appellate jurisdiction emerged from the conferences of the trial judges.]

AN ADDRESS

ON THE

History of the Supreme Court, . . .

. . . After four years of provisional government, with entire confidence of success, they proceeded, in 1769 [*sic*], to put into operation the extraordinary scheme called the Fundamental Constitutions of Carolina, fondly described by them as the "Grand Model." There could not possibly be a more striking proof of the truth that all good governments are slow growths, the product of the struggles and compromises of intelligent and well-meaning men, than this abortive product of Locke's metaphysical brain. Locke was a learned philosopher, and most of the Lords Proprietors were men of large experience and ability in various fields of human activity, one of them, Shaftesbury, of extraordinary genius, but their attempt at government was so unsuited to the people for whom it was intended, that it met with their scorn and resistance, and the historian's ridicule. . . .

By the act of 1804, the Court [of Conference] was made a permanent court of record, the judges were ordered to reduce their opinions to writing, and to deliver the same *viva voce* in open court. . . .

. . . In 1846 the lawyers of the western portion of the State induced the General Assembly to order a term of the Court to be held in Morganton on the first Monday in August for all cases in the counties west of Stokes, Davidson, Union, Stanly and Montgomery, and for cases from these counties, with consent of both parties. The experiment was not satisfactory to the Court or to the profession. Owing to a want of a law library, "Morganton decisions," as they were called, were regarded as less certainly sound than those at Raleigh. The Constitution of 1868 fixed the sessions of the Court "at the seat of government;" that of 1876 leaves the sessions at "the city of Raleigh, until otherwise ordered by the General Assembly.". . .

It was not until 1808 that there was any attempt made by law to furnish the people with the decisions of their highest legal tribunal. In that year the Clerk of the Supreme Court was directed to furnish the Secretary of State a report of the decisions of the preceding four years, and annually those made thereafter. There was no appropriation for the cost of publication, but advertisement was to be made for a printer to do the work at his own expense in consideration of the copyright for seven years, the State to have sixty-six copies free. In 1813, the same niggardly offer was made to the Clerk of the Court, the copyright being extended to the time granted by the laws of the United States. I think these laws led to no result, the reports of that day being published on private account.

In 1818 the Supreme Court was authorized to appoint a Reporter at a salary of $500, on condition he should furnish the State, free of charge, eighty copies of the reports, and the counties sixty-two copies. I presume, though it is not expressly so said, that he was entitled to the copyright. Afterwards he was allowed to print 101 copies for the State and counties at the public expense, and was allowed a salary of $300, and the copyright. In 1852 his salary was raised to $600, and the number of copies for the State increased, so as to supply the libraries of the different States and Territories, and a few others. In 1871 the office of Reporter was abolished, and the duties and emoluments given to the Attorney General. Afterwards the salary was increased to $1,000, and the State assumed all the expense of printing, distributing and selling the reports in excess of those donated, and covered into the treasury the receipts of sales, less five per cent. commission for selling. The office of Reporter has always been considered a very honorable one, and has been much sought after by aspiring lawyers. The list of reporters in the appendix shows the truth of this. . . .

These are the principal changes made, specially by law, in the functions of the Court. But there was a mighty mass of changes in the character of their work thrown on the judges, by the Constitution of 1868, and the transplanting to North Carolina the Code of Civil Procedure, first elaborated in New York. The Constitution of 1776, even as amended in 1835, was founded on the assumption that the agents of the people, the General Assembly, would be honest and have such stake in the soil that they could be intrusted with powers almost unlimited. They could tax any subject to any amount, and exempt any subject from any tax at all. They had boundless right to pledge the State credit. They had, as I have shown, vast powers in the control of the other departments of government. They had full discretion as to nearly all subjects of legislation.

The Constitution ratified in 1876, which is merely an amendment of that of 1868, is founded on the assumption that the representatives may be untrustworthy. Hence, the executive and judicial departments are made really independent of the legislative. Hence, there are limitations on the taxing power, and on the power of pledging the State credit. Hence, are made a part of the fundamental law numerous provisions, declaring what the General Assembly must do, what it may do, and what it may or may not do. Many provisions seem properly to belong to the statute books, to be modified or amended whenever the interests of the people require. . . .

Near the beginning of his long tenure on the Supreme Court of North Carolina, Walter Clark corresponded with famous codifier David Dudley Field of New York, who, in responding to Clark, wrote, "You seem to be the very man to take the lead as law-reformer in your State." Photograph of a portrait of Walter Clark. (*Credit:* State Archives of North Carolina, Raleigh)

Document IV–5 Field to Clark, 1892

[For decade upon decade in the nineteenth century, David Dudley Field was the moving force for codification in New York, his eventual nemesis being fellow New Yorker, James Coolidge Carter. In the thank you note transcribed below, the aged Field acknowledged that he had received a copy of *The Code of Civil Procedure of North Carolina, with Notes and Decisions to 1884* from its author, Justice Walter Clark. Field also worked up the energy to flatter Clark, noting that North Carolina's code of civil procedure was modelled on New York's code, that it would be good to see "all the codes prepared for New York adopted in North Carolina," and that Clark seemed "to be the very man to take the lead as law-reformer" in North Carolina.]

New York
January 21, 1892.

I have to thank you for a copy of your annotated Code of Civil Procedure, which you were good enough to send me. It is a monument to your labor and skill. New York has adopted three of the five codes prepared by her commissioners. Our code of Civil Procedure you took as a pattern for your own. Our Penal Code and Code of Criminal Procedure, which have been in practice some years, I will send you, if you wish. Perhaps you have them already in your library. The Civil Code and Code of Evidence I send you. They have passed both Houses more than once, but failed for want of the Governor's signature, having been generally passed in the last days of the Session.

The pamphlet, which I send you, being a reprint of an article I wrote for the American Law Review, will acquaint you with the progress of codification in this country. It would be a great pleasure to see all the codes prepared for New York adopted in North-Carolina. You seem to be the very man to take the lead as law-reformer in your State. Command me if I can help you. Please let me hear from you again on the subject, and oblige

---

Document IV–6 Clark's Preface, 1892

[In the second edition of his manual on *The Code of Civil Procedure*, published in 1892, Justice Walter Clark adopted the voice of the reformer—perhaps David Dudley Field's flattery had gone to Clark's head.[473] He was pleased with the turn civil procedure had taken in North Carolina: the new code was simpler than the old forms of action, which were "cumbersome" and "absurd," and the new philosophy on which the code was based rejected the artificial distinction between law and equity. In America, Clark reported, it was New York that had set off the rush to procedural reform, but as the turn of the century approached, this sort of reform had become a fashionable thing among states, and even among nations where Englishmen had planted the common law. So, Clark announced that codification had passed beyond the stage of experiment and into a practical reality—one that was here to stay. And yet, in order to justify an entire reference book about such utterly transparent and simple procedure, Clark had to admit a vast increase in the number of opinions touching upon civil procedure. Ironically, the increase in reported decisions was one of Clark's favorite reasons for disparaging the common law and for advocating for the complete codification of law,[474] even though it was apparent that codification itself was causing a great increase in the rate of publishing volumes of reported opinions.]

PREFACE TO THE SECOND EDITION.

To The Profession:

When the first edition of this work appeared, there were only twenty-six volumes of N. C. Reports which contained adjudications upon the Code of Civil Procedure. Since then, twenty-one additional volumes of our Reports have been issued. This edition has, therefore, been entirely re-written. The number of adjudications cited are about double in number those in the first edition. All the changes made by the last four Legislatures in the C. C. P. have also been incorporated in the text.

The new and simpler Code of Procedure, adopted in our State in 1868, is based upon the abolition of the cumbersome, not to say absurd, forms of action formerly in use and of the distinction between law and equity and the substitution of one form of action for the trial of all civil causes. Long discussed among thinking men, the reform first took practical shape by the adoption of the New York Code of Civil Procedure, in 1848. The reformed procedure is now in force in twenty-six States of this Union, in England, Ireland, Wales, India, Australia, in several provinces of Canada and in many other English colonies. It is no longer an experiment; it has come to stay.

The present work is simply a working-tool to save labor to the profession. It is intended for that purpose, and to be like the C. C. P. itself—a *practical* work.

One word as to the use of the volume. Many decisions are of such a character that they could be appropriately cited under many different sections. To avoid duplicating the same citation, as far as possible, each case has been put under the section which seemed most appropriate, and then, by a liberal system of cross-references, the repetition of the case has been saved. If a case is not found under the head where it is sought, it should be looked for in the *Index of Cases* at the end of the volume. It can then be found under the section selected for it, and, by following up the cross-references, all the cases on that and cognate matters will be found.

WALTER CLARK.

December 1, 1891.

Document IV-7 Rodman to Clark, 1892

[The elderly and ill William B. Rodman, former associate justice of the state supreme court and former code commissioner, responded to a letter from Associate Justice Walter Clark. Rodman enclosed a sketch of "the labors of [his] life." Perhaps Clark sought this information for an essay he hoped to publish about the history of procedural codification in North Carolina or for his biographical history of the supreme court.[475]]

Washington, N. C.
April 28, 1892

My son showed me your favor of 19th March last. I have been a long time without making a reply to it. I intended to comply with your request which I certainly appreciate the kindness of: but my health is such that I hate work of any sort, as much as I used to enjoy it. I am downright lazy, and half blind. I have proposed a sketch of the labors of my life however, which I enclose with this. I fear it is too long to suit your purpose, or rather that of the Periodical that you refer to. If so—strike out freely all that will not suit his views. The hardest work I ever did was in preparing the legislation which as one of the Committee to certify our laws, I reported to the Legislature in 1868–1869—including the Code of Criminal Procedure which they failed even to notice. I do think these Acts of Assembly will endure on our Statute Books and in every code hereafter, for many years, and it will never be known that I am entitled to any credit for them, unless I put up my claim to it now.

P. S. As to my opinions while on the bench, like all others, Coke's-Eldon's-Ruffin's-Gaston's, they will necessarily become obsolete,—as the buildings of each generation of men, are covered up by the accretions which the next builds over them. Where are the palaces of the Caesars in Rome? buried many feet under the surface, only occasionally dug up by antiquarians. I do not know that this thought has ever occurred to you, but it will do so, as you get old and it is the less sad—the older one grows.

Document IV-8 Office of the Reporter, 1893

[In the statute from 1893 excerpted below, the office of reporter of the decisions of the supreme court was brought once again under the authority of the supreme court, more than twenty years after the displacement of its duties to the office of attorney general in 1872.[476] That displacement had taken place when conservatives recaptured the general assembly a few years after adoption of the North Carolina Constitution of 1868, the constitution having placed the court on a constitutional basis, rather than leaving it on its traditional statutory basis. The excerpted statute also purported to remove any obligation of the court to write its opinions in full in every case.]

An act to amend The Code, sections thirty-three hundred and sixty-eight, thirty-seven hundred and twenty-eight and thirty-seven hundred and twenty-nine, in reference to the attorney general and supreme court reporter.

The General Assembly of North Carolina do enact: . . .

SEC. 4. The justices of the supreme court may employ a reporter of its decisions, who shall receive as compensation a sum to be fixed by said justices, not to exceed the sum of seven hundred and fifty dollars.

SEC. 5. That the supreme court justices shall not be required to write their opinions in full except in cases in which they deem it necessary.

SEC. 6. That this act shall be in force from and after its ratification.

Ratified the 6th day of March, A. D. 1893.

DOCUMENT IV-9   CLARK'S PREFACE, 1895

[Associate Justice Walter Clark prefaced his 1895 supplement to the second edition of his work on reform procedure even more shrilly than he had prefaced the second edition itself. He described the age in which he wrote as one of practicality and common sense. The title page to this supplement indicated just how practical Clark meant: it recorded that he had also written "Clark's Overruled Cases" and "Laws For Business Men." Clark described common law procedure, which grew up in England over the course of 700 years and spread across the globe with the rise of the British Empire, as a "vogue." This vogue required the student of law to burn time studying highly technical tomes and to "delve into the most useless waste and ashes of the past." By contrast, the new practice, which finds its place in our organic law, was useful, plain, and simple. Would the new practice promote justice? This question Clark did not pose.]

PREFACE.

The practical common sense of the age has swept away, in a large majority of English-speaking States and governments, the absurd and highly technical system of pleading and practice formerly in vogue. In 1868 this reform was enacted in North Carolina and placed in the organic law. In consequence of the Constitutional requirement, the Code of Civil Procedure was enacted the same year and has endured, with slight change, as we have it to-day. From that date, the time formerly wasted by the Profession and by law students on technical and ingenious works on pleadings, such as Stephens, Chitty, Tidd, and the like, has been economized for a study of useful principles of law, save by those curious to delve in the most useless waste and ashes of the past. The directions for the pleader and practitioner to follow are made plain and simple, and are compacted in one brief chapter of The Code for his ready reference. He need look no further in any case than that chapter and the decisions of our Court upon it.

This Supplement contains the changes which have been made in the Code of Civil Procedure by the Legislatures of 1893 and 1895, and the decisions of the Supreme Court upon the Code of Civil Procedure, as reported in the eight volumes—109 N. C. to 116 N. C., inclusive. It is only intelligible when used in connection with the Second Edition of the Annotated Code, issued in 1892. It refers to the *pages* of that work, where the additions should be made.

The paging of only a few cases in the 116 N. C. is given, as that volume has not yet been issued.

If my brethren of the Bench and Bar, who may have occasion to refer to the pages of this Supplement, shall find in it an alleviation of their labors, I shall not regret the not inconsiderable addition its compilation has been to mine.

WALTER CLARK.

Raleigh, N. C., 1 Aug., 1895.

DOCUMENT IV-10   MANNING'S COMMENTARIES, 1899

[Professor John Manning's *Commentaries on the First Book of Blackstone*, published posthumously by his son,[477] were notes intended to be the basis for a North Carolina version of Blackstone's *Commentaries on the Laws of England*, describing the state's law as it stood at the end of the nineteenth century. In the excerpt below, which defined "law," Manning included "proclaiming" as an essential feature of statute law and implied that customary common law had no such characteristic. It seems the professor meant that statute law may deviate from custom and so reside outside the consciousness of the people, while common law rests on the prevailing practice of the people and upon declarations of that practice by the courts.]

BLACKSTONE'S COMMENTARIES
BOOK FIRST
INTRODUCTION
OF THE NATURE OF THE LAWS IN GENERAL...

Sec. 6.—Definition of Law Considered.—Now for a moment let us consider this definition of Municipal Law....

4°. It is prescribed, viz: proclaimed beforehand in order that the people may know the law in advance. This word *prescribed* principally applies to the statute law: the common law is assumed to rest upon customs prevailing among the people, ascertained and announced from time to time by the courts and, when so announced, legally regarded as having existed from time immemorial, whether this is so in fact or not....

Document IV-11   Hinsdale on Codification, 1900

[In a committee report to the state bar association in 1900, Col. John W. Hinsdale provided a brief history of statutory revisals, compilations, and consolidations (lumping them under the term "codifications") in North Carolina. He praised the consolidation of the *Revised Code* of 1854 and suggested that the state codify its statutory laws once again, still in the manner of its past codifications, and not yet along the lines of codes found in states where Europe's civil law forms the basis of the jurisprudence. True reform, for Colonel Hinsdale, amounted to writing positive law more clearly, not in "tearing up the old and bringing in the new."]

REPORT OF COMMITTEE ON LEGISLATION AND LAW REFORM.

To the President and Members of the North Carolina Bar Association:

The Committee on Legislation and Law Reform beg leave to submit the following report:

In accordance with the duty imposed upon them by Section 5 of the By-laws of the Association, they have taken into consideration such amendments to the laws and of the judicial procedure as in their opinion will facilitate the administration of justice.

They suggest to the Association that the next General Assembly of this State be urged to legislate upon the following subjects.

CODIFICATION.

Before entering into a consideration of the present needs of codification it may not be without interest to make a hasty review of the history of codification of the laws of the State during the present century. Your Committee therefore beg your indulgence for a few moments to permit them to go back into the past and thereby the better to understand the present.

We find that at "A General Biennial Assembly held at the House of Capt. Richard Sanderson at Little River, begun on the 17th day of November, 1715, and continued by several adjournments until the 19th day of January, 1716," it was among other things provided,

"That the Chief Justice and the Clerks of each and every Precinct Court shall take care that the transcript or book of laws deposited in his or their custody shall be constantly laid open upon the Court Table during the sitting of the Court for the perusal of such members of the Court or other persons litigating causes therein as shall have occasion so to do."

The provision illustrates the care which the law-makers of that day took to give to all persons an opportunity to read for themselves the laws of the land and for those who were unable to read it was further provided, "That the Clerks of each Court shall at the next term after the receipt thereof, publicly and in open court read over the same and so yearly at the first Court next following the first day of May."

The labor involved in examining the numerous chapters of the several volumes of the laws, with in many cases, obscure indices, to ascertain the present condition of the statutes, consumes more time in this busy age that the citizen should be required to spare. We find that at the General Assembly of 1833 it is provided "That three Commissioners should be appointed by the Governor, to collate, digest and revise all public statutes of the State." The work thus provided for was done by Frederick Nash, James Iredell and Wm. H. Battle, Esqs., and printed and published under the supervision of Jas. Iredell and Wm. H. Battle, Esqs., in two volumes in 1837.

The 1st volume contained the general statutes in force. The 2d contained chapters on Railroads, Banks and other corporations and the boundaries of the several counties. To the 1st volume is a "Preface" in which is given an interesting sketch of the Legislation of the State from its earliest period. These volumes are known as the "Revised Statutes."

At the session of 1850 provision was made for another revisal of the statutes and pursuant thereto B. F. Moore, Asa Biggs and R. M. Saunders, Esqs., were appointed Commissioners. Judge Saunders resigned and the work was completed by Messrs. Moore and Biggs and reported to the session of 1854.

The Statutory law as thus compiled was printed and published under the supervision of Bartholomew F. Moore and W. B. Rodman in 1855, and is known as the "Revised Code."

In 1873 the General Assembly directed Judge Wm. H. Battle to revise the statutes of the State, and gave us in 1873 "Battle's Revisal" in one volume. The value of this work was seriously impaired by reason of the failure of the General Assembly to enact the Revisal in one Statute and repeal all acts not therein contained. See State vs. Cunningham, 72-469.

At the session of 1881, by Chapter 145, W. T. Dortch, John S. Henderson and John Manning, Esqs., were appointed Commissioners and directed to collect and reduce into one act the different acts and parts of acts which, from similarity of subject, ought, in their opinion, to be so arranged and consolidated; distributing them under such titles and sections as they shall think proper, with marginal notes of such statutes as may be collected and digested into one section, title or division, with full references under each section to the decisions of the Supreme Court pertaining thereto. Pursuant to the duty imposed upon them, the Commissioners proceeded to form and at the session of 1883 reported as a result of their labors the present Code. The report was accepted and enacted as one act, and the statute law of the State thus became collected, arranged and digested in the chapters and sections of the present Code. The work of these eminent lawyers was in all respects acceptable to the people and the profession.

Since the enactment of the present Code there has been held in the State nine sessions of the General Assembly and eighteen sittings of the Supreme Court, and we have a corresponding number of volumes of laws and reports. An examination of two volumes of the Public Laws shows that an average of fifty changes have been made at each session, thereby aggregating about 450 changes by which sections of the present Code have been "repealed, altered or amended." It would involve more time and labor than your Committee have been able to spare to ascertain the number of cases in which the various sections of the Code have been construed by the Court.

Thus we see that the present statute law of the State is contained in the two volumes of the Code and nine volumes of the Public Laws of the State, enacted since the Code. By this hasty review of the subject we may conclude that experience has shown that at periods of about twenty years apart there arises a necessity for "collecting, compiling and revising the statute law of the State." There will doubtless be a variety of opinion when the question comes for settlement as to the best manner in which to do this work and the extent of the power to be conferred upon the Commissioners.

An examination of the statutes whereby the Commissioners heretofore appointed were to be guided will show that they have been confined to the duty of "collecting, arranging and revising the statutes in force."

Messrs. Biggs and Moore, in their report to the General Assembly in 1854, stated "that they had departed in very essential respects from the course pursued by former Commissioners. That they had not only compiled and brought together the different acts and parts of acts on the same subject, but they had consolidated them by fusing them together and giving character as of a single enactment and as to a great many, indeed most of the acts, they had expunged the verbiage when it was cumbersome and imparted no aid to the meaning of the law."

It has always been conceded that the "Revised Code" was the most satisfactory work of the character which has ever been done in the State.

Of necessity many statutes are hastily drawn and but few of our legislators are skilled in the art of using the language of, the law, hence it frequently happens that acts of the General Assembly when subjected to the criticism of the Court in their application to cases fail to effectuate the intention of the lawmakers. Say the Commissioners hereinbefore quoted, "In not a few cases the known purpose of the laws have been defeated by judicial decision (a calamity which sometimes befalls the best considered statutes)."

The codification of the laws in the sense of embodying in one statute the entire body of the law as in the Codes of those States where the Civil law forms the basis of the jurisprudence, is hardly practicable at this time. It is by no means uncertain that this will not be undertaken at some time with success. It would seem that the extent to which we may codify at this time is to be measured by successful efforts in this direction in the past.

The Committee is of the opinion that the Association should recommend that the next General Assembly provide for the appointment of three Commissioners, eminent lawyers, who having the taste and talent for the work, shall undertake the task. The Assembly should mark out the lines upon which they shall work. They should carefully examine the present status of the statute law of the State and in connection therewith carefully study the decisions of the Court appertaining thereto. They should collect and revise the statutes under appropriate chapters and sections, which should be arranged in logical order. Where the language of the statute is obscure or where by judicial construction the reading of the same will not convey to the mind the true meaning thereof, the Commission should be empowered to so revise that the true ends and purposes of the statute will be obtained.

In those cases where, by construction of the Court, the sections or statutes work a hardship the Commission should have the power to modify and revise so as to meet the true intent of the Legislature.

The Commissioners should also, so far as possible, adhere to the arrangement of the Code of 1883. All sections which bear one upon the other should be referred to in the marginal notes and all cases of the Supreme Court should be annotated in the Code at the correct section. Of course the Commission will be required to report to the next session of the General Assembly.

In passing we would recommend that the statute appointing the Commission be carefully drawn and ample power in the premises be given them.

In the practical life of the North Carolina Lawyer he has to meet with many obscure statutes, we may say imperfect one. To remedy this, to point out the way to true reform, and not to reform simply for the sake of tearing up the old and bringing in the new, the Commissioners should devote their attention. . . .

JOHN W. HINSDALE,
For Committee.

DOCUMENT IV–12 CLARK'S PREFACE, 1900

[In his preface to yet a third edition of his manual on *The Code of Civil Procedure*, Walter Clark mentioned the numerous legislative changes that had been made to the code in North Carolina. The first edition of his book had appeared sixteen years after the adoption of reform procedure in the state, and his third edition now appeared sixteen years after that one. Clark noted that the number of adjudications about reform procedure cited in the third edition was three times greater than in the first edition. The quantity of amendments and level of confusion about this "plain and simple" system of civil procedure, then, appeared to be accelerating. In this preface from 1900, as well as in his prefaces from 1895,[478] 1892,[479] and 1884,[480] Clark addressed the practicing bar as his audience, which suggested that this plain and simple method of pleading had not made every person his own lawyer, as nineteenth-century advocates for the abolition of the common law forms of action had hoped it would.[481]]

PREFACE TO THE THIRD EDITION.

———

TO THE PROFESSION:

When the Second edition of this work appeared, there were 47 volumes of N. C. Reports which contained adjudications upon the Code of Civil Procedure. Since then, 17 additional volumes of our Reports have been issued. This edition has, therefore, been entirely re-written. The number of adjudications cited are more than three times the number of those in the First edition. All the changes made by the Legislature in the C. C. P. up to date have also been incorporated in the text. . . .

An Appendix beginning at p. 965, contains those cases in 125 and 126 N. C., which came out during the publication of this work but too late to be inserted in their proper places.

If my brethren of the Bench and Bar, who may have occasion to refer to the pages of this work shall find in it an alleviation of their labors, I shall not regret the not inconsiderable addition its compilation has been to mine.

WALTER CLARK.

Raleigh, N. C., 1 July 1900.

James E. Shepherd served as chief justice of the Supreme Court of North Carolina from 1892 to 1894. Shepherd thought little of codification, arguing instead for an increased respect for the doctrine of *stare decisis*. Photograph of portrait of James E. Shepherd. (*Credit*: State Archives of North Carolina, Raleigh)

DOCUMENT IV–13 SHEPHERD'S SPEECH, 1900

[In a speech to the bar association delivered in 1900, Chief Justice James Shepherd noted that North Carolina had no statutes which declare "great principles of substantive justice and equity." This observation matched James Coolidge Carter's notion that legislation is proper for areas of public administration and public interest, while unwritten law is proper for private law.[482] Shepherd's remark was also in accord with the thesis of Professor Richard Floyd Clarke that statutes should deal with matters of no ethical importance.[483] Shepherd discussed the danger of codifying all of the common law in the state. He thought that such a revolution would hinder the spontaneous development of law in society and that the uniformity of decisions would be agitated by conflicting decisions of the courts in sister states in the assemblage of a code. What would be better than a complete codification, Shepherd asserted, was an effort by the courts to "prevent obscurity" in the common law by "less dicta and a higher appreciation of the true principle and office of the doctrine of stare decisis."]

SOME LEAVES FROM COLONIAL HISTORY

By Jas. E. Shepherd, of Raleigh.

Mr. President, and Gentlemen of the North Carolina Bar Association: . . .

It will be observed that in this hasty reference to some of our old statutes, I have mentioned none which attempt to define and declare those great principles of substantive justice and equity, which, during all the colonial period, were applied by the courts in the determination of those private rights of persons and property which are incident to every social organism. I have not mentioned them because I can find none. The unwritten law with a few statutory modifications was during all these hundred years sufficient to meet the demands of this growing State, and thus furnishing, as I have before remarked, a most wonderful illustration of its wisdom and adaptability. It is this particular view that I have chiefly sought to impress in this imperfect paper. Not only here, but in all English speaking countries does this unwritten law constitute the great body of jurisprudence. I do not pretend to say that the system is perfect and that wholesome legislation is not needed in some directions, nor that even a codification of a part would not be attended with good results. When a branch of this customary law by reason of its constant use and application to a multitude and infinite variety of transactions has, like the law relating to negotiable instruments, approached somewhat near the line of complete development, I think it well to attempt a codification at least for the purpose of securing some degree of uniformity among the commercial people of different States. Of course this uniformity cannot be fully preserved in view of the probable diverse decisions by courts of different States. Still much may be done to correct these conflicts through associations, like the Bankers' Association, for instance, which are sufficiently interested and active and can from time to time by joint State action, influence the necessary legislation. Generally speaking, however, I feel quite sure that the time has not come when we should attempt an entire codification of the unwritten or Common Law of our State. Some special subjects may be treated in this way, but the idea of blending all of our written and unwritten law into a statute under the name of a Code would, I think, strike the mind of even of the least conservative lawyer with amazement and alarm. I have not the time to discuss such a proposition. Suffice it to say, that the one or two attempts in this direction that have been made in this country have not, in the estimation of some of the best writers, been very satisfactory. Such a revolution in our judicial system would necessarily obstruct that spontaneous development of the law with the progress of society, which is the distinctive characteristic of the English and American system of jurisprudence, and it is stoutly opposed by a very large majority of the profession under the leadership of James C. Carter and other distinguished lawyers. One of the arguments advanced in support of such a general codification is the immense volume of case-law, evidenced by about eight thousand law reports, and the difficulty of finding the law in the midst of so many conflicting decisions.

It must be remembered that this large number of reports include those of Great Britain and the various States of this Union, and that under our autonomous system of government it would be impossible to reduce them into one general or national Code. Even if this could be done, the uniformity would soon be disturbed by the conflicting decisions of the courts of the different States in the construction of such a Code, and in supplying its insufficiencies to meet the infinite number of new questions constantly arising and which cannot be anticipated. This consideration ought to be sufficient to meet any argument based upon the large number of reports. All the decisions outside of our State are but persuasive authority, and can be found in the digests. Those inside the State are comparatively small in number and as a general rule may easily be mastered with the aid of a good digest. What is most needed in a greater number of the States, in order to prevent obscurity in the unwritten law is a better opportunity for careful deliberation on the part of the courts,—less dicta and a higher appreciation of the true principle and office of the doctrine of *stare decisis*.

Retrospective laws, made by the reversal of decisions which have become rules of property, or have been so long followed as to have been contemplated by contracting parties, are as harmful and unjust as a retrospective act of the Legislature. "The doctrine of *stare decisis* is indeed one of the most important of the law; for in its simplicity it expresses man's reverence for civil authority, and the demand of his nature that it shall be obeyed; and this feeling is the surest foundation of social order. It is the expression of the people's expectation that all government shall be administered with great care and with a reasonable degree of consistency, and of their confidence that it is so; and it involves the injunction that functionaries shall not, for light reasons, abandon the expressed judgments of themselves, or of their predecessors, especially if any serious embarrassment of public order may be the consequence. It regards all governmental, and especially judicial decisions as the official representations of the public will in relation to civil rights and duties, and as being entitled to respect and reverence for this simple reason. To these feelings and principles we owe official reverence, and we desire to cherish it as a necessary element of social order and of judicial character." Callander vs. Ins. Co. 23 Pa. State, 474.

Wisely administered this unwritten law largely represents the experience, the intellect and the conscience of the greatest people on earth. It follows all who speak the English tongue, wherever they may be, even to the uttermost parts of the earth. Wherever it is planted, there you will find the rights of persons and of property guaranteed, and the principles of highest civilization advanced. As we have seen in this hurried sketch it is all sufficient to meet the demands of a State in its infancy, and we know that it is capable of expanding and adapting itself to the demands of society in its most complete development and organization.

From time to time it may be altered and supplemented in many respects by judicious legislation, but let not this great heritage, the growth of centuries, and so rich in blessings to the people, be marred by the iconoclast, who generally comes in the guise of the reformer.

This I feel sure will not be done in North Carolina as long as we cherish the memories of Taylor, Henderson, Nash, Ruffin, Pearson and other eminent jurists, whose labors have added a new and brighter lustre to our unwritten or Common Law.

Document IV–14   Revisal's Preface, 1905

[Since the commissioners for *The Code* in 1883 had not published a preface to that work, the preface from the state's *Revisal of 1905* brought up to date the history of statutory codification in North Carolina. One point of interest in this history was the implicit suggestion that the code commissioners of 1868 might have read their constitutional mandate too broadly insofar as they interpreted it to include the codification of the common law. The commissioners described the forty-six bills drafted by the code commissioners for the session of 1868–'69, some of them adopted by the general assembly, as "codifications."[484] And the commissioners noted another point of interest: the volume of legislation since the last official codification made it impracticable to publish the work in one volume. Thus, the *Revisal of 1905* showed the general assembly's slow shift from legislating by local, private, and special acts, which are not normally codified, to legislating by general statute[485] since the Civil War.[486] Finally, this preface concluded by stating the long-understood purposes of statutory codification: enlightenment of the people and improvement in the administration of justice.]

PREFACE.

The preface to the Revised Statutes, prepared by Messrs. James Iredell and William H. Battle, contains a brief history of legislation in North Carolina from the "Grand Assembly of the County of Albemarle," which convened in 1666 or 1667, to the legislation which resulted in "Potter's Revisal," prepared in 1821, and which was then known as the "New Revisal."

Mr. B. F. Moore and Judge W. B. Rodman, who published the Revised Code after it had been prepared by Messrs. Biggs and Moore, continued the history of the codification of our statute law in the preface of that publication, bringing it down to 1854.

The compilers and publishers of The Code in 1883 did not publish a preface, and it may not be inappropriate to now bring this history down to the present time.

In 1868 a new Constitution of the State was adopted, which greatly changed the State's judicial system and contemplated a complete codification of the statute laws, and possibly the unwritten law. By an ordinance of the Convention of 1868, Hon. Victor C. Barringer, Hon. A. W. Tourgee and Judge William B. Rodman were appointed commissioners to carry out the constitutional provisions, and on July 15, 1868, they submitted to the Legislature, then in session, a partial report, recommending (1) a Code of Civil Practise and Procedure, (2) a Code of Criminal Practise and Procedure, (3) a Political Code, (4) a Civil Code, (5) a Penal Code, (6) suggestions of alterations, amendments and revisions of laws necessary to carry out the provisions of the Constitution, (7) a general analysis of all the Codes.

These commissioners made a second report on August 31, 1868, and as a result of their labors The Code of Civil Procedure became a fixed part of our system of laws, although it will now be known merely as the chapter on Civil Procedure in the Revisal of 1905. These gentlemen also prepared a number of statutes, which were in fact codifications and are embodied in the Public Laws of 1868-'69. They prepared a Criminal Code, but it was never adopted by the Legislature.

The Legislature of 1871-'72 (chapter 210) passed an act to provide for the compilation of the public statutes, and appointed Judge William H. Battle a commissioner, with power to collate, digest and compile all the public statute laws of the State. Battle's Revisal was submitted to the General Assembly of 1872-'73, and Judge Battle was authorized and directed to publish it.

This compilation was never enacted into a law, and for that reason the Legislature, in eight years after its publication, provided for a new codification, and appointed Messrs. W. T. Dortch, John Manning and John S. Henderson to do the work.

By a provision in the Constitution of 1868 all existing laws, not repugnant to that instrument or to the Constitution of the United States, were declared to be in force. This made it necessary for the Code commissioners to use the Revised Code as the basis of their work, and for them to codify all statutes prior to 1868 not repugnant to the new Constitution, as well as those enacted between 1868 and 1883.

The Code published in 1883 was the result of their labors, and its satisfactory reception by the people of the State is attested by the fact that not until twenty years of legislation had practically emasculated it did the law-making body provide for another revision.

By chapter 314 of the Public Laws of 1903 the undersigned were appointed commissioners to compile, collate, revise and digest all the public statute laws of the State. They were to begin work the first of May, 1903, and were to deliver to the Secretary of State five hundred printed copies of their report by November 15, 1904, thus giving them a little more than eighteen months to prepare and publish their report. The hastily printed legislative edition was carefully scrutinized by a large joint legislative committee and adopted as a single act by the Legislature of 1905.

The commissioners were required to incorporate into the act all general public statutes of that session, and to submit the same, before publication, to a legislative committee composed of Senator A. C. Zollicoffer and Representatives A. W. Graham and R. B. Redwine, which was done.

This act became operative August 1, 1905, but, owing to the magnitude of the work, it could not be published by that date. It may not be amiss to call attention to the fact that the Revised Code was authorized by the Legislature of 1850. The commissioners made their report to the Legislature of 1854. The Code went into operation November 1, 1883, nearly eight months after the adjournment of the Legislature, and was not delivered for some months thereafter, although it was published by one of the largest law publishing houses in the United States. So the present delay is not without precedent.

The commissioners have adopted a new method of arrangement, which it is hoped will facilitate finding the law. In view of the prominent black-letter heads to all of the sections, and the information contained in the top line of each page, as well as the division of chapters into appropriate sub-chapters, it was considered that it would be a useless expense and unnecessarily add to the bulk of the volume to print at the beginning of the chapters the captions of sections, as was done in The Code and in the Revised Code.

No references have been made by foot or marginal notes to judicial interpretation of the statutes, as such notes were not contemplated or provided for by the legislation prescribing the duties of the commissioners.

The volume of legislation in the last twenty-two years, the period covered by our labors, made it impracticable to publish the work in one volume. The first volume contains the statutes of general application, and more particularly affecting our people as a whole, while in the second volume is collected those statutes relating largely to the political government of the commonwealth and of its several departments and institutions. There are also included in the second volume those statutes which it is customary to have printed and distributed in pamphlet form.

The original draft of the index is the work of the clerk of the commissioners, George P. Pell, Esq., and is much more elaborate and more carefully prepared than anything of the kind heretofore undertaken in any of our codifications.

An innovation has been made, in that for the first time the type metal from which the Revisal of 1905 is printed has been preserved, and will facilitate the publication of new editions as often as each recurring Legislature shall deem it wise, and at a minimum cost.

With these observations, the Revisal of 1905 (the name selected by the legislative committee) is submitted to a generous and appreciative public, trusting that, with the corrections and amendments which it received from the Legislature, and the sanction given to it by that body, it will contribute to an extension of the knowledge of our statutory law by our people, and to a just administration thereof by our courts.

THOMAS B. WOMACK,
NEEDHAM Y. GULLEY,
WILLIAM B. RODMAN.

DOCUMENT IV–15   TOURGÉE ON THE COMMON LAW, 1908

[In an article posthumously published in *The Green Bag: A Useless But Entertaining Magazine for Lawyers* in 1908, former North Carolina code commissioner and superior court judge, Albion W. Tourgée, followed a fashion by tracing the temporal roots of the common law to the Visigoths. He raced rapidly over the timeline, imagining the common law to be "untouched by Roman faith and uncorrupted by Roman thought" but "hidden in the heart of the Puritan." So much for the temporal roots of the common law. Jurisdictionally, he said, one border of the law of the land was equity, but Jeremy Bentham and John Austin in England, and Edward Livingston and David Dudley Field in America, he noted, had eliminated that arbitrariness. Procedurally, the common law suffered from weaknesses and unjustness in the forms of action. (Unfortunately, Tourgée admitted, modern code practice exacerbated these problems in some respects, "substituting for a half dozen forms of action, an infinity of inconclusive motions.") But one cannot define the common law by its cultural roots, its ever-changing scope of jurisdiction, or its procedural technicalities, wrote Tourgée. The distinctiveness of the common law arises from the fact that "it is linked in foundation and application with the common life." Its methodology is unique: it "has no 'rules' in the sense of fixed standards"; "it applies theoretically the universal principles of justice to every question coming within its scope, according to the conscience and wisdom of the judge, applied to specific conditions." Thus, the common law on Tourgée's view was always the same in principle and constantly changing in application, its flexibility arising from its adaptability to the ever-varying conditions of life.]

THE UNWRITTEN LAW AND WHY IT REMAINS UNWRITTEN
BY THE LATE ALBION W. TOURGÉE

THE babe that first sees the light within the domain of the English common law may well smile in its dreams. Above its cradle hovers a presence unmatched among human institutions for benignity and power. Already, before the breath of life had visited his nostrils, it had taken note of his existence and tenderly provided for his welfare and his rights. With the dawn of consciousness, it draws nearer to him. It hears his first inarticulate wail and provides for his proper nurture. It lays its behests on parent, guardian and nurse; protects him from neglect as well as malice, and even before he can speak himself, provides a friend who shall speak for him. As he grows in strength it puts into his hand a shield potent for his defence against all enemies. It makes the judge his servant to define his rights, and puts between him and the sovereign power the insurmountable presumption of incapacity. It will not hear his words, even of admission or self accusation, but puts in his baby hand the scepter and declares that "the king can do no wrong." Through childhood and youth it tenderly watches over his footsteps, clears the obstacles from his pathway and sees to it that he does not dash his foot against a stone. Little by little as he grows in power and discretion, it removes the barriers that restrict his action. It listens to his voice, trusts the testimony of his eyes, enlarges his capacity, enhances his responsibility, and prepares him by easy and successive steps for the more serious task and heavier burdens of manhood. It gives the power of the realm to enforce his rights, and demands concurrence of twelve of his peers before it will listen to any imputation of wrong doing against him.

In the battle of life it is with him. In the ancient mythology the "Queen of Heaven" watched over her favorite in the fierce onslaught of battle, warding off dangers which he did not see or was unable to prevent. Such a presence is the English Common Law to every champion in the arena of life. It clothes him in armor of proof; guards against surprise or ambush; bids him go boldly forward heedful only of his own footsteps and mindful of his own rectitude and watchfulness. It protects him from conspiracy and fraud, but refuses to shield him from the consequences of his own wrong, and requires him to come with clean hands to invoke its aid.

It guards him in slumber, but deserts him in sloth. In return for its faithfulness it demands vigilance, and of him to whom it grants relief it demands that he shall first do equity. While a reasonable doubt remains, the presumption of innocence is for him an impenetrable breastplate, warding off even the sting of imputation.

It puts a guardian angel at the threshold of the home, whose ever naked sword guards its holy mysteries against intrusion or inquisition. It protects the maiden in her love and the mother in her holiest right. It trudges with the child to school, gives the teacher authority and restrains his passion. Around the husband and the wife it folds the mantle of silence which none may penetrate, and which they themselves are powerless to lift. It protects the sanctuary but leaves the worshipper free. As many Mahometans as Christians enjoy its benefits and more believers in Brahma than Mahometans and Christians both. One-sixth of the habitable globe and one-third of its population acknowledges its sway. Twelve million square miles and four hundred million people constitute its empire. One-half the wealth of the world is in its keeping. It is the relentless foe of oppression and the sleepless guardian of individual right. Made the instrument of bondage, it serves unwillingly and with constant protest; as the nurse of liberty it is unfailing in assiduity. Tyrants hate its name; freemen bless its beneficence, and the world wonders at its mysterious potency.

Whence and what is this Common Law which is the distinguishing feature of Anglo-Saxon civilization the world over? Is it a peculiar system of rules, a specific part of the great field of jurisprudence which the English people have discovered and of which the rest of the world is ignorant? Such a presumption, though it is not lacking the authority of great names, is in the highest degree absurd. There is no striking difference in the so-called principles of the Common Law and the jurisprudence of other lands. The simple truth is, that legal principles are not a monopoly of any race or people—they belong to mankind. Almost every principle of the Common Law may be paralleled in the laws of other nations.

It is not a system of laws, but a method of applying law. Its distinctiveness does not arise from the excellence of its formulas or the eminence of its judges, but from the fact that it is linked in foundation and application with the common life. It is the impulse to self-judging which has made it so distinct. Born in the heart of the Visigoth on the rugged shores of the Caspian, it joined the functions of the judge and the legislator and devolved both upon the commune. The chief was president-judge and the whole tribe the court. In the Visigothic bund was the kernel of the American Republic.

Borne in barbaric triumph through the forests of central Europe, untouched by Roman faith and uncorrupted by Roman thought, it reached the shores of the North Sea. Pausing here awhile to gather strength, it poured over into Britain, from which it swept away every trace of Roman civilization and Celtic barbarism. Taking root upon the moors and under the greenwood trees of old England, nourished by Saxon frankness and made strong by Celtic stubbornness, holding its wittenagemote upon the village green and defending the common right against foes from without and usurpers from within; learning subtlety from the Roman and boldness from the Northman; guarded by the four seas that rage and foam about its white-walled home; softened by the light that shines from Calvary and strengthened by the echoes of the great Lawgiver's voice that comes to its ears across the slumbering centuries from the valley of curses and blessings; hidden in the heart of the Puritan; strengthened by the solitude and primeval grandeur of the New World's unsubdued expanse; blessing with unequaled prosperity those who proclaimed equality to all, the mainspring of English civilization is the Common Law we inherit, and which we have extended, harmonized, and replenished with unnumbered examples of its wisdom, beauty and beneficence. For this Common Law is no longer the Common Law of England, but the heritage and glory of Anglo-Saxon civilization.

But what are its limits? Of what is it composed? Where may its tenets be found? How may the Common Law be distinguished from that great mass of conventional regulation of human relations which constitutes the vast field of jurisprudence?

To no question which is met in preparation for the Bar is it so difficult to present a satisfactory and easily comprehended reply, unless it be that ever-to-remain unanswered query, "What is Equity?"

As to this latter question it is quite safe to say that nobody has been able to find a definition which would serve the subtlest legal practitioner under any other system, in determining where, in English law, Equity begins and where it ends. As a matter of fact its boundaries are as irregular as the line of a Virginia worm fence, and as unaccountable as the vagaries of the Mississippi on its winding way to the sea. Not only that, its boundaries are as shifting as the wave-lines on an ocean beach, and what constitutes a distinct and clearly defined equitable landmark to-day, by the course of legislation or decision disappears in the ocean of Common Law to-morrow. The nearest approach to a competent definition of this familiar legal term is the despairing conclusion of the father of American Equity-Jurisprudence, that "Equity is that portion of the law (he should have said the Common Law) which is cognizable only by a Court of Equity." In truth, Equity in a technical sense is simply a part of the Common Law which accident at first separated from the rest of its domain, and which a curious and unfounded fear of change has served to keep distinct in form in some jurisdictions, only in name in others, while in others still both form and name have been abandoned, and the law so divided in its functions has come at length to administer justice in the same form of action and by the same instrumentalities, no matter what the character of the relief sought.

In truth, Equity is best defined to be that portion of the Common Law which ignorance, stupidity and empiricism separated centuries ago from the body of legal principles and which it is one of the highest triumphs of modern learning under the lead of Bentham and Austin and their co-adjutors and disciples in England, and Livingstone, Field, and their co-workers in America, to have restored to proper relations with its long estranged kindred.

But what *is* this Common Law, of which the practitioner speaks so glibly, and very often, it is to be feared, very loosely, is still the question which constantly recurs to the puzzled student's thought?

It used to be said by the pilots on the great rivers of the West that one is never competent to take the wheel and be responsible for boat and passengers and cargo, until he could "put the river together,"—that is, begin at its source and give every landmark, its distance and bearing from any other to its mouth, or beginning at any point could go either way—in other words, to see the river from end to end. It is said, too, that no man can acquire this knowledge by the study of charts, but must gather it by constant observation, and has and can have no imitation of the progress he is making. After long experience and repeated failures, all at once, perhaps when walking the streets, lying in his bed or sometimes in a dream it flashes upon him, he "puts the river together"—the picture is complete—he sees the course and landmarks back and forth, up and down, and is ready for examination and license as a pilot.

There is some analogy between "putting the river together" and an adequate comprehension of what constitutes the Common Law.

There is probably no experienced practitioner who reads my words who does not remember the mist of uncertainty which hung over his early years of study, which no application to the text-books of the profession, no hint of any instructor, seemed able to penetrate. The Common Law was an incubus that hung over his consciousness, unsettled his conclusions, disappointed his hopes. He found himself baffled in every attempt to discover its nature, define its boundaries or assign it to its proper place in the science of judicature. Perhaps he even grew incredulous in regard to its existence, and came to regard it as a myth by which the elders of the profession consoled themselves for the existence of conditions for which they could not account. It is possible that—like an eminent practitioner who has pictured that period in unmistakable colors in a fancied life, they came to think of the "Common Law as a scientific term for unscientific nonsense."

Probably every practitioner recognizes the fact that a time came—he may not know how nor be able to specify time and place—when he thought and spoke of the Common Law with a certainty and comprehension he had never felt before, when he perceived, felt, knew, that it was a real factor of juridical thought and knowledge. All at once the pages of the reports were enlightened with it. He no longer felt surprised and confused by the opinions of the judges. He began to see the true significance of the maxim, "The law is what the judges judge it to be." He approved their reasonings with satisfaction, or controverted them with confidence. He *knew* the Common Law. He might not be able to define its limits, but found he had what he thought an instinctive knowledge of what it is and what it is not.

Under these circumstances it will not be expected that an absolutely exact definition of the Common Law will be attempted, though I by no means concur with those eminent jurists who believe such a definition impossible. I shall seek only to indicate some of the ordinary reasons for uncertainty, and consider some phases which I trust may enable the young practitioner more clearly and readily to apprehend the scope and character of our Common Law and understand how, without differing materially in the principles it enunciates, its effect upon the character of the peoples subjected to its influence are so remarkable as to justify the declaration that it is the keystone of Anglo-Saxon civilization.

And first I note as one of the reasons for this indistinctness of apprehension, the fact that the terms used in explanation or as synonymous equivalents, have been affected with a like indefiniteness. Leaving out of consideration that use of the term which makes the Common Law the equivalent of all English or American law, which is in fact only a synecdoche by which the distinguishing feature of Anglo-Saxon law is used to signify the whole, and that other use which applies the term to the general jurisprudence of any country, as well as that specific significance which is used to express the technical distinction between legal and equitable jurisdiction by designating the former as Common Law Courts, we find one term used almost universally in explanation of this most important factor of our jurisprudence, which is, if anything, a little more confusing than the term it is employed to explain. This term which I doubt not is on the lips of every professional hearer even before I utter it, is the *lex non scripta*. The Common Law we say first of all to the student, is the unwritten law of England.

One cannot but sympathize with the wondering incredulity with which the student listens to the astounding statement that the Common Law is that body of laws, principles, customs and traditions which have never been, and can never be reduced to writing, which yet may be found in the volumes of reports and which he is expected to glean from the works of elementary writers upon law. The idea of sending a man to search for unwritten law between the lids of a printed book is absurd enough to justify any sort of objurgation on the part of the student or the intelligent layman who would like to obtain, without a lifetime of application, some knowledge at least of the character, if not the extent, of the Common Law. Such a bit of self-contradictory explanation is small help to the learner, and it seems to be quite time that a profession boasting of its scientific character began to use definitions that really define. Yet, properly understood, the explanation throws not a little light upon the question under consideration. The unwritten portion of Anglo-Saxon judicature is indeed to be learned from books, yet those books do not declare the law. This unwritten law embraces, as every tyro knows, an immense proportion of our law. It is usually said to embrace all that has not been expressly formulated by some authorized law-making, or rather statute-prescribing, power.

But even this broad definition is too restricted. A very considerable portion of this *lex non scripta* is composed of the opinions of the courts construing specific statutes.

A very high authority has added materially to the complexity of the subject by declaring that the "*lex non scripta*" is law not written by the authority of law. Could confusion itself be worse confounding? If we keep on improving our definitions in this manner—and this is by a noted American judge—we shall soon have some conceited legal sensationalist asserting that the Common Law is unlawful law. The truth is that no law can be formulated except by authority of law. Common Law—the *lex non scripta*—is actually and truly unwritten still, just as much as it was when the opinions of the judges were perpetuated only by oral tradition, or in the case-book of the practitioner. But the volumes of the reports are not law. Neither are they, as has been sometimes declared, the evidence of what the law is. A paper-writing is *ipso facto*, evidence of a contract. The record of a court is evidence of what the court has done. But the volumes of reports are *not* evidence of what the unwritten law is, they are only evidence of what certain experts, at particular times and under certain conditions, believed the unwritten law to be.

The judge, so far as the construction of statutes or the formulation of non-statutory principles of law is concerned, is simply an authorized expert, while the text-writer is simply a voluntary or unauthorized expert. The process of development in the Common Law—the evolution of what we call Common Law principles—is of the simplest and most natural character. A decides that under certain conditions the law is thus and so: B endorses his opinion in a similar case, C in another and so on it may be for years, it may be for certain centuries, until there is established a line of decisions from which a general principle is deducible. This is said to be the law; yet it loses the character of law as soon as the conditions on which it rests are changed or its underpinning of logic fails. Such formulations are properly termed "opinions"—the opinions of experts. They hold good in the cases determined and are what we term authority in certain others, but their foundations are always open to assault.

By keeping this fundamental fact in view you will perceive that the whole field of equitable jurisdiction is a part of the *lex non scripta*, a part of that Common Law which distinguishes English judicature from all other systems, and which, though it may be gathered from books, has never been written and never can be written—meaning by the term "written" finally and authoritatively formulated.

But is nothing then ever settled at the Common Law? Theoretically, never: practically, a long line of decisions is much more difficult to flex or modify than a statute. A judge who would not hesitate to construe a statute out of all resemblance to what he may well know to be the legislative intent, upon the ground that the law-making power must have intended to act *justly*—knowing all the time that they really meant to act unjustly—would shrink back appalled from an attempt to overthrow a strong line of decided cases, though he might see clearly enough that the logic on which they rested, if it was ever good, had ceased to be conclusive.

As pertinent examples of this fact may be cited the Common Law forms of action. They were nearly always within the control of the court which administered them—always in England and usually in the United States. Every judge knew that they were harsh, unnecessary, unjust and oppressive. He knew that he was violating the highest function of the judge when he kicked a suiter [*sic*] out of court and made him pay costs for his attorney's error in declaring in covenant when he ought to have sued in assumpsit. He knew, too, that Equity was only another name for injustice when it required law to be asserted by piecemeal and the judge and chancellor played at shuttlecock with the suitor's rights, and the lawyer pocketed an equal fee for good or bad advice. If these forms had been newly prescribed by statute the court would unhesitatingly have pronounced them barbarous and intolerable outrages against the right of the citizen. But the fact that generations of judges had sanctioned this wrong lulled the voice of conscience, and permitted the ever-growing company of black-robed banditti. It is this fact which has made the administration of justice in almost all Anglo-Saxon nations more costly and burdensome than in any other land. The statement has recently been made, and I do not doubt its correctness, that the administration of justice in any leading city of the United States costs the people more than in the whole of France. The Common Law is a terrible enemy to the man whose rights are of small value and whose opponent has a long bank account. The corrupt judge is happily almost unknown to the Common Law, but its machinery must be lubricated with gold—its pinions like those of fine watches run smoothly only when pivoted on diamonds. And this defect the Code has in many cases increased rather than diminished by substituting for a half dozen forms of action, an infinity of inconclusive motions.

But a still more confusing element is that idea so easily obtained and so hard to be eradicated, that it is a body of usages and customs derived from days "to which the memory of man runneth not to the contrary," and deriving force and validity from the fact of ancientness. Indeed, the presumption of universal concurrence based on their contiguity is cited by almost every one who has written upon the subject, as the real basis of authority for the Common Law element of our jurisprudence.

Even a cursory examination of the present state of the law is sufficient to show neither of these presumptions is correct. Aside from ordinary principles of universal justice common to all systems of jurisprudence, there is but very little of the Common Law which derives any especial sanction from antiquity. What was the Common Law of ancient times has gradually crystallized into statutes, been negatived by express enactment, or rejected by the more enlightened judgment of modern times. Indeed it may be doubted if this familiar view of the source, character, and reason of the Common Law was ever anything more than a mythical theory intended to account for a system so unique that no juridical writer of any other land has been able to comprehend its character or operation. To the mind of the continental jurist, the Common Law is without sense or reason. He listens to the explanation of its beauties with a pitying smile. To the claim that the chiefest excellence of the Common Law lies in the fact that its rules are flexible, he responds with the unanswerable query, "What is the use of flexibility in a rule?" The idea is at variance not only with his notions of scientific accuracy, but also with ideas of law regarded as a rule or standard. What would one say of an elastic yardstick—one that gave sometimes a yard and sometimes an ell? Indeed, the Common Law itself regarded such variable yardsticks with such abhorrence that when used in traffic their employment became a crime.

The truth is that Common Law has no "rules" in the sense of fixed standards—the only sense, by the way, in which the term is properly used in judicature. It is on this fact that its distinctiveness depends.

Instead of employing fixed rules, it applies theoretically the universal principles of justice to every question coming within its scope, according to the conscience and wisdom of the judge, applied to specific conditions—this conscience being not a simple uniform, unmodulated impulse, but a judgment enlightened and informed by the actions of those under circumstances and conditions more or less analogous. In some cases analogies are so nearly identical that a continuous line of harmonious decisions result and we have what is termed a rule of the Common Law. By and by a new element is injected, a new condition arises which is inconsistent with the former determination, and the so-called rule disappears by the same process which called it forth.

Instead of being a finished product of a remote past, therefore, we see that the Common law is a constantly growing and constantly changing increment of all Anglo-Saxon law. What was the Common Law yesterday is not the Common Law to-day, and what is so accepted to-day, to-morrow's conditions may reverse. The flexibility of the Common Law is not then a flexibility of rule, but an inexhaustible adaptability of its machinery to the formulation of new rules to fit the ever-varying conditions of life. It is this fact that makes the Common Law not always the guarantor of liberty or the instrument of beneficent results, but a most efficient agent of oppression and the bulwark against which the tide of human progress not unfrequently breaks for long periods with unavailing force.

The Common Law is not a system of principles or maxims, but a peculiar system by which legal principles are formulated and applied. It is this fact which makes judicial power in any Anglo-Saxon society—in any English-descended community—so much more an important and notable element than in any other.

The judge has been the constant creator of law. About every constitution, ordinance, statute, has grown up a little system of law based upon continuous, conflicting, and perhaps finally settled adjudication. New social and scientific conditions have overthrown conclusions apparently the most securely fixed. The law-making power has been held in check by the fact that the power to construe rests in the hands through which alone its edicts can be enforced, and that justice, vague, intangible, undefined as it may be, controlling the mind of the judge, forbids it to do evil. It makes the judge also the reflection of the thought and manhood of his age and of the moral tone of his environment, which he in turn makes part and parcel of the Common Law he creates in the daily performance of his duties. The Common Law is not a specific, definable portion of English jurisprudence as so many commentators have sought to regard it, but is that over-rulingspirit, that genius of Anglo-Saxon individuality which subjects formulated law to restrictional and enabling construction, and creates or adapts whatever may be found needful to meet new conditions or supply the deficiencies of the enactments of the law-making power. It created Equity Jurisprudence; it formulated and has adapted popular government to all social conditions. It is the supplement—apparently a necessary and indispensable supplement—of parliamentary legislation and government by the people. It is a growth, not a creation—a continuing force, not a perfected science.

It is possible that this view of that distinguishing element of Anglo-Saxon civilization which we call the Common Law, may seem so new and incongruous with preconceived ideas to some, that a few illustrations of its continuing operation may be desirable to fix the truth more firmly in the mind. The volumes of the reports are so full of testimony upon this point that even the tyro could hardly go amiss in the search for them.

A hundred years or more ago a group of English colonists, having cut loose from the mother-country undertook the hazardous task, not merely of founding a new nationality, but of establishing one upon a new plan—to invent, indeed, a new form of government. They named the result the United States of America. Our government has sometimes been said to have been modelled on the constitution of Great Britain. English arrogance and American sycophancy have repeated this so often that there was actually danger of its being accepted as a fact had not one Englishman of wider views and truer knowledge shown its absurdity. Really, except the system of Common Law as a constructive, adaptive and harmonizing force, we derive very little of our governmental system from any source except the two centuries of experience of the American colonies. The most important feature and the one in which our government differs from all other systems, is that it put the judicial power above all others and authorized it to mark out and define the limits of executive and legislative power and distinguish between State and National authority. For twelve years that most august tribunal which the world has ever known—the Supreme Court of the United States—groped its way weakly and uncertainly along the path of its new duties. Eminent and able men sat upon its bench. The greatest negotiator of our revolutionary epoch, John Jay, and the brightest and most practical legal mind of the convention, James Wilson, were among its first judges. In four years it decided five causes. After ten years it had learned almost nothing of its own powers and duties. Twelve years after its organization a man of great brain, great will, and invincible integrity, John Marshall, was put at its head. The duty of defining State and National authority early claimed his attention and he enunciated this rule: "The Constitution of the United States must be strictly construed as regards the grant of power, but liberally construed as to the means by which such power may be exercised." Around this principle the government of the United States has crystallized. What was it? Simply a new principle of the Common Law—an application of the principle of justice to absolutely new conditions.

A decade and a half afterward the same great mind, dominated perhaps in some degree by the overwhelming personality of Webster, forged a chain which is fast growing to be shackle, in the definition of the relation of a private corporation to the State authority and applying to it without restriction or modification the inhibition of the National constitution in regard to the inviolability of contracts.

Around the Dartmouth College case has grown up a mass of Common Law adjudications having no other basis, which would of themselves probably fill a score of volumes, and whose influence on the business of the world during the last half century is simply incalculable.

The mass of Common Law decisions based on this opinion is hardly to be excelled in the history of English jurisprudence, except by that unwritten mercantile law which Mansfield half a century before had half borrowed and half invented to meet the exigencies of British commerce, then just developing into the leading interest of the British realm.

Another phase of our history offers a curious illustration of the continuing adaptability of the Common Law, not by the flexibility of its rules but by the adaptability of its organic character to the formulation of new ones. Slavery two centuries ago became, and until within a few years remained, the most important economical, social, and political factor of a large portion of the Union. In some of the Northern states it was, almost from the adoption of the Constitution, so restricted, antagonized, and subordinated by other interests, that its effect upon their legal development is hardly traceable. At the South, however, it left a peculiar impress, not more upon its statutory than on its unwritten law. Up to 1800 it had been, for some centuries at least, an accepted part of the unwritten Common Law that the presumption of freedom existed in favor of every man. The judges of the South in the due and proper exercise of the functions of the Anglo-Saxon jurist, because of the supreme importance of the institution of slavery and because of the fact that the slave was usually a person having a visible admixture of colored blood, reversed this rule as to such, and declared that the presumption as to them was that they were bondmen and the onus of proving that they were entitled to be free devolved upon them. In like manner the rule as to self-defence and provocation in case of assault were modified, impertinent language from a colored man, although he might be free, being held to afford and to be the same excuse for an assault, as a blow from a white man.

On these and other adjudications of similar character was built up the Common Law of slavery, the influence of which is to-day the most dangerous sentiment which yet remains to threaten the power of the Republic.

Another instance of like character, remarkable for its boldness yet accepted because of its justice and propriety, was the assertion by a distinguished judge of a Common Law admiralty jurisdiction over the commerce of the great lakes without any statutory authority.

It is but a few years since the new conditions of railroad transportation of passengers required the Supreme Court of the United States to reverse the former rule of the Common Law and make a new one. "The carrier of passengers by the dangerous instrumentality of steam," said the Court, "must be held to the highest degree of diligence consistent with existing and practicable safeguards." This has now become the Common Law of all English-speaking peoples.

In the arid regions of the West where questions affecting the distribution and supply of water are frequent, the courts by common consent apparently, have recognized and accepted the legal rules governing such transactions in India, where systems of irrigation have been in operation for thousands of years. But in daily practice the practitioner sees these rules reversed, modified, or new ones substituted in these days of scientific progress with a frequency that ought long ago to have shown the most unobservant that the Common Law was not a specific system of legal rules, but a universal method of formulating and applying legal principles adapted to infinitely varying conditions as seen by men of varying inheritance or acquired impulses.

A *ni si prius* judge in New Jersey decided that a bequest to Henry George to enable him to extend the knowledge of his Single Tax system was contrary to Common Law as tending to the subversion of good government. A hundred years ago this same principle was held to defeat the action of one of the most distinguished English scholars seeking to recover for the destruction of books and manuscripts by a mob. Fortunately, in the latter case, the appellate court had advanced far enough to declare that the Common Law needed a new rule, and that it was lawful always to advocate a change of political methods.

Thousands of such instances might be cited from the volumes of American reports showing clearly that this Common Law of which we boast is not a mere system of rules, but a method of formulating legal rules to which English jurisprudence owes the whole volume of its equity, and which is still enlarging, enriching, modifying, restricting and adapting the unwritten law to the swiftly changing conditions of modern life, is as stable as the human conscience and alert as the eye of science. As is always true of judicature it is at once a cause and consequence. Having its root in the peculiar individuality of the Visigoth, it both strengthened and was strengthened by British insularity. It nourished the colonizing spirit that sent continuous swarms from the parent hive, each having in it the strange instinctive germ of independent organization and self-directing power. The Common Law which was derived from the mother country has already received its fullest development in that newer England which rose out of the sea to protest against violation and debasement. What its future will be depends upon the character of those who administer it and the sentiment of the peoples whose servant it becomes. It is the mainspring of Anglo-Saxon progress and liberty, not because of any peculiar and inherent excellence, but because it offers a free and untrammeled opportunity for the expression of the popular will and conscience in the construction of laws and the adjustment of the individual rights to new conditions.

Thus far it has proved an insurmountable obstacle to eminence in our jurisprudence of men of alien birth. The Old World has sent us many brilliant minds which have deservedly taken the highest rank in other callings and professions, but hardly one has been able to surmount the obstacles which the Common Law jealously puts in the path of those who seek to approach her shrine without comprehending the spirit it represents. At every point where it has touched other systems of jurisprudence it has maintained its own distinctive character, but has drained them dry of every adaptable quality. On the plains of India it has assimilated the customs of a hundred peoples and the wisdom of a thousand ages. At the Cape of Good Hope it has ensnared the Dutchman in its toils and applied the law of Holland to the arid holding of the Boer. In Canada it has overcome the tenacious grip of French custom and tradition. Louisiana has become the land of its re-birth in that code which had its beginning in America in the brain of Livingstone, the young New Yorker toiling in his dingy office in the Crescent City.

It is worth something to be enlisted in the service of such a power, and it is well to remember that while one may be a fair practitioner and from a business point of view a successful one with but scant comprehension of the scope and glory of the Common Law, yet he can never become eminent at any English bar, or worthily administer the law in any tribunal of English-speaking people until the unwritten law is written in his heart, and the Common Law rises instinctively in his mind when he hears the tale of injustice or misfortune.

It is not the facts of the Common Law that have made it a priceless boon to humanity and the beacon light of civilization, but its spirit. It adopts the truth whether it be found in palace or hovel. It bows submissively to the verdict of the twelve—it matters not how humble, but bids defiance to the fiat of the king.

A noted American jurist when asked near the close of a long and honorable career what facts connected with it afforded him the most gratification, replied: "I have corrected one error which crept into the Common Law more than a century ago, which had received the endorsement of all English courts during that time—and that correction has now been accepted at Westminister." It may not be the privilege of every practitioner to heal so ancient an error, but it is within the power of the humblest to strengthen and confirm some beneficent tendency of that spirit which is a guardian angel to the brave and free and a malign influence only to the sluggard, the craven and the slave.

MAYVILLE, NEW YORK.

Document IV–16   Winston's Speech, 1913

[Judge Robert W. Winston in this address to the state bar association in 1913 focused on whether North Carolina should embark upon procedural reforms, ones along the lines of procedural reform in England and in a few leading states in America. He pointed out that *The Code of Civil Procedure* had not met expectations because it regulated too many details and thus became the subject of technical construction. He observed that the judicature acts of England in the last quarter of the nineteenth century allowed the judges to make all rules and regulations governing the details of practice and emphasized that this new provision was the key change in English procedure. And he concluded that North Carolina should adopt the same approach: "All statutes regulating the mere details of practice should be summarily repealed and the Supreme Court should formulate and promulgate rules regulating such details for the guidance of the courts."[487]]

"POPULAR DISCONTENT WITH JUDICIAL PROCEDURE."

Gentlemen of the North Carolina Bar Association: . . .

EFFORTS TO SIMPLIFY PROCEDURE.

The North Carolina Constitution of 1868 abolished feigned issues and wiped out the old distinction between actions at law and suits in equity. It likewise made provision for a Code Commission of three members to prepare rules of practice and procedure accordingly. V. C. Barringer, A. W. Tourgee and W. B. Rodman were chosen by the Convention as such Code Commissioners. They forthwith entered upon the discharge of their duties and as a result North Carolina fell into line with New York as a Code State. The old practitioner stood aghast at this innovation; while the heart of the reformer was made glad in anticipation of speedy trials, quick justice and the end of legal jargon and quibbles.

Both have been disappointed. The Code has not met the expectation of its friends. This is perhaps due to the fact that it came in under alien political conditions. Its adoption was in the face of strong opposition and its early interpretation by Bench and Bar was, for the most part, by no means in accord with its principles. Nor did we then know what we have since learned from experience and from the smooth-running English judicature act; that any Code of procedure which undertakes to regulate all the details of practice may "itself become the subject of technical construction and lead to the miscarriage of justice." A special committee of the American Bar Association in their report on the causes of delay and uncertainty in our judicial administration declared, in ten words, the chief causes of such conditions, to be: "Complex Procedure, Inadequate Judicature, Procrastination, Retrials, Unreasonable Appeals and Uncertain Law." A sad commentary to be sure, upon Code practice!

The average life of a law suit in America is from one and half to six years. How sharp a contrast these conditions present to what we find in the Mother Country. In the English Digest for full twenty years the title "Appellate Procedure" does not appear. There is no Appellate Procedure. New trials in England upon points of evidence are unknown; whereas in America, as Prof. Wigamore points out, the "sporting theory of justice," the instinct of "giving the game fair play" is so rooted in the profession that most of us take it as a fundamental legal tenet, and the judges are but umpires in the great legal game which is degenerating into a quest for error.

The Bar Association of nearly every State in the Union and particularly the American Bar Association, together with learned law professors and writers, are at this time earnestly endeavoring to correct these evils which have fastened themselves upon the administration of justice to its great reproach.

We shall presently come to consider and discuss the 1912 civil practice acts of New Jersey, and a similar act recommended to Governor Sulzer by a committee of five distinguished New York lawyers appointed by the Legislature of that State, and to contrast them with the procedure and practice in North Carolina. Just now I beg to call your attention to some of the merits of the Code of Procedure in this State. Let it be understood that in the administration of the law in North Carolina we now have some of the best things for which enlightened and patriotic members of the Bar elsewhere are so stoutly contending. For example, we have but one form of action; we have no trouble with parties to an action. If a person interested will not join as plaintiff we make him defendant. Our pleadings are few and simple. They consist of complaint and answer and occasionally of a demurrer, if a legal point is presented. Our Supreme Court has generally construed pleadings very liberally in the interest of substantial justice. The law governing counter-claims is likewise very liberal, but not so much so as modern practice acts provide. We have no writs of error and no bills of exception. The party desiring to appeal excepts in open court and gives notice of appeal. The trial judge settles the case and the Clerk sends the case so settled and a copy of the record to the Supreme Court. It may be observed that in England not only the notes of the Court Stenographer but of the trial judge are printed and the latter control on appeal. So also one may examine his adversary before the trial, or he may call on him before trial to admit a certain piece of evidence, and, if he refuse, his adversary is taxable with the cost of making the necessary proof. If a controversy arises, the parties to it may agree upon the facts, and by a simple affidavit without summons or pleadings, the matter is called to the attention of the Court and judgment entered, which is binding upon all the parties and is the final determination of the matters set forth therein.

The State Bar Association of Missouri through a select committee has recently submitted tentative suggestions for expediting business and administering justice in the courts of that State. Among other recommendations we find the following:

"That term bills-of-exception be abolished; that motions in arrest of judgment be abolished; that motions for new trials before the trial court be abolished; that the distinction between the record and the record proper be abolished, and that affidavits for appeal be likewise abolished."

In North Carolina we are troubled with none of these matters; they have long since been abolished. True, we have troubles and difficulties in the administration of the law, and these we shall presently consider and suggest some remedies. But first let us see how other jurisdictions have simplified their procedure, expedited trials and dealt with purely technical objections.

MODERN ENGLISH PRACTICE.

Prior to the year 1873 miscarriages of justice and delays in the courts of England had become so intolerable and proverbial that novelists and satirists found fertile fields for their caustic pens. The public conscience became aroused and in that year a reform of the judicial procedure of England was instituted. The judicature act which was then enacted and subsequently amended, has operated so well that English Courts are now models both as to the speedy trials of cases and the administration of substantial justice. An English "Court House" is strictly a business affair, at least those in London are. Imagine a long hallway ten feet wide, on either side rooms of very plain construction and about 30 by 80 feet—large enough to hold in the neighborhood of only about 100 people besides judge, jury, litigants and lawyers, and all these sitting on benches and not upon chairs, and you have a picture of the High Court and of the Court of Appeals of England.

In these rooms, some forty or fifty in number, all courts are in simultaneous session—both the High Court or Trial Courts, and the Court of Appeals. The case of Jesup vs. Jessup and another was on trial before Mr. Justice Buckmill, as I entered one of these high courts. The plaintiff was suing his wife for divorce and in the same action had joined as co-respondent a wealthy Scotch nobleman, charging him with alienating her affections and asking damages on account thereof. Mr. Marshall Hall was the plaintiff's solicitor, while Mr. Duke, K. C., was for the defendant. These gentlemen summed up for about 30 minutes each. The case was called at noon and before adjournment the day following it had ended in a verdict for the defendant. You may be sure that there was no delay in the trial of this case.

The judicature acts of England made a clean sweep of all the existing procedure, substituting a few simple statutes relating to the general principles of procedure, and at the same time empowered and directed the judges themselves to make all rules and regulations governing the details of practice. *This provision is the real change in English procedure.* These rules are not rigid and inflexible. They may be changed and are changed each year as the experience of the judges dictates, or as justice demands. The theory of an English trial is that a case is always in the same court, whether it be the High Court in which the case originated, or the Court of Appeals to which it is finally carried. The result is that no case can be dismissed because it is in the wrong court; nor because, in the Court of Appeals, some portion of the record or of the evidence has not been certified to said tribunal. Under the practice in England there are practically no exceptions to evidence and a new trial is never granted unless the court of last resort find not only error but prejudicial error. The judges of the highest courts announce their opinions orally from the Bench, citing but few authorities, and the opinion so announced is taken down by the court reporter. It will thus be seen that the secret of the reformation of court procedure in England lies in the fact that much power, authority and responsibility is given to the judges to whom is committed the entire procedure of the Kingdom. These judges are appointed for life and are men specially trained for the work, and who act not only as judges, but in a large measure as law givers. The rules of practice in our Federal Equity Courts recently promulgated by the Supreme Court of the United States, are modeled after the modern English Equity practice. Three of the judges of our Supreme Court were appointed a committee to investigate English procedure. They did so and the result is a few simple rules which expedite the business of the courts and take the place of the 94 cumbersome, involved, and prolix rules of equity which had clogged the Equity Dockets since the foundation of our government. It is indeed a long step from the bill, cross-bill, supplemental bill, amended bill and the other mazes of old equity practice, to these new business-like rules. Congress will undoubtedly pass House Resolution 26462, vesting power in the Supreme Court of the United States to prescribe rules for the simplification of Pleading and Procedure in the inferior Federal Courts.

MODERN CODE PROCEDURE IN THE UNITED STATES.

Five years ago it would not have been thought a thing credible that New Jersey, the contented home of trusts and the sheltering rock for fatherless corporations generally, would today be a pioneer in reform of judicial procedure; yet such is a fact. The "Practice Act" of New Jersey is a thorough and drastic statute regulating court procedure, simplifying the administration of the law and expediting the trial of causes. Let us now consider some of the most advanced features of this "Practice Act" of New Jersey.

Its aim is to prevent delays in trials; to abolish technicalities and to simplify procedure in courts.

. . . It likewise provides that the Supreme Court shall prescribe rules for that Court, for the circuit courts and courts of common pleas, to give effect to the provisions of the Practice Act, and for otherwise simplifying judicial procedure, and that the rules of the court so promulgated shall supersede all statutory and common law regulations heretofore existing. . . .

It likewise provides that an appeal is a step in the cause and is deemed to remove to the appellate court the entire record of the cause, and all orders, proceedings and documents, whether or not they are included in the transcript of the record, sent to that court. . . . The rules of court prepared by the New Jersey Court of Appeals under the Practice Act partake of the spirit of the act itself: they declare that these rules are to facilitate business to advance justice, and that they may be relaxed or dispensed with by the Court in any case where it shall be manifest that a direct adherence will work surprises or injustice. Forms of Pleadings accompany the rules. . . .

This in substance is the Practice Act of New Jersey. In it one may see much of the directness and single-mindedness of that student of history, the former Governor of New Jersey, the now President of the United States. The States of Kansas, Connecticut, New York, and others are either now considering or have already passed similar acts.

SOME TENTATIVE SUGGESTIONS.

I have now arrived at the most delicate and difficult part of what I dare to say to this Association. Can North Carolina profit by the Practice Acts of England and of New York, New Jersey, Connecticut and other States? Are the conditions in this State such that we can adopt some or most of their provisions? Do North Carolina people, "the freest of the free," says Bancroft, still worship liberty to such an extent that they are unwilling to entrust power and authority to their judges, even at the price of the abolition of technicalities and of securing more speedy trials in the courts?

Are we not reforming over-much? It is not the function of the judge to declare the law according to the golden metewand of the law and not by the crooked cord of discretion? The masters of the law have said that to avoid an arbitrary descretion [sic] in courts, it is indispensable that they should be bound down by strict rules and precedents which serve to point their duty in any particular case that comes before them. And "Ubi jus incertum, ibi jus nullum" comes sounding down the ages. Nor should we forget that Montesquieu, the father of modern enlightened jurisprudence, cautions law-makers against too hasty adoption of laws unsuited to the genius of a people. In his "Spirit of Laws" he declares that "men are governed by various things,—climate, religion, law, governmental maxims, precedents, morals, manners, and from all of these are formed as a resultant the general social spirit." The laws are the nerves of this body politic; they must correspond to the nature and uses of the Organs they animate. They are dependent on certain elements which man cannot change, and on certain others which he can change only after many efforts, and very slowly.

"They must have relations to the physical characteristics of a country, the climate, frigid, torrid or temperate—to the nature of the land, its situation, its extent, to the people's mode of life—they must have relations to the degree of liberty that the constitution can admit of; to the religion of the inhabitants, their inclinations, their wealth, their number, their commerce, their morals, their manners. Finally, they have relations one to another, their origin, to the aim of the legislature to the order of things under which they were established." All of these relations taken together form what Montesquieu calls "The Spirit of the Law."

Keeping steadily in view this admonition of the masters of the law, we approach a consideration of this delicate question. With much diffidence and due regard for the opinion of others who may differ with me, I submit the following suggestions as to the necessary changes in our court procedure. No action should be dismissed because it has been begun in the wrong court. . . . Nor should an action be dismissed because the plaintiff has mistaken his remedy; he should be allowed to amend. . . . All statutes regulating the mere details of practice should be summarily repealed and the Supreme Court should formulate and promulgate rules regulating such details for the guidance of the courts. . . .

SONS OF ZERUIAH MUST BE DETHRONED.

When Cromwell made an ineffectual attempt to reform the law and procedure of his country, he was driven to confess with a sigh that "the sons of Zeruiah are too hard for us." How technical and barbarous those old days were, to be sure. Thus we read that the Court of Common Pleas would not consider an affidavit because the barrister referred to therein was not designated as "esquire," *Messer v. Molynex*, cited in *Lee v. Brough, I Wis.* 245. The room in which the Court of Common Pleas had always been held became very cold and "if it might have been done, the court had been moved a little into a warmer place." But the Lord Chief Justice would not hear of it, conceiving it "against Magna Charta which says that the Common Pleas shall be held *in certo loco*, or in a certain place with which the distance of an inch from that place is inconsistent, and all the pleas would be *coram non judice*." *North, Life of Lord Keeper Guilford* (2d ed.) i 185. When the judges of England met to pass upon the points of law involved in the trial of Lord Morley for murder, the first question discussed was how they ought to dress for such an occasion, *Kelyng* 53. On the trial of the regicides for high treason, the point which gave the judges the most trouble was whether the indictment ought to charge that Charles I was killed in his own reign or in the reign of his successor. *Kelyng* 10.

But the day of Red Tape and the circumlocution office is gone and the whole world is instinct with a desire for equal and exact justice unhampered by formalism or over-refinement. Nor can the pains-taking legal reformer be longer laughed out of court. Such eminent, and practical scholars as Roscoe Pound of the Law Department of Harvard and others are devoting their best energies to this great problem, with much success; and, as we have seen such conservative jurisdictions as England, New York, and New Jersey in actual practice, are demonstrating the wisdom of the new and modern procedure. In this upward and unselfish movement the Bar will not be laggards. The real lawyer has ever been the conservative force of civilization and he will continue to be this. But he will be something more. He it is who will guide and direct the movement of that righteous remnant of our State in its quest for truth, justice and equality and which must not fail, for "as a terebinth tree and as an oak, whose substance is in them, though they be cut down, so the stock of that burned tenth shall be a holy seed."...

Document IV–17 Clark's Speech, 1914

[Chief Justice Walter Clark suggested in this speech that it was time to revert to the original intent of *The Code of Civil Procedure*, abandoning rotation of superior court judges and deciding all pre-trial matters of law through the county clerk of court with an appeal to the superior court judge in chambers. He also advocated a doctrine of harmless error to reduce the number of new trials.

Why did North Carolina need these and other reforms in the administration of justice? According to Clark, "[c]ivilization is simply a search for greater efficiency." Perhaps by "civilization," he was thinking of businesses. So, he explained, "our courts do not measure up, in their actual operation, to the economic demand of the age for efficiency." Apparently, doing justice took much time, and, as Clark noted, "[t]ime is money." Thus, there was "popular disapproval of [the] obsolete methods" of the courts.

As Clark's adages implied, "scientific," legislatively-authorized, judicial procedure arose in the aid of jurisdictions (whatever their traditions and their peoples) which had industrialized and citified during the nineteenth century in America. This was why the code did not suit North Carolina's ravaged economy in 1868. Perhaps reform procedure would have aided the administration of justice for anonymous teeming masses who drove the age of assembly lines and bureaucracies in the early 20th century, as it had purportedly suited Northern industrialization in prior decades. But did the people of North Carolina live homeless lives in heartless cities when Clark spoke to our state's lawyers in 1914? Was this former candidate for national political office thinking rather on a national or an international scale when he spoke of these things to state leaders?

Clark also alluded to reforms he would recommend, had he more time to elaborate on them, including the end of citation to precedents, the codification of substantive law, the abandonment of teaching the common law in law schools, and the rejection of judicial review.[488]]

Address of Chief Justice Clark on Reform in Law and Legal Procedure Before the State Bar Association at Wrightsville, June 30, 1914.

Mr. President and Gentlemen of the North Carolina Bar Association— ...

Civilization is simply a search for greater efficiency.... Success depends upon it.... In all the world there is but one profession which stands still, and that is ours....
I have only time to point out some of the things in which, in North Carolina, we are lacking in efficiency... Our system of rotating the judges is utterly indefensible....

When the Code of Civil Procedure was adopted in 1868, it provided, as it still does in most of the Code States, that the complaint should be served within twenty days after the issuance of summons, and that all the pleadings should be made up before the clerk, and that only issues of fact should be transferred to the docket at term time to be passed upon by the jury, and that the judgment of the clerk upon issues of law should be appealed to the judge at chambers. This was stricken out in 1870 because, owing to the condition of the country, instead of expediting the trial of causes it was considered advisable to delay judgment. We should now revert to the original system of permitting the clerk to pass upon the pleadings and all other matters until issues of fact are made up, when the cause should be transferred to the trial docket at term. There should be an appeal to the judge at chambers from the decision of the clerk on issues of law. This could readily be done should we revert to the system which then obtained of the judge holding only the courts of his own district.

There should be, as already said, stringent prohibition against any appellate court granting a new trial for any error, unless it is apparent that such error reasonably brought about the verdict and judgment appealed from.

For many centuries under the English law justice was denied or made dilatory and expensive by a system which divided causes of action into trover, detinue, replevin, case, assumpsit, covenant and many other forms of action, and divided remedies into actions at law and suits in equity by means of which if the plaintiff's lawyer should guess the wrong form of remedy the case was thrown out of court at great loss of time and expense, with the right to guess again at a new form of action. It is difficult to conceive how any intelligent people could have endured this state of things. In 1868, when the system was abolished here, the older lawyers felt greatly aggrieved at the destruction of the technical learning which they had spent many years in acquiring and which gave them a great advantage over new comers at the bar. They looked forward to Democratic success to restore the old system, but when that came in 1872, the younger members of the bar understood the situation and prevented the Code of Civil Procedure from being abolished. The friends of the older system, however, obtained from the courts a ruling by which if a case was erroneously brought before the clerk when it should have been brought to term, or vice versa, the action would be dismissed at term and the party would bring his new action in the court from which he had just been dismissed. This was cured by a statute. But we have another relic of the former system still with us in the fact that, if an action is brought before a justice of the peace and on appeal it is adjudged that it should have been brought to term, instead of going on to try the cause in that court the action is dismissed and the plaintiff has to bring a new action to the same court from which he is dismissed. The Supreme Court has held both ways upon the point, but the matter should be settled by a statute similar to that which applies when an action brought before the clerk which should have been brought to term is on appeal or otherwise before the judge at term.

There should also be a statute which will enable parties to make the summons returnable before the clerk, as all summonses should be, with power to the clerk to enter judgment when there is no real defense. In this way many actions to foreclose mortgages, to recover judgment upon debt or personal property and the like would not go upon the docket of the Superior Court at term at all.

Another statute might require the plaintiff in ejectment to set out his title upon which he seeks to recover and require the defendant to answer, admitting or denying the allegations of the complaint and setting out specifically his chain of title, giving the judge power to impose costs upon the defendant when he denies an allegation which he ought to have admitted.

This might be made broad enough to cover other actions.

There is one most potent cause in the delay in the trial of causes in the statute passed since the war know[n] as the "Spears Act," which restricts the judge in limiting the length of speeches by counsel. In England and all the States of this country, except Iowa and North Carolina, the judges are charged with the duty of restricting the length of the speeches of counsel. The statute depriving the judges of this power was passed at a time when the occupants of the bench were not in accord with the majority of the bar, and, indeed, with the majority of the white people of the State. There is no longer any cause to continue it. It has caused untold expense to the public by trebling and quadrupling the time required in the trial of causes, and at the same time has entailed upon counsel a vast amount of useless labor since clients now expect all their counsel to speak and for as long a time as clients desire. This extra work is a waste of time and a useless tax both upon the bar and the public. We cannot too soon restore the former system which prevails everywhere else except in Iowa, and there, according to the American Law Review, when counsel begin to address the jury the judge retires to a billiard room or sometimes hears causes at chambers; indeed, we have heard that a similar practice has sometimes obtained in this State. Judges here, as elsewhere, come from the bar and are in sympathy with their brethren, and have never been overdisposed to unduly restrict the length of speeches of counsel.

There are many other details in the administration of both the civil and criminal dockets which it would be useless to elaborate at this time. They have been suggested in the letters which I have received from my brethren and will readily occur to every practitioner. I think that the remedies I have suggested are the chief ones, and if adopted will bring about all the others.

The best system that has ever been devised for the ascertainment of disputed issues of facts is trial by jury, especially when it has been stripped of its most objectionable feature by the substitution of a verdict by three-fourths approved by the judge in lieu of the unanimity formerly required and when the jurors have been selected with proper care. But the spectacle often presented of days taken to procure a jury in capital cases strikes all intelligent men as inexcusable. It shows an utter lack of efficiency. The best remedy for this is what is known as a struck jury. In capital cases, and, indeed, in all other cases where either party desires it or the judge shall so order, a venire is drawn, in the presence of parties or their counsel, by the clerk beforehand. As each name comes out of the box, objections for cause may be shown until there are twenty-four names left on the panel, and then each side, whether in criminal or civil cases, has the right to strike off six names without cause shown, and the twelve remaining jurors are certified and summoned to be in the court room when the case is called for trial. In this way no one loses time from his business to attend court because he is on a venire. Only the twelve attend who are selected. To prevent the possible absence by unavoidable cause of any of the twelve, fourteen or even sixteen may be left on the panel and summoned, of whom at the trial the parties can alternately reject without cause until twelve are left.

In regard to the reforms which we need we may well recall that President Wilson says that "Back of every reform is the means of getting it."

To this end there will be necessary to submit an amendment adding to Article IV of our Constitution (which article covers the Judicial Department) an amendment similar to that which we have added to the last section of Article VII, to-wit: "The General Assembly shall have full power by statute to modify, change, or abrogate any and all the provisions of this article and substitute others in their place except Section 1 (abolishing the distinctions between law and equity and feigned issues) and Section 21 (fixing the terms of the Judges of the Supreme and Superior Court)." This would leave it open to the people through their legislature to abolish the rotating system and make the other changes which I have suggested, and all others which from time to time may commend themselves to public approval.

A great cause of delay and provocative misunderstandings between counsel is the present system of settling cases on appeal. Instead of lengthening, as we have been doing, the time within which the case on appeal and counter case should be served and the time in which the judge should settle the case, we should shorten those periods. With the requirement that each judge shall ride his own circuit we could return to the original requirement of the Code that the case on appeal shall be served within five days, the countercase within three days, and that the judge should settle the case, if there is disagreement, within ten days. We should add the provision which obtains in England and Germany that the case on appeal shall be docketed in the Supreme Court within twenty days after adjournment of the trial court.

There are collateral matters which I have not now the time to discuss. For instance, in all other countries than those which derive their legal system from England precedents are not allowed to be cited. Under our system of reports the accumulation of volumes is such that no private library can have them all and but few public libraries. We not only have digests but we have digests of digests. No lawyer can consult all the precedents, and if he did he can find about as many on one side of any question as on the other. We must some day come to the remedy which was adopted by Justinian and Napoleon in their Codes and which obtains in all the continental countries of Europe. We must codify our laws. In North Carolina we have 166 volumes of reports and these are already being added to at the rate of 3 or 4 volumes per year. In some States they are adding 10 volumes or more per year. A committee of three well-informed lawyers could condense all the law of our 166 volumes of reports into about 3 volumes. This will be done some day, but it is useless to discuss this now, for the profession has not yet taken hold of this necessity.

Our law schools are necessarily not progressive. Its teachers are hampered by the fact that they cannot say what the law ought to be, but merely what the courts have held it to be; still our court has been asked by some of the teachers to restore Blackstone in its entirety to the course, when all of Blackstone that is still law is in the course. Feudal tenures were abolished in 1660, more than two and a half centuries ago, and yet Blackstone with all the minutiae of those tenures with information as to *de donis*, *quia emptores* and other obsolete matter was required to be memorized by law students in this State up to a recent period.

Another matter which I have not time to discuss is the power exercised by the courts, without any authority named in the Constitution of setting aside statutes on the ground that they are unconstitutional. If a legislature should not observe the Constitution in the enactment of statutes the supervision lies with the people in electing another legislature or congress. It is impossible that we should continue to permit 3 judges at Raleigh or 5 judges at Washington to set up their views in opposition to the Executive, to the legislature and the public opinion that is behind the latter and by a majority of one vote negative the public will. This situation has brought about the adoption of the recall of the judges in eight States and the movement will spread unless this assumption of authority is abandoned. Some years ago in an address before your body at Morehead I expressed the opinion that the safest remedy was a constitutional amendment that the judges should not set aside an act of the legislature if more than one judge dissented. This provision has since been incorporated into the Constitution of Ohio. Some day the question may be presented in North Carolina. We had a narrow escape a dozen years ago when it was contemplated that a majority of the Supreme Court of this State might hold the suffrage amendment, known as the "Grandfather Clause," unconstitutional and invalid. It may be well for thoughtful lawyers to consider what is the most appropriate remedy before it is sharply and unexpectedly presented.

That our courts do not measure up, in their actual operation, to the economic demand of the age for efficiency is well known. Our judges are rarely lacking in legal knowledge. Sometimes they are lacking in executive ability, and those who have this ability are hampered by the customs and practice of past ages. The evil is here. Time is money and nowhere is this more true than in the trial of causes. Every moment of the time of the court costs money and it has been estimated that three-fourths of that time could be saved. I think Mr. Taft is one of those who have made this statement. There is not only the time of the parties and witnesses in a case on trial, but the time of the parties and witnesses of cases that are waiting for trial, or who have to attend court term after term without a trial. To render the courts more efficient is the demand which the people are making and the bar must respond.

When I was on the Superior Court, a witness was ruled out because his evidence was merely hearsay. Counsel protested, saying that the witness was one of the best men in the county. I remarked that the objection was not to the character of the witness, but to nature of his testimony, that the law required the "best evidence the nature of the case would admit of." He replied, "It is the very best I could get and I have ransacked the neighborhood." I may not have suggested the best remedies but they are the best I could find. It devolves upon our profession, in their wisdom and great experience, to discuss the evils of our present system and to discover and present the best remedies to the legislature for adoption.

Brethren, I thank you for your attention.

Document IV–18   Prohibition on Local Acts, 1917

[Law reformers during the Progressive Era in North Carolina jump-started the displacement of the common law by advocating for an amendment to the state constitution that required the general assembly to engage primarily in legislation by general statute on many matters of local government law, rather than to run the state by private, local, and special acts.[489] This amendment was ratified and the prohibition on local acts on many subjects of local government went into effect on January 10, 1917. The same amendment forbade the creation of most corporations by special act.]

AN ACT TO AMEND THE CONSTITUTION OF THE STATE OF NORTH CAROLINA.

The General Assembly of North Carolina do enact:

SECTION 1. That the Constitution of the State of North Carolina be and the same is hereby amended in manner and form as follows:

I. By adding at the end of Article II a new section, to wit:

"SEC. 29. The General Assembly shall not pass any local, private or special act or resolution:

"Relating to the establishment of courts inferior to the superior court:

"Relating to the appointment of justices of the peace:

"Relating to health, sanitation and abatement of nuisances:

"Changing the names of cities, towns and townships;

"Authorizing the laying out, opening, altering, maintaining or discontinuing highways, streets or alleys;

"Relating to ferries or bridges;

"Relating to non-navigable streams;

"Relating to cemeteries;

"Relating to the pay of jurors;

"Erecting new townships, or changing township lines, or establishing or changing the lines of school districts;

"Remitting fines, penalties and forfeitures, or refunding moneys legally paid into the public treasury;

"Regulating labor, trade, mining or manufacturing;

"Extending the time for the assessment or collection of taxes or otherwise relieving any collector of taxes from the due performance of his official duties or his sureties from liability;

"Giving effect to informal wills and deeds;

"Nor shall the General Assembly enact any such local, private or special act by the partial repeal of a general law, but the General Assembly may at any time repeal local, private or special laws enacted by it.

"Any local, private or special act or resolution passed in violation of the provisions of this section shall be void.

"The General Assembly shall have power to pass general laws regulating matters set out in this section."

II. By adding at the end of section eleven of Article IV the following: "and the General Assembly may by general laws provide for the selection of special or emergency judges to hold the superior courts of any county or district, when the judges assigned thereto by reason of sickness, disability, or other cause, is unable to attend and hold said courts, and when no other judge is available to hold the same. Such special or emergency judges shall have the power and authority of regular judges of the superior courts, in the courts which they are so appointed to hold; and the General Assembly shall provide for their reasonable compensation."

III. By striking out section one of Article VIII and substituting therefor the following:

"SECTION 1. No corporation shall be created nor shall its charter be extended, altered, or amended by special act, except corporations, for charitable, educational, penal, or reformatory purposes that are to be and remain under the patronage and control of the State; but the General Assembly shall provide by general laws for the chartering and organization of all corporations, and for amending, extending, and forfeiture of all charters, except those above permitted by special act. All such general laws and special acts may be altered from time to time or repealed; and the General Assembly may at any time by special act repeal the charter of any corporation."

IV. By striking out section four of Article VIII, and substituting therefor the following:

"It shall be the duty of the Legislature to provide by general laws for the organization of cities, towns, and incorporated villages, and to restrict their power of taxation, assessment, borrowing money, contracting debts, and loaning their credit, so as to prevent abuses in assessment and in contracting debts by such municipal corporations." . . .

Document IV–19 Clark/Mordecai Exchange, 1917

[In this exchange of notes in 1917, Chief Justice Walter Clark deprecated the influence in American legal education of Sir William Blackstone and Sir Edward Coke, two favorites of Trinity law professor, Samuel Mordecai, while Professor Mordecai graciously and wittily deflected the barbs.]

November 17, 1917.

Dean S. F. Mordecai,

My dear Dean: You have already read it doubtless, but if not, I think you will find it interesting to read the article on Sir William Blackstone in the 11th. (latest) Ed. of Encyclopedia Brittanica. It may interest your Law Class also to call it to their attention.

There are two other matters in regard to Blackstone which are characteristic, but which are not mentioned in this article. When he was elected to Parliament, nominally by a constituency of less than 300 voters but in reality appointed by the owner of the borough, the most strenuous thing he did was to oppose the passage of an Act to repeal the law requiring Court records and pleadings to be in dog latin, and to substitute therefor English, upon the ground that "It would make lawyers less learned." You will recall also that in the 4 Commentaries he said that burning witches to death was required by Scripture and that it was to contradict Divine Revelation to contend that there were not witches. This too on the very eve of the American Revolution.

I have always felt that the influence of Blackstone and Coke has had a very narrowing effect upon our Profession. It may interest your students at least to see the estimation in which these two writers have been held in England.

I hope you are having a pleasant and successful session.

Most truly yours,

Walter Clark.

Durham, N. C., Nov. 23d, 1917.

My dear Judge Clark: I am obliged to you for your letter and inclosure. It would be of no use my reading the article on Blackstone. . . .

I don't doubt that my stomach would be turned should I read the article in the Enc. Brit., but it would not be turned against Blackstone. . . .

Blackstone is not to be judged by his career in parliament. . . .

. . . He may have been wrong in his interpretation of the scriptures as to witches and witchcraft, but he was not wrong in his views as to the folly and wrong of human laws aimed at witches.

Well, I have thrown out these few remarks to show that in re Blackstone I stand by my prejudices, and if the facts be against me, so much the worse for the facts. I won't read 'em. . . .

First kill the shepherd and the sheep become an easy prey. There seems to be a "proper-gander," as Mrs. Partington would say, going around to make a prey of the liberties of the people by defaming the ancient and modern champions of their rights. I regard you as one of the shepherds. Sincerely yours,

S. F. M.

Document IV–20   Winston's Speech, 1919

["Statutes have no roots, we are taught, but judicial decisions are seldom without them." So said Judge Robert W. Winston at the 100-year anniversary of the Supreme Court of North Carolina. One such rootless statute was *The Code of Civil Procedure*, which was "[a]dopted at the end of the Civil War, [having been] brought to this State by carpet-baggers and scalawags against the wish of bench and bar. . . ." And yet, Winston had kind words for code pleading and encouraged our judges to be more progressive and far-sighted in their decisions and opinions.]

A CENTURY OF LAW IN NORTH CAROLINA.

By Hon. Robert W. Winston. . . .

Remedial Statutes—The Code.

Statutes of a general character have also been passed to facilitate the administration of justice. Statutes have no roots, we are taught, but judicial decisions are seldom without them. And yet, behind many a remedial statute is some dissent of a virile minority, or some impossible situation into which the law has been thrown by an ill-considered decision. There may be, and often is, a long struggle between the forces of reaction and of progress, but the end may be seen from the beginning. . . .

Napoleon was no doubt the most versatile of the children of men. He reformed everything—war, finance, arts, government, religion, and the law. On his Code Napoleon his fame rests secure. To simplify and perfect the law has been the labor of mankind from Lycurgus to David Dudley Field and Roscoe Pound. The problem is how to so simplify the law as to avoid technicalities and delays and yet preserve

Robert W. Winston was a judge and an author. He was a mild critic of codification who in an address to the supreme court remarked that, "Statutes have no roots . . . but judicial decisions are seldom without them." Photograph of portrait of Robert W. Winston. (*Credit:* State Archives of North Carolina, Raleigh)

personal and property rights. This great task has had the attention of this Court and of this Association and much free advice has been offered by enthusiastic reformers both on and off the bench. I submit, with becoming diffidence, that *the only remedy is the trial judge*. Continuances are too easy, cross-examinations too prolix, and speeches too long—and these are evils the trial judge can correct. There are no delays in this our Supreme Court. With each recurring first Tuesday in February and last Tuesday in August, as that faithful old timepiece ticks out its ten of the o'clock, a brand new bill of fare, *a la carte*, is ready for the expectant brethren whose speeches of three-hours length, cut to thirty minutes under Rule 33, come forth under high pressure.

It is the sense of the lawyers of this State generally, I think, that the Code of Civil Procedure, together with the amendments, under the liberal construction of this Court, gives the framework for the speedy and safe dispatch of the business of courts. The Code of Civil Procedure is an improvement on common-law pleading and practice, as cases are now tried on their merits and upon the main issue. The Code may not be so accurate or scientific as common-law practice, and undoubtedly it gives this Court great leeway to affirm or reverse in the interest of substantial justice without doing violence to any well-recognized legal principle. Adopted at the end of the Civil War, brought to this State by carpet-baggers and scalawags against the wish of bench and bar, the fact that it is still with us is the best evidence of its worth. . . .

. . . In addition to the codification of our Civil Procedure, we have codified most wisely the law of "Negotiable Instruments," "Corporations," "Partnerships," and "Executors and Administrators." . . .

Attitude of Courts to Statutes.

Let us now consider the attitude of this Court towards the work of the lawmakers. Has this Court heard the voice of the people? The late Col. Tazewell Hargrove used to tell the story of an old man who lay dying. His two sons, one weak-minded, having been called to his bedside, he said, "My dear boys, to Thomas I am going to leave the bulk of my fortune, and I will appoint you, Richard, his trustee." "Father," said the weak-minded youth, "won't you give Dick the bulk of the estate and make me *his trustee?*"

We recall that Jefferson wrote to Roane, "If the judges have the power to annul statutes in conflict with the Constitution, then the Constitution and laws are a mere thing of wax which they may twist and shape into any form they please." The power of courts so to do has been disputed at all times. North Carolina, though "the freest of the free," was a pioneer in upholding such power. In 1787 the highest Court in this State declared an act of the Legislature unconstitutional and void, Judge Iredell upholding the power and Governor Richard Dobbs Speight championing the opposition. Iredell addressed an open letter to Speight, which text-writers pronounce the ablest and most complete exposition of the power of the judiciary over unconstitutional legislation which had appeared in the whole literature on the subject. Governor Speight maintained that the judiciary had usurped all the functions of government. Judge Iredell replied that when a judge took an oath to support the Constitution, this oath ought to bind him, and that if an act of the Legislature conflicted with the Constitution, to sustain it would be to do violence not only to the Constitution but to the oath he had taken.

The members of this Court, at its organization in January, 1819, were of the Iredell school of thought. Chief Justice Taylor and Judge Hall were graduates of William and Mary College, the college of John Marshall, with whom they, as well as Judge Henderson, the ablest judge on the bench, were in full accord. They maintained that it is the duty of a judge to exercise his judgment, and not his will, and that judges should be free and independent.

We read in John Quincy Adams' Diary a remark of Senator Giles of Virginia, that he and men of the Jefferson school treated with the utmost contempt this idea of an independent judiciary.

In a few months after this Court was organized, the epoch-making opinion of Marshall in the *Dartmouth College case* was delivered, holding that the charter of a college was a contract which the Legislature of New Hampshire had no right to alter in any material respect without the consent of the trustees. It may be remarked that Justice Gabriel Duvall, without writing a word, dissented himself into immortality.

North Carolina was soon confronted with a similar question in the famous case of *Hoke against Henderson*. The question here presented was whether an office is the private property of a citizen. This Court held that it was, and that he could be deprived of it only by the law of the land. *Hoke against Henderson* was not reversed until early in the present century, when it was held that an office is not based on contract, but is held by right of tenure and is subject to the control of the Legislature. Many vigorous dissents were filed before this consummation came about. When courts cease to be farseeing and give utterance to doctrines opposed to orderly and natural progress and development, as in the *Dartmouth College case*, the *Dred Scott* decision, the *Income Tax cases*, they invite attack. It is to be wished that judges may so administer the important trust committed to them, with an eye not only to precedent but to manifest destiny, to things not of today or tomorrow but of a hundred years hence, that further attacks upon the system of which they are exponents will not be made.

The doctrine of the recall of judicial decisions is so humiliating to an honest-minded judge that an office held subject to such thralldom would have as little of honor as of emolument. Our judges were first appointed by the Crown, afterwards by the Executive (together with the Council of State), then by the Legislature, and since 1868 they have been elected by the people. In some States the final plunge has been made and judges and their opinions are subject to popular recall. What a commentary upon the fickleness and instability of the people or upon the narrowness of the courts! The dignity of our judiciary has been upheld because the courts have usually, in the first instance, planted themselves upon the immutable principles of justice and right, having due regard to the rights of property and of the individual. . . .

Document IV–21   Consolidated Statutes' Preface, 1920

[In their preface to the *Consolidated Statutes* in 1920, the commissioners offered very little that was new to the student of the history of statutory codification. One point worth recording was made: the commission had secured the copyright of the annotations which had been prepared by Judge George Pell for his unofficial revisal in 1908 and had those annotations brought up to date by Professor Atwell Campbell McIntosh.[490] In so doing, the commission corrected a weakness in the *Revisal of 1905*.[491]]

PREFACE

The history of previous revisions of the statutes of North Carolina is given in the preface to the Revisal of 1905 and earlier compilations, and it seems unnecessary to insert this matter here.

The Consolidated Statutes has been prepared under the direction of a committee of the General Assembly of 1917 appointed under chapter 252 of the Public Laws of 1917. On the part of the Senate, Messrs. Stahle Linn of Rowan and Lindsay C. Warren of Beaufort were selected; and on the part of the House, Messrs. Harry W. Stubbs of Martin, Harry P. Grier of Iredell, and Carter Dalton of Guilford. A short time after their appointment the Commission met and organized and elected Harry W. Stubbs, Esq., as chairman, and appointed Hon. T. H. Calvert of Raleigh as Revision Commissioner charged with the actual compiling, collating, and revising all of the public statutes of the State. Mr. Calvert, after collecting the material for the work, was appointed by Governor Bickett as Superior Court Judge, and thereupon tendered his resignation as Revision Commissioner. Mr. L. P. McGehee, Dean of the School of Law of the University of North Carolina, was selected as his successor.

The Commission desires to give full and entire credit for this work to Mr. McGehee. It realizes what a stupendous labor it has been, and he is rightly entitled to whatever approbation this work may bring. The Commission felt it was peculiarly fortunate in securing his services, and the splendid results that have been obtained have fully justified the wisdom of his selection.

The Commission desires to make acknowledgments to Prof. A. C. McIntosh, of the School of Law of the University of North Carolina, who has rendered invaluable aid in the preparation of this work. Several chapters were prepared by Messrs. Dalton and Warren of the Commission. The index was prepared by Mr. W. H. Grimes, who has also devoted unremitting care to getting the work through the press. Other members of the Bar who have collaborated in the work are Messrs. T. E. Didlake, M. B. Fowler, and Moses Shapiro.

The work of the Commission was accepted and enacted into law by the General Assembly of 1919 by an act entitled "An Act for Revising and Consolidating the Public and General Statutes of the State of North Carolina," approved March 10, 1919, and embodying the Compiled Statutes as prepared by the Commission, with amendments. See File No. 1030, House Bill 1321, Senate Bill 136.

Under chapter 238, Public Laws 1919, a copy of which is added to this preface, the General Assembly made provision for the completion and publication of the work by the insertion therein of the Public

Statutes of 1919. It is the Consolidated Statutes of 1919 as completed in accordance with this chapter which is herewith submitted to the public. Under the same act it was provided that the work should be accepted by a Legislative Committee, and this committee, composed of Senator Dorman Thompson of Iredell, Representative O. M. Mull of Cleveland, and Representative D. B. Teague of Lee, met with the Commission in Raleigh in November, 1919, and ordered that the work be accepted and printed.

In conformity with the last mentioned statute, the Consolidated Statutes are published in two editions, the Magistrates' Edition omitting the second volume of the completed work and containing the statutes without annotation, and the Annotated Edition containing all the statutes annotated to date and a full index.

The Commission secured the copyright of the annotations prepared by Judge Pell for Pell's Revisal. These annotations have been brought up to date under the direction of Professor McIntosh.

HARRY W. STUBBS.
LINDSAY C. WARREN.
HARRY P. GRIER.
STAHLE LINN.
CARTER DALTON.

JANUARY 14, 1920.

DOCUMENT IV–22   POUND ON THE COMMON LAW, 1920

[Dean Roscoe Pound argued before the North Carolina Bar Association that the Puritan conception of law in America was eventually replaced by a pioneer conception, the latter holding that "courts exist[ed] chiefly to work out rules for a new country." In fact, said Pound, judicial hierarchies were established in the nineteenth century to make over the common law of England for our pioneer communities. While the demand was high for "rule and system," i.e., uniform and certain justice with very limited judicial discretion, Pound thought that this sort of scientific development of American law lagged due to the "frontier spirit surviving the frontier." Ultimately, the vigorous good sense of the judges made for a good American common law, but its rapid development "left a bad mark on our administration of justice." In order to make progress in remedying this administrative blight, though, what was needed in 1920 was respect for the judge as an "expert specialist" so as to make the courts and the bar "efficient agencies for justice."]

ADDRESS OF ROSCOE POUND.

THE PIONEERS OF THE COMMON LAW.

Few institutions of the modern world show such persistence and vitality as the Common Law. Indeed, persistence and vitality have marked its history from the beginning. In the twelfth century it came into conflict with the Church, the most powerful antagonist of that time and succeeded in establishing itself as the law of the land. It is true a like struggle between State-law and Church-law went on all over Europe. But the Canon Law left much less mark upon the law of England than upon the law of Continental Europe, and today there is nothing beyond a separate probate court in most of our jurisdictions and a few peculiarities of probate practice to remind us of the conflict. In the sixteenth century the Common Law was again threatened by the onward march of the Roman law in western Europe. Renaissance, Reformation and Reception of Roman law seemed, as Maitland has shown us, an irresistible conjunction. Elsewhere the local law gave way before it. The common law of England was the only body of Germanic law that withstood the movement and survived as a whole. Again, in the seventeenth century, with the rise of absolute governments, the common law came into conflict with the most powerful movement of the time and emerged victorious. The contests between courts and crown in Stuart England insured the survival of English public law and further development in American public law of the most characteristic of common-law institutions. In the new world, at the end of the eighteenth century and at the beginning of the nineteenth century came another conflict, to be spoken of presently, which had for its result to make the common law of England a law of the world. Still later in the nineteenth century, in the legislative reform movement, the common law was threatened by legislative activity, the capital fact, it has been said, in modern politics. Yet as we look back over a century and a quarter of American State legislation, we are bound to admit that it has wrought no essential change in what truly goes to make up the common law. . . .

Moreover, the characteristic common-law institution, the supremacy of law, in the form in which it has reached its highest development in America, is commending itself to the most diverse peoples, when they find themselves living under written constitutions. Thus we find courts in South America deciding constitutional questions on the basis of Cooley's Constitutional Limitations; we find Dutch judges in South Africa, trained in Roman-Dutch law, holding legislation void for infringing the fundamental law, and citing *Marbury* v. *Madison* on the same page with commentators on the Pandects; we find continental publicists lamenting that their polity does not provide for judicial interpretation of their constitutions.

. . . It is the spirit of our [law] that has made it the law of the world. It [i]s the spirit of our law that will endure. And this spirit of English law, like the English people itself, is composite. One factor in making it was feudalism, whence we took the idea of relation—from the analogy of the relation of lord and man—and made it the most fruitful of our legal institutions, as the double titles in our treatises and digests bear abundant witness. A second factor was Puritanism, with its idea of consociation rather than subordination and its rooted distrust of magisterial discretion. A third factor was the body of politico-legal ideas developed in the seventeenth-century contests between courts and crown, giving us our American bills of rights and identification of the common-law rights of Englishmen with the natural rights of man. A fourth factor was the idealistic philosophy of the nineteenth century, the formative period in which the common law of England became the law of the new world; a philosophy which put the individual human will at the very center of law and politics and confirmed and intrenched the individualism inherent in Germanic law, already fortified by Puritanism and given dogmatic form in the contest between courts and crown. Finally, a fifth factor operated in the new world, namely, the ideas and ideals of the pioneer. It is of this factor and its effects upon our law that I would speak to you this morning. . . .

Our judicial organization, then, and the great body of our American common law are the work of the last quarter of the eighteenth century and the first half of the nineteenth century. On the other hand our great cities and the social and legal problems to which they give rise are of the last half of the nineteenth century, and, indeed, the pressing problems do not become acute until the last quarter of that century. . . .

To understand the administration of justice in American cities at the end of the nineteenth century, we must perceive the problems of the administration of justice in a homogeneous pioneer or rural community of the first half of the nineteenth century and the difficulties with which lawyers and jurists had to contend in meeting those problems; we must perceive the attitude of such a community toward legal procedure and its conception of the nature and function of a trial; we must perceive its attitude toward government and administration and its rooted objection to supervision and restraint.

In the homogeneous pioneer or rural community of the first half of the nineteenth century, the administration of justice involved three problems: (1) To receive the English common law, or to find somewhere else a basis for legal development, and to work out upon the basis adopted a system of principles and rules adapted to America; (2) to decentralize the administration of justice so as to bring justice to every man's door; and (3) to devise a criminal law and criminal procedure sufficient to deal with the occasional criminal and the criminal of passion in a homogeneous community, of vigorous pioneer race, restrained already for the most part by deep religious conviction and strict moral training. . . .

After the Revolution the public was extremely hostile to England and to all that was English and it was impossible for the common law to escape the odium of its English origin. Judges and legislators were largely influenced by this popular feeling, and there was no well-trained bar to resist it. . . . Moreover, a large and influential party were enthusiastically attached to France and not only denounced English law because it was English, but were inclined to call for a reception of French law. "The citation of English decisions in the opinions of the courts," says Loyd, "greatly exasperated the radical element. What were these precedents but the rags of despotism, who were the judges that rendered them but tyrants, sycophants, oppressors of the people and enemies of liberty." The legal muckraker of today wields but a feeble pen in comparison with his predecessor of the first half of the last century. Under the influence of such ideas, New

Jersey, Pennsylvania and Kentucky legislated against citation of English decisions in the courts. There was a rule against such citations in New Hampshire, and more than one judge elsewhere had his fling at the English authorities cited before him.

In part, this opposition to the reception of the common law was political. In large part, however, it was but a phase of the opposition of the frontiersman to scientific law. . . . As numbers increase there is a greater interest in general security. But even then, in the rude pioneer community the main point is to keep the peace. Tribunals with power to enforce their judgments are the most pressing need. There the refined, scientific law that weighs and balances and deliberates and admits of argument is out of place. A few simple rules, which everyone understands and a swift and decisive tribunal best serve such a community. . . . In the next stage, as wealth increases, commerce develops and society becomes more complex, the social interests in the security of acquisitions and [in the security of transactions call imperatively for cer]tainty and uniformity in the administration of justice and hence demand rules. . . . The prime requirement was rule and system, whereby to guarantee uniformity, equality and certainty. And, since in the nature of things rules may not be laid down in advance for every case, this meant that a scientific development of law was inevitable.

Scientific development of American law was retarded and even warped by the frontier spirit surviving the frontier. . . . It will suffice here to recall the lack of interest in universality and fostering of local peculiarities which are so characteristic of our legal system. In part, Puritanism must share the responsibility. But in large part this spirit in American law is a remnant of the frontier repugnance to scientific law and the insistence of the pioneer that his judges decide offhand without study of what other judges may have done in European monarchies or in effete [sic] communities to the eastward.

Again, the insistence upon the exact working out of rules and the devotion to that end of the whole machinery of justice, which is so characteristic of nineteenth-century America, is due in great part to pioneer jealousy of governmental action. A pioneer or a sparsely settled rural community is content with and prefers the necessary minimum of government. . . . There must be no magisterial or administrative or judicial discretion. If men had to be governed, it must be by known rules of the law.

Thus the chief problem of the formative period of our American legal system was to discover and lay down rules, to develop a system of certain and detailed rules which on the one hand would meet the requirements of American life, and, on the other hand, would tie down the magistrate by leaving as little to his personal judgment and discretion as possible, would leave as much as possible to the initiative of the individual and would keep down all governmental and official action to the minimum required for the harmonious co-existence of the individual and of the whole. . . . Often it was less important to decide the particular cause justly than to work out a sound and just rule for the future. Hence for a century the chief energies of our courts were turned toward the development of our case law and the judicial hierarchy was set up with this purpose in view. It could not be expected that a system of courts constructed chiefly for such purposes would be able to deal effectively with the litigation of an urban community of today in which men look to legislatures to make rules and to courts to dispose of controversies.

A second problem in the formative period of American law was to decentralize the administration of justice so as to bring justice to every man in a sparsely settled community. . . .

. . . Thus one part of the English law of crimes, as our fathers found it, was harsh and brutal, as befitted a law made to put down murder by violence, robbery, rape and cattle stealing in a rough and ready community. Another part seemed to involve dangerous magisterial discretion, as might have been expected of a body of law made in the council of Tudor and Stuart kings in an age of extreme theories of royal prerogative. The colonists had had experience of the close connection of criminal law with politics. The pioneers who had preserved the memory of this experience were not concerned solely to do away with the brutality of the old law as to felonies. Even more, their constant fear of political oppression through the criminal law led them and the generation following, which had imbibed their ideas, to exaggerate the complicated, expensive and dilatory machinery of a common law prosecution, lest some safeguard of individual liberty be overlooked, to give excessive power to juries and to limit or even cut off the power of the trial judge to control the trial and hold the jury to its province. Nor did these enfeeblings of punitive justice work much evil in a time and in places where crime except possibly the feud and the duel, on which the community looked indulgently, was rare and abnormal, where, therefore, the community did not require the swift-moving punitive justice, adjusted to the task of enforcing a voluminous criminal code against a multitude of offenders, which we demand today.

. . . In other words, our common-law polity presupposes an American farming community of the first half of the nineteenth century; a situation as far apart as the poles from what our legal system has had to meet in the endeavor to administer justice to great urban communities at the end of the nineteenth and in the twentieth century.

American procedure, as it had developed through judicial decision, professional usage and legislation in the last century, shows the hand of the pioneer even more plainly. It requires no great study of our procedure to enable us to perceive that many of its features, taking the country as a whole, were determined by the conditions of rural communities of seventy-five or one hundred years ago. Many of its features are more appropriate to rural, agricultural communities, where in intervals of work, the farmer, remote from the distractions of city life, found his theater in the court house and looked to politics and litigation for amusement, than to modern urban communities. For instance, if I have read American judicial biography aright, no small part of the exaggerated importance of the advocate in an American court of justice, of the free reign, one might almost say the license, afforded him, while the judge must sit by and administer the rules of the combat, may be traced to frontier conditions and frontier modes of thought. When the farmers of the county have gathered to hear a great forensic display they resent the direction of a verdict on a point of law which cuts off the anticipated flow of eloquence. They resent judicial limitation of the time for argument, since the audience is to be considered as well as the court and the litigants. Hence legislation tying down the trial judge in the interests of untrammeled advocacy has its origin on the frontier. In particular it may be shown that legislation restricting the charge of the court has grown out of the desire of eloquent counsel, of a type so dear to the pioneer community, to deprive not merely the trial judge but the law of all influence upon trials and to leave everything to be disposed of on the arguments. Moreover, the frontier spectator in the forensic arena is not unlike his urban brother who looks on at a game of baseball. He soon learns the points of the game and knows and appreciates those who can play it. . . .

The pioneer has influenced American judicial procedure in another way. On the frontier "everyone that was in distress and everyone that was in debt and everyone that was discontented gathered themselves" to begin life anew. . . . The very spirit of procedure in some parts of the United States is so tinctured by frontier favor to debtors that improvements in the direction of increased effectiveness in the judicial machinery can come but slowly. All this is quite alien to common-law modes of thought. But it has affected common-law procedure in America not a little. . . .

How great a strain is put upon our legal and judicial institutions by the stamp of the pioneer, which they acquired in the formative period, may be seen by taking up the chief problems of administration of justice in the American city of today and perceiving how little our institutions are adjusted to them.

Demand for socialization of law, in the United States, has come almost wholly, if not entirely, from the city. . . . But our legal system has had to meet this demand upon the basis of rules and principles developed for rural communities or small towns—for men who needed no protection other than against aggression and overreaching between equals dealing in matters which each understood. . . .

Again, the demand for organization of justice and improvement of legal procedure comes from our cities. . . . A modern judicial organization and a modern procedure would, indeed, be a real service to country as well as to city. But the pressure comes from the city, to which we are vainly endeavoring to adjust the old machinery. . . .

A third problem of the administration of justice in the modern city is to make adequate provision for petty litigation, to provide for disposing quickly, inexpensively and justly of the litigation of the poor, for the collection of debts in a shifting population, and for the great volume of small controversies which a busy, crowded population, diversified in race and language necessarily engenders. . . .

. . . The other cause referred to is that our procedure, as has been seen, was largely determined by the conditions of rural communities of seventy-five or one hundred years ago. Hence when better provision for petty causes is urged, many repeat the stock, saying that litigation ought to be discouraged. It will not do to say to the population of modern cities that the practical cutting off of all petty litigation, by which theoretically the rights of the average man are to be maintained is a good thing, because litigation ought to be discouraged. Litigation for the sake of litigation ought to be discouraged. But this is the only form of petty litigation which survives the discouragements involved in American judicial organization and procedure. In truth, the idea that litigation is to be discouraged, proper enough, in so far as it refers to amicable adjustment of what ought to be so adjusted, has its roots chiefly in the obvious futility of litigation under the conditions of procedure which have obtained in the immediate past. It is much more appropriate to frontier and rural communities where a law suit was a game and a trial a spectacle than to modern urban communities. . . .

. . . In these communities [cities] the Puritan conception of law as a guide to the conscience and the pioneer conception that the courts exist chiefly to work out rules for a new country are wholly inadequate. The pioneer conception of enforcement through individual initiative is even more inadequate. Both the law and the agencies that administer the law, shaped by such conceptions, are unequal to the burden put upon them by the circumstances of city life and the modern feeling in a busy community that law is a product of conscious and determinate human will. This is the more apparent in application and enforcement of law in a heterogeneous community. . . .

Reviewing the influence of the pioneer upon our law, it may be conceded that we owe not a little to the vigorous good sense of the judges who made over the common law of England for our pioneer communities. Science might have sunk into pedantry where strong sense gave to America a practical system in which the traditional principles were made to work in a new environment. On the other hand this rapid development of law in a pioneer environment left a bad mark on our administration of justice. The descendants of the frontiersman have been slow to learn that democracy is not necessarily a synonym of vulgarity and provincialism; that the court of a sovereign people may be surrounded by dignity which is the dignity of that people; that order and decorum conduce to the dispatch of judicial business, while disorder and easy-going familiarity retard it; that a counsellor at law may be a gentleman with fine professional feelings without being a member of a privileged caste; that a trial may be an agency of justice among a free people without being a forensic gladiatorial show; that a judge may be an independent, experienced, expert specialist without being a tyrant. In the federal courts and in an increasing number of the states something has been done to secure the dignity of judicial tribunals. But the country over there is still much to do. Not the least factor in making courts and bar efficient agencies for justice will be restoration of common-law ideals and deliverance of both from the yoke of crudity and coarseness which the frontier sought to impose on them.

Document IV–23   Clark's History of Reprints, 1920

[In an oft-reprinted essay,[492] Chief Justice Walter Clark defended in 1920 his decades of work dedicated to the reprinting of the reports of the Supreme Court of North Carolina. He argued that reducing the page count of each volume by gutting many of the reported briefs and records was a financial necessity of the reprint project, even if increasing the page count by spreading annotations throughout the volumes was a marketing necessity.[493] Along the way of his defense he criticized past reporting practices and, under the guise of great erudition, pushed his "proper-ganders"[494] about case law. Thus, the legislature abolished the reporter's office in 1871 due to questionable editorial practices of past reporters,[495] not due to Reconstruction economics and politics; and it reinstated that office in 1893 for no assigned reason at all. Clark advanced his agenda. He repeated the modern mantra that appellate judges really make law, not declare it[496]; and since judges are akin to legislators making laws, rather than akin to wise folks meting out justice in light of an ancient and complicated tradition, opinions ought to be written in ordinary English and reports of opinions need not reference the lobbying efforts found in counsels' briefs. Still, Clark did not go so far as to *equate* judges with modern-day legislators. Perhaps the new gap-filling role of judges amounted to making private law instead of general statute. On this view, one would not treat holdings of appellate opinions as binding in other cases, that is, as precedents. By mistaking judicial decisions for precedents, Clark thought, we elevate gap-filling efforts, which proceed according to perceived legislative intent, to the level of democratic policymaking itself, and thereby place too much emphasis on the petty compromises of the past as reported in appellate decisions. Even if there were good reason to cite appellate opinions, no private library could keep up with the rapidly rising flood of reports—at least not if one invented an "American common law," or worse, the common law of all English-speaking jurisdictions, as the gap-filling legislation which one must consult as precedent, rather than the common law of an actual jurisdiction like North Carolina. Due to Clark's jurisdiction-less and legislative-like view of the judicial work-product, he imagined that national legal encyclopedias, like *Corpus Juris*, might serve as an adequate remedy for the dizzying melee of American precedents, at least until we either were submerged beneath the flood of opinions or adopted the proper precedent-less approach of civil law jurisdictions.]

HISTORY OF THE SUPREME COURT REPORTS OF NORTH CAROLINA AND OF THE ANNOTATED REPRINTS

BY THE ANNOTATOR

The annotated reprint of our Reports has been made under the authority conferred on the Secretary of State by Laws 1885, ch. 309, and subsequent statutes, now Revisal, 5361, which has been further amended by Laws 1917, chapters 201 andd [sic] 292.

It may be of interest to the profession and to the public to give some data as to our original Reports and the Annotated Edition. One hundred and sixty-three volumes have been reprinted with annotations, these being all the volumes from 1 to 164, inclusive, excepting only volume 148.

The first 7 volumes of N. C. Reports were not official, but, as in England till 1865, reporting was a private enterprise. When the N. C. Supreme Court as a separate tribunal was created in November, 1818, to take effect from 1 January, 1819, the Court was authorized to appoint a Reporter with a salary of $500 on condition that he should furnish free to the State 80 copies of the Reports and one to each of the 62 counties then in the State, and it seems that he was entitled to the copyright. Later this was changed to 101 copies for the State and counties and a salary of $300 and the copyright. In 1852 the salary was raised to $600 and the number of free copies to the State and counties and for exchange with the other States was increased, 103 N.C., 487.

The price charged by the Reporter to lawyers and others was 1 cent a page, so that the 63 N. C. was sold at $7 per volume, the 64 N. C. at $9.50, and the 65 N. C. at $8. Being sold by the page, it was more profitable and much less labor to the Reporter to print the record and the briefs of counsel very fully without compression in the statement of facts. These prices being prohibitive, the Official Reporter was abolished, Laws, 1871, ch. 112, and the duties were put on the Attorney-General who was allowed therefor an increase of $1,000 in salary, and the State assumed all the expense of printing and distributing and selling, 5 per cent commission being allowed for selling. Code, 3363, 3728.

In 1893, ch. 379, the system was again changed and the Court was allowed to employ a Reporter for $750. This has been amended by subsequent acts, so that now the Reporter is allowed a salary of $1,500, and a clerk at $600 per annum.

When the small editions originally printed were exhausted many volumes of the Reports could not be had at all and others brought $20 per volume. To meet this condition, Laws 1885, ch. 309, with the amendments above referred to, being now Revisal, 5361, was passed to authorize the Secretary of State to reprint the volumes already out of print and such others as from time to time should become out of print, with a provision that no money should be used for the purpose except that derived from the sale of the Reports. As the price of the Reports had been reduced to $2 per volume, and later to $1.50, this work of reprinting could be done only by omitting briefs and by cutting out all the unnecessary matter in the statements of facts, as had been done by Judge Curtis of the U. S. Supreme Court when he reprinted the first 58 volumes of that Court in 21 volumes. In our Reports these statements of cases (until a very recent date) were always made by the Reporters, and not by the judges, and the briefs were already omitted in our current volumes.

The Secretary of State at first tried the experiment of reprinting a few volumes without eliminating the unnecessary matter and without annotations, and without correcting the numerous typographical errors; but this proving unsatisfactory to the Profession, and the expense entirely too great, after consultation with the Governor and Attorney-General, the then Secretary of State requested the writer to annotate the volumes in order to make them more salable and to reduce the expense of the work (which was necessary) by condensing prolix statements and omitting briefs of counsel. This has been done ever since. The annotations have been made, for the most part, without any aid, as Shephard's Annotations (which besides, required to be checked for possible errors) were not issued until 1913, after most of these reprints had been annotated. Besides this, in the first four volumes, as issued, there was no index of Reported Cases, and there was no reverse index to the Reported Cases till 84 N. C. There was no table of Cited Cases until 92 N. C., and no reverse Index of Cited Cases till 143 N. C. The Annotator had therefore to correct these defects by putting in full indices and reverse indices of Reported Cases and Cited Cases and has supervised the revised proof of all 163 volumes. For these labors, the payment at first was $25 per volume, including annotations, condensing the Reporter's statements of fact when unnecessarily prolix, and all work of every kind. But the later volumes being larger and the annotations more numerous, $50 per volume was allowed. Any lawyer will see that this work was undertaken in the interest of the profession and the State, and not for the compensation.

Owing to the fact that as to these *Reprints* there was no Reporter to be paid, either by profits of sale as formerly, or by salary as now, the reprints have all been issued at a considerable profit to the State. It is probably the only work of any kind from which the State has received any pecuniary profit. In November, 1915, the State lost by fire 47,000 of the Reports then stored in Uzzell's Bindery, with the result that many additional volumes were required to be reprinted, and others that had already been annotated and reprinted were reprinted a second time, the annotations, however, being brought down to date.

The current Reports were sold till recently at $1.50, from which the commission of 12½ per cent for selling is deducted, i. e., about 19 cents, making the net return to the State $1.31 per volume, while, owing largely to the increase in the cost of typesetting, presswork, paper and binding, the cost to the State of the 174 N. C. is $1.94 per copy, without charging into the cost of production any part of the compensation of the Reporter and his clerk. The next Legislature will doubtless raise the price of the current Reports, if not of the Reprints also.

In all the more recent volumes the statement of the cases has been made by the judges themselves in each case, and hence in reprinting those volumes there has been no abbreviation in the statement of the case. In the earlier volumes there has been a saving often of 50 per cent by condensation of the prolix statement or of the record, which was often used instead of a statement, and by the omission of the briefs. Even in using the original reports, notwithstanding the prolix matters printed therein, it has sometimes been found useful by the Court to refer to the original record.

In England there was no official reporter till 1865. Prior to that time all the reporters were volunteers without any supervision. As a result many of the English Reports were very inaccurate, as has been shown from investigations made in the Year Books and the Court Records by Professor Vinogradoff and others. See Holdworth's "Year Books"; Pollock & Maitland's History of English Law. These reporters were sometimes incompetent and more often careless, which is to be regretted, as the opinions of the English judges were usually, if not always, delivered orally from the bench and the reporters were not always careful to correct themselves by examination of pleadings and records. And as the common law is made up of these decisions of the judges, under the guise, it is true, of "declaring the law," it has been often changed from what was announced by the Bench. See Veeder's "English Reports." Besides, down till Blackstone's time, the pleadings and records were kept in dog Latin (and he strongly censured the change to English), and for several hundred years the oral pleadings and the decisions of the judges were in Norman French.

Nowhere outside of the English-speaking countries are the opinions of the Courts allowed to be quoted as precedents. In France and all other countries the Court makes a succinct statement of the facts, numbered under headings, and then merely cites the section of the Code applicable, without comment. In English-speaking countries, in which alone the Reports of decisions are allowed to be cited, the number of the volumes of the Reports in 1890 were 8,000. These have now increased to 30,000 volumes. This system is breaking down under its own weight. No private library and few public libraries can possibly keep up with the rapidly rising flood of Reports. It is only by the aid of compilations like "Cyc." and its second edition, the "Corpus Juris."; A. & E., and R. C. L., and the like, that we can have any access to the vast quantity of reported decisions.

In those countries where citations of former decisions are not allowed, the argument is that the Courts of the present day are more likely to be right than those in the past, and that to cite former decisions is simply a race of diligence in counting conflicting opinions, a precedent being readily found to sustain any proposition. We have been accustomed to the present system and are still able to wade through by use of the compilations cited; but this relief, in view of the steadily increasing output of Reports, is only temporary, and the profession and the Courts must inevitably be submerged beneath the flood. What the remedy will be is a matter engaging the attention and arousing discussion among the ablest men of the Bench and Bar.

On an average, the opinions of this Court now require three volumes a year. If the briefs and redundant statements were still inserted as in the earlier reports, it would require ten volumes per year, taxing the shelf room and purses of lawyers. It was therefore eminently proper in reprinting to cut out the briefs and reduce the superfluous records. This required the exercise of judgment and much labor, but it was absolutely necessary in order that the receipts might furnish funds for other Reprints as required by the statute. Many of the Reprints are consequently from a third to a half the size of the former volumes. The American Bar Association, voicing the general sentiment, has passed resolutions requesting all Courts to reduce the size of current Reports by the judges shortening their opinions, a request which has been presented to this Court through a distinguished member of the Association and of the Bar of this Court. The General Assembly had already given a similar intimation by providing that "The justices shall not be required to write their opinions in full, except in cases in which they deem it necessary." Rev., 1548.

RALEIGH, N. C., 1 August, 1920.

Walter Clark

DOCUMENT IV–24 VARSER'S ADDRESS, 1920

[In this address to the bar association in 1920, future associate justice, Lycurgus R. Varser, agreed that the bar association should support some amendments to current code pleading (even if not along the lines suggested by Chief Justice Walter Clark) but admitted that a return to common law procedure would not serve the interests of the state.]

"THE PRACTICE IN NORTH CAROLINA SINCE THE LAST WAR."

Mr. President, Ladies, and Gentlemen of the Bar Association of North Carolina: . . .

I pause here to state that I am satisfied that the bar of North Carolina feels that much success has attended the persistent efforts of the present Chief Justice in his effort to bring about simple and inexpensive procedure, and remove the causes of the congestion and furnish a speedy and fair trial, whether we take the particular rules that he marked out or not. The code as we now have it, although it bears little resemblance to the original Field Code of 1868, is a fine working practice system. As much as I admire the common law system of practice, and as much as I believe in the *profit*, that it made necessary, to-wit, the preparation of cases before they are instituted, I do not believe that the interest of the commonwealth of North Carolina would be subserved by changing from the code practice to the common law system. The code was fairly efficient when adopted, but on account of the conditions at that time it was soon found that its wheels ran too smoothly and that the oppressed debtors of the state did not desire judgments to be rendered so frequently upon their obligations. Hence it was changed so that the service of process and the maturing of the cases for trial should take place in term time. Then, of course, with the terms of the court widely separated, it was an easy matter for trials to be delayed. I believe the wisdom of the Code in North Carolina is fully established when compared with the very excellent compilation of rules adopted by the Supreme Court of the United States for the trial of equity causes in the federal court. I am satisfied that those who secured the adoption of the Code, builded far more wisely then [sic] they knew. In spite of the fact that it has worked long and well in most instances, the changes of the times and the needs of the people make a few changes profitable to consider. . . .

DOCUMENT IV–25 INVESTIGATION OF STATE PRINTING, 1923

[Near the end of his long judicial career, Chief Justice Walter Clark was hauled before a legislative committee which was investigating state printing.[497] The committee, on March 2, 1923, recommended reversing some of Clark's editorial decisions made in the reprints of the *"Supreme Court Reports."*]

IN THE MATTER OF INVESTIGATION OF CERTAIN:
CHARGES WITH REFERENCE TO STATE PRINTING AND:
THE STATE DEPARTMENT OF LABOR AND PRINTING:

To the Honorable the General Assembly
of North Carolina: . . .

With respect to the reprinting of the Supreme Court Reports:

We find that in the reprints so far made, more than twenty-three thousand pages of matter embodied in the original reports have been omitted. The responsibility for the omission of this has been assumed by the Editor, The Honorable Walter Clark, Chief Justice, in communications addressed to the Committee. We recommend that legislation be enacted which will prevent the omission of any part of the original matter from any reports to be hereafter reprinted, except the briefs of Counsel which were contained in the older reports, and that this law be so worded as that in reprinting for a second time such reprints shall be made from the original and not the reprinted editions.

The value of the Annotations has been considered and, in view of the fact that Shepard's Citation Service is available to all practitioners at a small cost and is in the hands of most of them and is continuously kept up-to-date, which cannot be done in annotated reprints, we are of opinion and recommend that further expenditure for the Annotation of reprints of the Supreme Court Reports should be discontinued.

A copy of the evidence heard, transcribed and considered by the Committee is herewith filed.

Respectfully submitted,

Committee on the part of the Senate:

Mark Squires
James L. Griffin
A. T. Castello
D. F. Giles
J. M. Boyett

Committee on the part of the House of Representatives;

Edward S. Parker Jr.
Frank D. Grist
T. M. Jenkins
Clayton Moore
J. F. Milliken
Zeb V. Turlington
T. E. Whitaker
N. A. Townsend
C. A. Gosney

Document IV-26 Adams's Evolution of Law, 1924

[In the year of Chief Justice Clark's death, Justice William J. Adams published "The Evolution of Law in North Carolina" in the nearly new *North Carolina Law Review*. The judges of our early supreme court, Adams wrote, had viewed the common law as the foundation upon which the laws of our state should rest and had respected its fundamental principles and scientific classification, perhaps with too little room for relief by equity. By the common law, Adams surely meant the post-Reformation epitomes of Sir Edward Coke, Sir Matthew Hale, Thomas Wood, and especially Sir William Blackstone. And while the law received at statehood was not identical to law described in these treatises, our early judges not only presumed the common law as the foundation of law in North Carolina, but also adopted the doctrine of stare decisis. Finally, Adams asserted that our first judges showed respect for the economic independence of the individual and of rights in private property. Did this early jurisprudence hold up? Adams acknowledged that over the intervening 100 years, the common law had come under bitter attack, individualism ceding ground to governmental energy, and common law precedents being gradually displaced by codification or restatement of law.]

The North Carolina Law Review

Volume Two   April, 1924   Number Three

EVOLUTION OF LAW IN NORTH CAROLINA

WILLIAM J. ADAMS

ASSOCIATE JUSTICE OF THE NORTH CAROLINA SUPREME COURT . . .

These influences may be regarded as incidental; but other forces, more active and more potential were at work in formulating the juristic policy of the State. Among them may be mentioned:

1. The attitude of the Court toward the common law. The orthodox view that the colonists brought the common law with them and that the English law has obtained in this country from the beginning is only a legal theory. In 1715 the colonists of North Carolina approved an act entitled "An act for the better observing of the queen's peace," which declared the colony to be "a member of the crown of England" and provided that the common law should be in force "so far as shall be compatible with our way of living and trade." This provision was modified by subsequent legislation and culminated in the following statute: "All such parts of the common law as were heretofore in force and use within this state, or so much of the common law as is not destructive of, or repugnant to, or inconsistent with, the freedom and independence of this state and the form of government therein established, and which has not been otherwise provided for in whole or in part, not abrogated, repealed, or become obsolete, are hereby declared to be in full force within this state."

The theory of this legislation accords with the conclusion of Mr. Justice Story: "The common law of England is not to be taken in all respects to be that of America. Our ancestors brought with them its general principles, and claimed it as their birthright; but they brought with them and adopted only that portion which was applicable to their situation." With respect to the colonists' estimate of the common law as a system of positive and subsidiary law applying when not replaced by statute or local custom, Professor Reinsch has said: "While this legal theory has obtained acceptance as a satisfactory explanation of the jurisprudence of to-day, it is not complete enough to afford an adequate synthesis of colonial legal facts for the historian. It contains, of course, the great truth that men cannot all at once cut themselves loose from a system of thought or action under which they have lived; that, though they may transfer themselves entirely to new conditions, their notions and institutions must necessarily be circumstanced and colored by their former experience. Thus, of course, the more simple, popular, general parts of the English common law were from the first of great influence on colonial legal relations. This is, however, very far from declaring the common law of England a subsidiary system in actual force from the beginning of colonization. On the contrary, we find from the very first, originality in legal conceptions, departing widely from the most settled theories of the common law, and even a total denial of the subsidiary character of English jurisprudence."

It was under these conditions that the courts of North Carolina essayed the task of adapting parts of the common law to the economic, social, and political status of a commonwealth recently created. That the task was not altogether grateful is manifest from the difficulty encountered in marking the boundary beyond which the common law should not extend. It was not to be doubted that such boundary must be fixed, for the entire body of the common law could not be transferred to the new commonwealth. Yet the law of England was recognized as the foundation upon which the laws of the State should rest. It was natural that with its importation there should come, not only the dross of pedantry, but a profound appreciation of its fundamental principles and their scientific classification. The Supreme Court from time to time expressed approbation of many of its features. For instance Judge Pearson uttered the following special tribute: "One excellence of the common law is that it *works itself pure* by drawing from the fountain of reason, so that if errors creep into it, upon reasons which more enlarged views and a higher state of enlightenment, growing out of the extension of commerce, and other causes, prove to be fallacious, they may be worked out by subsequent decisions." The interrelation of the common law, the canon and civil law, and the rules of the ecclesiastical courts was thus expressed by Judge Ruffin: "That the rules of the ecclesiastical courts, although most sensible deductions of facts, are not parts of the law of this country, but only of the law of those courts, we deduce, not only from the manner in which the judges of those tribunals speak upon this question, but from the nature of the subject itself." "But it is an entire mistake to say that the canon and civil laws, as administered in the ecclesiastical courts of England, are not parts of the common law. Judge Blackstone following Lord Hale, classes them among the unwritten laws of England and as parts of the common law, which by custom are adopted and used in peculiar jurisdictions. They were brought here by our ancestors as parts of the common law, and have been adopted and used here in all cases to which they were applicable, and whenever there has been any tribunal exercising a jurisdiction to call for their use."

The whole of the common law, of course, could never have been adapted to conditions prevailing here, and the courts were not reluctant to reject many of its characteristics, among them, for example, such antiquities as the demurring of the parol, outlawry, special custom, fine and common recovery, and the merger in felony of a civil trespass.

To the common law the Supreme Court generally adhered—sometimes, we think, too rigidly. Upon no other theory can be explained such lapses, infrequent to be sure, as the anachronistic arrest of judgment in *State* v. *Carter*, because in an indictment for murder the letter "a" had been omitted from the word "breast." Judge Johnston, "bound by all the authorities which required the greatest strictness and accuracy in all capital proceedings," intimated that the decision "attained a degree of critical exactness not easily to be reconciled to good sense or sound understanding," but was unwilling to run counter to the opinion of "the most learned and respectable judges who had written or decided in like cases." Two of the judges concurred, but Judge Taylor dissented on the ground that the alleged defect was the "omission of a single letter, a vowel, which if inserted could not be sounded in articulation, and the want of which could not possibly mislead the jury who found the bill, or any one who read it, as to the true meaning of the word."

Such deference to technical interpretation was intensified by a feeling akin to reverence for the common law; and although the application of equitable doctrines professed to keep pace with the demand of civil and social needs the dominant judicial thought had frequent recourse to the maxim, "Equity follows the law." Indeed, this characteristic, easily discernible in the earlier opinions of the Court, continued during several succeeding years.

2. Another characteristic of the earlier decisions was pronounced respect for precedent. The doctrine of judicial precedent, said Judge Dillon, is this: "That a decision by a court of competent jurisdiction of a point of law lying so squarely in the pathway of judicial judgment that a case could not be adjudged without decision, is not only binding upon the parties to the cause or judgment, but the point so decided becomes, until it is reversed or overruled, evidence of what the law is in like cases, which the courts are bound to follow not only in cases precisely like the one which was first determined, but also in those, which, however different in their origin or special circumstances, stand or are considered to stand upon the same principle."

Accordingly the Court, approving the doctrine that judicial precedent is an established and essential part of the English and American systems of law, assimilated this saying of Lord Kenyon's: "I cannot legislate, but by my industry I can discover what my predecessors have done and I will tread in their footsteps." The judges resolved to adhere to decided cases and settled principles. They had scant respect for the theory that because in the alien systems of continental Europe a judicial decision has no authoritative force in any other case, judicial precedents should be abolished and every question decided upon the basis of reason and common sense. In their minds, no doubt, arose the inquiry as to whose reason or whose common sense should become the ultimate arbiter in case of litigation. To undertake to avoid the multiplicity of precedents in this way would entail an appeal in every case and substitute whim, caprice, vagary for law and orderly procedure. To go in search of a reason for this aberrant fancy reminds one of Milton's quaint remark: "It is as the Prophecy of Isaiah was to the Eunuch, not to be understood without a guide." Fearne answered the proposal years ago: "If rules and maxims of law were to ebb and flow with the tastes of the judge, or to assume that shape which in his fancy best becomes the times; if the decisions of one case were not to be ruled by or dependent at all upon the former determinations in cases of a like nature, I should like to know what person would venture to purchase an estate without first having the judgment of a court of justice respecting the identical title which he means to purchase."

Upon this subject a wholesome lesson may be drawn from two historic incidents. It is said that a Roman soldier, awed into silence when he approached the image of a deity, afterwards defiantly struck it down with his battleaxe and suffered no harm; but when the Thasians erected a statue to Theogenes, a victor in the games, one of his rivals went to it by night and endeavored to throw it down by repeated blows, until at last he moved it from its pedestal and was crushed to death beneath its fall.

3. The third characteristic may be called the individualistic tendency in the opinions of the Courts,—a trend toward an individualism having all the features characteristic of the economic independence of the individual. In the civil law there was stressed the right of private property in capital, the right to accumulate wealth, and the freedom of rivalry in individual effort, while in the criminal law one of the ever recurring problems was the suppression of an individual self-assertion which in practical affairs frequently claimed exemption from social control.

What of the future? Beyond doubt a contest is waging. It is idle to deny that changing conditions have produced new conceptions of the common law and of its adaptability to progressive thought. Notwithstanding its triumph and its establishment as a law of the world by the side of the Roman law, the common law in certain aspects has become the subject of bitter attack. The doctrine of individualism is giving way to the theory that individual effort must be supplemented, if not supplanted, by governmental energy. Relief from the multiplicity of precedent is sought in codification or restatement of the law. We may not foresee what the future holds in store, but with confidence we await the result. Underlying all laws and all governments worthy of preservation are the fundamental principles of justice which may be likened to a "gyroscope that through storm and stress keeps the ship on a steady course and an even keel."

Document IV–27   About Chief Justice Clark (1846–1924)

[Judge Robert W. Winston raised his wicked pen yet again, this time in review of a biography of Chief Justice Walter Clark.[498] According to Winston, Clark was "a boy Colonel in Lee's army, editor, scrapper, duelist, breaker of images, radical of the radicals, at-outs with the past, critical of the Constitution—a device to enable plutocrats such as Washington and Hamilton to hold their ill-gotten gains—advocating a national convention to tear the thing to pieces and put the Declaration of Independence in its place." And here Winston recorded the famous jest that President William H. Taft "would not trust the Constitution with Clark over-night,"[499] as well as the similar sentiment expressed by United States Chief Justice Edward D. White.[500] Not only did figures of the national government not trust Clark, reported Winston, but neither did the people of North Carolina when Clark ran for United States Senator. "[Clark] the radical reformer, the forerunner of a political revolution which has since well nigh destroyed constitutional government, was mistrusted."]

Walter Clark, Fighting Judge. By Aubrey Lee Brooks. University of North Carolina Press. 1943. Pp. x, 278. $3.00.

This is an interesting work, of excellent style except when dealing with controversial or highly personal matters, and then far from accurate and objective. . . .

Sometimes Judge Clark's strange, radical notions had a ludicrous conclusion. On a certain occasion, in the Judges' chambers, Clark was expounding his pet idea that no court had the right to nullify an act of the legislature. Justice Allen interposed. "Suppose," said Allen in his soft, unanswerable manner, "Suppose, Judge Clark, the Legislature in violation of the Constitution should cut our salaries from $5,000 to $500. Should that law stand." "You suppose an impossibility, Judge Allen," retorted Clark. . . .

It is said that Chief Justice Taft was jesting when he declared that he would not trust the Constitution with Clark over-night. This may have been a jest, but a remark of U. S. Chief Justice White along the same line was no jest. The story is told by Murray Allen. Allen applied to White for a Writ of Error to the Supreme Court of North Carolina in a damage suit against a railroad. "Who wrote the opinion?" queried the Chief Justice. "Judge Clark," Allen replied. "Hand me your Writ," said White. And he signed, certifying error, without reading the record.

The climax of the Fighting Judge came in 1912 when he ran for the Senate. That he would be swept in on the Wilson tidal wave of liberalism, he had little doubt. Without resigning the judgeship he took the stump, delivered fifty-five political speeches and freely circulated his pamphlets, including "The Dream of John Ball." . . . Judge Clark did not carry a single county . . . He received only ten percent of the total vote in the state.

Why did Clark lose out in his first and only real election contest? . . . Clark on the bench, the people admired; but Clark, the radical reformer, the forerunner of a political revolution which has since well nigh destroyed constitutional government, was mistrusted. . . .

After about five years on the Superior Court bench Clark was appointed to the highest court by the governor. Here he remained the balance of his life. During this long service he was the acknowledged champion of labor and of women and children. He was also recognized as the leading authority on administrative or adjective law, the law of pleading, practice and the like. In regard to substantive law—body of the common law—he was not so strong. Truth to relate, Clark detested the law—"that codeless myriad of precedent, that wilderness of single instances"—and said of it that it was the only profession that had never made any progress. Coke and Blackstone, fathers of English and American jurisprudence, Clark held in derision and utter contempt. Perhaps had he paid a little more attention to Blackstone and a little less to "The Dream of John Ball" he might have ranked with Ruffin and Pearson.

Undoubtedly Aubrey Brooks has won his case and made good his point. Walter Clark was a fighting judge, but what of it? Is fighting an attribute of the model judge? We had thought of a judge as a detached, impartial personage, learned, just and merciful.

ROBERT W. WINSTON.

Chapel Hill, N. C.

Document IV–28 About Chief Justice Shepherd (1847–1910)

[One may contrast the idealism and conservativism of Chief Justice James Edward Shepherd with the progressivism of the judges who sat on our supreme court immediately following his defeat in 1894. How traditionalist was Shepherd? He found code pleading distasteful because it displaced the certitude of common law pleading and practice—now here was a sure sign of a reactionary! Worse, Shepherd continued to operate on the old maxim that law was the perfection of reason. For the new occupants of judicial office, who followed upon Shepherd's term of service, a sound judicial philosophy was less a matter of reason and more a matter of sloughing off the past. "[T]he people will not only make but interpret the laws," said they. For the new radical, precedent was anathema because "[w]hatever is is wrong": law must make daily adjustments to human needs. As in the physical sciences, so in the moral sciences: we must migrate our methodology to experimentation. In short, the pragmatism of William James, exalting the maxim, "Try it out and see if it will work," made over our judges into politicians. According to Judge Robert W. Winston in this 1925 vignette about Chief Justice Shepherd, Justice Merrimon's dissent in *S. Barksdale v. Commissioners of Sampson County*, 93 N.C. 472, 477 (1885) (Smith, C. J.), divided our old and our new jurisprudence. Shepherd was unable to comprehend this new jurisprudence, and he was unable to comprehend that "sociological, politicopragmatist, Chief Justice Walter Clark," under whom the Supreme Court itself, whenever Chief Justice Clark could dominate, was an "incubator for remedial legislation, adviser of progressive political parties, defender and maintainer of radical propaganda."]

The
North Carolina Law Review

Volume Three	February, 1925	Number One

CHIEF JUSTICE SHEPHERD AND HIS TIMES*

ROBERT WATSON WINSTON...

Because Judge Shepherd's mind worked in this way, from within a subject out, and not from without in, he could not abide individual cases—mere photographic views of life. For example, he was never interested in the law of torts with its uncertainties and variations, or in rules of practice and procedure, or indeed in any subject incapable of categorization. Little "pints" of law, discretionary rulings on the sufficiency of code pleadings, equally with trumpet-blowing, experimental decisions to catch the populace, these were for others, not for him. Code pleading, which someone likened to one old woman scolding another old woman, made its appearance the year Judge Shepherd came to the Bar. Displacing the certitude of and practice, it was especially distasteful to the old lawyer.

I could never tell exactly how Judge Shepherd relished the change from common law to code pleading, but from the zest with which he used to tell a story on Chief Justice Smith and my father, I concluded that he was in sympathy with them. In a case in Martin County about 1870, a defective complaint had been filed and the two above named lawyers wished to file a demurrer, not "going to the case," but to a matter of form. Now they thoroughly understood the old common law demurrer with well-defined meaning and consequences, but the new code demurrer, resting so largely in the judge's discretion and with direful results if he was against you, why that was quite another matter. "So," said Judge Shepherd, "Smith and Winston, in a great quandary, put their heads together, finally coming into court and cautiously announcing: 'Your Honor please, we desire to file this paper: a plea in the nature of a demurrer.'"

. . . More diligent, more painstaking, and with a larger concept of the law than his fellows—except the learned Chief Justice Smith—Shepherd was a high priest in the conservative temple. . . .

How well Judge Shepherd succeeded in maintaining a system of jurisprudence suitable to the needs of the times, depends upon the point of view. The conservative recognizes in Judge Shepherd's concept of law the only security of liberty and property—the enduring foundation of the Republic; the radical, on the other hand, calls him a reactionary and hails the coming of a better day when the people will not only make but interpret the laws. But neither conservative nor radical will deny that the princip[l]es which Judge Shepherd stood for, were those of Henderson, Ruffin and Smith, under which order was maintained and justice administered.

In 1894, when Chief Justice Shepherd was defeated by a combination of Populists and Republicans, the old order was passing away to give place to the new. The day of the idealistic judge who concurred with Hooker that law is the perfection of reason, her seat the bosom of God, was soon to end; the time for testing and trying out all things was come. As science had been changed from mere ratiocination to experimentation, so law, cut loose from precedent, should adjust itself to human needs from day to day. Whatever is, is wrong, became the slogan of the radical members of the Supreme Court, now divided 2–2 on disputed social and political issues, putting it up to a fifth judge to break the tie. Consciously or unconsciously, the doctrine of William James: "Try it out and see if it will work"—the "Monte Carlo doctrine"—was supplanting idealistic philosophy. Because of the conflict involved in this change, in 1902 when the position of Chief Justice was again to be filled by popular election, Shepherd, though urged by friends to do so, refused to enter the race.

Of this "bread and butter" philosophy, of this thing that James calls pragmatism, it must be said that it came with a crash upon "tender-minded" judges like Shepherd, who had been taught to regard the judicial office as a sacred affair. A political judge! What could be worse! The first of the new order, the first of those "tough minded" individuals who had occupied the Supreme Bench was Shepherd's predecessor, Chief Justice Merrimon. Merrimon's dissent in the *Barksdale case* may be said to mark the dividing line between the old and the new in our juristic thought. Previous to that dissent, education had been considered a luxury, a privilege of the rich; thereafter, it was to be considered a necessity; the common heritage of poor and rich alike. . . .

If Shepherd could not follow Merrimon in blazing new trails, he was quite unable to comprehend the views of that sociological, politico-pragmatist, Chief Justice Walter Clark—who counted that day lost when he did not prepare some bill enacting a dissent of his into law or write an opinion overruling some hoary precedent. What glory to Clark greater than overruling Ruffin in the *Rockingham will* case; how gleefully he whetted his blade for the sacrifice, as, concurring in Connor's great opinion overruling *Hoke* v. *Henderson*, he exclaimed: "There is no peculiar sacredness attaching to *Hoke* vs. *Henderson!*" North Carolina has had but one image smasher.

The contrast indeed between Shepherd and Clark is nowhere more clearly seen than in dealing with precedent. To Shepherd precedent was grateful—to him the Constitution was as sacred as to Marshall or Hamilton; on the other hand, Clark was never happier than in destroying precedent: to him the Constitution was anything but a palladium of liberty; it was a device of the rich to enable them to pocket and protect their ill-gotten gains, and the sooner blotted out and a brand new one substituted, the better.

The struggle between the forces of progress and conservatism was slow to develop in North Carolina, but when it came it came in earnest, reversing the do-nothing policy of a century. Every department of state government was shaken to the center; the Supreme Court itself, whenever Chief Justice Clark could dominate,

Samuel F. Mordecai, dean of the law school at Trinity College, was a defender of the common law as it was described in William Blackstone's work. Photograph of portrait of Samuel F. Mordecai. (*Credit:* State Archives of North Carolina, Raleigh)

becoming incubator for remedial legislation, adviser of progressive political parties, defender and maintainer of radical propaganda. What cared Clark, the Chief Justice, though his Court were more often overruled than affirmed, by the Supreme Court at Washington; to be overruled in a "progressive" cause was itself an honor.

If Shepherd lost out in this struggle, he went down without sacrifice of principle. A conservative to the last, it was due to him and to other conservative judges that North Carolina escaped the unbaked jurisprudence of certain northwestern states. Let us put ourselves in Shepherd's place and ask: Are the principles of law fixed and certain? Shall we visualize an Ideal and strive to attain it, or shall we each day try out something new? Are there Ultimates? Those who lived before the philosophy of William James, answer there are; those who have come on the stage since, say there are not. As in religion and politics, so in law, the New advances, the Old recedes: the conservative and the radical each alike being necessary to maintain the balance. . . .

In 1899, when the inspiring teacher and gentleman, John Manning, died, the Trustees and Faculty of the University were desirous that Judge Shepherd should succeed him as head of the Law School. Indeed Dr. Manning and Judge Shepherd together, a few years before, had conducted the school with marked success. The position of Dean—though it was not then called Dean—was accordingly tendered the Chief Justice, and during several months he took the matter under consideration, hoping to accept. Finally with that consideration for others so characteristic, the Chief Justice declined; his first duty was to continue the practice until his son, Sylvester Brown Shepherd, just come to the Bar, could establish himself. Carrying out this arrangement Judge Shepherd and his son practiced law in the city of Raleigh until the death of the Judge in 1910. . . .

Document IV–29   About Dean Samuel Mordecai (1852–1927)

[Like Chief Justices James Shepherd and Walter Clark, the professional life of Samuel Mordecai, dean of Trinity College School of Law, which became Duke University School of Law in 1924, spanned from the old jurisprudential outlook to the new pragmatic view of law. He was born in 1852, licensed to practice law in 1875, hired to teach law in 1900, and passed away in 1927. Mordecai had a classical education, knowing "his humanities as he knew his humanity." He practiced law successfully, but his fame was as a law teacher and legal writer. He knew and loved the monuments of English common law, from Littleton to Blackstone, and left with us *Mordecai on Blackstone*, among other precious works. The state supreme court cited him often as authority on the common law, though Chief Justice Walter Clark thought little of that common law and told Mordecai as much.[501]]

Samuel Fox Mordecai
(By Sidney S. Alderman)

Samuel Fox Mordecai was born in Richmond, Virginia, December 12, 1852, and accordingly he had just entered his seventy-sixth year when he died as Dean of the Duke University Law School at his home on the University campus at Durham on the twenty-ninth day of December, 1927.

He was the son of Samuel Fox Mordecai and Ellen Mordecai. His education was begun at private schools in Virginia and North Carolina and at the University of Virginia but was continued unremittingly, under the impulsion and guidance of his own native genius, through a long and diligent life as a practitioner, a student, a writer, and a teacher of the law. The degree of Doctor of Laws was conferred upon him by Trinity College, Durham, in June, 1911.

On November 10, 1875, he married Miss Bettie Grimes, of Grimesland. To them there were born nine children, seven of whom, together with his widow, survive him. . . .

He was admitted to the bar by the Supreme Court of this state in 1875 and he began and continued the practice of law at Raleigh. . . . In 1900 he began to deliver lectures in the Law School of Wake Forest College and for four years he divided his time between his office and the classroom.

His fame as a law teacher rapidly spread and in 1904 he was offered and accepted the position of Dean of the newly established Trinity College Law School. He moved to Durham and his life from then until its end was devoted to his work as Dean of this school and its successor, Duke University Law School, and to his authorship of legal text books. . . .

But it is as a teacher of law that we know him and revere him. . . .

And such profound learning! He knew his humanities as he knew his humanity. He was at home, took his ease in his inn, in Greek, in Latin, in French, in English old and new, in the masters of many ages and tongues. He was one of the few men who can quote accurately whole pages of prose. . . .

Dean Mordecai had a profound disrespect for pedantry . . . By his strictures on professors and doctors of philosophy he filled them with a real passion to become practicing lawyers. . . .

He had no peer in his familiarity with the monuments of English law, Littleton, Coke, Blackstone, Fearne. In his Preface to his First Edition of his *Law Lectures* he says: "I would like to say a word to express my love and reverence for Blackstone." And then he excuses himself with an anecdote which constrains us, in turn, to forbear entering into any encomium on that master. But at least we may say, "Thank God that he gave us no Ewell's Essentials, no dehydrated pabulum passed through the dessicating process of extraction, but Blackstone *tout pur*, and then 'Mordecai on Blackstone.'"

As he says again in the same preface, he did not always treat "apotheosized legal dogmas with that deferential solemnity and 'reverential gloom' which is usual in law books." He had no more patience with sham and pretense in his own profession than in that of the "professors" of the academic school. And his dissent from unsubstantial legal dogmas was as caustic as any of his utterances. But he had a firm faith that the common law would, in the picturesque language of one of our judges, "work itself pure." . . .

He himself was his law school. He had worthy and able associates, but the spirit of Mordecai was the leaven that leavened the whole lump. It was his aim to turn out no graduate who would drift out of the law into the more easily lucrative fields of the realtor and the insurance agent and the loan broker. A few have been beguiled away by the richer rewards of commerce and industry. But most of his students are now laboriously and devotedly following the craft of that most "jealous mistress" to whom he introduced them. And one and all, be they rich or be they poor, they love and revere Dean Mordecai....

Document IV-30 Winston's Autobiography, 1937

[Judge Robert Watson Winston was a mild critic of codification, yet in his autobiography he told interesting tales about his use of *The Code of Civil Procedure* during his early years as a lawyer. This short excerpt hinted at the sentiments of the time.]

CHAPTER XI
"WELL, LAWYER, YOU'VE LOST YOUR CLIENTS"...

I likewise discovered that my opponents were quite out of date. They clung to the old common-law practice and refused to accept the new-fangled Code which the Yankee Colonel Tourgee had brought down from New York and superimposed upon our jurisprudence. This pig-headed attitude gave me a decided advantage....

... So signal was my success along this line, and so often did my Code and statutes trip up the older lawyers, that they resented my conduct and charged me with taking short cuts.

Document IV-31 Pound's Speech, 1958

[Late in his life, Dean Roscoe Pound visited North Carolina to speak to its bar association about law reform. At that time, both the bar association[502] and the governor[503] had formed commissions on law reform. In his speech, Pound bemoaned that in 1957, as in 1868, questions of civil procedure dominated the appellate docket. The remedy, he said, was discovered 50 years ago by the American Bar Association: encourage the courts to make rules of procedure, instead of having the legislature make them. Such a shift, he thought, would be less revolutionary than the legislative codes themselves, which arguably violate separation of powers.]

TOWARD IMPROVING THE ADMINISTRATION OF JUSTICE IN NORTH CAROLINA...

... In 1868, volume 68 of the North Carolina Reports discloses 58 cases decided upon points of pleading and practice. This was by far the leading title in the index to the volume, the next being criminal law with 43 cases, evidence with 30 and wills with 20. In 1957, in 245 North Carolina, criminal law leads, but pleading and practice is a close second with 34, insurance third with 23, and negligence fourth with 17.... Even more than in the formative era the courts are being confronted with new and difficult questions of substantive law to which the judges ought to be able to devote their undivided attention. That a court should have to give over sixteen per cent of its time and attention to hearing arguments upon and deciding points of civil procedure is a gross and inexcusable waste of judicial power....

Fifty years ago, the report of the special committee of the American Bar Association on Delay and Expense in the Administration of Justice urged unification of the courts, organizing of the administrative work of the courts, and use of the rule-making power of the courts instead of detailed codes of procedure. The progress made along these lines since 1915 amply justifies what was then said and you are simply falling into line in the progress that has been going on. Indeed, there is nothing revolutionary in these propositions. They follow established lines of common-law development. What was revolutionary was rather the expectation of the legislative law reformers of 1848 and thereafter to make everything over by minutely detailed codes.

Indeed it has always been a weakness of history that since the entrance is easy many persons immature in knowledge, without training or experience and lacking in materials, have nevertheless rushed into the field and undertaken historical studies for which they are not prepared. To write or teach history is supposed to be within the reach of every man. This is perhaps the chief reason for so much inferior historical work. They write in simple ignorance of the subject, but in this North Carolina can claim no monopoly.... In this search for truth the historians of North Carolina have been often handicapped by lack of training and experience, more often by the lack of documentary materials, and sometimes by preconceived opinions....

—Stephen B. Weeks

As has been said, philosophy without history is empty. But to this must be added that history without philosophy is meaningless.

—Harold J. Berman

Afterword

In this compilation, we have collected documents that have lain dormant, scattered, and neglected. By reprinting excerpts of these materials under one title, we hope to have brought to the attention of students and scholars of legal history evidence of the early penetration of positivist jurisprudence in North Carolina and to have offered inspiration for picturing in additional detail the history of law reform in the state during the nineteenth century.

Having now studied this history, we believe that one might profitably associate three paradigmatic figures—Chief Justice John Louis Taylor, Judge Albion W. Tourgée, and Chief Justice Walter Clark—with the three main eras for which we have collected documents—Antebellum Period, Code Commission Era, and Applied Democracy, respectively. During the early decades of the nineteenth century, Taylor not only contributed importantly to the development of the state common law, but also to the acceptance of statutory codification. Tourgée stood victorious during Reconstruction in the fight to merge law and equity and to replace common law pleading with code pleading. And Clark at the end of the century fought stoutly to undermine reverence for the common law and to promote the codification of private substantive law.

We also think that students and scholars who study the documents excerpted here in the arrangement offered will identify fundamental changes in public law and private law that took place over the course of the nineteenth century in North Carolina. At the opening of the nineteenth century, the 1776 Constitution of North Carolina had long been in force, with its English-style declaration of rights and its government by assembly[504] through local, private, and special acts[505] and through legislatively elected governors and judges. Early in the twentieth century, the 1868 Constitution of North Carolina as amended had long been in force, with its "assumption that the representatives may be untrustworthy,"[506] its popularly elected government officials (assembly members, governors, and judges), its code-like provisions on corporations, education, and homesteads, and its restrictions on government by local, private, and special act.[507] In private law, the contrast is as stark. In antebellum North Carolina, when one spoke of the state's "laws," one might chiefly have meant its "common laws," inherited at the American Revolution from the state's colonial experience and taught locally to aspiring lawyers through the study of William Blackstone's *Commentaries on the Laws of England* and of English and American tomes digesting the incrementally developing precedents of case law.[508] Late in the century, when one spoke of the state's "laws," one might as easily have meant its "statute laws," inherited from nowhere[509] and revised extensively and continuously by the state legislature.[510]

Beyond suggesting paradigmatic figures and fundamental legal changes, these documents also raise several questions that have given us pause. For instance, was Chief Justice Taylor on sure ground when he read the word "Protestant" to mean "Anglican" in the 1776 Constitution of North Carolina (as one might have read the word in a constitution or a law from much earlier in the eighteenth century) and when he treated the Declaration of Rights as paramount to the remaining provisions of that constitution?[511] Was "Civis," writing for the *Wilmington Daily Journal* in 1868, merely inflammatory when he sneered that "in reducing all the old forms of action to one" the purpose of the code commissioners "evidently was to do away with the necessity of legal learning" so that freedmen and Northerners might be "qualified to come to the bar, or sit upon the bench," or did he, in spewing his vitriol, hit upon a truth—that the commissioners and their political allies in fact denied the worth of the state's common law?[512] Did Mr. Justice Grier, in an opinion of the United States Supreme Court, indulge in hyperbole when he accused law-reforming "sciolists" of bucking the "nature of things," or did he lay bare their methodology: to accept as scientific only the genus (the civil action of code pleading) and to reject as irrational the species (the forms of action of common law pleading)?[513] Did Kemp P. Battle speak misleadingly in his technical correctness in describing the "Constitution ratified in 1876" by convention of the people as "merely an amendment of that of 1868,"[514] given the massive shift in political power which had engendered the drive for amendments after 1868—including the call for a convention in 1870[515] and the repeated efforts to disband the code commission?[516] Was there sincerity in Chief Justice Clark's implication that the office of reporter was abolished in 1871 due to its occupants having printed "the record and the briefs of counsel very fully without compression in the statement of facts"[517] in their reports of cases "argued and adjudged" or "argued and determined" in the Supreme Court of North Carolina?

Other paradigms, contrasts, and provocative questions will occur to readers of this compilation. We wish students and scholars of legal history well in their investigations and urge them to cleave closely to the documents that reveal the story of law reform in North Carolina during the nineteenth century.

Tom Davis
Raleigh, N.C.
June 2024

Bibliography

Acts Passed by the General Assembly of the State of North-Carolina, at Its Session, Commencing on the 15th of November, 1824. Raleigh, N.C.: J. Gales & Son, 1825.

Acts Passed by the General Assembly of the State of North Carolina, at the Session of 1828–29. Raleigh, N.C.: Lawrence & Lemay, 1829.

Acts Passed by the General Assembly of the State of North Carolina, at the Session of 1829–30. Raleigh, N.C.: Lawrence & Lemay, 1830.

Adams, Henry. *History of the United States of America during the First Administration of Thomas Jefferson* Vol. 1. New York: Charles Scribner's Sons, 1891.

Adams, William J. "Evolution of Law in North Carolina." *North Carolina Law Review* 2, no. 3 (April 1924): 133–145.

———. "The Life and Influence of John Manning." *North Carolina Law Review* 2, no. 4 (December 1924): 218–224.

Alderman, Ernest Hamlin. "The North Carolina Colonial Bar." In vol. 13, no. 1 (January 1913) of *The James Sprunt Historical Publications*. Published under the direction of the North Carolina Historical Society, 5–31. Durham, N.C.: Seeman Printery, 1913.

Alderman, Sidney S. "Samuel Fox Mordecai." In London, *Proceedings of the Thirtieth Annual Session of the North Carolina Bar Association [. . .] June 28, 29, 30, 1928*, 68–73.

Allen, Oliver H. Address of Judge Oliver H. Allen: My Recollections of the Bench and Bar. In Andrews, *Proceedings of the Twenty-Second Annual Session of the North Carolina Bar Association [. . .] June 29, 30, and July 1, 1920*, 157–186.

Allen, W. R. "A Table of Cases Overruled in Whole or in Part, or Modified, or Reversed by the Supreme Court of the United States." In Strong, *Cases Argued and Determined in the Supreme Court [. . .] Fall Term, 1915 (in part) [and] Spring Term, 1916*, 857–866. [171 N.C. 857]

Andrews, A. B., ed. *Proceedings of the Twenty-Second Annual Session of the North Carolina Bar Association Held at United States Court Room Asheville, North Carolina June 29, 30, and July 1, 1920*. Raleigh, N.C.: North Carolina Bar Association, [1921].

[Anonymous], "The Independent Citizen (1787)." In Boyd, *Some Eighteenth Century Tracts*, 454–486.

Arnold, Matthew. *Culture and Anarchy and Other Writings*. Edited by Stefan Collini. Cambridge: Cambridge University Press, 1993.

Ashe, Samuel A., Stephen B. Weeks, and Charles L. Van Noppen. *Biographical History of North Carolina from Colonial Times to the Present*. 8 vols. Greensboro, N.C.: Charles L. Van Noppen, 1905–1917.

Ashe, Samuel A'Court. *History of North Carolina: Volume 1: From 1584 to 1783*. Greensboro, N.C.: Charles L. Van Noppen, 1908.

———. "Presentation of the Portrait of Hon. George Davis to the Supreme Court of North Carolina." In Strong, *Cases Argued and Determined in the Supreme Court [. . .] Fall Term, 1915 (in part)*, 801–823. [170 N.C. 801]

"Atwell Campbell McIntosh: Professor of Law, 1904–1910." Duke Law (website). Accessed August 10, 2023. https://law.duke.edu/history/faculty/mcintosh/.

Babbitt, Irving. *Rousseau and Romanticism*. Boston: Houghton Mifflin, 1919.

Bacon, Francis. *The Works of Francis Bacon, Lord Chancellor of England. A New Edition: With a Life of the Author by Basil Montagu, Esq. in Three Volumes*. Philadelphia, Pa.: Parry & McMillan, 1854. https://babel.hathitrust.org/cgi/pt?id=njp.32101068998481&seq=11; https://babel.hathitrust.org/cgi/pt?id=njp.32101068998499&seq=7; https://babel.hathitrust.org/cgi/pt?id=njp.32101068998507&view=1up&seq=7

Bailey, W. H., and W. B. Rodman. Report of the Code Commissioners. [November, 1870]. Doc. No. 5. In *Executive and Legislative Documents [. . .] 1870–'71*, 1–7.

Baker, Sir John. *The Oxford History of the Laws of England, Volume 6, 1483–1558*. Oxford: Oxford University Press, 2003.

Balanoff, Elizabeth. "Negro Legislators in the North Carolina General Assembly, July, 1868–February, 1872." *North Carolina Historical Review* 49, no. 1 (Winter 1972): 22–58.

Barringer, Victor C., Will: B. Rodman, and Albion W. Tourgee. *The Code of Civil Procedure of North Carolina, to Special Proceedings*. Raleigh, N.C.: N. Paige, 1868.

Barringer, Victor C., Wm. B. Rodman, and A. W. Tourgee, comms. Response by Code Commissioners to Senate Resolutions, January 25, 1870. In [Documents of Code Commission, 1868–1871], 1–6.

Bassett, John Spencer. *The Constitutional Beginnings of North Carolina (1663–1729)*. Johns Hopkins University Studies in Historical and Political Science, 12th ser., vol. 3. Baltimore, Md.: Johns Hopkins Press, 1894.

Battle, Kemp P. "An Address on the History of the Supreme Court, Delivered in the Hall of the House of Representatives, February 4th, 1889, at the Request of the Members of the Court and of the Bar, in Commemoration of the First Occupancy by the Court of the New Supreme Court Building, March 5th, 1888." In Davidson, *Cases Argued and Determined in the Supreme Court* [. . .] *February Term, 1889*, 445–516. [103 N.C. 445]

———. *History of the University of North Carolina*. 2 vols. Raleigh, N.C.: Edwards & Broughton, 1907–1912. https://docsouth.unc.edu/nc/battle1/menu.html, https://docsouth.unc.edu/nc/battle2/menu.html.

Battle, William H. "Memoir of John Louis Taylor, the First Chief Justice of the Supreme Court of North Carolina." *North Carolina University Magazine* 9, no. 7 (March 1860): 385–394. https://ia804707.us.archive.org/22/items/northcarolinauni18591860/northcarolinauni18591860.pdf.

———. "Memoir of Leonard Henderson." *North Carolina University Magazine* 9, no. 4 (November 1859): 193–202.

———. "William Gaston." In Peele, *Lives of Distinguished North Carolinians*, 150–160.

Bell, J. Spencer, chair. *Report of the Committee on Improving and Expediting the Administration of Justice in North Carolina*. Raleigh, N.C.: North Carolina Bar Association, December 1958.

Bentham, Jeremy. "Circular.—To the Governor of the State of." No. VII. In Bowring, *Works of Jeremy Bentham*, 4:476–477.

———. *Codification Proposal, Addressed by Jeremy Bentham to All Nations Professing Liberal Opinions*. London: J. M'Creery, 1822.

———. *An Introduction to the Principles of Morals and Legislation*. London: T. Payne and Son, 1789. https://www.google.com/books/edition/An_Introduction_to_the_Principles_of_Mor/vCIoAQAAMAAJ?hl=en&gbpv=1.

———. *Jeremy Bentham to His Fellow-Citizens of France, On Houses of Peers and Senates*. London: Robert Heward, 1830. https://www.google.com/books/edition/Jeremy_Bentham_to_His_Fellow_citizens_of/XwtAAAAAYAAJ?hl=en&gbpv=1&bsq=citizen.

———. *The Limits of Jurisprudence Defined: Being Part Two of an Introduction to the Principles of Morals and Legislation*. New York: Columbia University Press, 1945.

Berman, Harold J. "The Historical Foundations of Law." *Emory Law Journal* 54, no. 5 (2005): 13–24.

———. "Law and Belief in Three Revolutions." *Valparaiso University Law Review* 18, no. 3 (Summer 1984): 569–629.

———. *Law and Revolution, II: The Impact of the Protestant Reformations on the Western Legal Tradition*. Cambridge, Mass.: Harvard University Press, 2003.

Biggs, J. Crawford, ed. *Report of the Second Annual Meeting of the North Carolina Bar Association, Held at Battery Park Hotel, Asheville, N.C., June 27th, 28th and 29th, 1900*. Durham, N.C.: Seeman Printery, 1900.

———. *Report of the Fifth Annual Meeting of the North Carolina Bar Association, Held at Morehead City, N. C., July 1, 2, 3, 1903*. Durham, N.C.: Seeman Printery, 1903.

———. *Report of the Seventh Annual Meeting of the North Carolina Bar Association Held at the Toxaway Inn, Lake Toxaway, N.C., July 5th, 6th, 7th, 1905*. Durham, N.C.: Seeman Printery, 1905.

Bishop, Joel Prentiss. *Commentaries on the Criminal Law*. 3rd ed. 2 vols. Boston: Little, Brown, 1865.

———. *New Commentaries on Marriage, Divorce, and Separation: As to the Law, Evidence, Pleading, Practice, Forms and the Evidence of Marriage in All Issues on a New System of Legal Exposition*. 2 vols. Chicago: T. H. Flood, 1891.

Bizzell, Oscar M., ed. *The Heritage of Sampson County, North Carolina*. Sampson County, N.C.: Sampson County Historical Society, 1983.

Blackstone, William. *Commentaries on the Laws of England in Four Books*. Edited by William Draper Lewis. 4 vols. Philadelphia, Pa.: Rees Welsh, 1902. First published in 1765–1769 by Clarendon Press (Oxford).

Bowring, John. *The Works of Jeremy Bentham*, 11 vols. Edinburgh: William Tait, 1843. https://play.google.com/books/reader?id=mG1YAAAAMAAJ&pg=GBS.PA39

Boyd, William K., ed. *Some Eighteenth Century Tracts Concerning North Carolina*. Raleigh, N.C.: Edwards & Broughton, 1927.

Breem, W. W. S. "Primary Sources: Law Reports." In Moys, *Manual of Law Librarianship*, 157.

Brooks, Aubrey Lee, and Hugh Talmage Lefler, eds. 2 vols. *The Papers of Walter Clark*. Chapel Hill, N.C.: University of North Carolina Press, 1948–1950.

Brownson, Orestes Augustus. *The American Republic: Constitution, Tendencies, and Destiny*. Rockville, Md.: ARC Manor, 2007. First published in 1866 by P. O'Shea (New York).

———. "Cooper's *Ways of the Hour* (July 1851)." In Brownson, *Works in Political Philosophy*, 4:18–19, 22–26.

———. "Cuban Expedition (October 1850)." In Brownson, *Works in Political Philosophy*, 3:366.

———. *Essays and Reviews Chiefly on Theology, Politics, and Socialism*. New York: D. & J. Sadlier, 1887.

———. "Legitimacy and Revolution (October 1848)." In Brownson, *Works in Political Philosophy*, 3:258.

———. "Political Constitutions (October 1847)." In Brownson, *Works in Political Philosophy*, 3:232.

———. "Republic of the United States (April 1849)." In Brownson, *Works in Political Philosophy*, 3:302–303.

———. "Temporal Power of the Pope (October 1855)." In Brownson, *Works in Political Philosophy*, 4:449.

———. *Works in Political Philosophy: Volume 3: 1842–1850*. Gregory S. Butler, series editor. Stafford, Va.: St. Isidore Press, 2016.

———. *Works in Political Philosophy: Volume 4: 1851–1855*. Gregory S. Butler, series editor. Stafford, Va.: St. Isidore Press, 2016.

Bryant, Victor S., chair. *Report of the North Carolina Constitutional Commission to the Governor and Members of the General Assembly of the State of North Carolina*. Raleigh, N.C.: North Carolina Constitutional Commission, 1959. https://babel.hathitrust.org/cgi/pt?id=nc01.ark:/13960/t5bc5pr3j&view=1up&seq=7.

Busbee, Perrin. *Reports of Cases at Law Argued and Determined in the Supreme Court of North-Carolina, from December Term, 185[2], to August Term, 1853*. Raleigh, N.C.: W. W. Holden, 1853.

Cain, Robert J., ed. *The Church of England in North Carolina: Documents, 1699–1741*. Vol. 10 of *The Colonial Records of North Carolina [Second Series]*. Raleigh, N.C.: Division of Archives and History, 1999.

Cain, Robert J., and Jan-Michael Poff, eds. *The Church of England in North Carolina: Documents, 1764–1789*. Vol. 12 of *The Colonial Records of North Carolina [Second Series]*. Raleigh, N.C.: Office of Archives and History, 2020.

Cantwell, Edward. *Swaim's Justice—Revised, the North Carolina Magistrate, a Practical Guide to the Laws of the State, and the Decisions of the Supreme Court, Defining the Duties and Jurisdiction of Justices of the Peace Out of Court under the Revised Code, 1854-'55, Together with Full Instructions and Numerous Forms and Precedents*. Raleigh, N.C.: Henry D. Turner, 1856.

Carolina Law Repository, The. Containing Biographical Sketches of Eminent Judges; Opinions of American and Foreign Jurists; and Reports of Cases Adjudged in the Supreme Court of North-Carolina. 2 vols. Raleigh, N.C.: Joseph Gales, 1814, 1816.

Carter, James Coolidge. *Argument of James C. Carter in Opposition to the Bill to Establish a Civil Code, before the Senate Judiciary Committee, Albany, March 23, 1887*. Albany, N.Y.: Senate Judiciary Committee, 1887.

———. "*The Proposed Codification of Our Common Law.*" *A Paper Prepared at the Request of the Committee of the Bar Association of the City of New York, Appointed to Oppose the Measure*. New York: Evening Post Job Printing Office, 1884. https://books.google.com/books?id=CxOkvfvuZYEC&printsec=frontcover&source=gbs_ge_summary_r&cad=0#v=onepage&q&f=false.

———. *The Provinces of the Written and the Unwritten Law. An Address Delivered at the Annual Meeting of the Virginia State Bar Association, at White Sulphur Springs, July 25, 1889*. New York: Banks & Brothers, 1889. https://play.google.com/books/reader?id=gT4uAAAAIAAJ&pg=GBS.PP1.

Cheney, John L., Jr., ed. *North Carolina Government, 1585–1979: A Narrative and Statistical History (An Updated Edition of North Carolina Government, 1585–1974)*. Raleigh, N.C.: North Carolina Department of the Secretary of State, 1981.

Clark, Walter. "Address of Chief Justice Clark on Reform in Law and Legal Procedure Before the State Bar Association at Wrightsville, June 30, 1914." In Davis, *Proceedings of the Sixteenth Annual Session of the North Carolina Bar Association [. . .] June 29–30 and July 1, 1914*, 46–61.

———, ed. *Cases Argued and Determined in the Supreme Court of North Carolina: December Term, 1859 to August Term, 1860 (Inclusive)*, second annotated edition. Vol. 52 of the *North Carolina Reports*. Raleigh, N.C.: Mitchell Printing, 1920.

———. *The Code of Civil Procedure of North Carolina: With Notes and Decisions to 1884*. 1st ed. Raleigh, N.C.: Edwards, Broughton, 1884.

———. *The Code of Civil Procedure of North Carolina: With Notes and Decisions to December, 1891 (Including Some Decisions in the 109 N.C. Reports), with the Rules of the Supreme and Superior Courts, and the Adjudications Thereon*. Raleigh, N.C.: Edwards & Broughton, 1892.

———. *The Code of Civil Procedure of North Carolina, with Notes and Decisions to July 1900, with the Rules of the Supreme and Superior Courts, and the Adjudications Thereon, and an Appendix*. 3rd ed. Goldsboro, N.C.: Nash Brothers, 1900.

———. "History of the Supreme Court of North Carolina." In Strong, *Cases Argued and Determined in the Supreme Court [. . .] Spring Term, 1919*, 617–635. [177 N.C. 617]

———, ed. "History of the Supreme Court Reports of North Carolina and of the Annotated Reprints." In Clark, *Cases Argued and Determined in the Supreme Court* [. . .] *December Term, 1859 to August Term, 1860 (inclusive)*, xxi–xxiv. [52 N.C. xxi]

———. "Response by Chief Justice Walter Clark [to Addresses of Judge Winston, Mr. Hicks, and Mr. Haywood at the Proceedings of the North Carolina Bar Association in the Supreme Court Room, Raleigh, 4 January 1919, on the Occasion of the Centennial Celebration of the One Hundredth Anniversary of the Establishment of the Supreme Court of North Carolina]." In Strong, *Cases Argued and Determined in the Supreme Court* [. . .] *Fall Term, 1918*, 821–830. [176 N.C. 821]

———, ed. *The State Records of North Carolina*. 16 vols. Raleigh, N.C.: State of North Carolina, 1895–1907.

———. *Supplement to the Annotated Code of Civil Procedure of North Carolina, Containing Amendments to the Text by the Legislatures of 1893 and 1895, and the Decisions of the Supreme Court on the Code of Civil Procedure Embraced in Volumes 109 to 116 North Carolina Reports, Inclusive*. Raleigh, N.C.: Edwards & Broughton, 1895.

———. "The Supreme Court of North Carolina." *The Green Bag: A Useless But Entertaining Magazine for Lawyers* 4, no. 11 (November 1892): 521–538.

Clarke, Richard Floyd. *The Science of Law and Lawmaking: Being an Introduction to Law, a General View of Its Forms and Substance, and a Discussion of the Question of Codification*. New York: Macmillan, 1898.

Coates, Albert. "Standards of the Bar." *North Carolina Law Review* 6, no. 1 (December 1927): 34–63.

Coke, Edward. *The First Part of the Institutes of the Laws of England; or, a Commentary upon Littleton: Not the Name of the Author Only, But of the Law Itself*. 16th ed. Revised and corrected by Francis Hargrave and Charles Butler. London: Luke Hansard & Sons, 1809. First published in 1628 by [Adam Isip] (London).

Conkin, Paul. "The Church Establishment in North Carolina, 1765–1776." *North Carolina Historical Review* 32, no. 1 (January 1955): 1–30.

Connor, R. D. W. *Proceedings and Addresses of the Fifteenth Annual Session of the State Literary and Historical Association of North Carolina, Raleigh, December 1–2, 1914*. Raleigh, N.C.: Edwards & Broughton, 1915.

The Constitution or Form of Government Agreed to and Resolved upon by the Representatives of the Freemen of the State of North Carolina, Elected and Chosen for That Particular Purpose, in Congress Assembled, at Halifax, the Eighteenth Day of December, in the Year of Our Lord One Thousand Seven Hundred and Seventy-Six. In *State Records*, 23:980–984.

Constitution of the State of North-Carolina, Together with the Ordinances and Resolutions of the Constitutional Convention, Assembled in the City of Raleigh, Jan. 14th, 1868. Raleigh, N.C.: Joseph W. Holden, 1868.

Cook, Charles M. *The American Codification Movement: A Study of Antebellum Legal Reform*. Westport, Conn.: Greenwood Press, 1981.

Cooley, Thomas M. Preface to Blackstone, *Commentaries on the Laws of England*, by Sir William Blackstone, v–xxxii. 2 vols. Chicago: Callaghan and Cockcroft, 1871.

Cooper, James Fenimore. *The American Democrat*. New York: Barnes & Noble, 2004. First published 1835 by H. and E. Phinney (Cooperstown, N.Y.).

Cooper, Thomas, ed. *The Statutes at Large of South Carolina*. 5 vols. Columbia, S.C.: A. S. Johnson, 1836–1839.

Coughlin, John J. "Family Law: Natural Law, Marriage, and the Thought of Karol Wojtyla." In Scaperlanda and Collett, *Recovering Self-Evident Truths: Catholic Perspectives on American Law*, 275–291.

Craig, Burton. "The Medlin Commission's Proposed Reforms of the Civil Justice System." *Trial Briefs* (Summer 1997): 18–22.

Dallas, A. J., *Reports of Cases Ruled and Adjudged in the Several Courts of the United States, and of Pennsylvania, Held at the Seat of the Federal Government*, Vol. 3. Philadelphia, Pa.: J. Ormrod, 1799.

Davidson, Theodore F. *Cases Argued and Determined in the Supreme Court of North Carolina: February Term, 1889*. Vol. 103 of the *North Carolina Reports*. Raleigh, N.C.: Edwards & Broughton, 1889.

Davis, J. C. Bancroft. *Cases Adjudged in the Supreme Court at October Term, 1895*. Volume 163 of the *United States Reports*. New York and Albany: Banks & Brothers, 1896.

[Davis, James]. *A Collection of All the Acts of Assembly of the Province of North-Carolina, Now in Force and Use, since the Revisal of the Laws of the Year 1751*. 2 vols. Newbern, N.C.: James Davis, 1765.

[———]. *A Complete Revisal of All the Acts of Assembly, of the Province of North-Carolina, Now in Force and Use.* [. . .]. Newbern, N.C.: James Davis, 1773.

Davis, Joseph J. "Address of Hon. J. J. Davis." In *Proceedings of the North Carolina Bar Association* [. . .] *the 14th of October, 1885*, 7–12.

Davis, Thomas P. "From Aristocracy to Democracy: The Legislative Ascent to General Statute in the Moral Science of the Law in North Carolina." *Campbell Law Review* 42, no. 2 (Spring 2020): 215–255.

———. "Government Publishing of North Carolina Law." *North Carolina State Bar Journal* 5, no. 1 (Spring 2000): 20–25.

———. "Precedents on Precedent." *North Carolina State Bar Journal* 29, no. 2 (Summer 2024): 8–12, 19.

———. "Reading *Smith v. Campbell* at the 200th Anniversary of the Supreme Court of North Carolina: The Constitutional Right to Trial by Jury in Original Proceedings in Civil Cases in North Carolina." *Journal of Southern Legal History* 27 (2019): 1–77.

———. "School Days: The Supreme Court of North Carolina and the Moral Science of the Law, 1819–1931." *North Carolina Historical Review* 96, no. 4 (October 2019): 373–407.

———. "Summer Session: The Morganton Decisions, 1847–1861." *North Carolina State Bar Journal* 23, no. 4 (Winter 2018): 12–17.

Davis, Thomas W., ed. *Proceedings of the Fifteenth Annual Session of the North Carolina Bar Association Held at Battery Park Hotel, Asheville, N.C., July 2, 3 and 4, 1913*. Wilmington, N.C.: Jackson & Bell, [1913].

———. *Proceedings of the Sixteenth Annual Session of the North Carolina Bar Association Held at Seashore Hotel, Wrightsville Beach, N.C., June 29–30 and July 1, 1914*. Wilmington, N.C.: Wilmington Stamp and Printing, [1914].

———. *Proceedings of the Twentieth Annual Session of the North Carolina Bar Association Held at Harbor Island Auditorium Wrightsville Beach, North Carolina June 25, 26, 27, 1918*. Raleigh, N.C.: Edwards & Broughton, 1918.

Denny, Emery B. "History of the Supreme Court of North Carolina from January 1, 1919, until January 1, 1969." In Partin and White, *Cases Argued and Determined in the Supreme Court [. . .] Spring Term 1968 [to] Fall Term 1968*, 611–630. [274 N.C. 611]

Devereux, Thomas P. *Cases Argued and Determined in the Supreme Court of North Carolina, from December Term, 1833, to June Term, 1834*. Vol. 4. Raleigh, N.C.: Joseh Gales & Son, 1836.

———. *Equity Cases Argued in the Supreme Court of North-Carolina, from June Term, 1828, to December Term, 1830*. Vol. 1. Raleigh, N.C.: J. Gales & Son, 1831.

———. ["Note by the Reporter following *Pike v. Armstead & Thomas Turner*,"]. In Devereux, *Equity Cases Argued in the Supreme Court [. . .] June Term, 1828, to December Term, 1830*, 114–115.

Devereux, Thomas P., and William H. Battle. *Reports of Cases at Law, Argued and Determined in the Supreme Court of North Carolina, from December Term, 1834, to June Term, 1836, Both Inclusive*. Vol. 1. Raleigh, N.C.: Turner & Fisher, 1837.

Dick, Robert P. *Memorial Address on the Life and Character of Richmond Mumford Pearson, Chief Justice of North Carolina, Delivered by Hon. R. P. Dick at Raleigh, N.C., on the Occasion of the Unveiling of the Statue Erected to His Memory in Oakwood Cemetery, June 8th, 1881*. Raleigh, N.C.: Pearson Memorial Association, News and Observer Book and Job Print, [1881?].

[Documents of the Code Commission, 1868–1871:] A collection bound together with the above cover title. Raleigh, N.C.: N.p., 1868–1871. Microfilmed by the Photographic Services Section, University of North Carolina Library at Chapel Hill. North Carolina Collection. Wilson Special Collections Library, University of North Carolina at Chapel Hill, Chapel Hill N.C.

Dortch, William T., John Manning, and John S. Henderson, commissioners. *The Code: In One Volume*. [Legislative Edition]. Raleigh, N.C.: Ashe & Gatling, 1883.

[Duer, John, Benjamin F. Butler, and John C. Spencer]. "Appendix, Containing Extracts from the Original Reports of the Revisers, Exhibiting the Form in Which the Provisions of the Several Chapters of the Revised Statutes Were Submitted to the Legislature, and Including All the Material Notes and References Subjoined by the Revisers; With Explanatory Remarks, Showing the Alterations Made by the Legislature in the Course of Enactment, and by Subsequent Provisions." In *Revised Statutes of the State of New-York*, 3:401–863.

Eaton, William, Jr. *Book of Practical Forms, with Explanatory Notes and References to Authorities; Intended As a Manual to the Practising Lawyer in the State of North Carolina*. Philadelphia, Pa.: Lindsay and Blakiston, 1854.

———. "Memoir of the Honorable John Hall." *North Carolina University Magazine* 9, no. 8 (April 1860): 449–455.

Edwards & Broughton Printing Company. "Answer of Edwards & Broughton Printing Company to Memorandum As to the Reprinting of the Supreme Court Reports, by Chief Justice Walter Clark, Said Memorandum Having Been Referred to and Made a Part of the Answer Filed by J. W. Bailey, Attorney for the Department of Labor and Printing." In *In the Matter of the Investigation of State Printing by the Joint Legislative Committee*, 67–71.

Ekins, Richard, ed. *Judicial Power and the Balance of Our Constitution: Two Lectures by John Finnis.* London: Policy Exchange, 2018. https://judicialpowerproject.org.uk/judicial-power-and-the-balance-of-our-constitution-2/.

Encyclopedia Americana: International Edition, Complete in Thirty Volumes; First Published in 1829. 30 vols. Danbury, Conn.: Grolier, 1992.

Ervin, Sam J., Jr., chair, and Harold Shepherd, secretary. "Report of the Commission for the Improvement of the Administration of Justice [to His Excellency R. Gregg Cherry, Governor of North Carolina, Supplemental to the Interim Report of November 1, 1948]." [1949].

Everett, C. W. "Bentham in the United States of America." In Keeton and Schwarzenberger, *Jeremy Bentham and the Law*, 185–201.

Executive Documents, Convention, Session 1865. Constitution of North-Carolina, with Amendments, and Ordinances and Resolutions Passed by the Convention, Session, 1865. Raleigh, N.C.: Cannon & Holden, 1865.

Executive and Legislative Documents Laid before the General Assembly of North Carolina, Session 1869–'70. Raleigh, N.C.: Jo. W. Holden, 1870.

Executive and Legislative Documents Laid before the General Assembly of North Carolina. Session 1870–'71. Raleigh, N.C.: James H. Moore, 1871.

Executive and Legislative Documents Laid before the General Assembly of North Carolina, Session 1872–'73. Raleigh, N.C.: Stone & Uzzell, 1873.

Farmer, Fannie Memory. "Legal Practice and Ethics in North Carolina, 1820–1860." *North Carolina Historical Review* 30, no. 3 (July 1953): 329–353.

Fay, John W., ed. *The Cyclopædia of American Biography*. Vol. 8. Edited by James E. Homans. New Enlarged Edition of *Appleton's Cyclopædia of American Biography* originally edited by James Grant Wilson and John Fiske. New York: Press Association Compilers, 1918.

The Federal Cases Comprising Cases Argued and Determined in the Circuit and District Courts of the United States. Book 17. St. Paul, Minn.: West Publishing, 1895.

Field, David Dudley. "The Code of Civil Procedure of the State of New-York: Reported Complete by the Commissioners on Practice and Pleadings." In *New York Field Codes*, 1:4.

Finnis, John. *Human Rights and Common Good: Collected Essays*. Vol. 3. Oxford: Oxford University Press, 2011.

———. "Human Rights and Their Enforcement." In Finnis, *Human Rights and Common Good*, 19–46.

———. "Judicial Power: Past, Present and Future." In Ekins, *Judicial Power and the Balance of Our Constitution*, 26–61.

First Report of the Commissioners of the Code [for the State of New-York] .Albany, N.Y.: Weed, Parsons, 1858, [3]. https://www.google.com/books/edition/First_Report_of_the_Commissioners_of_the/qpFSAAAAcAAJ?hl=en&gbpv=1&dq=First+Report+of+the+Commissioners+of+the+Code+of+the+New+York+Commissioners+(Albany,+1858)&pg=PA1&printsec=frontcover.

Fisher, H. A. L., *The Collected Papers of Frederic William Maitland:* Volume 1. Cambridge: Cambridge University Press, 1911.

Flint, John E., and Glyndwr Williams, eds. *Perspectives of Empire: Essays Presented to Gerald S. Graham*. London: Longman, 1973.

Ford, Paul Leicester, ed. *The Works of Thomas Jefferson*. Federal Edition. 12 vols. New York: G. P. Putnam's Sons, 1904–1905. https://oll.libertyfund.org/title/ford-the-works-of-thomas-jefferson-12-vols.

The Friends of Liberty and Equality. *An Address to the People of North Carolina, on the Evils of Slavery*, Greensborough, N.C.: William Swaim, 1830.

Furches, D. M. "Judge Anderson Mitchell." In Biggs, *Report of the Seventh Annual Meeting of the North Carolina Bar Association [. . .] July 5th, 6th, 7th, 1905*, 185–193.

Galligan, D. J., ed. *Constitutions and the Classics: Patterns of Constitutional Thought from Fortescue to Bentham*. Oxford: Oxford University Press, 2014.

Garner, Bryan A., ed. *Black's Law Dictionary*. 11th ed. Eagan, Minn.: Thomson Reuters, 2019.

General Assembly Session Records, Jan.–Mar., 1923. State Archives of North Carolina, Raleigh, N.C.

Gierke, Otto. *Natural Law and the Theory of Society, 1500 to 1800*. 2 vols. Translated by Ernest Barker. Cambridge: University Press, 1934.

Gilmore, Grant. *The Ages of American Law*. New Haven, Conn.: Yale University Press, 1977.

———. Review of *Justice Joseph Story and the Rise of the Supreme Court*, by Gerald T. Dunne. *University of Chicago Law Review* 39, no. 1 (Fall 1971): 244–253.

Graham, William A. "Discourse in Memory of the Life and Character of the Hon. Geo. E. Badger, Delivered by William A. Graham, of Orange (by Request of the Bar of Wake County,) at Raleigh, July 19th, 1866." In Hamilton, Williams, and Peacock, *Papers of William Alexander Graham.* 7:161–183.

Graveson, R. H. "The Restless Spirit of English Law." In Keeton and Schwarzenberger, *Jeremy Bentham and the Law*, 101–122.

Greensboro Patriot and Times, vol. 30/7, no. 47, Thursday, December 24, 1868. https://newspapers.digitalnc.org/lccn/sn91068360/1868-12-24/ed-1/seq-2.pdf.

Grey, Thomas C. Review of *Patterns of American Jurisprudence*, by Neil Duxbury. *Yale Law Journal* 106, no. 2 (November 1996): 493–517.

Grimké, Thomas Smith. "An Oration of the Practicability and Expedience of Reducing the Whole Body of the Law to the Simplicity of a Code. Delivered to the South Carolina Bar Association, March 17, 1827." In Miller, *Legal Mind in America*, 147–159.

Grossberg, Michael, and Christopher Tomlins, eds., *The Cambridge History of Law in America: Early America (1580–1815).* Vol. 1. Cambridge: Cambridge University Press, 2008.

Guthrie, W. K. C. *The Sophists.* Pt. 1 of Vol. 3 of *A History of Greek Philosophy: The Fifth-Century Enlightenment.* New York: Cambridge University Press, 1971.

Hamilton, J. G. de Roulhac, ed. *The Papers of Thomas Ruffin.* Raleigh, N.C.: North Carolina Historical Commission, 1918.

Hamilton, J. G. de Roulhac, Max R. Williams, and Mary Reynolds Peacock, eds. *The Papers of William Alexander Graham.* 8 vols. Raleigh, N.C.: State Department/Division of Archives and History, 1957–1992.

Hand-book for County Officers: A Guide for Justices of the Peace, Superior Court Clerks, County Commissioners, Township Officers, Sheriffs, Coroners, and Other County Officials, Containing the Laws Prescribing the Respective Duties and Powers of Each, under the New Constitution, Together with Approved Forms and Precedents, Also the Acts of the General Assembly of 1868–'69, Relating to County Officers and County Police. 2nd ed. Raleigh, N.C.: Nichols & Gorman, 1869.

Hargrove, Tazewell L. *Cases Argued and Determined in the Supreme Court of North Carolina, January Term, 1874.* Vol. 70 of the *North Carolina Reports*. Raleigh, N.C.: Josiah Turner Jr., 1874.

———. *Cases Argued and Determined in the Supreme Court of North Carolina, January Term, 1875.* Volume 72 of the *North Carolina Reports*. Raleigh, N.C.: Josiah Turner, 1875.

Hawks, Francis L. *A Digested Index of the Reported Cases Adjudged in the Courts of North Carolina from the Year, 1778 to 1826.* Raleigh, N.C.: Bell & Lawrence, 1826.

———. *History of North Carolina: With Maps and Illustrations.* 2nd ed. 2 vols. Fayetteville, N.C.: E. J. Hale & Son, 1858.

———. *Reports of Cases Argued and Adjudged in the Supreme Court of North-Carolina, during the Years 1822 & 1823.* Vol. 2. Raleigh, N.C.: J. Gales & Son, 1824.

———. *Reports of Cases Argued and Adjudged in the Supreme Court of North-Carolina, during the Years 1824 and 1825.* Vol. 3. Hillsborough, N.C.: D. Heartt, 1826.

Haywood, Edward Graham. "Bartholomew Figures Moore." In Peele, *Lives of Distinguished North Carolinians*, 378–388.

Haywood, John. *A Manual of the Laws of North-Carolina, Arranged under Distinct Heads in Alphabetical Order. With References from One Head to Another, When a Subject Is Mentioned in Any Other Part of the Book Than under the Distinct Head Where It Is Placed.* 2nd ed. Raleigh, N.C.: J. Gales and W. Boylan, 1808.

———. *Reports of Cases Adjudged in the Superior Courts of Law and Equity, Court of Conference, and Federal Court, for the State of North-Carolina: From the Year 1797 to 1806.* Vol. 2. Raleigh, N.C.: William Boylan, 1806.

———. *Reports of Cases Adjudged in the Superior Courts of Law and Equity of the State of North-Carolina, from the Year 1789, to the Year 1798.* [Vol. 1]. Halifax, N.C.: Abraham Hodge, 1799.

Haywood, Marshall De Lancey. *Calvin Jones, Physician, Soldier and Freemason, 1715–1846: Being an Account of His Career in North Carolina and Tennessee.* Bolivar, Tenn.: James W. Jones, 1919.

Hill, D. H. "The Old South." [Speech to the] Comrades of the Society of the Army and Navy of the Confederate States in the State of Maryland. In Peele, *Lives of Distinguished North Carolinians*, 564–587.

Hilty, Hiram H. *Toward Freedom for All: North Carolina Quakers and Slavery.* Richmond, Ind.: Friends United Press, 1984. https://archive.org/details/towardfreedomfor00hilt/page/42/mode/2up.

Hinsdale, John W. "Report of Committee on Legislation and Law Reform." In Biggs, *Report of the Second Annual Meeting of the North Carolina Bar Association [. . .] June 27th, 28th and 29th*, 1900, 97–105.

Holden, W. W. "[Provisional] Governor's Message [of November 30, 1865]." In [*North Carolina Legislative Documents for Session of 1865–'66*]. Document No. 1, 1–5.

House, R. B., ed. *Public Letters and Papers of Thomas Walter Bickett, Governor of North Carolina, 1917–1921*. Compiled by Santford Martin, private secretary to the governor. Raleigh, N.C.: Edwards & Broughton Printing, 1923.

House Journal—1790. At a General Assembly Begun and Held at Fayetteville, on the First Day of November, in the Year of Our Lord One Thousand Seven Hundred and Ninety, and in the Fifteenth Year of the Independence of the United States of America, Being the First Session of This Assembly. In *State Records*, 21:871–1083.

Howard, Benjamin C. *Reports of Cases Argued and Adjudged in the Supreme Court of the United States. December Term, 1857*. Washington, D.C.: W. H. & O. H. Morrison, 1858.

Hoyt, William Henry, ed. *The Papers of Archibald D. Murphey*. 2 vols. Raleigh, N.C.: E. M. Uzzell, 1914.

Humphreys, James. *Observations on the Actual State of the English Laws of Real Property; With the Outlines of a Code*. London: John Murray, 1826.

———. *Observations on the Actual State of the English Laws of Real Property; With Outlines of a Systematic Reform*. London: John Murray, 1827.

Hunt, James L. "Dissent on the North Carolina Supreme Court." *Juridicus: Journal of the North Carolina Supreme Court Historical Society* 2 (January 1997): 31–33.

Hunter, Thomas. "The Institutionalization of Legal Education in North Carolina, 1790–1920." In Sheppard, *History of Legal Education in the United States*, 1:406–485.

Hutcheson, Harry James, *North Carolina Reports, Volume 368, Supreme Court of North Carolina, 10 April 2015 [to] 10 June 2016*. Raleigh, N.C.: N.p., 2017.

Hyde, Joseph L. " 'The Common Law Cut Down': Homicide and Human Property in Post-Colonial North Carolina." *Australian Bar Review* 36 (October 2012): 176–188.

In the Matter of the Investigation of State Printing by the Joint Legislative Committee, Pursuant to Joint Resolution of the 1923 General Assembly. Raleigh, N.C.: Edwards & Broughton, 1923.

Iredell, James. *Laws of the State of North-Carolina*. Edenton, N.C.: Hodge & Wills, 1791.

Iredell, James, Jr. *Reports of Cases in Equity, Argued and Determined in the Supreme Court of North Carolina, from December Term, 1851, to August Term, 1852, Both Inclusive*. Vol. 8. Raleigh, N.C.: Seaton Gales, 1852.

———. *Reports of Cases at Law, Argued and Determined in the Supreme Court of North Carolina, from December Term 1848, to June Term 1849, Both Inclusive*. Vol. 9. Raleigh, N.C.: Seaton Gales, 1849.

———. *Reports of Cases in Law, Argued and Determined in the Supreme Court of North Carolina, from June Term, 1850 to December Term, 1850, Both Inclusive*. Vol. 11. Raleigh, N.C.: Seaton Gales, 1851.

———. *Reports of Cases in Law, Argued and Determined in the Supreme Court of North Carolina, June Term, 1851, to August Term, 1851, Both Inclusive*. Vol. 12. Raleigh, N.C. Seaton Gales, 1851.

———. "Terms [for Subscription to the North-Carolina Supreme Court Reports]." In Iredell, *Reports of Cases in Equity, Argued and Determined in the Supreme Court [. . .] December Term, 1851, to August Term, 1852*, 316. [43 N.C. 316]

———. *A Treatise on the Law of Executors and Administrators in North Carolina*. Raleigh, N.C.: N.C. Institution for the Deaf and Dumb and the Blind, 1851.

Iredell, James, and William H. Battle. *The Revised Statutes of the State of North Carolina, Passed by the General Assembly at the Session of 1836–'7 [. . .]*. Raleigh, N.C.: Turner and Hughes, 1837.

Johnson, Guion Griffis. *Ante-bellum North Carolina: A Social History*. Chapel Hill: University of North Carolina Press, 1937.

Joint Committee [of the General Assembly]. "[Report of the Special Committee of the General Assembly Formed under a Joint Resolution for the Investigation of the State Printing]." Box 17, Committee Reports Folder, H.R. 73 S.R. 86 of General Assembly Session Records, Jan.–Mar., 1923. State Archives of North Carolina, Raleigh.

Jones, H. C., and P. H. Winston. *North Carolina Reports, Vol. 60. Embracing Winston's Law Reports*, Vols. 1. and 2. *and Winston's Equity Reports, or Cases Argued and Determined in the Supreme Court of North Carolina, from June Term, 1863, to December Term, 1864, Inclusive*. 2nd ed. Raleigh, N.C.: News Publishing, 1878.

Jones, Hamilton C. *Reports of Cases at Law Argued and Determined in the Supreme Court of North Carolina, from December Term, 1854, to August Term, 1855, Both Inclusive*. [Vol. 2]. Salisbury, N.C.: J. J. Bruner, 1855.

———. *Reports of Cases at Law Argued and Determined in the Supreme Court of North Carolina, from December Term, 1855, to August Term, 1856, Both Inclusive*. Vol. 3. Salisbury, N.C.: J. J. Bruner, 1856.

———. *Reports of Cases at Law Argued and Determined in the Supreme Court of North Carolina, from December Term, 1856, to August Term, 1857, Inclusive*. Vol. 4. Salisbury, N.C.: J. J. Bruner, 1857.

Jones, Johnstone, and John Reilly. *Amendments to the Constitution of North Carolina, Proposed by the Constitutional Convention of 1875, and the Constitution As It Will Read As Proposed to Be Amended*. Raleigh, N.C.: Josiah Turner, 1875.

Journal of the Constitutional Convention of the State of North-Carolina, at Its Session 1868. Raleigh, N.C.: Joseph W. Holden, 1868. https://docsouth.unc.edu/nc/conv1868/menu.html.

Journal of the Convention of the State of North-Carolina, at Its Adjourned Session of 1866. Raleigh, N.C.: Cannon & Holden, 1866.

Journal of the House of Commons, at Its Special Session of 1866. [At a Session of the General Assembly of North Carolina, Begun and Held in the City of Raleigh, on Thursday, the 18th Day of January, in the Year of Our Lord One Thousand Eight Hundred and Sixty-Six, and in the Ninetieth Year of the Independence of the United States of America, Convened by Proclamation of the Governor of the State]. [Raleigh, N.C.?: N.p., 1866?].

Journal of the House of Commons of the State of North-Carolina. At a General Assembly, Begun and Held at the City of Raleigh, on Monday the Twentieth Day of November, in the Year of Our Lord One Thousand Eight Hundred and Nine, and in the Thirty-Fourth Year of the Independence of the United States of America: It Being the First Session of This General Assembly. [Raleigh, N.C.: Gales & Seaton, 1810?].

Journal of the House of Representatives of the General Assembly of the State of North Carolina, at Its Session of 1868–'69. Raleigh, N.C.: M. S. Littlefield, 1869.

Journal of the House of Representatives of the General Assembly of the State of North Carolina, at Its Session of 1870–'71. Raleigh, N.C.: James H. Moore, 1871.

Journal of the Senate of the General Assembly of the State of North Carolina, at Its Session of 1869–'70. Raleigh, N.C.: M. S. Littlefield, 1869.

Journal of the Senate, at Its Special Session of 1866. At a Session of the General Assembly of North Carolina, Begun and Held in the City of Raleigh, on Thursday, the 18th Day of January, in the Year of Our Lord One Thousand Eight Hundred and Sixty-Six, and in the Ninetieth Year of the Independence of the United States of America, Convened by Proclamation of the Governor of the State. [Raleigh, N.C.: N.p., 1866?].

Journals of the Senate and House of Commons, of the General Assembly of North-Carolina: At Its Session in 1819. Raleigh, N.C.: Thomas Henderson, 1820.

Journals of the Senate and House of Commons of the General Assembly of the State of North Carolina at Its Session in 1825. Raleigh, N.C.: Bell & Lawrence, 1826.

Journals of the Senate & House of Commons of the General Assembly of the State of North-Carolina, at the Session of 1826–27. Raleigh, N.C.: Lawrence & Lemay, 1827.

Journals of the Senate & House of Commons of the General Assembly of the State of North-Carolina, at the Session of 1827–28. Raleigh, N.C.: Lawrence & Lemay, 1828.

Journals of the Senate & House of Commons of the General Assembly of the State of North-Carolina, at the Session of 1828–29. Raleigh, N.C.: Lawrence & Lemay, 1829.

Journals of the Senate & House of Commons of the General Assembly of the State of North Carolina, at the Session of 1829–30. Raleigh, N.C.: Lawrence & Lemay, 1830.

Journals of the Senate & House of Commons of the General Assembly of the State of North-Carolina, at the Session of 1830–31. Raleigh, N.C.: Lawrence & Lemay, 1831.

Keeton, George W. and Georg Schwarzenberger, eds. *Jeremy Bentham and the Law: A Symposium*. London: Stevens & Sons, 1948.

Kelly, Alfred H., Winfred A. Harbison, and Herman Belz. *The American Constitution: Its Origins and Development*. 7th ed. 2 vols. New York: W. W. Norton, 1991.

Kent, James. *Commentaries on American Law*. Edited by Oliver Wendell Holmes Jr. 12th ed. 4 vols. Boston: Little, Brown, 1896. First published in 1826–1830 by O. Halsted (New York).

Kirk, Russell. *The Conservative Mind: From Burke to Santayana*. Chicago: Henry Regnery, 1953.

———. *John Randolph of Roanoke: A Study in American Politics: With Selected Speeches and Letters*. 4th ed. Indianapolis, Ind.: Liberty Fund, 1997.

———. *Orestes Brownson: Selected Essays*. Chicago: Gateway Editions, 1955. Distributed by Henry Regnery.

Laws of North-Carolina, At a General Assembly, Begun and Held at Newbern, on the Fifth Day of December, in the Year of Our Lord One Thousand Seven Hundred and Ninety-One, and in the Sixteenth Year of the Independence of the Said State: Being the First Session of the Said Assembly. Raleigh, N.C.: Hodge and Wills, 1792.

Laws of North-Carolina, At a General Assembly, Begun and Held at Raleigh, on the Eighteenth Day of November, in the Year of Our Lord One Thousand Seven Hundred and Ninety-Nine, and in the Twenty-Fourth Year of the Independence of the Said State: Being the First Session of the Said Assembly. Raleigh, N.C.: Arnett & Hodge, 1799.

Laws of North-Carolina, At a General Assembly, Begun and Held at Raleigh, on the Sixteenth Day of November, in the Year of Our Lord One Thousand Eight Hundred and One, and in the Twenty-Sixth Year of the Independence of the Said State. Raleigh, N.C.: Arnett & Hodge, 1801.

Laws of the State of North-Carolina, Enacted in the Year, 1817. Raleigh, N.C.: Thomas Henderson, 1818.

Laws of the State of North-Carolina, Enacted in the Year, 1818. Raleigh, N.C.: Thomas Henderson, 1819.

Laws of the State of North Carolina, Passed by the General Assembly, at the Session of 1836–37. Raleigh, N.C.: Thos. J. Lemay, 1837.

Laws and Resolutions of the State of North Carolina, Passed by the General Assembly at Its Session of 1883. Raleigh, N.C.: Ashe & Gatling, 1883.

Lefler, Hugh Talmage and Albert Ray Newsome. *North Carolina: The History of a Southern State.* 3rd ed. Chapel Hill: University of North Carolina Press, 1973.

[*Legislative Documents Printed by Order of the General Assembly of North Carolina at Its Sessions of 1835–1839*]. Raleigh, N.C.: Philo White, 1835.

Livingston, Edward. *A System of Penal Law, for the State of Louisiana: Consisting of a Code of Crimes and Punishments, a Code of Procedure, a Code of Evidence, a Code of Reform and Prison Discipline, a Book of Definitions.* Philadelphia, Pa.: James Kay Jun., 1833. https://archive.org/details/systemofpenallawooliviiala/page/368/mode/2up?view=theater.

London, H. M., ed., *Proceedings of the Thirtieth Annual Session of the North Carolina Bar Association: Held at Grove Park Inn, Asheville, N.C., June 28, 29, 30, 1928.* Raleigh, N.C.: Edwards & Broughton, 1928.

MacClamroch, James G. W. "Ancestors of the Consolidated Statutes." *Popular Government* 5 no. 7 (July 1938): 7–15.

MacDonald, William, ed. *Select Charters and Other Documents Illustrative of American History: 1605–1775.* New York: MacMillan, 1899.

Madden, A. F. McC. "1066, 1776, and All That: The Relevance of English Medieval Experience of 'Empire' to Later Imperial Constitutional Issues." In Flint and Williams, *Perspectives of Empire*, 9–26.

Maitland, Frederic W., and Francis C. Montague. *A Sketch of English Legal History.* New York: G. P. Putnam's Sons, 1915.

Maitland, Frederic William. "A Historical Sketch of Liberty and Equality as Ideals of English Political Philosophy from the Time of Hobbes to the Time of Coleridge." In Fisher, *Collected Papers of Frederic William Maitland*, 1:47, 79, 82.

Manning, John. *Commentaries on the First Book of Blackstone.* Chapel Hill, N.C.: University Press, 1899.

Martin, François-Xavier. *A Collection of the Private Acts of the General Assembly of the State of North-Carolina, from the Year 1715, to the Year 1790, Inclusive, Now in Force and Use.* Newbern, N.C.: François-Xavier Martin, 1794.

———. *A Collection of the Statutes of the Parliament of England in Force in the State of North-Carolina.* Newbern, N.C.: From the Editor's Press, 1792.

———. *Notes of a Few Decisions in the Superior Courts of the State of North-Carolina, and in the Circuit Court of the U. States, for North-Carolina District. To Which Is Added a Translation of Latch's Cases.* Newbern, N.C.: François-Xavier Martin, 1797.

———, reviser. *The Public Acts of the General Assembly of North-Carolina.* 2 vols. Newbern, N.C.: Martin & Ogden, 1804. https://play.google.com/books/reader?id=RTFRAQAAMAAJ&pg=GBS.PP4&hl=en.

———. *Treatise on the Powers and Duties of Executors and Administrators, According to the Law of North-Carolina.* Raleigh, N.C.: J. Gales, 1820. First published in 1803 by Martin & Ogden (Newbern).

Martinez, Albert J., Jr. "The Palatinate Clause of the Maryland Charter, 1632–1776: From Independent Jurisdiction to Independence." *American Journal of Legal History* 50, no. 3 (July 2008–2010): 305–325.

McClellan, James. *Liberty, Order, and Justice: An Introduction to the Constitutional Principles of American Government.* 3rd ed. Indianapolis, Ind.: Liberty Fund, 2000.

McFarland, Daniel Miles. "North Carolina Newspapers, Editors, and Journalistic Politics, 1815–1835." *North Carolina Historical Review* 30, no. 3 (July 1953): 376–414.

McGehee, L. P. *Consolidated Statutes of North Carolina*, 2 vols. Raleigh, N.C.: Commercial Printing, 1920.

McIlwain, Charles Howard. *Constitutionalism: Ancient and Modern.* Indianapolis, Ind.: Liberty Fund, 2007. First published in 1940 by Cornell University Press.

McRee, Griffith J. *Life and Correspondence of James Iredell, One of the Associate Justices of the Supreme Court of the United States.* 2 vols. New York: D. Appleton, 1857–1858.

Medlin, John G., Jr., chair. *Without Favor, Denial or Delay: A Court System for the 21st Century.* Raleigh, N.C.: Commission for the Future of Justice and the Courts in North Carolina, 1996.

Michie, A. Hewson, Chas. W. Sublett, and Beirne Stedman. *The General Statutes of North Carolina of 1943*. 4 vols. Charlottesville, Va.: The Michie Company, 1943.

Miller, Perry, ed. *The Legal Mind in America: From Independence to the Civil War*. Ithaca, N.Y.: Cornell University Press, 1969.

Miller, Robert D. "Samuel Field Phillips: The Odyssey of a Southern Dissenter." *North Carolina Historical Review* 58, no. 3 (July 1981): 263–280. https://www.jstor.org/stable/23534961.

Miller, William. Governors' Letter Books. State Archives of North Carolina, Raleigh.

Milsom, S. F. C. *Historical Foundations of the Common Law*. London: Butterworths, 1969.

———. *A Natural History of the Common Law*. New York: Columbia University Press, 2003.

Moore, Bartholomew F., and William B. Rodman. *Revised Code of North Carolina, Enacted by the General Assembly at the Session of 1854*. Boston: Little, Brown, 1855.

Mordecai, Samuel F. *Law Lectures: A Treatise, from a North Carolina Standpoint, on Those Portions of the First and Second Books of the Commentaries of Sir William Blackstone Which Have Not Become Obsolete in the United States*. [2nd ed.] 2 vols. Raleigh, N.C.: Commercial Printing, 1916.

———. *Mordecai's Miscellanies*. [Durham, N.C.]: Privately printed, [1927].

Moys, Elizabeth M., ed. *Manual of Law Librarianship: The Use and Organization of Legal Literature*. 2nd ed. Boston: G. K. Hall, 1987.

Murray, John Courtney. *We Hold These Truths: Catholic Reflections on the American Proposition*. Lanham, Md.: Rowman & Littlefield, 2005. First published in 1960 by Sheed & Ward (New York).

Nash, Frederic, Jas. Iredell, and Will. H. Battle, *Report of the Commissioners, Appointed to Revise and Consolidate the Public Statutes, of North Carolina*. House of Commons. No. 6. [Raleigh, N.C.: N.p., 1836].

New York Field Codes 1850–1865. Union, N.J.: Lawbook Exchange, 1998.

[*North Carolina Legislative Documents for Session of 1865–'66*]. [Raleigh, N.C.]: Wm. E. Pell, [1866?].

Olsen, Otto H. *Carpetbagger's Crusade: The Life of Albion Winegar Tourgée*. Baltimore, Md.: Johns Hopkins Press, 1965.

Ordinances Passed by the North Carolina State Convention, at the Sessions of 1865–'66. Raleigh, N.C.: Wm. E. Pell, 1867.

Orth, John V. *How Many Judges Does It Take to Make a Supreme Court?: And Other Essays on Law and the Constitution*. Lawrence: University Press of Kansas, 2006.

———. *The North Carolina State Constitution: A Reference Guide*. Westport, Conn.: Greenwood Press, 1993.

———. *The Tree of Legal Knowledge: Imagining Blackstone's Commentaries*. Singapore: Springer Nature, 2023.

———. "When Analogy Fails: The Common Law & *State v. Mann*." *North Carolina Law Review* 87, no. 3 (March 2009): 979–990.

Osborne, Francis I. "Presentation of the Portrait of Mr. Joseph Harvey Wilson to the Supreme Court of North Carolina." In Strong, *Cases Argued and Determined in the Supreme Court* [. . .] *Spring Term, 1915 (in Part) Fall Term, 1915 (in Part)*, 755–765. [169 N.C. 755]

Pagden, Anthony. "Law, Colonization, Legitimation, and the European Background." In Grossberg and Tomlins, *Cambridge History of Law in America*, Volume 1, *Early America (1580–1815)*, 1–31.

Parker, Mattie Erma Edwards, ed. *North Carolina Charters and Constitutions, 1578–1698*. Raleigh, N.C.: Carolina Charter Tercentenary Commission, 1963.

Partin, Wilson B., and Ralph A. White, Jr. *Cases Argued and Determined in the Supreme Court of North Carolina: Spring Term 1968 [to] Fall Term 1968*. Vol. 274 of the *North Carolina Reports*. Raleigh, N.C.: Bynum Printing, 1969.

———. *North Carolina Supreme Court Reports: Volume 275; Fall Term 1968, Spring Term 1969, Fall Term 1969*. Raleigh, N.C.: [Commercial Printing], 1970.

Peele, W. J., comp. *Lives of Distinguished North Carolinians: With Illustrations and Speeches*. Raleigh, N.C.: North Carolina Publishing Society, 1898.

Phillips, S. F. *Cases Argued and Determined in the Supreme Court of North Carolina, January and June Terms, 1870*. Vol. 64 of the *North Carolina Reports*. Raleigh, N.C.: Nichols & Gorman, 1870.

Philo Florian [pseud.]. "Sketch of the Character of Archibald Henderson as a Lawyer." In Hoyt, *Papers of Archibald D. Murphey*, 2:312–319.

Pierce, Edward L. *Memoir and Letters of Charles Sumner*. 4 vols. Boston: Roberts Brothers, 1877–1893.

Pollock, Frederick. *The Expansion of the Common Law*. Boston: Little, Brown, 1904.

Postema, Gerald J. "Classical Common Law Jurisprudence (Part I)." *Oxford University Commonwealth Law Journal* 2, no. 2 (Winter 2002): 155–180.

Potter, Henry. *The Office and Duty of a Justice of the Peace, and a Guide to Sheriffs, Coroners, Clerks, Constables, and Other Civil Officers. According to the Laws of North-Carolina. With an Appendix, Containing the Declaration of Rights and Constitution of This State, the Constitution of the United States, with the Amendments Thereto; and a Collection of the Most Approved Forms*. Raleigh, N.C.: Joseph Gales, 1816.

Potter, Henry, J. L. Taylor, & Bart. Yancey, revisers. *Laws of the State of North-Carolina, Including the Titles of Such Statutes and Parts of Statutes of Great Britain As Are in Force in Said State; Together with the Second Charter Granted by Charles II. to the Proprietors of Carolina; the Great Deed of Grant from the Lords Proprietors; the Grant from George II. to John Lord Granville; the Bill of Rights and Constitution of the State, Including the Names of the Members of the Convention That Formed the Same; the Constitution of the United States, with the Amendments; and the Treaty of Peace of 1783; with Marginal Notes and References*. 2 vols. Raleigh, N.C.: J. Gales, 1821.

Potter, Robert. *An Argument Addressed to the Supreme Court of North-Carolina at June Term, 1825. On the Constitutionality of the Civil Jurisdiction Conferred by the Legislature of North-Carolina on Single Justices of the Peace*. Raleigh, N.C.: J. Gales & Son, 1826.

Pound, Roscoe. "The Pioneers and the Common Law." In Andrews, *Proceedings of the Twenty-Second Annual Session of the North Carolina Bar Association [. . .] June 29, 30, and July 1, 1920*, 188–206.

———. "Toward Improving the Administration of Justice in North Carolina." June 12, 1958. Housed in the Special Collection of the North Carolina Supreme Court Library.

Powell, William S., ed. *Dictionary of North Carolina Biography*. 6 vols. Chapel Hill: University of North Carolina Press, 1979–1996.

———., ed. *Encyclopedia of North Carolina*. Chapel Hill: University of North Carolina Press, 2006.

Pratt, Walter F., Jr. "The Struggle for Judicial Independence in Antebellum North Carolina: The Story of Two Judges." *Law and History Review* 4, no. 1 (Spring 1986): 129–159.

"Proceedings of the Legislature. Called Session. House of Commons. Thursday, Feb. 1, 1866. Special Order." *Raleigh Weekly North-Carolina Standard*, vol. 32, no. 6, Raleigh, N.C., February 7, 1866. https://chroniclingamerica.loc.gov/lccn/sn85042148/1866-02-07/ed-1/seq-2/.

"Proceedings of the Legislature. Called Session. House of Commons. Friday, Feb. 2, 1866. Special Order." *Raleigh Weekly North-Carolina Standard*, vol. 32, no. 6, Raleigh, N.C., February 7, 1866. https://chroniclingamerica.loc.gov/lccn/sn85042148/1866-02-07/ed-1/seq-2/.

"Proceedings of the Legislature. Called Session. House of Commons. Thursday, Feb. 8th, 1866, Special Order." *Raleigh Weekly North-Carolina Standard*, vol. 32, no. 7, Raleigh, N.C., February 14, 1866. https://chroniclingamerica.loc.gov/lccn/sn85042148/1866-02-14/ed-1/seq-2/.

Proceedings of the North Carolina Bar Association, at a Meeting Held in Raleigh, the 14th of October, 1885, 7–12. Raleigh, N.C.: Edwards, Broughton, 1886.

Public Laws and Resolutions of the State of North Carolina Passed by the General Assembly at Its Session of 1893, Begun and Held in the City of Raleigh on Wednesday, the Fourth Day of January, A. D. 1893. Raleigh, N.C.: Josephus Daniels, 1893.

Public Laws and Resolutions of the State of North Carolina Passed by the General Assembly at Its Session of 1915 Begun and Held in the City of Raleigh on Wednesday, the Sixth Day of January, A. D. 1915, Raleigh, N.C.: Edwards & Broughton, 1915.

Public Laws and Resolutions, Together with the Private Laws, of the State of North Carolina, Passed by the General Assembly at Its Session 1872–'73, Begun and Held in the City of Raleigh, on Monday, the Eighteenth Day of November, A. D. 1872. Raleigh, N.C.: Stone & Uzzell, 1873.

Public Laws of the State of North-Carolina, Passed by the General Assembly at Its Called Session of 1863. Raleigh, N.C.: W. W. Holden, 1863.

Public Laws of the State of North Carolina, Passed by the General Assembly at the Session of 1866. Raleigh, N.C.: Wm. E. Pell, 1866.

Public Laws of the State of North Carolina, Passed by the General Assembly at Its Session 1868–'69, Begun and Held in the City of Raleigh on the Sixteenth of November, 1868. Raleigh, N.C.: M.S. Littlefield, 1869.

Public Laws of the State of North Carolina, Passed by the General Assembly at Its Session 1870–'71, Begun and Held in the City of Raleigh on the Sixteenth of November, 1870. Raleigh, N.C.: James H. Moore, 1871.

Public Laws of the State of North Carolina, Passed by the General Assembly at Its Session 1871–'72, Begun and Held in the City of Raleigh, on the Twentieth Day of November, 1871. Raleigh, N.C.: Theo. N. Ramsay, 1872.

Rakove, Jack N. *Declaring Rights: A Brief History with Documents*. Boston: Bedford Books, 1998.

Raleigh Daily Sentinel, vol. 3, no. 311, Saturday, August 8, 1868. https://newspapers.digitalnc.org/lccn/sn84026569/1868-08-08/ed-1/seq-2.pdf.

Raleigh Daily Sentinel, vol. 4, no. 74, Friday, November 6, 1868. https://newspapers.digitalnc.org/lccn/sn84026569/1868-11-06/ed-1/seq-2.pdf.

Raleigh Daily Sentinel, vol. 4, no. 101, Wednesday, December 9, 1868. https://newspapers.digitalnc.org/lccn/sn84026569/1868-12-09/ed-1/seq-2.pdf.

Raleigh Daily Sentinel, vol. 4, no. 102, Friday, December 18, 1868. https://newspapers.digitalnc.org/lccn/sn84026569/1868-12-18/ed-1/seq-2.pdf.

Raleigh Daily Sentinel, vol. 4, no. 110, Saturday, December 19, 1868. https://newspapers.digitalnc.org/lccn/sn84026569/1868-12-19/ed-1/seq-2.pdf.

Raleigh Daily Sentinel, vol. 5, no. 294, Saturday Evening, July 30, 1870. https://newspapers.digitalnc.org/lccn/sn84026569/1870-07-30/ed-1/seq-2.pdf.

Raleigh Daily Sentinel, vol. 6, no. 30, Raleigh, N.C., Thursday, September 29, 1870. https://newspapers.digitalnc.org/lccn/sn84026569/1870-09-29/ed-1/seq-2.pdf.

Raleigh North Carolina Standard, vol. 11, no. 569, Wednesday, October 1, 1845. https://newspapers.digitalnc.org/lccn/sn85042147/1845-10-01/ed-1/seq-3/.

Raleigh North Carolina Standard, vol. 2, no. 306, Friday, January 8, 1869. https://newspapers.digitalnc.org/lccn/sn85042144/1869-01-08/ed-1/seq-2.pdf.

Raleigh North Carolina Standard, vol. 2, no. 320, Monday, January 25, 1869. https://newspapers.digitalnc.org/lccn/sn85042144/1869-01-25/ed-1/seq-2.pdf.

Raleigh North Carolina Standard, vol. 3, no. 371, Thursday, March 25, 1869. https://newspapers.digitalnc.org/lccn/sn85042144/1869-03-25/ed-1/seq-2/.

Raper, Horace W., ed. *The Papers of William Woods Holden:* Volume I: *1841–1868*. Raleigh, N.C.: Division of Archives and History, North Carolina Department of Cultural Resources, 2000. https://digital.ncdcr.gov/Documents/Detail/papers-of-william-woods-holden/2149063?item=2239608.

Reinsch, Paul Samuel. "The English Common Law in the Early American Colonies." In Zane, et al., *Select Essays in Anglo-American Legal History*, 1:367–415.

Report of the Commission to Investigate Charges of Fraud and Corruption, under Act of Assembly, Session 1871–'72. Raleigh, N.C.: James H. Moore, 1872.

Report of Will. H. Battle [Nov. 18th, 1872]. Doc. No. 14. In *Executive and Legislative Documents* [. . .] *1872–'73*, 1–4.

Reppy, Alison, ed. *David Dudley Field: Centenary Essays Celebrating One Hundred Years of Legal Reform*, 17–54. New York: New York University School of Law, 1949.

———. "The Field Codification Concept." In Reppy, *David Dudley Field*, 17–54.

The Revised Statutes of the State of New-York, As Altered by the Legislature; Including the Statutory Provisions of a General Nature, Passed from 1828 to 1835 Inclusive; With References to Judicial Decisions; To Which Are Added, Certain Local Acts Passed Before and Since the Revised Statutes; All the Acts of General Interest Passed during the Session of 1836; And an Appendix, Containing Extracts from the Original Reports of the Revisers to the Legislature, All the Material Notes Which Accompanied Those Reports, and Explanatory Remarks, 3 vols. Albany, N.Y.: Packard and Van Benthuysen, 1836. https://play.google.com/books/reader?id=QIA4AAAAIAAJ&pg=GBS.PP10.

The Revised Statutes of the State of North Carolina, Passed by the General Assembly at the Session of 1836-7, Including an Act Concerning the Revised Statutes and Other Public Acts, Passed at the Same Session; Together with the Second Charter Granted by Charles the 2d to the Proprietors of Carolina—the Great Deed of Grant from the Lords Proprietors—the Grant from George the 2d to John Lord Granville—the Bill of Rights and Constitution of the State, with the Amendments Thereto—the Constitution of the United States, with the Amendments—the Treaty of Peace of 1783—the Mecklenburg Declaration of Independence, with a Short Narrative Thereof. Raleigh, N.C.: Turner and Hughes, 1837.

Rivers, William J. *A Sketch of the History of South Carolina to the Close of the Proprietary Government by the Revolution of 1719: With an Appendix Containing Many Valuable Records Hitherto Unpublished*. Charleston, S.C.: McCarter, 1856.

Robbins, Wm. M., and C. T. Murphy. Report of the Special Committee on the Senate Bill to Provide for Calling a State Convention. Doc. No. 34. In *Executive and Legislative Documents* [. . .] *1869–'70*, 1–16.

Rodman, Will. B., and W. H. Bailey. Report of the Code Commissioners, December 18, 1870. In Rodman Papers, Collection No. 329, Item 329.16d.

Rodman, Will. B., V. C. Barringer, and A. W. Tourgee. Report of the Code Commissioners. [March 12th, 1870]. Doc. No. 28, in *Executive and Legislative Documents* [. . .] *1869–'70*, 1–4.

Rodman, William Blount. William Blount Rodman Papers, Collection No. 329. East Carolina Manuscript Collection. J. Y. Joyner Library, East Carolina University. Greenville, N.C.

Rommen, Heinrich A. *The Natural Law: A Study in Legal and Social History and Philosophy*. Translated by Thomas R. Hanley. Indianapolis, Ind.: Liberty Fund, 1998. First published in 1936 by Verlag Jakob Hegner (Leipzig).

Ruffin, Thomas, and Francis L. Hawks. *Reports of Cases Argued and Adjudged in the Supreme Court of North-Carolina, during the Years 1820 & 1821: The Former Part by Thomas Ruffin, Esquire. The Latter by Francis L. Hawks*. Vol. 1. Raleigh, N.C.: J. Gales & Son, 1823.

[Rush, Richard]. "American Jurisprudence." In *Carolina Law Repository*, 2:347–363.

Salisbury North-Carolina Mercury and Salisbury Advertiser, vol. 2, no. 87, Salisbury, Thursday, December 26, 1799. https://newspapers.digitalnc.org/lccn/sn83025836/1799-12-26/ed-1/seq-2.pdf.

Santayana, George. *Dominations and Powers: Reflections on Liberty Society and Government*. New York: Charles Scribner's Sons, 1951.

———. *The Life of Reason or the Phases of Human Progress: Reason in Science*. New York: Charles Scribner's Sons, 1906.

———. *Persons and Places: Fragments of Autobiography*. Edited by William G. Holzberger and Herman J. Saatkamp Jr. Cambridge, Mass.: MIT Press, 1986.

———. *Realms of Being*. One-volume edition. New York: Charles Scribner's Sons, 1942.

———. *Santayana on America: Essays, Notes, and Letters on American Life, Literature, and Philosophy*. Edited by Richard Colton Lyon. New York: Harcourt, Brace & World, 1968.

———. *Winds of Doctrine: Studies in Contemporary Opinion*. New York: Charles Scribner's Sons, 1913.

Saunders, William L., ed. *The Colonial Records of North Carolina*. 10 vols. Raleigh, N.C.: P. M. Hale [etc.] State Printer, 1886–1890.

Scaperlanda, Michael A., and Teresa Stanton Collett, eds. *Recovering Self-Evident Truths: Catholic Perspectives on American Law*. Washington, D.C.: Catholic University of America Press, 2007.

Schall, James V. *Reason, Revelation, and the Foundations of Political Philosophy*. Baton Rouge: Louisiana State University Press, 1987.

Schenck, David. David Schenck Papers, Collection No. 652. Southern Historical Collection. Wilson Special Collections Library, University of North Carolina at Chapel Hill. Chapel Hill, N.C.

Scruton, Roger. *Kant: A Very Short Introduction*. Oxford: Oxford University Press, 2001.

Senate Journal—1790. At a General Assembly Begun and Held at Fayetteville, on the First Day of November, in the Year of Our Lord One Thousand Seven Hundred and Ninety, and in the Fifteenth Year of the Independence of the United States of America: Being the First Session of This Assembly. In *State Records*, 21:729–869.

Session Laws and Resolutions Passed by the General Assembly at the Regular Session [. . .] *February, A.D. 1961*. Raleigh, N.C.: Observer Printing House, 1961.

Session Laws and Resolutions Passed by the General Assembly at the Extra Session [. . .] *November 15, A.D. 1965 and the Extra Session* [. . .] *January 10, A.D. 1966 and the Regular Session* [. . .] *February 8, A.D. 1967*. Raleigh, N.C.: Observer Printing House, 1967.

Shepherd, James E. "Some Leaves from Colonial History." In Biggs, *Report of the Second Annual Meeting of the North Carolina Bar Association* [. . .] *June 27th, 28th and 29th, 1900*, 143–164.

Sheppard, Steve, ed. *History of Legal Education in the United States: Commentaries and Primary Sources*. Pasadena, Calif.: Salem Press, 1999.

Sioussat, St. George Leakin. "The Theory of the Extension of English Statutes to the Plantations." In Zane, et al., *Select Essays in Anglo-American Legal History*, 416–430.

Smith, James. *Civil Practice in the Court of Pleas and Quarter Sessions of North Carolina, in Ordinary Cases*. New York: A. S. Gould, 1846.

Stanlis, Peter J. *Edmund Burke & the Natural Law*. New Brunswick, N.J.: Transaction Publishers, 2003. First published in 1958 by the University of Michigan Press (Ann Arbor, Mich.).

Statutes and Parts of Statutes of Great Britain, Reported as Being in Force in This State, By the Commissioners Appointed under the Act of 1817, Entitled, "An Act for the Revision of the Acts of the General Assembly." In Potter, Taylor, & Yancey, *Laws of the State of North-Carolina*, 1:85–93.

Story, Joseph. *Commentaries on the Constitution of the United States; with a Preliminary Review of the Constitutional History of the Colonies and States, before the Adoption of the Constitution*. 3 vols. Boston: Hillard, Gray, 1833.

Strong, Robert C. *Cases Argued and Determined in the Supreme Court of North Carolina: Fall Term, 1908 (in part)*. Vol. 149 of the *North Carolina Reports*. Raleigh, N.C.: Commercial Printing, 1908.

———. *Cases Argued and Determined in the Supreme Court of North Carolina: Spring Term, 1915 (in Part) Fall Term, 1915 (in Part)*. Vol. 169 of the *North Carolina Reports*. Raleigh, N.C.: Edwards & Broughton, 1916.

———. *Cases Argued and Determined in the Supreme Court of North Carolina: Fall Term*, 1915 (in part). Vol. 170 of the *North Carolina Reports*. Raleigh, N.C.: Edwards & Broughton, 1916.

———. *Cases Argued and Determined in the Supreme Court of North Carolina: Fall Term*, 1915 (in part) *[and] Spring Term, 1916*. Vol. 171 of the *North Carolina Reports*. Raleigh, N.C.: Edwards & Broughton, 1916.

———. *Cases Argued and Determined in the Supreme Court of North Carolina: Fall Term, 1918*. Vol. 176 of the *North Carolina Reports*. Raleigh, N.C.: Mitchell Printing, 1919.

———. *Cases Argued and Determined in the Supreme Court of North Carolina: Spring Term, 1919*. Vol. 177 of the *North Carolina Reports*. Raleigh, N.C.: Mitchell Printing, 1919.

Swaim, Benjamin. *The North Carolina Executor: Containing the Statutes and Common Law of This State, Together with the Decisions of the Supreme Court and All the Necessary Forms and Precedents*. Asheborough, N.C.: Southern Citizen, 1841.

[Swain, David L.] *Message of the Governor of North Carolina, to the General Assembly of the State, at the Commencement of the Session, November 18, 1833: [Document] No. 1, Legislature of North Carolina, 1833*. Raleigh, N.C.: Charles B. Ramsay, 1833.

———. *Message from His Excellency the Governor, to the General Assembly, Transmitting a Communication from the Commissioners Appointed to Revise the Public Statute Laws of North Carolina. December 4th, 1834: [Document] No. 6, Legislature of North Carolina, 1834*. Raleigh, N.C.: Philo White, 1834.

———. "A Sketch of the Judicial History of North Carolina, with a List of the Judges and Attorney Generals Since the Adoption of the Constitution." In *Revised Statutes of the State of North Carolina, Passed by the General Assembly [. . .] 1836–7*, 2:527–532.

Swan, Joseph R. *Commentaries on Pleading under the Ohio Code. With Precedents of Petitions, Answers, Demurrers and Replies*. Cincinnati, Ohio: Robert Clarke, 1860.

[Swann, Samuel]. *A Collection of All the Public Acts of Assembly, of the Province of North-Carolina: Now in Force and Use. Together with the Titles of All Such Laws As Are Obsolete, Expir'd, or Repeal'd. And Also, an Exact Table of the Titles of the Acts in Force. Revised by Commissioners Appointed by an Act of the General Assembly of the Said Province, for That Purpose; and Examined with the Records, and Confirmed in Full Assembly*. Newbern, N.C.: James Davis, 1751.

Taylor, John L., reviser. *A Revisal of the Laws of the State of North-Carolina, Passed from 1821 to 1825 (Both Years Inclusive) with Marginal Notes and References*. Raleigh, N.C.: J. Gales & Son, 1827.

Taylor, John Louis. *A Digest of the Statute Law of North-Carolina, Relative to Wills, Executors and Administrators, the Provision for Widows, and the Distribution of Intestates Estates*. Raleigh, N.C.: J. Gales & Son, 1824.

Taylor, Raymond M. "History of the North Carolina Supreme Court Library." In Partin and White, *North Carolina Supreme Court Reports [. . .] Fall Term 1968, Spring Term 1969, Fall Term 1969*, 713–728. [275 N.C. 713]

Testimony Taken by the Joint Select Committee to Inquire into the Condition of Affairs in the Late Insurrectionary States: North Carolina. House of Representatives. Report No. 22, pt. 2. 42d Cong., 2d sess. Washington, D.C.: Government Printing Office, 1872.

Tourgée, Albion W. *The Code of Civil Procedure of North Carolina, with Notes and Decisions*. Raleigh, N.C.: John Nichols, 1878.

———. "The Unwritten Law and Why It Remains Unwritten." *The Green Bag: A Useless But Entertaining Magazine for Lawyers* 20, no. 1 (January 1908): 8–17.

Tourgée, Albion Winegar. Albion Winegar Tourgée Papers, 1801–1924, Collection 1-2383. Davis Library, University of North Carolina at Chapel Hill.

Tushnet, Mark V. *The American Law of Slavery 1810–1860: Considerations of Humanity and Interest*. Princeton, N.J.: Princeton University Press, 1981.

[Unknown]. Review of *An Address Delivered before the Law Association of the City of New York, October 21, 1836*, by James Kent. *American Jurist and Law Magazine* 16, no. 32 (January 1837): 471–481.

[Unknown]. Review of *The Statute Laws of Tennessee, of a Public and General Nature*, by John Haywood and Robert L. Coobs, revisers. *American Jurist and Law Magazine* 8, no. 16 (October 1832): 298–315.

Valentine, Patrick M. "Useful Books: Community Libraries in Antebellum North Carolina." *North Carolina Libraries* 64, no. 3 (Fall/Winter 2006): 60–69.

Versteeg, Mila. " 'Perfection in Imperfection': Joseph de Maistre and the Limitations of Constitutional Design." In Galligan, *Constitutions and the Classics*, 312–326.

Warren, Charles. *A History of the American Bar*. New York: Howard Fertig, 1966.

Weber, Michael. Introduction to *The Code of Civil Procedure of the State of New-York. Reported Complete by the Commissioners on Practice and Pleadings*. Vol. 1 (1850) of *New York Field Codes 1850–1865*. Union, N.J.: Lawbook Exchange, 1998.

Weeks, Stephen B., ed. *Index to the Colonial and State Records of North Carolina, Covering Volumes 1–25: Published under the Supervision of the Trustees of the Public Libraries, by Order of the General Assembly with an Historical Review*. 4 vols. Raleigh, N.C.: E. M. Uzzell, 1914.

———. "The North Carolina Historians." In Connor, *Proceedings and Addresses of the Fifteenth Annual Session of the State Literary and Historical Association of North Carolina, Raleigh, December 1–2, 1914*, 71–86.

———. *Southern Quakers and Slavery: A Study in Institutional History*. Baltimore, Md.: Johns Hopkins Press, 1896.

Whatley, L. McKay. "Benjamin Swaim and the 'Man of Business'." *Notes on the History of Randolph County, NC*. Accessed August 3, 2023. https://randolphhistory.wordpress.com/2012/01/17/benjamin-swaim-and-the-man-of-business/.

Whichard, Willis P. *A Consequential Life: David Lowry Swain, Nineteenth-Century North Carolina, and Their University*. Chapel Hill: University of North Carolina at Chapel Hill Library, 2022.

———. *Justice James Iredell*. Durham, N.C.: Carolina Academic Press, 2000.

Wild, John. *Plato's Modern Enemies and the Theory of Natural Law*. Chicago: University of Chicago Press, 1953.

Wilmington Daily Journal, vol. 17, no. 258, Wednesday Morning, July 29, 1868. https://newspapers.digitalnc.org/lccn/sn84026521/18680729/ed1/seq2.pdf.

Wilmington Daily Journal, vol. 17, no. 271, Thursday Morning, August 13, 1868. https://newspapers.digitalnc.org/lccn/sn84026521/1868-08-13/ed-1/seq-2.pdf.

Winston, R. W. "Presentation of Portrait of Chief Justice Leonard Henderson." In Strong, *Cases Argued and Determined in the Supreme Court* [. . .] *Fall Term, 1908*, 595–616. [149 N.C. 595]

Winston, Robert W. "A Century of Law in North Carolina [at the Proceedings of the North Carolina Bar Association in the Supreme Court Room, Raleigh, 4 January 1919, on the Occasion of the Centennial Celebration of the One Hundredth Anniversary of the Establishment of the Supreme Court of North Carolina]." In Strong, *Cases Argued and Determined in the Supreme Court* [. . .] *Fall Term, 1918*, 763–791. [176 N.C. 763]

———. "Popular Discontent with Judicial Procedure." In Davis, *Proceedings of the Fifteenth Annual Session of the North Carolina Bar Association* [. . .] *July 2, 3 and 4, 1913*, 24–44.

———. Review of *Walter Clark, Fighting Judge*, by Audrey Lee Brooks. *North Carolina Law Review* 22, no. 2 (1944): 181–185.

Winston, Robert Watson. "Chief Justice Shepherd and His Times." *North Carolina Law Review* 3, no. 1 (February 1925): 1–13.

———. *It's a Far Cry*. New York: H. Holt, 1937.

Womack, Thomas B. "Report of the Committee on Legislation and Law Reform." In Biggs, *Report of the Seventh Annual Meeting of the North Carolina Bar Association* [. . .] *July 5th, 6th, 7th, 1905*, 68–82.

Womack, Thomas B., Needham Y. Gulley, and William B. Rodman. *Revisal of 1905 of North Carolina*. 2 vols. Raleigh, N.C.: E. M. Uzzell, 1905.

Worth, Jonathan. "[Address to the Gentlemen of the Convention May 25th, 1866]. In *Journal of the Convention of the State of North-Carolina at Its Adjourned Session of 1866*. Raleigh, N.C.: Cannon & Holden, 1866.

Yancey, Bartlett. "Letters to Bartlett Yancey." In vol. 10, no. 2 of *The James Sprunt Historical Publications*. Published under the direction of the North Carolina Historical Society, 25–76. Chapel Hill: University [of North Carolina], 1911. https://archive.org/details/bartlettyanceypooooogeor/page/n1/mode/2up.

Zane, John Maxcy, James Bryce, Frederic William Maitland, Frederick Pollock, and William Searle Holdsworth. *Select Essays in Anglo-American Legal History*. Compiled and edited by a committee of the Association of American Law Schools. 3 vols. Boston: Little, Brown, 1907.

Further Reading

Adams, William J., Jr. "Recodification of the North Carolina Statutes." *North Carolina Law Review* 19, no. 1 (December 1940): 27–46.

Battle, R. H. "Hon. Samuel Field Phillips, LL. D." *North Carolina Journal of Law* 1, no. 1 (January 1904): 22–29.

Calnan, Alan. *A Revisionist History of Tort Law: From Holmesian Realism to Neoclassical Rationalism.* Durham, N.C.: Carolina Academic Press, 2005.

Carter, James C. *The Ideal and the Actual in the Law. The Annual Address Delivered by James C. Carter, of New York, at the Thirteenth Annual Meeting [of the American Bar Association], August 21, 1890.* Philadelphia, Pa.: Dando Printing and Publishing, 1890.

———. "Independence of the Judiciary." Address Delivered at the Grand Central Palace Meeting, Thursday Evening, November 3d, 1898. [New York?]: [1898?].

———. *Law: Its Origin Growth and Function: Being a Course of Lectures Prepared for Delivery before the Law School of Harvard University.* New York: G. P. Putnam's Sons, 1907.

Coquillette, Daniel R. *The Anglo-American Legal Heritage: Introductory Materials.* Durham, N.C.: Carolina Academic Press, 1999.

———. "The Nineteenth Century: Legal Instrumentalism, Codification and Utilitarianism." In Coquillette, *Anglo-American Legal Heritage.*

Dibble, Roy Floyd. *Albion W. Tourgée: A Thesis with a Bibliography.* New York: Lemcke and Buechner, 1921.

Dillon, John F. "Codification." *American Law Review* 20, no. 1 (January–February 1886): 1–47.

Elliott, Mark. *Color-Blind Justice: Albion Tourgée and the Quest for Racial Equality from the Civil War to* Plessy v. Ferguson. Oxford: Oxford University Press, 2006.

Elliott, Mark, and John David Smith, eds. *Undaunted Radical: The Selected Writings and Speeches of Albion W. Tourgée.* Baton Rouge: Louisiana State University Press, 2010.

Field, David Dudley. "Annual Address of the President of the American Bar Association." *American Law Review* 23, no. 6 (November–December 1889): 946–957.

———. "Codification—Mr. Field's Answer to Mr. Carter." *American Law Review* 24, no. 2 (March–April 1890): 255–266.

———. "Reasons for Codification." In Honnold, *Life of the Law,* 113–115.

Field, David Dudley, and Alexander Bradford. "Introduction to the Completed Civil Code (1865)." In Honnold, *Life of the Law,* 109–113.

Frank, Jerome. "Codification and the Command Theory of Law." Chap. 17 in Frank, *Law and the Modern Mind.*

———. *Law and the Modern Mind.* New York: Brentano's, 1930.

Gordon, Robert W. Review of *The American Codification Movement: A Study of Antebellum Legal Reform,* by Charles M. Cook. *Vanderbilt Law Review* 36, no. 2 (March 1983): 431–458.

Gray, William C. Review of *Law: Its Origin, Growth and Function* [. . .], by James Coolidge Carter. *The Green Bag: A Useless But Entertaining Magazine for Lawyers* 20, no. 6 (June 1908): 321.

Grossman, Lewis A. "Essay: Codification and the California Mentality." *Hastings Law Journal* 45, no. 3 (March 1994): 617–639.

———. "James Coolidge Carter and Mugwump Jurisprudence." *Law and History Review* 20, no. 3 (Fall 2002): 577–629.

———. "Langdell Upside-Down: James Coolidge Carter and the Anticlassical Jurisprudence of Anticodification." *Yale Journal of Law & the Humanities* 19, no. 2 (Summer 2007): 149–219.

Hall, A. Oakey. "Reminiscences of David Dudley Field." *The Green Bag: A Useless But Entertaining Magazine for Lawyers* 6, no. 5 (May 1894): 209–213.

Hamilton, Edith, and Huntington Cairns, eds. *The Collected Dialogues of Plato Including the Letters.* Bollingen Series 71. Princeton, N.J.: Princeton University Press, 1961.

Henderson, Archibald. "Democracy and Literature: Address [. . .] before the State Literary and Historical Association, December 4, 1912." In Poe, *Proceedings of the Thirteenth Annual Session of the State Literary and Historical Association of North Carolina,* 62–73.

Holmes, Oliver Wendell. "Codes, and the Arrangement of the Law." *American Law Review* 5, no. 1 (October 1870): 1–13.

Honnold, John, ed., *The Life of the Law: Readings on the Growth of Legal Institutions*. New York: Free Press of Glencoe, 1964.

Lang, Maurice Eugen. *Codification in the British Empire and America*. Clark, N.J.: Lawbook Exchange, 2005. First published in 1924 by H. J. Paris (Amsterdam).

LaPiana, William P. "Just the Facts: The Field Code and the Case Method." *New York Law School Law Review* 36, no. 2 (1991): 287–336.

Lerner, Gerda. *The Grimké Sisters from South Carolina: Pioneers for Women's Rights and Abolition*. Chapel Hill: University of North Carolina Press, 2004.

Lewis, William Draper, ed. *Great American Lawyers: The Lives and Influence of Judges and Lawyers Who Have Acquired Permanent National Reputation, and Have Developed the Jurisprudence of the United States. A History of the Legal Profession in America*. 8 vols. South Hackensack, N.J.: Rothman Reprints, 1971. First published in 1909 by John C. Winston (Philadelphia, Pa.).

Lieberman, David. *The Province of Legislation Determined: Legal Theory in Eighteenth-Century Britain*. Cambridge: Cambridge University Press, 1989.

Madison, James. "To Thomas S. Grimke, Montpellier, January 15, 1828." In Rives, *Letters and Other Writings of James Madison*, 3:611–612.

Mallonee, L. Dee. "Revised Statutes and Codes." *American Law Review* 48, no. 1 (January–February 1914): 37–49.

Miller, George Alfred. "James Coolidge Carter 1827–1905." In Lewis, *Great American Lawyers*, 8:1–41.

Morris, Sylvanus. "Thomas Reade Rootes Cobb 1823–1863." In Lewis, *Great American Lawyers*, 7:309–320.

Nelson, William E. *Americanization of the Common Law: The Impact of Legal Change on Massachusetts Society, 1760–1830*. Cambridge, Mass.: Harvard University Press, 1975.

Orth, John V. Review of *Toward a Usable Past: Liberty under State Constitutions*, edited by Paul Finkelman and Stephen E. Gottlieb. *Constitutional Commentary* 10, no. 1 (Winter 1993): 203–211.

Plato. "The Laws." Translated by A. E. Taylor. In Hamilton and Cairns, *Collected Dialogues of Plato Including the Letters*, 1225–1513.

Platt, Charles M. "The Proposed Civil Code of New York." *American Law Review* 20, no. 5 (September–October 1886): 713–717.

Poe, Clarence. *Proceedings of the Thirteenth Annual Session of the State Literary and Historical Association of North Carolina, Raleigh, December 3–4, 1912*. Raleigh, N.C.: Edwards & Broughton Printing, 1913. https://digital.ncdcr.gov/Documents/Detail/proceedings-of-the-...-annual-session-of-the-state-literary-and-historical-association-1912-13th/2310412.

Pomeroy, John Norton, Jr. "John Norton Pomeroy. 1828–1885." In Lewis, *Great American Lawyers*, 8:89–135.

Postema, Gerald J. *Bentham and the Common Law Tradition*. 2nd edition. Oxford, UK: Oxford University Press, 2019.

Pound, Roscoe. "The Advisability of Codifying Anglo-American Law." In Honnold, *Life of the Law*, 140–143.

———. "Codification in Anglo-American Law." In Schwartz, *Code Napoleon and the Common-Law World*, 267–297.

Rives, William C., ed. *Letters and Other Writings of James Madison, Fourth President of the United States. In Four Volumes. Published by Order of Congress. 1816–1828*. Philadelphia, Pa.: J. B. Lippincott, 1865.

Schwartz, Bernard, ed. *The Code Napoleon and the Common-Law World*. Westport, Conn.: Greenwood Press, 1956.

Schweber, Howard. "The 'Science' of Legal Science: The Model of the Natural Sciences in Nineteenth-Century American Legal Education." *Law and History Review* 17, no. 3 (Autumn 1999): 421–466.

Shapiro, Barbara. "Codification of the Laws in Seventeenth-Century England." *Wisconsin Law Review* (1974): 428–465.

Skinner, Robert W., Jr. Review of *Law: Its Origin, Growth, and Function* [. . .], by James Coolidge Carter. *Columbia Law Review* 8, no. 6 (June 1908): 515–517.

Smith, Joseph. *A Descriptive Catalogue of Friends' Books, or Books Written by Members of the Society of Friends, Commonly Called Quakers, from Their First Rise to the Present Time,* [. . .]. 2 vols. London: Joseph Smith, 1867. https://archive.org/details/desccatalo1smit; https://archive.org/details/desccatalo2smit.

Stone, Ferdinand Fairfax. "A Primer on Codification." *Tulane Law Review* 29, no. 2 (February 1955): 303–310.

Story, Joseph, Theron Metcalf, Simon Greenleaf, Charles E. Forbes, and Luther S. Cushing. "Codification of the Common Law of Massachusetts." *American Jurist and Law Magazine* 17, no. 33 (April 1837): 17–51.

Swisher, Carl B. "Fringes of the Codification Movement." Chap. 14 in Swisher, *History of the Supreme Court*.

———. *History of the Supreme Court of the United States*. Vol. 5, *The Taney Period, 1836–64*. New York: Macmillan, 1974.

Telkampf, J. Louis. "On Codification, or the Systematizing of the Law." *American Jurist and Law Magazine* 26, no. 51 (October 1841): 113–144.

Tocqueville, Alexis de. *Democracy in America*. Translated by Henry Reeve. New York: Adlard and Saunders, 1838.

Tushnet, Mark V. *Slave Law in the American South:* State v. Mann *in History and Literature*. Lawrence: University Press of Kansas, 2003.

Whichard, Willis P. "A Place for Walter Clark in the American Judicial Tradition." *North Carolina Law Review*, 63, no. 2 (January 1985): 287–337.

Wiecek, William M. *The Lost World of Classical Legal Thought: Law and Ideology in America, 1886–1937*. New York: Oxford University Press, 1998.

Yelle, Robert A. "Bentham's Fictions: Canon and Idolatry in the Genealogy of Law." *Yale Journal of Law & the Humanities* 17, no. 2 (January 2005): 151–179.

Table of Cases and Acts Cited

Federal Cases	**Documents**
Calder v. Bull, 3 U.S. 386 (1798).	I–27, n. 177 I-27, n. 178 I-27, n. 179
Minge v. Gilmour, 17 F. Cas. 440 (No. 9631) (C.C.N.C. 1798).	I–27, n. 180
McFaul v. Ramsey, 61 U.S. 523 (1857).	III–33, n. 418 III–33, n. 513
Plessy v. Ferguson, 163 U.S. 537 (1896).	III–49, n. 459 IV–23, n. 495
North Carolina Cases	**Documents**
Walton v. Gatlin, 60 N.C. 310, 321, 1 Win. 318, 328–329 (1864)	Gen. Intro., n. 40
Bayard v. Singleton, 1 N.C. 5, 1 Mart. 48 (1787).	I–23, n. 161 I–23, n. 163 I–23, n. 164
Hoke v. Henderson, 15 N.C. (4 Dev.) 1 (1833).	II–11, n. 214
Lewis v. Williams, 2 N.C. (1 Hayw.) 150 (1795).	II–15, n. 227
State v. Williams, 47 N.C. (2 Jones) 257 (1855).	II–14, n. 223
State v. Will, 18 N.C. (1 Dev. & Bat.) 121 (1834)	II-14, n. 224
State v. Cunningham, 72 N.C. 469 (1875).	III–44, n. 443
State ex rel. Armfield v. Brown, 70 N.C. 27 (1874).	III–47, n. 453
Keener v. Finger, 70 N.C. 35 (1874).	III–47, n. 453
In re Burke, 368 N.C. 226 (2015).	III–27, n. 397
North Carolina Acts	**Documents**
An Act for Establishing Courts of Law, and for Regulating Proceedings Therein. Ch. 2, § 1, at a General Assembly Begun and Held at New Bern on the Fifteenth Day of November, in the Year of Our Lord One Thousand Seven Hundred and Seventy-Seven, and in the Second Year of the Independence of the Said State: Being the Second Session of this Assembly. In *State Records* 24:48, 49.	I–21, n. 159
An Act to Empower the Court of Admiralty of this State to Have Jurisdiction in All Cases of Capture of the Ships and Other Vessels of the Inhabitants and Subjects of Great Britain, to Establish the Trial by Jury in the Said Court in Cases. Ch. 16, at a General Assembly Begun and Held at New Bern on the Fifteenth Day of November, in the Year of Our Lord One Thousand Seven Hundred and Seventy-Seven, and in the Second Year of the Independence of the Said State, Being the Second Session of This Assembly. In *State Records* 24:119–123.	I–21, n. 158
An Act Directing the Sale of Confiscated Property. Ch. 6, § 19, at a General Assembly, Begun and Held at Hillsborough, on the Thirteenth Day of April, in the Year of Our Lord One Thousand Seven Hundred and Eighty-Two, and in the Sixth Year of the Independence of the Said State, Being the First Session of This Assembly. In *State Records*, 24:424–429.	I–23, n. 160
An Act for Allowing Salaries to the Governor, Secretary and Other Officers of State, and for Other Purposes. Ch. 19, § 5, at a General Assembly Begun and Held at Hillsborough, on the Eighteenth Day of April, in the Year of Our Lord, One Thousand Seven Hundred and Eighty-Three, and in the Seventh Year of the Independence of the United States of America, Being the First Session of This Assembly. In *State Records*, 24:501–502.	I–23, n. 160

An Act Authorizing James Davis, Esquire, to Revise, Print and Publish All the Laws Now in Force and Use in This State, for Appointing a Public Printer, and Other Purposes. Ch. 46, at a General Assembly Begun and Held at Hillsborough, on the Eighteenth Day of April, in the Year of Our Lord, One Thousand Seven Hundred and Eighty-Three, and in the Seventh Year of the Independence of the United States of America, Being the First Session of This Assembly. In *State Records*, 24:537.	I–24, n. 166
An Act for Encreasing the Jurisdiction of the County Courts of Pleas and Quarter Sessions, and of the Justices of the Peace Out of Court, and Directing the Time of Holding the Several Courts of this State. Ch. 2, § 4, at a General Assembly, Begun and Held at New Bern on the Nineteenth Day of November, in the Year of Our Lord One Thousand Seven Hundred and Eighty-Five, and in the Tenth Year of the Independence of the Said State, it Being the First Session of This Assembly. In *State Records*, 24:716–718.	I–23, n. 160
An Act to Secure and Quiet in Their Possessions All Such Persons, Their Heirs and Assigns Who Have Purchased, or May Hereafter Purchase Lands and Tenements, Goods and Chattels, Which Have Been Sold, or May Hereafter Be Sold by Commissioners of Forfeited Estates, Legally Appointed for That Purpose. Ch. 25, at a General Assembly, Begun and Held at New Bern on the Nineteenth Day of November, in the Year of our Lord One Thousand Seven Hundred and Eighty-Five, and in the Tenth Year of the Independence of the Said State, it Being the First Session of This Assembly. In *State Records*, 24:731–732.	I–23, n. 160
An Act to Amend an Act, Entitled, "An Act to Secure and Quiet in Their Possessions All Such Persons, Their Heirs and Assigns, Who Have Purchased or May Hereafter Purchase Lands and Tenements, Goods and Chattels, Which Have Been Sold or May Hereafter Be Sold by the Commissioners of Forfeited Estates Legally Appointed for That Purpose." Ch. 6, § 1, at a General Assembly, Begun and Held at Fayetteville on the Eighteenth Day of November, in the Year of Our Lord One Thousand Seven Hundred and Eighty-Six, and in the Eleventh Year of the Independence of the Said State, Being the First Session of the Said Assembly. In *State Records*, 24:794–795.	I–23, n. 160
An Act to Amend an Act Passed at New Bern, in December, One Thousand Seven Hundred and Eighty-Five, Entitled, "An Act for Encreasing the Jurisdiction of the County Courts of Pleas and Quarter Sessions, and of the Justices of the Peace Out of Court, and Directing the Time of Holding Courts in This State." Ch. 14, § 7, at a General Assembly, Begun and Held at Fayetteville on the Eighteenth Day of November, in the Year of Our Lord One Thousand Seven Hundred and Eighty-Six, and in the Eleventh Year of the Independence of the Said State, Being the First Session of the Said Assembly. In *State Records*, 24:804–807.	I–23, n. 160
An Act to Confirm the Revisal of the Laws of This State, Made by James Iredell, Esquire, Commissioner Appointed by an Act of the General Assembly, Entitled, "An Act for Revising and Collecting the Acts of the General Assembly of the General Assembly of the State of North-Carolina." Ch. 1, at a General Assembly, Begun and Held at Newbern, on the Fifth Day of December, in the Year of Our Lord One Thousand Seven Hundred and Ninety-One, and in the Sixteenth Year of the Independence of the Said State: Being the First Session of the Said Assembly. 1791 N.C. Laws 1.	I–24, n. 171 II–10, n. 205
An Act to Confirm a Revisal of Certain Acts of Assembly. Ch. 1, at a General Assembly, Begun and Held at Raleigh, on the Nineteenth Day of November, in the Year of Our Lord One Thousand Eight Hundred and Four, and in the Twenty-Ninth Year of the Independence of the Said State. 1804 N.C. Laws 1.	I–26, n. 173
An Act Supplemental to the Act Concerning the Supreme Court. Ch. 2, § 13, Enacted by a General Assembly Begun and Held at Raleigh, on the Seventeenth Day of November, in the Year of Our Lord One Thousand Eight Hundred and Eighteen, and in the Forty-Second Year of the Independence of the Said State. 1818 Laws of N.C. 5, 8.	III–43, n. 437

Act Directing the Publication of the Revisal of the Laws of this State, Made under the Act Passed in 1817, Entitled ["]An Act for the Revision of the Acts of the General Assembly.["] Ch. 9, Enacted at a General Assembly Begun and Held at Raleigh, on the Twentieth Day of November, in the Year of our Lord One Thousand Eight Hundred and Nineteen, and in the Forty-Fourth Year of the Independence of the Said State. 1819 Laws of N.C. 13–14.	II–10, n. 206
An Act to Give Effect to the "Revised Statutes," as the Same Have Been Published by the Commissioners Appointed for That Purpose. Ch. 37, Passed by the General Assembly, at Their Session Which Commenced on Monday the Nineteenth of November, One Thousand Eight Hundred and Thirty-Eight, and Ended on Tuesday the Eighth of January, One Thousand Eight Hundred and Thirty-Nine. 1838–'39 Laws of N.C. 73.	II–42, n. 307
An Act to Amend Chapter 55 of Revised Code. Ch. 5, 1863 N.C. Pub. Laws Called Session 5.	III–1, n. 358
An Act to Allow Citizens of North Carolina to Practice in the Courts of the State. Ch. 46, Passed by the General Assembly at Its Session 1868–'69, Begun and Held in the City of Raleigh on the Sixteenth of November, 1868. 1868–'69 N.C. Pub. Laws 118–119.	Preface, n. 28
An Act in Relation to the Public Library. Ch. 70, § 3, Passed by the General Assembly at Its Session 1870–'71, Begun and Held in the City of Raleigh on the Sixteenth of November, 1870. 1870–'71 N.C. Pub. Laws 133, 134.	IV–1, n. 469
[An Act to Repeal Chapter 46, Laws of 1868, Re Practice of Law]. Ch. 120, Passed by the General Assembly at Its Session 1870–'71, Begun and Held in the City of Raleigh on the Sixteenth of November, 1870. 1870–'71 N.C. Pub. Laws 189.	III–27, n. 399
An Act to Alter the Constitution of North Carolina. Ch. 53, Passed by the General Assembly at Its Session 1871–'72, Begun and Held in the City of Raleigh, on the Twentieth Day of November, 1871. 1871–'72 N.C. Pub. Laws 81.	III–45, n. 444
An Act to Provide a Compilation of the Public Statutes. Ch. 210, Passed by the General Assembly at Its Session 1871–'72, Begun and Held in the City of Raleigh, on the Twentieth Day of November, 1871. 1871–'72 N.C. Laws 373.	III–44, n. 441
An Act to Provide for the Printing and Publication of "Battle's Revisal" of the Public Statute Laws of North Carolina, and for Other Purposes. Ch. 74, Passed by the General Assembly at Its Session 1872–'73, Begun and Held in the City of Raleigh, on Monday, the Eighteenth Day of November, A. D. 1872. 1872–'73 N.C. Laws 92.	III–44, n. 441
An Act to Amend the Constitution of North Carolina by Rewriting Article IV Thereof and Making Appropriate Amendments of Other Articles So As to Improve the Administration of Justice in North Carolina. Ch. 313, Passed by the General Assembly at the Regular Session Held in the City of Raleigh Beginning on Wednesday, the Eighth Day of February, A.D. 1961. 1961 N.C. Sess. Laws 436, 439.	III–46, n. 448
An Act to Create a Court of Appeals in the Appellate Division of the General Court of Justice; To Allocate Jurisdiction between the Supreme Court and the Court of Appeals; To Provide for the Retirement and Recall to Temporary Service of Certain Justices and Judges; and for Other Purposes. Ch. 108, Passed by the General Assembly at the [...] Regular Session Held in the City of Raleigh Beginning on Wednesday, February 8, A.D. 1967. 1967 N.C. Sess. Laws 144, 151.	III–46, n. 447
N.C. Gen. Stat. § 4-1 (1943).	I–5, n. 94

Table of Documents Excerpted

I–1	The First Charter Granted by King Charles the Second, to the Lords Proprietors of Carolina, *Colonial Records*, 1:20–33.
I–2	The Second Charter Granted by King Charles the Second, to the Proprietors of Carolina, Dated the Thirtieth Day of June, in the Seventeenth Year of His Reign, A. D., 1665, *Colonial Records*, 1:102–114.
I–3	The Fundamental Constitutions of Carolina, Drawn Up by John Locke, March 1, 1669, *Colonial Records*, 1:187–206.
I–4	Acts of the Assembly of Albemarle Ratified and Confirmed by the Proprietors, 20 January, 1669–1670, *State Records*, 25:119–122.
I–5	An Act for the Better and More Effectual Preserving the Queen's Peace, and the Establishing a Good and Lasting Foundation of Government in North Carolina. Ch. 1, Laws of North Carolina—1711, *Colonial Records*, 1:787–790 and *State Records*, 25:152–154.
I–6	An Act for the Confirmation of the Laws Passed This Session of Assembly & for Repealing All Former Laws Not Herein Particularly Excepted. Ch. 66 At a General Assembly of November 17, 1715–January 19, 1716, *State Records*, 23:94–96.
I–7	An Act for the More Effectual Observing of the Queen's Peace, and Establishing a Good and Lasting Foundation of Government in North Carolina. Ch. 31. At a General Assembly of November 17, 1715–January 19, 1716, *State Records*, 23:38–40.
I–8	Report by George Burrington Concerning Acts of the North Carolina General Assembly, 1731, *Colonial Records*, 3:175–179.
I–9	An Act for Appointing Commissioners to Revise and Print the Laws of This Province, and for Granting to His Majesty, for Defraying the Charge Thereof, a Duty on Wine, Rum and Distilled Liquors and Rice Imported into This Province. Ch. 1, §§ 1–4. At a General Assembly, Held at New Bern, the Seventh Day of March, in the Year of Our Lord One Thousand Seven Hundred and Forty Six, *State Records*, 23:268–272.
I–10	An Act to Put in Force in This Province, the Several Statutes of the Kingdom of England, or South-Britain, Therein Particularly Mentioned. Ch. 1, § 2. At a General Assembly, Held at New Bern, the Sixteenth Day of October, in the Year of Our Lord One Thousand Seven Hundred and Forty Nine, *State Records*, 23:317–329.
I–11	An Act, for Establishing Superior Courts of Pleas and Grand Sessions, and Regulating the Proceedings Therein. Ch. 1, § 57. At an Assembly, Begun and Held at New Bern, the Twenty-Fourth Day of April, in the Thirty-Third Year of the Reign of Our Sovereign Lord George the Second, by the Grace of God, of Great Britain, France, and Ireland, King, &c., and from Thence Continued, by Prorogation, to the Twenty-Sixth Day of May in the Year of Our Lord One Thousand Seven Hundred and Sixty: Being the Second Session of This Present Assembly, *State Records*, 25:433–449.
I–12	"Declaration and Resolves of the First Continental Congress, October 14, 1774," MacDonald, *Select Charters and Other Documents*, 356–361.
I–13	A Declaration of Rights Made by the Representatives of the Freemen of the State of North Carolina. At a Congress of the Representatives of the Freemen of the State of North Carolina, Assembled at Halifax, the Seventh Day of December, in the Year of Our Lord One Thousand Seven Hundred and Seventy-Six, for the Purpose of Establishing a Constitution or Form of Government of the Said State, *State Records*, 23:977–979.
I–14	The Constitution or Form of Government Agreed to and Resolved Upon by the Representatives of the Freemen of the State of NorthCarolina, Elected and Chosen for That Particular Purpose, in Congress Assembled, at Halifax, the Eighteenth Day of December, in the Year of Our Lord One Thousand Seven Hundred and Seventy-Six, *State Records*, 23:980–984.
I–15	An Ordinance to Appoint Certain Commissioners to Revive the Statutes and Acts of Assembly Heretofore in Force and Use in North Carolina and to Prepare Bills for the Consideration of the Next Assembly, *State Records*, 23:987.

I–16	An Ordinance to Inforce the Statute Laws and Such Part of the Common Law and Acts of Assembly Heretofore in Use Here, Also to Enforce the Resolve of the Convention and Congresses of This State Which Have Not Had Their Effect. Ordinances of Convention, 1776, *State Records*, 23:992.
I–17	An Act for Enforcing the Statute Laws and Such Parts of the Common Law and Acts of Assembly Heretofore in Use Here, and Also for Enforcing the Resolves of the Conventions and Congresses of This State, Which Have Not Had Their Effect, and for Other Purposes Therein Mentioned. Ch. 25. At a General Assembly, Begun and Held at New Bern, on the Eighth Day of April, in the Year of Our Lord One Thousand Seven Hundred and Seventy-Seven, and in the First Year of the Independence of the Said State, Being the First Session of This Assembly, *State Records*, 24:36.
I–18	An Act for Establishing Courts of Law, and for Regulating the Proceedings Therein. Ch. 2. At a General Assembly Begun and Held at New Bern on the Fifteenth Day of November, in the Year of Our Lord One Thousand Seven Hundred and Seventy-Seven, and in the Second Year of the Independence of the Said State: Being the Second Session of This Assembly, *State Records*, 24:48–75.
I–19	An Act to Enforce Such Parts of the Statute and Common Laws as Have Been Heretofore in Force and Use Here, and the Acts of Assembly Made and Passed When This Territory Was under the Government of the Late Proprietors, and the Crown of Great Britain; and for Reviving the Several Acts Therein Mentioned. Ch. 14. At a General Assembly Begun and Held at New Bern on the Fifteenth Day of November, in the Year of Our Lord One Thousand Seven Hundred and Seventy-Seven, and in the Second Year of the Independence of the Said State: Being the Second Session of This Assembly, *State Records*, 24:113.
I–20	An Act to Enforce Such Parts of the Statute and Common Laws As Have Been Heretofore in Force and Use Here; and the Acts of Assembly Made and Passed When This Territory Was under the Government of the Late Proprietors and the Crown of Great Britain, and for Reviving the Several Acts Therein Mentioned. Ch. 5. At a General Assembly, Begun and Held at New Bern on the Fourteenth Day of April, in the Year of Our Lord One Thousand Seven Hundred and Seventy Eight, and in the Second Year of Our Independence: Being the First Session of This Assembly, *State Records*, 24:162–163.
I–21	An Act for Giving an Equity Jurisdiction to the Superior Courts. Ch. 11. At a General Assembly, Begun and Held at Hillsborough, on the Thirteenth Day of April, in the Year of Our Lord One Thousand Seven Hundred and Eighty Two, and in the Sixth Year of the Independence of the Said State: Being the First Session of This Assembly, *State Records*, 24:439–442.
I–22	An Act to Amend an Act Passed at New Bern, in December, One Thousand Seven Hundred and Eighty-Five, Entitled, "An Act for Encreasing the Jurisdiction of the County Courts of Pleas and Quarter Sessions, and of the Justices of the Peace Out of Court, and Directing the Time of Holding Courts in This State." Ch. 14. At a General Assembly, Begun and Held at Fayetteville on the Eighteenth Day of November, in the Year of Our Lord One Thousand Seven Hundred and Eighty-Six, and in the Eleventh Year of the Independence of the Said State, Being the First Session of the Said Assembly, *State Records*, 24:804–807.
I–23	[Anonymous], "The Independent Citizen (1787)," Boyd, *Some Eighteenth Century Tracts*, 454–486.
I–24	An Act for Revising and Collecting the Acts of the General Assembly of the State of North Carolina. Ch. 4. At a General Assembly, Begun and Held at Tarborough on the Eighteenth Day of November, in the Year of Our Lord One Thousand Seven Hundred and Eighty-Seven, and in the Twelfth Year of the Independence of the Said State, Being the First Session of the Assembly, *State Records*, 24:888–889.
I–25	Preface to Iredell, *Laws of the State of North-Carolina*, [iii]–iv.
I–26	Preface to Martin, *Collection of the Statutes of the Parliament of England*, iii–iv.
I–27	Calder *et* Wife, *versus* Bull *et* Wife, in Dallas, *Reports of Cases Ruled and Adjudged in the Several Courts of the United States*, 3:386–401. [3 U.S. (3 Dall.) 386 (1798)]
II–1	An Act Directing the Judges of the Superior Courts to Meet Together to Settle Questions of Law or Equity Arising on the Circuit, and to Provide for the Trial of All Persons Concerned in Certain Land Frauds, ch. 4, *Laws of North-Carolina* [. . .], 2–4. [1799 N.C. Laws 2–4]
II–2	"Court of Errors and Appeals," *Salisbury North-Carolina Mercury and Salisbury Advertiser*, vol. 2, no. 87, December 26, 1799, p. 2, col. 1.

II–3	An Act to Continue Longer in Force, and to Amend an Act Passed in the Year One Thousand Seven Hundred and Ninety-Nine, Entitled "An Act Directing the Judges of the Superior Courts to Meet Together to Settle Questions of Law or Equity Arising on the Circuit, and to Provide for the Trial of All Persons Concerned in Certain Frauds," ch. 12, *Laws of North-Carolina* [...], 9. [1801 N.C. Laws 9]
II–4	Preface to Haywood, *Manual of the Laws of North-Carolina*, [iii]–iv.
II–5	*Journal of the House of Commons* [...] [1809], 12–16.
II–6	[Rush], "American Jurisprudence," *Carolina Law Repository*, 2:347–363.
II–7	Bentham, "Circular.—To the Governor of the State of," Bowring, *Works of Jeremy Bentham*, 4:476–477.
II–8	An Act for the Revision of the Acts of the General Assembly. Ch. 16, [Enacted by a General Assembly Begun and Held at Raleigh, on the Seventeenth Day of November, in the Year of Our Lord One Thousand Eight Hundred and Seventeen, and in the Forty-Second Year of the Independence of the Said State], *Laws of the State of North-Carolina* [...] *1817*, 3, 17–18. [1817 N.C. Laws 17]
II–9	An Act Supplemental to the Act Concerning the Supreme Court. Ch. 2, § 13 [Enacted by a General Assembly Begun and Held at Raleigh, on the Seventeenth Day of November, in the Year of Our Lord One Thousand Eight Hundred and Eighteen, and in the Forty-Second Year of the Independence of the Said State], *Laws of North-Carolina* [...] *1818*, 5, 8. [1818 N.C. Laws 5]
II–10	Report of the Commissioners Appointed by an Act of the Legislature of 1817, to Revise the Laws of North-Carolina, Potter, Taylor, & Yancey, *Laws of the State of North-Carolina*, 1:[iii]–vi.
II–11	[Report of the Select Joint Committee on the Judiciary.] Journal of the Senate. At a General Assembly Begun and Held in the City of Raleigh, on Monday the Fifteenth Day of November, in the Year of Our Lord One Thousand Eight Hundred and Nineteen, and in the Forty-Fourth Year of the Independence of the United States of America: It Being the First Session of This General Assembly, *Journals of the Senate and House of Commons* [...] *1819*, 112–118.
II–12	The State v. Tackett, in Ruffin and Hawks, *Reports of Cases Argued . . . in the Supreme Court* [...] *1820 & 1821*, 210–220. [The State v. Tackett, 8 N.C. (1 Hawks) 210 (1820)]
II–13	Statutes and Parts of Statutes of Great Britain, [...] Entitled, "An Act for the Revision of the Acts of the General Assembly," Potter, Taylor, & Yancey, *Laws of the State of North-Carolina*, 1:85–93.
II–14	State *v.* Hale} From Cumberland, in Hawks, *Reports of Cases Argued and Adjudged in the Supreme Court* [...] *1822 & 1823*, 582–587. [State v. Hale, 9 N.C. (2 Hawks) 582 (1823)]
II–15	Preface to Ruffin and Hawks, *Reports of Cases Argued and Adjudged in the Supreme Court* [...] *1820 & 1821*, [iii].
II–16	Preface to Taylor, *Digest of the Statute Law of North-Carolina*, [5].
II–17	An Act to Provide for Revising and Consolidating the Acts of the General Assembly Concerning Administrators and Executors. Ch. 15, [Enacted by a General Assembly, Begun and Held at Raleigh, on the Fifteenth Day of November, in the Year of Our Lord One Thousand Eight Hundred and Twenty-Four, and in the Forty-Eighth Year of the Independence of the Said State], *Acts Passed by the General Assembly* [...] *1824*, 14. [1824–'25 N.C. Acts 14]
II–18	Smith *v.* Campbell} From Halifax, in Hawks, *Reports of Cases Argued and Adjudged* [...] *in the Supreme Court* [...] *1824 and 1825*, 590–598. [Smith v. Campbell, 10 N.C. (3 Hawks) 590 (1825)]
II–19	Potter, *Argument Addressed to the Supreme Court of North-Carolina at June Term, 1825*, 1, 3–4, 10–11.
II–20	Preface to Hawks, *Digested Index of the Reported Cases Adjudged in the Courts of North Carolina from the Year, 1778 to 1826*, [v]–vii.
II–21	Matthias Evans Manly to William Alexander Graham, August 31, 1827, New Bern, Hamilton, Williams, and Peacock, *Papers of William Alexander Graham*, 1:152–154.
II–22	["Note by the Reporter following *Pike v. Armstead & Thomas Turner*"], Devereux, *Equity Cases Argued in the Supreme Court* [...] *from June Term, 1828, to December Term, 1830*, 114–115.
II–23	Resolution on Motion of Mr. Swain, Tuesday, January 2, 1827. Journal of the House of Commons. At a General Assembly, Begun and Held in the City of Raleigh, on Monday, the Twenty-Fifth Day of December, A. D. 1826, and in the Fifty-First Year of the Independence of the United States, It Being the First Session of This General Assembly, *Journals of the Senate & House of Commons* [...] *1826–27*, 132–133.

II–24	Resolution on Motion of Mr. Foy, Tuesday, November 27, 1827. Journal of the House of Commons. At a General Assembly, Begun and Held in the City of Raleigh, on Monday, the 19th of November, in the Year of Our Lord 1827, and in the Fifty Second Year of the Independence of the United States of America, It Being the First Session of This General Assembly, *Journals of the Senate & House of Commons* [...] *1827–28*, 139–140.
II–25	Resolution on Motion of Mr. Shober, Friday, December 7, 1827. Journal of the Senate. At a General Assembly, Begun and Held in the City of Raleigh, on Monday, the 19th Day of November, in the Year of Our Lord One Thousand Eight Hundred and Twenty Seven, and in the Fifty-Second Year of the Independence of the United States of America, It Being the First Session of This General Assembly, *Journals of the Senate & House of Commons* [...] *1827–28*, 36.
II–26	Resolution on Motion of Mr. Salmons, Wednesday, December 12, 1827. Journal of the House of Commons. At a General Assembly, Begun and Held in the City of Raleigh, on Monday, the 19th of November, in the Year of Our Lord 1827, and in the Fifty Second Year of the Independence of the United States of America, It Being the First Session of This General Assembly, *Journals of the Senate & House of Commons* [...] *1827–28*, 173, 175.
II–27	[Floor of the House], Monday, January 7, 1828. Journal of the House of Commons. At a General Assembly, Begun and Held in the City of Raleigh, on Monday, the 19th of November, in the Year of Our Lord 1827, and in the Fifty Second Year of the Independence of the United States of America, It Being the First Session of This General Assembly, *Journals of the Senate & House of Commons* [...] *1827–28*, 244.
II–28	Resolution on Motion of Mr. Newland, Wednesday, November 26, 1828. Journal of the House of Commons. At a General Assembly, Begun and Held in the City of Raleigh on Monday, the 17th Day of November, in the Year of Our Lord One Thousand Eight Hundred and Twenty Eight, and Fifty-Third of the Independence of the United States of America, It Being the First Session of This General Assembly, *Journals of the Senate & House of Commons* [...] *1828–29*, 155, 156.
II–29	[Floor of the House], Saturday, November 22, 1828 to Tuesday, December 16, 1828. Journal of the House of Commons. At a General Assembly, Begun and Held in the City of Raleigh on Monday, the 17th Day of November, in the Year of Our Lord One Thousand Eight Hundred and Twenty Eight, and Fifty-Third of the Independence of the United States of America, It Being the First Session of This General Assembly, *Journals of the Senate & House of Commons* [...] *1828–29*, 152–153, 168–169, 186–188, 194–201 passim.
II–30	An Act for Revising, Digesting and Amending the Laws Relating to Executors and Administrators. Ch. 38 [Enacted by a General Assembly, Begun and Held at Raleigh on the Seventeenth Day of November, in the Year of Our Lord One Thousand Eight Hundred and Twenty-Eight, and in the Fifty-Third Year of the Independence of the Said State], in *Acts Passed by the General Assembly* [...] *1828–29*, 22–23. [1828–'29 N.C. Acts 22]
II–31	John Owen to Thomas Ruffin and George E. Badger, May 22nd, 1829, in Hamilton, *Papers of Thomas Ruffin*, 1:498–499.
II–32	Resolution on Motion of Mr. Shipp, Saturday, December 12, 1829. Journal of the House of Commons. At a General Assembly, Begun and Held on Monday, the 16th of November, in the Year of Our Lord One Thousand Eight Hundred and Twenty-Nine, and Fifty-Fourth of the Independence of the United States, It Being the First Session of This General Assembly, *Journals of the Senate & House of Commons* [...] *1829–30*, 206, 207.
II–33	Index [to Acts], *Acts Passed by the General Assembly* [...] *1829–30*, 95–98.
II–34	Bill presented by Mr. M'Kay, Thursday, December 9, 1830. Journal of the Senate. At a General Assembly, Begun and Held in the City of Raleigh, on Monday, the 15th Day of November, in the Year of Our Lord One Thousand Eight Hundred and Thirty, and in the Fifty-Fifth Year of the Independence of the United States of America, It Being the First Session of This General Assembly, *Journals of the Senate & House of Commons* [...] *1830–31*, 49, 50.
II–35	Friends of Liberty and Equality, *Address to the People of North Carolina*, [title page verso], 3, 10–24 passim, 68.
II–36	[Unknown], Review of *Statute Laws of Tennessee*, 298–315.
II–37	[Swain, *Message of the Governor of North Carolina, to the General Assembly* [...] *1833*, 9–10.
II–38	The State *v.* Negro Will, Slave of James S. Battle, Devereux and Battle. *Reports of Cases at Law, Argued* [...] *in the Supreme Court of North Carolina, from December Term, 1834, to June Term, 1836*, 121–172 [18 N.C. (1 Dev. and Bat.) 121 (1834)]

II–39	[Swain, David L.] *Message from His Excellency the Governor, to the General Assembly* [...] *1834*, [title page verso].
II–40	Report of the Joint Select Committee, on the Subject of the Revised Statutes. [Document] No. 14, Legislature of North Carolina, 1835, [*Legislative Documents Printed by Order of the General Assembly* [...] *1835–1839*].
II–41	Nash, Iredell, and Battle, *Report of the Commissioners, Appointed to Revise and Consolidate the Public Statutes, of North Carolina*, 1–2.
II–42	An Act Concerning the Revised Statutes. Ch. 26 [Passed by the General Assembly, at Their Session Which Commenced on Monday, the Twenty First of November, One Thousand Eight Hundred and Thirty-Six, and Ended on Monday, the Twenty Third of January, One Thousand Eight Hundred and Thirty-Seven], *Laws of the State of North-Carolina, Passed by the General Assembly* [...] *1836–37*, 138–146. [1836–'37 N.C. Laws 138–146]
II–43	Preface to Iredell and Battle, *Revised Statutes of the State of North Carolina* [...] *1836–'7*, 1:[v]–xvi.
II–44	Swaim, *North Carolina Executor*, 5–7.
II–45	"The Administration of Justice in North Carolina.—(No. 4.)." *Raleigh North Carolina Standard*, vol. 11, no. 569, Wednesday, October 1, 1845, p. 3, cols. 3–4.
II–46	Preface to Smith, *Civil Practice in the Court of Pleas and Quarter Sessions*, [iii]–vii.
II–47	The State *vs.* Cæsar, a Slave. Iredell, *Reports of Cases at Law* [...] *December Term 1848, to June Term 1849*, 391, 406, 411. [State v. Cæsar, 31 N.C. (9 Ired.) 391, 406, 411 (1849) (Nash, J., concurring)]
II–48	The State *vs.* Atlas Jowers, in Iredell, *Reports of Cases in Law* [...] *June Term, 1850 to December Term, 1850*, 555, 557. [State v. Jowers, 33 N.C. (11 Ired.) 555, 557 (1850)]
II–49	Elijah Gaskill *v.* William C. King, Iredell *Reports of Cases in Law* [...] *from June Term, 1851, to August Term, 1851*, 211, 222. [Gaskill v. King, 34 N.C. (12 Ired.) 211, 222 (1851)]
II–50	A. J. Patton *vs.* William Marr, Busbee, *Reports of Cases at Law* [...] *from December Term, 185[2], to August Term, 1853*, 377, 378. [Patton v. Marr, 44 N.C. (1 Busbee) 377, 378 (1853)]
II–51	Preface to Moore and Rodman. *Revised Code of North Carolina* [...] *1854*, [v]–xvi.
II–52	Preface to Eaton, *Book of Practical Forms, with Explanatory Notes and References to Authorities*, [v]–x.
II–53	Thomas Jones *vs.* Timothy Ward, Jones, *Reports of Cases at Law* [...] *December Term, 1855, to August Term, 1856*, 24, 25–26. [Jones v. Ward, 48 N.C. (3 Jones) 24, 25–26 (1855)]
II–54	H. M. Shaw et al. propounders *vs.* John A. Moore et al. caveators, Jones, *Reports of Cases at Law* [...] *December Term, 1856, to August Term, 1857*, 25, 27. [Shaw v. Moore, 49 N.C. (4 Jones) 25, 27 (1856)]
II–55	Cantwell, *Swaim's Justice—Revised, the North Carolina Magistrate*, 226–229, 271.
II–56	C. D. Smith *v.* North Carolina Railroad Company, Jones and Winston. *North Carolina Reports, Vol. 60* [...] *from June Term, 1863, to December Term, 1864*, 202–205. [Smith v. N. Carolina R. Co., 60 N.C. 202, 1 Win. 203 (1864)]
II–57	Battle, "Memoir of Leonard Henderson," 193–202.
II–58	Eaton, "Memoir of the Honorable John Hall," 449–455.
II–59	Philo Florian [pseud.]. "Sketch of the Character of Archibald Henderson as a Lawyer," Hoyt, *Papers of Archibald D. Murphey*, 2:312–319.
II–60	Battle, "Memoir of John Louis Taylor," 385–394.
II–61	Graham, "Discourse in Memory of the Life and Character of the Hon. Geo. E. Badger," Hamilton, Williams, and Peacock, *Papers of William Alexander Graham*. 7:161–183.
III–1	An Ordinance Declaring What Laws and Ordinances Are in Force, and for Other Purposes, in *Executive Documents* [...] *Passed by the Convention, Session, 1865*, 56–59.
III–2	Report of Committee [to Prepare and Report to the Legislature a System of Laws upon the Subject of Freedmen, &c.], [*North Carolina Legislative Documents for Session of 1865–'66*], 1–21.
III–3	An Act Concerning Negroes and Persons of Color or of Mixed Blood, ch. 40, in *Public Laws of the State of North Carolina* [...] *1866*, 99–105. [1866 N.C. Laws Special Session 99]
III–4	Plan for Organization of the Judicial Department, Reported by the Committee on That Subject, *Journal of the Constitutional Convention* [...] *1868*, Tuesday, February, 25th, 1868, 258–264.

III–5	An Ordinance Appointing Commissioners to Prepare a Code of Practice and Procedure in the Different Courts of the State, *Journal of the Constitutional Convention* [...] *1868*, Friday, March 13th, 1868, 439–441.
III–6	Article IV. Judicial Department, *Constitution of the State of North-Carolina* [...] *1868*, 18–20, 23, 24.
III–7	William B. Rodman to William W. Holden, May 5, 1868, Raper, *Papers of William Woods Holden*, 1:309–310.
III–8	Albion W. Tourgée to William B. Rodman, June 8, 1868, Rodman Papers, Collection No. 329, Item 329.3g.
III–9	David Dudley Field to Albion W. Tourgee, New York City, [Oct.?] 20, 1868. Tourgée Papers, Collection 1-2383, Reel 9, Item 1472[40].
III–10	First Report of the Code Commissioners, July 15th, 1868, Barringer, Rodman, and Tourgee, *Code of Civil Procedure of North Carolina to Special Proceedings*, [ix]–xiii.
III–11	"The New Judicial System—The Commission on 'Rules of Practice and Procedure'—The Recent 'Corporation Act.'" *Wilmington Daily Journal*, vol. 17, no. 258, Wednesday Morning, July 29, 1868, p. 2, col. 2.
III–12	Richmond M. Pearson to William B. Rodman, August 6, 1868. Rodman Papers, Collection No. 329, Item 329.4g.
III–13	"The Code Commission," *Raleigh Daily Sentinel*, vol. 3, no. 311, Saturday, August 8, 1868, p. 2, col. 2.
III–14	"Our Raleigh Correspondence," *Wilmington Daily Journal*, vol. 17, no. 271, Thursday Morning, August 13, 1868, p. 2, col. 2.
III–15	Preface to Barringer, Rodman, and Tourgee, *Code of Civil Procedure of North Carolina to Special Proceedings*, [iii]–iv.
III–16	"Second Report of the Code Commissioners, August 31st, 1868," Barringer, Rodman, and Tourgee, *Code of Civil Procedure of North Carolina to Special Proceedings*, xiv–xvii.
III–17	Richmond M. Pearson to William B. Rodman, September 24, 1868, Rodman Papers, Collection No. 329, Item 329.3g.
III–18	"State Affairs," *Raleigh Daily Sentinel*, vol. 4, no. 74, Friday, November 6, 1868, p. 2, col. 1.
III–19	"The Code Commission," *Raleigh Daily Sentinel*, vol. 4, no. 101, Raleigh, N.C., Wednesday, December 9, 1868, p. 2, col. 1.
III–20	"Mismanagement and Incompetency," *Raleigh Daily Sentinel*, vol. 4, no. 102, Friday, December 18, 1868, p. 2, col. 1.
III–21	"The Code," *Raleigh Daily Sentinel*, vol. 4, no. 110, Saturday, December 19, 1868, p. 2, col. 2.
III–22	"New Code—Other Iniquities, December 23, 1868," Schenck Papers, p. 25.
III–23	"A Meeting of the Bench and Bar of North Carolina," *Greensboro Patriot and Times*, vol. 30/7, no. 47, Thursday, December 24, 1868, p. 2, col. 2.
III–24	"Publishers' Notice," *Hand-book for County Officers: A Guide* [...] *Containing the Laws* [...] *under the New Constitution* [...] *Also the Acts of the General Assembly of 1868-'69*, 3–4.
III–25	"The Meeting of the Bench and Bar," *Raleigh North Carolina Standard*, vol. 2, no. 306, Friday, January 8, 1869, p. 2, col. 2.
III–26	"Our Courts," *Raleigh North Carolina Standard*, vol. 2, no. 320, Monday, January 25, 1869, p. 2, cols. 4–5.
III–27	An Act to Allow Citizens of North Carolina to Practice in the Courts of the State, Ch. 46, in *Public Laws* [...] *Passed by the General Assembly* [...] *1868-'69*, 118–119. [1868-'69 N.C. Pub. Laws 118–119]
III–28	"New Code—Fish Pond—Children &c, March 8th, 1869." Schenck Papers, p. 30.
III–29	"Report of the Code Commissioners, Session of 1868-'9," *Raleigh North Carolina Standard*, vol. 3, no. 371, Thursday, March 25, 1869, p. 2, col. 7 & p. 3, col. 1.
III–30	William B. Rodman to Albion W. Tourgée, July 21, 1869. Tourgée Papers, Collection 1-2383, Reel 9, Item 1472[91].
III–31	V. C. Barringer to William B. Rodman, November 15, 1869. Rodman Papers, Collection No. 329, Item 329.4a.
III–32	Rodman, W. B., V. C. Barringer, and A. W. Tourgee, comms. The Penal Code, [Documents of the Code Commission, 1868–1871], 3–6, 20–21, 111–115.
III–33	Robbins and Murphy, Report of the Special Committee on the Senate Bill to Provide for Calling a State Convention, doc. no. 34, in *Executive and Legislative Documents* [...] *1869-'70*, 1–16.

III–34	L. A. Tate *v.* W. E. Powe and Others, Phillips, *Cases Argued and Determined in the Supreme Court* [...] *January and June Terms, 1870*, 644–648. [Tate v. Powe, 64 N.C. 644 (1870)]
III–35	Barringer, Rodman, and Tourgee, Response by Code Commissioners to Senate Resolutions, January 25, 1870, in [Documents of the Code Commission, 1868–1871], 1–6.
III–36	Rodman, Barringer, and Tourgee, Report of the Code Commissioners. [March 12th, 1870], doc. no. 28, in *Executive and Legislative Documents* [...] *1869–'70*, 1–4.
III–37	"New Code Commissioner," *Raleigh Daily Sentinel*, vol. 5, no. 294, Saturday Evening, July 30, 1870, p. 2, col. 4.
III–38	"Civil Code Commission," *Raleigh Daily Sentinel*, vol. 6, no. 30, Raleigh, N.C., Thursday, September 29, 1870, p. 2, col. 2.
III–39	Bailey and Rodman, Report of the Code Commissioners, [November, 1870], doc. no. 5, in *Executive and Legislative Documents* [...] *1870–'71*, 1–7.
III–40	Rodman and Bailey. Report of the Code Commissioners, December 18, 1870, in Rodman Papers, Collection No. 329, Item 329.16d.
III–41	An Act in Relation to the Public Library, ch. 70, § 3, in *Public Laws of the State of North Carolina* [...] *1870–'71*, 133–134. [1870–'71 N.C. Pub. Laws 133–134]
III–42	David F. Caldwell to William A. Graham, March 7, 1871, Hamilton, Williams, and Peacock, *Papers of William Alexander Graham*, 8:180.
III–43	An Act to Abolish the Office of Supreme Court Reporter and for Other Purposes, ch. 112, *Public Laws* [...] *Passed by the General Assembly* [...] *1871–'72*, 159–160. [1871–'72 N.C. Pub. Laws 159–160]
III–44	Report of Will. H. Battle [Nov. 18th, 1872], doc. no. 14, in *Executive and Legislative Documents* [...] *1872–'73*, 1–4.
III–45	An Act to Alter the Constitution of North Carolina in Relation to Code Commission. Ch. 87. In *Public Laws and Resolutions* [...] *Passed by the General Assembly* [...] *1872–'73*, 117. [1872–'73 N.C. Pub. Laws 117]
III–46	An Ordinance to Abrogate and Annul Sections Fifteen, Sixteen and Seventeen, of Article Four, of the Constitution, ch. 17, Jones and Reilly, *Amendments to the Constitution of North Carolina, Proposed by the Constitutional Convention of 1875*, 15.
III–47	Preface to Tourgee, *Code of Civil Procedure of North Carolina*, [iii]–v.
III–48	Will. B. Rodman to A. W. Tourgee, January 8, 1878, Tourgée Papers, Collection 1-2383, Reel 16, Item 2208.
III–49	S[amuel] F. Phillips to [Not given], Washington, D.C., July 18, 1878, Tourgée Papers, Collection 1-2383, Reel 16, Item 2221.
III–50	Allen, Address of Judge Oliver H. Allen: My Recollections of the Bench and Bar, Andrews, *Proceedings of the Twenty-Second Annual Session of the North Carolina Bar Association* [...] *June 29, 30, and July 1, 1920*, 157–186.
III–51	Furches, "Judge Anderson Mitchell," Biggs, *Report of the Seventh Annual Meeting of the North Carolina Bar Association* [...] *July 5th, 6th, 7th, 1905*, 185–193.
III–52	Dick, *Memorial Address on the Life and Character of Richmond Mumford Pearson*, 1, 8, 10–15 passim, 20, 21.
III–53	Osborne, "Presentation of the Portrait of Mr. Joseph Harvey Wilson to the Supreme Court of North Carolina," in Strong, *Cases Argued and Determined in the Supreme Court* [...] *Spring Term, 1915 (in Part) Fall Term, 1915 (in Part)*, 755–765.
III–54	Adams, "Life and Influence of John Manning," 218–224.
III–55	Graham, "Some Events in My Life," Davis, *Proceedings of the Twentieth Annual Session of the North Carolina Bar Association* [...] *June 25, 26, 27, 1918*, 76–96.
IV–1	An Act to Authorize and Empower the Trustees of the Supreme Court Library to Appoint a Librarian and for Other Purposes. Ch. 100, Begun and Held in the City of Raleigh on Wednesday, the Third Day of January, A. D. 1883, *Laws and Resolutions* [...] *Passed by the General Assembly* [...] *1883*, 153–154. [1883 N.C. Sess. Laws 153]
IV–2	Report of Commissioners, in Dortch, Manning, and Henderson, *The Code*, [iii]–iv.
IV–3	Preface to Clark, *Code of Civil Procedure of North Carolina*, [v]–vi.
IV–4	Battle, Address on the History of the Supreme Court," Davidson, *Cases Argued and Determined in the Supreme Court* [...] *February Term, 1889*, 445–516. [103 N.C. 445]

IV–5	David Dudley Field to Walter Clark, New York, January 21, 1892, Brooks and Lefler, *Papers of Walter Clark*, 1:249.
IV–6	Preface to Second Edition, in Clark, *Code of Civil Procedure of North Carolina* [...] *1891*, [v]–vi.
IV–7	William B. Rodman to Walter Clark, Washington, N.C., April 28, 1892, Brooks and Lefler, *Papers of Walter Clark*, 1:251.
IV–8	An Act to Amend the Code, Sections Thirty-Three Hundred and Sixty-Eight, Thirty-Seven Hundred and Twenty-Eight and Thirty-Seven Hundred and Twenty-Nine, in Reference to the Attorney General and Supreme Court Reporter, ch. 379, *Public Laws and Resolutions* [...] *Passed by the General Assembly* [...] *1893*, 383. [1893 Pub. Laws 383]
IV–9	Preface to Clark, *Supplement to the Annotated Code of Civil Procedure* [...] *Containing Amendments* [...] *by the Legislatures of 1893 and 1895*, [3].
IV–10	Manning, *Commentaries on the First Book of Blackstone*, 1, 6, 7.
IV–11	Hinsdale, "Report of Committee on Legislation and Law Reform," Biggs, *Report of the Second Annual Meeting of the North Carolina Bar Association* [...] *June 27th, 28th and 29th, 1900*, 97–105.
IV–12	Preface to Clark, *Code of Civil Procedure of North Carolina* [...] *July 1900*, [v]–vi.
IV–13	Shepherd, "Some Leaves from Colonial History," Biggs, *Report of the Second Annual Meeting of the North Carolina Bar Association* [...] *June 27th, 28th and 29th, 1900*, 143–164.
IV–14	Preface to Womack, Gulley, and Rodman, *Revisal of 1905 of North Carolina*, [vii]–x.
IV–15	Tourgée, "Unwritten Law and Why It Remains Unwritten," 8–17.
IV–16	Winston, "Popular Discontent with Judicial Procedure," Davis, *Proceedings of the Fifteenth Annual Session of the North Carolina Bar Association* [...] *July 2, 3 and 4, 1913*, 24–44.
IV–17	Clark, "Address [...] on Reform in Law and Legal Procedure," Davis, *Proceedings of the Sixteenth Annual Session of the North Carolina Bar Association* [...] *June 29–30 and July 1, 1914*, 46–61.
IV–18	An Act to Amend the Constitution of the State of North Carolina, ch. 99, § 1, in *Public Laws and Resolutions* [...] *Passed by the General Assembly* [...] *1915*, 148–149. [1915 N.C. Pub. Laws 148]
IV–19	Mordecai, *Mordecai's Miscellanies*, 3–5.
IV–20	Winston, "Century of Law in North Carolina," Strong, *Cases Argued and Determined in the Supreme Court* [...] *Fall Term, 1918*, 763–791.
IV–21	Preface to McGehee, *Consolidated Statutes of North Carolina*, 1:[iii]–[iv].
IV–22	Pound, "Pioneers and the Common Law," Andrews, *Proceedings of the Twenty-Second Annual Session of the North Carolina Bar Association* [...] *June 29, 30, and July 1, 1920*, 188–206.
IV–23	Clark, "History of the Supreme Court Reports of North Carolina and of the Annotated Reprints," Clark, *Cases Argued and Determined in the Supreme Court* [...] *December Term, 1859 to August Term, 1860*, xxi–xxiv.
IV–24	Varser, "Practice in North Carolina since the Last War," Andrews, *Proceedings of the Twenty-Second Annual Session of the North Carolina Bar Association* [...] *June 29, 30, and July 1, 1920*, 140–156.
IV–25	Joint Committee [of the General Assembly], [Report of the Special Committee [...] Formed under "A Joint Resolution for the Investigation of the State Printing"], Box 17, Committee Reports Folder, General Assembly Session Records, Jan.– Mar., 1923.
IV–26	Adams, "Evolution of Law in North Carolina," 133–145.
IV–27	Winston, Review of *Walter Clark, Fighting Judge*, 181–185.
IV–28	Winston, "Chief Justice Shepherd and His Times," 1–13.
IV–29	Alderman, "Samuel Fox Mordecai," London, *Proceedings of the Thirtieth Annual Session of the North Carolina Bar Association* [...] *June 28, 29, 30, 1928*, 68–73.
IV–30	Winston, *It's a Far Cry*, 123–124.
IV–31	Pound, "Toward Improving the Administration of Justice in North Carolina," 8, 11.

Document Credits

Chautauqua County Historical Society

The following documents excerpted or cited in this compilation—available on microfilm at Davis Library, University of North Carolina at Chapel Hill—are reproduced with permission of the Chautauqua County Historical Society, Westfield, N.Y.:

III–9	David Dudley Field to Albion W. Tourgée, New York City, [?] 20, 1868, Tourgée Papers, Collection 1-2383, Reel 9, Item 1472[40],
III–30	William B. Rodman to Albion W. Tourgée, July 21, 1869. Tourgée Papers, Collection 1-2383, Reel 9, Item 1472[91].
III–48	William B. Rodman to Albion Winegar Tourgée, January 8, 1878. Tourgée Papers, Collection 1-2383, Reel 16, Item 2208.
III–49	Samuel F. Phillips to [Not given], Washington, D.C., July 18, 1878. Tourgée Papers, Collection 1-2383, Reel 16, Item 2221.
Note 385	David Dudley Field to Albion W. Tourgée, New York City, [September?] 30, 1868, Tourgée Papers, Collection 1-2383, Reel 9, Item 1472[22] (former item 905),
Note 385	David Dudley Field to Albion W. Tourgée, New York City, April 26, 1887, Tourgée Papers, Collection 1-2383, Reel 19, Item 2657, ("...you are, I think, a firm believer in codification & in my code.").
Note 385	David Dudley Field to Albion Winegar Tourgée, Stockbridge, Mass., Tourgée Papers, Collection 1-2383, Reel 57, Item 10,992.
Note 401	V. C. Barringer to Tourgée, Raleigh, 1869, Tourgée Papers, Collection 1-2383, Reel 8, Item 1210.

East Carolina Manuscript Collection

The following documents excerpted or cited in this compilation are reproduced with permission of the East Carolina Manuscript Collection. J. Y. Joyner Library, East Carolina University, Greenville, N.C.:

III–8	Albion W. Tourgee to William B. Rodman, June 8, 1868. Rodman Papers, Collection No. 329, Item 329.3g.
III–12	Richmond M. Pearson to William B. Rodman, August 6, 1868. Rodman Papers, Collection No. 329, Item 329.4g.
III–17	Richmond M. Pearson to William B. Rodman, September 24, 1868. Rodman Papers, Collection No. 329, Item 329.3g.
III–31	V. C. Barringer to William B. Rodman, November 15, 1869. Rodman Papers, Collection No. 329, Item 329.4a.
III–40	"Report of the Code Commissioners, December 18, 1870." Rodman Papers, Collection No. 329, Item 329.16d.

State Archives of North Carolina

The following documents excerpted or cited in this compilation are reproduced with permission of the State Archives of North Carolina, Raleigh, N.C.:

Note 195	John Quincy Adams to William Miller, August 25, 1817, Gov. William Miller Letter Book, Book 22, Part II, p. 369.
Note 196	John Quincy Adams to William Miller, November 10, 1817, Gov. William Miller Letter Book, Book 22, Part II, p. 393.
Note 197	William Miller to John Quincy Adams, November 17, 1817, Gov. William Miller Letter Book, Book 22, Part II, p. 394.
IV–25	Joint Committee [of the General Assembly], ["Report of the Special Committee of the General Assembly Formed under "A Joint Resolution for the Investigation of the State Printing"], Box 17, Committee Reports Folder, H.R. 73 S.R. 86, General Assembly Session Records, Jan.– Mar., 1923.

About the Epigraphs

Opposite Title Page (nineteenth-century mind)

"Our people have taken fast hold..."

> Document III–29 (Report of the Code Commissioners, March 20, 1869)

"We live in a period of uncommon excitement...."

> [Unknown], review of *An Address Delivered before the Law Association of the City of New York, October 21, 1836*, by James Kent, 472.

"I labored under the comfortable illusion that..."

> Kirk, *Orestes Brownson: Selected Essays*, 193.

"[T]he liberal and socialistic revolutions of Europe..."

> Kirk, *Orestes Brownson: Selected Essays*, 135–136.

"The imagination of the age was intent on history..."

> Santayana, *Winds of Doctrine*, 8.

Beneath Dedication (ordering and preserving law)

"If government is to be "of laws and not of men,..."

> Taylor, "History of the North Carolina Supreme Court Library," in Partin and White, *North Carolina Supreme Court Reports: Volume 275*, 713. [275 N.C. 713]

Opposite Preface (sentiment of reform)

"The legal muckraker of today..."

> Document IV–22 (Pound on the Common Law, 1920)

"During the first fifty years of this Court..."

> Clark, "Response by Chief Justice Walter Clark [to Addresses of Judge Winston, Mr. Hicks, and Mr. Haywood] at the Proceedings of the North Carolina Bar Association," in Strong, *Cases Argued and Determined in the Supreme Court [...] Fall Term, 1918*, 821. [176 N.C. 821]

"The enactment of that Code of Procedure..."

> Carter, *Argument of James C. Carter in Opposition to the Bill to Establish a Civil Code*, 5–6.

"From time to time [the common law] may be altered..."

> Document IV–13 (Shepherd's Speech, 1900)

Opposite General Introduction (Science of Common Law and Science of Statute Law)

"[N]either the common law, nor any other code yet devised by man..."

DOCUMENT II–14 (TAYLOR ON THE COMMON LAW, 1823)

"[C]odification is... philosophically impossible."

CARTER, *PROVINCES OF THE WRITTEN AND THE UNWRITTEN LAW*, 26.

"Enactment has taken the place of living social instinct..."

SANTAYANA, *DOMINATIONS AND POWERS*, 81–82.

"The law is... a complex science...."

[UNKNOWN], REVIEW OF *AN ADDRESS DELIVERED BEFORE THE LAW ASSOCIATION OF THE CITY OF NEW YORK, OCTOBER 21, 1836*, BY JAMES KENT, 473.

"[N]othing, except matters of mere form and arbitrary regulations..."

DOCUMENT II–36 (UNWRITTEN CODE OF THE PEOPLE, 1832)

"A judge has a discoverable generic character..."

SANTAYANA, *DOMINATIONS AND POWERS*, 116.

"... morals do not of necessity advance... with the sciences."

ADAMS, *HISTORY OF THE UNITED STATES DURING THE FIRST ADMINISTRATION OF JEFFERSON: VOL. 1*, 179 (QUOTING THOMAS JEFFERSON IN 1815).

Opposite Introduction to Early Documents

"[T]he... common Law is and shall be in force..."

DOCUMENT I–5 (THE QUEEN'S PEACE, 1711)

"Whereas... the ancient standing laws of this Government have been carefully revised."

DOCUMENT I–6 (REVISAL, 1715)

"An Act... to revise and print the Laws of this Province..."

DOCUMENT I–9 (REVISAL, 1746)

"Be it ordained by the representatives of the Freemen of North Carolina in Congress assembled..."

DOCUMENT I–15 (REVISAL ORDINANCE, DECEMBER 21, 1776)

"[T]he said commissioner... in revising and collecting said Acts..."

DOCUMENT I–24 (REVISAL, 1787)

Opposite Introduction to Antebellum Period

"He said, the rules of pedantry did not suit this country..."

DOCUMENT II–59 (ABOUT MR. ARCHIBALD HENDERSON (1768–1822))

"The [early] judges resolved to adhere to decided cases..."

DOCUMENT IV-26 (ADAMS'S EVOLUTION OF LAW, 1924)

"Permit me to call your attention to an act..."

DOCUMENT II-31 (COMMISSIONS FOR COMMON AND STATUTE LAW SUBJECT REVISAL, MAY 1829)

"The truth is ... our statute Law [is] 'as undiscoverable as the sources of the Nile.'"

DOCUMENT II-37 (GOVERNOR SWAIN'S MESSAGE, 1833)

"[T]he revisal now published ... differs..."

DOCUMENT II-43 (REVISED STATUTES' PREFACE, 1837)

OPPOSITE INTRODUCTION TO CODE COMMISSION ERA

"From the beginning of the thirteenth [there is nothing so revolutionary] as the Judicature Acts in England or ... 'code pleading' [in] American states."

POLLOCK, EXPANSION OF THE COMMON LAW, 29.

"Such cautious progress..."

DOCUMENT III-29 (REPORT OF THE CODE COMMISSIONERS, MARCH 20, 1869)

"The New York system..."

DOCUMENT III-33 (CALL FOR CONVENTION, 1869–1870)

"These acts, with many others [drafted by the Code Commission]..."

DOCUMENT III-36 (REPORT OF THE CODE COMMISSIONERS, MARCH 1870)

"[I]t is admitted by all, that the Constitution and Code—are [Tourgée's]."

OLSEN, CARPETBAGGER'S CRUSADE, 130N6 (QUOTING A LETTER OF TOURGÉE TO HIS WIFE, JANUARY 12, 1873, IN WHICH TOURGÉE QUOTES GEORGE V. STRONG).

"[My opponents] clung to the old common-law..."

WINSTON, IT'S A FAR CRY, 123–125.

OPPOSITE INTRODUCTION TO APPLIED DEMOCRACY

"It would be a great pleasure to see all the codes ... adopted in North Carolina."

DOCUMENT IV-5 (FIELD TO CLARK, 1892)

"The codification of the laws ... is hardly practicable at this time."

DOCUMENT IV-11 (HINSDALE ON CODIFICATION, 1900)

"Generally speaking ... [it is too soon to] attempt an entire codification..."

DOCUMENT IV-13 (SHEPHERD'S SPEECH, 1900)

"A very high authority..."

DOCUMENT IV-15 (TOURGÉE ON THE COMMON LAW, 1908)

"All the laws should be burned every thirty years."

MacClamroch, "Ancestors of the Consolidated Statutes," 7 (attributing the quotation to Chief Justice Walter Clark).

"We must some day [follow European countries and] codify our laws."

Document IV–17 (Clark's Speech, 1914)

"Demand for socialization of law . . . has come . . . from the city . . ."

Document IV–22 (Pound on the Common Law, 1920)

"What was revolutionary was rather . . . codes."

Document IV–31 (Pound's Speech, 1958)

Opposite Afterword (legal history)

"Indeed it has always been a weakness of history . . ."

Weeks, "North Carolina Historians," in Connor, *Proceedings of the Fifteenth Annual Session of the State Literary and Historical Association of North Carolina*, 84.

"As has been said, philosophy without history is empty. . . ."

Berman, "Historical Foundations of Law," 23.

About the Compilers

Thomas P. Davis has worked in the law library of the Supreme Court of North Carolina since 1994, serving as librarian since 1999. He is a graduate of the University of North Carolina at Chapel Hill and Duke University School of Law and has been licensed to practice law in North Carolina since 1992. He lives in Cary, North Carolina.

J. Barrett Fish, a native of Willow Spring, North Carolina, has worked in the law library of the Supreme Court of North Carolina since 1999, serving as assistant librarian for public services since 2005. He earned an undergraduate degree in history at North Carolina State University and a master's degree in library science from North Carolina Central University.

NOTES

1. According to Battle, "Address on the History of the Supreme Court, 481: the legislatively created supreme court was "a wide departure from the old English system, and from that of our general government, in that its judges do not try cases in the courts below." In his report to the general assembly defending the newly created supreme court, Document II–11 (Gaston's Report, 1819), Senator Gaston wrote: it is the hope that this new court would "receive those weighty and numerous equity suits, which have for so many years slept unheaded on the dockets of the courts in the west, and which the committee learn, are in preparation for their journey hither." This highly charged issue of administration of justice in the western counties soon resulted in bills designed to alter the operation of the supreme court. On the question of the court being "holden in several places" to better handle the backlog of equity cases, for example, see Journal of the House of Commons, Friday, December 12, 1828, 192, 193; Journal of the House, Wednesday, December 24, 1828, 222; Journal of the House, Monday, December 29, 1828, 234–235, all in *Journals of the Senate & House of Commons* [...] *1828–29*.
2. Document II–35 (Friends of Liberty Address, 1830) (advocating abolition of slavery); Document II–55 (Cantwell on Criminal Law, 1856) (exploring reform of capital punishment).
3. While our focus in this compilation is speculative, we do not suggest that the jurisprudential sea-change toward codification was not driven by Jeremy Bentham's intense dissatisfaction with the court administration and substantive law of eighteenth-century England. Bentham viewed the systematic written arrangement of public-general acts of a sovereign authority in force in a jurisdiction, i.e., codification, as a remedy for the arbitrary accretions of the unwritten law. In fact, his reforms would forewarn even the layperson of the requirements of the law, while the unwritten law, he thought, had predictive value only for a narrow, aristocratic class of experts in legal reasoning, and then only insofar as precedent limited judicial discretion. The science of legislation—Bentham's alternative to the law under Western moral-religious traditions—would reorganize the court system on a transparently rational scheme, mitigate the penal law, and transfigure the law of contracts, marriage, land, conveyancing, and succession. See Graveson, "Restless Spirit of English Law," in Keeton and Schwarzenberger, *Jeremy Bentham and the Law*, 113–120.
4. For example, see Wild, *Plato's Modern Enemies and the Theory of Natural Law*, 147: "We must not confuse what is good with our own opinions and wishes. We are in no position to legislate what is really good and bad. This humanistic pride is a delusion of utilitarianism. It is nature that first legislates independent of all arbitrary human decree."
5. For example, see Murray, *We Hold These Truths*, 270: "At about the turn of the century it was rather generally believed in professional circles that the Scholastic idea of natural law, as an operative concept in the fields of ethics, political theory, and law and jurisprudence, was dead. In other words, it was generally assumed that the great nineteenth-century attack on natural law had been successful."
6. For example, see Kirk, *Conservative Mind*, 42–43: "At a time when the world was infatuated with constitution-manufacture, . . . when every coffee-house had its philosopher qualified to revise the statutes of the nation on a rational plan, when America had just got up fourteen new constitutions and was thinking of more, Burke declared that men do not make laws: they merely ratify or distort the laws of God. He said that men have no rights to what they please: their natural rights are only what may be directly deduced from their human nature. [He said] that there is indeed an immutable law, and there are indeed inalienable rights, but they are of origins and character profoundly different from what *philosophes* and levellers take them for."; Kirk, *John Randolph of Roanoke*, 61–62: "Proper constitutions[, according both to Edmund Burke and John Randolph,] are the product of social experience; they are rooted in custom and prescription, which have a deeper validity than mere positive law. . . . Social compacts . . . do not take precedence of the *real* rights of humanity. . . . Similarly, Burke and Randolph denied the validity of the rights of man as erected into abstract absolutes by Paine and his fellows; they affirmed natural laws of a very different sort—natural laws in the Christian tradition, the moral view of politics which we may trace back to Hooker and Aquinas and the Stoics. Burke defines the *real* rights of men upon the classical predicate of justice, 'to each his own.'"; Arnold, *Culture and Anarchy and Other Writings*, 219–221:

   > French equality appeals to this abstract natural right [i.e., equality] as its support. It goes back to a state of nature where all were equal, and supposes that 'the poor consented,' as Rousseau says, 'to the existence of rich people,' reserving always a natural right to return to the state of nature. . . . The principle of abstract right . . . is

false.... The natural right to have work found for one to do, the natural right to have food found for one to eat—rights sometimes so confidently and so indignantly asserted—seem to me quite baseless. It cannot be too often repeated: peasants and workmen have no natural rights, not one. Only we ought instantly to add, that kings and nobles have none either.... It is assumed... that our signal inequality of classes and property is expedient for our civilisation and welfare.... Civilisation is the humanisation of man in society. To be humanised is to comply with the true law of our human nature."

Brownson, *American Republic*, 76: "The Abbe Sieyes pronounced politics a science which he had finished, and he was ready to turn you out constitutions to order... Many in the last century... confounded the written instrument with the constitution itself. No constitution can be written on paper or engrossed on parchment. What the convention may agree upon, draw up, and the people ratify by their votes, is no constitution, for it is extrinsic to the nation, not inherent and living in it... The constitution of the state is not a theory, nor is it drawn up and established in accordance with any preconceived theory.... The French people adopted constitution after constitution of the most approved pattern... all to no effect; for they had no authority for the nation, no hold on its affections, and formed no element of its life."; Versteeg, "'Perfection in Imperfection'," in Galligan, *Constitutions and the Classics*, 313: attributing to de Maistre the position that "a nation's true constitution is *indigenous* and particular to the nation. It is neither universal nor rational, but grows from each nation's past and best remains unwritten."; Cooper, *American Democrat*, 37: "They who fancy it possible to frame the institutions of a country, on the pure principles of abstract justice, as these principles exist in theories, know little of human nature, or of the restraints that are necessary to society."

7. For a contemporary overview of the classical common law tradition, see Postema, "Classical Common Law Jurisprudence (Part I)," 155–180. According to Postema, 170–171: jurists have at times tightly linked the jurisprudential norms of common law and natural law:

> Most common lawyers were inclined to accept some version of the idea that the long experience exemplified in the continuous tradition of common law was on the whole one of the common law's greatest assets. Even Hale, who took a far more modest view, gave time its due. '[L]ong and iterated experience', he allowed, is 'the wisest expedient among mankind, and discovers those defects... which no wit of man could either at once foresee or aptly remedy.' But the less modest common law contingent went further, arguing that through the trial of time common law approximated natural law, and, indeed it was, in Coke's phrase, 'the perfection of reason.' While not rejecting Coke's immodest claim, Davies argued that time's testing and trying had a different, but equally important, consequence: time made common law 'fit and agreeable to the nature and disposition of the people.' Indeed, 'it is so framed and fitted to the nature and disposition of this people, as we may properly say it is connatural to the nation.'

Professor Postema reiterates the point on page 176: "This close association of law with reason strongly suggests that classical common law jurisprudence sought to wrap itself in the mantle of classical natural law theory. However, the relationship between common law and natural law jurisprudence is a complex matter." Not only is common law linked historically and theoretically with natural law, but it is also equally the target of modern positivist legal reform, as described in Coughlin, "Family Law: Natural Law, Marriage, and the Thought of Karol Wojtyla," in Scaperlanda and Collett, *Recovering Self-Evident Truths*, 275, 280–282:

> The eighteenth-century view of law was in harmony with the liberal theory. Government was by the consent of individuals... The era witnessed a gradual shift away from the traditional conception of the common law as a fixed and determinate body of rules reflecting ancient custom and divinely designed principles. Supreme Court Justice James Wilson delivered a series of lectures in 1791 in which he "acknowledged the obligations derived from natural law," but "reduced them to private questions of conscience." Wilson's view reflected the predominant conception of law, which held that it was the voluntary consent of individual men, instead of the authority of some higher law, that formed the obligatory basis of statutes, custom, and even the natural law itself. The view was consistent with the theory of John Austin, who held that the state creates the law. It marked the waning of the medieval and common-law solution that the sovereign had power over the positive law, but was bound by the higher principles of natural justice. Statutory law passed by the legislature was increasingly viewed as supreme, as it best reflected the consent of the people. No longer would judges understand their role as the guardians and interpreters of a higher, transcendent, and immutable corpus of law. Nor would they continue to understand the common law as primarily derived from these higher principles in order to furnish justice in individual cases.

8. Graveson, "Restless Spirit of English Law," in Keeton and Schwarzenberger, *Jeremy Bentham and the Law*, 104: "His first and most famous broadside . . . was his 'Comment on the Commentaries,' a considered statement of his revulsion of feeling against the publication of Blackstone's 'Commentaries on the Laws of England.' . . . [W]hat Bentham refused to admit, and at times may have failed to perceive, was the accuracy, for the most part, of Blackstone's statements of law . . . Blackstone, like most of his contemporaries, saw in English law the embodiment of the law of nature."

9. The bottomless contempt for natural law and customary common law of those waving the banner of codification is multi-faceted. After reviewing contemporaneous events on the continent, for instance, one might contend that the Napoleonic Code of 1804 codifies the principles of the French Revolution, thereby linking some modern natural rights doctrines with socialism, utilitarianism, and transcendentalism in combat against Western jurisprudential orthodoxy. A contrast of the revolutionary movement spawning these doctrines with the scholasticism that preceded it is provided in Santayana, *Dominations and Powers*, 223–224:

> But the French Revolution and the whole movement, still not quite spent, which proceeded from it, was not liberal except verbally and by accident. The world was to be freed from Christianity and feudalism; it was not to be free to become Christian and feudal again. These were not regarded as normal episodes in human history, as forms of civilisation as legitimate as any others; they were regarded as fiendish inventions foisted by tyrants on human helplessness and ignorance. . . . What the Revolution was really making for, though hardly expressed with frankness before Nietzsche, was . . . liberty without foundations in nature or history . . . Custom, law, privilege, and religion were not to command allegiance, but to be themes only for criticism and invective. . . . Thus while politically the Revolution led to nationalism, industrialism, and absolute democracy, intellectually it ended in romantic egotism.

10. Rommen, *Natural Law*, 110–111: "Positivism as a method was already present in the historical school of law. It developed with the victorious advance of scientism, of natural-science modes of thought. This approach to reality became the standard methodological pattern for all scientific thinking, as was once the case of deductive, mathematical rationalism which insisted on conceiving and handling ethics and law *more geometrico*."; Stanlis, *Edmund Burke*, 248: "The eighteenth-century rationalists . . . constructed a priori social projects, based on infallible mathematics and moral computation, without reference to history or to human nature . . ."; Babbitt, *Rousseau and Romanticism*, 27–28: "In fact one may ask if any doctrine has ever appeared so fatal to every form of tradition—not merely literary but also religious and political—as Cartesianism. The rationalist of the eighteenth century was for dismissing as 'prejudice' everything that could not give a clear account of itself in the Cartesian sense. This riot of abstract reasoning (*la raison raisonnante*) that prepared the way for the Revolution has been identified by Taine and others with the classic spirit. A more vicious confusion has seldom gained currency in criticism."

11. Rommen, *Natural Law*, 109–110: "Empiricism, which dismisses metaphysics as epistemologically impossible (agnosticism), believed that, since it had won such great triumphs in the natural sciences, it is also the right method to follow in the socalled cultural sciences. . . . The will of the state, the formal general will of the citizens, is the source and criterion of law. Sociology thereupon explains . . . the further question of why this particular norm is chosen by the will."; Stanlis, *Edmund Burke*, 17: "Thus, Hobbes's philosophy is the great dividing line between medieval and modern secular thought; his revolutionary break with the past, his destruction of the primacy of 'law' or 'reason' in favor of 'power' or 'will' is the fountainhead of revolutionary social thought. . . . Hobbes's attitude toward tradition in human affairs was as revolutionary as that of Bacon in scientific method. Hobbes's addiction in middle age to Euclid led to his conviction that the methods of physical science, particularly of mathematics, could be applied to social and political thought."

A similar extension of method from the physical sciences to the moral sciences is documented by Professor Guthrie in describing the Greeks of the fifth century B.C. in his *Sophists*, 100:

> Necessity (*ananké*) as a cosmological force runs right through Presocratic thought, in the Western tradition (Parmenides, Empedocles, the Pythagoreans) with almost mystical or theological overtones, but in Ionian rationalism, which reached its culmination in Leucippus and Democritus, appearing as a mindless natural force equated with the chance collisions of the atoms and the cosmic vortices which they form. Two passages in the *Clouds* of Aristophanes parody the jargon of the scientists and illustrate the way in which it was transferred to human life as a justification for immorality. *Ananké* fills the clouds with moisture and governs the motions by which they collide and cause thunder; and the author of this necessity is no longer a personal Zeus but 'the

celestial whirl.' Later in the play the Unjust Argument speaks of 'the necessities of nature' with reference to adultery, and calls shamelessness and self-indulgence 'exercising one's nature.' Democritus himself made the transfer to human life in a less provocative way when he said that the begetting of children is looked upon as one of the necessities arising from nature."

12. Santayana, *Santayana on America*, 206: "And what authority can the dominant morality retain? Evidently none: yet it is wonderful how long it has taken the liberal world to discover that it has deliberately abandoned mankind to moral anarchy. It has been only in recent years that the Russian revolution, Madam Caillaux, D. H. Lawrence, and André Gide have openly and conscientiously written down robbery, murder, adultery, and sodomy among the inalienable rights of man."

13. Schall, *Reason, Revelation, and the Foundations of Political Philosophy*, 38–39: "[T]he political theory of the modern era has attempted to replace Aristotle's metaphysical analysis . . . Indeed, this modern adaptation . . . has considered all natural distinction, even heredity and talent, as an 'alienation' imposed upon men from outside themselves. This is the basis for the modern attack on classic natural law and order, with the shift in emphasis from law to 'human rights,' themselves presupposed to nothing but man's self-definition. Man's reality must be taken not from the highest faculties but from the lowest instincts . . ."

14. One oft-attacked corollary of moral realism is the discovery theory of law, which is typically dismissed as a carry-over from pre-Enlightenment thought, for example, see Kelly, Harbison, and Belz, *American Constitution*, 1:39: "This sharing of power, as we have seen, was characteristic of mixed government. Conceptually, it was rooted in the medieval belief that the purpose of government was essentially judicial—to declare and carry out the word of God. Thus law was not made by human agency, but was discovered."

Moral realism implies that every aspect of life, not merely its political government, is a pursuit of the good by art, and thus the discovery theory extends beyond jurisprudence to all the moral sciences, including the medieval queen of the sciences, philosophy, as stated in the "Introduction [to the Compact Edition]," Santayana, *Realms of Being*, xxvii–xxviii: "I had no thought of constructing any rival [philosophical] system; yet my sincere reaction to one system after another gradually revealed to me the unformulated principles that guided my judgment; so that my system, if system it can be called, was not so much formed by me as discovered within me." There is nothing essentially medieval, mystical, or metaphysical about moral realism or the discovery theory in the cultural or moral sciences. Moral realism necessarily holds only that knowledge and love are theoretically, logically, and practically conditioned, and that these conditions are "not made by human agency" and may be understood, respected, and expressed by humans. This definition of moral realism does not preclude the doctrine that in the political realm, discovered principles of natural law are specified by the positive laws of a people, whether specified by legislators, jurists, or executive officials of a particular jurisdiction.

15. For example, see Brownson, *Essays and Reviews*, 307–308:

> The modern spirit is in every thing the direct denial of the practical reason. It reverses every thing which has received the sanction of the race. In former times, it was universally held that authority was a good . . . ; morals were binding, were the law imposed by religion; . . . But the modern spirit reverses all this. . . . It asserts the universal and absolute supremacy of man, and his unrestricted right to subject religion, morals, and politics to his own will, passion, or caprice. . . . It calls government government, because it is *not* government; morals morals, because they are *not* morals, that is, not obligatory upon the will; religion religion, because it is *not* religion, that is, does *not* bind man to God; law law, because it is *not* law; and reason reason, because it is *not* reason. Marvellous is the age we live in! Marvellous the light and progress of the modern world! We have extinguished the light of reason, and therefore are reasonable; reduced wisdom to folly, and therefore are wise; substituted nonsense for sense, and therefore are intelligent, and have the right to call all who went before us fools and madmen, which assuredly they were,—unless we are.

See also Carter, *Provinces of the Written and the Unwritten Law*, 32: "No; those who insist that the body of the private law shall be expressed in writing really *seek* to make rules for all future cases. Their real purpose is to stop the processes of [practical] reason and to substitute in the determination of particular cases the simple inquiry 'what has been written?' in the place of 'what is right?' Their great apostle Jeremy Bentham had the courage of his convictions."

16. Everett, "Bentham in the United States of America," in Keeton and Schwarzenberger, *Jeremy Bentham and the Law*, 185: "Bentham certainly meant his work to form a system, and a complete one, extending the scientific principle into

law and morals. He was to be, in his own phrase, the 'Newton of legislation'." Contrasting this modern utilitarian approach in morals with preceding orthodox approaches to the good life, Professor Santayana writes, in his *Persons and Places*, 259: "Epicurus had a different notion of happiness from that of Solon, but it was just as much a form of wisdom, a choice among possible lives; in neither sage was it a calculus of quantitative pleasures and pains."

17. Santayana, *Winds of Doctrine*, 8–9: "The imagination of the age was intent on history; its conscience was intent on reform. Reform! This magic word itself covers a great equivocation. To reform means to shatter one form and to create another; but the two sides of the act are not always equally intended nor equally successful. Usually the movement starts from the mere sense of oppression, and people break down some established form, without any qualms about the capacity of their freed instincts to generate the new forms that may be needed."

18. "Reception" means "[t]he adoption in whole or in part of the law of one jurisdiction by another jurisdiction," Garner, *Black's Law Dictionary*, s.v. "Reception," 1523.

19. Document IV–5 (Field to Clark, 1892): "It would be a great pleasure to see all the codes prepared for New York adopted in North-Carolina. You seem to be the very man to take the lead as law-reformer in your State."

20. Miller, *Legal Mind in America*.

21. Warren, *History of the American Bar*, 523–531. Regarding statutory codification, Warren's survey includes New York (1828), Pennsylvania (1830), Massachusetts (1836), and Ohio (1834). North Carolina is ignored, even though it revised its statutes similarly and contemporaneously.

22. Cook, *American Codification Movement*.

23. It seems to the compilers, looking back on this project after having gathered these materials, that political figures in North Carolina reacted to the debates on codification in an extraordinarily ordinary way, and that Cook's perfunctory references to North Carolina sources were appropriate for his study. As far as Professor Miller's grand work is concerned, we had as much trouble as he must have had in finding any extended oration on codification in North Carolina sources or by North Carolina speakers. Warren's neglect remains unclear to us.

24. Document III–47 (Tourgée's Notes, 1878) (comment under section 12): "It is somewhat remarkable that the court, by construing our constitutional provisions so as to make a jury trial in all actions a matter of right, seems likely to have overcome the only impediment hitherto unsurmounted in the development of the civil action."; Document III–47 (Tourgée's Notes, 1878) (comment under section 219):

> In *Gragg v. Wagoner*, 77 N.C. 246, [a]n equitable defence was set up in an action in the nature of *covenant* at the common law, and issues thereon tried by a jury. Whether under the Constitution as amended, Article IV, Section 8, the court can review the *findings of fact by a jury*, is the very delicate question presented, but not determined by the court. Under the old equity practice the court could review the findings by the *judge* below, in regard to facts. They might also refer issues to a jury, whose finding, they were not bound to follow, but might modify or reverse. In those cases, however, there was no constitutional right to a trial by jury. Now, there is, and such provision would seem to be altogether useless if the court may review and reverse the decision of the jury. . . . That the constitution should, as it unquestionably does, guarantee a jury trial, upon all '*issues of fact*,' and then allow their findings to be modified and overturned, upon a necessarily incomplete statement of the evidence before them, without even the sworn statement of a single witness, but only the case as made up by the judge, who presided at the trial below, seems somewhat absurd and untenable. Surely no court should review the decision of a tribunal specially empowered to try such issues, upon such testimony.

25. Document IV–4 (Battle's History, 1889). The process of appeal and removal in the early days of the new supreme court is described in Battle, "Address on the History of the Supreme Court," 490:

> By act of 1810, any party dissatisfied with the ruling of the Superior Court had a right to remove it to the Supreme Court. By the act of 1818 the judges were to have all the powers of the Superior Court Judges, except that of holding a Superior Court. Any party could appeal from the final judgment, sentence or decree of the Superior Court on giving security to abide the judgment or decree of the Supreme Court, which was authorized to give such judgment as should appear to them right in law, to be rendered on inspection of the whole record. Equity cases could be removed to the Supreme Court for hearing, upon sufficient cause appearing, by affidavit or otherwise, showing that such removal was required for purposes of justice, but no parol evidence was received before the court, or any jury impaneled to try issues, except witnesses to prove exhibits or other documents. Under this provision it became customary to remove all important equity causes, so that the Superior Court Judge escaped

the responsibility of giving any opinion in the matter. The Constitution of 1868 and that of 1876 put a stop to these proceedings by confining the jurisdiction of the Supreme Court to appeals on matters of law or legal inference.

26. Document IV–17 (Clark's Speech, 1914). In this compilation's excerpt of Chief Justice Clark's speech is found the following historical explanation of the changing powers of the clerk under *The Code of Civil Procedure*:

    When the Code of Civil Procedure was adopted in 1868, it provided . . . that all the pleadings should be made up before the clerk, and that only issues of fact should be transferred to the docket at term time to be passed upon by the jury, and that the judgment of the clerk upon issues of law should be appealed to the judge at chambers. This was stricken out in 1870 because, owing to the condition of the country, instead of expediting the trial of causes it was considered advisable to delay judgment. We should now revert to the original system of permitting the clerk to pass upon the pleadings and all other matters until issues of fact are made up, when the cause should be transferred to the trial docket at term. There should be an appeal to the judge at chambers from the decision of the clerk on issues of law. This could readily be done should we revert to the system which then obtained of the judge holding only the courts of his own district.

27. Adams, "Life and Influence of John Manning," 222: "Hence it is easy to see that transition from the old procedure to the new required mental readjustment; but one can hardly appreciate the difficulty experienced by the ante-bellum lawyers in actually applying the novelties of the Code of Civil Procedure."
28. An Act to Allow Citizens of North Carolina to Practice in the Courts of the State, ch. 46, *Public Laws* [. . .] *Passed by the General Assembly* [. . .] *1868–'69*, 118–119. [1868–'69 N.C. Pub. Laws 118–119] (ratified 15 February 1869): "That any citizen of this State, by establishing a good moral character, and paying a license tax of twenty dollars, shall be allowed to practice law in the courts of North Carolina."
29. On the difficulty with understanding some of these reported appellate opinions, see Document III–47 (Tourgée's Notes, 1878) (criticizing many opinions issued in the first decade under code pleading, for example, at section 187, page 149 n.*a* criticizing *Boyleston Ins. Co. v. Davis*, 74 N.C. 78 (1876)), and see Document IV–16 (Winston's Speech, 1913): "The Code has not met the expectation of its friends. This is perhaps due to the fact that it came in under alien political conditions. Its adoption was in the face of strong opposition and its early interpretation by Bench and Bar was, for the most part, by no means in accord with its principles."
30. For a list of the many instances of stillborn initiatives in statutory codification in the 1820s in North Carolina, see note 191. For the success of statutory codification in the 1830s in North Carolina, see, for example, Document II–43 (Revised Statutes' Preface, 1837).
31. For instance, a remark by official reporter Thomas P. Devereux pits his views about reforms in property law against the opinions of the judges of the supreme court in 1827. See Document II–22 (Devereux on Humphreys, 1827). And an Act of 1829 commissions a revisal of the common and statute law of executors and administrators. See Document II–30 (Common and Statute Law on Subject Revisal, January 1829).
32. A speech by Thomas Smith Grimké is excerpted in Miller, *Legal Mind in America*, 147 (reprinting an oration of Grimké in support of codification), and a speech by Robert Rantoul Jr. is excerpted in Miller, 220 (reprinting an 1836 oration of Rantoul against the common law).
33. On the theme of the agricultural character of antebellum North Carolina, see Document III–26 (Superior Courts and Clerks, January 25, 1869): "Our old laws were conformed to the life and habits of our people, and executions were made returnable, as far as possible, in accordance with the agricultural pursuits of our population.", and Document III–33 (Call for Convention, 1869–1870): "Our present Judicial system is a servile copy of that of New York, a State less like ours than almost any other in the Union. New York is densely populated, North Carolina sparsely. New York is full of large towns and cities, and her people are extensively engaged in commercial and maritime pursuits. North Carolina is an agricultural State with a rural people." The more casual common law practice in North Carolina's sparsely-populated, deep-rooted agricultural communities allowed for "chimney corner law"—see Document III–28 (Schenck's Diary, March 8, 1869), presumably leaving its people less susceptible than citizens in the metropolitan melting pots of large, mid-nineteenth-century port cities to agitation for law reform in court procedure.
34. Document IV–5 (Field to Clark, 1892) (implying Clark had expressed an interest in codification of private substantive common law).
35. Document IV–17 (Clark's Speech, 1914): "We must codify our laws."
36. This role of the Institute of Government is discussed in Davis, "From Aristocracy to Democracy," 215.

37. The establishment and maintenance of an institution to settle difficult points of law and conflicting judgments of the superior courts was a continuing point of debate in the general assembly early in the Antebellum Period. See Document II–1 (Meetings of the Judges, November 18, 1799), Document II–2 (Court of Errors and Appeals, December 26, 1799), Document II–3 (The Court of Conference, 1801), and Document II–11 (Gaston's Report, 1819).
38. See, for example, Document II–7 (Bentham's Letter, 1817).
39. Regarding statutory codification, see the documents listed for Part II in the table in note 204. Regarding common law codification during the Antebellum Period, see, for example, Document II–22 (Devereux on Humphreys, 1827) and Document II–30 (Common and Statute Law on Subject Revisal, January 1829).
40. Document III–6 (Constitution, April 21–23, 1868). On the dependence of the antebellum state supreme court on the general assembly, see Edward S. Walton v. T. H. Gatlin, Jones and Winston, *Cases Argued and Determined in the Supreme Court* [...] *June Term, 1863, to December Term, 1864*, 321. [60 N.C. 310, 321, 1 Win. 318, 328–329 (1864) (Manly, J., dissenting)]: "It [the antebellum state supreme court] is the creature of statute law, and has its powers limited and defined by that law.... It is created by statute and clothed with powers there specially defined. With a range of jurisdiction, in the very highest regions of power exercised by human tribunals, it is nevertheless a limited range, defined by the written law."
41. Regarding the scope of the "code of the law of North-Carolina" which the commissioners were to report to the general assembly, see, for example, Document III–5 (Code Commissioners, March 13, 1868).
42. Document III–6 (Constitution, April 21–23, 1868).
43. Document IV–14 (Revisal's Preface, 1905). This increase in legislative output occurred during the gradual abandonment of governing by private, special, and local act and the gradual acceptance of governing by administrative regulation in accordance with general statute. Davis, "From Aristocracy to Democracy," 223–229.
44. Document IV–28 (About Chief Justice Shepherd (1847–1910)): "As science had been changed from mere ratiocination to experimentation, so law, cut loose from precedent, should adjust itself to human needs from day to day. Whatever is, is wrong, became the slogan of the radical members of the Supreme Court, now divided 2–2 on disputed social and political issues, putting it up to a fifth judge to break the tie." In 1916, the supreme court published a table of its overruled cases in the reports of the Supreme Court of North Carolina. See Allen, "Table of Cases Overruled," 857. Additionally, a marked increase in the number of dissents during the period of Applied Democracy paved the way for future overrulings. Hunt, "Dissent on the North Carolina Supreme Court," 31.
45. Davis, "School Days," 406: "By the end of the century, though, a disaffection with the moral science of the common law had set in. The judges no longer taught the science of the common law, and abridged versions of Enlightenment treatises crept onto the court's reading list."
46. See the mention of "The Code of Justinian" in Document III–40 (Report of the Code Commissioners, December 18, 1870).
47. Schwarzenberg's work was the first modern code of criminal law. Berman, *Law and Revolution II*, 138–139.
48. See the mention of "the Code Napoleon" in Document III–40 (Report of the Code Commissioners, December 18, 1870).
49. Bentham, *Jeremy Bentham to His Fellow-Citizens of France*, 3.
50. For evidence of Bentham offering his services to the world, see Bentham, *Codification Proposal*, as well as Document II–7 (Bentham's Letter, 1817).
51. On the treatment of classification as a form of scientific thinking, see Santayana, *Life of Reason*, 98: "[S]cience is nothing but common knowledge extended. It is willing to reckon in any terms and to study any subject-matter; where it cannot see necessity it will notice law; where laws cannot be stated it will describe habits; where habits fail it will classify types; and where types even are indiscernible it will not despise statistics. In this way studies which are scientific in spirit, however loose their results, may be carried on in social matters . . ."
52. For an article that relies on the work of two Enlightenment expositors of English common law—Thomas Wood and Sir William Blackstone—see Davis, "Reading *Smith v. Campbell*. For a brief discussion about a codifier of English property law—James Humphreys—see Document II–22 (Devereux on Humphreys, 1827).
53. Bentham, *Introduction to the Principles of Morals and Legislation*, 9: "[T]ruths that form the basis of political and moral science, are not to be discovered but by investigations as severe as mathematical ones, and beyond all comparison more intricate and extensive.... There is no *King's Road* . . . to legislative, any more than to mathematical science." On the ideal of extending the scientific method of the physical sciences to the moral or cultural sciences, see also notes 10, 11, 16, and 51.

54. On the notion of statutes being outside the consciousness of a people, see Document IV–10 (Manning's Commentaries, 1899) (recording the need to proclaim statute law so the people may know it in advance, no such need arising for customary common law). On the idea of statutes being applicable in theory to all peoples, see note 50.
55. See, for example, Maitland, "Historical Sketch of Liberty and Equality as Ideals of English Political Philosophy," in Fisher, *Collected Papers of Frederic William Maitland*, 1:47, 79, 82: noting that Rousseau, who goes further toward democracy than Locke and who sets up the will of the majority as an idol, "does try to insist that the popular assembly must do nothing but pass general laws, for *la volonté générale* cannot descend to particulars"; Scruton, *Kant: Very Short Introduction*, 123: "The business of government consists in ... enabling the 'general united will' of the people to find expression in the legislative assembly."; Rommen, *Natural Law*, 110: "The will of the state, the formal general will of the citizens, is the source and criterion of law."
56. In the case of North Carolina, see, for example, Document I–16 (Reception Ordinance, December 22, 1776) and Document I–20 (Reception Statute, 1778).
57. In the case of North Carolina, see Document I–14 (Constitution, December 18, 1776).
58. In the case of North Carolina, see Document I–13 (Declaration of Rights, December 17, 1776) (containing section 12, which is rooted in clauses 39 and 40 of Magna Carta, 1215 (clause 29 of Magna Carta, 1297), and which demands that no person be deprived of life, liberty, or property but by the law of the land, rather than by the arbitrary will of the governing sovereign).
59. McIlwain, *Constitutionalism*, 78–79.
60. In the case of North Carolina, Attorney Robert Potter advanced this sort of radical understanding of popular sovereignty in his argument to the state supreme court. Document II–19 (R. Potter on Social Contract, 1825). During North Carolina's period of Applied Democracy, Chief Justice Walter Clark would express the sentiment, radically contemptuous of legal tradition, that "All the laws should be burned every thirty years," quoted in MacClamroch, "Ancestors of the Consolidated Statutes," 7. Presumably, Clark here followed Thomas Jefferson, who from Paris at the outbreak of the French Revolution asserted to James Madison that one generation had no right to bind another by a perpetual constitution or law, as found in Thomas Jefferson to James Madison, Paris, September 6, 1789, Ford, *Works of Thomas Jefferson*, 6:3–8.
61. Brownson, "Cuban Expedition (October 1850)," in Brownson, *Works in Political Philosophy*, 3:366: suggesting that "French Jacobins, and English and Scotch radicals, have sought to give our [republican American] institutions a democratic interpretation in the modern sense of the word"; Brownson, "Cooper's *Ways of the Hour* (July 1851)," in Brownson, *Works in Political Philosophy*, 4:18–19 (distinguishing the use of "sovereignty of the people" in the "pure democracy" of the "Jacobinical revolutions" from the use of the phrase in American states at their declared independence from England).
62. Regarding the will of the people as the source of law, see for example notes 11 and 55 (citing Rommen, *Natural Law*). Regarding the importance of public opinion in law, see Berman, "Law and Belief in Three Revolutions," 570, as well as Document II–14 (Taylor on the Common Law, 1823), Document II–38 (Moore's Argument, 1834), and Document II-60 (About Chief Justice Taylor (1769–1829)) for its importance to the law of North Carolina.
63. These secular philosophies, with the generality or universality of their purely logical or speculative-theoretical reasoning, might be employed by the state to remake not merely the law of all peoples, but likewise the morality, economics, politics, and technical arts of all peoples, that is, all aspects of their practical living. Perhaps such uses or abuses of these sorts of rationality are presumed by the code commissioners in Document III–10 (First Report of the Code Commissioners, July 15, 1868), where it asserts that: "Public order, sound morals, all advancement in the arts of civilization, and all growth in true prosperity, are dependent, in a great degree, upon those rules of action, which the state prescribes for the conduct of its citizens."
64. Maitland and Montague, *Sketch of English Legal History*, 103: "The need for legislation [in the early days of the English common law], however, was occasioned (so men thought) not by any fated progress of the human race, but by the perversity of mankind. Ideally there exists a perfect body of law, immutable, eternal, the work of God, not of man. Just a few more improvements in our legal procedure will have made it for ever harmonious with this ideal; and, indeed, if men would but obey the law of the land as it stands, there would be little for a legislator to do."
65. In the case of North Carolina, see Davis, "Precedents on Precedent," 8, for a short discussion of the doctrine of precedent as applied by the Supreme Court of North Carolina in three cases from the twentieth century.
66. Kirk, *Orestes Brownson: Selected Essays*, 193. Brownson abandoned transcendentalism and converted to Catholicism in the early 1840s. He is considered to be among the more profound political thinkers of nineteenth-century America.

While Brownson wrote from New England and described the plan of attack of radical secularists generally, attacks on the judiciary and on the common law it expounded are evident in North Carolina documents from the period of Applied Democracy. For example, see Document IV–17 (Clark's Speech, 1914), where Chief Justice Walter Clark speaks of collateral matters which he does not have sufficient time to discuss.

67. In the case of North Carolina, see Document III–6 (Constitution, April 21–23, 1868).
68. In the case of North Carolina, see Document III–27 (Practice of Law, February 15, 1869) concerning the abandonment of the educational requirements to practice law. Regarding the revamping of educational requirements to practice law, see Davis, "School Days," 399–402.
69. In the case of North Carolina, a more subtle attack on the tradition-focused training of the state's bevy of lawyers was the denigration of their central role in the appellate process (e.g., invoking the jurisdiction of the court; settling the record for review; participating in written and oral arguments), thereby promoting the appearance that the professional responsibility to settle—or to unsettle—the common law of the state rested solely in the hands of a few popularly elected justices of the supreme court. See text accompanying note 517 and Document IV–23 (Clark's History of Reprints, 1920) (evidencing an implied attack by Chief Justice Walter Clark on the state's antebellum reporters of appellate opinions, as well as describing his role, played during his lengthy service as editor of the *Reprints* of the *North Carolina Reports*, in removing "unnecessary matter" from the cases argued and determined in the Supreme Court of North Carolina, both the implied criticism of the original reporters and the removal of material from the reprints concerning contributions of counsel to the development of the state's common law).
70. Brownson, "Cooper's *Ways of the Hour* (July 1851)," in Brownson, *Works in Political Philosophy*, 4:22–26 (describing reforms affecting judges and lawyers, and reform of the common law by codification, in American jurisdictions). Regarding reform by codification, in the case of North Carolina, see note 39 concerning codification during the Antebellum Period, the text accompanying notes 41–42 concerning codification during the Code Commission Era, and Document IV–5 (Field to Clark, 1892), for example, concerning codification in the period of Applied Democracy. What role would courts serve were systematized public-general acts to displace common law rules? Perhaps when properly knocked off their precedent-setting pedestal by law reformers, the courts might take up some part of the role abandoned by the assemblies—judgment in special, public-local, or private matters, such as ruling on divorce. Davis, "From Aristocracy to Democracy," 223: describing stages in the legislative ascent to general statute, "each stage consisting of an initiative in the codification of the law and a restriction on the general assembly's power to enact private, special, or local acts." Or perhaps the courts might fill gaps in the legislative schemes of assemblies. See Davis, "Reading *Smith v. Campbell*," 64n158 (citing Grey, Review of *Patterns of American Jurisprudence*, 513–514).
71. The second paragraph of the 1663 charter names (1) Edward Earl of Clarendon, (2) George Duke of Albemarle, (3) William Lord Craven, (4) John, Lord Berkley, (5) Anthony Lord Ashley, (6) Sir George Carteret, (7) Sir William Berkley, and (8) Sir John Colleton as proprietors. Parker, *North Carolina Charters*, 76.
72. The patent to Sir Robert Heath by King Charles I in 1629 was declared void in 1663. Parker, *North Carolina Charters*, 63. While Parker's work provides a scholarly treatment of the founding documents of the colony, including the charter to Walter Raleigh in 1584, one may read a rapidly moving summary history of the colony in Story, *Commentaries on the Constitution of the United States*, 1:14: "The Carolinas were originally proprietary governments. In 1721 a revolution was effected by the people, who shook off their obedience to the proprietors, and declared their dependence immediately on the crown. The king, however, purchased the title of those, who were disposed to sell." For a short discussion of the division of the province into North and South Carolina, see Story, *Commentaries*, 1:124–125. As to the formation of Georgia, see Story, *Commentaries*, 1:128–131.
73. For sources discussing the meaning of the "bishop of Durham" clause, see note 79.
74. Whether the king by his charter declared a just war that might have conferred title by conquest is discussed in Pagden, "Law, Colonization, Legitimation, and the European Background," in Grossberg and Tomlins, *Cambridge History of Law in America*, 1:5–14.
75. The 1665 charter ostensibly enlarged the territory granted in the 1663 charter but may also have cured a defect in the earlier grant, that defect being that the 1629 charter had not properly been voided before issuance of the 1663 charter. Parker, *North Carolina Charters*, 90.
76. The charter of 1665 associated "liege" with "denizen" and "subject." A liege was one who owed allegiance to a lord in England's feudal system, or more technically, "[a] loyal subject of a monarch or other sovereign," Garner, *Black's Law Dictionary*, s.v. "Liege," 1107.

77. Free and common socage was the species of tenure to which almost all English common law tenures of higher dignity, such as knight's service and tenure *in capite*, were converted in 1660, Garner, *Black's Law Dictionary*, s.v. "Socage," 1672 (describing free and common socage).
78. Story, *Commentaries on the Constitution*, 1:118.
79. Kelly, Harbison, and Belz, *American Constitution*, 1:11 (discussing the proprietary grant for Maryland, and in particular, the grant to Lord Baltimore of the rights, privileges, and immunities possessed then or in the past by the bishop of Durham); Martinez, "Palatinate Clause of the Maryland Charter," 305, 321 (describing the failure in the new world of governments based on the ancient palatinate clause). It has been said that "Durham is important to the Commonwealth historian, for it links the medieval empire with the American." Madden, "1066, 1776, and All That," in Flint and Williams, *Perspectives of Empire*, 21.
80. Regarding the vociferous attack on tradition by nineteenth-century reformers, see generally Part II (Antebellum Period) and Part III (Code Commission Era). Regarding *reason* and *custom* as suggesting the common law tradition, note that expressions like "laws and customs" mimic the titles of famous medieval treatises, one known as Glanville and the other known as Bracton. The compilation known as Glanville is entitled, *Tractatus de legibus et consuetudinibus regni Angliae*, or Treatise on the laws and customs of the Kingdom of England, while the compilation known as Bracton is entitled, *De Legibus Et Consuetudinibus Angliæ*, or On the Laws and Customs of England. They were compiled during the reigns of Henry II and Henry III, respectively, and may survive as the most respected evidences of the early common law in England. Laws of the province of Carolina must, under the 1665 charter, approach conformity to English laws and customs, this medieval common law being a special application of practical reason; and these local laws must also approach conformity to the general application of practical reason embodied in the *jus gentium* and the natural law.
81. For a summary description of *Fundamental Constitutions of Carolina*, often referred to as the *Grand Model*, see Cheney, *North Carolina Government*, 123. On the different versions of this constitution, see Bassett, *Constitutional Beginnings of North Carolina*, 43n1: "There were five editions of the Constitutions: (1) the original draft, signed July 21, 1669; (2) that of March 1, 1670, a slight revisal; (3) that of January 12, 1682; (4) one issued at some unknown date between 1682 and 1698; and (5) that of 1698 (Hawks, II., 183–4, and Ramsay: Hist. of S. C., II., 123, *note*)."
82. Reinsch, "English Common Law," in Zane, et al., *Select Essays in Anglo-American Legal History*, 1:367, 407: "The purpose of this code was to 'establish the interest of the proprietor with equality and without confusion that the erecting of a numerous democracy may be avoided.'"
83. Kelly, Harbison, and Belz, *American Constitution*, 1:17. Document I–3, *Colonial Records*, 1:188: Section 4 of *Fundamental Constitutions of Carolina* divided the province into counties and divided each county between the proprietors (1/5), the hereditary nobility (1/5), and the people (3/5), "so that in setting out and planting the lands, the balance of government may be preserved."
84. Kelly, Harbison, and Belz, *American Constitution*, 1:71. The authors distinguish mixed government from separation of powers in 1: 28–29: "The basic point of mixed-government theory was to give a distinct role in the governmental structure to the constituent elements of society. Modern constitutional theory . . . is premised on the division of government into three essential functions. . . . In the theory of mixed government, however, no such functional distinction existed. . . . The key distinction was not between separate governmental functions, but rather, as in medieval theory, between the sphere of government power (or *gubernaculum*) on the one hand and the rights and liberties of subjects (or *jurisdictio*) on the other." The constituent elements of society were evident in section 77 of the March 1, 1670 version of *Fundamental Constitutions of Carolina*, where it mentioned the four estates of proprietors, landgraves, casiques, and freeholders. And the faith in and respect for the separate and distinct interests of these elements of society is evident in the power of any estate to prevent by majority vote the passage of an act due to its conflict with the fundamental written law. See Parker, *North Carolina Charters*, 179.
85. For sources that point out the link of a constitution and the life of its people, see notes 87–90.
86. Pierce, *Memoir and Letters of Charles Sumner*, 1:189 (from letter of March 27, 1837 to Professor Mittermaier, Heidelberg, appearing in a chapter entitled, "Codification of the Common Law"). Other sources that identify constitutions as a type of code include Reinsch, "English Common Law," 1:407 (describing *Fundamental Constitutions of Carolina* as an early instance of a code), and Orth, *How Many Judges Does It Take to Make a Supreme Court?*, 118: "Codes confine judicial discretion, and the advent of written constitutions, a form of constitutional code, might have threatened the common-law tradition."

87. For example, the author of the document excerpted at Document II–36 (Unwritten Code of the People, 1832), condemns theoretical constitutions: "Thus Locke's celebrated constitution of Carolina is only a monument of the utter futility of hypothetical (it does not deserve the name of theoretical,) legislation,—a lively memento of the singular preposterousness of attempting to form a people by laws." Similarly, the famed nineteenth-century critic, Orestes Brownson, in his *American Republic*, 76, stresses that constitutions are not theoretical constructs: "The constitution of the state is not a theory, nor is it drawn up and established in accordance with any preconceived theory. . . . The French people adopted constitution after constitution of the most approved pattern . . . all to no effect; for they had no authority for the nation, no hold on its affections, and formed no element of its life. . . ." Elsewhere Brownson explains that constitutions are generated, like organisms, and he refers specifically to the failure of the "constructed" constitution of provincial Carolina. See Brownson, "Legitimacy and Revolution (October 1848)," in Brownson, *Works in Political Philosophy*, 3:258.
88. Story, *Commentaries on the Constitution*, 1:123: "Thus perished the labours of Mr. Locke; . . . Perhaps in the annals of the world there is not to be found a more wholesome lesson of the utter folly of all efforts to establish forms of governments upon mere theory; and of the dangers of legislation without consulting the habits, manners, feelings, and opinions of the people, upon which they are to operate."
89. Document IV–4 (Battle's History, 1889), Battle, "Address on the History of the Supreme Court," 446: "There could not possibly be a more striking proof of the truth that all good governments are slow growths, the product of the struggles and compromises of intelligent and well-meaning men, than this abortive product of Locke's metaphysical brain."
90. For an argument adopting this theme by the most celebrated opponent of codification in nineteenth-century America, see Carter, *"Proposed Codification of Our Common Law,"* 5–9.
91. Instructions to the Governor and Councell of Albemarle, *Colonial Records*, 1:181–183.
92. *Colonial Records*, 1:183–187. The nine confirmed laws are also reprinted at "Laws of North Carolina—1669, and Prior Thereto," *State Records*, 25:119–122.
93. Prefatory notes to *State Records*, 23:i: asserting that the "collection [of laws] begins with the 'Six Confirmed Laws' of 1715, which were really a codification (the first codification of laws in this State) of all the statutes prior to 1715 which were not deemed obsolete." Putting aside the editor's (Walter Clark's) report of the obsolescence of three of the confirmed laws, his use of "codification" is loose, and his assertion that the six confirmed laws were Carolina's first codification is perhaps misleading. One might argue that the Nine Confirmed Laws of 1669[–1670] were the first *compilation* of laws in force in Carolina, or alternatively, one might argue that the sixty-six acts confirmed in 1715, which includes six of the nine confirmed laws, were the first compilation of laws in force in Carolina, but it would be an abuse of language to say that the six confirmed laws were the first such compilation even when hemming in the assertion with the language, "prior to 1715," and it would be to speak very loosely to describe them as the first *codification*.
94. See, for example, the history note accompanying the 1943 version of chapter 4, section 1, of the *North Carolina General Statutes*, which lists as its first entry, "1715, c. 5, ss. 2, 3," this entry pointing to chapter 5 of *Potter's Revisal* of 1819, wherein is reprinted the 1715 act for the queen's peace insofar as it remained in force in 1819.
95. Regarding the recovery of lost acts, such as the 1711 act for the Queen's Peace, editor and Chief Justice Walter Clark wrote in the *State Records*, 25:iii: that he "finds great satisfaction in being able to publish in this volume with the Acts of 1789 and 1790, many of the earlier Acts which, not accessible when Volumes XXIII and XXIV were being printed, have since been found, by careful search, in the British Archives. These lost Acts are printed as a supplement to this volume—'Omitted Acts 1669–1783.'"

    Sixteen years earlier, the Honorable Kemp Battle had written in his "Address on the History of the Supreme Court," 453–454: "It is to be remarked in passing that the Colonial Records show that the act of the General Assembly, expressly declaring that the common law is and shall be in force in this government, except the 'part of the practice in the issuing out and return of writs and proceedings in the Court of Westminster,' &c., which Hawks and others say was first passed in 1715, was certainly passed as early as 1711."
96. While the title to the act as it appears in the *State Records* limited its force to North Carolina, rather than extending its applicability to the entire province, the text did not do so. This lack of limitation in the text is one of the features that distinguished the declaration of the Queen's Peace in 1711 from that declaration in the *Revisal* of 1715.

    In 1712, an act concerning English law in force passed for the southwest portion of the province, which included in Section 5 a declaration that the English common law is in force. An Act to Put in Force in This Province the

Several Statutes of the Kingdom of England or South Britain, Therein Particularly Mentioned, No. 322, A. D.1712, in Cooper, *Statutes at Large of South Carolina*, 2:413. Section 15 of the 1712 act repeals an act of 1694 on the same subject. An Act to Put in Force the Several Acts of the Kingdom of England Therein Particularly Mentioned, No. 109, A. D. 1694, Cooper, *Statutes at Large of South Carolina*, 2:81 (stating that "The original Act [of 1694] not now to be found.").

97. Writing decades after Carolina had become a dominion of George II, and on the eve of colonial revolt against his grandson, George III, Sir William Blackstone wrote that according to the law of nature, or at least the law of nations, the common law followed Englishmen to the uninhabited lands they discovered, while the ancient laws of conquered or ceded lands (with some caveats) remained in force until varied by the king, though the king's power remained subordinate to those acts of parliament which named such lands with particularity. Applying this rule, Blackstone classified the American plantations as conquered or ceded lands where the common law of England had no authority. See Blackstone, *Commentaries* 1:*106–109.

Joseph Story, American jurist and professor of law, disagreed with Blackstone's classification. Story concluded that the colonial lands in America fell under the category of uninhabited territories, and thus the colonists carried with them the common law of England. Story, *Commentaries on the Constitution*, 1:132–142. Among the arguments he advanced was the one set forth in the act of 1711 concerning the Queen's Peace: that the provincial charter of Carolina presumed, as did provincial charters of other colonies, that the common law was in force by its restrictions on the provincial power to legislate. Story, *Commentaries* 1:139. Another argument he advanced in support of the common law following the colonists to America was that the charter of Carolina contained "an express declaration, that all subjects and their children inhabiting therein shall be deemed natural-born subjects, and shall enjoy all the privileges and immunities thereof. . . ." Story, *Commentaries* 1:139. Parker, *North Carolina Charters*, 96: the 1665 Charter stated, "And we will also, and, of our especial grace, for us, our heirs and successors, do straitly enjoin, Ordain, Constitute, and Command, that the said Province or Territory shall be of our allegiance; And that all and singular the Subjects and Liege people of us, our heirs and successors, transported or to be transported into the said Province, and the Children of them and such as shall descend from them there, born or hereafter to be born, be and shall be Denizens and Lieges of us, our heirs and successors, of this our Kingdom of England; and be in all things held, treated, and reputed as the liege, faithful People of us, our heirs and successors, born within this our said Kingdom or any other of Our Dominions; . . . Any Act, Statute, Ordinance, provision, to the contrary notwithstanding." The Charter of March 24, 1663 had contained almost identical language. Parker, *North Carolina Charters*, 80–81. "Liege" means "A loyal subject of a monarch or other sovereign." Garner, *Black's Law Dictionary*, s.v. "Liege," 1107. This provision of the charter concerning subjects and their children being deemed "natural-born subjects," though, need not be read to support Justice Story's conclusion that the common law followed the colonists, since allegiance to the English king may make one a subject without denying the king's absolute discretion in his royal demesne, for instance. Rather, constitutional limitations on the English monarchy won throughout the centuries by parliaments may have been implicitly rejected in the restoration charters, the power to issue charters presuming royal patrimony outside the purview of Parliament.

Joel Bishop was yet another nineteenth-century commentator who disputed Blackstone's interpretation of the law, rejecting it with less discussion than had Story. See Bishop, *New Commentaries on Marriage, Divorce, and Separation*, 1:52: "[A]nd though Blackstone considered the American colonies to be of the latter class [conquered territories], his opinion is manifestly erroneous; and both the reason of the thing, and the judicial decisions, English and American, are the other way."

For persons who took the position that Carolina operated under the common law of England from its establishment, through its revolutions and rebellions during its proprietary period, and up through the American Revolution, the act of 1711 was merely declaratory in nature. According to Professor John Manning, in his *Commentaries on the First Book of Blackstone*, 18, a declaratory statute might be enacted when "the Common Law has . . . become disputable, in which case the legislature *in perpetuum rei testimonium* has thought proper to declare what the Common Law is and ever shall have been." And in fact folks did debate the scope of the force of English law in Carolina, as the province's act concerning the Queen's Peace recounts. The question of what portion of laws of England were in force in America was controversial and politically explosive. See Sioussat, "Theory of the Extension of English Statutes to the Plantations," in Zane, et al., *Selected Essays in Anglo-American Legal History*, 1:418: "As settlement in the new world progressed, . . . we find all the charters save one granting to the colonists the rights of English citizens, and the claim to these rights maintained by the inhabitants of every colony, whether in possession of a charter or not. As to the interpretation of these rights, and the determination of their extent, discussion and dispute were more or less continuous." Settling such a controversy as this was the *sine qua non* of a recognized class of declaratory act. On this reading, an act declaring the common law in force does not deny that the common law followed the colonists to the province, it does not limit which principles of the common law and which applications of those principles have authority locally, and it does not transform unwritten law into a portion of the written law. Rather, it aims to settle controversy. Nonetheless, Professor Samuel Mordecai of Trinity College in Durham, North Carolina, suggested that no act concerning the force of English law would have been enacted in North Carolina unless Blackstone's assessment that the common law had no authority in the conquered lands of the American plantations had been correct. See Mordecai, *Law Lectures*, 1:5.

98. Though the act of 1711 declaring the common law in force distinguished statute law from common law, the statute law of England was often subsumed under the definition of the common law. Postema, "Classical Common Law Jurisprudence (Part 1)," 166: "The orthodox lawyer's view in the 17th century was that the common law of England was found primarily in three places: judicial decisions, Acts of Parliament, and local custom."

99. For a reference to the naming doctrine of the English common law and to a counter-doctrine popular in the colonies, see Kent, *Commentaries on American Law*, 2:6–7n(a).

100. A manuscript volume—probably a presentation copy made in the nineteenth century—of the *Revisal* of 1715 held by the North Carolina Supreme Court Library, like the one referenced in Hawks's *History of North Carolina*, provides the dates of this general assembly. This history, published in 1858, relied on one of "three . . . manuscript volumes of our statute law still extant, the most perfect of which, through the kindness of a friend, is now in the possession of the author." See Hawks, *History of North Carolina*, 2:145. Hawks identified that friend as William B. Rodman, who assisted with the *Revised Code* of 1854, was elected in 1868 to the Supreme Court of North Carolina, and served along with Judge Albion W. Tourgée as commissioner on the code commission during Reconstruction. Though by 1858 there remained three known copies of this manuscript, at one time there had been twelve, according to Weeks, "Historical Review of the Colonial and State Records," *Index to the Colonial and State Records*, 4:2: "The first Revisal was made by the Assembly of 1715. As there was no printing press in the colony, no attempt was made to print this compilation, but twelve manuscript copies were made and distributed one to each county. These copies were kept on the clerk's table during the sitting of the precinct court and were audibly read from beginning to end during the first term in each year. It will be seen that copies of this Revisal were necessarily scarce and that many discrepancies would soon creep into them."

101. Ashe, *History of North Carolina*, 1:198. The *Revisal* of 1715 is reprinted in *State Records*, 23:1–96.

102. Document I-6 (Revisal, 1715).

103. Document I-8 (Provincial Laws in Force, 1731).

104. Hawks, *History of North Carolina*, 2:145–146 (emphasis added).

105. This document was omitted from the initial publication of the state records but was acquired later and then included in the last volume of that series. See *State Records*, 25:159–161. According to Chief Justice Walter Clark, it was by "diligent research in the British Archives and elsewhere the following laws have been discovered in MMS. form." See *State Records*, 25:118.

106. See section 13 of the excerpt. These confirmed laws are six of the nine laws which had been re-enacted and sent to England for confirmation in 1669. See prefatory notes to *State Records*, 25:iii. Chief Justice Walter Clark provided this description of the "Six Confirmed Laws" in the prefatory notes to the *State Records*, 23:[i]:

> A vast deal of the history of a people is to be found in its laws. . . . The collection begins with the "Six Confirmed Laws" of 1715, which were really a codification (the first codification of laws in this State) of all the statutes prior to 1715 which were not deemed obsolete. There was a subsequent codification reported to the Legislature in 1749 (the "Yellow Jacket"), by Samuel Swann, but first printed in 1752 by James Davis, and private codifications printed by the latter in 1765 and again in 1773, and another codification by legal authority by James Iredell printed in 1791. Each of these collections omitted laws or parts of laws which had then become obsolete, and the original statutes in many instances were never printed or all copies have been lost in the process of time. . . . There have been several codifications since "Iredell's Revisal" in 1791, but these do not concern us.

107. See section 7 of the excerpted document.

108. See section 8 of the excerpted document.

109. See section 10 of the excerpted document.

110. The acts, or parts of acts, specifically saved in sections 9, 11, 12, and 14 of the Act of Confirmation did not have their text laid out in chapters of the revisal and were not listed in the ratifying document. It seems likely that these

acts—concerning (1) the building of a courthouse, (2) the appointing of commissioners to discuss Indian affairs with commissioners from Virginia, (3) the raising of money to defray the cost of government, and (4) the acts concerning public funds, bills of credit, and naturalization, or any other private acts—were private or special acts, and thus properly omitted from a revisal of public laws.

111. Queen Anne was succeeded by King George I in 1714. Rivers, *Sketch of the History of South Carolina*, 256.
112. *South Carolina Act of 1712*.
113. North Carolina did not attempt a list of English statutes in force in the colony until 1749. Document I–10 (English Laws in Force, 1749).
114. Prefatory notes in *Colonial Records*, 3:iii: noting also that these laws passed in November 1729, though declared null and void, "were regularly brought forward as valid in all of our [North Carolina's] Revisals."
115. "Commission Captain George Burrington to Be Governor of North Carolina, 15 Jan^{ry} 1729/30," *Colonial Records*, 3:66–73.
116. "Instructions for Our Trusty and Welbeloved George Burrington Esqre Our Captain Genera and Governor in Chief in & Over Our Province of North Carolina in America. Given at Our Court at St. James's the Fourteenth Day of December 1730 in the Furth Year of Our Reign," *Colonial Records*, 3:90.
117. Document I–4 (Nine Confirmed Laws, 1669[–1670]).
118. Document I–5 (The Queen's Peace, 1711).
119. Powell, *Encyclopedia of North Carolina*, s.v. "Cary Rebellion," 190.
120. Document I–7 (The Queen's Peace, 1715).
121. In the decade prior to the 1746 act, the general assembly commissioned a revisal that did not come to fruition. Regarding the commissioners for this revisal, Professor William Powell noted that, "In February or March 1738/39 the Assembly appointed Swann to a commission charged with revising the laws of the colony, which had last been codified in 1715. Swann's brother John and his uncle-in-law Edward Moseley also were on the commission." Powell, *Dictionary of North Carolina Biography*, s.v. "Swann, Samuel," 5:489. The fact of this commission appears in the minutes of the upper house of the North Carolina General Assembly for February 06, 1739–March 06, 1739. *Colonial Records*, 4:379. Many other pages of this volume of the *Colonial Records* relate to this proposed revisal.
122. Ashe, *History of North Carolina*, 1:273.
123. In *Swann's Revisal*, repealed and obsolete provisions of the public laws were removed and the statutes were compiled for the years prior to 1746. The statutes collected for the sessions after 1745 and up through the printing of the revisal in 1751, though, do not evidence elimination of repealed provisions. For instance, chapter 7 of the laws passed in the October 7, 1748 session altered and amended chapter 1 of the laws passed in the March 7, 1746 session, both concerning the commissioning of *Swann's Revisal*, but the statutes compiled for 1746 do not evidence those alterations or amendments.
124. *South Carolina Act of 1712*. South Carolina was made a royal colony in 1719. Rivers, *Sketch of the History of South Carolina*, 3.
125. Mordecai, *Law Lectures*, 1:6–7: "It would seem that the board of trade in London—which was a committee of the privy council on colonial affairs, I believe—recommended the repeal of the act of 1749 upon the ground that it was too sweeping in its repeal of British statutes."; *Colonial Records*, 5:81, 105–106 (printing a memorandum from the Board of Trade to King George II relating to its examination of *Swann's Revisal* and recommending the repeal of the act of 1749 contained therein).
126. Uncommissioned updates to *Swann's Revisal* by James Davis omitted the Act of 1749 and indicated that it had been repealed. [Davis], *Collection of All the Acts of Assembly*, 1:158; [Davis], *Complete Revisal of All the Acts of Assembly*, 1:127. Later compilations and codifications also omitted the act of 1749. For example, see Iredell, *Laws of the State of North-Carolina*, 127n*(a)*: "I think myself justified in not inserting this Act, as it is universally acknowledged to have been repealed or disallowed by the King in Council, though I have no authentic Evidence of it."
127. For the resolution of the issue of reception of English statute law, see Document II–42 (Revised Statutes, 1837).
128. Only the title, not the text, of the Act of 1715 was included in *Swann's Revisal*, chapter 31, the margin note there pointing the reader to the Act of 1749.
129. *State Records*, 23:327.
130. See note 129.
131. Alderman, "North Carolina Colonial Bar," 5.
132. Alderman, "North Carolina Colonial Bar," 17. Alderman surveys various other initiatives related to the control of the bar in colonial North Carolina. Alderman, 5 (mentioning the provision in the *Grand Model* regarding pleading

for money); Alderman, 12 (discussing two acts of 1715 relating to attorney fees); Alderman, 15 (laying out the Act of 1743 about attorney fees); Alderman, 16 (noting a failed bill concerning admission to the bar in 1743); Alderman, 17 (noting the same failure in 1753); Alderman, 28 (mentioning the fee-regulating act of 1770).

133. Document IV–4 (Battle's History, 1889).
134. For North Carolina, the delegates were William Hooper, Joseph Hewes, and Richard Caswell. Lefler and Newsome, *North Carolina*, 202.
135. For a general discussion of the *Declaration and Resolves*, see McClellan, *Liberty, Order, and Justice*, 117–119. While independence was not declared by the First Continental Congress, the delegates issued an ultimatum aimed at the repeal of offensive actions by the English Parliament. Rakove, *Declaring Rights*, 62–63.
136. McClellan, *Liberty, Order, and Justice*, 172; see also Rakove, *Declaring Rights*, 63: "[T]he Declaration also corresponded to the traditional notion that bills of rights were acts of negotiation or compacts, as had been the case with Magna Carta in 1215 and the Declaration of Rights in 1689."
137. McClellan, *Liberty, Order, and Justice*, 172.
138. For example, see Kirk, *Orestes Brownson: Selected Essays*, 196–197: objecting to the democratic principle advanced by nineteenth-century reformers which grounds government merely in human convention and consent and which rejects the *jus gentium* as understood in pre-modern times and accepts Benthamite international law in its stead; asserting that the American constitution, by contrast, recognizes "the rights of man, and, therefore, the rights of God" and that the American people maintain a link to Western tradition by "the common law and the judicial department of the government. . . ."
139. For example, see Gierke, *Natural Law and the Theory of Society*, 1:xlviii–xlix: "[A]nd Nature could be used to consecrate the monarch as well as the people. All through the history of the [post-medieval] School of Natural Law we can find advocates of the Sovereignty of the Ruler as well as of the Sovereignty of the People. . . ."
140. For the distinction between mixed government and separation of powers, see note 84.
141. For thoughts about separation of powers in the English constitution, see Finnis, *Judicial Power*, 28, 39–40, 48, 58–59.
142. Document I–13 (Declaration of Rights, December 17, 1776).
143. The senate and house of commons, when assembled for the purpose of legislation, were called the general assembly under the state's original constitution. Constitution of North Carolina of 1776, § 4. And it was the general assembly that appointed life-tenured judges by joint ballot, Constitution of North Carolina of 1776, § 13. On the other hand, it was the senate and the house of commons jointly, not the general assembly, that elected a governor each year, Constitution of North Carolina of 1776, § 15; and it was the senate and house of commons that appointed officials of the militia and army of the state, Constitution of North Carolina of 1776, § 14.
144. Document I–5 (The Queen's Peace, 1711); Document I–7 (The Queen's Peace, 1715); Document I–10 (English Law in Force, 1749).
145. Joseph Story contrasted Thomas Jefferson's view on the question of whether the common law was a cause of the American Revolution with the view of the First Continental Congress of 1774 in its resolves. In his *Commentaries on the Constitution*, 1:140n1, he quoted Jefferson as having said: "I deride with you the ordinary doctrine, that we brought with us from England the common law rights. This *narrow notion* was a *favourite* in the first moment of rallying to our rights against Great Britain." (citing "Journal of Congress, Declaration of Rights of the Colonies, Oct. 14, 1774, p. 27 to 31"). The Congress had "*unanimously* resolved, 'That the respective colonies are entitled *to the common law of England*, and more especially to the great and inestimable privilege of being tried by their peers of the vicinage according to the course of that law.' Furthermore, the Congress resolved that the colonies were 'entitled to the benefit of such of the English statutes, as existed at the time of their colonization . . .' and 'that their ancestors at the time of their emigration were 'entitled . . . to all the rights, liberties, and immunities of free and natural born subjects within the realm of England.'"
146. Document I–13 (Declaration of Rights, December 17, 1776).
147. Document I–16 (Reception Ordinance, December 22, 1776).
148. See note 147.
149. [Swain], "Sketch of the Judicial History of North Carolina," in vol. 2 of Nash, Iredell, and Battle, *Revised Statutes of the State of North Carolina [. . .] 1836–7*, 528. Although this sketch is unsigned, according to Justice William H. Battle, it was written by Gov. David Swain. Battle, "Memoir of John Louis Taylor," 385–386.
150. Document II–43 (Revised Statutes' Preface, 1837).

151. Document I–11 (Court Act, 1760); Document I–22 (Court Act, 1786).
152. For an example of a reception statute listing evils to be remedied, see Document I–19 (Reception Statute, December 24, 1777).
153. Document I–16 (Reception Ordinance, December 22, 1776).
154. Battle, "Address on the History of the Supreme Court," 467: "On November 15, 1777, the new court law was adopted. It is so nearly a copy of the act of 1767 as to suggest the probability of having been drawn by the same lawyer. The term 'Superior Court' was used when it was manifestly proper to use the constitutional term 'Supreme Court,' which would not have been a misnomer, as it had supreme jurisdiction. In another section the draftsman forgot to omit the words 'or commander-in-chief' after the word Governor, as should have been done. In the oath are phrases copied from the old oath, which are out of place in a government where the judges are in no danger from the arbitrary action of the executive."
155. Document I–14 (Constitution, December 18, 1776).
156. See note 155.
157. Document I–17 (Reception Statute, May 9, 1777); Document I–16 (Reception Ordinance, December 22, 1776).
158. This Act on equity jurisdiction is discussed in a letter from William Gaston to Bartlett Yancey, July 15, 1821, in Yancey, "Letters to Bartlett Yancey," 29–31. Another unusual jury provision of the eighteenth century applied to admiralty courts in cases of capture. An Act to Impower the Court of Admiralty [. . .] in all Cases of Capture of the Ships and other Vessels of the Inhabitants and Subjects of Great Britain, to establish the Trial by Jury [. . .] in *State Records*, 24:119. This procedure was adopted at the recommendation of the Continental Congress.
159. According to An Act for Establishing Courts of Law, and for Regulating the Proceedings Therein, *State Records*, 24:49: in law, as contrasted with equity, the general assembly required two or more judges only on "Demurrers, Cases agreed, special Verdicts, Bills of Exception to Evidence, and Motions in Arrest of Judgment."
160. One series of statutes mentioned in this pamphlet dealt with juries in cases of small claims. The 1785 Jurisdiction Act extended jurisdiction of certain courts to debts and demands of ten pounds and under, see An Act for Encreasing the Jurisdiction of the County Courts of Pleas and Quarter Sessions, and of the Justices of the Peace out of Court, *State Records*, 24:716–718, while the 1786 Act to Amend the Jurisdiction Act of 1785 expanded this jurisdiction to debts and demands of twenty pounds and under, see An Act to Amend [. . .] "An Act for Encreasing the Jurisdiction of the County Courts of Pleas and Quarter Sessions, and of the Justices of the Peace Out of Court [. . .]" *State Records*, 24:804–807. The editor of the work containing the pamphlet excerpted in the text of this compilation, William K. Boyd, suggested that the anonymous author of the pamphlet had ignored the fact that the statute which increased jurisdiction to twenty pounds also contained a jury provision.

    Another series of acts mentioned by the pamphlet dealt with juries in cases of confiscated property. These were: (1) the 1782 Confiscated Property Act (containing a jury provision), see An Act Directing the Sale of Confiscated Property, *State Records*, 24:424–429; (2) the 1783 Act repealing the 1782 Confiscated Property Act, see An Act for Allowing Salaries to the Governor, Secretary and Other Officers of State, and for Other Purposes, *State Records*, 24:501–502, and (3) the 1785 Quiet Title Act (requiring dismissal of suits on affidavit), see An Act to Secure and Quiet in Their Possessions All [. . .] Who Have Purchased [. . .] Lands and Tenements, Goods and Chattels, [. . .] Sold by Commissioners of Forfeited Estates [. . .], *State Records*, 24:730–731. Boyd suggested that in pursuing his argument, the anonymous author of the pamphlet had ignored the decision in *Bayard* and had ignored also the 1786 Act to Amend the Quiet Title Act of 1785, see An Act to Amend [. . .] "An Act to Secure and Quiet in Their Possessions All [. . .] Who Have Purchased [. . .] Lands and Tenements, Goods and Chattels, [. . .] Sold [. . .] by the Commissioners of Forfeited Estates [. . .]," *State Records*, 24:794–795. Arguably, though, the pamphlet addressed this last statute, albeit with contempt. [Anonymous], "Independent Citizen (1787)," in Boyd, *Some Eighteenth Century Tracts*, 468.
161. Den, *on the demise of* Bayard & Wife, *vs.* Singleton, *Notes of a Few Decisions [. . .] in the Circuit Court of the U. States, for North-Carolina District*, 48–52. [1 N.C. 5, 1 Mart. 48 (1787)] The case was first heard in May Term, 1786, the court taking the matter under advisement at the end of this term. In August 1786, James Iredell published an essay entitled, "To the Public," in which he defended the power of judicial review. McRee, *Life and Correspondence of James Iredell*, 2:145. According to Boyd, *Some Eighteenth Century Tracts*, 456, when the legislature convened in November 1786, "there was an unsuccessful attempt to impeach the judges." *State Records*, 18:42, 136–142, 167, 194–195, 212–217, 362, 420, 421–425, 428–429, 461, 477–483. In July 1787, the pamphlet called "Independent Citizen" was published, it being notably addressed to W. R. Davie, a co-counsel for the plaintiffs. Argument in *Bayard* had resumed at May

Term, 1787 and a decision on a motion to dismiss was given separately but unanimously at that term, followed by a trial. Decision on the trial, given *seriatim* but unanimously by Judges Samuel Ashe, Samuel Spencer, and John Williams were published at "NEW BERN, *November Term*, 1787," which is after the publication of the pamphlet.

162. Boyd, *Some Eighteenth Century Tracts*, 457.
163. At this time W. R. Davie was not only co-counsel with James Iredell Sr. for plaintiffs in *Bayard*, but also a member of the Federal Convention.
164. James Iredell Sr., also involved in the litigation in *Bayard*, did take a stance on the enforcement of natural law under North Carolina law. Iredell was listed as counsel for the plaintiff in the official report of *Bayard v. Singleton*, though he had been hired initially by the defendant and ultimately may have been merely an amicus. Whichard, *Justice James Iredell*, 11. Although acknowledging the impiety in the abstract notion of legislative omnipotence (while failing to acknowledge impiety in the speculative notion of the omnipotence of the people), Iredell argued in, "To the Public," that the constitution defined and bound the legislature. McRee, *Life and Correspondence of James Iredell*, 2:145–146. Iredell described the constitution as "a law of the State," thereby freeing the judiciary to declare void those acts passed in derogation of the fundamental law. While Iredell would allow the judiciary to review legislative acts for conformity to the constitution, in later writings he would deny the judiciary the power to review legislative acts for conformity to natural law. Document I–27 (Iredell on Natural Justice, 1798) (arguing that a legislative body is presumed to act morally—i.e., per the natural law—and that only the sovereign people—not the judiciary—has the power to judge that presumption to be overcome).
165. Document I–15 (Revisal Ordinance, December 21, 1776).
166. An Act Authorizing James Davis, Esquire, to Revise, Print and Publish All the Laws Now in Force and Use in This State [. . .], *State Records*, 24:537. According to a note in the state records (copied from Martin, *Public Acts of the General Assembly of North-Carolina*, 1:339n(*a*)): this "revisal was never executed" by James Davis.
167. "*Swann's Revisal*" is the popular name for the revisal of the laws of North Carolina published in 1751. [Swann], *Collection of All the Public Acts of Assembly*. For discussion of *Swann's Revisal*, see Document I–9 (Revisal, 1746).
168. James Iredell Sr. was named the sole commissioner under this act for a revisal of the laws and had been named one of eleven commissioners under the 1776 ordinance on statutes in force.
169. One eye-catching addendum to the commissioned revisal required by this act was described by the general assembly as: "the confederation of the United States existing at the time such revisal shall be published." Apparently, the general assembly did not simply require Commissioner James Iredell to include the Articles of Confederation as an addendum to the revisal because it questioned whether the articles would be in force at the date of printing of the revisal. The federal convention had adjourned on September 17, 1787; its report was transmitted to the states on September 28, 1787; and North Carolina's Governor Richard Caswell alerted the general assembly of his receipt of "Papers respecting the Federal Constitution" on November 21, 1787. Minutes of the North Carolina House of Commons, November 19, 1787–December 22, 1787, *State Records*, 20:119, 128–129. The act commissioning a revisal was introduced the next Monday, November 26, 1787. Minutes of the North Carolina Senate, November 19, 1787–December 21, 1787, *State Records*, 20:301, 328.
170. Commissioner James Iredell Sr. found some provisions of his commission difficult to execute. See Document I–25 (Iredell's Preface, 1791).
171. An Act to Confirm the Revisal of the Laws of this State, Made by James Iredell [. . .], ch. 1, *Laws of the State of North-Carolina*, 1. [1791 N.C. Laws 1]
172. See note 126 for mention of these unofficial collections of laws.
173. Martin, *Public Acts of the General Assembly of North-Carolina*. The second volume of this work, completed in June 1804, supplemented *Iredell's Revisal* with the acts of subsequent sessions, while volume one, printed in November 1804, revised again the acts of 1715 to 1790, some of which had been repealed since *Iredell's Revisal*. Martin's work was approved by the general assembly. An Act to Confirm a Revisal of Certain Acts of Assembly, ch. 1, *Laws of North-Carolina*, 1. [1804 N.C. Laws 1 (ratified December 12, 1804)]
174. Martin, *Notes of a Few Decisions*.
175. Martin extracted and reprinted at the front of his collection of private acts a committee report, originally printed in Journals of the General Assembly, House of Commons, 4th January, 1794, which said, among other things, that "they think it absolutely necessary, that these laws [private acts] should be collected and placed within the reach of *every individual*." Martin, *Collection of the Private Acts of the General Assembly of the State of North-Carolina*. (emphasis added).

176. For entries regarding François X. Martin, see Monday, November 15, 1790, in House Journal—1790. At a General Assembly Begun and Held at Fayetteville, on the First Day of November, in the Year of Our Lord One Thousand Seven Hundred and Ninety [...], *State Records*, 21:920–921; and Tuesday, November 16, 1790, in Senate Journal—1790. At a General Assembly Begun and Held at Fayetteville, on the First Day of November, in the Year of Our Lord One Thousand Seven Hundred and Ninety [...], *State Records*, 21:769.

177. Calder *et* Wife, *versus* Bull *et* Wife, Dallas, *Reports of Cases Ruled and Adjudged in the Several Courts of the United States*, 3:386–401. [3 U.S. 386, 398, 399 (1798) (Iredell, J.)]

178. See note 177 at 398–399. [3 U.S. 398–399]

179. See note 177 at 399 [3 U.S. 399 (citing "1 *Bl. Com.* 91")]. Iredell's citation to Blackstone for this example is suspect. The incapacity of the king's courts to void a judgment of the sovereign parliament in a mixed government of estates which knew nothing of the modern theory of separation of powers seems a poor analogy on which to consider the interactions of American branches of governments. On these distinctions between the two societies, Brownson, in his *American Republic*, 248, said this: "Theoretically the constitution of Great Britain is feudal, and there is, properly speaking, no British state; there are only the estates, king, lords, and commons, and *these three estates constitute the Parliament*, which is held to be omnipotent; that is, has the plenitude of political sovereignty. The British Parliament, composed of the three estates, possesses in itself all the powers of the convention in the American constitution, and is at once the convention and the government." (emphasis added). On the distinction between mixed government and separation of powers, see generally note 84.

180. Similar arguments denying natural justice as a basis for the judiciary declaring statutes void were advanced by Justice Iredell in *Minge v. Gilmour, Federal Cases* [...] *in the Circuit and District Courts of the United States*, 443–446 [17 F. Cas. 440, 443-444 (No. 9631) (C.C.N.C. 1798)]:

> It is, however, further urged by the counsel for the plaintiff that this act is contrary to natural justice, and therefore void. Some respectable authorities do, indeed, countenance such a doctrine—that an act against natural justice is void. Others maintain a different one, with at least an equal claim to respect. Under these circumstances, I can only consult my own reason; and I confess I think no court is authorized to say that an act is absolutely void merely because, in the opinion of the court, it is contrary to natural justice.
>
> Two principles appear to me to be clear: If an act be unconstitutional, it is void. If it be constitutional, it is valid. In the latter case it must be admitted that the legislature have exercised a trust confided to them by the people. In doing so they necessarily are left to their own discretion, and it is to be presumed they will have a due regard to justice in all their conduct. It is, however, I conceive, left to them so far without control; and if they abuse their trust in the execution of an acknowledged power, they are indeed responsible, in the only way in which a legislature can be responsible, for not exercising their authority properly; but still, having exercised an authority confided to them, their act is legal in the same manner as a judgment given by this court would be, in a case confessedly within its jurisdiction, however erroneous the principles may be on which the court decided. The words 'against natural justice' are very loose terms, upon which very wise and upright members of the legislature and judges might differ in opinion. If they did, whose opinion is properly to be regarded—those to whom the authority of passing such an act is given, or a court to whom no authority, in this respect, necessarily results? This case is surely different from an unconstitutional act which the courts must certainly declare to be void, because passed without any authority whatever. The constitution, by saying that the legislature shall have authority in certain cases, but shall not have in others, as plainly declares everything valid done in pursuance of the first provision, as everything void that is done in contradiction of the last; and it may surely be inferred that if, in addition to other restrictions on the legislative power, such a restriction as that in question was intended, so as to leave it to the courts, in all instances, to say whether an act was agreeable to natural justice or not, this restriction would have been inserted, together with others. All courts, indeed, as being bound to give the most reasonable construction to acts of the legislature, will, in construing an act, do it as consistently with their notions of natural justice (if there appears any incompatibility) as the words and context will admit; it being most probable that, by such construction, the true design of the legislature will be pursued; but, if the words are too plain to admit of more than one construction, and the provisions be not inconsistent with any articles of the constitution, I am of opinion, for the reason I have given, that no court has authority to say the act is void because in their opinion it is not agreeable to the principles of natural justice.
>
> Admitting, however, that this is a ground upon which a court has authority to decide, I am of opinion that this act is not contrary to the principles of natural justice.

181. These meetings served as a remedy for a variety of ills caused by changes to the superior court in 1790. Davis, "Summer Session," 12–13.
182. The primary purpose of the meeting of the superior court judges was the trial of alleged land frauds. Ashe, Weeks, and Van Noppen, *Biographical History of North Carolina*, s.v. "James Glasgow," 7:115, 120: "This court afterward passed out of existence, having been created chiefly for the purpose of trying those charged with land frauds." Governor David Swain, in his sketch of the judicial history of North Carolina, which is published in the second volume of *The Revised Statutes*, seemed to agree that the Legislature had not contemplated this tribunal operating beyond the trials associated with the North Carolina land frauds. Swain, "Sketch of the Judicial History of North Carolina."
183. While this debate of December 26, 1799 killed a bill to establish a court of error and appeals, the court of conference had been established the preceding month, and its operation would be extended in 1801. This court of conference was the predecessor to the modern Supreme Court of North Carolina, established in 1818. Davis, "Summer Session," 12–13.
184. Davis, "Summer Session," 12–13.
185. Document II–1 (Meeting of the Judges, November 18, 1799).
186. Document II–2 (Court of Errors and Appeals, December 26, 1799).
187. For documents relating to *The Revised Statutes*, see Document II–39 (Commission Report, 1834); Document II–40 (Joint Select Committee Report, 1835); Document II–41 (Commission Report, 1836); Document II–42 (Revised Statutes, 1837); Document II–43 (Revised Statutes' Preface, 1837).
188. Haywood published his reports in two volumes. Haywood, *Reports of Cases Adjudged in the Superior Courts of Law and Equity* [. . .] *1789, to the Year 1798*; Haywood, *Reports of Cases Adjudged in the Superior Courts of Law and Equity* [. . .] *1797 to 1806*.
189. The librarian of the Supreme Court of North Carolina who served from 1918 to 1930 wrote a biography of Jones. See Haywood, *Calvin Jones, Physician, Soldier and Freemason*.
190. For a list of documents in this compilation pertaining to revisals and for a few observations concerning the vocabulary associated with such initiatives, see note 204.
191. Document II–17 (Revisal on Administrators and Executors, 1825), Document II–23 (Resolution on Full Revisal, January 2, 1827), Document II–24 (Resolution on Full Revisal, November 27, 1827), Document II–25 (Resolution on Subject Revisal, December 7, 1827), Document II–26 (Resolution on Subject Revisal, December 12, 1827), Document II–27 (Bill on Subject Revisal, January 7, 1828), Document II–28 (Resolution on Subject Revisal, November 26, 1828), Document II–29 (Bill on Full Revisal, December 1828), Document II–30 (Common and Statute Law on Subject Revisal, January 1829), and Document II–32 (Resolution on Subject Revisal, December 1829).
192. General Rush, who lived from 1780 to 1859, served in a variety of respected state and federal offices and was an avid Republican with strong ties to the Madison administration. Rush is remembered also for having compiled an early-nineteenth-century edition of the laws of the United States. *Encyclopedia Americana: International Edition*, s.v. "Rush, Richard," 23:872.
193. This epigraph, found in the writings of John Locke, appears on the title page of the second volume of the *Carolina Law Repository*, 2:[i]: "The mind of man not being capable of having many ideas under view at once, it was necessary to have a Repository to lay up those ideas."
194. Regarding the related roles of Blackstone and Bentham in nineteenth-century law reform, see Milsom, *Natural History of the Common Law*, 22: "[Blackstone's] exposure of the artificialities [of common law procedure] so horrified one of his listeners, the young Bentham, that Blackstone can be said to have inspired not only the textbooks of the nineteenth century but also that century's drive for legislative reform of the law."
195. John Quincy Adams to William Miller, August 25, 1817, Gov. William Miller Letter Book, Book 22, Part II, p. 369.
196. John Quincy Adams to William Miller, November 10, 1817, Gov. William Miller Letter Book, Book 22, Part II, p. 393.
197. William Miller to John Quincy Adams, November 17, 1817, Gov. William Miller Letter Book, Book 22, Part II, p. 394.
198. For a list of documents in this compilation pertaining to revisals and a few observations concerning the vocabulary associated with such initiatives, see note 204.
199. See the remarks preceding the excerpt at Document I–26 (Martin's Preface, 1792) concerning the separation of the revisals of British statutes in force in North Carolina and local statutes in force in the state prior to the revisal commissioned in 1817.

200. Document I–25 (Iredell's Preface, 1791).
201. Document II–20 (Hawks's Digested Index, 1826).
202. For a discussion of the degradation of practical reason to a mere battle of public opinions, and of the rise of legislative activity in nineteenth-century America, see Brownson, "Temporal Power of the Pope (October 1855)," in Brownson, *Works in Political Philosophy*, 4:449 (arguing that American Christian sects practicing a nineteenth-century philanthropic substitute for true Protestantism left themselves subject to a public opinion that sought to embody itself in legislative enactments).
203. Document I–24 (Revisal, 1787).
204. Document II–8 (Revisal, 1817). The term "revise" describes the duties of those who would be commissioned to compile the public laws in force in North Carolina since as early as 1715. The term "digest" is first used in the 1820s in legislative initiatives to codify the positive law of executors and administrators, much as Chief Justice John L. Taylor had used the term in the title of his treatise on that subject. See Document II–16 (Taylor's Preface, 1824). With the commission for *Potter's Revisal* in 1817, the term "consolidate" is added to "revise" to describe the duties of the commissioners. In preparing the *Revised Statutes* of 1837, the commissioners would "collate, digest, and revise" the public laws in force, consolidating into one act the different acts on a similar subject. "Consolidate" apparently takes on a stronger meaning by mid-century, when the commissioners of the *Revised Code* of 1854 use it to mean "fuse" in describing the distinction between their work and the work of their immediate predecessors. See Document II–43 (Revised Statutes' Preface, 1837).

In this compilation, revisals of statutory law are an important subject in the following documents:

PART-DOCUMENT	TITLE
I–6	Revisal, 1715
I–8	Revisal, 1746
I–14	Revisal Ordinance, December 21, 1776
I–23	Revisal, 1787
I–24	Iredell's Preface, 1791
II–5	State Military Laws, 1808
II–8	Revisal, 1817
II–10	H. Potter's Report, 1819
II–17	Revisal on Administrators and Executors, 1825
II–23	Resolution on Full Revisal, January 2, 1827
II–24	Resolution on Full Revisal, November 27, 1827
II–25	Resolution on Subject Revisal, December 7, 1827
II–26	Resolution on Subject Revisal, December 12, 1827
II–27	Bill on Subject Revisal, January 7, 1828
II–28	Resolution on Subject Revisal, November 26, 1828
II–29	Bill on Full Revisal, December 1828
II–32	Resolution on Subject Revisal, December 1829
II–34	Bill on Full Revisal, December 1830
II–37	Governor Swain's Message, 1833
II–39	Commission Report, 1834
II–40	Joint Select Committee Report, 1835
II–41	Commission Report, 1836
II–42	Revised Statutes, 1837
II–43	Revised Statutes' Preface, 1837
II–51	Revised Code's Preface, 1854

III–2	Report on Freedmen's Code, January 22, 1866
III–3	Freedmen's Code, March 10, 1866
III–5	Code Commissioners, March 13, 1868
III–10	First Report of the Code Commissioners, July 15, 1868
III–15	C.C.P. Preface, August 25, 1868
III16	Second Report of the Code Commissioners, August 31, 1868
III–29	Report of the Code Commissioners, March 20, 1869
III–36	Report of the Code Commissioners, March 1870
III–39	Report of the Code Commissioners, November 1870
III–40	Report of the Code Commissioners, December 18, 1870
III–44	Battle's Report on Revisal, 1872
IV–2	Commission Report on The Code, 1883
IV–14	Revisal's Preface, 1905
IV–21	Consolidated Statutes' Preface, 1920

205. An Act to Confirm the Revisal of the Laws of This State, Made by James Iredell [...], *Laws of North-Carolina* [...], 1791, 1. [1791 N.C. Laws 1] Section 1 of this act, which allows *Iredell's Revisal* to be given in evidence in all the courts of law and equity in the state, is summarized in its margin note as "Iredell's Revisal of the laws of the state confirmed."
206. An Act Directing the Publication of the Revisal of the Laws of This State, ch. 9, *Laws of the State of North-Carolina* [...] *1819*, 13–14. [1819 Laws of N.C. 13–14] (directing the printing and binding of this revisal). This act did not declare that the laws inserted and retained in *Potter's Revisal* "shall be held, deemed and taken to be and remain in full force," that this revisal could be given in evidence, or that this revisal was confirmed, as the general assembly had said of *Iredell's Revisal* in 1791. See note 205 for points relating to *Iredell's Revisal*.
207. Document II–4 (Haywood's Preface, 1808).
208. For information about the modern Supreme Court of North Carolina, see Document II–11 (Gaston's Report, 1819).
209. Potter, *Office and Duty of a Justice of the Peace*.
210. While the compilers have not located legislative sanction for *Taylor's Revisal*, a resolution by Mr. Nash directs that the secretary of state procure copies of the title. Journal of the House of Commons, Monday, December 28, 1829, *Journals of the Senate & House of Commons* [...] *1829–30*, 243. This resolution passed its first reading and then after amendment passed its second reading. Journal of the House, Wednesday, December 30, 1829, 250–251.
211. Document II–16 (Taylor's Preface, 1824).
212. Document IV–4 (Battle's History, 1889).
213. See note 212.
214. Professor Pratt writes of a dozen sessions of the general assembly that attacked the supreme court in the 1820s and 1830s. Pratt, "Struggle for Judicial Independence," 130: "Democrats [of the various states in the first half of the nineteenth century] preferred a system of courts patterned after the Court of King's Bench which had no superior appellate court." William Gaston had reported the same phenomenon soon after the general assembly established the supreme court. William Gaston to Bartlett Yancey, July 15, 1821, Yancey, "Letters to Bartlett Yancey," 31: noting that the "Supreme Court has its enemies to encounter." Gaston's 1819 committee report puts the question of the continuance of the judge's salaries as a question of contract at best and of mere morality more likely, but does not make an argument from property in office under the law of the land. Document II–11 (Gaston's Report, 1819). Chief Justice Thomas Ruffin would make the latter argument in John D. Hoke *v.* Lawson Henderson, Devereux, *Cases Argued and Determined in the Supreme Court of North-Carolina from December Term, 1833, to June Term, 1834*, 1–31. [15 N.C. (4 Dev.) 1 (1833)] When reading Pratt's analysis of *Hoke*, then, one must presume that Ruffin was aware of arguments from contract made since the founding of the court. Pratt, "Struggle for Judicial Independence," 129.
215. Document IV–4 (Battle's History, 1889).
216. In addition to John Louis Taylor, the contributions of two other of the nominative reporters, François-Xavier Martin and John Haywood, fill out that foundation of the state's developing law.

217. Davis, "School Days," 383.
218. Document II–8 (Revisal, 1817).
219. See Taylor, *Revisal of the Laws of the State of North-Carolina, Passed from 1821 to 1825*.
220. Document II–16 (Taylor's Preface, 1824).
221. Document II–42 (Revised Statutes, 1837).
222. Even if it were true that English law did not recognize slavery in the Realm, English law has not been innocent of treating people as property. Milsom, *Historical Foundations of the Common Law*, 94 (like villeinage, military wardship treats people as property); Baker, *Oxford History of the Laws of England*, 6:598n16: "Richard Hesketh, following *Bracton*, held that a captive in a just war against a foreign prince was a villein both by the law of arms and 'by the common law called *jus gentium*, which is derived immediately from the law of nature' . . . But contemporary [Tudor] prisoners of war were more akin to slaves."
223. Can a judge rely on principles or rules of the common law to resolve apparent gaps in a despotic institution prevailing under local law but explicitly rejected by the common law and contrary to natural law? Justice Richmond Pearson posed an inversion of this sort of question rhetorically in *State v. Williams*, asking if a judge can apply principles or rules of the civil law to resolve apparent gaps in the common law concerning the roles of judge and jury. State *vs.* Joseph T. Williams, Jones, *Reports of Cases at Law Argued and Determined in the Supreme Court* [. . .] *December Term, 1854, to August Term, 1855*, 262, 271 [47 N.C. (2 Jones) 257, 262, 271 (1855) (emphasis added)]:

> TAYLOR, Ch. Justice, [in *State v. Jim*, 12 N.C. (1 Dev.) 508, 511,] also comes to the conclusion that the Judge below erred: but he puts his opinion upon a different ground, to wit, "our faith cannot be *partial* or *fractional*, the maxim being *falsum in uno*, &c.:" and the Judges agree, that as the jury may have been misled by the charge, and the case affects the life of the prisoner, there should be a *venire de novo*.
>
> No authority is cited by the counsel, or by either of the Judges, and the question is, was it their intention and the scope of the decision, merely to say that the Judge erred in telling the jury that they might reject part of a witness' [sic] testimony, which they believed to be corruptly false, and act on such part as they did believe? Or, did the Judges <u>intend to import and make a part of the Common Law, a maxim</u> of the Civil Law, which is not applicable to a trial by jury, and <u>for which there is no authority, analogy or principle?</u> . . .
>
> Should it be asked, how did it happen that the counsel and the Judge, who took part in the trial of Jim's case, all used language which, it is assumed, did mislead the profession? we would venture to suggest this answer: it was the result of a misconception, whereby a maxim or "general rule," which had been adopted and acted on by the fixed tribunals for the decision of facts, according to the civil law and by the Judges in the Ecclesiastical Courts, and the Courts of Admiralty, and the Courts of Equity, which are fixed tribunals, for the decision of questions of fact, and mere emanations from the Civil Law, was assumed to be a rule of evidence in the courts of Common Law, without referring to the authorities or the legal analogy, or to the principle and "reason of the thing" growing out of the difference between the trial of facts by a jury, "a casual tribunal" selected for that particular trial, and the trial of facts by a fixed tribunal, the tendency of which is to generalise and reduce every case to an artificial system or rule formed by study.

In a recent law review article, Professor John V. Orth also took up this sort of question. See Orth, "When Analogy Fails."
224. The reliance on public opinion, as well as public feeling and manners, as a political, moral, and legal authority, crops up in Chief Justice Taylor's speech for Jacob Henry, excerpted in Document II–60 (About Chief Justice Taylor, 1769–1829). Such reliance appears also in B. F. Moore's argument for the prisoner in The State *v.* Negro Will, Slave of James S. Battle, Devereux and Battle, *Reports of Cases at Law, Argued and Determined in the Supreme Court* [. . .] *December Term, 1834, to June Term, 1836*, 121–172 [18 N.C. (1 Dev. & Bat.) 121 (1834)], which is excerpted at Document II–38 (Moore's Argument, 1834). The importance of public opinion in legal history is discussed by Professor Harold Berman in his description of "The Enlightenment, the French Revolution, and the Napoleonic Codes," Berman, "Law and Belief in Three Revolutions," 613, 619–621, 628.
225. For discussions of *Hale*, see generally Hyde, " 'Common Law Cut Down,' 185; Orth, "When Analogy Fails," 979–981.
226. One contemporary historian, Guion Griffis Johnson, had this to say about Hawks's history in *Ante-bellum North Carolina*, 820:

> Of a far different caliber was Francis L. Hawks's two-volume history of North Carolina which Edward J. Hale published in 1857 and 1858. The work brought the historical narrative only to the close of the proprietary period in 1730, but, unlike his predecessors, Hawks had attempted to write an unbiased history of the colonial period,

including social and economic data as well as stories of war and politics. Hawks had studied law under Judge Gaston and had been a reporter of the North Carolina Supreme Court, but he decided to become a clergyman and in 1829 left the State for New Haven where he began his services in the Episcopal Church. He had already written several other books when his *History of North Carolina* appeared. He spent most of the remaining years of his life in New York, but North Carolina always boasted of him as one of her most distinguished sons.

227. For example, Lewis *against* Williams, Haywood, *Reports of Cases Adjudged in the Superior Courts of Law and Equity* [...] *1789, to the Year 1798*, 150–154 [2 N.C. (1 Hayw.) 150 (1795) (1st prtg. 1799)] the reporter's note was eight times longer than the opinion itself and was spaced more tightly and in smaller font than the opinion. This note is omitted from the reprint volume currently sold by the North Carolina Administrative Office of the Courts (4th prtg. 1921).

228. For example, the original printing of Chief Justice Taylor's two volumes of the *Carolina Law Repository* contained biographies, English case law, and reprints of statutes, as well as opinions of the early Supreme Court of North Carolina. The North Carolina opinions would one day be included in volume four of the *North Carolina Reports*, other matter from the original printings being omitted.

229. Document II–17 (Revisal on Administrators and Executors, 1825).

230. Document II–10 (H. Potter's Report, 1819).

231. The dedication, in Taylor, *Digest of the Statute Law of North-Carolina*, reads: "To the Honourable Alfred Moore, Esq. Speaker of the House of Representatives, Is Inscribed This Attempt to Systematize an Interesting Portion of the Labours of the Legislature, over a Branch of Which He Presides, with Equal Urbanity, Dignity, and Intelligence."

232. For example, the act of 1829 regarding executors and administrators (Document II–30 (Common and Statute Law on Subject Revisal, January 1829)) used "code or system." Also, as noted in this compiler's remarks about Reporter Thomas Devereux's reference in the *North Carolina Reports* to Professor James Humphreys' book (Document II–22 (Devereux on Humphreys, 1827)), Humphreys changed "code" in the title of his first edition to "systematic reform" in the title of his second edition due to the offensiveness of the term "code."

233. Document II–4 (Haywood's Preface, 1808).

234. Martin, *Treatise on the Powers and Duties of Executors and Administrators*.

235. Document II–57 (About the Judges of Our First Supreme Court (1819–1829)).

236. An earlier treatise displaying the drive to systematically present the English common law was Thomas Wood's common law institute from 1820, discussed in Davis, "Reading *Smith v. Campbell*" (showing the comparative support of the works of Wood and Blackstone in the argument of counsel and in the majority opinion in *Smith v. Campbell*).

237. Document I–25 (Iredell's Preface, 1791) (explaining the difficulty in finding some acts passed after the publication of *Swann's Revisal*). *Swann's Revisal* was the first book printed in North Carolina, arranging colonial acts of assembly chronologically, while omitting repealed acts and repealed sections of acts. [Swann], *Collection of* [...] *Public Acts*. For further description of this work, see generally Powell, *Encyclopedia of North Carolina*, s.v. "Swann's Revisal," 1099. For a more precise description of *Swann's Revisal*, see note 123.

238. Document II–42 (Revised Statutes, 1837). See also note 123.

239. For a list of documents in this compilation pertaining to revisals and for a few observations concerning the vocabulary associated with such initiatives, see note 204.

240. Gaston served in the state senate in 1800 and 1812 and served for three terms in the house of commons. He had also served in the United States Congress from 1813 to 1817. The general assembly elected him to the state supreme court in 1833. Powell, *Dictionary of North Carolina Biography*, s.v. "Gaston, William," 2:283.

241. Battle, "William Gaston," in Peele, *Lives of Distinguished North Carolinians*, 153: "In the year 1808 [Gaston] drew up the 'Act regulating the descent of inheritances,' which, with scarcely any alteration or addition, remains the law on that subject to this day [1898]."

242. Communication from Governor Burton, Journal of the House of Commons, Tuesday, November 22, 1825, in *Journals of the Senate and House of Commons* [...] *1825*, 100: "You will herewith receive a communication from William Gaston, Esq. in which he 'declines altogether the task of revising and consolidating the laws concerning the duties of Executors and Administrators,' for reasons which will be found in his letter herewith submitted."

243. Hawks served as reporter to the newly-created state supreme court from 1820 to 1826, publishing the first modern subject-arranged digest of the opinions of the supreme court in 1826. Many of Hawks's successors also produced digests of the opinions they reported. Davis, "Government Publishing of North Carolina Law," 21.

244. Mordecai was the grandfather of Samuel Fox Mordecai II, who would one day serve as dean of Trinity Law School, which eventually became Duke School of Law. Powell, *Dictionary of North Carolina Biography*, s.v. "Mordecai, Samuel Fox II," 4:318.

245. Librarian and Keeper of the Manuscripts at the Honourable Society of the Inner Temple, W. W. S. Breem, said this about the modern English digest in "Primary Sources: Law Reports," Moys, *Manual of Law Librarianship*, 157: "Charles Petersdorff's *Practical and Elementary Abridgment of Cases in the Courts of King's Bench, Common Pleas, Exchequer, and at Nisi Prius*, 15 volumes, 1825–30, was the first to approximate to a modern digest, containing as it did a series of catchwords or phrases under each title."
246. Davis, "School Days," 383 (describing Taylor's margin notes as the first headnotes used in reports of North Carolina opinions).
247. The digest covered the cases reported in the ten volumes of unofficial reports produced by various North Carolina judges, Davis, "School Days," 383, as well as four volumes of the official reports published between 1819 and 1826.
248. While the second edition (published in 1849) to what became volume 16 of the *North Carolina Reports* also contained Devereux's note, the printing in 1900 did not contain it, having been excised by Chief Justice Walter Clark during his editorship of the reprint series of the *North Carolina Reports*. That this late-century historian, codifier, and progressive reformer, Walter Clark, should remove such a significant sign of respect for a radical codifier like Mr. Humphreys is difficult to explain. The most innocuous explanation for such editing must be the desire of the editor to reduce the bulk and cost of the volumes reprinted.
249. Humphreys, *Observations with the Outlines of a Code*.
250. Humphreys, *Observations with Outlines of a Systematic Reform*.
251. "Appendix," *Revised Statutes of the State of New-York*, 3:571–572 (describing the confluence of Mr. Humphreys' work and the modification of the rule against perpetuities proposed by the commissioners of the *Revised Statutes* in New York, for example).
252. Humphreys, *Observations with Outlines of a Code*, 172: "Take the two systems just alluded to [that of personal property and of the Code Napoleon]; and, with the only material variation, which equally pervades both, of partibility of succession for primogeniture, they would furnish the outline of a code of real property embracing every legitimate object, without a trace of the excrescences of tenures, uses, or passive trusts."
253. Battle, *History of the University of North Carolina*, 1:250–251.
254. Battle, *History of the University of North Carolina*, 1:258.
255. For a list of documents in this compilation pertaining to revisals and observations concerning the vocabulary associated with such initiatives, see note 204.
256. Document II–16 (Taylor's Preface, 1824).
257. Legislative commissions and confirmations of revisals failed to employ the term "digest" for the official revisals of 1715, 1749, 1791, 1792, 1794, 1804, and 1819. For a list of documents in this compilation pertaining to revisals and for a few observations concerning the vocabulary associated with such initiatives, see note 204.
258. Journal of the House of Commons, Thursday, January 18, 1827, 168 (bill reported and passed first reading); Journal of the House, Wednesday, January 24, 1827, 183–184 (bill to lie on table); Journal of the House, Thursday, February 8, 1827, 217 (bill postponed indefinitely), all in *Journals of the Senate & House of Commons [...] 1826–27*.
259. For a list of documents in this compilation pertaining to revisals and for a few observations concerning the vocabulary associated with such initiatives, see note 204.
260. Journal of the House of Commons, Monday, December 31, 1827, Mr. Spruill, 221: "Mr. Spruill, from the Judiciary committee, to whom was referred the resolution instructing them to inquire into the expediency of providing by law for arranging, revising and digesting the whole body of public and statute law of North-Carolina, reported that the committee had considered the said resolution, and instructed him to recommend that it be rejected. The report was read and concurred in." *Journals of the Senate & House of Commons [...] 1827–28*.
261. For a list of documents in this compilation pertaining to revisals and for a few observations concerning the vocabulary associated with such initiatives, see note 204.
262. Journal of the Senate, Saturday, December 22, 1827, Mr. Pickett, 72 (allowing discharge of committee and resolution to lie on table). *Journals of the Senate & House of Commons [...] 1827–28*.
263. For a list of documents in this compilation pertaining to revisals and for a few observations concerning the vocabulary associated with such initiatives, see note 204.
264. Journal of the House of Commons, Wednesday, December 19, 1827, Mr. Hill, 193 (committee discharged from these duties). *Journals of the Senate & House of Commons [...] 1827–28*.
265. Journal of the House of Commons, Monday morning, December 24, 1827, Mr. Spruill, 204. *Journals of the Senate & House of Commons [...] 1827–28*. For a list of documents in this compilation pertaining to revisals and for a few observations concerning the vocabulary associated with such initiatives, see note 204.

266. Journal of the House of Commons, Saturday, January 5, 1828, 243. *Journals of the Senate & House of Commons* [. . .] *1827–28*.
267. Journal of the Senate, Saturday Evening, January 5, 1828, 119–120. *Journals of the Senate & House of Commons* [. . .] *1827–28*.
268. For a list of documents in this compilation pertaining to revisals and for a few observations concerning the vocabulary associated with such initiatives, see note 204.
269. See note 268.
270. Document II–37 (Governor Swain's Message, 1833).
271. This act was passed just weeks after the election of Andrew Jackson as President of the United States, which began the era of Jacksonian Democracy. *Encyclopedia Americana*, s.v. "Jackson, Andrew," 15:642.
272. Document II–16 (Taylor's Preface, 1824).
273. Document II–17 (Revisal on Administrators and Executors, 1825).
274. Document II–31 (Commissions for Common and Statute Law Subject Revisal, May 1829).
275. Later that year, the general assembly elected Ruffin to the supreme court. Journal of the House of Commons, Tuesday, November 24, 1829. *Journals of the Senate & House of Commons* [. . .] *1829–30*, 165 (electing Ruffin).
276. See Document II–61 (About Mr. George Badger (1795–1866)).
277. Journal of the House of Commons, Friday, November 26, 1830, 184. At the governor's suggestion, a representative introduced a new bill for revising and digesting the laws relating to executors and administrators, but it was ultimately laid on the table. Journal of the House, Monday, January 3, 1831, 261. *Journals of the Senate & House of Commons* [. . .] *1830–31*.
278. For a list of documents in this compilation pertaining to revisals and for a few observations concerning the vocabulary associated with such initiatives, see note 204.
279. Journal of the House of Commons, Tuesday, December 22, 1829, 229 (reporting the inexpediency of legislating on the topics of the resolution and discharging the judiciary committee from further consideration of the issue). *Journals of the Senate & House of Commons* [. . .] *1829–30*.
280. While subject terms comprise the top level of the index to the 1829–1830 acts, beneath each subject term are short titles of acts arranged by order of passage (i.e., in page-number order). That is, the acts were assigned chapter numbers according to the chronology of passage before they were indexed by subject. By contrast, for the session of 1833–1834 the general assembly tried to place its acts in subject order before assigning chapter numbers, though the execution did not perfectly comply with this principle. This sort of practice varied in subsequent sessions.
281. See Document II–4 (Haywood's Preface, 1808).
282. The private acts of 1817, 1818, and 1819, on the other hand, provided a subject index.
283. See Document II–10 (H. Potter's Report, 1819).
284. For a list of documents in this compilation pertaining to revisals and for a few observations concerning the vocabulary associated with such initiatives, see note 204.
285. Journal of the Senate, Wednesday, January 5, 1831, 139. *Journals of the Senate & House of Commons* [. . .] *1830–31*.
286. Journal of the Senate, Friday, January 7, 1831, 147 (receiving a message from the house of the postponement indefinitely of the senate's engrossed bill for revising and digesting the public statute laws of the state). *Journals of the Senate & House of Commons* [. . .] *1830–31*.
287. A well-known American writer of the nineteenth century, Orestes Brownson, steadfastly rejected one classical justification of slavery under a natural law tradition. Brownson, *American Republic*, 177: While Brownson accepted Justinian's assertion of "the equality of all men by the natural law," he rejected Justinian's defense of slavery "as a commutation of the punishment of death. . . ." Thus, in Brownson, 160: he thought that the "abolitionists were right in opposing slavery, but not in demanding its abolition on humanitarian or socialistic grounds." In Brownson, 163: he rejected the "socialistic or humanitarian democracy represented by Northern abolitionists as hostile alike to the Church and to civilization," and in Brownson, 157–158: he rejected the Jeffersonian, personal, egotistical, individualistic democracy as well, which he held had characterized the Confederacy. He supported what he called a territorial democracy based on a refined natural law jurisprudence. In Brownson, 161: he was Catholic and held that the "infusion of the Christian dogma of the unity and solidarity of the race into the belief, the life, the laws, the jurisprudence of all civilized nations, has doomed slavery and every species of barbarism. . . ." In Brownson, 160: he thought slavery a "barbaric element" which stood "in direct antagonism to American civilization."
288. McFarland, "North Carolina Newspapers," 389: "Although not actually a Quaker, [William] Swaim often fought for their causes"; McFarland, 389n44: "In the *Patriot*, May 9, 1822, [William] Swaim says he is not a Quaker. It is

clear, however, that many of his family were Friends." Other authorities, though, report that Swaim was a Quaker. Fay, *Cyclopædia of American Biography*, s.v. "Porter, William Sidney (O. Henry)," 8:371: "Apparently, Sidney Porter's remarkable literary abilities were inherited from his maternal grandfather, William Swaim, whose ancestor, also named William Swaim, came from Holland to New York, about 1700, and whose descendants removed to North Carolina some ten years before the Revolution. William Swaim, Sidney Porter's grandfather, a Quaker, was editor of the Greensboro 'Patriot' after 1827, and through its columns uttered his vehement protests against the institution of slavery."

289. Weeks, *Southern Quakers and Slavery*, 240.

290. Powell, *Dictionary of North Carolina Biography*, s.v. "Swaim, Benjamin," 5:480; McFarland, "North Carolina Newspapers," 389; Valentine, "Useful Books," 64. Another source asserts that the men were not cousins, but brothers. Johnson, *Ante-Bellum North Carolina*, 769, 795n88 (asserting that William's cousin was Lyndon Swaim and William's brother was Benjamin Swaim).

291. Document II–4 (Haywood's Preface, 1808).

292. Powell, *Dictionary of North Carolina Biography*, s.v. "Haywood, John", 3:87 (noting that Haywood served in North Carolina as attorney general and judge, and served in Tennessee as judge and statutory commissioner; Haywood also reported opinions in both states, compiled a manual of North Carolina's statute laws, and published a handbook for North Carolina public officers).

293. See Document I–3 (The Grand Model, 1669).

294. For a biography of Governor Swain, see Whichard, *Consequential Life: David Lowry Swain*. Whichard outlines the governor's address of 1833, which mentions revision of the state's statutes. Whichard, 55–57.

295. For a list of documents in this compilation pertaining to revisals and for a few observations concerning the vocabulary associated with such initiatives, see note 204.

296. Hill, "The Old South," Peele, *Lives of Distinguished North Carolinians*, 569: "Hence the people of the Old South maintained slavery and devoted themselves almost exclusively to agriculture. . . . The Old South labored under a more serious disadvantage; there were few literary and scientific men among them."

297. Document II–46 (Smith's Preface, 1846).

298. Davis, "Reading *Smith v. Campbell*," 74n199 (noting the widespread use of juries in colonial proceedings in North Carolina).

299. For references on the relation of public sentiment and law, see note 224.

300. On the relation of ontology and axiology, contemporary philosopher John Finnis would sharply distinguish theoretical (or speculative) reason, whose flights of contemplation include ontology, from practical reason, but would not deny the relevance of human nature to good reasons for action. For example, see Finnis, "Human Rights and Their Enforcement," in his *Human Rights and Common Good*, 39: one cannot "identify rights without proceeding from an understanding of human goods (which feeds and is fed by an understanding of human nature)."

301. For a list of documents in this compilation pertaining to revisals and for a few observations concerning the vocabulary associated with such initiatives, see note 204.

302. Powell, *Dictionary of North Carolina Biography*, s.v. "Graham, William Alexander," 2:337.

303. This legislative edition is held in the Special Collection of the North Carolina Supreme Court Library. The legislature would have used this volume in passing the acts which would comprise the chapters of *The Revised Statutes*. This legislative edition contains the full text of all acts listed in the Act Concerning the Revised Statutes, as well as the text of the 68th item, An Act Concerning Public Printing, which was skipped in that list.

304. The marginal notes of *The Revised Statutes* ultimately shed their history notes, relegating that information to footnotes.

305. The volume of session laws for 1836–1837 is unusual. Acts are assigned a subject, arranged with an eye to subject, and then assigned a chapter number. However, in nine instances there are acts labeled "[Revised Statute.]" that have no chapter numbers and that are anomalously inserted between chapters. Between chapters 18 and 19 are inserted four acts, each concerning the courts. These four acts are listed 90th, 66th, 67th, and 69th in the Act concerning the Revised Statutes (which is excerpted in the text of this compilation). Similarly, between chapters 35 and 36 is inserted the 38th listed item, and between chapters 37 and 38 is inserted the 4th listed item. Additionally, between chapters 49 and 50 is inserted the 18th, 17th, and 15th listed items, each of which deals with money matters. The subjects of these extraneously inserted acts, then, in order of appearance in this volume of session laws, are:

- County Courts (90th listed act)
- Supreme Court (66th listed act)

- Courts of Equity (67th listed act)
- Justices of the Peace (69th listed act)
- Miscellaneous (Pilots and Commissioners of Navigation) (38th listed act)
- Militia (4th listed act)
- Revenue (18th listed act)
- Treasurer of State (17th listed act)
- Comptroller (15th listed act)

No explanation for the unusual placement of these nine acts in the session laws of 1836–1837 is evident.

306. *The Revised Statutes* places "References to Adjudged Cases" at the end of statutory sections (see, for example, the references under the section entitled "Partition"). No annotations are provided with these references, but the subsection of the statutory section to which the case refers is indicated.
307. An Act to Give Effect to the "Revised Statutes," As the Same Have Been Published by the Commissioners Appointed for That Purpose, ch. 37, *Laws of the State of North Carolina, Passed by the General Assembly* [...] *1838–'39*, 73. [1838–'39 Laws of N.C. 73]
308. For a list of documents in this compilation pertaining to revisals and for a few observations concerning the vocabulary associated with such initiatives, see note 204.
309. Whatley, "Benjamin Swaim and the 'Man of Business'."
310. Document II–35 (Friends of Liberty Address, 1830).
311. Hilty, *Toward Freedom for All*, 43.
312. The five other documents on the subject of executors and administrators are: (1) a preface to a treatise (Document II–16 (Taylor's Preface, 1824)); (2) a statute (Document II–17 (Revisal on Administrators and Executors, 1825)); (3) a bill (Document II–27 (Bill on Subject of Revisal, January 7, 1828)); (4) an act (Document II–30 (Common and Statute Law on Subject Revisal, January 1829)); and (5) a letter (Document II–31 (Commissions for Common and Statute Law Subject Revisal, May 1829)). The last two of these items addressed codification of both the statute and common law on a narrow subject. The first item initiated a sort of treatise that was continued after Swaim's entry by James Iredell Jr., in 1851. Iredell, *Treatise on the Law of Executors and Administrators in North Carolina*.
313. Interest in assisting the layman with his legal needs is a recurring and important theme in law reform in North Carolina. That theme relates to at least three prominent values: (1) diffusion of law to subjects and citizens, (2) common sense in law, and (3) transparency of legal practice and procedure. The first of these values, for instance, appears even in *The Fundamental Constitutions*, where it is required that the constitutions be kept in a "great book," read before every parliament, and subscribed to by adults in an oath of allegiance. Document I–3 (The Grand Model, 1669). The second value also appears in a peculiar way in the constitutions, where "comments and expositions" on the constitutions are prohibited. These values, which appear even in these medieval-sounding constitutions of the Restoration period in English history, also characterize the thunderous modern drive toward a more democratic society, which was unleashed during the French Revolution. Regarding the value of transparency in legal practice and procedure, at least four documents from the Antebellum Period record the loose procedure and practice in courts in North Carolina, which shows that the technicalities of English common law pleading were not prized here and that the arcane and scholastic qualities of English common law pleading were not an obstacle to the layperson or new attorney in the state. Document II–45 (Administration of Justice, 1845); Document II–46 (Smith's Preface, 1846); Document II–50 (Nash on Local Practice), and Document II–52 (Eaton's Preface, 1854). Even if English practice was mangled in North Carolina, the local traditions in pleading and practice which prevailed here shrouded the profession in mystery that only the local practitioner and local official might penetrate, thus undermining the third value in a different way.
314. Farmer, "Legal Practice and Ethics in North Carolina," 345.
315. Document II–59 (About Mr. Archibald Henderson (1768–1822)).
316. Document III–47 (Tourgée's Notes, 1878).
317. The theme of looseness in North Carolina legal practice is raised in Document II–45 (Administration of Justice, 1845), Document II–46 (Smith's Preface, 1846), Document II–50 (Nash on Local Practice), and Document II–52 (Eaton's Preface, 1854).
318. See note 317.
319. Tushnet, *American Law of Slavery 1810–1860*, 94–95.

320. Other aspects of Justice Pearson's idea of the common law appear in Document II–49 (Pearson on the Common Law, 1851) and in Document II–54 (Pearson on the Common Law, 1856).
321. Pearson's objections to codification appear in letters exchanged with Justice Rodman at Document III–12 (Pearson to Rodman, August 6, 1868) and Document III–17 (Pearson to Rodman, September 24, 1868), and are not too subtly concealed in Document III–34 (Pearson on Judicial Legislation, 1870).
322. Other aspects of Justice Pearson's idea of the common law appear in Document II–48 (Pearson on the Common Law, 1850) and Document II–54 (Pearson on the Common Law, 1856).
323. Document II–45 (Administration of Justice, 1845).
324. Document II–46 (Smith's Preface, 1846).
325. Document II–52 (Eaton's Preface, 1854).
326. Haywood, "Bartholomew Figures Moore," in Peele, *Lives of Distinguished North Carolinians*, 384: describing the *Revised Code* as "far more than a bare compilation of statutes—far more than a codification of existing acts of Assembly," and admiring that it "has amended and perfected every such act in those particulars in which it has been proved by experience to be imperfect" under "every principle which had been established, and every decision which had then been made by our courts...."
327. Document IV–14 (Revisal's Preface, 1905). For a list of documents in this compilation pertaining to revisals and for a few observations concerning the vocabulary associated with such initiatives, see note 204.
328. For a passing description of William Eaton Jr., see Davis, "Address of Hon. J. J. Davis," *Proceedings of the North Carolina Bar Association [...] the 14th of October, 1885*, 11: "Mr. Hugh Waddell, chivalrous and eloquent, brave, generous and scholarly; John Kerr, sometimes a torrent of eloquence, never so happy as when denouncing with withering scorn some act of meanness; Wm. Eaton, gentle as a woman, a lawyer of great learning, and one of the best of pleaders under the old system; Wm. H. Battle, my own beloved preceptor, learned, laborious and safe counsellor, and one of the gentlest, purest and best men I ever knew—all attended the Granville bar."
329. The theme of looseness in North Carolina legal practice is raised in Document II–45 (Administration of Justice, 1845), Document II–46 (Smith's Preface, 1846), Document II–50 (Nash on Local Practice), and Document II–52 (Eaton's Preface, 1854).
330. Other aspects of Justice Pearson's idea of the common law appear in Document II–48 (Pearson on the Common Law, 1850) and Document II–49 (Pearson on the Common Law, 1851).
331. In 1829, a codification of the statute and common law on a particular subject was called for by the general assembly. Document II–30 (Common and Statute Law on Subject Revisal, January 1829). In 1827, official supreme court reporter, Thomas Devereux, had excerpted a contemporary English codification of property law, printing it below an opinion of the court. Document II–22 (Devereux on Humphreys, 1827).
332. Document II–35 (Friends of Liberty Address, 1830).
333. Document II–12 (Taylor on the Common Law, 1820); Document II–14 (Taylor on the Common Law, 1823). Looking at these documents of the early nineteenth century, one might conclude that Judge Taylor would fill gaps in statutory schemes that deviate from the common law by application of fundamental principles and particular rules of the common law, which in the case of slavery would ameliorate injustices at least to some small degree. In other words, Taylor took the common law as the law of the state and as a system complete in principle whose rules the courts would develop case by case, unless the general assembly affirmatively deviated from that system. By contrast, in the document excerpted here, Document II–56 (Battle on the Common Law, 1864), Battle suggests that a case might arise where "no principle of the common law [is] applicable," forcing the court to await legislative intervention to devise a pertinent legal principle. Though the justice here says "principle," perhaps his opinion should be read to mean that there existed in 1864 in North Carolina no common law *rule* excepting plaintiff in the sort of case on appeal from the common law *principle* or maxim that "no one is allowed to be a witness in his own cause," and that the court had no authority to develop such an exception. In other words, in the last years of its existence as a statutory court, the supreme court allowed that the common law is not a system complete in itself and that the state's adjectival law of evidence, at least, must develop by legislative action.
334. Document II–53 (Battle on the Common Law, 1855).
335. Winston, "Presentation of the Portrait of Chief Justice Leonard Henderson," in Strong, *Cases Argued and Determined in the Supreme Court [...] Fall Term, 1908*, 604. [149 N.C. 595, 604]
336. See note 335 at 605–606. [149 N.C. 605–606]
337. Document II–58 (About Judge John Hall (1767–1833)).

338. Johnson, *Ante-bellum North Carolina*, 783 (noting that "Philo Florian" was a pseudonym of Archibald D. Murphey).
339. Potter, Taylor, and Yancey, *Laws of the State of North-Carolina*, 2:1439 (empowering the supreme court to appoint a reporter).
340. Powell, *Dictionary of North Carolina Biography*, s.v. "Murphey, Archibald DeBow," 4:345.
341. Archibald D. Murphey sat on the Supreme Court in 1819 and 1820 by letters missive of the governor under the act supplemental to the act that created the modern supreme court. Apparently, this requisition occurred because Supreme Court Judge Leonard Henderson had conflicts of interest that prevented him from sitting for some cases during those terms. Denny, "History of the Supreme Court of North Carolina from January 1, 1919, Until January 1, 1969," in Partin and White, *Cases Argued and Determined in the Supreme Court [. . .] Spring Term 1968 [to] Fall Term 1968*, 626.
342. Hunter, "The Institutionalization of Legal Education in North Carolina, 1790–1920," in Sheppard, *History of Legal Education in the United States*, 1:406, 410.
343. Document I–13 (Declaration of Rights, December 17, 1776); Document I–14 (Constitution, December 18, 1776).
344. See the excerpt of this document for where Henry says, "It is undoubtedly a natural right, and when it is declared to be an inalienable one by the people in their sovereign and original capacity, any attempt to alienate it either by the Constitution, or by law, must be vain and fruitless."
345. Document I–13 (Declaration of Rights, December 17, 1776).
346. Constitution of North Carolina of 1776, § 44.
347. Orth, *North Carolina State Constitution*, 161: "The state's first constitution, drafted and adopted by a provincial congress and never thereafter referred to the voters, included no provision for amendment."; Kirk, *John Randolph*, 211–212 (describing Randolph's fight to save Virginia's old constitution and his objection to provision for constitutional amendment).
348. For an elaboration on the doctrine that a constitution cannot be amended in its essentials, such an amendment by definition destroying the polity, see, for example, Brownson, "Republic of the United States (April 1849)," in Brownson, *Works in Political Philosophy*, 3:302–303. On the same theme, see Document I–3 (The Grand Model, 1669): "120th. These fundamental constitutions, in number a hundred and twenty, and every part thereof, shall be and remain, the sacred and unalterable form and rule of government of Carolina forever."
349. Whether enumerating additional natural rights in the declaration of rights is to amend that declaration is a fine question. The source of the inalienable rights being human capacities and not the accident of declaration in a document, one might argue that the enumeration of rights in 1776, if in fact partial, may not be construed to deny or disparage others retained by the people. That is, one might argue that all natural or human rights are implicitly recognized in the state's fundamental law, those initially selected for enumeration in the declaration of rights being rights vindicated historically after their violation in England or its American colonies. On the other hand, one might argue that the text of the codification should be taken as the comprehensive rule from which only the authorized writer can acknowledge exceptions or elaborations by further writings. For an argument to this effect, see Carter, *Provinces of the Written and the Unwritten Law*, 25–28 (comparing the methods of common law adjudication and codification in the handling of the first case of an infant ratifying a contract).
350. Were Taylor interpreting a text from the early eighteenth century in the province, when supporters of established Anglicanism in Carolina blocked Quakers from public office, see, for example, Document I–5 (The Queen's Peace, 1711), his identification of "Protestant" and "Anglican" would certainly carry weight. At that time, Anglicanism was the established protestant religion in North Carolina. Cain, *Church of England in North Carolina*, 10:xxiii–xxiv: "The establishment of Anglicanism as the officially sanctioned faith in North Carolina came in November, 1701, with the enactment of the first of a succession of so-called 'vestry acts.'"
351. On the relation of public opinion to law in the nineteenth century, see note 224.
352. Document I–14 (Constitution, December 18, 1776).
353. See note 352.
354. Anti-Catholic sentiment, for instance, was expressed in North Carolina in the years leading up to the vestry act of 1765. Conkin, "Church Establishment in North Carolina, 1765–1776," 2: "While in 1759 there was a common sentiment in North Carolina that the Protestant religion should be legally established, there was a wide difference of opinion as to the form the Establishment should take. . . . The dissenters wanted to retain almost complete religious freedom within an establishment that would do little more than definitely exclude Catholics." The unlikelihood that the 1776 state constitution meant to exclude non-Anglican Protestants—dissenters—from public office seems high

given the instigating role played by the dissenters leading up to and during the revolution that led to the adoption of the constitution. According to a letter from Rev. Andrew Morton to Secretary, SPG, August 25, 1766 in Cain and Poff, *Church of England in North Carolina*, 12:112: dissenters in Mecklenburg County, for instance, "look'd upon a Law lately enacted in this Province for the better Establishment of the Church [the vestry act], as oppressive as the Stamp Act. . . ." And after the Revolutionary War, the dissenters were credited with having brought the revolution about. In a letter from Rev. Daniel Earl to Secretary, SPG, June 1, 1784 in Cain and Poff, *Church of England in North Carolina*, 12:393: "[T]he Dissenters seem to have gained all public favour, as they are thought to be very Instrumental in bringing about the Revolution."

355. Document I–5 (The Queen's Peace, 1711).
356. Document I–7 (The Queen's Peace, 1715).
357. Document I–16 (Reception Ordinance, December 22, 1776); Document I–17 (Reception Statute, May 9, 1777); Document I–19 (Reception Statute, December 24, 1777); and Document I–20 (Reception Statute, 1778).
358. Amendment of the *Revised Code* occurs frequently in the legislation of North Carolina passed after secession. For example, see An Act to Amend Chapter 55 of Revised Code, ch. 5, *Public Laws* [. . .] *Passed by the General Assembly* [. . .] *1863*, 5 [1863 N.C. Pub. Laws Called Session 5] (concerning habeas corpus).
359. The codification of the reception of the common law appears in the twenty-second chapter of the *Revised Code*.
360. An Ordinance Prohibiting Slavery in the State of North Carolina, ch. 2, in *Ordinances Passed by the North Carolina State Convention, at the Sessions of 1865–'66*, 4 (ratified October 9, 1865). While the committee report refers to a "resolution of the recent Convention," the compilers have located only an ordinance of the Convention on this topic.
361. Holden, "[Provisional] Governor's Message [of November 30, 1865]," Document No. 1, [*North Carolina Legislative Documents* [. . .] *1865–'66*], 3–4: appointing "the Hon. B. F. Moore, the Hon. Richard S. Donnell, and William S. Mason, Esquire, Commissioners to prepare and report to the Legislature a system of laws upon the subject of freedmen, and to designate such laws and parts of laws, now in force, as should be repealed. . . ."
362. *Journal of the House of Commons at Its Special Session of 1866*, Friday, January 19, 1866, 21 (emphasis added).
363. Ashe, *Biographical History of North Carolina*, s.v. "William Woods Holden," 3:197.
364. Balanoff, "Negro Legislators," 41n78 (using the name, "Black Codes of 1866").
365. For the record of the introduction of these nine bills in the house, see *Journal of the House of Commons at Its Special Session of 1866*, Tuesday, January 23, 1866, 34–35.
366. The death penalty provision of the proposed Freedmen's Code was section 13 of the original bill and section 11 of the act. The evidence provision was section 11 of the original bill and section 9 of the act.
367. For the bill history of the main bill in the senate, see *Journal of the Senate at Its Special Session of 1866*, Wednesday, February 28, 1866, 163–164; Friday, March 2, 1866, 176–179; Saturday, March 3, 1866, 187–188; and Friday, March 9, 1866, 240–242.

For the bill history of the main bill in the House of Commons, see *Journal of the House of Commons at Its Special Session of 1866*, Tuesday, January 23, 34–35; Monday, January 29, 1866, 60; Tuesday, January 30, 1866, 63–64; Wednesday, January 31, 1866, 67; Thursday, February 1, 1866, 70; Friday, February 2, 1866, 73; Monday, February 5, 1866, 82; Thursday, February 8, 1866, 96; Friday, February 9, 1866, 98–99; Thursday, February 15, 1866, 116; Monday, February 19, 1866, 133; Wednesday, February 21, 1866, 147–151; and Monday, February 26, 173–174.

The limited right to testify in court, which the bill extended to the freedmen, was characterized by Representative William A. Jenkins of Warren County as a "franchise," while Representative Samuel F. Phillips of Orange County in opposition characterized the right to testify as a "privilege" which was not a political right, but a natural right. "Proceedings of the Legislature," Thurs., Feb. 1, 1866, in *Raleigh Weekly North-Carolina Standard*, Feb. 7, 1866, p. [2], col. 2. Representative Neil McKay of Harnett County urged that the right to testify was not a political right and argued that recognition of this right as a necessary implication of the abolition of slavery would be a reason for the national government to withdraw the Freedmen's Bureau from North Carolina. "Proceedings of the Legislature," Thurs., Feb. 2, 1866, in *Raleigh Weekly NorthCarolina Standard*, Feb. 7, 1866, p. [2], cols. 3–4; "Proceedings of the Legislature," Thurs., Feb. 8, 1866, in *Raleigh Weekly North-Carolina Standard*, Wed., Feb. 14, 1866, p. [2], col. 1, Representative Atlas J. Dargan of Anson County asserted that he would not extend the right to testify to the freedmen until they were "educated and christianized," and that no reason existed to believe that extension of this "franchise" would lead the Freedmen's Bureau to leave North Carolina, while extension of the right to testify might lead to "negro suffrage" and "negro equality."

368. An Ordinance Repealing the Provisions of Section Nine, of an Act of the General Assembly, Entitled "An Act Concerning Negroes and Persons of Color or of Mixed Blood," and for Other Purposes, ch. 37, in *Ordinances Passed by the North Carolina State Convention, at the Sessions of 1865–'66*, 59 (ratified June 10, 1866); An Ordinance Concerning the Crime of Assault, with Intent to Commit Rape, ch. 21, in *Ordinances Passed by the North Carolina State Convention, at the Sessions of 1865–'66*, 39 (ratified June 12, 1866); "Worth, [Address to the Gentlemen of the Convention, May 25th, 1866], in *Journal of the Convention* [...] *at Its Adjourned Session of 1866*, 6: reporting that Brevet Major-General Ruger, Military Commandant of North Carolina, "would gladly transfer to the civil Courts of the State full jurisdiction in all matters relating to freedmen, but that he feels embarrassed in doing so, consistently with his instructions, on account of certain provisions and conflicting constructions of the act of the General Assembly, passed at its late session, entitled 'An act concerning negroes, persons of color, or of mixed blood.' His difficulties are understood to grow out of the 9th [right to bear evidence] and 11th [unequal punishment for assault with intent to commit rape] sections of the act."
369. Balanoff, "Negro Legislators," 41n78: "... apparent removal, with the acceptance of the 1868 Constitution, of all discrimination [on the basis of color] required by the Black Codes of 1866...."
370. Under sections 2 and 3 of article 4 of the Constitution of 1868, the commissioners were guaranteed a reasonable compensation, and vacancies on the commission were filled by the governor. Document III–6 (Constitution, April 21–23, 1868).
371. Document III–45 (Constitutional Amendment Dissolving Code Commission, 1873) (ratified by the general assembly February 24, 1873; ratified by the people August 7, 1873).
372. The codification of the entire body of the common law had been under way in New York since the late 1840s. Weber, introduction to *New York Field Codes*, vi–vii. The question of whether to adopt the civil and political codes would be a vicious battle beginning in the 1860s, one eventually won by opponents of codification. Weber, vii–viii.
373. Document III–5 (Code Commissioners, March 13, 1868).
374. Document III–4 (Merger of Law and Equity, February 25, 1868).
375. Document III–6 (Constitution, April 21–23, 1868).
376. The Reconstruction constitution, article 4, section 3, stated that "The same Commissioners shall also report to the General Assembly as soon as practicable, a code of the law of North-Carolina." Document III–6 (Constitution, April 21–23, 1868).
377. According to Bentham, *Limits of Jurisprudence Defined*, 233n11: "*procedure*" is a term of art introduced by philosopher Jeremy Bentham in the late eighteenth century, as a more precise expression of the traditional notion of "*practice*" in court proceedings or "*rules of practice*" made by judges.
378. The penal code would not only provide for punishments, but would define crimes, i.e., it would codify the common law of crimes. Document III–32 (Bill for Penal Code, 1869): for example, defining blasphemy as "wantonly uttering or publishing words contumelious reproach or profane ridicule upon God, Jesus Christ, the Holy Ghost, the Holy Scriptures or the Christian religion."
379. Document II–37 (Governor Swain's Address, 1833).
380. Act for the Appointment of Commissioners under the Seventeenth Section of the First Article of the Constitution, to Prepare a Civil Code, Passed April 6th, 1857, in *First Report of the Commissioners of the Code [for the State of New-York]*, [3]. The statute implemented a New York constitutional provision, much as North Carolina's ordinance elaborated on a constitutional provision of its 1868 Constitution.
381. Field modelled his analysis for the codification of "the whole body of the law" of New York on the outline of the common law used by Sir William Blackstone in his *Commentaries on the Laws of England*.
382. Document III–10 (First Report of the Code Commissioners, July 15, 1868).
383. For the usage of the term "jurisprudence," see the compiler's remarks for Document III–17 (Pearson to Rodman, September 24, 1868) quoting Charles Sumner's letter, which uses "*jurisprudence* des arrets" to refer to a vast body of case law. See also Document III–54 (About Judge Manning, 1830–1899) (describing Blackstone's work as influential in engrafting the common law upon the *jurisprudence* of American states); and Document IV–11 (Hinsdale on Codification, 1900) (referring to "States where the Civil law forms the basis of the *jurisprudence*").
384. Document II–51 (Revised Code's Preface, 1854).
385. For example, the following three letters are also from Field to Tourgee: David Dudley Field to Albion W. Tourgee, New York City, [September?] 30, 1868, Tourgée Papers, Collection 1-2383, Reel 9, Item 1472[22] (formerly Item 905); David Dudley Field to Albion W. Tourgee, New York City, April 26, 1887, Tourgée Papers, Collection 1-2383,

Reel 19, Item 2657: "... you are, I think, a firm believer in codification & in my code."; David Dudley Field to Albion Winegar Tourgée, Stockbridge, Mass., Tourgée Papers, Collection 1-2383, Reel 57, Item 10,992.

386. *First Report of the Commissioners of the Code [for New-York]*, 6.
387. Document III–32 (Bill for a Penal Code, 1869).
388. Document III–5 (Code Commissioners, March 13, 1868).
389. See note 388.
390. Beyond the excerpt in Document III–17 (Pearson to Rodman, September 24, 1868) at least three other sources suggest what Pearson's opinion on codification was, including:

- Document III–12 (Pearson to Rodman, August 6, 1868): requesting that the commissioners not abolish the common law and equity, but instead use these evidences of law as a foundation from which to understand modifications of the common law and statutes,

- Document III–23 (Meeting of Bench and Bar, December 24, 1868): referring perhaps to Pearson's views on codification when it reported about the meeting of bench and bar on the newly adopted code of civil procedure, stating that "An interesting and able communication was read from Chief Justice Pearson, which on motion of Judge Mitchell was referred to the above Committee," and

- Olsen, *Carpetbagger's Crusade*, 139: mentioning that Pearson declined a position on the Code Commission in 1870 "with the assertion that Rodman and Tourgée desired to reduce the entire common law to a written code, which he considered an 'impossibility.'"

391. Document I–3 (The Grand Model, 1669).
392. Pierce, *Memoir and Letters of Sumner*, 1:189 (quoting a letter of March 27, 1837 to Professor Mittermaier, Heidelberg, in a chapter entitled, "Codification of the Common Law").
393. This maxim appeared in Coke's commentary on Littleton. Coke, *First Part of the Institutes of the Laws of England*, sect. 227b. This maxim is also mentioned in Document IV–16 (Winston's Speech, 1913). The Latin expression may translate comfortably as: "Where the law is uncertain, there is no law."
394. Professor Grant Gilmore distinguished the American codification movement at the state level from the English Benthamite movement, the former more concerned with freeing Americans from English law and from lawyers, and American lawyers from the ever-accumulating mass of case reports, than with "jurisprudential enthusiasms." Gilmore, review of *Justice Joseph Story*, 247; Gilmore, *Ages of American Law*, 26: "The movement in favor of codification at the state level—a proposal which was eloquently supported by Justice Story as early as 1821—was not Benthamite either in its inspiration or in its detail." Gilmore quoted at length an address given by Story to the members of the Suffolk Bar in 1821, *Progress of Jurisprudence*, for the details of the less radical view of codification in America—a view that perhaps Rodman had in mind in codifying North Carolina's law of homicide. In Gilmore's review of *Justice Joseph Story*, 249: Story would support a " 'gradual digest, under legislative authority, of those portions of our jurisprudence, which, under the forming hand of the judiciary, shall from time to time acquire scientific accuracy'" which, he thought, would " 'pave the way to a general code, which will present, in its positive and authoritative text, the most material rules to guide the lawyer, the statesman, and the private citizen'"; and "[s]uch a code, ... would require periodic revisions 'to reflect all the light which intermediate decisions may have thrown upon our jurisprudence.'" For a similar distinction made by Professor Alison Reppy in discussing the concept of codification understood by David Dudley Field, see notes 416 and 449.
395. *Journal of the House of Representatives [...] 1868–'69*, Tuesday, December 1st, 1868, 47 (recording that Mr. Malone introduced a resolution concerning the code commission and that it was laid over).
396. Document III–23 (Meeting of Bench and Bar, December 24, 1868).
397. In the Matter of Lynn Marie Burke, Hutcheson, *North Carolina Reports, Volume 368, Supreme Court of North Carolina, 10 April 2015 [to] 10 June 2016*, 226–233. [368 N.C. 226 (2015)] (appeal from the decision of the North Carolina Board of Law Examiners denying application to sit for the bar examination on the grounds of the applicant's failure of general fitness and good moral character expected of attorneys licensed to practice law in North Carolina).
398. *Journal of the Constitutional Convention [...] 1868*, 188 (session of Thursday, February 13, 1868).
399. An Act to Repeal Chapter Forty-Six, Laws re Practice of Law, ch. 120, *Public Laws [...] Passed by the General Assembly [...] 1870–'71*, 189 [1870–'71 N.C. Pub. Laws 189] (ratified March 11, 1871). For a historical overview of law licensing in North Carolina, see Coates, "Standards of the Bar," 34.
400. The orthodox view, that the laws never make a people, is expressed in Document II–36 (Unwritten Code of the People, 1832): "Thus Locke's celebrated constitution of Carolina is only a monument of the utter futility of hypothetical

(it does not deserve the name of theoretical,) legislation,—a lively memento of the singular preposterousness of attempting to form a people by laws." The same view is expressed in Document III–33 (Call for Convention, 1869–1870): "They [the people of North Carolina] ought to have a system of internal government in accord with [their native] . . . characteristics; and this they will have, if they are permitted to come together and make a government for themselves, the true type and embodiment of their own genius, instead of having a government made for them."

401. V. C. Barringer to Tourgée, Raleigh, 1869, Tourgée Papers, Collection 1-2383, Reel 8, Item 1210.
402. Document III–31 (Barringer to Rodman, November 15, 1869).
403. For journal entries of the general assembly relevant to this postponement, see note 421.
404. Another portion of the state's public law—that is, constitutional law—had been reduced to writing in 1776 and in 1868, but the code commission participated in neither accomplishment, the commission having been created by the 1868 constitution.
405. Carter, *Argument of James C. Carter*, 12–13: agreeing that public law—"everything that relates to the organization of the State"—must be codified but objecting that private law—"our *unwritten common law*"—cannot possibly be codified.
406. For discussion of the significance of bills submitted by the code commissioners to the 1868–'69 general assembly, see note 484.
407. See the compiler's remarks introducing Document III–40 (Report of the Code Commissioners, December 18, 1870).
408. Document III–15 (C.C.P. Preface, August 25, 1868).
409. Document III–6 (Constitution, April 21–23, 1868).
410. Under title eight (Of Crimes Against Public Justice), chapter five (Perjury and Subornation of Perjury), this North Carolina bill for a penal code includes in section 162 the following draft text and comment:

> §162. An unqualified statement of that which one does not know to be true is equivalent to a statement of that which one knows to be false.
> The Commissioners are not aware that this question has been adjudicated in this State [of North Carolina]. It is one of those questions undecided at the common law. We give the American decisions as cited by the N. Y. Commissioners: [citations to various decisions follow].

411. Livingston, *System of Penal Law, for the State of Louisiana*, 357.
412. For example, section 332 of this bill for a penal code, which concerns abortion and is here reprinted, references the *Revised Code* of 1854.
413. For example, the comment to section 5 of the preliminary provisions of the bill for a penal code, concerning disqualification to hold and enjoy any office of trust or profit under the State, looks to Blackstone and to Chitty, among others, in discussing the terms "crime," "felony," offense," and "misdemeanor"; and the comment to section 255 concerning maiming looks first to Blackstone and to Coke, and then to the statutes of various American jurisdictions.
414. For example, the comment to section 1273 concerning robbery references volume two, section 1108, of Bishop's *Commentaries on the Criminal Law*, which would have been the third edition from 1865.
415. The rejection of vengeance and of retribution as theories of punishment for crime is characteristic of the penal code of 1810, adopted in France during the French Revolution, and of utilitarian philosophy generally, which adopts rehabilitation and deterrence of crime by penalty and intimidation as the proper ends of punishment. Crimes are to be punished because they are socially harmful, not because they are morally wrong and against local tradition. Berman, "Law and Belief," 624.
416. According to one authority, perhaps focusing on codification of procedural law, the codifications by David Dudley Field in New York, on which North Carolina's codifications were based, involved the "digesting and restatement of the existing law," viewing "[d]eviations from this conservative policy in the form of amendment of the existing law" as merely experimental. See Reppy, "The Field Codification Concept," in Reppy, *David Dudley Field: Centenary Essays*, 30.
417. The latter part of the penal code, preserved in the same microform as Part I, included such titles as "Of Crimes Against the Public Health and Safety," which contained a provision against exposing persons with contagious disease in any public place (section 54), for example, and "Of Crimes Against the Public Peace," which contained provisions defining riot (section 2), rout (section 4), unlawful assembly (section 5), and assembly of disguised persons (section 6).
418. Eneas McFaul, Plaintiff in Error, *v.* James C. Ramsey, Howard, *Reports of Cases Argued and Adjudged in the Supreme Court of the United States. December Term, 1857.* 523–527. [61 U.S. 523, 525 (1857)] (emphasis added by code commissioners).

419. See note 6 and Brownson, *American Republic*, 123:

> The division of powers of government between a General government and particular governments, rendered possible and practicable by the original constitution of the people themselves, as one people existing and acting through State organizations, is the American method of guarding against the undue centralism. . . . The system is no invention of man, is no creation of the convention, but is given us by Providence in the living constitution of the American people. The merit of the statesmen of 1787 is that they did not destroy or deface the work of Providence, but accepted it, and organized the government in harmony with the real orders the real elements given them. They suffered themselves in all their positive substantial work to be governed by reality, not by theories and speculations. In this they proved themselves statesmen, and their work survives; and the republic, laugh as sciolists may, is, for the present and future, the model republic—as much so as was Rome in her day; and it is not simply national pride nor American self-conceit that pronounces its establishment the beginning of a new and more advanced order of civilization; such is really the fact.

420. Document IV–31 (Pound's Speech, 1958).
421. The first part of the penal code had been introduced in the senate and referred to the judiciary committee, which recommended that consideration of the bill be postponed until the next session. *Journal of the Senate* [. . .] *1869–'70*, Wednesday, March 16th, 1870, 569: "Mr. Cook introduced Code bill entitled Procedure in Criminal Actions; also, Code bill entitled First Part of the Penal Code. On motion of Mr. Cook, the bills were read by their title and referred to the Judiciary Committee."; Thursday, March 17th, 1870, 578: "The Judiciary Committee recommended that the following bills be postponed until the next session: Code bill entitled Procedures in Criminal Actions; Code bill entitled Part 1st of the Penal Code."
422. The senate received from the code commission a bill entitled, "Procedure in Criminal Actions" and referred it to the judiciary committee, which recommended that consideration of the bill be postponed until the next session. *Journal of the Senate* [. . .] *1869–'70*, Thursday February 3rd, 1870, 283: "A bill was received from the Code Commission entitled, 'Procedure in Criminal Actions.' Read first time and referred to the Judiciary Committee."; Wednesday, March 16th, 1870, 569: "Mr. Cook introduced Code bill entitled Procedure in Criminal Actions; also, Code bill entitled First Part of the Penal Code. On motion of Mr. Cook, the bills were read by their title and referred to the Judiciary Committee."; Thursday, March 17th, 1870, 578: "The Judiciary Committee recommended that the following bills be postponed until the next session: Code bill entitled Procedures in Criminal Actions; Code bill entitled Part 1st of the Penal Code."
423. Document III–5 (Code Commissioners, March 13, 1868).
424. A similar sentiment had been expressed by Commissioner William B. Rodman from the moment of his appointment to the commission. Document III–7 (Rodman to Holden, May 5, 1868). Chief Justice Pearson also advocated for a role for the courts in developing procedural rules. Document III–34 (Pearson on Judicial Legislation, 1870).
425. Carter, "Proposed Codification of Our Common Law," 84: "[O]ur Code of Civil Procedure . . . has been so incessantly changed by legislation that even its principal author disowns and contemns [*sic*] it, and few pretend to understand it."
426. Document III–10 (First Report of the Code Commissioners, July 15, 1868): "Nothing within the range of government, can exceed in magnitude the task of collecting, condensing and arranging the jurisprudence of a people."; Document III–29 (Report of the Code Commissioners, March 20, 1869): "Our aim has been, from the beginning, to fashion our work on a consistent plan of construction, with a view to the ultimate result of our labors—a complete Code of the law of the State."
427. Document III–5 (Code Commissioners, March 13, 1868) (appointing code commissioners).
428. Document III–37 (New Code Commissioner, July 30, 1870); Document III–38 (Bill Dissolving Code Commission, September 29, 1870).
429. Document III–37 (New Code Commissioner, July 30, 1870).
430. It has been asserted that Commissioner Tourgée resigned in the hope of inducing Chief Justice Pearson to join the code commission after Pearson had already rejected the governor's offer. Olsen, *Carpetbagger's Crusade*, 139.
431. In the code commission's fifth report, the commissioners speak of the "new code of civil practice and procedure"—meaning a replacement for the code passed in 1868—as a bill they will "propose to present to your body for action in a few days." Though journal entries are not perfectly clear on its submission, William Battle's report on his revisal

of the public laws (Document III–44 (Battle's Report on Revisal, 1872)) asserted that this "new code" was submitted to the "last" general assembly, was reported favorably by the house judiciary committee, but was not adopted. Since Battle dated his report November 18, 1872, which is the first day of the general assembly of 1872–1874, his reference to the "last" general assembly meant the general assembly of 1870–1872.

432. It has been suggested by a biographer of Tourgée, Otto Olsen, that the report of November 1870, signed by W. H. Bailey and W. B. Rodman, was the last report of the code commissioners to be submitted to the legislature. Olsen goes on to say, though, that Rodman made one more unsuccessful attempt to secure acceptance of the revised code. Olsen, *Carpetbagger's Crusade*, 139.

433. Document III–35 (Commissioners' Response, January 25, 1870).

434. Document III–39 (Report of the Code Commissioners, November 1870).

435. *Journal of the House of Representatives* [. . .] *1870–'71*, Friday, January 20th, 1871, 214: "Mr. Speaker offered report from Code Commission. Mr. Sparrow moved to receive the report and refer to Judiciary committee. Mr. Robinson moved to lay the matter on the table. . . . The motion was sustained and the matter tabled."

436. For a history of legislation pertaining to the library of the Supreme Court of North Carolina, see Taylor, "History of the North Carolina Supreme Court Library," Partin and White, *North Carolina Reports: Volume 275*, 714n4.

437. From 1818 through 1871, the judges of the Supreme Court of North Carolina appointed the official reporter of decisions who controlled the publication of the court's opinions. In addition to his state salary, the reporter held copyright to the volumes he published. An Act Supplemental to the Act Concerning the Supreme Court, ch. 2, § 13, *Laws of the State of North-Carolina* [. . .] *1818*, 5, 8. [1818 Laws of N.C. 5, 8 (consolidated in *Potter's Revisal*, ch. 963, § 13)].

438. This legislation transferred the duties of the official reporter of decisions of the supreme court from Reporter James M. McCorkle to Attorney General William M. Shipp, the state taking over the right to print, distribute, and sell the *North Carolina Reports*. The office of reporter was re-established as a judicial office in 1893. See Document IV–8 (Office of the Reporter, 1893).

439. Long before the transfer of the reporter's duties to the attorney general during Reconstruction, the official reports of the opinions of the Supreme Court of North Carolina included in each volume many pages of argument by counsel and were priced at 1¢ per page. Iredell, "Terms [for Subscription to the North-Carolina Supreme Court Reports]," in Iredell, *Reports of Cases in Equity* [. . .] *from December Term, 1851, to August Term, 1852*, 316. The titles of the reports themselves made clear the central role of counsel's argument in declaring common law in antebellum North Carolina: not just determination of cases but rather *argument* and determination both were noted in the titles. The Honorable William H. Battle, former reporter of opinions of the supreme court, confirms this central place of counsel's argument in the efforts of the first supreme court of the state to develop the state's common law in Document II–57 (About the Judges of Our First Supreme Court (1819–1829)). The reporters of opinions in the Supreme Court of North Carolina were not alone in this concept of bench and bar declaring law. In an admired antebellum address, famed author and judge James Kent of New York also presumed the joint venture of bench and bar in the science of law. [Unknown], review of Kent, *Address Delivered before the Law Association of the City of New York*, 473: "The law, as a science, is only a collection of general principles, founded on the moral law, and in the common sense of mankind, and applied to particular cases as they arise, by the diligence of the bar and the erudition of the courts."

During his defense before the general assembly of his editorial practice of cutting many of counsel's arguments in reprinting these volumes, see Document IV–25 (Investigation of State Printing, 1923), and in his history of official reporting in North Carolina, see Document IV–23 (Clark's History of Reprints, 1920), Chief Justice Walter Clark suggested that the practices and pricing by the reporters had been questionable, if not abusive. Clark included his "History of the Supreme Court Reports" in his reprints of volumes 2, 22, 52, 104, 115, 133, and 148 of the *North Carolina Reports*.

This account by Clark of the abolition of the office of reporter failed to describe the political climate of 1871 and vilified past reporters in bolstering Clark's legal defense. While acknowledging that antebellum reporters of decisions held copyright to the volumes they published, and without offering a firm alternative explanation of the transfer of duties of the reporter, one might note events of possible import in the transfer of the duties of reporter to the attorney general. For example, control of the legislature shifted dramatically in the fall of 1870 from the Republican Party to the Democratic Party. The code commission, a creation of the Republican initiative in the 1868 Convention, at this time lost much of its political clout, finally being abolished in 1873. The Commission on Fraud was put in motion at this time, too, attacking Commissioner Albion W. Tourgée and many other officials. Shipp, Batchelor, and Martin, *Report of the Commission to Investigate Charges of Fraud and Corruption* [. . .] *1871–'72*, 22. Gov. William Holden had just been impeached, being found guilty on March 22, 1871; while Chief Justice Richmond Pearson had barely escaped impeachment, having last been accused of the impeachable offense of public drunkenness on January 16, 1871. Ashe, *Biographical History of North Carolina*, s.v. "William Woods Holden," 3:203; Powell, *Dictionary of North Carolina Biography*, s.v. "Pearson, Richmond Mumford," 5:51.

The reporter of the opinions of the supreme court, James M. McCorkle, was an employee of the court (and thus closely associated with Chief Justice Pearson) and one of Holden's attorneys during the impeachment trial. Additionally, McCorkle was a prominent Republican himself, as evidenced by the record of Congress's investigation into the state of affairs in the South. See *Testimony Taken [...] to Inquire into the Condition of Affairs in [...] North Carolina*, 332: "There was, though, an idea among the members of the bar that Judge Logan would resign; and he has been advised to resign by prominent republicans. The supreme court advised him to resign. Judge Pearson moved, in a meeting in Governor Caldwell's office at Raleigh, that Judge Logan be advised to resign. Mr. McCorkle, a prominent republican of Salisbury, told me in Raleigh, some time ago, that it was the intention of the individual members of the supreme court to advise Judge Logan to resign. Mr. Bynam, who is a very prominent republican in the county, signed this petition to the legislature; and so did General Barringer. It is the universal belief that Judge Logan is incompetent; and it is also, I think, the general belief that he is corrupt."

McCorkle also served as secretary to the "meeting of the bench and bar of North Carolina," which, "[i]n accordance with previous notice, a considerable number of the Judges and Attorneys of the State met in the Senate Chamber at 2 o'clock P.M., of the 16th instant." Document III–23 (Meeting of Bench and Bar, December 24, 1868) and Document III–25 (Meeting of Bench and Bar, January 8, 1869).

Beyond being a prominent Republican just when that party was losing its sway, and beyond being so strongly associated with public figures who were the subject of fierce attack by the general assembly, it may also be significant that Reporter McCorkle was new to office, having replaced Samuel F. Phillips in the very year the office of reporter was abolished. Phillips himself was a Radical Republican who was associated strongly with the reviled code commissioner, Albion W. Tourgée. Phillips's term of office as reporter was 1866–1870, after which he ran against William M. Shipp, Democrat, for the office of attorney general. Powell, *Dictionary of North Carolina Biography*, s.v. "Phillips, Samuel Field," 5:93. Shipp won that close race. During 1871, Shipp chaired the Commission on Fraud. Powell, *Dictionary of North Carolina Biography*, s.v. "Shipp, William Marcus," 5:337. In February 1872, the general assembly assigned to Shipp the duties of reporter of decisions of the Supreme Court of North Carolina.

In short, the general assembly may have expressed its disapproval of the reporters, Phillips and McCorkle, of Chief Justice Pearson, or even of the supreme court itself—now secured from interference by the general assembly by the state constitution of 1868—by removing one of the traditional offices of the judiciary from the court's control. Alternatively, the general assembly might have moved the office of reporter in order to reduce the number of state offices when the state debt was severe—so severe it had caused the creation of the Commission on Fraud (Document III–33 (Call for Convention, 1869–70)). Since the Attorney General was a state officer required to attend every argument of the supreme court, perhaps the expense of a second state officer attending court could be spared.

Both politics and economics, then, may serve as alternative explanations for the elimination of the office of reporter to Clark's suggestion of the reporters' seeking profits by unnecessarily increasing the page count of reports.

440. Document IV–23 (Clark's History of Reprints, 1920); Document IV–25 (Investigation of State Printing, 1923).
441. The authority for *Battle's Revisal* is found in two acts: An Act to Provide a Compilation of the Public Statutes, ch. 210, *Public Laws [...] Passed by the General Assembly [...] 1871–'72*, 373. [1871–'72 N.C. Laws 373], and An Act to Provide for the Printing and Publication of "Battle's Revisal" of the Public Statute Laws of North Carolina, and for Other Purposes, ch. 74, *Public Laws and Resolutions [...] Passed by the General Assembly [...] 1871–'72*, 92–96. [1872–'73 N.C. Laws 92]
442. Document III–6 (Constitution, April 21–23, 1868).
443. Document IV–11 (Hinsdale on Codification, 1900): "The value [of *Battle's Revisal*] was seriously impaired by reason of the failure of the General Assembly to enact the Revisal in one Statute and repeal all acts not therein contained. See State vs. Cunningham, 72-469."; State *v.* G. W. Cunningham in Hargrove, *Cases Argued and Determined in the Supreme Court [...] January Term, 1875*, 477. [72 N.C. 469, 477 (1875) (Bynum, J.)]: the court read section two of the act for the "printing and publication" of the revisal as repealing only those public statutes digested by Battle in his revisal and noted that "the Revisal never passed through the process of legislative scrutiny and enactment."
444. This act relied upon an act of 1872. An Act to Alter the Constitution of North Carolina, ch. 53, *Public Laws [...] Passed by the General Assembly [...] 1871–'72*, 81. [1871–'72 N.C. Pub. Laws 81] (ratified January 19, 1872).

445. On August 7, 1873, the vote to approve the constitutional amendment to disband the code commission was 70,315 to 20,080. Cheney, *North Carolina Government*, 872.
446. Document III–5 (Code Commissioners, March 13, 1868).
447. While it is unclear whether the scope of "methods of proceeding" in the 1875 amendment is narrower or coextensive with the scope of "practice and procedure" under the 1868 constitution, presumably its scope is not broader, as the people had reacted in 1873 against the complete textual control of adjective law by the general assembly when they amended the constitution to eliminate the code commission. Even if "methods of proceeding" were coextensive with "practice and procedure," though, the scope of the former expression remains unclear because the scope of the latter expression is arbitrary. Certainly, civil procedure and criminal procedure fell within the purview of practice and procedure in 1868, as the 1868 Ordinance said so in describing the new code of practice to be drafted by the code commission. But why did the 1868 Ordinance omit the law of evidence from its description of this new code of practice? The field of evidence was classified as adjective law by nineteenth-century codifiers, but presumably the convention in North Carolina omitted evidence from its code of practice because the legislature in New York had failed to adopt a code of evidence along with its Field Code. Reppy, "Field Codification Concept," 35–36, 45. Field had included the law of evidence as Part IV of his revision of December 31, 1849. Field, "The Code of Civil Procedure of the State of New-York," *New York Field Codes*, 1:4. Apparently, no amendments or recommendations in North Carolina pertinent to practice in the courts below the supreme court explicitly mentioned evidence until after a code of evidence was adopted by the general assembly in 1983. Medlin, *Without Favor, Denial or Delay*, 33–34.

While the 1868 Ordinance probably envisioned complete legislative control of "practice and procedure," and the 1875 Ordinance permitted legislative interference with "methods of proceeding" as necessary, a 1962 amendment to the constitution allowed the general assembly to make rules of "procedure and practice" (or to delegate that authority to the supreme court), thus virtually returning to the 1868 description of the scope of this provision, whatever that scope may have been in the interim. Not long after ratification of the 1962 amendment, the legislature delegated to the Supreme Court the authority "to prescribe rules of practice and procedure for the Superior and District Courts supplementary to, and not inconsistent with, Acts of the General Assembly." See An Act to Create a Court of Appeals in the Appellate Division of the General Court of Justice; To Allocate Jurisdiction between the Supreme Court and the Court of Appeals; To Provide for the Retirement and Recall to Temporary Service of Certain Justices and Judges; and for Other Purposes, ch. 108, *Session Laws and Resolutions Passed by the General Assembly at the Extra Session [. . .] November 15, A.D. 1965 and the Extra Session [. . .] January 19, A.D. 1966 and the Regular Session [. . .] February 8, A.D. 1967*, 144–158. [1967 N.C. Sess. Laws 144, 151]

448. While the 1868 Ordinance perhaps envisioned complete legislative control of law (adjective and substantive law; private and public law) and the 1875 Ordinance had permitted only such legislative interference in the methods of proceeding in the courts below the supreme court as was necessary, twentieth-century constitutional initiatives on adjective law would flip and flop on the necessity of intrusion in court procedure by the general assembly:

- A 1949 report recommended that the supreme court be empowered to prescribe rules of practice and procedure, particularly rules of civil procedure, the legislature retaining a power to reject them. Ervin and Shepherd, "Report of the Commission for the Improvement of the Administration of Justice," 10.

- The North Carolina Constitutional Commission of 1958 recommended that the general assembly shall provide by law for the regulation of methods of proceeding in the inferior courts. Part II: "Text of Proposed Constitution for the State of North Carolina," in Bryant, *Report of the North Carolina Constitutional Commission*, 21. The Commission, though, would allow the general assembly to delegate this authority. Part III: "Commentary on Proposed Changes in Constitution," in *Report of the North Carolina Constitutional Commission*, 56.

- In 1962, the people amended the constitution, giving authority to the general assembly to make rules of procedure and practice for the inferior courts, as well as the ability to delegate this authority to the supreme court. An Act to Amend the Constitution of North Carolina by Rewriting Article IV Thereof and Making Appropriate Amendments of Other Articles So As to Improve the Administration of Justice in North Carolina, ch. 313, *Session Laws and Resolutions Passed by the General Assembly at the Regular Session [. . .] February, A.D. 1961*, 436–439. [1961 N.C. Sess. 436, 439]

- In 1996, the Commission for the Future of Justice and the Courts in North Carolina recommended that "authority over the rules of civil and criminal procedure, and the rules of evidence, be vested in the Supreme Court," leaving a veto power with the general assembly. See Medlin, *Without Favor, Denial or Delay*, 34; Craig, "Medlin Commission's Proposed Reforms of the Civil Justice System," 18, 20.

449. An example of such a restatement or digest of common law rules is the bill for a Code of Criminal Procedure described by the code commissioners in their Fourth Report to the general assembly in March 1870 (Document III–36 (Report of the Code Commissioners, March 1870)). This bill, apparently the second one submitted on the topic of criminal procedure, did not pass into law, but it is interesting that this "mere digest" of an area of adjective law accompanied a report that abandoned the idea of a complete codification of private law. In this same report, the commissioners justified their failure to submit any substantial amendment to improve *The Code of Civil Procedure* on the ground that the "duty can now be much better performed by the Courts than it is likely to be by the Legislature. . . ." If before its dissolution even the code commissioners had abandoned the mantra of topdown control by the legislature of adjectival law, it would not be unreasonable to interpret the intent of the people in 1875 to be based on the same retreating premise. In fact, the codifications by David Dudley Field in New York, on which North Carolina's codifications were based, involved the "digesting and restatement of the existing law," viewing "[d]eviations from this conservative policy in the form of amendment of the existing law" as merely experimental. See Reppy, "Field Codification Concept," 30.
450. Document IV–15 (Tourgée on the Common Law, 1908) (describing the difficulty for "the student or the intelligent layman" of finding unwritten law in printed books).
451. Document III–47 (Tourgée's Notes, 1878): "There were many "forms of action" at common law. In equity there was but one "form of action." Under the operation of the Constitution we have now but one form of action. . . ."
452. See generally Davis, "Reading *Smith v. Campbell*," 27.
453. Justice William B. Rodman recorded the change in the duties of the jury under reform procedure in two of his dissenting opinions: State on the relation of H. B. Armfield and another v. John D. Brown and Others, Hargrove, *Cases Argued and Determined in the Supreme Court of North Carolina, January Term, 1874*, 32–33. [70 N.C. 27, 32–33 (1874) (Rodman, J., dissenting)]: "While a jury was thought the best and safest tribunal to try one, or only a few simple issues of fact, such as were those raised by the pleadings at common law, it was thought obviously inadequate to try the numerous issues arising on a single disputed account, if complicated, or on mutual accounts. These were referred in the common law courts to auditors and in chancery to a master. This long established practice had its origin in the nature of things, and I fear our experience will show that it cannot be wisely changed."; Joseph Keener and Others v. Daniel Finger and Peter Keener, Adm'rs, Hargrove, *Cases Argued and Determined in the Supreme Court of North Carolina, January Term, 1874*, 48. [70 N.C. 35, 48 (1874) (Rodman, J., dissenting)] (citing "3 Bl. Com., chap. 20" and "3 Com. ch. 21, p. 314,"): "It is trite learning, that in actions at common law, the rules of pleading were so framed as to compel the parties by their respective allegations and denials finally to come to some single, certain and material fact, alleged on one side and denied on the other. Then the parties were said to be at issue, and the question so raised was called an issue of fact. It was called 'an issue' because it was the '*exitus*' or end of the pleadings. At common law but a single plea was allowed and there could be but a single issue."
454. Document III–47 (Tourgée's Notes, 1878): "It is somewhat remarkable that the court, by construing our constitutional provisions so as to make a jury trial in all actions a matter of right, seems likely to have overcome the only impediment hitherto unsurmounted in the development of the civil action. Mr. Pomeroy says: '*Remedies and Remedial Rights*, § 64.—Absolute unity in the judicial methods by which remedies are to be obtained, is practically impossible so long as the jury trial is required in certain classes of causes and dispensed with in others. In respect to all other features the theoretical unity is attainable.'"
455. Document III–47 (Tourgée's Notes, 1878): "I cannot refrain from again calling the attention of the profession, in this State, to the very admirable discussion of the Civil Action, given by Mr. Pomeroy in his excellent work entitled 'Remedies and Remedial Rights.' This is the only systematic work upon the Reformed Procedure, and it is not too high praise to say that no one can obtain a full knowledge of that system, in no manner so easily and well, as by the study of the work."
456. The compilers suspect that Judge Tourgée here referred to Swan, *Commentaries on Pleading under the Ohio Code*.
457. Document III–47 (Tourgée's Notes, 1878).
458. Document IV–3 (Clark's Preface, 1884).
459. Plessy v. Ferguson, Davis, *Cases Adjudged in the [United States] Supreme Court at October Term, 1895*, 537–564. [163 U.S. 537 (1896)]

460. *Journal of the Constitutional Convention [. . .] 1868*, (Friday, March 13) 438–439.
461. Olsen, *Carpetbagger's Crusade*, 132–133 (citing the letter of "Phillips to D. L. Swain, August 20, 1868, Spencer Papers"); Miller, "Samuel Field Phillips," 273n37.
462. Miller, "Samuel Field Phillips," 273n37 (referencing letters between Phillips and Tourgée of May 12, 1873 and June 20, 1874 found in the Tourgée Papers, Collection No. 870, Southern Historical Collection.)
463. The address in the *North Carolina Reports* described "Lucien Holmes" as of the "Wilmington Bar," while an address in the proceedings of the bar association described "Mr. Lucien Holmes" as the "head of the Sampson bar," which raises the question of whether the two references describe the same person. The birth and death dates used in this compilation for "Mr. Hardy Lucien Holmes" were taken from Bizzell, *Heritage of Sampson County*. In the history of the University of North Carolina, a graduate of the class of 1817 named "Hardy Lucian Holmes" is identified as being from "Sampson Co." and is said to be "a well-known lawyer." Battle, *History of the University of North Carolina*, 1:789.
464. Ashe, "Presentation of the Portrait of Hon. George Davis," in Strong, *Cases Argued and Determined in the Supreme Court [. . .] Fall Term, 1915 (in part)*, 801–823.
465. Document II–7 (Bentham's Letter, 1817).
466. Document III–47 (Tourgée's Notes 1878) (describing the abolition of the distinction between actions at law and suits in equity in the comment under section 12).
467. Manning, *Commentaries on Blackstone*.
468. Battle wrote about the link of the library to sound law in the context of the supreme court's summer sessions in Morganton. See Battle, "Address on the History of the Supreme Court," 485: "In 1846 the lawyers of the western portion of the State induced the General Assembly to order a term of the Court to be held in Morganton on the first Monday in August for all cases in the counties west of Stokes, Davidson, Union, Stanly and Montgomery, and for cases from these counties, with consent of both parties. The experiment was not satisfactory to the Court or to the profession. Owing to a want of a law library, 'Morganton decisions,' as they were called, were regarded as less certainly sound than those at Raleigh." For a short overview of the Morganton Term, see Davis, "Summer Session," 12.
469. An Act in Relation to the Public Library, ch. 70, § 3, *Public Laws [. . .] Passed by the General Assembly [. . .] 1870–'71*, 134. [1870–'71 N.C. Pub. Laws 133, 134].
470. In 1873, William H. Battle completed a commission for a revisal of the state's public laws, but the general assembly neither enacted it as a single statute, nor repealed all acts not contained therein. Document III–44 (Battle's Report on Revisal, 1872).
471. Document III–47 (Tourgée's Notes, 1878).
472. Bacon, preface to *Works of Francis Bacon*, 3:221: "I hold every man a debtor to his profession; from the which, as men of course do seek to receive countenance and profit, so ought they of duty to endeavour themselves, by way of amends, to be a help and ornament thereunto."
473. Document IV–5 (Field to Clark, 1892).
474. Clark, "Address of Chief Justice Clark on Reform in Law and Legal Procedure," in Davis, *Proceedings of the Sixteenth Annual Session of the North Carolina Bar Association*, 59.
475. Clark, "Supreme Court of North Carolina," 524; Clark, "History of the Supreme Court of North Carolina," in Strong, *Cases Argued and Determined in the Supreme Court [. . .] Spring Term, 1919*, 623.
476. Document III–43 (Supreme Court Reporter Abolished, 1872).
477. James Manning (1859–1938) was John Manning's second son. James was a lawyer who, among his many accomplishments, finished an unexpired term on the state supreme court and served as state attorney general. Powell, *Dictionary of North Carolina Biography*, s.v. "Manning, James Smith," 4:213.
478. Document IV–9 (Clark's Preface, 1895).
479. Document IV–6 (Clark's Preface, 1892).
480. Document IV–3 (Clark's Preface, 1884).
481. Carter, "Proposed Codification of Our Common Law," 92: "I will not stop to answer the insincere assertion that if the law be written in a Code laymen can comprehend it and become their own lawyers."; Thomas M. Cooley, preface to *Commentaries on the Laws of England*, 1:xxvii: "Any expectation which may have existed, that the code was to banish technicality and substitute such simplicity that any man of common understanding was to be competent, without legal training, to present his case in due form of law, has not been realized."; Grimké, "An Oration of the Practicability and Expedience of Reducing the Whole Body of the Law to the Simplicity of a Code," in Miller, *Legal Mind in America*, 158 (suggesting that while codification will not make every man his own lawyer, it will aid educated

men in their "public and private usefulness"); Document–16 (Taylor's Preface, 1824): "... opening to all descriptions of persons, a ready access to the knowledge they seek...."; Document II–44 (Swaim's Preface, 1841): "... to render every man his own counselor in matters of business.").

482. Carter, "Proposed Codification of Our Common Law," 16–21.

483. Clarke, *Science of Law and Lawmaking*, 449: "... Statute Law should be confined to such questions as are: first, of no ethical importance; or second, changes in ethical rules laid down by mistake; or third, questions of convenience...."

484. Commissioners Womack, Gulley, and Rodman probably meant in 1905 that the list of forty-six bills appended to the code commission report of 1869, see Document III–29 (Report of the Code Commissioners, March 20, 1869), pointed to "codifications" of statute law on various subjects, rather than to codifications of statute and common law on those subjects. Whether these acts did go beyond statutory codification is a question for further study. For instance, one might compare the eighteenth listed bill, proceedings in habeas corpus, which became law in the 1868–1869 session as chapter 116, with the lengthy chapter on the same subject in the *Revised Code* of 1854 and with the common law precedents on that subject. One might supplement that comparison with study of a bill meant for the planned civil code and with one meant for the planned political code, such as the thirty-seventh listed item, an act concerning the powers and duties of state officers, which passed into law during the same session as chapter 270, and the forty-second listed item, an act concerning guardian and ward, which passed into law during that session as chapter 201. Whatever the conclusion drawn from such an endeavor, it seems unlikely that one could fairly describe these forty-six acts as comprising an entire civil code or an entire political code in displacement of statute and common law on those dense subjects, as the code commission's bill for a penal code, see Document III–32 (Bill for a Penal Code, 1869), could be fairly described as having attempted. If David Dudley Field was accurate when writing to Walter Clark in 1892, see Document IV–5 (Field to Clark, 1892), North Carolina had not adopted during Reconstruction all the codes prepared in New York. The code commissioners themselves say in 1869, see Document III–29 (Report of the Code Commissioners, March 20, 1869), that they aimed with these forty-six acts "[t]o bring the body of our civil and political law, including appropriate modes of proceeding therein, into harmony with the organic changes of the Constitution and the existing judicial order of the State[, seeking] to depart as little as possible from the 'old paths, which is the good way,' either in the substance or in the language of the Statutes...."

485. See generally Davis, "From Aristocracy to Democracy," 226n53.

486. Womack, "Report of the Committee on Legislation and Law Reform," in Biggs, *Proceedings of the Seventh Annual Meeting of the North Carolina Bar Association*, 68: "[T]he last Legislature enacted more general public statutes than any previous Legislature in the twenty-two years since the Code [of North Carolina, Enacted March 2, 1883."

487. Perhaps Judge Winston is here inspired in part also by the code commissioners themselves, who in their report of 1870, see Document III–36 (Report of the Code Commissioners, March 1870), had argued that further amendment of *The Code of Civil Procedure* "can now be much better performed by the Courts than . . . by the Legislature...."

488. Compare Chief Justice Clark's recommendation here in 1914 for American jurisdictions to abandon judicial review with Dean Roscoe Pound's observation about the desire of European jurisdictions to adopt that practice. Document IV–22 (Pound on the Common Law, 1920): "Moreover, the characteristic common law institution, the supremacy of law, in the form in which it has reached its highest development in America, is commending itself to the most diverse peoples, when they find themselves living under written constitutions. Thus . . . we find continental publicists lamenting that their polity does not provide for judicial interpretation of their constitutions."

489. See generally Davis, "From Aristocracy to Democracy," 216.

490. McIntosh served as instructor at this time on the Trinity College law faculty (later re-founded as the Duke School of Law). In 1910, he joined the faculty of the UNC School of Law as a professor. "Atwell Campbell McIntosh."

491. Document IV–14 (Revisal's Preface, 1905).

492. Clark included his essay on the history of the supreme court reports and reprints in eight of his reprint volumes, each printing of the essay carrying a date. The eight volume numbers of the reprints, and the dates of the essays' printings, are: 163 (May 1, 1918), 52 (August 1, 1920), 104 (December 1, 1920), 148 (December 1, 1920), 115 (January 1, 1921), 2 (September 1, 1921), 133 (September 1, 1921), and 22 (May 1, 1922).

493. Clark's apology did not convince everyone familiar with the reprint project. See, for example, Edwards & Broughton Printing Company, "Answer of Edwards and Broughton Printing Company to Clark Memorandum," in *In the Matter of the Investigation of State Printing*, 68: "The position of Judge Clark that the act of the Legislature in 1885 required that the paging of the reprint should be marginal, justifies some condensation or omissions, is in our opinion an unsound, improper, and unreasonable construction of the Act."; Document IV–25 (Investigation into State Printing,

1923): "We [the investigative joint committee of the general assembly] recommend that legislation be enacted which will prevent the omission of any part of the original matter from any reports to be hereafter reprinted, except the briefs of Counsel which were contained in the older reports. . . ."

494. For Dean Mordecai's use of "proper-gander" in describing Chief Justice Clark's attack on the works of Sir William Blackstone and Sir Edward Coke on the common law, see Document IV–19 (Clark/Mordecai Exchange, 1917).

495. Clark does not specify whether the abusive practices of the reporters had been undertaken by future chief justice Thomas Ruffin, Reverend Francis Hawks, or former governor James Iredell Jr., all of whom had held the office of reporter in the court's early years. Or perhaps Clark confined his attack to the reporters who held office during Reconstruction, such as Samuel F. Phillips, who later served as Solicitor General of the United States and who sat as second chair for defendant in Plessy v. Ferguson, Davis, *Cases Adjudged in the [United States] Supreme Court at October Term, 1895*, 537–564. [163 U.S. 537 (1896)] or James M. McCorkle, who held the office of reporter in 1871 and published just one volume of the reports before his duties were transferred to the attorney general. Clark does point to volumes 63, 64, and 65 of the *North Carolina Reports*—these volumes reported by Phillips and then McCorkle—as examples of excessive printing of the record and of counsel's arguments to up the page count in order to increase profit, but the reporting of full arguments of counsel was not new to these two reporters (see, for example, Document II–38 (Moore's Argument, 1834)) and the price per page they charged was no more than pre-Civil War prices, see note 439.

496. For a discussion of law declaration within the discovery theory of law, see note 14.

497. See Document IV–23 (Clark's History of Reprints, 1920) and notes 493–495 for Clark's defense of his editorial work on the *North Carolina Reports* and for evidence of skepticism of that defense by some of his opponents. For political and economic factors that might suggest a defense of the reporters of opinions of the supreme court against Clark's suggestion, see note 439.

498. In his autobiography, Judge Winston also touched upon the life of Walter Clark, describing the chief justice, in Winston, *It's a Far Cry*, 174–176: as "the North Carolina puzzle, a man without emotion and without friendship."

499. This story about President Taft's remark is also recorded by Gov. Thomas Bickett in a speech from June 26, 1920. House, *Public Letters and Papers of Thomas Walter Bickett*, 313: "At a banquet given him in the city of Durham, Ex-President Taft said in the presence of Judge Clark that he would not be willing to trust the Chief Justice with the Constitution over night."

500. This story about Chief Justice White's remark is also recorded in Winston's autobiography. See Winston, *It's a Far Cry*, 174.

501. Mordecai, *Mordecai's Miscellanies*, 3.

502. See, for example, Bell, *Report of the Committee on Improving and Expediting the Administration of Justice in North Carolina* (popularly known as the "Bell Commission").

503. See, for example, Bryant, *Report of North Carolina Constitutional Commission* (popularly known as the "Bryant Commission").

504. "Political Constitutions (October 1847)," in Brownson, *Works in Political Philosophy*, 3:232: "The commons alone emigrated [at the colonization of the states], and consequently our constitution recognized only commons. When, therefore, the foreign authority [Britain] was thrown off, and we were left to our own constitution, we had only the government of the commons, that is to say, the representative democracy, or the elective aristocracy, if we may use the term, which we brought here from the mother country. Our government is simply the British house of commons, without the king and house of lords, divided for the sake of convenience into an upper and lower chamber, and with such few changes and modifications as were necessary to provide for an executive authority. . . ."

505. Davis, "From Aristocracy to Democracy," 215, 222n38.

506. Document IV–4 (Battle's History, 1889). Perhaps the observation that the 1868 Constitution presumes untrustworthy representatives shows that document to be an assault on the notion of an "elective aristocracy," see note 504, and a demand that the representatives abide by the weight of the public opinion of their electors, see note 62, rather than by the experience and judgment of the representatives on behalf of their electors.

507. Davis, "From Aristocracy to Democracy," 226nn52–53.

508. See generally Davis, "School Days." For a short treatise tracing the history of a locally-developed study aid for *Blackstone's Commentaries*, see Orth, *Tree of Legal Knowledge*.

509. Document IV–20 (Winston's Speech, 1919): "Statutes have no roots, we are taught, but judicial decisions are seldom without them." The English statutes inherited with the colonial common law in 1776, and absorbed in *The Revised Statutes of the State of North Carolina* in 1837, see Document II–43 (Revised Statutes' Preface, 1837), were essentially

alterations of the common law designed to preserve and defend its principles, see note 64, rather than rootless scientific social initiatives designed to enlighten society, its government, and its law on how to progress beyond the common law tradition.

510. The increased volume of legislation is alluded to in Document IV–14 (Revisal's Preface, 1905): "The volume of legislation in the last twenty-two years, the period covered by our labors, made it impracticable to publish the work in one volume." In discussing the course of study for law students, Judge Winston, at a meeting of the state bar association in 1901, alluded to the continual changes made to the state's statute laws. Biggs, *Report of the Fifth Annual Meeting of the North Carolina Bar Association*, 22: "The statute law of a State changes with each changing wind, to teach it to the young aspiring law student, lowers his ideals and makes of him a mere clerk."

511. Document II–60 (About Chief Justice Taylor (1769–1829)).

512. Document III–11 (The Judicial System, July 29, 1868).

513. Document III–33 (Call for Convention, 1869–1870) (quoting *McFaul v. Ramsey*, 61 U.S. 523, 525 (1857)). In order to defend the thesis that a refusal to descend to the multiplicity of species characterized the "sciolist" methodology, one would have to distinguish the multiplicity of statutory special proceedings, which along with the statutory "civil action" falls under the constitutional "civil action" of reform procedure, see Document III–47 (Tourgée's Notes, 1878) (discussing special proceedings in section 6), from the multiplicity of the common law forms of action, and would have to account for the multiplicity of motions under reform procedure, see Document IV–15 (Tourgée on the Common Law, 1908).

514. Document IV–4 (Battle's History, 1889).

515. Document III–33 (Call for Convention, 1869–1870). The *Report of the Special Committee*, excerpted in Document III–33 (Call for Convention, 1869–1870), includes this paragraph:

> A very large portion of our citizens, who voted to ratify our present Constitution, did not approve many of its prominent features. But we were in an anomalous and disagreeable position. A restoration of the State to the Union, and relief from the yoke of military government, were ardently longed for. These happy results were expected to follow a ratification of the Constitution; so shutting their eyes to its faults, stopping their ears to objections, and preferring *any* form of civil government to military, the majority voted to ratify it, with the general expectation and intention of having it amended soon. The necessity of its amendment is now apparent to a very great majority of the people, without respect to party or race. They desire a constitution more in conformity with their circumstances and their true spirit and character. The people of North Carolina have always been distinguished for the simplicity of their tastes, their frugality and economy, their honesty and integrity, their scorn of empty pretension, and their sturdy independence. They ought to have a system of internal government in accord with these characteristics; and this they will have, if they are permitted to come together and make a government for themselves, the true type and embodiment of their own genius, instead of having a government made for them.

516. Regarding efforts to disband the code commission, see Document III–37 (New Code Commissioner, July 30, 1870), Document III–38 (Bill Dissolving Code Commission, September 29, 1870), and Document III–45 (Constitutional Amendment Dissolving Code Commission, 1873). On the misleading aspect of Battle's characterization of the "Constitution of 1876," consider that even if the 1875 constitutional convention did no more than offer amendments to the 1868 Constitution, the state constitution as it stood in 1876 consolidated not only the thirty amendments of the convention that the people had ratified, but also the eight amendments that the people had overwhelmingly ratified in 1873, at least one of which, the amendment abolishing the code commission, significantly altered the 1868 Constitution.

517. Document IV–23 (Clark's History of Reprints, 1920).

Index

The excerpted documents have not been indexed. Most of the front matter, all of the compiler's remarks, the epigraphs, the afterword, and the notes have been indexed.

A

Acts of assembly: colonial, 22, 26–28, 30, 357n237; concerning roads, bridges, and ferries, 81; early 18th-century, xvii; N.C. followed N.Y. in codifying its, xxiii; revisal and consolidation of the, 16, 26, 80

Adams, Secretary of State John Quincy, 54

Adams, Justice William J., xxii, 42, 233, 283

Adjectival law, 135, 362n333, 372n449

Amendment of constitutions, 128, 363nn347–348

American Revolution, 33, 293, 346n97, 349n145, 364n354

Anarchy, 22, 338n12

Anglican(s), 128, 293, 363nn350, 354

Anglicanism, 128, 363n350

Anne, Queen, 9, 13, 22, 348n111. *See also* Queen's Peace

Anson County, 364n367

Aquinas, [Thomas], 335n6

Aristocracy, xiii, 20, 375nn504, 506

Aristophanes, 337n11

Aristotle, 338n13

Ashe, Samuel, 136, 350–351n161

Attorney(s): the common man might be his own, 110; conservative, 89; continued to abuse and distress the people, 31; distrust of, xxi, 3, 17, 43, 46; early opinions on code pleading cause difficulty for contemporary, xxii; fees, 349n132; firebrand, 75; good moral character was expected of, 366n397; during impeachment trial of governor, 370n439; named, 77, 78, 83, 91, 114, 123, 127, 130, 159, 163, 342n60; practicing, xiii; reading law under an established, 76; select group of, 27; were not permitted to attend biannual meetings of judges of superior courts, 43, 46. *See also* Lawyer(s)

Attorney general: duties of court reporter were transferred to the, 194, 245, 369n439, 375n495; named, 91, 360n292, 369–370nn438–439, 373n477; U.S., 51

Austin, John, 254, 336n7

B

Bacon, Sir Francis, 241, 337n11, 373n472

Badger, George, 78, 83, 130

Baltimore, Lord, 344n79

Bar: admission to the, 162, 348–349n132; association, 235, 251, 282, 291, 373n463; attention of, to *The Code of Procedure*, 198; control of, in colonial N.C., 348n132; diligence of the, 369n439; as an efficient agency for justice, 275; examination, 366n397; leader of the, 127; members of the, 120, 369–370n439; protests against the, 17; qualifications for the, 233, 293. *See also* North Carolina Bar Association

Barringer, Victor C.: advocated the adoption of an inflexible "state code," 156; drafted the bill for a penal code in N.C., 167–169; pictured, front cover; resigned from the code commission, 185; signed a petition advising a judge to resign, 369–370n439; was replaced on the code commission, 183

Battle, Kemp Plummer: believed that good government is by slow growth, 239, 241; characterized the 1876 constitution, 295, 376n516; noticed that law must be naturally concomitant with the society it characterizes, 6; quote by, concerning the supreme court, 335n1; wrote about the link between the library and sound law, 373n468

Battle, Judge William Horn: assisted in the development of the state's common law, 122, 125, 362n333; attributed a historical sketch to a former governor, 349n149; characterized the 1876 constitution, 376n516; description of, 362n328; marked off the realms of legislature and supreme court in an opinion, 126; pictured, 125; prepared reports, 95, 195, 368–369n431; published a revisal of N.C. statute law, xiii, 26–27, 195, 373n470; served as a code commissioner, 115, 373n470; served as reporter of opinions of the supreme court, 369n439; treated English case law as the persuasive authority in N.C., 122; wrote a memoir about a chief justice of the state supreme court, 126, 128

Bayard v. Singleton, 31, 350nn160–161, 351nn163–164

Bench and bar: *The Code of Civil Procedure* was adopted against the wishes of the, 271; declaring law as a concept, 369n439; going against the opinions of the leading lights of the N.C., 79; interpretation of the code by the, 340; meetings of the, 159, 161, 366n390, 369–370n439; might induce legal rules, 76; placed a high value on the "writtenness of law," xiii; skipped phase of procedural law reform became a flashpoint for the, xxiii

Bentham, Jeremy: attempted to frame a *de novo* code for people, 6; extended the scientific principle into law and morals, 338–339n16; introduced the term "procedure," 365n377; objected to the arbitrary distinction between common law and equity jurisdiction, 254; offered his services as a codifier, xiii, xxv, 341n50; rejected Mansfield's liberties in common law judging, 230; views of, differed from contemporaries, 337n8, 353n194; was dissatisfied with the court administration and substantive law of 18th-century England, 335n3; was enamored with codification, 126; wrote a letter to the N.C. governor, 53; wrote publications, 54

Berman, Harold J., 292
Bickett, Gov. Thomas, 375n499
Biggs, Asa, 118
Bill of rights, 349n136
Bishop, Joel, 346n97
"Black Codes," 137, 139, 364n364, 365n369. *See also* "Freedmen's Code"
Blackstone, Sir William: attack on the works of, 375n494; classical common law was articulated by, xxi; considered the American colonies to be conquered territories, 346n97; influence in American legal education by, 270; inspired the drive for legislative reform of the law, 353n194; presented a rational synthesis of the English common law, 230, 341n52; restated the unwritten law of England in a treatise, 54, 156; saw in English law the embodiment of the law of nature, 337n8; work of, among the post-Reformation epitomes of the common law, 283; work of, was a monument of English common law, 290
Blackstone's Commentaries on the Laws of England, 73, 168, 230, 246, 293, 337n8
Bracton (treatise), 344n80, 356n222
Branch, Gov. John, 54, 59
Breem, W. W. S., 358n245
British Empire, 246
British Parliament, 352n179
British statutes: Americanization of colonial acts and, 26; repeal of the, 15, 55, 348n125; still in force were compiled under state authority, 36, 95; a table listing the, 64; were divided into two periods, 56
Brownson, Orestes Augustus, xii, 171, 342–343n66, 345n87, 352n179, 359n287
Bryan, James West, 77
Buncombe County, 81
Burke, Edmund, 335n6
Bynum, Mr., 370n439

C
Caldwell, David Franklin, xiii, 193
Cantwell, Edward, 123
Carolina Law Repository, 51, 353n193, 357n228
Carter, James Coolidge, Esq., xx, xxiv, 244, 251
Cartesianism. *See* Descartes
Caswell, Richard, 349n134
Catholic Church, xx
Catholicism, 128, 342n66
Charles I, 343n72
Charles II, 3, 22
Charleton, Jasper, 2
"Chimney corner law," 135, 163, 340n33
Chitty, 120
Christianity, 3, 70, 337n9
Church of England, 17
Circuits, 59, 73

Civil law, 238
Civil procedure: calls for stricter attitudes about, 123; code of, 145, 185, 188, 198, 199, 366n390; code commissioners had success at the general assembly with their codes of, 168; codification of, xxv, 167, 232, 244; fell within the purview of practice and procedure, 371n447; increase in the number of opinions relating to, 244; newly adopted code of, 366n390; objection to the vast change in, 160; questions of, 291; reform of, in N.Y., xxiii; rules of, 371n448; scientific arrangement of, 164; simple system of, 249; supreme court was empowered to prescribe rules of, 371n448. *See also Code of Civil Procedure, The*
Clark, Associate/Chief Justice Walter: addressed the bar association, 249, 266; adopted the voice of the reformer, 244; agitated for further reform in the administration of law, 239; appeared before a legislative committee investigating state printing, 282; assessed that court procedure was inefficient and obsolete, 239; attacked reporters of appellate opinions, 343n69; biography of, 286; continued annotated version of amended code of civil procedure, 227, 244; described common law procedure, 246; description of, 287, 375n498; edited many of the reprints of the *North Carolina Reports*, 194, 279; fought to undermine reverence for common law and to promote codification of private substantive law, 295, 340n34; letters to and from, 245, 270, 271, 374n484; pictured, 243; published digested cases about reform procedure in N.C., 241; quotes by, xx, 238; recommended that American jurisdictions abandon judicial review, 374n488; revived the notion of codification, xxii, xxiii; suggested a legislative motive to abolish the supreme court reporter office, 194; suggested that practices and pricing by reporters had been questionable, 369–370n439, 375n495; was radically contemptuous of legal tradition, 342n60
Clarke, Professor Richard Floyd, 251
Clerk of the superior court, xxii
Code of Civil Procedure of North Carolina, to Special Proceedings, The (1868): adoption of, 163, 271; amendments to, 159, 181, 372n449, 374n487; changing powers of the clerk under, 340n26; clarification of, 144; committee considered changes to, 161; description of, 228; inaugurates a complete revolution in the system of practice and proceeding in courts, 134; legislature suspended parts of, 160; meeting of the bench and bar regarding, 159; modified when executions were returnable, 161; need of today's lawyers to gain understanding of the state's, xxii; opposition to, xiii, 193; original intent of, 266; page from, pictured, 209; perhaps anyone could be his own lawyer before adoption of, 111; preface of, reveals the hastiness of its preparation, 152, 185; regulated too many details, 262; remained in force, 197; support for, 163
Code commission: authority for, placed in the judicial article of the constitution, 143; drafted modern rules of

practice and procedure, 141; elimination of the, 158, 183–185, 196, 197, 239, 295, 369n439, 371nn445–447, 376n516; establishment of the, xxv, 135, 367n404; members of the, 198, 347n100; moderated excesses of the general assembly, 156; opposition to the, 152, 158; report of the, 374n484; resolution concerning the, 366n395; the scope of codification of the common law was left to the discretion of the, 181; sent a bill to the senate, 368n422; strong tie between procedural codification accomplished in N.Y. and N.C.'s, 146; successfully introduced codifications of civil and criminal procedure, xxv

Code commissioners: bills submitted to the general assembly by, 367n406; contempt for the, 150; copied language from N.Y.'s code in the report to the general assembly, 142, 146, 153; did not attempt to codify portions of the common law understood to be private law, 168; discussed amending *The Code of Civil Procedure*, 372n449, 374n487; handwritten report of, pictured, 192; the last report made by the, 369n432; named, 145, 146, 152, 167–169, 183, 185, 188, 195, 227–229, 239, 240, 245, 254, 347n100, 368n424, 368n430, 369–370n439, 374n484; pictured, front cover; questions surrounding the scope of codification engaged by, 155, 156, 252, 341n41; quotes by and about, xii, 134, 135, 163, 164, 185, 238, 342n63, 365n376, 368n431, 374n484; recommended changes to existing statute law, 139; reported to the general assembly, 168, 181, 185, 188; responsibilities of the, 136, 137, 141–142, 144, 178, 293; were challenged by a senate resolution to account for their time, 178; were guaranteed a reasonable compensation under the Constitution of 1868, 365n370; were ousted by constitutional amendment before they could codify private substantive law, xxiii; were requested not to abolish the common law and equity, 366n390

Code of criminal procedure: a bill for a, 188, 372n449; fell within the purview of practice and procedure in 1868, 371n447; remained in force, 197; successful introduction of a, xxv; was submitted to the general assembly, 178, 181. *See also* Crime

Code of New York, 153

Code pleading: adjustment to, 233; amendments to, 282; civil action of, 295; a code commission was established to adopt, 135; displaced the certitude of common law pleading and practice, 287, 293; father of, 198; introduction of, 134; many opinions issued in the first decade under, were criticized, 340n29; might make all persons their own lawyers, 249, 373n481; opponents, 287; perhaps promoted litigation, 199; promoted common sense and justice, 199; provisions for, were hastily prepared for publication, 152; role of clerk of court in, 340n26; still required how-to books, 199; support for, 271; views of, 271, 287; was compared to common law pleading, 184, 198, 199; was foreign to jurists and practitioners in late 1868, xxii

Codification: of adjectival law and substantive law, 135; caused a great increase in the rate of publishing volumes of reported opinions, 244; of common law, xxiii, xxv, xxvi, 6, 43, 89, 141, 142, 156, 181, 252; common law precedents were gradually being displaced by, 283; debates, 15, 17, 53, 57, 116, 130, 135, 146, 339n23; of the entire body of the laws, 238, 361n312, 362n331; of fundamental public law, 128, 129; had passed into a practical reality, 244; jurisprudential sea-change toward, 335n3; legislative, 181, 239; mild critics of, 6, 118, 272, 291; opposition to, 158, 167, 250, 251, 345n90, 362n321, 365n372; of private and substantive law, 135, 168, 188, 266, 293, 340n34, 372n449; of procedural law, 146, 171, 197, 232, 245, 367n416; question as to the scope of, 155; radical side of the movement for, 78, 82–83; reform and, xxi, 4, 343n70; scientifically rational, 230; simplification of the law through, 36, 99, 149, 193, 373n481; statutory, 43, 50, 63, 84, 97, 107, 188, 233, 252, 274, 293, 339n21, 340n30, 341n39, 374n484; support for, xiii, 51, 111, 123, 126, 135, 160, 193, 335n3, 337n9, 340n32, 366n385, 366n394; views on, xiii, xxii, 78, 82–83, 366n390, 366n394; was based on that of N.Y., 153, 168, 244, 365n372, 365n381

Coke, Sir Edward: attack on the works of, 375n494; described classical common law in the seventeenth century, xxi; influence of, on American legal education, 270; phrase of, 336n7; post-Reformation epitomes of, 283; treatises of, were viewed as a less rigid code, 156; was referenced, 155, 168, 366n393, 367n413

Colonial acts/laws. *See* Acts of assembly

Colored people/free people of color, 116, 136, 137, 365n369. *See also* Freedmen

Commission on Fraud, 369–370n439

Commission for the Future of Justice and the Courts in North Carolina, 372n448

Common law: an act authorized commissioners to revise, digest, alter, and amend all the statute and, 42; codification of, xxii, xxiii, xxv, 6, 43, 51, 83, 128, 155, 156, 178, 181, 251, 252, 341n39, 361n312, 364n359, 365n372, 374n484; colonial, xxvi, 20, 26, 375n509; description of, 116, 122; development of, 43, 44, 72, 117, 125, 126; English, xxv, xxvi, 30, 74, 233, 290, 342n64, 357n236; may be altered and supplemented by judicious legislation, xx; mystery taken out of the, 76; opposition to, 73, 111; and positive laws must harmonize with and acquiesce in divine law and the law of nature, 86; practice, 118; principles and rules of, 63, 70, 90, 115, 116, 122, 126, 127; professionals, 78; relation of statute law and, 130; revision of, 95; statutory displacement of, 51, 82; tradition, xxi, xxvi, 4, 75, 241, 336n7, 344n80, 376n509; was in force in N.C., 9, 10, 15, 18, 22, 345n95, 346n97, 347n98; was known as unwritten law, xx, xxii, xxiv, xxv, 6, 22, 54, 56, 155, 238, 251, 335n3, 346–347n97, 367n405, 372n450; who shall put in execution, 17; worship of custom by, blamed for toleration of slavery, 85; written law and, 31

Common law pleading: in antebellum probate matters, 184; appreciation of the certitude of, 287; elimination/repeal of, xxv, 120, 135, 141, 185; English, 361n313; entailed many forms of action, 198, 295; hope for restoration of, 158; jury tried a single issue of fact raised by, 372n453; loose practice of, in N.C. perhaps allowed persons to be their own lawyers on some matters, 111, 361n313; perhaps could not speak to non-professionals like the code of civil procedure could, 198; replacement of, with code pleading, 285, 293; scholasticism of, 89; should not be abandoned for code pleading, 120; some aspects of, were better understood by laypersons than was code pleading, 184; stricter enforcement of, 111; views of/opinions about, 31, 89, 111, 134, 199, 287, 361n313; was invented by sciolists, 171

Conservative(s), 63, 89, 127, 245, 367n416, 372n449

Constitution of North Carolina (1776): a declaration of rights was prepended to the, 19, 20, 70, 128, 295; defined and bound the general assembly/legislature, 22, 349n143, 351n164; freedmen were considered freemen under the, 137; perhaps did not mean to exclude non-Anglican Protestants from holding public office, 363n354; provided for judges appointed by joint ballot of the general assembly, 28; was described as evidence of a social compact, 75, 335n6; was divided into articles, 143; was silent as to the fount of the people's political power, 19–20

Constitution of North Carolina (1868): abrogated common law procedure, 168; code commission was dissolved by amendment to the, 141, 185, 196; confined the jurisdiction of the supreme court to appeals on matters of law or legal inference, 339–340n25; conservatives recaptured the general assembly a few years after adoption of the, 245; contained a provision that the revised code of 1854 and subsequent legislation would be in force unless it conflicted with the, 195; eliminated common law pleading and united law and equity, 141; established a code commission, 135, 367n404; Freedmen's Code was precluded by the, 139; guaranteed reasonable compensation to the code commissioners, 365n370; is primarily the work of Tourgée, 134; mandates were introduced in the, 188; need of contemporaries to gain understanding of the state's, xxii; organic changes of the, 374n484; presumes untrustworthy representatives, 375n506; provided for popular election of supreme court justices, xxv; requirements and restrictions of the general assembly in the, xxiii, 197, 269, 371n447; and trial by jury, 232, 339n24; was amended to eliminate the code commission, 371n447

Constitution of North Carolina (1876 amendments), 242, 376n516

Constitution, English, 18, 349n141, 352n179

Constitution, provincial, 9, 344n81, 345n87, 361n313, 363n348. *See also Fundamental Constitutions of Carolina, The*; Grand Model

Constitution, U.S., 54, 286, 342n60, 349n138
Constitutional Convention (1865–1866), 136
Constitutional Convention (1868), xiii, 135, 142, 143, 162, 193
Constitutional Convention (1875), 376n516
Constitutional convention, state, 139, 141, 153, 171, 228, 235. *See also by date*
Continental Congress, 18, 22, 349n135, 349n145, 350n158
Cook, Mr., 368nn421, 422
Cook, Mr. Charles, xxii, 339n23
County courts, 114, 149
"Court of Conference, The," 46, 47, 63, 353n183
Court of errors, 46
Crime: capital, 123; common law of, 70, 168, 169; defined, 142, 167, 168, 365n378; punishment for and deterrence of, 136, 367n415; statutes in respect to, 134, 169. *See also* Code of criminal procedure

Criminal procedure. *See* Code of criminal procedure

Custom(s): call for reform is a rejection of sacred, xxi; common law of England was found in local, 347n98; common law worship of, 85; by courts, xxvi; declarations of law were rooted in an upright people's, 56; framing a new system of laws requires consultation of the previous, 6, 155; had modified the common law of the colony, 15; law, privilege, and religion were to be themes for criticism and invective, 337n9; laws of Carolina must reasonably conform to English laws and, 4, 9, 344n80; new statutory provisions called for by an altered state of, 96; prevailing upon a people, 239; proper constitutions are rooted in, 335n6; statute law may deviate from, 247; traditional conception of the common law as a fixed and determinate body of rules reflecting ancient, 336n7

D

Darwin, Charles, 130
Davie, W. R., 31, 350n161, 351n163
Davis, James, 32, 351n166, 347n106, 348n126
Declaration of Independence, 286
Declaration of rights: contained natural rights that were inalienable, 128, 363n349; distinguished N.C. from some aspects of its English heritage, 20; English-style, 295; N.C. adopted a, xiii; regarding freemen, 70; in 1689, 349n136; was prepended to N.C.'s first constitution, 19

Democracy: erecting a, 344n82; Jacksonian, 56; lovers of, 43; philosophers and, 342n55; pure, 342n61; representative, 375n504; the Revolution led to, 337n9; rising tide of, 128; support of territorial, 359n287

Democritus, 337–338n11
Descartes, 337n10
Devereux, Thomas P., 78, 79, 340n31, 358n248, 362n331
Digest(s): as scientifically-arranged summaries of opinions of the supreme court, 76, 193, 241, 357n243, 358n245, 358n247; as scientifically-arranged text of session laws with annotations, 63, 72–74, 110, 198; as summaries of sections of acts, 118; commissioned codifiers prepared,

79–82, 88, 95, 97, 181, 195, 354n204, 358nn257–260, 359n277, 359n286, 370n443, 372n449; of military laws, 50; and a scientific way of thinking, 76, 126, 366n394, 367n416

Discovery theory of law, 338n14, 375n496

Dissenters, 363–364n354

Divine law, xxvi, 20, 86

Durham, bishop of, 3, 4, 343n73, 344n79

Durham, N.C., 347n97, 375n499

E

Eaton, William, Jr., 111, 118, 120, 127

Economics, 279, 342n63, 370n439

Economy, 266, 376n515

Edwards, Jonathan, 79

Edwards & Broughton Printing Company, 374n493

Emigration, 111, 349n145

Empedocles, 337n11

England: American states declared independence from, 342n61; common law of, 15, 18, 22, 73, 127, 246, 275, 310, 344n80, 346n97, 347n98, 349n145; customs of, 4, 9; feudal system of, 343n76; laws of, xiii, 2, 11, 58, 89, 335n3, 346n97, 347n106; legal tradition of, 54, 120; modern digest for case law was produced in, 76; monarchs of, xvii, 3, 4, 9, 13–15, 18, 22, 33, 343nn72–74, 346n97, 348n111, 348nn125–126, 375n504; post-Revolution, 156; reform in, 52, 262; residents of, 254; statutes of, 10, 63, 64, 347n98; system of pleading in, 111; unwritten law of, 54; violation of natural or human rights in, 363n349

English Bill of Rights, 18

English law(s): codification of, 185; did not recognize slavery, 356n222; the extent to which, were in force in N.C., 9, 13, 345n96, 346n97, 347n97; influence of, on the province and state, 3, 344n80; list of, 17; scope of the reception of, 15, 348n127; state codification movements were concerned with freeing Americans from, 366n394; were seen as the embodiment of the law of nature, 337n8

English Parliament, 349n135

English Revolution, 20

Enlightenment: alternative, 126; discovery theory of law is typically dismissed as a carry-over from pre-, 338n14; expositors of English common law, 341n52; reasoning, xxv; secular philosophies were spawned during the, xxvi; treatises, 75, 341n45

Enslaved person(s), 70, 90, 136. *See also* Slavery

Epicurus, 338–339n16

Equality, xxi, 136, 162, 335n6, 359n287, 364n367

Equity: controversies in, 139; courts of, 356n223, 361n305; great principles of, 251; infrequent use of, by early statutory supreme court, 283; is artificially distinguished from law, 244, 254; jurisdiction, 350n158; merger of law and, xxv, 135, 141, 143, 295, 372n451; pleading, xxv; practice, 339n24; proceedings, 3, 30; relief by, 283; there was one form of action in, 372n451; use of juries, 3, 339n24; was one border of the law of the land, 254. *See also* Law and equity

Equity cases/suits: backlog of, 61, 335n1; distinction between actions at law and, 199, 373n466; reached the newly established supreme court, 73; removal jurisdiction of the supreme court for, xxii, 59, 335n1, 339n25

Ethics, 335n5, 337n10

F

Farmer, Fannie Memory, 110

Federal Convention, 351n163

Federal district court judge, 57

Federalist, 59, 126

Feudalism, 146, 337n9

Field, David Dudley: codifications by, involved digesting and restatement of existing law, 367n416, 372n449; on the common law, 254; corresponded regarding law reform, xxii; flattery of, 244; letters to and from, 146, 244, 365n385; modelled his analysis for the codification of the law of N.Y. on the outline of the common law used by Blackstone, 142, 365n381; N.C. code of civil procedure relied heavily upon the work of, 199; quote by, 238; was a famous codifier, 243; was the moving force for codification in N.Y., 244

Finnis, John, 360n300

Free Blacks/Negroes. *See* Colored people/free people of color

Freedmen: should be governed by whatever laws had governed free Blacks, 137; simplification of legal procedure served the needs of, 149, 293, 364n367; a system of laws concerning the, 136, 139, 364n361; transfer to the civil courts full jurisdiction in all matters relating to, 365n368. *See also* Colored people/free people of color

Freedmen's Bureau, 136, 364n367

"Freedmen's Code," 136, 137, 139, 364n366. *See also* "Black Codes"

Freemen: a declaration of rights was made by the, 70; landed, 22; Lords Proprietors were to enact constitutions with the assent of the local, 4; representatives of the, 2, 20, 26; the same common law existed for both races of, 137

French Jacobins, 342n61

French Revolution, 337n9, 361n313, 367n415

Freud, Sigmund, 130

Friends, 110, 360n288. *See also* Friends of Liberty; Quakers

Friends of Liberty, 85, 86. *See also* Friends; Quakers

Fundamental Constitutions of Carolina, The: criticism of, 88, 135; divided the province into counties, 344n83; evidenced a distrust of lawyers, of the multiplicity of laws, and of commentary and exposition on the law, 7; a later version of, 344n84; summary description of, 344n81; was chiefly a political code, 155; was described as an early instance of a code, 239, 344n86; was often referred to as the *Grand Model*, 6, 9, 344n81, 348–349n132; were required to be kept in a great book, read before every parliament, 361n313

Fundamental law: all natural or human rights are implicitly recognized in the state's, 363n349; commands in 1868 that a code be prepared, 184; constitutions are understood by some to be codifications of, 54; hierarchy of, 128; the judiciary declared void those acts passed in derogation of, 351n164; the jurisdiction of the supreme court was grounded in, xxv; must be naturally concomitant with the society it characterizes, 6; under an English-style customary constitution, 185; written, 3

Furches, Chief Justice David, 230

G

Gaston, Judge William: declined serving as commissioner to revise and consolidate the acts in force on administrators and executors, 74, 357n242; drew up an act regulating the descent of inheritances, 357n241; introduced a bill to create the modern supreme court, 59; letters to and from, 350n158, 355n214; men studied law under, 357n226; positions held by, 78, 357n240; quote by, 335n1; was given a legislative commission, 73; wrote for the court, 91

General assembly (in general), xxv

General assembly (prior to statehood), 9, 10, 14, 348n121

General assembly (under 1776 constitution): amended the laws relating to executors and administrators, 81; antebellum state supreme court depended on the, 341n40; appointed life-tenured judges, 349n143; appointed a replacement commissioner, 95; bills for consideration by the, 26; called for a codification of the statute and common law on a particular subject, 362n331; chair of the joint select committee of the, 97; commissioned a compilation of the state's private acts, 36; commissioned a revision and consolidation of the acts in force on administrators and executors, 74; confirmed revisals, 33, 355n206; debates in the, 343n37; elected all judges, 63, 70, 127, 357n240; established the antebellum supreme court, xxv, 43, 355n214; established biannual meetings of the judges of the superior courts, 43; established a superior court consisting of three judges, 28; exercised fundamental control over public functionaries, 22; extended the biannual meetings of the judges, 46; members debated a bill to establish a court to review judgments and decrees of the trial courts, 43; passed many acts and repealed or superseded others, 55, 101; recommendation that the military laws be revised by the, 50; repealed all the British acts, 10; reports to the, 335n1; representative to the, 127; revisal and consolidation of the public acts and parts of acts of the, 56; selected public officers to perform non-legislative functions of government, 22; the senate and house of commons were called the, 349n143; should allow an elected Jew to sit as a member, 128; took great care with public monies, 30; was presumed to act justly, 39

General assembly (under 1868 constitution): bills were adopted by the, 150, 252; code commission moderated excesses of the, 156; code commissioners enjoyed some success at the, 168; a code was submitted to and approved by the, 240, 369n431; commissioners presented a new code of civil practice and procedure to the, 185; commissioners reported that they had engaged in bill drafting for the, 178; commissioners submitted a code of criminal procedure to the, 181; conservatives recaptured the, 245; the 1868 constitution was amended to restrict the power of the, xxiii; the first part of a draft penal code was submitted to the, 168; passed public laws, 142; removed one of the traditional offices of the judiciary from the court's control, 370n439; reports to the, 135, 136, 146, 163, 188, 341n41; 372n449; sought to amend the constitution to eliminate the code commission, 371n447; was more firmly on the track of legislating by general statute in displacement of the common law, 239, 269

General statute: describing stages in the legislative ascent to, 343n70; general assembly legislated by, 239, 252, 269; governing by administrative regulation in accordance with, 341n43; passed in displacement of the common law, xxiii; primacy of, xxvi

George I, 13, 22, 348n111

George II, 14, 22, 346n97

George III, 22, 346n97

Gilmore, Professor Grant, 366n394

Glanville (treatise), 344n80

Graham, Gov. William A., xiii, 77, 97, 98, 130, 193

Grand Model. See Fundamental Constitutions of Carolina, The

Great Britain, xxv, 64, 352n179

Grier, Mr. Justice[Harry P.], 293

Grimké, Thomas, xxiii, 340n32

Gulley, [Needham Y.], 374n484

Guthrie, Professor [W. K. C.], 337n11

H

Hale, Sir Matthew, xxi, 155, 156, 283, 336n7

Hall, Judge John, xix, 78, 126, 127

Harnett County, 364n367

Hawks, Francis L.: described the "book of Laws," 10, 11; positions held by, 71, 357n243, 375n495; published a digested index of N.C. judicial decisions, 76; quote about, 345n95; studied law, 357n226; wrote a history of N.C., 347n100, 356n226

Haywood, Judge John: authored a manual of the laws of N.C., 47, 88; positions held by, 43, 47, 355n216, 360n292; published his reports of cases adjudged in the superior courts of law and equity, 353n188

Henderson, Archibald, 110, 127, 128

Henderson, John S., 240

Henderson, Judge Leonard: pictured, front cover; xx, 74, 126, 127, 363n341

Henderson, Judge Richard, 127

Henry II, 344n80

Henry III, 344n80

Henry, Mr. Jacob, 128, 356n224

Hewes, Joseph, 349n134

Higher law, 336n7

Hinsdale, Col. John W., xxii, 238, 247

Hobbes, [Thomas], 337n11

Hogg, Gavin, 78, 95

Holden, Gov. William Woods, 136, 137, 144, 183, 369–370n439

Holmes, Justice Oliver Wendell, Jr., xiii

Holmes, Mr. Lucien, 228, 373n463

Hooker, [Richard], 335n6

Humphreys, James, 78, 79, 341n52, 357n232, 358n248, 358n251–252

I

Immutable law, 18, 335n6

Impeachment, 350n161, 369–370n439

Inalienable rights, 128, 335n6, 338n12, 363n349

Individualism, 283

Institute of Government, xxiii, 340n36

Internal improvements, 80, 181, 188

Iredell, Justice James: pictured, 34; prepared a report, 95; published an essay defending judicial review, 350n161; revised state law, xiii, 108, 347n106; served as counsel in *Bayard v. Singleton*, 351n164; and views of natural justice, 39, 352n180; was appointed to revise the laws, 2, 26, 33, 351n168; was appointed to the Supreme Court of the U.S., 38;

Iredell, James, Jr., 95, 106, 115, 361n312, 375n495

Iredell's Revisal (1791): collected, compiled, and revised the whole body of the laws of the state, 56; several codifications since, 347n106; supplement to, 351n173; update to, 36, 38, 55; was allowed to be given in evidence in all the courts of law and equity, 355nn205–206

J

Jackson, President Andrew, 359n271

Jacksonian thought/democracy, 56, 107, 359n271

James, William, 287

Jefferson, President Thomas, xxiv, 126, 127, 349n145

Jenkins, William A., 364n367

Johnson, Guion Griffis, 356n226

Johnston, Samuel, 2

Jones, Dr. Calvin, 50, 353n189

Judge(s) (in general): distrust of, xxi, 30; in England, made all rules and regulations governing the details of practice according to the judicature acts of the 19th century, 262; good sense of, 275; had differing opinions regarding natural justice, 352n180; named, 228, 272, 360n292, 369n439; reforms affecting, 343n70; resolved to adhere to decided cases and settled principles, 42; role of, no longer to interpret higher, transcendent, and immutable corpus of law, 336n7; of the superior court, rotating, 43; traditionally, made rules of practice, 365n377;

under 1868 constitution, popular election of, xxvi, 295; were encouraged in the 20th century to be more progressive and far-sighted in their decisions and opinions, 271

Judge(s) (under 1776 constitution): in biannual meetings, argued and determined open questions of law and equity from the circuits, 43; in cases at law, the general assembly sometimes required two or more, 350n159; general assembly appointed life-tenured, 349n143; general assembly established a superior court consisting of three, 28; general assembly exercised fundamental control over, 22; legislatively elected, 295; meetings of the superior court, 46; opinions of, reported unofficially before 1818, 358n247; power and authority of, defined, 28; powers of antebellum supreme court judges were like superior court, 339n25; salaries of, 355n214; some early precedents were set by trial court, 73; after statehood, colonial common law developed by, 74; supreme court, did not try cases in the courts below, xxv, 335n1; unsuccessful attempt to impeach the superior court, 350n161; were in no danger from the arbitrary action of the executive, 350n154;

Judge(s) (under 1868 constitution), 135, 156, 279, 287, 340n26, 341n45

Judicature acts, 134, 262

Judicial review: in *Bayard v. Singleton*, 31, 350–351n161, 351n164; court can void an *ultra vires* enactment, 38–39; and declaration of rights, 128, 352n180; of legislation for conformity to constitution, 266, 350n161, 374n488; rejecting the doctrine of, 266, 374n488; in *Smith v. Campbell*, 75

Judiciary: accountability of the, xxvi; and the legislature, 39; contributed to an attacks on the, xxvi, 342–343n66; the code commission had done little good for the, 156; code commissioners offered the codes of practice and procedure and of law to officials the, for criticism, 142; committee, 80, 81, 359n279, 368n421, 368n422; construction of statutes by the, 96; general assembly removed one of the traditional offices of the, 369–370n439; and jurisprudence, 366n394; reviewed legislative acts for conformity to natural law, 351n164, 352n180; understanding of the law, 73

Jurisprudence: addition to the lore of N.C., xiii; classical common law, 336n7; code of general principles of, 185; collecting, condensing, and arranging the, of a people, 368n426; criminal, 134; discovery theory extends beyond, 338n14; division of old and new, 287; early call for, 283; Europe's civil law forms the basis of the, 238, 247; fathers of English and American, 287; natural law, 335n5, 359n287; noble science of, 230; of a people was to be arranged by code commissioners, 146; positivist, 293; support of a digest of portions of the, 366n394; use of the term, 51, 142, 365n383;

Jurisprudence des arrets, 6, 155, 365n383

Jury/juries: change in the duties of the, under reform procedure, 372n453; extension of, to equity proceedings, 3; the impact of codification of civil procedure in N.C. on the role of the, 232; only issues of fact should be passed upon by the, 340n26; provision, 350n158, 350n160; the rigid system of pleading in England maintained the distinction between law and fact which prevented the, from usurping the role of judge, 111; role of, 356n223; trial, 75, 89, 232, 339n24, 372n454; widespread use of, in colonial proceedings in N.C., 360n298. *See also* Trial by jury

Jus gentium, 344n80, 349n138, 356n222

Justinian (emperor), xxv, 238

K

Kent, Chancellor James, xxiv, 369n439

Kerr, John, 362n328

L

Land fraud, 43, 353

Law and equity: committee report would eliminate common law pleading and united, 141; constitutional merger of, xxii, xxv, 135, 141, 143, 295; judges argued and determined open questions of, 43; judges in the same courts would handle cases of both, 30; the new philosophy on which the code was based rejected the distinction between, 244; revisal could be given in evidence in all courts of, 56, 355n205; weightier precedent would soon settle puzzles and cabin discretion as suits in equity and appeals in, reached the supreme court, 73. *See also* Equity

Law licensing, 366n399

Law of nature, 86, 337n8, 346n97, 356n222. *See also* Natural law

Law reform: agitation for, in court procedure, 340n33; commissions on, 291; control of, during the antebellum period, 63; elimination of slavery was one focus of, 85; evidenced a strong preference for plain, clear, published criminal laws, 169; history of, 295; lessons about, gleaned from the state's history, 241; in the 17th and 18th centuries, 3; in the 19th century, xxi, xxv, 110, 239, 353n194; in the 20th century, 239; skipped phase of procedural, was quickly imposed on N.C. during Reconstruction, xxiii, themes of, xxii, 97, 361n313

Lawyer(s): anyone could be his own, before adoption of the *Code of Civil Procedure*, 111; committee of, were appointed to consider changes to *The Code of Civil Procedure*, 161; contemporary, 70; criminal, 127; efforts at codification were controversial among judges and, 135; experienced difficulty in actually applying the novelties of the code of civil procedure, 340n27; feudal judges were not, xx; named, 71, 110, 127, 228, 362n328, 373n463, 373n477; number of, was limited in court, 31; people must go to, in order to understand the simplest matters of process under reform procedure, 151, 184; protests were made against, 17; reforms affecting judges and, 343n70; the simple method of code pleading had not made every person his own, 249, 373n481; training of, 343n69; were appointed as commissioners, 27; were appointed to study what amendments to the code would be beneficial, 159; were assigned to revise the statutes and acts, 26. *See also* Attorney(s)

Legal education, xxv, xxvi, 230, 270, 343n68, 376n510

Legislators, xiii, 43, 279, 338n14, 342n64

Leucippus, 337n11

Liberty, 70, 99, 337n9, 342n58

Littleton (treatise), 155, 290

Livingston, Edward, 168, 254

Locke, John: another philosopher went further toward democracy than, 342n55; attempted to frame a *de novo* code for people, 6, 155; pictured, 7; prepared a code known as the *Fundamental Constitutions*, 6; quote by, 353n193; quotes about, 345nn87, 88, 89, 366n400

Lords Proprietors: each county was divided between the, 344n83; instructed the governor and council to make laws for the province, 9; the king granted the province of Carolina to the, 4; the king purchased the province from the, 15; named, 343nn71–72; surrendered the government of N.C. to King George II, 14; would relate legally to the King of England, 3

M

Macay, Judge Spruce, 43

Madison, President James, xiii, 342n60, 353n192

Magna Carta, 342n58, 349n136

Manly, Mr. Matthias Evans, 77

Manning, James, 373n477

Manning, Professor John, 233, 240, 246, 247, 346n97, 373n477

Mansfield, Chief Justice Lord, 54, 230

Manumission Society, 86, 110

Martin, François-Xavier, 36, 38, 55, 351n173, 355n216

McCorkle, J. M., 194, 369n438, 370n439, 375n495

McIntosh, Professor Atwell Campbell, 274, 374n490

Military laws: revision of, 50

Miller, Professor Perry, xxii, 339n23

Miller, Gov. William, 54, 59

Mitchell, Anderson, xiii, 230, 366n390

Mixed government, 6, 20, 338n14, 344n84, 352n179

Montesquieu, Baron de, 20

Moore, Bartholomew Figures, 90, 118, 136, 364n361

Moral realism, xxi, 338n14

Moral science(s): codification of procedural law related to the movement for a new, 171; of the common law, 230, 341n45; discovery theory extends beyond jurisprudence to all the, 338n14; an extension of method from the physical sciences to the, 337n11; must migrate methodology to experimentation, 287; the notion of, 130; rejection of sacred custom and traditional, xxi; truths form the basis of political and, 341n53

Morality, 86, 338n12, 342n63, 355n214

Mordecai, Moses, 76, 357n244

Mordecai, Professor Samuel Fox, II: began a systematic commentary on Blackstone, 233, 346–347n97; biographical sketch of, 290–291; disagrees with attacks on classical common law, xxii; letters to and from, 270; opposed certain views on reform in the administration of law, 239; pictured, 289; served as dean of Trinity Law School, 357n244

Morganton, N.C., 118

Morton, Rev. Andrew, 364n354

Moseley, Edward, 348n121

Murphey, Judge Archibald DeBow: description of, 128; pseudonym of, 127, 363n338; quote by, 42; sat on the Supreme Court, 363n341; served as an official reporter of opinions of the Supreme Court of N.C., 71; sponsored a bill as senator, 59

N

Napoleon/Napoleonic code, xxv, 123, 238, 337n9

Nash, Associate Judge Frederick, 115, 117, 355n210

Natural justice, 38, 39, 336n7, 352n180

Natural law: attack on, 335n6; in the Christian tradition, 335n6; codification in the 19th century is a phase of positivism that related to classical common law traditions and, xxi; colonists claimed entitlement to certain rights and liberties by English constitutional law, positive foundational law of the colonies, and, 18; common law tradition emerged from, 4; contempt for, 337n9; detractors of codification generally agree with the universality of divine and, 135; the judiciary was denied the power to review legislative acts for conformity to, 351n164; jurisprudence of, 54; legal tradition specified under, xxvi; link between the jurisprudential norms of common law and, 336n7; local laws approached conformity to the general application of practical reason embodied in, 344n80; modern attack on classic, 338n13; modern views of, 85; principles of, 340; reform by codification contrasts with, xxi; relation between common law and, 336n7, 356n223; relation of popular sovereignty to divine law, colonial common law, and, 20; territorial democracy based on a refined, 359n287; written law was placed in the bosom of, 31. *See also* Law of nature

Natural rights: are only what may be directly deduced from their human nature, 335n6; asserted that no social classes have any, 336n6; in the declaration of rights, 363n349; of mankind, 86; modern rights doctrines were linked with socialism, utilitarianism, and transcendentalism, 337n9; theories, 85; were inalienable, 128

New York: codes, 238; commissioners received shipment of the codes of procedure from, 146; differences between N.C. and, 340n33; drafted a penal code based on the law of, 168; law would be of great use to the legislature, 146, 153; legislature in, 371n447; moderate codification had broken with the past in, 118; N.C. followed, in codifying acts of assembly, xxiii, 120, 241, 244, 339n19, 365n372, 365n381; N.C. would not rely solely on the code of practice of, 145, 374n484; resident of, xxii, 243, 244, 356–357n226, 369n439; statute to appoint commissioners to prepare a civil code, 142; system of laws, 134

"Newton of legislation," 338–339n16

Nietzsche, [Friedrich], 337n9

North Carolina Bar Association, xxii, xxiii, 275

North Carolina Board of Law Examiners, 162, 366n397

North Carolina Constitutional Commission of 1958, 371n448

North Carolina Reports, xxii, 194, 228, 232

Northerners, 149, 293

O

Olsen, Otto, 369n432

Orth, Professor John V., 356n223

Owen, Gov. John, 42, 83

P

Paine, Thomas, 335n6

Parmenides, 337n11

Pasteur, Edward, 50

Pearson, Judge/Chief Justice Richmond: advocated for a role for the courts in developing procedural rules, 178, 368n424, 368n430; asked if a judge can apply principles or rules of the civil law to resolve gaps in the common law, 356n223; cited a maxim about discretion, 155; conceded the usefulness of the less rigid "codes" of Coke and Hale, 156; declined an offer to serve on the code commission, 185; described common law, 116, 122; the governor proposed a seat on the code commission for, 183; the idea of the common law by, 362nn320–322, 330; memory of, xx; moved that a judge resign, 369–370n439; opinion of, on codification, 366n390; pictured, 157; remarks about, 230; wrote to other justices, 150

Penal code: bill for a, 167–169, 367nn410–414, 374n484; characteristics of the, 367n415; commissioners failed to resubmit the, 188; commissioners had nearly completed the remainder of the, 178; a general analysis of the, 146; had been introduced in the senate and referred to the judiciary committee, 368n421; would not only provide for punishments, but would define crimes, 365n378

Philo Florian, 127

Philosopher(s): English, xiii, xxv, 53; named, 6, 7, 20, 78, 88, 89, 95, 155, 265, 335n6, 337nn9, 11, 338n13, 342n55, 345nn87, 353n193, 360n300, 365n377, 366n400. *See also* by name

Pleading: England had a rigid system of, 111; hope for a quick restoration of the old system of practice and, 158; ignorance of arcane, scholastic forms of, 31; the invention of new codes and systems of, 171, 232; for money,

348–349n132; plain and simple method of, 249; rules of, 111, 372n453. *See also* Code pleading; Common law pleading

Pomeroy, Professor John Norton, 199, 372nn454–455

Popular sovereignty, xxvi, 342n60

Positive law: an act commissioned a revisal and consolidation of the, 44; being written more clearly, 247; codification of the, 76, 107, 354n204; and common law must harmonize with divine law and the law of nature, 86; discovered principles of natural law are specified by the, 338n14; legislative initiatives to codify the, 354n204; proper constitutions are rooted in custom and prescription, which have a deeper validity than mere, 335n6; revisal and consolidation of the, 55; the revisal would have the status of, 14; true reform amounted to clearly writing, 247

Postema, Professor Gerald J., 336n7

Potter, Henry, 57, 63, 107, 108

Potter, Robert, 75, 342n60

Potter's Revisal (1819), 56, 64, 72, 73, 84, 354n204

Pound, Dean Roscoe: argued before the N.C. Bar Association, 275, 291; essay by, 178; inclusion of speech by, xxii; observed the desire of European jurisdictions to adopt judicial review, 374n488; quotes by, xx, 238

Practical reason, xxv, 56, 338n15, 344n80, 354n202, 360n300

Practice of law: an act allowing citizens of good moral character to engage in the, 340n28; character requirements for the, 162, 366n397; educational requirements for the, xxvi, 343n68; license for the, 290; while *The Code of Civil Procedure* was in effect, some men would not participate in the, 193

Pratt, Professor Walter F., Jr., 355n214

Precedents: call for abolition of authority of, 42, 78, 266, 279–280, 343n70; carried less weight pre-1819, 73; cited in statutory digest, 73, 82; controls arbitrariness in exercise of discretion by judges, 155, 335n3; doctrine of, xxvi, 342n65; English constitutional, 22; gradual displacement of, xxiii, xxv, 283; law cut loose from, 287, 341n44; in period of applied democracy, overruling of, xxv; revered, xxvi; statutory supreme court established in 1818 to reinvigorate, 43; undermined in the 1790s, 43; undermined, perhaps, by power of code commission, xxv

Private substantive common law: abandonment of the idea of a complete codification of, 372n449; cannot possibly be codified, 367n405; Clark's interest in codification of, 293, 340n34; code commission fails to codify, 135, 188, 197; codification of, 7, 168, 181; fundamental changes in, 293; instead of general statute, judges made, 279; not extensively considered for codification before 1868, xxiii; question concerning, 22; shall be expressed in writing, 338n15; unwritten law is proper for, 251. *See also* Substantive law

Privileges and immunities, 4, 344n79, 346n97

Progressive Era, 269

Progressivism, 287

Property law, 340n31, 341n52, 362n331

Proprietors, 22, 344n84

Protestant(s), xxi, 22, 128, 295, 363n350, 363n354

Protestantism, 128, 354n202

Public acts, 11, 47, 56, 84, 107

Punishment, 139, 169, 335n2, 359n287, 365n368, 367n415

Pythagoreans, 337n11

Q

Quakers, 86, 359n288, 360n288. *See also* Friends; Friends of Liberty

"Queen's Peace," 2, 13, 15, 346n97. *See also* Anne, Queen

R

Raleigh, Walter, 343n72

Rantoul, Robert, xxiii, 340n32

Rationalism, 337nn10–11

Reception: of British acts, 73, 89; of colonial law, 27, 28; of the common law, 15, 364n359; conundrum, xxi; definition of, 339n18; of English statute law, 15, 348n126; ordinances, 27, 29, 30; problem of, 57; question of, 57; statutes, 27, 29, 30, 56, 350n152

Reconstruction: advocates of codification during, 295; code commissioner during, 145, 228, 347n100; constitution, xxii, 143, 195, 232, 365n376; description of, 164; law school at UNC was re-established after, 233; not all codes prepared in N.Y. were adopted in N.C. during, 374n484; reporter's duties were transferred to the attorney general during, 369n439; a skipped phase of procedural law was quickly imposed on N.C. during, xxiii; superior court judge during, 198

Reform procedure, 241, 246, 249, 266, 372n453, 376n513

Reformation, xxv, 283

Religion: Anglicanism was the established Protestant, 363n350; Christian, 365n378; dominion in, 42; modern belief that man has a right to subject, to his own will, 338n15; Protestant, 363n354; relation of law to, 130; sketch about an attorney touched upon the theme of, 127; was no longer to command allegiance, 337n9

Reporter: named, 36, 47, 71, 76, 78, 79, 106, 228, 229, 340n31, 357n226, 357n243, 362n331, 369n439; official duties of, were transferred to the attorney general, 369n438, 369n439; position abolished and re-established, 194, 293; practices and pricing were questionable/abusive, 369n439, 375n495; supplemental act created the judicial office of, 56; supreme court was empowered to appoint a, 363n339, 369n437; was brought under the authority of the supreme court, 245; was an employee of the court, 370n439

Restoration, 22, 361n313

Revisal (1715), 2, 10–11, 13, 14, 345n96, 347nn100–101

Revisals: description of, 80; did not "digest" the statute laws, 358n257; in general, xiii, 47, 56, 73, 195, 247, 354n204

Revised Code (1854): amendment of the, 364n358; a bill for a penal code references the, 367n412; commissioner who assisted with preparation of the, 347n100; constitutional convention ordinance encompassed statute laws as reflected in the, 135; description of the, 362n326; fused disparate acts on the same subject, 118, 354n204; lengthy chapter on proceedings in habeas corpus was found in the, 374n484; praise for the consolidation of the, 247; provisions in effect under the, 163, 168; updating the, 142, 178, 188

Revised Statutes, The (1837): adopted an alphabetic arrangement, 47; an annotated code of the state's statute law was envisioned well before the general assembly commissioned, 73; code commissioners for, 99, 106, 115, 117, 125, 145, 195; commentary on, 97; differed from earlier revisals, 107, 118; English statutes inherited with the colonial common law were absorbed in, 375n509; the general assembly commissioned, 81; preface to, 26–27; prior revisals did not measure up to, 56; repealed all the statutes of England, 64; report by two commissioners of the, 95; a sketch of the judicial history of N.C. is published in the, 353n182; was published in a volume separate from the session laws, 101–102

Revised Statutes of New York, 78

Rodman, Commissioner/Justice William B.: accepted the duties of a code commissioner, 144; apparently described the list of bills appended to the March 1869 code commission report as codifications of statute law on various subjects, 374n484; assisted with the *Revised Code* of 1854, 347n100; letters to and from, 145, 150, 155, 227, 245, 362n321; not clear whether he advocated the adoption of an inflexible "statute code," 156; opinion of, on codification, 366nn390, 394; pictured, front cover, 145; recorded the change in the duties of the jury under reform procedure, 372n453; reported on behalf of the code commission, 185; signed the last report of the code commission, 369n432; suggested that the supreme court opposed codification of civil procedure, 167; was associated with re-codifying the public laws of the state, 118

Rousseau, [Jean-Jacques], 335n6, 342n54

Ruffin, Thomas: accepted a commission to codify the statute and common law of executors and administrators, 83; memory of, xx; questioned the salaries of the supreme court judges, 355n214; served as a reporter of opinions of the supreme court, 71; was elected to the supreme court, 70, 359n275

Rush, Attorney General Richard, 51, 353n192

S

Santayana, Professor George, xii, xxiv, 338–339n16
Saunders, Romulus Mitchell, 118
Schenck, David, 159, 163
Schwarzenberg, Johann von, xxv, 341n47

Scientific thinking, xxv, 337n10, 341n51
Sciolist(s), 171, 293, 368n419, 376n513
Secession, 43, 135, 193, 364n358
Secretary of state (N.C.): files of the, 33; original version of the codification was placed in the office of, 102; 355n210
Secretary of State (U.S.), 54
Separation of powers, 20, 143, 291, 344n84, 349n141, 352n179
Session laws. *See* Statute law(s)/session law(s)
Shepherd, Chief Justice James E., xx, xxii, 238, 250, 251, 287
Shipp, William M., 369n438, 370n439
Sieyes, Abbe, 335–336n6
Slavery: abolition of, 85, 123, 137, 139, 335n2, 364n367; cases involving, 70; deviated from the common law, 63, 362n333; English law did not recognize, 356n222; protests against the institution of, 86, 360n288; quote about, 360n296; rejection of one classical justification of, 359n287. *See also* Enslaved persons
Smith, Hon. W. N. H., 137
Social classes, xii, 335–336n6
Social compact(s), 75, 335n6
Socialism, xxvi, 337n9
Solon, 338–339n16
South Carolina, xxiii, 15, 343n72, 348n124
Statute law(s)/session law(s) (in general): the antebellum state supreme court is the creature of, 341n40; common law was sometimes distinguished from, 347n98; a judge compiled a manual of N.C.'s, 360n292; may deviate from custom and reside outside the consciousness of the people, 247, 342n54; proclaiming was seen as an essential feature of, 246
Statute law(s)/session law(s) (early documents): colonial, 26; concerning reception was allowed to endure until the end of the next general assembly, 27; of England were in force in N.C., 10, 15; English, 348n127; first authentic general collection of, 33; a reception statute included both English common law and, 30; revisal of the whole body of, 11, 26
Statute law(s)/session law(s) (antebellum period): appointment to revise the, 63; bill for revising the, 84; bills pointed to codifications of, on various subjects, 374n484; changing relation between common law and, 130; codification of, xxv; codification of both common law and, 83; commission to revise the, 38; commissioners aimed to revise the public, 95; contemplations of an official revisal of the entire body of, 79, 80; early innovator in the movement for codification of, 43; envisioning of an annotated code of the state's, 73; a failed bill had aimed to revise and digest the public, 81; governor called for a codification of the whole body of public, 142; is undiscoverable, 42; periodic revisals of, addressed the problem of repeal, 73; plan for an unofficial, annotated manual of the entire state, 77; postponement indefinitely of a bill for revising and digesting the public,

359n286; rejection of a law for arranging, revising, and digesting the whole body of public and, 358n260; resolution sought a revisal and consolidation of a narrow subject of, 84; simplification of the, 107

Statute law(s)/session law(s) (code commission era and applied democracy): commissioner for the codification of N.C.'s, 233; commissioners focused on, 178; commissioners would end their work after submitting to the legislature a codification of the whole, 181; commissioning act required the collating, digesting, and compiling of all the public, 195; continual changes were made to the state's, 376n510; convention called for a re-codification of the, 141; declaration in ordinance encompassed both the common laws and the, 135; recommended changes to conform existing, 139; was revised extensively and continuously by the state legislature, 293

Stoics, 335n6

Stone, Gov. David, 50

Story, Justice Joseph, 6, 346n97, 349n145, 366n394

Substantive law, xxi, 135, 168, 266, 335n3, 371n448. *See also* Private substantive common law

Superior court judges: biannual meetings of, 43; meeting of, to try alleged land frauds, 353n182; named, 47, 127, 198, 254; powers of the, 339n25; rotation of, abandoned, xxii, 266

Supreme court (in general): acknowledged the looseness of common law practice in N.C., 118; differentiation between the realms of the legislature and the, 126; law library of the, 193, 239; the N.C.B.A. encouraged reliance of the, on restatement of the "American" common law, xxiii; published revised statutes were to be enhanced by references to decisions of the state, 101, 118; quote about the, xx; relative importance of, in development of law in N.C., xxv; reporter of decisions for the, 127, 245, 369n438; reporter of opinions for the, 369–370n439, 375n497

Supreme court (under 1818 statute): an act created the modern, 363n341; depended on the general assembly, 341n40; English common law was the essence of the colonial common law inherited at statehood and developed thereafter by the decisions of the, 74; judges viewed the common law as the foundation upon which the laws of the state should rest, 283; members viewed the common law as a system, 73; Potter's arguments to the state, 342n60; questioned late in the antebellum period whether adjectival law was a common law system complete in itself, 362n333; the radical side of the codification movement was acknowledged by an officer of the state, 78; removal jurisdiction in equity cases, xxii, 59; reporter of, excerpted a contemporary English codification of property law, 362n333; reporter's digested index was published not long after the founding of the modern, 76; sessions of the general assembly attacked the, 355n214; traditionalism of the judges of the state's first, 126; was empowered to appoint a reporter, 363n339; was established by the general assembly, 43; was a wide departure from the old English system, 335n1; weightier precedent would soon settle suits in equity and appeals in law and equity when they reached the newly established, 73; Yancey's role in creation of the modern state, 57

Supreme court (under 1868 constitution): address to the, 272; associate justice of the state, 245; cited Mordecai as an authority on the common law, 290; clerk of the, 239; construed the Reconstruction constitution to secure a jury trial in all actions, civil and criminal, 232; jurisdiction of, is grounded in fundamental law, xxv; progressivism in the 1890s of the judges who sat on the, 287; published a table of its overruled cases, 341n44; was empowered to prescribe rules of practice and procedure, 371nn447–448

Supreme Court judges (under 1818 statute), 56, 126, 283, 357n243

Supreme court judges/justices (in general): appointed the official reporter of decisions, 369n437; assisted in the development of the state's common law, 125; named, 43, 57, 70, 115, 119, 126, 127, 357n240, 359n275, 373n477

Supreme Court justices (under 1868 constitution), xxv, 287, 343n69

Supreme Court of the United States, 34, 38, 171, 228, 295

Swaim, Benjamin, 86, 110, 123, 360n290

Swaim, Mr. William, 86, 359n288, 360n288

Swain, Gov. David L.: as a member of the house of commons contemplated an official revisal of all the statute laws in force, 79–81; complained about the conundrum of the reception of British acts in N.C., 89; justified his proposed reorganization of the state's revised laws, 89; made a resolution concerning revisal of statute laws, 79; quote by, 42; reported that the first two general assemblies revised all of the statute law, 26; resolution by, 80; served as governor and lobbied for an act commissioning the revised statutes, 81; wrote a sketch of the judicial history of N.C., 353n182

Swann's Revisal: general assembly aimed to update, 33; repealed and obsolete provisions of the public laws were removed from, 348n123; served as a foundation to Iredell's collection of public statutes in force, 33; title page of, pictured, 16; updates to, 348n126; was the first book printed in N.C., 15, 357n237; would supersede the laws on which it was based, 14–15. *See also* "Yellow Jacket"

T

Taft, President William H., 286, 375n499

Taylor, Chief Justice John Louis: anonymous publication by, 51, 357n228; did not think his statutory appellate court had jurisdiction to contradict the general assembly, 70; envisioned an annotated code of the state's statute law, 73; made a tremendous contribution to the development of the law in the early 19th century, 63; memory of, xx; narrowed the definition of Protestant to Anglican, 128; opinions by, 78; pictured, 72, front cover; published a statutory digest, 72, 73, 79, 82; quote by, xxiv; respected the principles and rules of the common law, 63; served as first chief justice of the supreme court, 43, 57; served as a superior court judge, 43, 63; speech by, 356n224; struggled to do justice in a society based in significant part on gross injustice, 69; unofficial nominal reports of, 63, 76

Tourgée, Judge Albion W.: accusations against, xiii, 193, 369n439; as a pivotal figure in the 19th century, xxii; biographer of, 369n432; close friend of, pictured, 229; compiled an annotated digest-treatise on civil procedure, 198, 199, 227, 241; criticized opinions of the Supreme Court of N.C., 209, 232; description of, 152, 228, 235; is responsible for the Constitution of 1868 and the new code, 134; led the law reform effort, 135; letters to and from, 145, 146, 167, 227; perhaps desired to reduce the entire common law to a written code, 366n390; pictured, front cover, 198; resigned, 185, 368n430; served as commissioner on the code commission, 347n100; stood victorious in merging law and equity, 295; traced the roots of common law, 254; was reviled, 369–370n439; was run out of the state, 239; was a staunch advocate of codification, xiii, 156

Tradition: advent of written constitutions might have threatened the common-law, 344n86; ancient, 279; Christian, 335n6; civil practice is a matter of, 114; common law, xxvi, 4, 75, 239, 241, 336n7, 344n80, 375–376n509; crimes are morally wrong and against local, 367n415; crimes listed in the bill for a penal code did not break dramatically with, 169; disavowels of European, 22; first supreme court judges respected, 126;-focused training of lawyers, 343n69; Jefferson would divorce law from, 126; legal, 54, 135, xxvi; natural law, 4, 359n287; nineteenth-century reformers attacked, 344n80; of state statutory revisals, 56; Western, 337n11, 349n138; writers who classified the rules of the English common law courts held tightly to the thread of, xxv

Transcendentalism, xxvi, 337n9, 342n66

Treatises: on civil practice, 114, 120, 198, 241; common law, xxv, 73, 75, 76, 156, 167, 168, 283, 341n45, 344n80, 357n236; on executors, 63, 73, 110, 361n312; and a scientific way of thinking, 54, 76, 126, 357n236. *See also by title or common reference*

Trial by jury, xxii, 30, 31, 339n24, 356n223. *See also* Jury/juries

Trial court judge, 230, 241

Trinity College (later Duke School of Law), 233, 346–347n97, 357n244, 374n490

Tushnet, Professor Mark, 116

U

United States Supreme Court. *See* Supreme Court of the United States

University of North Carolina: history of the, 373n463; law school at the, 233; president, 6, 239, 241; professor at the, 86; students at the, 77; trustee of the, 79

Unwritten law: codification was seen as a remedy for the arbitrary accretions of the, 335n3; of England, 54; failure to explain the constitution's relation to, 22; had arisen out of reasonable customary practices, xxv; is proper for private substantive law, 251; official reporting of opinions gave the impression of more writtenness of the, 56; in printed books, 372n450; was not transformed into a portion of the written law, 346–347n97

Utilitarianism, xxvi, 335n4, 337n9

W

Warren, Professor Charles, xxii, 23, 339nn21–23

Washington, President George, 34, 38, 286

Weeks, Stephen, 86, 292

Whichard, Willis P., xiii–xiv, 360n294

Williams, Justice/Judge John, 43, 351n161

Wilson, Justice James, 336n7

Winston, Judge Robert W.: addressed the bar association, 262; expressed opinion about codification, xxii; opposed further reform in the administration of law, 239; pictured, 272; quotes by, 126, 134, 271, 286, 375n498, 376n510; reviewed a biography of one of the chief justices of the supreme court, 286–288; was a conservative moving toward moderation about court procedure, 239; was a mild critic of codification, 291; was inspired in part by the code commissioners, 374n487

Wood, Thomas, xxi, 283, 341n52, 357n236

Worth, Gov. Jonathan, 136

Y

Yancey, Bartlett, 57, 59, 63, 350n158

"Yellow Jacket," 347n106. *See also Swann's Revisal*

www.ingramcontent.com/pod-product-compliance
Lightning Source LLC
Chambersburg PA
CBHW080723300426
44114CB00019B/2469